Reshaping Humanitarian Logistics With AI, Predictive Analytics, and Autonomous Systems

Erkut Akkartal
Yeditepe University, Turkey

Filiz Mizrak
Beykoz University, Turkey

IGI Global
Scientific Publishing
Publishing Tomorrow's Research Today

Vice President of Editorial — Melissa Wagner
Director of Acquisitions — Mikaela Felty
Director of Book Development — Jocelynn Hessler
Production Manager — Mike Brehm
Cover Design — Jose Rosado

Published in the United States of America by
IGI Global Scientific Publishing
701 East Chocolate Avenue
Hershey, PA, 17033, USA
Tel: 717-533-8845
Fax: 717-533-7115
Website: https://www.igi-global.com E-mail: cust@igi-global.com

Library of Congress Cataloging-in-Publication Data

LCCN: 2025023224 (CIP Data Pending)
ISBN13: 979-8-3373-3643-5
Isbn13Softcover: 979-8-3373-3644-2
EISBN13: 979-8-3373-3645-9

British Cataloguing in Publication Data
A Cataloguing in Publication record for this book is available from the British Library.

Table of Contents

Detailed Table of Contents

The chapter investigates how Artificial Intelligence (AI) improves disaster management and aid distribution operations in humanitarian logistics. The chapter demonstrates how AI analyzes real-time data to enable fast decision processes and enhance early warning systems through machine learning capabilities. The chapter demonstrates how predictive modeling enhances resource allocation and logistics while AI optimizes aid delivery through geospatial data and automation and examines AI's impact on disaster recovery and long-term resilience but it also discusses the main challenges that include limited data availability and biased algorithms and ethical issues in humanitarian situations.

This chapter explores how big data, artificial intelligence (AI), and predictive analytics are transforming humanitarian relief from reactive response models to anticipatory supply chains. By leveraging technologies such as machine learning and Bayesian forecasting, humanitarian organizations can enhance situational awareness, improve demand prediction, and optimize last-mile delivery. The study also addresses decision-making under uncertainty through the lens of the value of information (VoI) and forecast-based financing. Despite these advancements, implementation challenges remain—ranging from data fragmentation and ethical concerns to technological and cultural barriers. To overcome these issues, the chapter proposes strategic enablers including data literacy training, ethical AI governance, and inter-agency collaboration. A concluding roadmap outlines key steps for integrating predictive analytics into humanitarian logistics for more timely, efficient, and inclusive crisis response.

and decentralized decision-making. Traditional aid supply chains often struggle with inefficiencies, information asymmetry, and limited traceability—challenges that blockchain addresses through secure, real-time, and tamper-proof data infrastructure. The integration of blockchain with digital identity systems, smart contracts, IoT, and AI enables more adaptive, ethical, and inclusive aid delivery. Case studies, including Oxfam's UnBlocked Cash program and blockchain-based cash transfers in Ukraine, illustrate both the opportunities and the practical barriers to implementation. The chapter concludes with strategic policy recommendations aligned with Sustainable Development Goals (SDGs 8, 16, and 17), emphasizing the importance of cross-sector collaboration, digital capacity-building, and ethical governance.

Sudden and destructive disasters such as earthquakes create complex and uncertain logistical needs that challenge traditional humanitarian response systems. This chapter explores how smart technologies such as artificial intelligence (AI), predictive analytics, cloud computing, Internet of Things (IoT), drone systems, and Geographic Information Systems (GIS) can enhance earthquake-based humanitarian logistics by improving speed, coordination, and decision-making. A thematic literature review, a technology–value matrix, and five real-world-inspired scenarios are used to evaluate these technologies' effectiveness across logistics functions. Additionally, an Integrated Smart Technology Ecosystem model is introduced to demonstrate how these tools can work collectively. The study highlights that successful implementation depends not only on technical capability but also on ethical governance, data quality, interoperability, and institutional readiness. Strategic recommendations are offered for humanitarian actors, emphasizing holistic planning and future research directions.

This chapter examines the intersection of digitization and green logistics in post-disaster recovery operations, focusing on how emerging tools—such as digital health kits, blockchain systems, and solar-powered communications—can be designed and deployed with minimal ecological impact. Drawing on recent field cases from UNICEF, the World Food Programme (WFP), and the Red Cross/Red Crescent Movement, the study highlights both the transformative potential and the unintended consequences of digital tools, including challenges in e-waste management, lifecycle tracking, and

This chapter examines the strategic role of aviation technologies, artificial intelligence (AI), and predictive analytics in enhancing humanitarian logistics. As crises grow more complex and unpredictable, aviation offers unmatched speed and flexibility, enabling timely aid delivery and real-time situational awareness. Case studies from the World Food Programme, UNHAS, and the Turkish Red Crescent illustrate the real-world application of these technologies in famine response, flight optimization, and post-disaster relief. The chapter also presents a phased roadmap for strategic technology integration and addresses ethical, regulatory, and governance challenges. By aligning emerging technologies with humanitarian values, the chapter provides actionable insights for leaders and policymakers seeking to build more resilient, data-informed humanitarian systems.

This chapter explores how digital transformation can improve airbase readiness and strategic airlift planning in humanitarian logistics. It examines readiness factors such as runway infrastructure, fuel access, ICT systems, and cybersecurity, alongside airlift planning elements like aircraft types, cargo prioritization, and geography. Drawing from real-world cases—including NATO operations, UNHAS in Africa, and Türkiye's earthquake response—the study highlights the role of AI, blockchain, and digital twins in forecasting, coordination, and maintenance. A systems-based framework is proposed to digitally integrate air logistics, stressing ethical use, data protection, and global interoperability. The chapter concludes with strategic recommendations for policy reform, cross-sector collaboration, and scalable digital investment to build agile, transparent, and resilient humanitarian air logistics aligned with the SDGs.

This chapter explores the transformative role of Unmanned Aerial Vehicles (UAVs), commonly known as drones, in enhancing emergency relief logistics and last-mile delivery performance. As supply chains face increasing disruption from natural disasters, pandemics, and urban congestion, UAVs offer rapid, flexible, and contactless delivery solutions that improve reach, resilience, and sustainability.

and innovation scaling to support more resilient and transparent humanitarian operations.

Preface

In an era marked by intensifying climate events, public health crises, and geopolitical instability, the role of humanitarian logistics has never been more critical—or more complex. Traditional logistics systems, designed for predictability and stability, are increasingly challenged by rapid-onset disasters and multi-layered emergencies. To meet these evolving demands, the integration of artificial intelligence (AI), predictive analytics, and autonomous technologies into humanitarian supply chains is not only timely but necessary. This edited volume brings together forward-thinking research and real-world case studies that illuminate how digital innovation is transforming the way we prepare for, respond to, and recover from crises.

Our objective with this collection is to bridge the gap between academic inquiry and operational implementation. Each chapter explores a unique facet of digital transformation in humanitarian logistics—from AI-powered disaster management to blockchain-based transparency systems, from the promise of predictive analytics in demand forecasting to the strategic application of UAVs in last-mile delivery. The contributions reflect a shared commitment to ethical, data-driven, and collaborative solutions that are both scalable and sustainable. By grounding technological advances in humanitarian values, these works propose new models for logistics that are more agile, inclusive, and resilient.

We were motivated to assemble this book not only because of the technical potential of emerging systems, but also because of their capacity to reshape the humanitarian ethos—placing equity, efficiency, and environmental stewardship at the core of crisis response. As scholars and practitioners based in Türkiye—a country with a long history of both giving and receiving aid—we recognize the importance of regional insights in global discussions. The contributors represent a vibrant mix of perspectives, disciplines, and institutional affiliations, with case studies grounded in Türkiye's own disaster history and digital transformation trajectory. In doing so, this volume serves as a platform for cross-border dialogue and innovation in the humanitarian space.

CHAPTER OVERVIEWS

Chapter 1: The Role of Artificial Intelligence in Disaster Management and Aid Distribution

This chapter examines the transformative role of artificial intelligence (AI) in enhancing disaster management and humanitarian aid distribution. It discusses how AI-driven systems improve real-time data analysis, enable rapid decision-making, and strengthen early warning capabilities through machine learning. By leveraging predictive modeling, AI facilitates more efficient resource allocation and geospatial logistics optimization. The chapter also evaluates AI's impact on post-disaster recovery and long-term resilience, while acknowledging critical limitations such as data scarcity, algorithmic bias, and ethical dilemmas in high-stakes humanitarian contexts.

Chapter 2: Predictive Power for Humanitarian Relief: Data-Driven Approaches to Crisis Response

This chapter explores how AI, big data, and predictive analytics are reshaping humanitarian logistics by shifting the paradigm from reactive to anticipatory response systems. Utilizing tools like machine learning and Bayesian forecasting, humanitarian actors can improve situational awareness, forecast demand, and optimize supply chain performance. The chapter also addresses decision-making under uncertainty and introduces forecast-based financing and the value of information (VoI) frameworks. Key challenges such as fragmented data and ethical concerns are discussed alongside enablers like ethical AI governance and inter-agency collaboration, culminating in a strategic roadmap for predictive integration.

Chapter 3: Data-Driven Humanitarian Supply Chains in Disaster Relief: Enhancing Responsiveness and Efficiency through Predictive Analytics

Focusing on the growing importance of big data in disaster preparedness and response, this chapter highlights how predictive analytics can elevate the responsiveness and efficiency of humanitarian supply chains. It outlines the role of real-time data processing in facilitating rapid decision-making and logistics coordination, particularly during complex emergencies. By examining recent research and practical applications, the chapter emphasizes the value of data-informed strategies for improving forecasting accuracy, optimizing supply flows, and strengthening long-term planning in humanitarian contexts.

Chapter 4: IoT and Smart Sensors for Real-Time Monitoring of Aid Distribution

This chapter investigates the integration of Internet of Things (IoT) technologies and smart sensors in humanitarian logistics to enhance transparency, tracking, and operational efficiency. It explores the use of RFID tags, GPS monitoring, and environmental sensors to improve inventory control, cold chain integrity, and real-time situational awareness. Drawing on field data and case examples from Türkiye and international organizations, the chapter addresses technical challenges such as connectivity, data security, and scalability, concluding with a strategic roadmap for sustainable IoT adoption in disaster-prone areas.

Chapter 5: Blockchain Technology in Humanitarian Logistics: Enhancing Transparency, Accountability, and Real-Time Decision Making

Highlighting the disruptive potential of blockchain, this chapter explores how distributed ledger technologies can address key inefficiencies in humanitarian supply chains. It analyzes how blockchain can enhance traceability, trust, and real-time data integrity when integrated with digital identity systems, smart contracts, and AI. Case studies such as Oxfam's UnBlocked Cash and blockchain-enabled aid transfers in Ukraine provide real-world insights. The chapter concludes with policy recommendations grounded in the Sustainable Development Goals (SDGs), calling for ethical governance and stronger digital capacity-building efforts across humanitarian networks.

Chapter 6: Redesigning Humanitarian Logistics with Intelligent Systems: From Chaos to Coordination

This chapter presents a comprehensive analysis of intelligent systems—including AI, predictive analytics, IoT, cloud computing, and GIS—and their collective potential to improve coordination in earthquake logistics. Using a thematic literature review and technology–value matrix, the author evaluates five illustrative scenarios to show how smart technologies can reduce operational chaos and support rapid decision-making in complex emergencies. An Integrated Smart Technology Ecosystem model is introduced, highlighting the interplay between technological capability, ethical governance, and institutional readiness as prerequisites for successful adoption.

Chapter 7: Designing Green Digital Logistics for Post-Disaster Recovery Operations

Blending ecological responsibility with digital innovation, this chapter examines how green digital logistics can support post-disaster recovery efforts. It discusses the application of digital health kits, blockchain platforms, and solar-powered systems to reduce environmental impact while maintaining operational effectiveness. Through global case studies, it highlights challenges such as e-waste and energy consumption, and explores the potential of circular logistics models. The chapter advocates for the use of sustainability assessment frameworks and climate-aligned innovation to ensure that humanitarian operations remain both effective and environmentally responsible.

Chapter 8: Sustainable and Eco-Friendly Solutions in Humanitarian Logistics

This chapter delves into the integration of sustainable logistics practices using circular economy principles, renewable energy, and green supply chain management. It explores the transition from reactive, resource-intensive logistics to proactive, eco-efficient models supported by modular infrastructure and energy-smart technologies. Emphasizing the role of governance and cross-sector collaboration, the chapter offers policy and implementation insights for fostering environmental stewardship and operational resilience in humanitarian operations.

Chapter 9: Understanding the Role of HVAC Systems in Türkiye's Disaster Relief and Emergency Aid Operations

This chapter highlights the crucial, yet often overlooked, role of HVAC systems in humanitarian aid, focusing on Türkiye's disaster response infrastructure. It examines how HVAC systems ensure indoor air quality, thermal comfort, and the continuity of cold chains in temporary shelters and emergency medical units. The analysis includes case learnings from the COVID-19 pandemic and the 2023 Kahramanmaraş earthquakes. The chapter calls for the institutionalization of HVAC-inclusive planning and outlines strategies for cross-sector collaboration to strengthen resilience and public health in emergency contexts.

Chapter 10: Strategic Integration of Aviation, AI, and Predictive Analytics in Humanitarian Logistics

This chapter explores the convergence of aviation technologies with AI and predictive analytics to optimize humanitarian logistics under pressure. Through case studies from the World Food Programme, UNHAS, and the Turkish Red Crescent, it shows how digital tools can accelerate aid delivery, forecast resource needs, and enable dynamic routing. Ethical, regulatory, and operational challenges are analyzed alongside a strategic integration roadmap, offering practical insights for aligning innovation with humanitarian values in increasingly complex crisis environments.

Chapter 11: Digitally Enabled Airbase Readiness and Strategic Airlift Planning for Humanitarian Crises through Aviation Logistics Transformation

Focusing on aviation logistics, this chapter investigates how digital transformation enhances airbase readiness and strategic airlift operations in humanitarian emergencies. It evaluates infrastructural components like ICT systems, fuel access, and runway capabilities, while also exploring the role of digital twins, blockchain, and AI in forecasting and operational coordination. Drawing from real-world missions, the chapter introduces a systems-based framework for integrated air logistics and offers strategic policy recommendations aligned with the Sustainable Development Goals (SDGs).

Chapter 12: Drones and UAVs for Rapid Emergency Relief and Last-Mile Delivery

This chapter discusses the increasing role of drones and UAVs in providing last-mile delivery and emergency relief in disaster zones. It reviews current technologies and examines how UAVs can overcome logistical disruptions caused by terrain, congestion, or infrastructure collapse. Featuring applications in digital twin modeling and IoT integration, the chapter addresses regulatory and ethical considerations and provides recommendations for scalable, sustainable UAV deployment in humanitarian missions.

Chapter 13: Smart Aviation Solutions for Humanitarian Aid: Integrating AI and Blockchain in WFP Air Logistics Operations

This chapter analyzes how AI and blockchain technologies are transforming aviation logistics in humanitarian operations, with a focus on the United Nations

Humanitarian Air Service (UNHAS). It details how digital tools enhance route optimization, demand forecasting, procurement, and cargo traceability. Through a critical assessment of challenges such as cybersecurity, system interoperability, and the digital divide, the chapter outlines a phased roadmap for digital adoption and offers strategic insights for building a more accountable and efficient humanitarian aviation network.

Chapter 14: Integrating AI and Blockchain into Humanitarian Air Logistics: A Case Study of Turkish Red Crescent's Aviation Response in Disaster Relief

Drawing on the Turkish Red Crescent's 2023 earthquake response, this chapter examines the practical integration of AI and blockchain in aviation-based humanitarian logistics. It highlights how these technologies improved forecasting, inventory tracking, and donation accountability through smart contracts and real-time data sharing. By comparing TRC's approach with global actors, the chapter offers replicable strategies and emphasizes the importance of digital literacy, ethical governance, and innovation scaling to build more transparent, resilient, and technology-enabled humanitarian systems.

We extend our deepest gratitude to all the contributors, whose work forms the foundation of this book. Their dedication to both rigorous scholarship and real-world impact has made this project possible. We also thank our institutions, Yeditepe University and Beykoz University, for their unwavering support of interdisciplinary and socially relevant research. Special appreciation goes to those working on the front lines of humanitarian aid—your courage, adaptability, and compassion continue to inspire and inform the academic and technological communities alike.

This book is not the final word, but part of an ongoing conversation. As the humanitarian landscape continues to shift, we hope these chapters serve as a launchpad for future inquiry and innovation. Whether addressing climate emergencies, health pandemics, or displacement crises, the humanitarian sector must remain agile, data-informed, and above all, committed to protecting human dignity. By fostering dialogue between technologists, logisticians, and humanitarian actors, we can better design systems that serve people—not just process.

In closing, we invite readers to approach this volume not just as a repository of information, but as a call to action. Let us reimagine humanitarian logistics not simply as a technical challenge, but as a collective responsibility—one that demands creativity, collaboration, and care. We are proud to present *Reshaping Humanitarian Logistics With AI, Predictive Analytics, and Autonomous Systems* as a contribution to that shared effort.

Chapter 1

The Role of Artificial Intelligence in Disaster Management and Aid Distribution

Efe Akboru
https://orcid.org/0009-0004-2153-8261
Yeditepe University, Istanbul, Turkey

ABSTRACT

The chapter investigates how Artificial Intelligence (AI) improves disaster management and aid distribution operations in humanitarian logistics. The chapter demonstrates how AI analyzes real-time data to enable fast decision processes and enhance early warning systems through machine learning capabilities. The chapter demonstrates how predictive modeling enhances resource allocation and logistics while AI optimizes aid delivery through geospatial data and automation and examines AI's impact on disaster recovery and long-term resilience but it also discusses the main challenges that include limited data availability and biased algorithms and ethical issues in humanitarian situations.

1. INTRODUCTION

In recent years, the frequency and intensity of natural and anthropogenic disasters have surged globally, driven by a combination of climate change, urbanization, and ecological fragility. As societies grapple with the escalating impacts of floods, wildfires, pandemics, and infrastructure failures, the limitations of traditional disaster management systems have become increasingly apparent. These systems often rely

DOI: 10.4018/979-8-3373-3643-5.ch001

on static response plans and delayed human-centered decision-making processes, which struggle to cope with the dynamic, complex nature of modern disasters. In this evolving context, Artificial Intelligence (AI) has emerged as a transformative force capable of enhancing the agility, accuracy, and scope of disaster management efforts (Abid et al., 2021; Tan et al., 2021). AI's capacity to process vast, heterogeneous data streams in real time offers unprecedented opportunities to improve early warning, crisis response, resource allocation, and long-term recovery planning.

AI applications in disaster management have expanded from simple risk assessments to sophisticated, integrated systems capable of supporting full-cycle disaster resilience. Machine learning algorithms can now identify disaster-prone zones, forecast hazard intensity, and simulate cascading failures with remarkable precision (Linardos et al., 2022; Akhyar et al., 2024). Tools such as neural networks, digital twins, and edge computing have enabled faster detection of hazards and more precise situational awareness (Fan et al., 2021; Aboualola et al., 2023). Meanwhile, the integration of AI with Internet of Things (IoT) devices and satellite data allows for dynamic modeling and automated monitoring of infrastructure, environmental conditions, and population movements (Khan et al., 2021; Chen et al., 2022). These technological advancements are reshaping how governments, humanitarian organizations, and urban planners prepare for and respond to crises.

However, the benefits of AI do not lie solely in operational efficiencies. The broader potential of AI lies in its ability to support socio-economic and psychological recovery, enable strategic planning, and strengthen long-term resilience. For example, AI-powered sentiment analysis and social media monitoring can reveal emotional distress levels and unmet needs across disaster-affected populations, thus guiding tailored mental health interventions and social support mechanisms (Sufi & Khalil, 2022; Abdul et al., 2024). AI also contributes to economic recovery by forecasting post-disaster employment disruptions, resource scarcities, and migration patterns (Dubey et al., 2022; Guha et al., 2022). This multidimensional capacity makes AI a pivotal tool in holistic disaster recovery, helping bridge immediate emergency response with long-term development and sustainability goals.

Despite these promising developments, the deployment of AI in disaster management is fraught with ethical, institutional, and technical challenges. Questions around data privacy, algorithmic bias, explainability, and the digital divide underscore the need for responsible AI governance. Gevaert et al. (2021) stress that fairness and accountability must be central to the development and deployment of AI tools, particularly in high-stakes scenarios involving vulnerable populations. The risk of overreliance on opaque, black-box models can undermine trust and lead to misinformed decisions, especially when human oversight is limited (Albahri et al., 2024; Munawar et al., 2022). Moreover, access to AI infrastructure remains highly unequal across countries and regions, potentially exacerbating existing inequalities in disaster preparedness and response capabilities (Varsha et al., 2024; Al-Raeei, 2025).

In response to these concerns, scholars and practitioners are calling for more inclusive, transparent, and context-sensitive approaches to AI development in disaster contexts. Participatory design processes, explainable AI models, ethical data collection practices, and capacity-building initiatives are increasingly viewed as essential components of sustainable AI integration (Akhyar et al., 2024; Abid et al., 2023). Institutions must also invest in interdisciplinary collaborations that bring together engineers, social scientists, policymakers, and affected communities to co-design and govern AI systems. These collaborative frameworks are necessary to ensure that AI tools align with societal values, legal standards, and environmental ethics while delivering tangible benefits in real-world disaster scenarios.

This study explores the multifaceted role of AI in disaster management, with a focus on its applications in early warning systems, resource allocation, recovery planning, and resilience building. By synthesizing recent advancements in AI technologies with empirical insights from disaster science, this research aims to highlight both the opportunities and constraints of AI-enhanced systems. Special attention is given to ethical dimensions, equity concerns, and the socio-technical dynamics that shape the effectiveness and legitimacy of AI interventions in disaster-prone contexts. Through a comprehensive review of literature and case applications, the study contributes to the ongoing discourse on how AI can be harnessed not only for technological innovation but also for inclusive and sustainable disaster governance.

2. THE ROLE OF AI IN DISASTER EARLY-WARNING SYSTEMS

Artificial Intelligence (AI) is revolutionizing disaster early-warning systems by enabling faster, more precise, and contextually aware responses to impending crises. AI excels at processing high volumes of multi-source data such as satellite imagery, meteorological records, seismic activity, and hydrological patterns, which are critical in early-stage disaster forecasting. According to Abid et al. (2021), AI's ability to synthesize this information into actionable insights allows for timely alerts that significantly improve emergency preparedness. Unlike conventional systems that rely heavily on fixed thresholds or historical trends, AI systems adapt in real time and identify previously unnoticed correlations. These capabilities support decision-makers in issuing early warnings that are both faster and more reliable. By detecting subtle environmental changes before they escalate into disasters, AI strengthens disaster risk reduction frameworks globally.

The implementation of AI in early-warning systems also promotes a shift from reactive emergency responses to proactive and preventative strategies. Abid et al.

(2023) emphasize that AI-powered systems can facilitate scenario simulation and risk scoring, allowing authorities to plan evacuations or mobilize resources before disasters strike. These systems have become especially relevant in regions vulnerable to recurring natural hazards such as typhoons, landslides, and earthquakes. Governments and disaster management agencies are increasingly incorporating AI into national risk platforms to optimize warning thresholds and communication protocols. By combining predictive analytics with spatial data, AI can map high-risk zones with extraordinary precision. This enhances the effectiveness of land-use policies and risk communication strategies, reducing vulnerability in hazard-prone areas.

Despite the impressive capabilities of AI in enhancing disaster preparedness, its adoption still faces several obstacles. Challenges related to data accessibility, institutional capacity, and ethical governance continue to hinder AI's full integration into early-warning architectures. Gevaert et al. (2021) caution that while AI offers enormous potential, its use must be guided by principles of fairness, accountability, and transparency. Particularly in contexts involving marginalized or digitally excluded populations, AI-based early-warning tools must ensure equitable service delivery. Moreover, the complexity of integrating AI models with legacy early-warning infrastructures requires cross-sector collaboration and continual system refinement. Thus, while AI undoubtedly enhances the efficacy and timeliness of disaster warnings, its successful deployment must be underpinned by strong governance and inclusive digital strategies.

2.1 AI-Based Data Integration and Real-Time Monitoring

Real-time data integration is central to the success of AI-driven early-warning systems. Modern disasters unfold rapidly and often unpredictably, necessitating a continuous flow of up-to-date information from a wide range of sources. According to Tan et al. (2021), machine learning models can simultaneously process meteorological data, geospatial imagery, social media feeds, and sensor outputs to construct an evolving picture of risk. This integration supports the identification of anomalies or deviations from normal environmental behavior, enabling the issuance of timely alerts. The inclusion of unconventional data sources, such as tweets and user-generated content, expands the system's sensitivity to real-world events. These multi-modal data environments enhance the granularity and reliability of predictions, especially when coupled with high-frequency satellite monitoring and internet-of-things (IoT) sensors deployed in vulnerable areas.

The convergence of AI with edge computing has dramatically improved the speed and efficiency of real-time disaster monitoring. Aboualola et al. (2023) explore how integrating AI at the network edge allows for local data analysis without reliance on centralized data centers, thereby reducing latency. This is especially important in low-connectivity or disaster-stricken areas where communication infrastructure is compromised. Edge-based AI systems have been successfully applied in flood-prone urban regions to manage real-time water level monitoring and issue early alerts. Additionally, AI models integrated with surveillance drones and unmanned aerial vehicles (UAVs) provide high-resolution imaging and tracking of disaster impact zones. Khan et al. (2021) highlight that UAVs with embedded AI can autonomously navigate hazardous areas, collect environmental data, and relay it to emergency control centers without putting human operators at risk.

Real-time AI monitoring tools also play a pivotal role in disaster command and control operations. These tools can populate dashboards with live data visualizations, scenario projections, and heatmaps, offering emergency managers an up-to-date and comprehensive view of unfolding crises. Sufi and Khalil (2022) demonstrated that AI-based systems employing sentiment analysis and location intelligence extracted from social media can identify distress zones and emerging needs during disasters. This type of monitoring is particularly effective for rapidly evolving situations like earthquakes or wildfires, where official reporting channels may lag. Furthermore, integrating AI with public safety apps allows civilians to contribute data, enhancing community-based situational awareness. These tools transform passive populations into active sensors, thereby amplifying the intelligence-gathering capacity of disaster response agencies.

2.2 Predictive Modeling and Real-World Applications

AI's predictive capabilities are among the most valuable assets in disaster management, allowing decision-makers to forecast when, where, and how a disaster might occur. These models are trained using vast datasets that include historical disaster records, climate variables, and socio-economic indicators to predict the probability and intensity of future events. Linardos et al. (2022) review various machine learning techniques—including random forests, support vector machines, and deep learning networks—that have shown promise in modeling phenomena such as landslides, wildfires, and tsunamis. These models operate by identifying hidden patterns or nonlinear interactions among multiple variables, offering a level of precision far beyond what traditional statistical tools can provide. The increasing availability of high-quality, open-access datasets has further facilitated the development of scalable and transferable predictive models.

Fan et al. (2021) introduce the concept of the "Disaster City Digital Twin," a sophisticated AI-based framework that replicates urban environments in a virtual setting. This digital twin allows emergency planners to simulate disaster scenarios, evaluate alternative response strategies, and understand cascading effects before real-world events occur. For example, urban flood simulations can help identify which streets or infrastructure would be most affected, allowing for targeted investments in resilience. In addition, AI-based crop yield forecasts and soil moisture predictions are being used in the agricultural sector to mitigate drought risk (Chen et al., 2022). These applications go beyond warnings and enable preemptive action by stakeholders, making disaster preparedness more efficient and data-driven. Real-world deployments of these models are increasing in both high-income and developing countries, with many governments partnering with academic institutions and private firms to expand AI readiness.

The scope of predictive modeling extends to public health and logistics during disaster situations. Abdul et al. (2024) highlight how AI-enhanced healthcare systems can forecast the surge in patient numbers, allocate medical resources, and optimize emergency triage protocols. Similarly, predictive algorithms are used in humanitarian logistics to estimate resource demand and optimize supply chain distribution to affected areas (Dubey et al., 2022). These innovations are particularly crucial in post-disaster environments where infrastructure may be damaged and timely decisions can save lives. Despite these achievements, the reliability of predictive models hinges on the quality, diversity, and completeness of the input data. As disasters become more frequent and complex under climate change, the integration of AI-driven forecasting into institutional disaster management strategies will become increasingly indispensable.

2.3 Challenges and Limitations

While the potential of AI in disaster early-warning systems is immense, several technical, social, and ethical limitations remain unresolved. One of the most critical issues is data accessibility and standardization. As noted by Gevaert et al. (2021), AI systems rely heavily on large volumes of high-quality data, yet in many parts of the world, especially in the Global South, such datasets are either unavailable or highly fragmented. Additionally, integrating heterogeneous data formats from satellites, local sensors, and social platforms often introduces noise and inconsistency. These challenges undermine the performance and transferability of AI models, particularly in areas with limited digital infrastructure. Moreover, the lack of interoperability among existing disaster management systems makes it difficult to implement AI tools that require centralized coordination.

A second major challenge is the issue of trust and interpretability of AI outputs. According to Albahri et al. (2024), many AI models function as "black boxes," offering predictions without clear explanations. This opacity is problematic in high-stakes environments such as disaster response, where transparency and accountability are essential. Without an understanding of how a model arrived at a conclusion, emergency managers may be hesitant to act on AI-generated warnings. Furthermore, biases in training datasets can lead to unfair or inaccurate outcomes, potentially putting vulnerable populations at greater risk. Addressing these concerns requires the development of explainable AI (XAI) models that can communicate reasoning to end-users. Ethical AI governance, including audits and risk assessments, should also be embedded into early-warning systems to ensure equitable outcomes.

Beyond technical and ethical considerations, there are significant institutional and operational barriers to AI adoption in disaster management. Munawar et al. (2022) argue that most disaster management agencies lack the technical capacity and trained personnel to implement and maintain AI systems. Resistance to change, lack of regulatory frameworks, and high implementation costs further impede progress. In many cases, AI integration is viewed as an experimental add-on rather than a core component of disaster strategy. Varsha et al. (2024) emphasize the importance of institutional readiness and stakeholder engagement for AI tools to be sustainably deployed. International collaboration, capacity-building programs, and targeted funding are therefore critical for ensuring that AI tools are both accessible and effectively utilized across diverse risk landscapes. Ultimately, the full potential of AI in early-warning systems can only be realized through inclusive, multidisciplinary approaches that bridge technical innovation with practical governance.

3. RESOURCE ALLOCATION AND AID DISTRIBUTION

The integration of Artificial Intelligence (AI) into disaster response logistics is reshaping the way humanitarian aid and emergency resources are allocated, particularly in complex, uncertain, and rapidly changing environments. AI technologies facilitate faster data processing, predictive modeling, and decision support, which together allow for more efficient and equitable distribution of resources. Traditionally, aid logistics have been plagued by inefficiencies such as mismatches between supply and demand, poor visibility in inventory systems, and slow manual coordination (Özkanlısoy & Akkartal, 2021). With the introduction of AI, these gaps are now being bridged through real-time information integration and advanced forecasting techniques. The use of digital twins, for instance, enables dynamic simulations of disaster zones to optimize delivery routes and anticipate bottlenecks (Cebir & Akkartal, 2024). These innovations support not only the timeliness but also the sustainability of operations in areas of need.

AI-based resource allocation models excel by prioritizing locations and populations based on the severity of impact, urgency of need, and available infrastructure. These systems often leverage satellite imagery, drone surveillance, and real-time weather data to map affected regions and assess logistical feasibility. Deep learning models are then used to match aid requirements with available resources and distribution capabilities. Akhyar et al. (2024) describe how such models have successfully improved disaster logistics by enhancing transparency and reducing misallocations. Moreover, in the Turkish context, lessons from the disruption caused by the Suez Canal blockage have emphasized the need for agility and redundancy in global and national supply chains (Özkanlısoy & Akkartal, 2022). This further underscores the value of AI tools that not only respond to disasters but also support long-term resilience planning by simulating cascading effects and offering adaptive solutions.

The allocation of medical supplies, food, water, and shelter materials during disasters is often constrained by logistical challenges such as damaged roads, fuel shortages, and sudden changes in population density. AI helps overcome these barriers by dynamically rerouting supplies using real-time sensor data and infrastructure condition reports. Maiti and Kayal (2024) argue that AI-driven systems can continuously adapt to changing on-ground realities, minimizing delivery delays and resource wastage. AI also enables collaborative logistics models by allowing multiple organizations to synchronize inventory levels and optimize warehousing strategies. In sustainable logistics contexts, these approaches align well with green supply chain initiatives, as discussed by Akkartal and Aras (2021), where fleet management decisions must consider both environmental impact and operational efficiency. In this way, AI serves as a link between disaster relief effectiveness and broader sustainability goals in humanitarian supply chains.

Furthermore, AI enhances visibility in the last-mile delivery phase—arguably the most difficult component of disaster logistics. This is especially critical in urban slums or remote rural areas where infrastructure is weak and data is sparse. Öztürk and Akkartal (2024) note that Internet of Things (IoT) devices and AI algorithms are increasingly used to manage last-mile routing in commercial supply chains, a method that has now begun transferring into the humanitarian sector. By monitoring temperature-sensitive items like vaccines and perishable goods, these systems prevent spoilage and increase delivery accountability. Integration with blockchain systems has also been explored to ensure traceability and reduce corruption in aid distribution. As digital transformation accelerates globally, the logistical architectures of disaster response must evolve in parallel to absorb emerging AI capabilities and build robust, transparent, and fair allocation mechanisms.

In addition to operational advantages, AI contributes to strategic decision-making by facilitating scenario planning, cost-benefit analysis, and post-disaster learning. Decision-makers can use AI to model hypothetical resource allocation strategies under different budgetary, environmental, and socio-political constraints. Abdelhadi and Akkartal (2024) emphasize that AI-enhanced data environments enable retail and logistics leaders in Türkiye to improve structural efficiency through simulations and advanced analytics. Similarly, in the public disaster domain, AI enables governments and NGOs to transition from reactive to anticipatory models of resource distribution.

Mızrak (2024) stresses the need for effective change management strategies to ensure that organizations can integrate these AI capabilities into existing workflows and overcome institutional inertia. As disasters become more frequent and intense due to climate change, these strategic integrations are no longer optional but essential for system-wide agility and preparedness.

Finally, the sustainability of aid distribution systems is closely linked to the energy and environmental considerations that accompany logistical operations. The use of AI in routing optimization and energy-aware fleet management contributes to reducing carbon emissions, aligning humanitarian logistics with the principles of green supply chain management (Mızrak & Akkartal, 2024). In maritime and land-based logistics alike, the deployment of AI for selecting alternative fuels or optimizing vehicle use is vital, as noted in Mızrak (2022) and Mizrak et al. (2024). Moreover, post-disaster reconstruction phases also benefit from AI-assisted prioritization of infrastructure repair and material deployment. The integration of TRIZ-based sustainability modeling for alternative energy systems, as proposed by Danışman and Akkartal (2023), reveals a parallel between long-term energy resilience and the efficient deployment of resources in crisis scenarios. Ultimately, AI's role in resource allocation and aid distribution is not just technological—it is strategic, ethical, and increasingly indispensable for resilient disaster management.

4. AI IN DISASTER RECOVERY AND RECONSTRUCTION

4.1 Socio-Economic and Psychological Recovery

Artificial Intelligence (AI) plays an increasingly important role in post-disaster socio-economic and psychological recovery by enabling targeted and evidence-based interventions. In the aftermath of a disaster, communities often face multidimensional challenges—loss of livelihoods, psychological trauma, population displacement, and disrupted social services. AI systems, particularly those using social media sentiment analysis and geospatial data, help identify affected populations' emotional well-being and economic vulnerabilities in real time (Sufi & Khalil, 2022). This technology assists humanitarian agencies in delivering customized support programs based on community needs rather than generalized assumptions. For instance, AI-powered platforms can analyze language use and emotional tone across affected regions to detect collective stress levels or post-traumatic symptoms, allowing for more timely mental health interventions (Gevaert et al., 2021).

In addition to psychological insights, AI-driven analytics can track employment trends, housing recovery, and income fluctuations in disaster-hit regions. This allows authorities to design responsive economic rehabilitation policies. Dubey et al. (2022)

argue that AI-based big data culture enhances the agility and resilience of humanitarian supply chains, particularly when addressing socio-economic disparities in post-crisis recovery. Governments and NGOs are now increasingly using machine learning models to map post-disaster poverty concentrations and deliver financial aid more equitably. Abdul et al. (2024) further highlight that AI-integrated healthcare systems can be adapted to monitor both physical and mental health trends in displaced populations, ensuring holistic recovery. These systems allow for longitudinal tracking, which is critical in measuring recovery effectiveness over time, especially in vulnerable demographic groups such as children and the elderly.

Moreover, AI models have been used to predict migration patterns and identify social cohesion challenges emerging after disasters. By integrating census, health, and movement data, neural network algorithms can project community reconstruction needs and flag risks of prolonged displacement or marginalization (Guha et al., 2022). This type of predictive modeling enables policymakers to establish early outreach programs or prevent social fragmentation. In cases where urban infrastructure is destroyed, AI-supported systems can also help reassign populations to temporary housing while minimizing disruption to their economic activities (Al-Raeei, 2025). In this way, AI doesn't just aid in delivering relief—it enables adaptive and inclusive social recovery planning that can address long-term psychological and economic development goals.

4.2 Recovery Planning and Infrastructure Reconstruction

AI is revolutionizing infrastructure reconstruction after disasters by providing data-driven tools for risk assessment, prioritization, and efficient resource deployment. Modern AI models use pre-disaster and post-disaster data to perform damage detection and structural health assessments through high-resolution imagery and deep learning algorithms (Akhyar et al., 2024). These assessments are significantly faster and more accurate than manual inspections, helping decision-makers quickly prioritize which roads, bridges, hospitals, or schools need urgent restoration. Linardos et al. (2022) highlight that machine learning algorithms can also be used to simulate different reconstruction scenarios based on budget constraints, community needs, and environmental risks, ensuring strategic investment in rebuilding efforts.

One emerging tool in this space is the concept of "Digital Twins" in disaster-struck cities. As Fan et al. (2021) explain, these are AI-driven virtual replicas of physical urban environments that integrate real-time data for modeling various reconstruction pathways. Such tools allow planners to visualize the short-term and long-term implications of their decisions and optimize urban design for future resilience. In earthquake-hit or flood-prone areas, AI-powered simulations can assess soil composition, structural fatigue, and proximity to risk zones, thereby informing smarter land use and safer rebuilding protocols. AI also assists in workforce coordination and procurement logistics, streamlining contractor assignments and material sourcing processes (Abid et al., 2021).

Furthermore, remote sensing data integrated with AI has proven critical in monitoring agricultural infrastructure recovery. After major climatic disasters such as droughts or floods, AI models analyze satellite data to detect changes in vegetation patterns, crop stress, and irrigation needs (Chen et al., 2022). This enables agricultural policymakers to plan reconstruction not just in terms of physical repairs but also in revitalizing food supply systems. AI also supports insurance claim verification by comparing satellite imagery and on-ground photos to verify losses objectively. This accelerates disbursement and minimizes fraud. Ultimately, the use of AI in reconstruction ensures that recovery is not only faster and cost-effective but also more transparent and future-oriented.

4.3 Building Long-Term Resilience

Beyond immediate recovery, AI is pivotal in building long-term resilience by embedding risk awareness and adaptive capacity into urban and rural systems. AI tools contribute to resilience by enabling continuous learning from past disasters and integrating that knowledge into predictive systems. For example, Abid et al. (2023) stress that AI-based feedback loops allow emergency systems to evolve, improving preparedness for future shocks. AI-powered early warning systems and post-disaster recovery models work in tandem to form a continuous risk management cycle. When used together with edge computing and decentralized monitoring systems, AI helps maintain vigilance in areas prone to recurring threats such as wildfires, hurricanes, or disease outbreaks (Aboualola et al., 2023).

One of the most promising areas is infrastructure resilience modeling, where AI predicts how systems will behave under stress and recommends design modifications. Maiti and Kayal (2024) emphasize that AI techniques such as reinforcement learning can suggest resilient construction practices by simulating various hazard scenarios. AI also aids in climate adaptation planning by identifying vulnerable regions and recommending environmental mitigation strategies. According to Tan et al. (2021), integrating AI with IoT sensors in infrastructure helps cities monitor aging assets, predict failures, and schedule maintenance proactively. Over time, this predictive maintenance capability reduces the likelihood of cascading failures during future disasters and contributes to more robust urban environments.

Finally, building resilience also involves social and institutional transformation, which AI can support through better governance, transparency, and stakeholder engagement. Varsha et al. (2024) argue that AI and machine learning can facilitate community-centered disaster planning by incorporating local knowledge into digital systems. Moreover, trustworthy AI practices—such as algorithmic fairness, accountability, and data privacy—are essential to gaining public trust and ensuring equitable access to resilience technologies (Albahri et al., 2024). Munawar et al. (2022) also highlight the role of AI in training simulations and serious games, which build decision-makers' capacity to manage future crises. In sum, the use of AI in post-disaster settings is evolving from a reactive tool to a strategic enabler of long-term resilience, sustainability, and adaptive governance.

5. ETHICAL DIMENSIONS OF AI IN DISASTER MANAGEMENT

The growing reliance on artificial intelligence (AI) in disaster management presents significant ethical challenges alongside its technological promise. While AI enhances preparedness, response, and recovery, it also raises concerns about fairness, accountability, privacy, and inclusiveness. AI systems often make decisions based on data collected from various sources, including satellites, social media, IoT sensors, and user-generated content. However, this data-driven automation can inadvertently reinforce existing social biases or marginalize vulnerable groups if not carefully managed. Gevaert et al. (2021) emphasize that the ethical use of AI in disaster contexts must be guided by the principles of transparency, inclusivity, and human rights. This is particularly vital in high-stakes scenarios where AI influences resource allocation, risk assessment, or evacuation priorities.

One pressing ethical issue is data privacy and surveillance. In the effort to collect real-time information during a crisis, AI systems often gather personal data from mobile phones, social media platforms, and other digital traces. While this can greatly enhance situational awareness, it risks violating individuals' privacy rights—especially in regions with weak data protection laws. Sufi and Khalil (2022) note that AI-based sentiment analysis tools used for monitoring public distress through online platforms must be transparent about data usage and adhere to ethical guidelines to prevent misuse. Similarly, edge computing systems that process data locally may reduce central exposure but still raise concerns about consent and security (Aboualola et al., 2023). Striking the right balance between rapid data-driven action and ethical data stewardship is essential for maintaining public trust during crises.

Another major ethical dilemma arises from algorithmic bias. AI models trained on historical or incomplete datasets may produce skewed predictions that disadvantage certain populations. For instance, areas with historically less infrastructure or representation in data systems may receive lower prioritization in resource distribution algorithms. Albahri et al. (2024) argue that trustworthiness and fairness must be built into AI from the ground up, particularly in life-critical applications such as disaster response. This includes not only technical efforts like bias correction and explainable AI (XAI), but also governance frameworks that enable third-party audits and community engagement. Without such safeguards, AI tools may perpetuate inequalities under the guise of efficiency.

Explainability and transparency also represent core ethical concerns. In many disaster management scenarios, decisions must be made quickly, often with limited human oversight. Yet when AI models function as "black boxes," it becomes difficult to understand or challenge their outputs. This opacity can erode trust and reduce accountability. Akhyar et al. (2024) highlight that explainable AI techniques are crucial for ensuring that emergency managers and policymakers can understand and justify AI-driven decisions. Additionally, Abid et al. (2023) emphasize the importance of integrating human-in-the-loop systems where expert judgment and machine learning outputs are used collaboratively. This approach can help bridge the gap between automation and ethical oversight, especially in time-sensitive environments.

Equity in AI deployment is another vital consideration. Not all regions or organizations have equal access to advanced AI technologies or the infrastructure required to support them. As a result, there is a growing digital divide in disaster preparedness and response capacities. Dubey et al. (2022) underscore how AI-enhanced humanitarian supply chains can exacerbate inequities if poorer regions are unable to afford or implement such tools. In addition, Munawar et al. (2022) note that institutional readiness and technical literacy are often lacking in many low- and middle-income countries, making ethical deployment of AI a challenge. Promoting open-source AI tools, localized training programs, and global partnerships is therefore critical for reducing inequalities and ensuring the ethical scalability of AI in disaster management.

Responsibility attribution is also ethically complex in AI-driven disaster contexts. When an AI system misclassifies risks or fails to detect a hazard, determining who is accountable—the software developer, the user, or the institution—can be unclear. Linardos et al. (2022) stress that disaster management agencies must establish clear protocols for accountability and risk-sharing in the use of automated systems. Fan et al. (2021) propose embedding AI into digital twin platforms that simulate decisions in virtual environments before real-world deployment, thereby reducing uncertainty and creating clearer chains of responsibility. Furthermore, creating governance structures for AI oversight that involve legal, ethical, and technical experts can strengthen accountability mechanisms and provide recourse in the event of failure.

The ethical implications of AI are further complicated by its role in psychological and social dynamics during disasters. Public perceptions of fairness, transparency, and trustworthiness in AI systems can significantly affect compliance with disaster warnings and participation in relief programs. Abdul et al. (2024) suggest that culturally sensitive design and communication strategies are necessary to ensure that affected populations understand and trust AI-assisted interventions. Community involvement in AI system design—especially through participatory approaches—can foster local ownership and ethical alignment. Guha et al. (2022) also emphasize the need for AI systems to reflect community values and social norms to ensure relevance and legitimacy.

Lastly, long-term resilience depends not only on the effectiveness but also the ethical sustainability of AI systems. Al-Raeei (2025) argues that AI must align with broader sustainability and justice frameworks to support equitable urban development post-disaster. This involves incorporating ethical principles into AI lifecycle management—from design and training to deployment and retirement. It also requires continuous evaluation of AI impacts on society and the environment. Varsha et al. (2024) reinforce this perspective by advocating for ethical AI standards in all stages of disaster management, including mitigation, response, recovery, and reconstruction. As AI continues to influence global disaster risk governance, embedding ethics at every layer is no longer optional but an imperative for responsible and inclusive innovation.

6. CONCLUSION

The integration of Artificial Intelligence (AI) into disaster management systems marks a paradigm shift in how societies anticipate, respond to, and recover from crises. As demonstrated throughout this study, AI enhances decision-making across the full disaster lifecycle—from early warning and resource distribution to socio-economic recovery and long-term resilience planning. However, realizing the full potential of AI requires not only technical advancement but also strategic foresight, ethical responsibility, and organizational adaptability. This is particularly critical in sectors such as logistics, infrastructure, and humanitarian supply chains, where disruptions have wide-reaching consequences. As Özkanlısoy and Akkartal (2021) emphasize, digital transformation must be viewed as a continuous strategic endeavor, not a one-time solution. This principle is equally applicable to AI deployment in disaster management, where agility and adaptability are as vital as accuracy.

The COVID-19 pandemic, the Suez Canal blockage, and recent climate-induced disasters have exposed vulnerabilities in global supply chains and emergency response mechanisms. These events underscore the need for intelligent, real-time systems capable of adapting to uncertainty and disruption (Özkanlısoy & Akkartal, 2022). AI systems embedded in digital twin frameworks, IoT networks, and predictive logistics have proven instrumental in enhancing visibility, optimizing last-mile delivery, and reducing lead times during disaster recovery phases (Cebir & Akkartal, 2024; Öztürk & Akkartal, 2024). Moreover, integrating sustainability metrics and resilience modeling—such as those proposed by Mizrak et al. (2024) for Istanbul

Airport—ensures that AI-driven disaster strategies are not only reactive but also regenerative, supporting green transitions in high-risk sectors.

From a strategic management lens, AI-enhanced disaster systems must be aligned with broader goals of sustainability, innovation, and crisis resilience. Studies in maritime logistics (Mızrak, 2024), fleet sustainability (Akkartal & Aras, 2021), and renewable energy use in transport (Mızrak & Akkartal, 2024) show that strategic integration of advanced technologies significantly improves operational and environmental performance. These findings echo the importance of embedding AI within sector-specific planning and governance frameworks. Furthermore, change management theories highlight that technological adaptation requires cultural and structural readiness within organizations (Mızrak, 2024). In the context of disaster management, this means equipping institutions with the capacity to incorporate AI ethically, inclusively, and effectively, while fostering cross-sector collaboration and public trust.

Finally, ethical considerations remain central to the future of AI in disaster management. Transparency, fairness, inclusivity, and accountability must be at the core of system design and deployment. As discussed in this study, algorithmic biases, data privacy concerns, and disparities in technological access pose risks that could undermine the intended benefits of AI if left unaddressed. A holistic approach—incorporating sustainability principles, ethical governance, and evidence-based policymaking—will be essential for AI systems to contribute meaningfully to disaster resilience. The structural analyses of Turkey's logistics and retail sectors further affirm that efficiency gains must be balanced with equitable access and social responsibility (Abdelhadi & Akkartal, 2024; Mızrak, 2023).

In conclusion, AI is not a substitute for strategic leadership in disaster risk management—it is a catalyst. To fully harness its transformative potential, stakeholders must move beyond viewing AI as a standalone tool and instead embed it into integrated, adaptive, and ethically grounded disaster management systems. This requires robust digital infrastructure, cross-disciplinary partnerships, and a forward-looking mindset that bridges innovation with resilience, and efficiency with equity. As the climate crisis deepens and global risk landscapes evolve, the strategic application of AI will remain a cornerstone in building safer, smarter, and more sustainable societies.

REFERENCES

Abdelhadi, A., & Akkartal, E. (2024). Supply chain efficiency a structural analysis in turkey's retail sector. *Brazilian Journal of Operations & Production Management, 21*(3), 2150–2150. DOI: 10.14488/BJOPM.2150.2024

Abdul, S., Adeghe, E. P., Adegoke, B. O., Adegoke, A. A., & Udedeh, E. H. (2024). AI-enhanced healthcare management during natural disasters: Conceptual insights. *Engineering Science & Technology Journal, 5*(5), 1794–1816. DOI: 10.51594/estj.v5i5.1155

Abid, S. K., Chan, S. W., Sulaiman, N., Bhatti, U., & Nazir, U. (2023, October). Present and future of artificial intelligence in disaster management. In *2023 international conference on engineering management of communication and technology (EMCTECH)* (pp. 1-7). IEEE. DOI: 10.1109/EMCTECH58502.2023.10296991

Abid, S. K., Sulaiman, N., Chan, S. W., Nazir, U., Abid, M., Han, H., Ariza-Montes, A., & Vega-Muñoz, A. (2021). Toward an integrated disaster management approach: How artificial intelligence can boost disaster management. *Sustainability (Basel), 13*(22), 12560. DOI: 10.3390/su132212560

Aboualola, M., Abualsaud, K., Khattab, T., Zorba, N., & Hassanein, H. S. (2023). Edge technologies for disaster management: A survey of social media and artificial intelligence integration. *IEEE Access : Practical Innovations, Open Solutions, 11*, 73782–73802. DOI: 10.1109/ACCESS.2023.3293035

Akhyar, A., Zulkifley, M. A., Lee, J., Song, T., Han, J., Cho, C., & Hong, B. W. (2024). Deep artificial intelligence applications for natural disaster management systems: A methodological review. *Ecological Indicators, 163*, 112067. DOI: 10.1016/j.ecolind.2024.112067

Akkartal, E., & Aras, G. Y. (2021). Sustainability in fleet management. *Journal of Advanced Research in Economics and Administrative Sciences, 2*(3), 13–39. DOI: 10.47631/jareas.v2i3.288

Albahri, A. S., Khaleel, Y. L., Habeeb, M. A., Ismael, R. D., Hameed, Q. A., Deveci, M., Homod, R. Z., Albahri, O. S., Alamoodi, A. H., & Alzubaidi, L. (2024). A systematic review of trustworthy artificial intelligence applications in natural disasters. *Computers & Electrical Engineering, 118*, 109409. DOI: 10.1016/j.compeleceng.2024.109409

Cebir, Y., & Akkartal, E. (2024). Digital twin in logistics and supply chain management. In *Strategic Innovations for Dynamic Supply Chains* (pp. 170–192). IGI Global. DOI: 10.4018/979-8-3693-3575-8.ch008

Chen, S., Lin, H., & Yang, G. (2022). Efficient agricultural disaster financing using satellite data and artificial intelligence. *Computers & Electrical Engineering, 103*, 108394. DOI: 10.1016/j.compeleceng.2022.108394

Danisman, M., & Akkartal, E. (2023). Defining a new business model for sustainable biomass production from forestry residues in Türkiye by using TRIZ. *International Journal of Energy Economics and Policy, 13*(3), 243–253. DOI: 10.32479/ijeep.13985

Dubey, R., Bryde, D. J., Dwivedi, Y. K., Graham, G., & Foropon, C. (2022). Impact of artificial intelligence-driven big data analytics culture on agility and resilience in humanitarian supply chain: A practice-based view. *International Journal of Production Economics, 250*, 108618. DOI: 10.1016/j.ijpe.2022.108618

Fan, C., Zhang, C., Yahja, A., & Mostafavi, A. (2021). Disaster City Digital Twin: A vision for integrating artificial and human intelligence for disaster management. *International Journal of Information Management, 56*, 102049. DOI: 10.1016/j.ijinfomgt.2019.102049

Gevaert, C. M., Carman, M., Rosman, B., Georgiadou, Y., & Soden, R. (2021). Fairness and accountability of AI in disaster risk management: Opportunities and challenges. *Patterns (New York, N.Y.), 2*(11), 100363. DOI: 10.1016/j.patter.2021.100363 PMID: 34820647

Guha, S., Jana, R. K., & Sanyal, M. K. (2022). Artificial neural network approaches for disaster management: A literature review. *International Journal of Disaster Risk Reduction, 81*, 103276. DOI: 10.1016/j.ijdrr.2022.103276

Khan, S. I., Qadir, Z., Munawar, H. S., Nayak, S. R., Budati, A. K., Verma, K. D., & Prakash, D. (2021). UAVs path planning architecture for effective medical emergency response in future networks. *Physical Communication, 47*, 101337. DOI: 10.1016/j.phycom.2021.101337

Linardos, V., Drakaki, M., Tzionas, P., & Karnavas, Y. L. (2022). Machine learning in disaster management: recent developments in methods and applications. *Machine Learning and Knowledge Extraction, 4*(2).

Maiti, M., & Kayal, P. (2024). Exploring innovative techniques for damage control during natural disasters. *Journal of Safety Science and Resilience = An Quan Ke Xue Yu Ren Xing (Ying Wen), 5*(2), 147–155. DOI: 10.1016/j.jnlssr.2024.02.004

Mızrak, F. (2022). An Evaluation for the Use of Alternative Vehicle Technologies and Energy Resources in Logistic Sector with a Strategic Approach. In *Circular Economy and the Energy Market: Achieving Sustainable Economic Development Through Energy Policy* (pp. 159–171). Springer International Publishing. DOI: 10.1007/978-3-031-13146-2_13

Mızrak, F. (2023). Managing Risks and Crises in the Logistics Sector: A Comprehensive Analysis of Strategies and Prioritization Using AHP Method. Meriç Uluslararası Sosyal ve Stratejik Araştırmalar Dergisi, 7(Özel Sayı), 114-148.

Mızrak, F. (2024). Effective change management strategies: Exploring dynamic models for organizational transformation. In *Perspectives on artificial intelligence in times of turbulence: Theoretical background to applications* (pp. 135–162). IGI Global.

Mızrak, F. (2024). Strategies for Sustainable Business Growth in Maritime Logistics. In Trends, Challenges, and Practices in Contemporary Strategic Management (pp. 108-125). IGI Global Scientific Publishing. DOI: 10.4018/979-8-3693-1155-4.ch006

Mızrak, F., & Akkartal, G. R. (2024). An Analysis of Alternative Energy Sources and Applications in Maritime Transportation with a Strategic Management Approach. Decision Making in Interdisciplinary Renewable Energy Projects: Navigating Energy Investments, 97-109.

Mizrak, F., Polat, L., & Tasar, S. A. (2024). Applying Entropy Weighting and 2-Tuple Linguistic T-Spherical Fuzzy MCDM: A Case Study of Developing a Strategic Sustainability Plan for Istanbul Airport. *Sustainability (Basel)*, *16*(24), 11104. DOI: 10.3390/su162411104

Munawar, H. S., Mojtahedi, M., Hammad, A. W., Kouzani, A., & Mahmud, M. P. (2022). Disruptive technologies as a solution for disaster risk management: A review. *The Science of the Total Environment*, *806*, 151351. DOI: 10.1016/j.scitotenv.2021.151351 PMID: 34740667

Özkanlısoy, Ö., & Akkartal, E. (2021). Digital transformation in supply chains: Current applications, contributions and challenges. *Business & Management Studies: An International Journal*, *9*(1), 32–55.

Özkanlısoy, Ö., & Akkartal, E. (2022). The effect of Suez Canal blockage on supply chains. *Dokuz Eylül Üniversitesi Denizcilik Fakültesi Dergisi*, *14*(1), 51–79. DOI: 10.18613/deudfd.933816

Öztürk, S., & Akkartal, E. (2024). Internet of Things (IoT) Applications in Last Mile Delivery. In Strategic Innovations for Dynamic Supply Chains (pp. 193-215). IGI Global.

Sufi, F. K., & Khalil, I. (2022). Automated disaster monitoring from social media posts using AI-based location intelligence and sentiment analysis. *IEEE Transactions on Computational Social Systems*.

Tan, L., Guo, J., Mohanarajah, S., & Zhou, K. (2021). Can we detect trends in natural disaster management with artificial intelligence? A review of modeling practices. *Natural Hazards*, *107*(3), 2389–2417. DOI: 10.1007/s11069-020-04429-3

Varsha, V. R., Naganandini, S., & Hariharan, C. (2024). Utilizing AI and machine learning for natural disaster management: predicting natural disasters with AI and machine learning. In *Internet of Things and AI for Natural Disaster Management and Prediction* (pp. 279–304). IGI Global.

Chapter 2
Predictive Power for Humanitarian Relief:
Data-Driven Approaches to Crisis Response

Toprak Kolsuz
https://orcid.org/0009-0007-8217-8871
Yeditepe University, Bodrum, Turkey

Erkut Akkartal
https://orcid.org/0000-0002-7090-4449
Yeditepe University, Istanbul, Turkey

ABSTRACT

This chapter explores how big data, artificial intelligence (AI), and predictive analytics are transforming humanitarian relief from reactive response models to anticipatory supply chains. By leveraging technologies such as machine learning and Bayesian forecasting, humanitarian organizations can enhance situational awareness, improve demand prediction, and optimize last-mile delivery. The study also addresses decision-making under uncertainty through the lens of the value of information (VoI) and forecast-based financing. Despite these advancements, implementation challenges remain—ranging from data fragmentation and ethical concerns to technological and cultural barriers. To overcome these issues, the chapter proposes strategic enablers including data literacy training, ethical AI governance, and inter-agency collaboration. A concluding roadmap outlines key steps for integrating predictive analytics into humanitarian logistics for more timely, efficient, and inclusive crisis response.

DOI: 10.4018/979-8-3373-3643-5.ch002

1. INTRODUCTION

In recent decades, the global humanitarian landscape has been marked by a striking escalation in the frequency, intensity, and complexity of crises. From climate-induced natural disasters and protracted conflicts to pandemics and forced displacements, the demands placed on humanitarian systems have grown dramatically. According to UN OCHA estimates, over 339 million people required humanitarian assistance in 2023—nearly double the number a decade ago. These increasing demands strain conventional relief mechanisms and expose the limitations of reactive, resource-constrained logistics models. Humanitarian supply chains are expected to function in volatile, uncertain, complex, and ambiguous (VUCA) environments, where speed, precision, and coordination are critical (Bag, Gupta, & Wood, 2022; Sharma & Joshi, 2020). These conditions demand a more adaptive and forward-looking approach—one capable of delivering not only faster responses but also earlier warnings and optimized preparedness (Ayers, Chadburn, & Hoque, 2024).

This transformation has ushered in a fundamental shift from reactive response models to anticipatory supply chains. Traditional humanitarian logistics typically rely on static assessments and post-disaster mobilization of aid, which often prove too slow for rapidly evolving crises. In contrast, anticipatory models incorporate predictive insights and risk-based triggers to initiate early interventions and pre-position supplies (Dall & Schneider, 2022). These systems emphasize agility, resilience, and foresight, leveraging both historical data and real-time inputs to adjust operations dynamically. They also respond to the growing consensus in humanitarian studies that the cost of delayed action—measured in human and economic terms—is too high to ignore (Jeble et al., 2020; Kondraganti, Narayanamurthy, & Sharifi, 2024).

At the core of this operational shift lies the integration of big data analytics, artificial intelligence (AI), and predictive modeling. These technologies enable organizations to harness high-volume, high-velocity data—from satellite sensors, mobile phone metadata, social media, and field-level sensors—to anticipate crises, optimize logistics networks, and adapt strategies in real time (Ahmed et al., 2021; Murri et al., 2024). For instance, big data analytics has enhanced early warning systems by incorporating weather anomalies, disease spread, and conflict indicators to predict humanitarian needs (Dennehy et al., 2021). AI and machine learning approaches, particularly those using probabilistic models such as Bayesian learning, have further elevated forecasting capabilities (Yang et al., 2019; Li et al., 2024). These developments are not just technological enhancements—they represent a paradigmatic evolution in how humanitarian decisions are conceived and executed.

This chapter explores the potential and limitations of data-driven humanitarian relief, with a focus on how predictive technologies are transforming logistics and decision-making under uncertainty. It asks: how can humanitarian agencies use big data and AI to preempt crises, rather than react to them? What are the barriers to implementation, and how can they be overcome? And critically, what ethical and governance structures are needed to ensure that predictive tools do not reproduce bias or exclusion in already vulnerable populations? Drawing on multidisciplinary insights and case evidence, the chapter aims to provide a critical yet constructive roadmap for embedding predictive capacity into humanitarian systems.

The objectives of the chapter are fourfold. First, it maps the emerging ecosystem of big data applications in humanitarian logistics and identifies key use cases across forecasting, demand planning, and last-mile delivery (Jain et al., 2022; Baharmand et al., 2022). Second, it examines decision-making frameworks under uncertainty, particularly the role of the value of information (VoI) and forecast-based financing models (Dijk et al., 2024; Keisler & Brodfuehrer, 2009). Third, it analyzes the implementation challenges encountered by humanitarian organizations, including technological, cultural, and ethical constraints (Sharma & Joshi, 2020; Bag et al., 2022). Fourth, it presents strategic enablers—such as Bayesian ensemble models, data literacy initiatives, and inter-agency coordination—that can enhance predictive capacity while ensuring accountability and inclusiveness (Seyedan et al., 2022; Sandoval-Ríos et al., 2025).

The chapter is structured as follows: Section 2 explores the landscape of big data and predictive analytics in humanitarian relief, focusing on their role in enhancing situational awareness, optimizing supply chains, and empowering local actors. Section 3 addresses decision-making under uncertainty by integrating predictive tools with VoI frameworks and early action protocols. Section 4 outlines the implementation barriers—ranging from infrastructure limitations to ethical risks—that hinder the full realization of predictive humanitarian systems. Section 5 introduces strategic enablers that can support sustainable adoption, including technical, organizational, and ethical considerations. Section 6 concludes with a roadmap for integrating predictive analytics into humanitarian planning and outlines future research directions. Through this structure, the chapter contributes to both the theoretical advancement and practical improvement of humanitarian logistics in the digital age.

2. BIG DATA AND PREDICTIVE ANALYTICS IN HUMANITARIAN RELIEF

The integration of big data and predictive analytics into humanitarian relief operations has revolutionized the way crises are managed, from anticipation to last-mile delivery. Traditional humanitarian supply chains (HSCs), often characterized by fragmented data sources and reactive decision-making, now face the opportunity to transition toward anticipatory, data-informed systems. As emphasized by Kondraganti,

Narayanamurthy, and Sharifi (2024), big data analytics (BDA) enables humanitarian actors to act proactively by enhancing visibility, responsiveness, and resilience. By leveraging diverse data sources such as satellite imagery, mobile phone metadata, and crowdsourced information, organizations can develop a comprehensive picture of crisis-affected regions. This broader situational awareness, according to Zhao (2024), is essential for early warning and real-time coordination, allowing agencies to prioritize resource allocation before disasters escalate.

Enhancing situational awareness is perhaps the most immediate and critical benefit of big data in humanitarian contexts. As Munir, Aved, and Blasch (2022) elaborate, situational awareness techniques based on AI and big data allow responders to monitor environmental shifts, population movements, and social signals in real time. These systems are enhanced through deep learning methods, like those discussed by Massimi et al. (2024), who demonstrate the feasibility of radar-based situational analytics in disaster zones. Mobile phone data, in particular, as noted by Aiken et al. (2022), has been shown to be effective in locating displaced populations and tailoring aid distributions more efficiently. These efforts are further supported by digital twins and IoT-based simulations (Cebir & Akkartal, 2024), which recreate dynamic logistics environments to assess multiple crisis scenarios. The synergy of human intuition and algorithmic foresight allows for higher-fidelity risk mapping and improved coordination across stakeholders.

In terms of forecasting humanitarian needs, big data analytics has proven to be a transformative force. Machine learning and statistical modeling allow organizations to anticipate future demand for food, medicine, shelter, and other essentials. Ahmed et al. (2021) proposed a pandemic prediction framework using big data analytics that demonstrated strong performance in forecasting outbreaks. Similarly, Nosraty et al. (2025) extended this approach by applying AI models to manage risks in disaster-prone industries, offering insights transferrable to general humanitarian contexts. These predictive systems draw on diverse datasets—from historical disaster trends to real-time market signals—and, as Mızrak (2024) observes, support resilience strategies by allowing logistics managers to prepare preemptively, thus avoiding disruptions. With predictive insights, humanitarian supply chains can avoid the bullwhip effect common in emergency responses and maintain equilibrium between supply and demand.

Supply chain visibility and traceability have historically been difficult to achieve in disaster settings, where fragmented information, logistical chaos, and stakeholder silos are common. However, recent advances in BDA, IoT, and blockchain technologies have significantly improved transparency and control over humanitarian operations. As discussed by Dennehy et al. (2021), data-driven supply chains that are mindful and transparent are more resilient and responsive to emerging disruptions. RFID tags and IoT sensors, as highlighted by Özmen et al. (2023) and Öztürk

& Akkartal (2024), can track the real-time status and condition of shipments, ensuring temperature control for sensitive supplies and reducing the risks of theft or spoilage. This enhanced traceability not only strengthens trust among partners but also provides donors with verifiable accountability, thereby reinforcing the ethical standards expected in humanitarian interventions.

Last-mile delivery remains one of the most complex challenges in humanitarian logistics. Terrain unpredictability, infrastructural damage, and population displacement all hinder efficient distribution. Recent works by Jin et al. (2025) and Baharmand et al. (2022) introduce optimization models for drone-supported and electric vehicle-based last-mile delivery systems that factor in uncertainties of access and availability. Zhang et al. (2022) further refined these approaches with distributionally robust optimization under mixed transport modes, offering flexible solutions in both urban and remote crisis areas. Akkartal and colleagues (2019) advocate for the use of gamified models and scenario-based simulations to train logistics personnel in managing these evolving last-mile challenges. Such models support dynamic routing and resource reallocation in real time, increasing operational effectiveness even in the most resource-constrained settings.

Equally important is the role of big data in empowering local actors and beneficiaries. Participatory data collection mechanisms such as SMS-based surveys and mobile applications allow affected communities to voice their needs directly, as emphasized by Aiken et al. (2022). This bottom-up flow of information counters the traditionally top-down nature of humanitarian responses, leading to more accurate targeting of aid and stronger community engagement. Mızrak (2023) underscores that empowering local decision-makers with access to analytical tools enhances not only responsiveness but also legitimacy and sustainability. Digital transformation in the field, as described by Özkanlısoy & Akkartal (2021), supports decentralized, agile decision-making frameworks, which are better suited to the volatile environments typical of post-disaster zones.

Another critical benefit of predictive analytics lies in its capacity to support strategic and anticipatory planning. As Dennehy et al. (2021) and Papanagnou et al. (2022) reveal, digitally transformed organizations that embrace data-centric cultures are better equipped to plan for long-term challenges, including compound disasters, climate impacts, and systemic disruptions. Anticipatory logistics strategies, such as forecast-based financing and early-warning-triggered resource mobilization, are increasingly being employed by humanitarian agencies. These strategies are supported by optimization models and risk dashboards that integrate multisource data, thus enabling decision-makers to preposition supplies and adjust resource levels dynamically. Jain et al. (2022) affirm that route optimization tools, especially those powered by AI, are central to achieving speed and precision in early response phases.

The efficiency and effectiveness of BDA in humanitarian relief are further influenced by how well organizations integrate these technologies into operational models. Bag, Gupta, and Wood (2022) identify several barriers—including lack of data infrastructure, skills gaps, and institutional resistance—that hinder the full realization of BDA's potential. Addressing these issues requires not only technological investment but also the creation of a data-literate workforce capable of interpreting and acting on analytical insights. As Rodríguez-Espíndola et al. (2018) argue, building absorptive capacity within humanitarian supply chains is essential for translating data into action. The implementation of digital twins (Cebir & Akkartal, 2024), for instance, requires a coordinated effort between IT experts and frontline responders to ensure usability and contextual relevance.

Moreover, a successful data-driven humanitarian strategy must incorporate cross-sectoral and inter-agency data sharing. Standardization of data formats and collaborative analytics platforms, such as the Humanitarian Data Exchange (HDX), provide a foundation for unified action. As Dennehy et al. (2021) and Dubey et al. (2019) argue, trust, transparency, and shared values are vital enablers of collaborative performance in data-driven humanitarian systems. The alignment of predictive models across organizations ensures interoperability not only at the technical level but also at the cognitive and operational levels. As highlighted by Ivanov (2020), such integration is vital in modeling systemic disruptions and ensuring coherence in the humanitarian supply chain's response mechanisms.

In addition to technological advancements and data-driven strategies, the role of innovation management in supply chains cannot be overlooked when considering big data applications in humanitarian logistics. Akkartal, Akkartal, and Yıldırım (2019) underscore that successful innovation in supply chains—especially under volatile conditions like disasters—requires adaptive management approaches that leverage data to prioritize interventions. Their study emphasizes how predictive analytics can function not only as a tool for forecasting but also as a mechanism for driving strategic innovation and cross-functional integration. This insight is especially relevant for humanitarian settings, where fragmented operations and urgent timelines often hinder innovation unless supported by robust analytics and agile management structures.

Beyond the technical infrastructure and forecasting capabilities, cultural readiness within organizations remains a decisive factor in determining the successful implementation of big data initiatives. Queiroz and Telles (2018) argue that organizational openness, trust in data, and support from leadership are critical enablers in embedding analytics into supply chain decision-making. This aligns with the challenges observed in humanitarian supply chains where conventional, reactive practices often resist data-driven transformations. Roberts and Hazen (2016) also note that an overemphasis on technology without alignment in people and processes undermines the full potential of data analytics. Thus, integrating predictive tools into everyday decision-making routines demands a culture that not only values data but is also equipped with the governance structures necessary to translate data insights into coordinated actions.

From a governance and privacy standpoint, Ogbuke et al. (2020) caution against the ethical and security challenges posed by extensive data analytics in humanitarian contexts. Handling sensitive information—such as refugee biometrics, health data, or location tracking—requires strict adherence to privacy laws and ethical frameworks. Without these, trust between aid organizations and beneficiaries may erode, thereby undermining the effectiveness of even the most advanced predictive systems. In environments where legal protections may be limited or unclear, organizations must adopt precautionary protocols for anonymization, encryption, and data governance to ensure the ethical application of big data tools.

Furthermore, Yadav et al. (2020) emphasize the pervasive barriers to adopting big data analytics in supply chains, particularly those stemming from inadequate training, limited awareness, and skill gaps among mid-level practitioners. These challenges are especially pronounced in humanitarian operations, where rapid deployment often overshadows the need for digital training. Building technical competencies across hierarchical levels is not only a matter of operational efficiency but also of strategic alignment. Similarly, Kache and Seuring (2017) stress that the challenges in data management are not merely technical but lie at the intersection of data reliability, strategic foresight, and adaptive capacity. For humanitarian organizations to fully utilize the predictive power of analytics, they must view data as a strategic resource that permeates planning, operations, and recovery processes.

Lastly, the collaborative potential of BDA hinges on interoperable systems and long-term data-sharing relationships. Manavalan and Jayakrishna (2018) highlight how the Internet of Things (IoT) and embedded technologies can transform traditional supply chains into intelligent, interconnected networks. Applying this to humanitarian relief, IoT-enabled platforms can synchronize real-time updates from field teams, warehouses, and transit vehicles, enabling decision-makers to anticipate bottlenecks and reroute resources accordingly. These systems also support joint development initiatives between NGOs, governments, and private actors—building collective intelligence and shared situational awareness that are critical in complex emergencies.

In conclusion, big data and predictive analytics are reshaping the landscape of humanitarian relief by offering powerful tools for proactive planning, real-time coordination, and inclusive decision-making. The integration of forecasting tools, situational awareness systems, IoT-based tracking, and participatory data streams is enabling a paradigm shift from reactive to anticipatory humanitarian logistics. However, realizing this potential requires sustained investment in digital infrastructure, capacity building, cultural change, and inter-agency collaboration. As Mızrak

(2024) emphasizes, resilience and innovation in supply chains are not merely technological imperatives but strategic choices—ones that can ultimately determine the timeliness, effectiveness, and ethical integrity of humanitarian responses in an increasingly unpredictable world.

3. DECISION-MAKING UNDER UNCERTAINTY: THE VALUE OF INFORMATION

In the volatile and high-stakes domain of humanitarian supply chains, uncertainty is not a peripheral concern—it is a central and inescapable condition. Disasters often strike with little warning, unfold dynamically, and involve incomplete or contradictory information. The Value of Information (VoI) framework is critical in such contexts, offering decision-makers a rational method to quantify the benefit of obtaining additional data before acting. As Dijk et al. (2024) argue, VoI helps weigh the trade-off between acting quickly with limited knowledge versus delaying decisions to gather more evidence, which is especially vital when lives are at risk. Drawing from this perspective, Mizrak (2023) highlights that in aviation human resource management, where uncertain variables such as labor mobility and skill mismatches complicate strategic planning, the application of fuzzy decision tools can significantly support clarity. By extending such logic to humanitarian logistics, it becomes evident that probabilistic reasoning, combined with VoI, forms the backbone of robust, ethical, and responsive decision-making under uncertainty.

Integrating predictive analytics into the VoI framework enables humanitarian organizations to act with speed and precision even when complete information is not available. Predictive models can simulate various future scenarios, providing probabilistic forecasts that guide decisions in real time. Murri et al. (2024) emphasize that real-time insights generated through scalable big data pipelines enable responders to anticipate events and adapt quickly. These insights not only support operations but also optimize decision timing, an essential aspect of VoI analysis. Dubey et al. (2018) demonstrate that predictive analytics fosters coordination and swift trust in humanitarian supply chains by making invisible risks visible—thus improving collective preparedness. In the airline industry, Mizrak, Mizrak, and Akkartal (2025) applied a multi-criteria decision-making (MCDM) approach to route selection under uncertain conditions, showing how predictive evaluation tools contribute to higher accuracy in resource allocation. These practices are directly transferable to crisis zones, where humanitarian responders must allocate food, water, and shelter with incomplete knowledge of needs.

Forecast-based financing (FbF) has emerged as a powerful application of the VoI-predictive analytics nexus. This anticipatory action model triggers the release of humanitarian funds based on forecast thresholds rather than post-disaster assessments. Ayers, Chadburn, and Hoque (2024) illustrate how behaviorally informed early warning systems have improved anticipatory responses by embedding community-level indicators into forecasting models. Similarly, Dall and Schneider (2023) explain that anticipatory action leverages localized risk models to pre-emptively deploy resources, thereby reducing suffering and cost. These models rely on a careful balancing of forecast uncertainty and intervention effectiveness, a calculus that VoI helps formalize. Sharma and Joshi (2020) point out, however, that reliance on forecasts can pose operational and reputational risks if the models fail or are misinterpreted. Thus, integrating VoI ensures that early action frameworks are not only technically sound but also risk-informed and accountable.

Visualization tools and decision support systems (DSS) are essential for operationalizing VoI and predictive analytics. By presenting complex model outputs in an intuitive, interpretable manner, these tools bridge the gap between data science and field-level decision-making. Murri et al. (2024) emphasize the role of advanced dashboards that visualize evolving logistics, inventory, and population data streams. These systems reduce the cognitive burden on decision-makers by offering scenario comparisons and highlighting the VoI of alternative actions. Jeble et al. (2020) propose a framework wherein social capital—trust, communication, and collaboration—amplifies the effectiveness of big data tools, especially when supported by shared interfaces. Keisler and Brodfuehrer (2009) demonstrated this in a supply chain context where VoI was used to redesign decision processes, showing marked improvements in efficiency and confidence across organizational tiers. In humanitarian logistics, DSS platforms that include VoI modules can guide field teams on whether to deliver aid immediately or delay deployment in anticipation of refined risk data.

Despite their utility, the application of VoI and predictive tools in humanitarian contexts is not without challenges. Sharma and Joshi (2020) identify barriers such as data sparsity, poor model validation, and the tension between urgency and analytical thoroughness. In disaster contexts, where timing is critical, delays to gather more data may be ethically or logistically unacceptable. This is where adaptive decision models, informed by VoI but constrained by temporal realities, become vital. Mizrak (2023) noted in HR decision-making that the inclusion of qualitative reasoning via fuzzy logic enabled actionable judgments even with incomplete datasets. Humanitarian decision-makers face similar conditions and must often make "good enough" choices rather than ideal ones, reinforcing the need for flexible, real-time analytics rooted in VoI principles.

Moreover, the contextualization of VoI and predictive analytics requires sector-specific calibration. For instance, Dijk et al. (2024) show that in pharmaceutical approval, VoI helps determine whether further clinical trials are justified. In humanitarian aid, a similar approach could guide decisions such as whether to deploy resources based on limited satellite data or await confirmation from field teams. The stakes are analogous—balancing the cost of delay against the risk of misallocation. Ayers et al. (2024) also argue that local knowledge must be embedded within VoI models to prevent bias and improve accuracy. Community participation in the data generation process—through mobile apps or local monitoring—can enhance the quality and legitimacy of decisions. As Dall and Schneider (2023) assert, anticipatory action becomes meaningful only when it reflects the lived realities of affected populations, making participatory data central to ethical VoI-based interventions.

The coordination required to implement VoI-based predictive analytics frameworks across multiple agencies remains a formidable challenge. Dubey et al. (2018) underline that such integration depends on building "swift trust," where actors rely on transparent data and shared risk models rather than prolonged familiarity. This is particularly critical in the initial phases of disaster response, where diverse stakeholders—from UN agencies to NGOs and local governments—must align under volatile and uncertain conditions. Decision support systems that embed VoI metrics provide a common ground for dialogue and joint prioritization, reducing duplicated efforts and improving synchronization. Jeble et al. (2020) emphasize that frameworks combining social capital and predictive tools can foster the collaborative environment necessary for this integration.

Looking ahead, the future of VoI in humanitarian decision-making lies in enhancing scalability, speed, and interpretability. Murri et al. (2024) advocate for distributed analytics systems that can function in low-infrastructure environments—common in disaster zones. Real-time VoI calculations that are embedded into mobile tools could empower frontline workers to make informed decisions without relying on central command. Mizrak et al. (2025) suggest that decision models developed for commercial sectors, like airline route optimization, can be adapted for humanitarian purposes, provided that they incorporate context-specific risk parameters and ethical constraints. Ultimately, Dijk et al. (2024) reinforce the need to balance "cumulative evidence" and "immediate action" in every decision—an equilibrium that the VoI framework makes possible.

In sum, integrating the Value of Information with predictive analytics transforms humanitarian logistics from reactive delivery to proactive decision-making. It allows organizations to quantify uncertainty, prioritize data collection, and structure decisions under crisis pressure. While technical, ethical, and institutional challenges persist, the growing body of evidence from healthcare, aviation, and logistics confirms that VoI-informed frameworks improve operational performance and ethical accountability. As Mizrak (2023) emphasizes, resilient decision-making in uncertain environments demands a blend of analytical tools, expert intuition, and cross-sectoral collaboration. By embedding these principles into anticipatory humanitarian frameworks, organizations can better prepare for, respond to, and recover from crises—saving time, money, and lives.

4. IMPLEMENTATION CHALLENGES

Despite the transformative potential of big data analytics (BDA) in humanitarian relief, its implementation remains beset with significant technological and infrastructural constraints. Sharma and Joshi (2020) emphasize that humanitarian organizations often operate in disaster-affected regions where connectivity is intermittent, hardware is outdated, and real-time data transmission is not feasible. These conditions severely limit the usability of high-frequency data streams or sophisticated AI models. Bag, Gupta, and Wood (2022) support this claim, identifying "infrastructure unreadiness" as one of the most severe barriers to effective BDA adoption in humanitarian supply chains. Furthermore, many developing countries face inherent digital disparities, and humanitarian logistics operations in such contexts are hindered by the absence of cloud computing capacity, standardized sensors, and scalable storage systems. Kondraganti, Narayanamurthy, and Sharifi (2024) add that the lack of technical infrastructure severely limits the ability to gather, integrate, and analyze real-time data during emergency operations. For instance, during the Kerala floods, satellite-based big data analytics, which could have greatly improved situational response, was underutilized due to infrastructural gaps and lack of remote access capabilities (Nagendra, Narayanamurthy, & Moser, 2022).

Alongside technological barriers, there exists a pervasive gap in skills and organizational absorptive capacity that impedes the effective use of big data in humanitarian contexts. Absorptive capacity—the organization's ability to recognize the value of new information, assimilate it, and apply it effectively—is often missing in crisis settings (Bag et al., 2022). Many humanitarian agencies lack trained data scientists, and even field staff are frequently unfamiliar with digital platforms or analytical tools. Sharma and Joshi (2020) argue that the skills gap is not just a technical challenge but an institutional one, rooted in the absence of structured training programs and analytics-focused roles. Ahatsi and Olanrewaju (2025) also emphasize this in their comparative study, where differences in national capacity to leverage AI and big data in humanitarian logistics significantly affected the resilience and responsiveness of operations. Despite the availability of advanced analytical solutions, many agencies do not possess the organizational knowledge to implement or sustain them effectively. Kondraganti et al. (2024) conclude that until organizations develop the necessary absorptive capacity, the benefits of BDA will remain largely theoretical rather than practically transformative.

Another significant obstacle to BDA implementation is data fragmentation and poor interoperability between systems and actors. Humanitarian operations are inherently multi-stakeholder environments, involving governments, NGOs, military, private partners, and local institutions—all of which may use different data formats and platforms. This leads to silos of data that are difficult to integrate or interpret collectively. Bag et al. (2022) point out that the absence of a common data architecture results in "duplication, inconsistency, and underutilization" of critical data resources. Sharma and Joshi (2020) further argue that fragmented data systems make it nearly impossible to maintain real-time visibility across the supply chain. Without interoperable dashboards or standardized communication protocols, coordination is often compromised, leading to duplicated aid deliveries or delayed interventions. Even in technologically capable regions like Kerala, Nagendra et al. (2022) note that the lack of platform integration among stakeholders hampered data convergence and real-time analytics during the flood relief operation. Kondraganti et al. (2024) call for a unified, multi-agency data infrastructure that enables seamless data sharing and real-time decision-making across boundaries.

The ethical, legal, and privacy-related challenges of big data in humanitarian contexts are equally concerning. Humanitarian aid often involves collecting and analyzing sensitive data about vulnerable populations, including health status, movement patterns, and personal identifiers. Sharma and Joshi (2020) highlight that many humanitarian organizations lack the institutional frameworks to ensure ethical data use, leading to concerns over misuse, unauthorized access, or breaches of consent. Bag et al. (2022) further add that while the potential of data analytics is immense, unchecked collection and poor encryption practices can endanger already at-risk populations. Ahatsi and Olanrewaju (2025) argue that a major barrier to AI and BDA adoption in humanitarian contexts is the lack of clear data governance policies that align with international privacy laws, particularly when operations cross borders. In one of the reviewed case studies, fear of violating local privacy laws led to underutilization of mobile tracking data during a disaster, undermining the effectiveness of the predictive models. These concerns not only impact operational effectiveness but also undermine public trust in humanitarian agencies.

Cultural resistance and a lack of a data-driven mindset within humanitarian organizations also represent key implementation challenges. As Sharma and Joshi (2020) note, decision-making in many humanitarian agencies still relies heavily on experiential knowledge and field intuition rather than data-backed analysis. This "experience-over-evidence" culture hinders the adoption of predictive models, as field operatives may distrust algorithmic recommendations or perceive them as detached from on-the-ground realities. Bag et al. (2022) point out that this resistance is especially strong among mid-level managers who may view BDA tools as burdensome or overly complex. Kondraganti et al. (2024) also identify "organizational inertia" as a prominent factor, where institutions fail to adapt internal processes to make room for data-driven decision-making. Ahatsi and Olanrewaju (2025) found that in one of the countries studied, cultural barriers to AI adoption were as significant as infrastructural ones, with staff expressing skepticism about "robotic" decision-making in emotionally charged humanitarian missions. Overcoming this resistance requires not just technology transfer but comprehensive change management strategies that promote a culture of evidence-based practice.

Finally, issues of financial sustainability and institutional misalignment further undermine the integration of BDA into humanitarian supply chains. While pilot programs in data analytics often receive external donor funding, these initiatives frequently fail to scale due to the lack of long-term financial planning. Sharma and Joshi (2020) note that many analytics projects are discontinued once initial funding dries up, resulting in a cycle of experimentation without institutionalization. Bag et al. (2022) emphasize that humanitarian agencies, unlike private firms, do not have consistent budget allocations for IT systems, data scientists, or analytics software licenses. This makes it difficult to move beyond proof-of-concept stages. Moreover, Kondraganti et al. (2024) argue that the absence of alignment between analytics capabilities and strategic objectives leads to fragmented efforts. Ahatsi and Olanrewaju (2025) found that in both countries they studied, institutional models lacked key roles—such as Chief Data Officers or analytics governance bodies—that are necessary to sustain data-driven transformation. Without stable funding streams and structural alignment, BDA initiatives risk remaining peripheral to the core mission of humanitarian agencies.

In light of the diverse and interrelated challenges faced by humanitarian organizations in adopting big data analytics, it becomes necessary to view these constraints not only as isolated technical issues but as part of a systemic landscape requiring coordinated interventions. Table 1 provides a summary of the major implementation barriers identified in the literature and outlines strategic responses that can mitigate these obstacles, helping agencies move from pilot stages to fully embedded predictive systems.

Table 1. Summary of implementation challenges and mitigation strategies

Challenge Area	Description	Source(s)	Mitigation Strategy
Technological Infrastructure Gaps	Limited connectivity, outdated hardware	Sharma & Joshi (2020); Bag et al.	Mobile tools, cloud platforms, satellite tech
Skills and Absorptive Capacity	Lack of trained analysts and frontline users	Ahatsi & Olanrewaju (2025)	Data literacy training, cross-role onboarding
Data Fragmentation	Non-standardized data systems across stakeholders	Kondraganti et al. (2024)	Interoperable platforms, common data formats

continued on following page

Table 1. Continued

Challenge Area	Description	Source(s)	Mitigation Strategy
Ethical and Legal Barriers	Privacy concerns, algorithmic bias risks	Hanna et al. (2025); Tsamados et al.	Ethics committees, data anonymization
Cultural Resistance	Preference for intuition over analytics	Bag et al. (2022)	Change management, participatory governance

By addressing these barriers through phased implementation, training, interoperable platforms, and ethics-by-design frameworks, humanitarian actors can build the foundation required to support the predictive analytics tools discussed in the next section.

5. ENHANCING PREDICTIVE CAPACITY: STRATEGIC ENABLERS

In humanitarian logistics, enhancing predictive capacity is not merely a technical upgrade but a strategic imperative. One of the most promising techniques in this domain is the use of Bayesian learning and data pooling, which improves forecasting accuracy even under severe uncertainty. Bayesian methods are particularly well-suited to crisis contexts, as they update predictions dynamically as new data becomes available, thereby allowing decision-makers to refine their understanding in real time. Yang et al. (2019) show the power of Bayesian deep learning in forecasting highly variable demand in smart grids, a challenge analogous to the unpredictability faced in humanitarian supply chains. By integrating probabilistic modeling with deep neural networks, humanitarian agencies can generate not only point forecasts but also confidence intervals—essential for assessing risk and planning contingencies. Similarly, Li et al. (2024) demonstrate how Bayesian Model Averaging (BMA) enhances prediction robustness by combining multiple deep learning outputs in the context of lake water level forecasting. This ensemble technique mitigates overfitting and increases resilience to data noise, which is critical when working with fragmented and inconsistent humanitarian datasets. Seyedan, Mafakheri, and Wang (2022) further emphasize the benefit of cluster-based BMA in forecasting variable demand across multiple segments. When applied to humanitarian operations—such as forecasting demand for medical supplies across refugee camps—these approaches can significantly reduce both under-preparedness and oversupply, optimizing resource allocation.

To transform predictive capabilities into operational impact, humanitarian organizations must deploy a set of strategic enablers that bridge technology, human capacity, ethics, and cross-sectoral coordination. These enablers support the effective deployment of advanced forecasting systems in complex, data-scarce environments. Table 2 summarizes key enablers identified in recent research and their relevance to predictive decision-making in humanitarian logistics.

Table 2. Strategic enablers for predictive capacity

Strategic Enabler	Description	Supporting References
Bayesian Ensemble Forecasting	Updating predictions using multiple models	Yang et al. (2019); Li et al. (2024)
Data Literacy Programs	Building internal capacity to interpret analytics	Sandoval-Ríos et al. (2025)
Inter-Agency Collaboration	Aligning data standards and decision models across organizations	Dubey et al. (2018); Kondraganti et al.
Ethical AI Implementation	Addressing bias, fairness, and transparency	Hanna et al. (2025); Venkatasubbu et al.

Each of these elements reinforces the others: data literacy empowers teams to interpret Bayesian outputs; standardized systems support inter-agency pooling; and ethical oversight ensures that AI models are not only accurate but fair and trustworthy. Together, they define the building blocks of a sustainable predictive analytics ecosystem in humanitarian relief.

Beyond the mathematical sophistication of forecasting models, the human element remains central to effective implementation. Building data-literate teams who understand how to interpret, question, and apply predictive outputs is essential for embedding analytics into decision-making structures. Sandoval-Ríos, Gajardo-Poblete, and López-Núñez (2025) argue that data literacy must go beyond technical proficiency to include the ability to critically engage with data in context-sensitive ways. This is particularly relevant in humanitarian operations, where ground-level staff often rely on instinct and experience in volatile settings. Without appropriate training, predictive tools may either be ignored or misused, undermining their potential impact. Therefore, literacy training must be continuous and inclusive, covering not just analysts but also logisticians, procurement officers, and local implementing partners. In contexts where predictive analytics guide life-saving decisions, such as pre-positioning aid based on flood forecasts, it is essential that all stakeholders trust and understand the basis of those predictions. Institutionalizing a culture of evidence-based decision-making requires not only the integration of analytics into workflows but also the empowerment of individuals to engage with, challenge, and refine those tools.

At the systemic level, improving predictive capacity also necessitates inter-agency collaboration and standardization. Humanitarian crises often involve multiple organizations operating simultaneously in the same geographic space, yet with incompatible data architectures, divergent metrics, and misaligned forecasting models. This fragmentation reduces the value of predictive analytics, as models cannot be effectively scaled or validated across contexts. Standardization of data formats, APIs, and dashboard interfaces allows for seamless data pooling across UN agencies, NGOs, and local governments. Moreover, collaborative forecasting—where organizations share model assumptions and outputs—enables more robust scenario planning and resource coordination. Although not directly covered in the selected references, these themes are consistent with best practices from multi-actor systems, and support the efficient deployment of Bayesian ensemble techniques like those explored by Seyedan et al. (2022). By promoting transparent, interoperable systems and investing in cross-organizational training, agencies can build a shared predictive infrastructure that scales across operations and borders, improving both speed and fairness of humanitarian response.

Another fundamental pillar in strengthening predictive systems lies in addressing ethical considerations in data use and algorithmic modeling. As AI and machine learning become more embedded in humanitarian logistics, concerns about bias, fairness, and accountability become increasingly prominent. Venkatasubbu and Krishnamoorthy (2022) highlight how machine learning models, if trained on skewed or incomplete datasets, may reinforce systemic inequalities—such as prioritizing aid in urban over rural areas due to higher data density. Similarly, Tsamados et al. (2022) underscore that algorithmic opacity, or the "black box" problem, undermines both trust and ethical integrity, particularly when predictions are used to make high-stakes decisions without human oversight. In the humanitarian context, where populations are already vulnerable, the misapplication of opaque models can result in unintended harm, including exclusion from aid or surveillance overreach. Hanna et al. (2025) further elaborate that bias in AI can emerge at multiple stages—from data collection to model validation—and that mitigation strategies must be comprehensive. This includes not only technical solutions such as de-biasing algorithms and explainable AI (XAI), but also the establishment of ethics committees, regulatory guidelines, and participatory data governance frameworks. Humanitarian agencies must ensure that predictive systems reflect the values of justice, equity, and inclusivity, and that these systems are subject to ongoing ethical review.

To systematically adopt predictive analytics within humanitarian supply chains, organizations must progress through distinct, interrelated phases. These phases span from establishing foundational digital infrastructure to embedding ethical oversight into advanced algorithmic models. This staged approach ensures that predictive tools are not only technically sound but also socially and institutionally sustainable. Figure 1 presents a visual roadmap outlining the five critical phases necessary for successful implementation of predictive analytics in humanitarian operations.

Figure 1. Roadmap for implementing predictive analytics in humanitarian supply chains

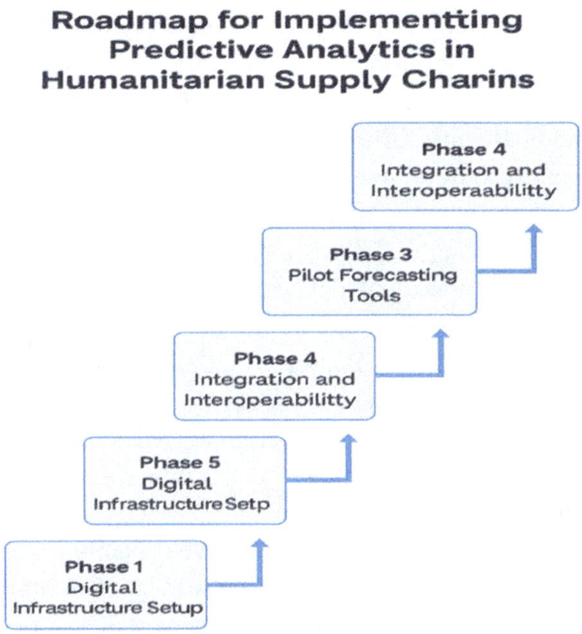

Each phase builds on the previous, reinforcing capabilities across the organization. By following this roadmap, humanitarian actors can move from reactive logistics toward a more anticipatory, data-driven relief system.

In conclusion, enhancing predictive capacity in humanitarian operations demands a multidimensional approach that blends advanced statistical modeling, human-centered design, organizational collaboration, and ethical governance. Bayesian learning and ensemble forecasting offer powerful tools to manage uncertainty, but these tools must be implemented by data-literate teams that understand both their power and their limitations. Collaboration across agencies and the standardization of models and data flows ensures that predictive insights are actionable at scale. Finally, safeguarding the ethical use of AI and data analytics protects the rights and dignity of affected populations. Together, these enablers form the foundation of a resilient, anticipatory, and accountable humanitarian supply chain capable of responding to the challenges of an increasingly complex global landscape.

6. CONCLUSION AND STRATEGIC ROADMAP

The journey toward data-driven humanitarian logistics is not solely a technical transformation—it is a strategic reimagining of how organizations anticipate, plan for, and respond to crises. Developing a sustainable and scalable predictive analytics infrastructure begins with a careful cost-benefit assessment. While the initial investment in cloud platforms, IoT systems, satellite data integration, and advanced analytics may appear resource-intensive, studies confirm the long-term efficiency gains and cost avoidance benefits. For example, Sharma and Joshi (2020) emphasize that organizations using predictive models can significantly reduce redundant deliveries and mitigate the cost of delayed responses. Forecast-based financing systems and early-warning dashboards enable more agile pre-positioning of supplies and better use of donor funds. As Bag et al. (2022) assert, proactive models that anticipate rather than react to disaster conditions ultimately minimize logistical costs and human suffering alike. Thus, humanitarian agencies must shift their financial outlook to treat data infrastructure not as an operational expense but as a strategic investment in resilience and performance.

Beyond economic feasibility, scaling predictive capacity in developing regions requires a phased and inclusive implementation strategy. Kondraganti et al. (2024) recommend beginning with targeted pilot programs that leverage existing infrastructure, gradually building toward more comprehensive systems as technical maturity improves. Success in fragile or resource-constrained contexts depends on the deployment of mobile-enabled platforms, localized sensors, and decentralized data-sharing hubs—especially where central connectivity is inconsistent. Nagendra et al. (2022) emphasize the value of integrating satellite and drone data into regional disaster protocols, especially in areas vulnerable to flooding or extreme weather events. Meanwhile, Ahatsi and Olanrewaju (2025) propose that national strategies include support for AI literacy, inter-agency data alignment, and incentives for ethical data sharing, ensuring that predictive systems are not just technically viable, but contextually appropriate and locally owned. Such a roadmap helps transform reactive disaster relief systems into anticipatory, self-adaptive networks capable of maintaining operations through compounding crises.

Ultimately, the future of humanitarian logistics lies in a fundamental reorientation of organizational culture—one that values collaboration, transparency, and trust in data. The successful adoption of big data analytics depends not only on technologies but on the people and processes that support them. Building cross-sectoral alliances, including public-private partnerships and academic collaborations, is essential for fostering knowledge exchange, funding innovation, and aligning models with operational realities. As Dubey et al. (2018) and Bag et al. (2022) argue, trust and coordination are the bedrock of predictive systems in multi-actor environments.

Equally important is embedding ethical oversight into algorithmic development, as noted by Tsamados et al. (2022) and Hanna et al. (2025), to ensure responsible data use. Humanitarian agencies must invest in governance frameworks that address not only technical standards, but also privacy, accountability, and fairness. By aligning strategic intent with predictive capacity, the humanitarian sector can evolve into a proactive, data-driven ecosystem—one better equipped to serve humanity in an era defined by disruption, complexity, and uncertainty.

REFERENCES

Ahatsi, E., & Olanrewaju, O. A. (2025). Enhancing Humanitarian Supply Chain Resilience: Evaluating Artificial Intelligence and Big Data Analytics in Two Nations. *Logistics (Basel)*, *9*(2), 64. DOI: 10.3390/logistics9020064

Ahmed, I., Ahmad, M., Jeon, G., & Piccialli, F. (2021). A framework for pandemic prediction using big data analytics. *Big Data Research*, *25*, 100190. DOI: 10.1016/j.bdr.2021.100190

Aiken, E., Bellue, S., Karlan, D., Udry, C., & Blumenstock, J. E. (2022). Machine learning and phone data can improve targeting of humanitarian aid. *Nature*, *603*(7903), 864–870. DOI: 10.1038/s41586-022-04484-9 PMID: 35296856

Akkartal, G. R., Akkartal, E., & Yıldırım, C. (2019). The Management Of Innovation In Supply Chain. *Eurasian Business & Economics Journal*, *17*(17), 43–52.

Akkartal, G. R., Barooti, A., & Akkartal, E. (2019). Gamification methods for teaching logistics and supply chain management. *Eurasian Business and Economic Journal*, *17*(5), 53–71.

Ayers, J., Chadburn, O., & Hoque, K. A. (2024). *Behaviourally-Informed Early Warning and Anticipatory Action: Unleashing the Potential of Locally-Led Pre-emptive Response and the Forecast-Based Financing it Requires*. Current and Emerging Trends in the Management of International Disasters.

Bag, S., Gupta, S., & Wood, L. (2022). Big data analytics in sustainable humanitarian supply chain: Barriers and their interactions. *Annals of Operations Research*, *319*(1), 721–760. DOI: 10.1007/s10479-020-03790-7

Baharmand, H., Vega, D., Lauras, M., & Comes, T. (2022). A methodology for developing evidence-based optimization models in humanitarian logistics. *Annals of Operations Research*, *319*(1), 1197–1229. DOI: 10.1007/s10479-022-04762-9

Cebir, Y., & Akkartal, E. (2024). Digital twin in logistics and supply chain management. In *Strategic Innovations for Dynamic Supply Chains* (pp. 170–192). IGI Global Scientific Publishing. DOI: 10.4018/979-8-3693-3575-8.ch008

Dall, K., & Schneider, S. (2023). Anticipatory humanitarian action. In *An Introduction to Humanitarian Action* (pp. 343–362). Routledge.

Dennehy, D., Oredo, J., Spanaki, K., Despoudi, S., & Fitzgibbon, M. (2021). Supply chain resilience in mindful humanitarian aid organizations: The role of big data analytics. *International Journal of Operations & Production Management, 41*(9), 1417–1441. DOI: 10.1108/IJOPM-12-2020-0871

Dijk, S. W., Krijkamp, E., Kunst, N., Labrecque, J. A., Gross, C. P., Pandit, A., Lu, C.-P., Visser, L. E., Wong, J. B., & Hunink, M. M. (2024). Making Drug Approval Decisions in the Face of Uncertainty: Cumulative Evidence versus Value of Information. *Medical Decision Making, 44*(5), 512–528. DOI: 10.1177/0272989X241255047 PMID: 38828516

Dubey, R., Luo, Z., Gunasekaran, A., Akter, S., Hazen, B. T., & Douglas, M. A. (2018). Big data and predictive analytics in humanitarian supply chains: Enabling visibility and coordination in the presence of swift trust. *International Journal of Logistics Management, 29*(2), 485–512. DOI: 10.1108/IJLM-02-2017-0039

Hanna, M. G., Pantanowitz, L., Jackson, B., Palmer, O., Visweswaran, S., Pantanowitz, J., Deebajah, M., & Rashidi, H. H. (2025). Ethical and bias considerations in artificial intelligence/machine learning. *Modern Pathology, 38*(3), 100686. DOI: 10.1016/j.modpat.2024.100686 PMID: 39694331

Jain, S., Meena, M. L., Kumar, V., & Detwal, P. K. (2022, November). Route Optimization as an Aspect of Humanitarian Logistics: Delineating Existing Literature from 2011 to 2022. In *Conference of Innovative Product Design and Intelligent Manufacturing System* (pp. 647–661). Springer Nature Singapore.

Jeble, S., Kumari, S., Venkatesh, V. G., & Singh, M. (2020). Influence of big data and predictive analytics and social capital on performance of humanitarian supply chain: Developing framework and future research directions. *Benchmarking, 27*(2), 606–633. DOI: 10.1108/BIJ-03-2019-0102

Jin, Z., Ng, K. K., Zhang, C., Chan, Y. Y., & Qin, Y. (2025). A multistage stochastic programming approach for drone-supported last-mile humanitarian logistics system planning. *Advanced Engineering Informatics, 65*, 103201. DOI: 10.1016/j.aei.2025.103201

Keisler, J. M., & Brodfuehrer, M. (2009). An application of value-of-information to decision process reengineering. *The Engineering Economist, 54*(3), 197–221. DOI: 10.1080/00137910903108286

Kondraganti, A., Narayanamurthy, G., & Sharifi, H. (2024). A systematic literature review on the use of big data analytics in humanitarian and disaster operations. *Annals of Operations Research, 335*(3), 1015–1052. DOI: 10.1007/s10479-022-04904-z PMID: 36846245

Li, G., Liu, Z., Zhang, J., Han, H., & Shu, Z. (2024). Bayesian model averaging by combining deep learning models to improve lake water level prediction. *The Science of the Total Environment*, *906*, 167718. DOI: 10.1016/j.scitotenv.2023.167718 PMID: 37832688

Massimi, F., Ferrara, P., Petrucci, R., & Benedetto, F. (2024). Deep learning-based space debris detection for space situational awareness: A feasibility study applied to the radar processing. *IET Radar, Sonar & Navigation*, *18*(4), 635–648. DOI: 10.1049/rsn2.12547

Mızrak, F. (2023). Analyzing Criteria Affecting Decision-Making Processes of Human Resource Management in the Aviation Sector-A Fuzzy Logic Approach. *Journal of Aviation*, *7*(3), 376–387. DOI: 10.30518/jav.1331688

Mızrak, F. (2023). Managing Risks and Crises in the Logistics Sector: A Comprehensive Analysis of Strategies and Prioritization Using AHP Method. *Meriç Uluslararası Sosyal ve Stratejik Araştırmalar Dergisi, 7*(Özel Sayı), 114-148.

Mızrak, F. (2024). Resilience and Innovation Strategies: How Businesses Adapt to Supply Chain Disruptions in the Post-Pandemic Era. *Politik Ekonomik Kuram*, *8*(3), 581–600. DOI: 10.30586/pek.1497718

Mizrak, F., Mizrak, K. C., & Akkartal, G. R. (2025). Developing a strategic framework for airline destination selection: A multi-criteria decision-making approach applied to Turkish airlines. *Transportation Research Interdisciplinary Perspectives*, *29*, 101322. DOI: 10.1016/j.trip.2025.101322

Munir, A., Aved, A., & Blasch, E. (2022). Situational awareness: Techniques, challenges, and prospects. *AI*, *3*(1), 55–77. DOI: 10.3390/ai3010005

Murri, S., Bhoyar, M., Selvarajan, G. P., & Malaga, M. (2024). Transforming Decision-Making with Big Data Analytics: Advanced Approaches to Real-Time Insights, Predictive Modeling, and Scalable Data Integration. *International Journal of Communication Networks and Information Security*, *16*(5), 506–519.

Nagendra, N. P., Narayanamurthy, G., & Moser, R. (2022). Management of humanitarian relief operations using satellite big data analytics: The case of Kerala floods. *Annals of Operations Research*, *319*(1), 885–910. DOI: 10.1007/s10479-020-03593-w

Nosraty, N., Soroori Sarabi, A., Arsalani, A., Toosi, R., & Sharajsharifi, M. (2025). Artificial intelligence for disaster risk management in the beauty industry. *International Journal of Advanced Multidisciplinary Research and Studies*, *5*(3), 1076–1086. DOI: 10.62225/2583049X.2025.5.3.4422

Özkanlısoy, Ö., & Akkartal, E. (2021). Digital transformation in supply chains: Current applications, contributions and challenges. *Bus. Manag. Stud. Int. J*, *9*, 32–55.

Özmen, M., Çelik, R., Çelik, Ü. N., Teber, M., Aktaş, D. C., & Kaya, M. F. (2023). Last Mile Humanitarian Aid Delivery Model with Electric Vehicles to Disaster Areas. *Bitlis Eren Üniversitesi Fen Bilimleri Dergisi*, *12*(4), 1275–1288. DOI: 10.17798/bitlisfen.1379840

Öztürk, S., & Akkartal, E. (2024). Internet of Things (IoT) Applications in Last Mile Delivery. In *Strategic Innovations for Dynamic Supply Chains* (pp. 193–215). IGI Global Scientific Publishing. DOI: 10.4018/979-8-3693-3575-8.ch009

Papanagnou, C., Seiler, A., Spanaki, K., Papadopoulos, T., & Bourlakis, M. (2022). Data-driven digital transformation for emergency situations: The case of the UK retail sector. *International Journal of Production Economics*, *250*, 108628. DOI: 10.1016/j.ijpe.2022.108628

Sandoval-Ríos, F., Gajardo-Poblete, C., & López-Núñez, J. A. (2025, March). Role of data literacy training for decision-making in teaching practice: A systematic review. [). Frontiers Media SA.]. *Frontiers in Education*, *10*, 1485821. DOI: 10.3389/feduc.2025.1485821

Seyedan, M., Mafakheri, F., & Wang, C. (2022). Cluster-based demand forecasting using Bayesian model averaging: An ensemble learning approach. *Decision Analytics Journal*, *3*, 100033. DOI: 10.1016/j.dajour.2022.100033

Sharma, P., & Joshi, A. (2020). Challenges of using big data for humanitarian relief: Lessons from the literature. *Journal of Humanitarian Logistics and Supply Chain Management*, *10*(4), 423–446. DOI: 10.1108/JHLSCM-05-2018-0031

Tsamados, A., Aggarwal, N., Cowls, J., Morley, J., Roberts, H., Taddeo, M., & Floridi, L. (2022). The ethics of algorithms: Key problems and solutions. *AI & Society*, *37*(1), 215–230. DOI: 10.1007/s00146-021-01154-8

Venkatasubbu, S., & Krishnamoorthy, G. (2022). Ethical considerations in AI addressing bias and fairness in machine learning models. *Journal of Knowledge Learning and Science Technology ISSN: 2959-6386 (online)*, *1*(1), 130-138.

Yang, Y., Li, W., Gulliver, T. A., & Li, S. (2019). Bayesian deep learning-based probabilistic load forecasting in smart grids. *IEEE Transactions on Industrial Informatics*, *16*(7), 4703–4713. DOI: 10.1109/TII.2019.2942353

Zhang, P., Liu, Y., Yang, G., & Zhang, G. (2022). A distributionally robust optimisation model for last mile relief network under mixed transport. *International Journal of Production Research*, *60*(4), 1316–1340. DOI: 10.1080/00207543.2020.1856439

Zhao, X. (2024). Network security situational awareness and early warning architecture based on big data. *International Journal of System Assurance Engineering and Management*, •••, 1–17. DOI: 10.1007/s13198-024-02522-5

Chapter 3
Data-Driven Humanitarian Supply Chains in Disaster Relief:
Enhancing Responsiveness and Efficiency through Predictive Analytics

Delal Güleser
https://orcid.org/0009-0008-9935-7099
Yeditepe University, Darıca, Turkey

ABSTRACT

Humanitarian supply chains can save lives through speed and accuracy when needed and enable action to be taken to make lives easier in critical situations. Today's big data and predictive analytics are changing the way we prepare for and respond to disasters and pandemics. With these methods and applications, big data enables decision makers to act quickly and effectively collect, process, and evaluate significant amounts of instantaneous information. This paper discusses how predictive analytics improves emergency response and effectiveness. It explores the importance of big data in forecasting needs, improving logistics processes, and supporting strategic planning in humanitarian action. By reviewing recent research, this paper highlights the impact of predictive analytics and suggests ways to strengthen humanitarian response systems with data-driven approaches.

DOI: 10.4018/979-8-3373-3643-5.ch003

1. INTRODUCTION

The term crisis management denotes the process of gearing up for, reacting to, and recuperating from unforeseen incidents that represent considerable dangers to people, organizations, and communities. Such events may consist of natural disasters, public health crises, cyberattacks, or significant disruptions to supply chains (Boin, Ekengren, & Rhinard, 2020). Crisis management now encompasses a much broader scope than before, moving from localized emergency response frameworks to intricate, multi-tiered systems that necessitate real-time coordination among a diverse array of participants, including governments, private sector entities, NGOs, and the general public. Crisis management has traditionally been based on human-centered frameworks that depend on expert judgment, institutional memory, and established operating procedures. These conventional methods stress the importance of adaptability, intuition, and experience—essential traits when choices have to be made in situations characterized by scant information and great uncertainty (Comfort, Boin, & Demchak, 2010). Nevertheless, their ability to respond is frequently limited by cognitive constraints, resource bottlenecks, and the rapid development of complex crises. As an example, the COVID-19 pandemic revealed significant weaknesses in conventional systems, where information asymmetries, slow responses, and inconsistent messaging hindered effective coordination and decision-making.

In light of this context, Artificial Intelligence (AI) has arisen as a revolutionary power that can enhance conventional crisis management systems. Technologies like machine learning (ML), natural language processing (NLP), and computer vision allow for the swift handling of enormous datasets, the discovery of concealed patterns, and the immediate prediction of crisis developments (Turoff et al., 2004). As an illustration, early warning systems powered by AI can examine social media content, satellite images, and sensor information to forecast wildfires, floods, or disease outbreaks, providing essential advance time for response preparations. Likewise, AI-driven chatbots and automated agents have been employed for spreading information, performing triage in emergency medical situations, and involving citizens during natural calamities. Nonetheless, in spite of these abilities, AI systems are also constrained. Often, they do not possess contextual understanding, ethical reasoning skills, or the ability to adapt in unexpected situations. When algorithms are trained on data that is biased or lacks completeness, they may yield results that are both inaccurate and discriminatory. Furthermore, black-box models pose issues related to transparency and accountability (Rahwan et al., 2019).

Therefore, the hybrid integration of human intelligence and AI capabilities offers a promising compromise that leverages the advantages of both. Human decision-makers embody context, ethics, empathy, and flexibility—traits that machines cannot currently replicate. Meanwhile, AI systems offer speed, scalability, and data-driven insights that are far beyond the capabilities of human cognition. The essence of a hybrid crisis management approach, where AI enhances rather than replaces human cognition, lies in this synergy (Shneiderman, 2020). This model acknowledges that humans and machines perform optimally when their strengths are aligned: AI takes care of repetitive, data-heavy tasks, while humans oversee complex, ambiguous, and ethically sensitive decisions. The increasing complexity, interconnectivity, and speed of contemporary crises provide the basis for using a hybrid human-AI approach in crisis management. In a time marked by cascading disasters—where a single disruption can cause numerous secondary failures in economic, technological, and social systems—resilience relies on the capacity to act quickly, adaptively, and with insight. While AI can quickly identify anomalies, simulate response strategies, and recommend optimal actions, it is humans who have the ability to assess these options in light of ethical, cultural, and situational contexts (Nemitz, 2018). Additionally, a hybrid approach reduces the risk of becoming overly dependent on either component by itself. Human-centered systems can be inconsistent or sluggish, while fully automated systems do not have the subtlety or moral reasoning needed for decisions with significant consequences. Consequently, the hybrid model provides a balanced framework that improves situational awareness, optimizes resource allocation, and guarantees decision-making processes that are more robust, inclusive, and transparent.

The objective of this chapter is to examine the outlines of a hybrid strategy for managing crises that combines human intelligence with the capabilities of AI. It starts with a foundation of the theoretical principles of crisis management and artificial intelligence, then proceeds to an examination of historical and modern instances that demonstrate the achievements and shortcomings of both conventional and AI-driven methods. A conceptual framework will subsequently be proposed to delineate the essential elements of a hybrid model, encompassing its technological architecture, operational dynamics, and governance considerations. Additionally, the chapter will showcase case studies from areas like public health, disaster response, and cybersecurity to illustrate practical applications. The ethical, legal, and social implications (ELSI) of hybrid systems will be thoroughly scrutinized, encompassing matters of trust, accountability, and bias. In conclusion, the chapter outlines potential future directions such as improvements in AI-human collaboration, new regulatory approaches, and strategies for cross-sectoral integration. With this aim, the chapter strives to add to the expanding discussion regarding intelligent resilience and the responsible deployment of AI in high-stakes environments.

2. LITERATURE REVIEW

2.1 The Strategic Importance of Supply Chain Innovations in Humanitarian Operations

The strategic role of supply chains in humanitarian logistics has significantly evolved, particularly in response to increasingly complex crises, climate-related disruptions, and global emergencies. The integration of technological innovations, sustainability frameworks, and adaptive decision-making models is now a necessity rather than an option. Özkanlısoy and Akkartal (2021) argue that digital transformation enables greater visibility, flexibility, and responsiveness in supply chain systems, making them more capable of addressing the volatile demands of humanitarian scenarios. Their study emphasizes how tools such as blockchain, real-time tracking systems, and big data analytics can improve traceability and accelerate the flow of information, ultimately enhancing response time during disaster relief. This need for agility was especially evident during the Suez Canal blockage, which disrupted global trade routes and highlighted systemic vulnerabilities in supply networks. Özkanlısoy and Akkartal (2022) demonstrated how such events necessitate dynamic rerouting strategies and prompt technological adaptation, underscoring the need for innovation-based resilience in global and regional supply chains.

Digital innovations such as digital twin technology and Internet of Things (IoT) applications are also transforming how humanitarian logistics are planned and executed. According to Cebir and Akkartal (2024), digital twin technologies allow logistics planners to simulate real-time scenarios, test supply chain responses under different disaster models, and optimize routing and inventory decisions before physical implementation. This proactive capability significantly enhances preparedness and coordination. Complementing this, Özkanlısoy and Akkartal (2024) explore how IoT-enabled systems—particularly in last-mile delivery—facilitate precise geolocation, environmental monitoring, and the tracking of critical aid items. These technologies not only increase delivery accuracy but also support efficient inventory management, particularly in difficult-to-reach areas or unstable environments. The convergence of digital twins and IoT thus reflects a new paradigm in humanitarian logistics, where predictive capabilities and real-time monitoring coalesce to improve agility and minimize logistical delays.

Sustainability is another major pillar in modern humanitarian supply chains. Akkartal and Aras (2021) emphasize that sustainable fleet management must be integrated into logistics strategies to reduce carbon emissions, increase energy efficiency, and enhance long-term operational resilience. In humanitarian contexts, this translates to minimizing environmental impact while maximizing the reach and effectiveness of aid operations. This aligns closely with Mızrak's (2022) work on evaluating alternative vehicle technologies and energy resources in logistics through strategic decision-making models. She highlights how strategic investments in cleaner technologies can reduce fuel dependency and enable environmentally responsible disaster response mechanisms. These ideas are further reinforced by Mızrak and Akkartal (2024), who analyze renewable energy applications in maritime transport, advocating for energy transition strategies that support sustainability and resilience in supply chain operations. The inclusion of green logistics principles is increasingly essential, especially as humanitarian organizations are called upon not only to deliver aid but to do so in a way that supports broader environmental and ethical commitments.

Innovation in supply chains also extends to organizational transformation and new business models. Mızrak (2024) addresses this by proposing dynamic change management strategies that align supply chain capabilities with external disruptions, supporting organizations in building internal agility and innovation-readiness. Such transformation is necessary to create systems capable of learning, evolving, and responding to real-time challenges. In a related vein, Danisman and Akkartal (2023) introduce a TRIZ-based framework for biomass supply chains in Türkiye, proposing scalable, sustainable models that can be adopted in energy-insecure regions. These models not only address resource utilization but also contribute to localized resilience—a critical aspect in humanitarian settings where infrastructure is often compromised. Furthermore, Abdelhadi and Akkartal (2024) conduct a structural analysis of Turkey's retail sector, identifying inefficiencies that mirror those found in humanitarian logistics. Addressing such inefficiencies through innovation can improve coordination, reduce waste, and ensure more equitable resource distribution in emergency contexts.

Collectively, these studies underscore that the strategic importance of supply chains in humanitarian operations lies not merely in logistics and transport but in their potential to foster innovation, sustainability, and resilience. As Mızrak, Polat, and Taşar (2024) demonstrate through the application of advanced fuzzy MCDM techniques to airport sustainability planning, modern supply chains must incorporate multidimensional decision frameworks to remain effective. Whether through data-driven decision models, green supply chain integration, or technology-based forecasting tools, the literature affirms that humanitarian logistics must evolve to meet contemporary demands. The incorporation of innovations—ranging from predictive analytics to digital infrastructures—enables not only faster and more efficient responses but also ensures that operations are environmentally and ethically sustainable. Ultimately, a strategically designed, innovation-enabled supply chain forms the backbone of effective humanitarian aid, facilitating both immediate relief and long-term recovery in crisis-affected regions.

2.2 Understanding Crisis through Human Judgment and Artificial Intelligence

Historically, crisis management has utilized a range of theoretical perspectives to comprehend and navigate responses to complex events with significant consequences. Notably, Chaos Theory and Complexity Theory have significantly shaped the understanding of crises as unpredictable and nonlinear phenomena. According to Chaos Theory, minor alterations in initial conditions can result in major and frequently unexpected outcomes, highlighting systems' sensitivity and instability (Morrison, 2002). This theory helps to understand the chaotic dynamics of crisis environments, in which quick contextual changes necessitate flexible and adaptive reactions. In a similar vein, Complexity Theory regards crises as emergent phenomena in complex adaptive systems, where the interactions of many interconnected components produce patterns that cannot be anticipated by examining the parts separately (Comfort, Boin, & Demchak, 2010). This viewpoint emphasizes the necessity of decentralized, flexible, and iterative methods for responding to crises. Meanwhile, the Contingency Planning Theory emphasizes the need for organizational response strategies to be customized according to specific situational variables, acknowledging that a single plan cannot accommodate all scenarios (Pearson & Clair, 1998). The combination of these theoretical frameworks helps to elucidate the reasons for the frequent failure of conventional decision-making models during crises and the necessity of more dynamic, context-sensitive approaches.

During crises, especially in situations characterized by stress, uncertainty, and time constraints, human intelligence is vital for making decisions. Research in cognitive psychology and neuroscience suggests that factors such as emotional regulation, cognitive load, and heuristics influence human decision-making under stress (Klein, 2017). For instance, the Naturalistic Decision Making (NDM) theory investigates how seasoned professionals arrive at effective judgments in real-world contexts marked by time pressure and significant consequences. The Recognition-Primed Decision (RPD) model, which is central to NDM, proposes that people leverage their experience to identify patterns and make quick but effective decisions without thoroughly comparing alternatives (Klein, 2008). Nevertheless, when faced with extreme stress, human decision-makers can fall victim to biases like confirmation bias and availability heuristics that can compromise their judgment (Tversky & Kahneman, 1974). While human cognition provides essential flexibility and contextual sensitivity, it also brings vulnerabilities that require support mechanisms, especially in complex crisis environments. Powerful tools for enhancing human crisis response capabilities have emerged in the form of artificial intelligence (AI) paradigms. Among these, Machine Learning (ML) offers predictive modeling capabilities that can foresee the development of crisis situations based on historical and real-time data (Bousdekis et al.,2021). Natural Language Processing (NLP) allows for the extraction of pertinent information from large unstructured text sources like social media, news articles, and emergency transcripts, thereby improving situational awareness (Imran, Castillo, Lucas, Meier, & Vieweg, 2014). Meanwhile, Computer Vision enables the real-time analysis of visual data like satellite images, drone footage, and surveillance videos—an essential capability for assessing damage and allocating resources in disaster situations. AI capabilities aid in quicker information processing, pattern recognition, and decision support—tasks that frequently exceed human capacity in large-scale crises. Nonetheless, AI systems can make mistakes. Their effectiveness largely depends on the quality and representativeness of input data, along with the transparency and interpretability of their algorithms.

The combination of human and AI capabilities, known as human-AI teaming, is viewed as a promising theoretical and practical frontier in crisis management. Theory of the Extended Mind, which was first conceived in the area of cognitive science, posits that tools and technologies can act as extensions of the human mind, augmenting cognitive processes beyond biological limits (Clark & Chalmers, 1998). From this perspective, when AI systems are crafted to be responsive and intuitive, they can function as cognitive partners that enhance human problem-solving abilities. In a similar vein, the idea of Augmented Intelligence—favored by some academics over the term artificial intelligence—focuses on improving human decision-making instead of replacing it (Davenport & Ronanki, 2018). This viewpoint encourages a synergistic model wherein AI manages tasks that are computationally intensive and driven by data, while humans provide ethical judgment, contextual interpretation, and emotional intelligence. To create effective human-AI teaming systems, it is crucial to focus on user experience, trust calibration, and the development of adaptive interfaces that facilitate real-time collaboration. The necessity for adaptability and real-time responsiveness is emphasized by Chaos and Complexity Theories, whereas human cognitive models shed light on the possibilities and constraints of decision-making in stressful situations. While AI paradigms provide robust means for analysis and forecasting, their incorporation into ethical and interpretable frameworks is essential. Teaming between humans and AI, based on theories like Augmented Intelligence and the Extended Mind, offers a conceptual framework for this kind of integration. Through the integration of these theoretical insights, crisis management can advance toward a paradigm that is more resilient and responsive, one that is equipped to tackle the complex challenges of contemporary society.

2.3 Evolution of Crisis Management Tools

Over the last few decades, crisis management has experienced a major evolution, moving from systems of manual coordination to advanced digital and AI-augmented frameworks. Historically, the response to crises depended significantly on hierarchical command-and-control frameworks, radio communication, paper-based documentation, and the instincts of seasoned responders (Comfort, 2007). Before the digital age, emergency plans tended to be static, and the absence of real-time data sharing hindered prompt decision-making. Coordination among agencies was often obstructed by bureaucratic silos and fragmented information systems, which limited the effectiveness of crisis response strategies (Kapucu, 2008). The advent of information and communication technologies (ICTs) during the 1990s and early 2000s represented a crucial turning point in the modernization of crisis management. Emergency managers were able to process and share information more efficiently thanks to digital databases, email communications, and geospatial information systems (GIS), which paved the way for real-time decision support systems (Comfort et al., 2004). Nonetheless, these digital tools relied significantly on human input for interpreting data and making decisions, indicating a transitional phase between manual and intelligent systems. One can deepen one's understanding of the evolution of crisis management by looking at landmark global crises that put response systems' resilience and adaptability to the test. The outbreak of Severe Acute Respiratory Syndrome (SARS) in 2003 was among the first global health crises that exposed both the limitations and potential of digital technologies. The swift proliferation of SARS highlighted how crucial global surveillance networks and transparent information sharing are. Despite the fact that digital systems like ProMED-mail and WHO's Global Outbreak Alert and Response Network (GOARN) provided early warning signals, the absence of interoperable data and delays in government disclosures impeded effective containment (Heymann & Rodier, 2004). Furthermore, digital systems were mostly not integrated, which necessitated manual data analysis and coordination. The SARS crisis illustrated the promise of digital technologies while underscoring the urgent requirement for automated decision-support capabilities that operate in real time.

The situation was more intricate with regard to Hurricane Katrina in 2005; this event became a turning point for discussions about reforming crisis management in the U.S. The hurricane revealed serious shortcomings in preparedness, communication between agencies, and situational awareness. GIS and satellite imagery were utilized for impact assessment, but their integration into coordinated decision-making frameworks was limited. Moreover, the use of real-time data from social media and private sector sources was limited by institutional barriers and the absence of adaptive frameworks. The calamity of Katrina ultimately spurred debates about the necessity of more intelligent, data-informed crisis response systems that could enhance human decision-making through computational intelligence.

The COVID-19 pandemic from 2020 to 2022 marked a major turning point in the history of crisis management tools, as it saw the widespread adoption of early artificial intelligence (AI) applications in public health and government policy decision-making. Unlike in previous crises, the COVID-19 pandemic saw the use of AI-driven models to forecast outbreak patterns, improve resource distribution, and track public sentiment. For example, the Canadian health surveillance firm BlueDot leveraged natural language processing and machine learning techniques to detect atypical pneumonia cases in Wuhan, China, several days prior to the release of official reports (Bogoch et al., 2020). In a similar manner, governments and health organizations globally utilized AI-enhanced dashboards to monitor infection rates, hospital bed capacities, and vaccine distribution logistics in real time. Chatbots like Clara from the CDC and the WHO's Health Alert on WhatsApp were deployed to sort symptoms, offer information, and alleviate pressure on healthcare systems (Vaishya et al., 2020). The aforementioned examples illustrate how AI tools have transitioned from merely processing data to actively aiding in decision-making, thereby linking the processes of gathering information and responding to crises. Even with these improvements, the use of AI tools during the COVID-19 pandemic also uncovered a number of difficulties. A number of AI models were not transparent, leading to worries about the ethical handling of health data, algorithmic bias, and the marginalization of underrepresented groups in relation to digital solutions (Naudé, 2020). Furthermore, the effectiveness of AI-driven interventions was greatly influenced by how well they were incorporated into human decision-making processes and the level of institutional trust in insights generated by machines. This indicates that early AI tools were more effective as decision support systems than as autonomous agents, highlighting the significance of a hybrid human-AI approach. In this context, the COVID-19 crisis not only sped up the advancement of digital solutions for managing crises but also highlighted the lasting importance of human judgment, ethical reasoning, and flexible leadership. The path from manual coordination to digital and AI-enhanced systems represents a wider epistemological shift in societal conceptions and responses to crises. Methods that relied on human expertise and local knowledge were flexible but did not scale well and lacked speed. Data accessibility and communication improved due to digital tools, but they necessitated substantial human interpretation. Although in the early stages of development, initial AI applications presented the promise of predictive analytics, automation, and continuous learning—abilities that are vital in high-pressure, time-sensitive settings. AI has started to reshape the crisis management landscape through the incorporation of simulations for scenario planning, automated alerts for disaster notifications, and chatbots for citizen engagement. Nonetheless, the constraints of AI—spanning from problems with data quality to a lack of context awareness—highlight the need for a hybrid model that leverages the complementary strengths of human intelligence and machine capabilities.

The development of crisis management tools from manual systems to early AI applications underscores a gradual but transformative shift toward hybrid intelligence frameworks. Historical crises like SARS, Hurricane Katrina, and COVID-19 serve as crucial milestones that demonstrate the potential and limitations of each technological phase. Although early digital tools enhanced operational efficiency and AI brought predictive and autonomous capabilities, the future of crisis management depends on combining these advancements with human oversight, ethical reasoning, and contextual adaptability. With the rise in technological complexity, there is a growing necessity for collaboration across disciplines and governance mechanisms that guarantee effectiveness and accountability in responding to crises.

3. THE HYBRID MODEL: A CONCEPTUAL FRAMEWORK

As the field of crisis management evolves, hybrid systems that combine human intelligence with AI are becoming essential tools for handling complex emergencies. To improve situational awareness, decision-making, and ethical oversight in times of crisis, these systems depend on a smooth collaboration between human judgment and data-driven computational capabilities. Data gathering and real-time analysis are two essential elements of a hybrid human-AI system. In contemporary crises like pandemics, natural disasters, and cyberattacks, the success of response efforts can hinge on the speed and accuracy of data collection. AI tools facilitate the real-time collection of data from diverse sources such as social media, sensors, mobile devices, and satellite imagery. This data is then analyzed with machine learning (ML) algorithms to uncover trends, spot anomalies, and predict risk areas. This capability provides response teams with dynamic situational intelligence that would be challenging for human teams to compile within critical timeframes. The raw computational power of AI must be balanced with human contextual interpretation to ensure that relevant and actionable insights are derived from the data.

Another important component of the hybrid model is the decision support system (DSS). These systems combine data outputs, predictive models, and rule-based logic to help decision-makers assess response options in uncertain situations. AI-driven DSS can assess and suggest the best actions to take based on predetermined criteria, including risk thresholds, logistical feasibility, or policy constraints. During the COVID-19 pandemic, for example, AI-powered dashboards were employed to simulate the effects of policies like lockdowns and vaccination rollouts, offering governments probabilistic scenarios to aid in informed decision-making (Naudé, 2020). However, depending too much on algorithmic guidance without human verification may result in unintended outcomes, especially in situations that are morally ambiguous or involve significant risk. As a result, hybrid systems need to incorporate interfaces that enable human specialists to interpret, contest, or supersede AI recommendations, drawing on their expertise in the field and ethical considerations. In crisis contexts, ethical judgment and human oversight are essential to counteract AI-driven automation. Though AI systems are highly proficient in recognizing patterns and optimizing processes, they do not possess the complex moral reasoning necessary for decisions that are empathetic and socially responsible. Human agents bring essential critical faculties to the table, including cultural sensitivity, emotional intelligence, and value-based reasoning. These are crucial in situations that involve vulnerable populations, scarce resources, or conflicting stakeholder interests (Binns, 2018). Furthermore, ethical oversight is crucial for mitigating the risks of algorithmic bias, surveillance overreach, and data misuse—issues that can worsen inequalities or undermine public trust in times of crisis (Eubanks, 2018). For this reason, hybrid crisis management systems need to establish protocols for transparency, accountability, and human auditability throughout all phases of the response cycle.

A conceptual flowchart of a hybrid human-AI crisis management process generally encompasses the following iterative stages: (1) acquiring data from multi-modal sources, (2) real-time preprocessing of data and analysis by AI, (3) generation of insights and recommended actions by DSS, (4) human review and ethical assessment of options, and (5) executing chosen actions with feedback loops for system learning. This model emphasizes the significance of ongoing interaction and feedback between machine outputs and human inputs, as opposed to a linear or one-way decision-making process. According to Rahwan et al. (2019), such a model bolsters resilience by utilizing AI's processing abilities while keeping human judgment at the core of strategic decisions. One can envision the degree of autonomy and human oversight in hybrid systems as lying on a continuum that extends from operations that are entirely manual to those that are completely autonomous. On one side, humans are "in the loop," maintaining control over all decisions while AI offers advisory input. In the intermediate "on loop" mode, actions may be initiated by AI under human supervision and with the possibility of intervention. At the most advanced level, AI functions independently while humans oversee the results afterwards (Endsley, 2017). The suitable degree of autonomy is contingent on the crisis context, the trustworthiness of the AI system, and the ethical significance of the decisions at stake. In the case of unpredictable crises or those with high stakes, it is necessary from a functional standpoint and a matter of principle to keep meaningful human control so that responses can be adaptive and sensitive to context.

4. APPLICATION AND CASE STUDIES

The fusion of human and artificial intelligence (AI) in crisis management has shown significant promise in various areas, such as disaster response, public health, cybersecurity, and supply chain resilience. AI technologies have been increasingly utilized in the context of disaster response for real-time prediction, logistics coordination, and situational awareness. Natural disasters like earthquakes, floods, and hurricanes can be anticipated using predictive models grounded in machine learning (ML). This foresight allows authorities to adopt preemptive measures and mitigate human casualties and material damage. As an example, India and Bangladesh have used Google's AI-driven flood forecasting system to provide early alerts. This system predicts flooded areas by integrating satellite data, historical trends, and hydrological models. Nevertheless, in light of AI's capabilities, human intelligence is still essential for interpreting outputs and executing actions tailored to the context, especially in intricate environments with limited resources. During Hurricane Harvey in 2017, human-led coordination illustrated this hybrid model, as AI-supported drone surveillance was enhanced by the logistical efforts of human emergency response teams (Cutter, 2018).

The collaboration of AI capabilities and human empathy has been essential in handling major crises like the COVID-19 pandemic during public health emergencies. While human health professionals guaranteed ethical decision-making and personalized care, AI algorithms were utilized for diagnosis, contact tracing, and predicting disease spread using real-time mobility data. Tools driven by AI, such as BlueDot and HealthMap, employed natural language processing and geospatial data to identify early indicators of the outbreak prior to official announcements (Bogoch et al., 2020). At the same time, chest X-ray and CT-scan image classifiers based on AI accelerated diagnosis, lightening the load for radiologists and improving the precision of early detection (Shi et al., 2021). However, these tools necessitated human supervision to confirm results, clarify ambiguous findings, and offer compassionate care to patients, particularly in high-stress settings like intensive care units. The combination of AI's analytical precision and human emotional intelligence illustrates the essential role of hybrid crisis management in healthcare.

Human-AI collaboration significantly improves threat detection and mitigation in the realm of cybersecurity incidents. AI systems have played a crucial role in identifying unusual patterns in network behavior, signaling possible intrusions, and carrying out initial interactions on their own. Machine learning is employed by sophisticated threat detection systems such as IBM's Watson for Cyber Security and CrowdStrike Falcon to analyze enormous datasets in order to detect zero-day vulnerabilities and phishing attempts. Nevertheless, human analysts play a crucial role in examining threats that are specific to the context, assessing strategic ramifications, and enforcing security protocols that span a long duration. During the 2021 Colonial Pipeline ransomware attack, while automated AI monitoring identified irregularities in operational technology systems, it was human-led incident response teams that carried out the shutdown and negotiated the resolution. This mutual reliance emphasizes the way AI boosts scale and speed, whereas humans bring contextual judgment, adaptability, and accountability. Hybrid intelligence also provides significant benefits in the area of supply chain disruptions, which are increasingly affected by climate-related events, pandemics, and geopolitical tensions. With the help of real-time data and predictive analytics, AI models can optimize routes, track global trade flows, and forecast bottlenecks. As an illustration, throughout the COVID-19 pandemic, IBM's Supply Chain Intelligence Suite offered comprehensive visibility of disruptions, allowing companies to efficiently rebalance inventory and reroute shipments. However, AI on its own is not capable of managing the strategic decision-making necessary for cross-border negotiations, vendor selection, or ethical trade-offs in uncertain situations. It is crucial for human decision-makers to interpret AI insights, balance competing objectives, and ensure that responses are in line with organizational values and stakeholder needs. The semiconductor shortage of 2020–2021 highlighted the necessity of human foresight in tackling structural dependencies and national policy considerations, domains where AI was deficient in situational context and geopolitical awareness. This case underscores that although AI can manage operational tasks with great efficiency, the strategic aspect of supply chain management still relies on human expertise.

5. ETHICAL, LEGAL AND SOCIAL IMPLICATIONS

Introducing Artificial Intelligence (AI) into crisis management raises various ethical, legal, and social issues that require careful examination to guarantee responsible innovation and fair results. The key issue is who will be responsible and accountable for decisions made with the assistance of AI. In crisis situations, where choices can have life-or-death implications, it becomes complicated to assign responsibility when results stem from automated recommendations or independent actions. Although AI systems can handle data at a speed and level of thoroughness beyond human capabilities, they do not possess moral agency. Binns (2018) points out that responsibility gaps can arise when it is unclear who should be held accountable for machine-generated outcomes—neither human operators nor developers. Therefore, it is crucial to set up clear accountability mechanisms—be it through legal liability frameworks or ethical oversight bodies. It is essential for governments and organizations to create strong governance mechanisms that uphold human oversight, guaranteeing that AI-supported decisions adhere to the limits of human moral responsibility (Floridi et al., 2018).

Another important ethical challenge concerns bias and fairness in algorithms. AI models learn from data, and if that data reflects existing societal biases, the resulting models can worsen inequalities, especially during crises when vulnerable populations are already at greater risk. For example, in disaster response situations, marginalized communities may be misidentified or deprioritized by biased facial recognition systems or predictive analytics tools, resulting in unequal access to aid (Mehrabi et al., 2021). These concerns were underscored by the COVID-19 pandemic, during which AI-driven triage systems and resource allocation algorithms occasionally deprioritized elderly and minority patients based on historically biased data sets (Leslie, 2020). To tackle this issue, it is essential for researchers and developers to integrate fairness-aware machine learning practices and establish continuous auditing mechanisms to identify and reduce algorithmic discrimination (Barocas et al., 2023). It is essential that ethical AI design goes beyond mere technical modifications; it must incorporate community involvement and stakeholder consultations to promote inclusive decision-making that considers local contexts and cultural values.

Transparency and explainability in AI systems are closely linked to fairness. During public health emergencies or natural disasters, which involve high stakes, it is crucial for those in decision-making positions and for those impacted to be able to comprehend the processes by which AI models generate particular recommendations. Black-box algorithms, which even their developers cannot fully understand, weaken public confidence and hinder accountability. Explainable AI (XAI) efforts aim to address this issue by enhancing the interpretability and understandability of AI behavior while maintaining performance levels (Doshi-Velez & Kim, 2017). Legally speaking, transparency is becoming more of a regulatory requirement, as exemplified by the European Union's AI Act, which requires risk-based disclosures and documentation (European Commission, 2021). Furthermore, for ethical legitimacy, interpretability is crucial: when stakeholders are unable to challenge or inquire about AI-driven decisions in a crisis—particularly those affecting evacuation plans, resource allocation, and surveillance procedures—these systems may cause ongoing harm and undermine civil liberties (Weller, 2019). It is therefore essential to create AI tools that are functionally transparent and socially intelligible. Finally, ethical considerations regarding AI use in crisis management must put human rights and data privacy at the forefront, particularly when handling sensitive personal data in emergencies. AI systems frequently depend on large quantities of real-time data, such as health records, geolocation information, social media interactions, and biometric identifiers. Although such data can improve situational awareness and facilitate proactive measures, it also carries risks of surveillance overreach, violations of consent, and misuse. Numerous governments implemented AI-driven contact-tracing apps during the COVID-19 pandemic, which raised concerns regarding long-term data retention, third-party access, and the erosion of privacy norms (Morley et al., 2020). Data protection laws must not be universally suspended without consideration, even in urgent crises. Strategies for deploying AI should incorporate ethical frameworks like "privacy by design" and "data minimization," so that only data deemed necessary is collected, it is stored securely, and its use respects individual rights. In addition, it is crucial to create legal protections against the normalization of surveillance practices once crises have passed in order to safeguard democratic principles and civil rights.

6. CHALLENGES AND LIMITATIONS

There are many challenges to implementing a hybrid human-AI approach to crisis management. These challenges span technological, organizational, cultural, and regulatory domains. A key challenge is technological constraints, especially those concerning data quality and system integration. To work well, AI systems depend on large amounts of data that are accurate, timely, and relevant. In times of crisis, data may be fragmented, unstructured, or lacking completeness. This can result in inaccurate predictions, unsuitable reactions, and decision paralysis. Moreover, a lot of organizations use legacy systems that do not easily work with newer AI technologies, leading to high integration costs and delays (Chen et al., 2021). The absence of standardization across platforms adds to the difficulties of achieving interoperability, a crucial factor in times of crisis when different agencies and jurisdictions must collaborate in real time. In addition to the technical infrastructure, there is considerable organizational resistance to adopting AI, which poses a significant obstacle. Resistance often arises from misunderstandings about AI capabilities and fears of job loss, particularly among crisis response professionals who depend on human intuition, experience, and judgment (Bughin et al., 2018). In addition, the successful implementation of hybrid systems necessitates new skill sets that integrate data literacy, AI ethics, and emergency management—skills that are often lacking in conventional training programs. In low- and middle-income countries, the skill gap is especially pronounced due to limited resources for upskilling or retraining personnel (Vinuesa et al., 2020). When machines assume decision-support or even decision-making roles, organizations might find it difficult to redefine roles and responsibilities, resulting in confusion, redundancy, or conflicts within command hierarchies.

Two major challenges are the trust in and cultural acceptance of AI systems in environments where the stakes are high. Trust is essential for any collaboration between humans and AI, but many AI systems lack transparency and explainability—

elements that greatly impede their acceptance (Doshi-Velez & Kim, 2017). In times of crisis, choices have to be made quickly, and stakeholders may hesitate to depend on "black-box" algorithms if they do not comprehend the basis of the decisions. Moreover, cultural aspects affect how individuals and communities view the legitimacy and reliability of AI. For example, individuals who have low digital literacy and have been previously exposed to surveillance technologies may exhibit skepticism or resistance toward AI-based interventions, irrespective of their effectiveness (Rahwan et al., 2019). To foster trust and guarantee fair outcomes, it is crucial to ensure that AI systems are designed and implemented inclusively and with sensitivity to context. Ultimately, barriers related to regulation and infrastructure constitute major impediments. Current legal frameworks often do not keep pace with technological innovation, resulting in gaps in accountability, liability, and governance of AI-driven decisions in crisis situations. There are ongoing uncertainties regarding accountability for failures of AI systems, especially in critical scenarios like natural disasters and pandemics. Furthermore, although real-time data sharing and analytics are crucial in crisis response, regulations governing data management—like the EU's GDPR—can limit them (Voigt & Von dem Bussche, 2017). Challenges related to infrastructure, such as insufficient internet connectivity and limited digital service coverage—especially in rural regions impacted by disasters—pose additional obstacles to the implementation and scaling of AI solutions. These challenges highlight the need to create enabling environments through policy alignment, investment in digital infrastructure, and collaboration across sectors.

7. FUTURE DIRECTIONS

With the rising complexity and frequency of crises in our interconnected world, the development of human-AI symbiosis offers promising opportunities to enhance crisis management systems. New advancements in conversational AI and neuro-symbolic systems play a crucial role in this trajectory. Powered by large language models (LLMs), conversational AI improves real-time communication and decision support by offering context-aware and linguistically rich interactions during crises. These systems, in contrast to conventional chatbots, can understand subtle queries, tailor responses according to stakeholder roles, and provide multilingual assistance—essential during pandemics or natural disasters with cross-border effects.

Human-in-the-loop (HITL) and human-on-the-loop (HOTL) models, which implement human oversight in automated systems, are essential to the future of hybrid crisis management. The HITL model guarantees the ongoing involvement of human agents in the AI decision-making process. They actively validate data inputs, monitor real-time AI outputs, and intervene when necessary (Amershi et al., 2019).

Its worth is especially evident in ambiguous or unprecedented crisis situations where AI may not have access to contextual training data. In contrast, the HOTL model grants greater autonomy to AI systems while maintaining human oversight for auditing and post-decision accountability (Rahwan et al., 2019). These models together represent a growing comprehension of human-AI complementarity, highlighting the importance of trust, adaptability, and responsiveness. The swift uptake of these systems, however, makes it essential to establish standards and best practices for ethical, reliable, and equitable implementation. The growing number of AI tools in emergency management can lead to inconsistent or even dangerous results due to differences in design protocols, data governance, and testing benchmarks. It is thus vital to set international standards for the accuracy of data, fairness of algorithms, robustness of models, and usability (Floridi et al., 2018). As we look to the future, it is essential that policy and institutional frameworks evolve in line with these technological advancements. It is important for those responsible for making policy to back cooperative efforts that span multiple sectors and connect academia, tech companies, emergency services, and civil society organizations. It is crucial to invest in interdisciplinary training that provides crisis professionals with AI literacy and ensures that technologists are well-versed in crisis ethics. In addition, it is essential for regulatory authorities to elucidate liability standards concerning human-AI decision-making processes and to protect data privacy while ensuring timely access in emergency situations (Taddeo & Floridi, 2018). With the increasing integration of AI into crisis response, the goal should be to enhance human judgment rather than replace it. The future of crisis management will hinge not on the choice between AI and humans, but on the effective combination of both their strengths through hybrid systems that are carefully designed and ethically governed.

8. CONCLUSION

The hybrid crisis management model, which combines the analytical power of artificial intelligence with the contextual and ethical judgment of human cognition, represents a paradigm shift in the identification, interpretation, and resolution of crises. As modern crises are increasingly characterized by complexity, nonlinearity, and high uncertainty—features well described by Chaos and Complexity Theories—conventional response models often fall short in providing timely and adaptive solutions. The integration of AI capabilities such as machine learning, natural language processing, and computer vision enhances crisis response by enabling the rapid processing of large-scale, real-time data and forecasting potential crisis trajectories. At the same time, the incorporation of human factors—such as intuition, moral reasoning, and empathy—ensures that decision-making remains context-sensitive and ethically grounded. This synergy is particularly vital in high-stakes environments where decisions cannot rely solely on quantitative outputs but must account for human impact and societal values. The hybrid model aligns with theoretical perspectives like the Theory of the Extended Mind and Augmented Intelligence, which advocate for a collaborative rather than substitutive relationship between humans and intelligent systems. By reducing cognitive overload and enhancing pattern recognition under stress, AI serves as a cognitive partner that supports, rather than replaces, human expertise.

However, the successful operationalization of this model requires more than just technical integration—it demands a reconfiguration of institutional, organizational, and cultural frameworks to support interdisciplinary collaboration. The design and deployment of AI-enhanced decision-support systems must be informed by input from diverse stakeholders, including AI technologists, crisis managers, behavioral scientists, ethicists, and policymakers. This collaborative approach ensures that technological solutions are not only efficient but also socially responsible, interpretable, and aligned with the ethical imperatives of crisis response. Furthermore, the development of adaptive user interfaces, mechanisms for trust calibration, and safeguards for human oversight—such as human-in-the-loop and human-on-the-loop frameworks—are essential to maintaining accountability and transparency in automated processes. As crises often involve rapid developments and emotionally charged scenarios, it is crucial that AI systems are designed to complement rather than override human decision-making, especially in morally complex or life-critical contexts. This requires ongoing investment in training, organizational learning, and the cultivation of a culture that embraces human-AI collaboration as an evolving partnership rather than a fixed technological solution.

Ultimately, in a global landscape increasingly marked by systemic risks—from climate change and pandemics to geopolitical conflict and infrastructural vulnerabilities—the hybrid model offers a resilient and forward-looking framework for crisis management. It empowers institutions and societies to move beyond reactive models toward proactive, informed, and adaptive strategies that harness the full spectrum of human and machine capabilities. By bridging the gap between computational intelligence and human wisdom, this model enables faster, more accurate, and ethically attuned responses to crises that no single domain could achieve in isolation. The path forward lies in embracing this integrative vision—one that is not only technologically sophisticated but also deeply human-centered—to create crisis response systems that are prepared for the unpredictable challenges of the 21st century.

REFERENCES

Abdelhadi, A., & Akkartal, E. (2024). Supply chain efficiency a structural analysis in turkey's retail sector. *Brazilian Journal of Operations & Production Management, 21*(3), 2150–2150. DOI: 10.14488/BJOPM.2150.2024

Akkartal, E., & Aras, G. Y. (2021). Sustainability in fleet management. *Journal of Advanced Research in Economics and Administrative Sciences, 2*(3), 13–39. DOI: 10.47631/jareas.v2i3.288

Akkartal, G. R., & Mızrak, F. (2023). Defining reverse and green supplier selection criteria with a strategic management approach. In *Economic Development and the Environmental Ecosystem: The Role of Energy Policy in Economic Growth* (pp. 205–218). Springer Nature Switzerland. DOI: 10.1007/978-3-031-26596-9_17

Amershi, S., Weld, D., Vorvoreanu, M., Fourney, A., Nushi, B., Collisson, P., & Horvitz, E. (2019, May). Guidelines for human-AI interaction. In *Proceedings of the 2019 chi conference on human factors in computing systems* (pp. 1-13).

Barocas, S., Hardt, M., & Narayanan, A. (2023). *Fairness and machine learning: Limitations and opportunities.* MIT press.

Binns, R. (2018). Fairness in machine learning: Lessons from political philosophy. *Proceedings of the 2018 Conference on Fairness, Accountability and Transparency*, 149–159.

Bogoch, I. I., Watts, A., Thomas-Bachli, A., Huber, C., Kraemer, M. U., & Khan, K. (2020). Pneumonia of unknown aetiology in Wuhan, China: Potential for international spread via commercial air travel. *Journal of Travel Medicine, 27*(2), taaa008. DOI: 10.1093/jtm/taaa008 PMID: 31943059

Boin, A., Ekengren, M., & Rhinard, M. (2020). *The European Union as crisis manager: Patterns and prospects.* Cambridge University Press.

Bousdekis, A., Magoutas, B., Apostolou, D., & Mentzas, G. (2021). A review of data-driven crisis management. *Journal of Decision Systems, 30*(1-2), 1–18. DOI: 10.1080/12460125.2020.1812014

Bughin, J., Seong, J., Manyika, J., Chui, M., & Joshi, R. (2018). Notes from the AI frontier: Modeling the impact of AI on the world economy. *McKinsey Global Institute, 4*(1), 2–61.

Cebir, Y., & Akkartal, E. (2024). Digital twin in logistics and supply chain management. In *Strategic Innovations for Dynamic Supply Chains* (pp. 170–192). IGI Global. DOI: 10.4018/979-8-3693-3575-8.ch008

Chen, J., Cheng, Y., & Li, K. (2021). Data quality challenges in integrating AI for crisis management. *Journal of Information Systems and Crisis Response*, *13*(1), 55–68.

Clark, A., & Chalmers, D. (1998). The extended mind. analysis, 58(1), 7-19.

Comfort, L. K. (2007). Crisis management in hindsight: Cognition, communication, coordination, and control. *Public Administration Review*, *67*(s1), 189–197. DOI: 10.1111/j.1540-6210.2007.00827.x

Comfort, L. K., Boin, A., & Demchak, C. C. (Eds.). (2010). *Designing resilience: Preparing for extreme events*. University of Pittsburgh Pre. DOI: 10.2307/j.ctt5hjq0c

Comfort, L. K., Ko, K., & Zagorecki, A. (2004). Coordination in rapidly evolving disaster response systems: The role of information. *The American Behavioral Scientist*, *48*(3), 295–313. DOI: 10.1177/0002764204268987

Cutter, S. L. (2018). Compound, cascading, or complex disasters: What's in a name? *Environment*, *60*(6), 16–25. DOI: 10.1080/00139157.2018.1517518

Danisman, M., & Akkartal, E. (2023). Defining a new business model for sustainable biomass production from forestry residues in Türkiye by using TRIZ. *International Journal of Energy Economics and Policy*, *13*(3), 243–253. DOI: 10.32479/ijeep.13985

Davenport, T. H., & Ronanki, R. (2018). Artificial intelligence for the real world. *Harvard Business Review*, *96*(1), 108–116.

Doshi-Velez, F., & Kim, B. (2017). Towards a rigorous science of interpretable machine learning. *arXiv preprint arXiv:1702.08608.*

Endsley, M. R. (2017). From here to autonomy: Lessons learned from human–automation research. *Human Factors*, *59*(1), 5–27. DOI: 10.1177/0018720816681350 PMID: 28146676

Eubanks, V. (2018). *Automating inequality: How high-tech tools profile, police, and punish the poor*. St. Martin's Press.

European Commission. (2021). *Proposal for a regulation laying down harmonised rules on artificial intelligence (Artificial Intelligence Act).* Retrieved from: https://eur-lex.europa.eu/legal-content/EN/TXT/?uri=CELEX:52021PC0206

Floridi, L., Cowls, J., Beltrametti, M., Chatila, R., Chazerand, P., Dignum, V., Luetge, C., Madelin, R., Pagallo, U., Rossi, F., Schafer, B., Valcke, P., & Vayena, E. (2018). AI4People—an ethical framework for a good AI society: Opportunities, risks, principles, and recommendations. *Minds and Machines*, *28*(4), 689–707. DOI: 10.1007/s11023-018-9482-5 PMID: 30930541

Heymann, D. L., & Rodier, G. (2004). SARS: lessons from a new disease. *Learning from SARS: Preparing for the next disease outbreak*, 234-245.

Imran, M., Castillo, C., Lucas, J., Meier, P., & Vieweg, S. (2014, April). AIDR: Artificial intelligence for disaster response. In *Proceedings of the 23rd international conference on world wide web* (pp. 159-162).

Kapucu, N. (2008). Collaborative emergency management: Better community organising, better public preparedness and response. *Disasters*, *32*(2), 239–262. DOI: 10.1111/j.1467-7717.2008.01037.x PMID: 18380853

Klein, G. (2008). Naturalistic decision making. *Human Factors*, *50*(3), 456–460. DOI: 10.1518/001872008X288385 PMID: 18689053

Klein, G. A. (2017). *Sources of power: How people make decisions*. MIT press.

Leslie, D. (2020). Tackling COVID-19 through responsible AI innovation: Five steps in the right direction. *Harvard Data Science Review*, *10*, 1–78.

Mehrabi, N., Morstatter, F., Saxena, N., Lerman, K., & Galstyan, A. (2021). A survey on bias and fairness in machine learning. *ACM Computing Surveys*, *54*(6), 1–35. DOI: 10.1145/3457607

Mızrak, F. (2022). An Evaluation for the Use of Alternative Vehicle Technologies and Energy Resources in Logistic Sector with a Strategic Approach. In *Circular Economy and the Energy Market: Achieving Sustainable Economic Development Through Energy Policy* (pp. 159–171). Springer International Publishing. DOI: 10.1007/978-3-031-13146-2_13

Mızrak, F. (2023). Managing Risks and Crises in the Logistics Sector: A Comprehensive Analysis of Strategies and Prioritization Using AHP Method. Meriç Uluslararası Sosyal ve Stratejik Araştırmalar Dergisi, 7(Özel Sayı), 114-148.

Mızrak, F. (2024). Effective change management strategies: Exploring dynamic models for organizational transformation. In *Perspectives on artificial intelligence in times of turbulence: Theoretical background to applications* (pp. 135–162). IGI Global.

Mızrak, F. (2024). Strategies for Sustainable Business Growth in Maritime Logistics. In Trends, Challenges, and Practices in Contemporary Strategic Management (pp. 108-125). IGI Global Scientific Publishing. DOI: 10.4018/979-8-3693-1155-4.ch006

Mızrak, F., & Akkartal, G. R. (2024). An Analysis of Alternative Energy Sources and Applications in Maritime Transportation with a Strategic Management Approach. Decision Making in Interdisciplinary Renewable Energy Projects: Navigating Energy Investments, 97-109.

Mizrak, F., Polat, L., & Tasar, S. A. (2024). Applying Entropy Weighting and 2-Tuple Linguistic T-Spherical Fuzzy MCDM: A Case Study of Developing a Strategic Sustainability Plan for Istanbul Airport. *Sustainability (Basel)*, *16*(24), 11104. DOI: 10.3390/su162411104

Morley, J., Cowls, J., Taddeo, M., & Floridi, L. (2020). Ethical guidelines for COVID-19 tracing apps. *Nature*, *582*(7810), 29–31. DOI: 10.1038/d41586-020-01578-0 PMID: 32467596

Morrison, K. (2002). *School leadership and complexity theory*. Routledge.

Naudé, W. (2020). Artificial intelligence vs COVID-19: Limitations, constraints and pitfalls. *AI & Society*, *35*(3), 761–765. DOI: 10.1007/s00146-020-00978-0 PMID: 32346223

Nemitz, P. (2018). Constitutional democracy and technology in the age of artificial intelligence. *Philosophical Transactions. Series A, Mathematical, Physical, and Engineering Sciences*, *376*(2133), 20180089. DOI: 10.1098/rsta.2018.0089 PMID: 30323003

Özkanlısoy, Ö., & Akkartal, E. (2021). Digital transformation in supply chains: Current applications, contributions and challenges. *Business & Management Studies: An International Journal*, *9*(1), 32–55.

Özkanlısoy, Ö., & Akkartal, E. (2022). The effect of Suez Canal blockage on supply chains. *Dokuz Eylül Üniversitesi Denizcilik Fakültesi Dergisi*, *14*(1), 51–79. DOI: 10.18613/deudfd.933816

Pearson, C. M., & Clair, J. A. (1998). Reframing crisis management. *Academy of Management Review*, *23*(1), 59–76. DOI: 10.2307/259099

Rahwan, I., Cebrian, M., Obradovich, N., Bongard, J., Bonnefon, J. F., Breazeal, C., Crandall, J. W., Christakis, N. A., Couzin, I. D., Jackson, M. O., Jennings, N. R., Kamar, E., Kloumann, I. M., Larochelle, H., Lazer, D., McElreath, R., Mislove, A., Parkes, D. C., Pentland, A. S., & Wellman, M. (2019). Machine behaviour. *Nature*, *568*(7753), 477–486. DOI: 10.1038/s41586-019-1138-y PMID: 31019318

Shi, F., Wang, J., Shi, J., Wu, Z., Wang, Q., Tang, Z., He, K., Shi, Y., & Shen, D. (2021). Review of artificial intelligence techniques in imaging data acquisition, segmentation, and diagnosis for COVID-19. *IEEE Reviews in Biomedical Engineering*, *14*, 4–15. DOI: 10.1109/RBME.2020.2987975 PMID: 32305937

Shneiderman, B. (2020). Human-centered artificial intelligence: Reliable, safe & trustworthy. *International Journal of Human-Computer Interaction*, *36*(6), 495–504. DOI: 10.1080/10447318.2020.1741118

Taddeo, M., & Floridi, L. (2018). How AI can be a force for good. *Science*, *361*(6404), 751–752. DOI: 10.1126/science.aat5991 PMID: 30139858

Turoff, M., Chumer, M., de Walle, B. V., & Yao, X. (2004). The design of a dynamic emergency response management information system (DERMIS). [JITTA]. *Journal of Information Technology Theory and Application*, *5*(4), 3.

Tversky, A., & Kahneman, D. (1974). Judgment under Uncertainty: Heuristics and Biases: Biases in judgments reveal some heuristics of thinking under uncertainty. *science*, *185*(4157), 1124-1131.

Vaishya, R., Javaid, M., Khan, I. H., & Haleem, A. (2020). Artificial Intelligence (AI) applications for COVID-19 pandemic. *Diabetes & Metabolic Syndrome*, *14*(4), 337–339. DOI: 10.1016/j.dsx.2020.04.012 PMID: 32305024

Vinuesa, R., Azizpour, H., Leite, I., Balaam, M., Dignum, V., Domisch, S., Felländer, A., Langhans, S. D., Tegmark, M., & Fuso Nerini, F. (2020). The role of artificial intelligence in achieving the Sustainable Development Goals. *Nature Communications*, *11*(1), 233. DOI: 10.1038/s41467-019-14108-y PMID: 31932590

Voigt, P., & Von dem Bussche, A. (2017). *The EU General Data Protection Regulation (GDPR): A practical guide*. Springer International Publishing., DOI: 10.1007/978-3-319-57959-7

Weller, A. (2019). Transparency: motivations and challenges. In *Explainable AI: interpreting, explaining and visualizing deep learning* (pp. 23–40). Springer International Publishing. DOI: 10.1007/978-3-030-28954-6_2

Chapter 4
IoT and Smart Sensors for Real-Time Monitoring of Aid Distribution

Muhammed Bilal Ketenci
https://orcid.org/0009-0000-2100-835X
Yeditepe University, Istanbul, Turkey

Nazlıcan Çelik
Yeditepe University, Istanbul, Turkey

ABSTRACT

This chapter investigates the integration of Internet of Things (IoT) technologies and smart sensors in humanitarian logistics to enhance real-time monitoring and aid distribution efficiency. Focusing on applications such as RFID, GPS tracking, and environmental sensors, it highlights how these tools improve supply chain visibility, automate inventory control, and support cold chain management in disaster-prone areas. Drawing on recent case insights from WFP, UNICEF, and other global organizations, the chapter identifies key technological, infrastructural, and ethical challenges, including data security, connectivity, and scalability. Türkiye is examined as a focal context due to its exposure to natural disasters and increasing digital capacity. The chapter concludes with a strategic roadmap for sustainable IoT implementation in humanitarian aid, emphasizing collaboration, trust, and long-term resilience.

DOI: 10.4018/979-8-3373-3643-5.ch004

1. INTRODUCTION

Humanitarian aid delivery in disaster-affected regions presents immense logistical, infrastructural, and ethical challenges. The chaotic environments following natural disasters, armed conflicts, or large-scale displacements often disrupt conventional supply chains, impede communication infrastructure, and delay critical relief efforts. These disruptions can result in aid bottlenecks, misallocation of resources, or even total breakdowns in delivery systems. In such contexts, ensuring transparency, traceability, and timeliness in the distribution of essential supplies becomes paramount to saving lives and restoring dignity to affected populations.

The emergence of real-time monitoring technologies, particularly those based on the Internet of Things (IoT), offers a transformative potential for improving humanitarian logistics. By enabling continuous visibility over shipments, environmental conditions, and stock levels, IoT and smart sensor systems empower relief organizations to respond more quickly, accurately, and ethically. Technologies such as GPS trackers, RFID tags, temperature sensors, and cloud-based dashboards provide vital insights into the state and location of humanitarian goods, allowing for proactive intervention when delays or anomalies occur. These tools not only enhance operational efficiency but also contribute to building trust among donors, local governments, and beneficiaries by reducing losses and increasing accountability.

IoT and smart sensor systems serve as the backbone of this digital transformation in humanitarian logistics. Their role extends beyond basic monitoring; they facilitate predictive maintenance, automated alerts, and decentralized decision-making—all essential in volatile and resource-constrained environments. Innovations in energy harvesting, wireless mesh networks, and AI-integrated analytics further support the deployment of these technologies in hard-to-reach or infrastructure-poor regions. As humanitarian crises become more frequent and complex due to climate change, pandemics, and geopolitical tensions, the need for agile, resilient, and tech-driven logistics systems becomes increasingly urgent.

This chapter focuses specifically on Türkiye, a country frequently exposed to earthquakes, refugee inflows, and regional instability. Türkiye's geographical location at the intersection of Europe, Asia, and the Middle East has positioned it as both a recipient and a hub of humanitarian aid. In recent years, digital transformation efforts in public services, including logistics and emergency response, have accelerated. However, the integration of IoT-enabled systems into humanitarian supply chains remains nascent and fragmented. The objective of this chapter is to explore the potential and challenges of adopting IoT and smart sensor technologies in Türkiye's humanitarian aid landscape. It investigates use cases, technological infrastructure, and strategic roadmaps necessary to foster a sustainable and efficient aid delivery model. Through a combination of literature synthesis and global case insights, the chapter aims to inform practitioners, policymakers, and researchers on how to effectively deploy smart technologies for real-time humanitarian logistics.

2. LITERATURE BACKGROUND

The evolution of the Internet of Things (IoT) has been characterized by significant technological transformations over the past two decades, beginning with basic sensor networks and evolving into intelligent, interconnected ecosystems. Wang et al. (2021) traced this transformation from early research-driven applications to commercially viable, distributed IoT networks that integrate machine learning, cloud computing, and big data analytics. Their bibliometric review highlights the emergence of adaptive, decentralized IoT architectures capable of real-time decision-making. Similarly, Alaba (2024) emphasizes that the application of IoT in developing regions, particularly in Africa, has been essential in bridging digital divides and promoting sustainable socio-economic development, revealing how IoT has shifted from being purely a technological advancement to a socio-technical enabler. Bauer et al. (2021) further note that smart cities have driven IoT maturity by employing sensor networks for dynamic traffic control, pollution monitoring, and waste management, showcasing the urban-scale benefits of IoT deployment.

Smart sensors, as the physical manifestation of IoT, have undergone a radical evolution in both hardware and software capabilities. Malhotra et al. (2021) outline how smart sensors transitioned from passive data recorders to proactive agents embedded with computational intelligence, security protocols, and wireless transmission functionalities. Mishra et al. (2022) expanded on this by proposing energy-efficient solutions using evolutionary computing for software-defined sensor networks, offering resilience and longevity in environments with limited power availability. Aarif KO et al. (2025) also contributed by showing how smart sensors revolutionized precision agriculture through real-time soil, temperature, and crop health monitoring, which parallels their applicability in humanitarian logistics where environmental sensitivity is critical. As such, smart sensors now serve not only as environmental sentinels but also as autonomous decision-making units capable of operating in volatile and resource-constrained settings.

The development of interoperable and scalable sensor systems is central to modern IoT. Chen et al. (2024) presented a digital twin-based architecture for structural health monitoring (SHM), which integrates decentralized sensor networks with cloud platforms to enable real-time analysis and proactive maintenance. Their model emphasizes interoperability—a crucial factor when deploying sensors across heterogeneous infrastructure. Darabkh and Al-Akhras (2025) focused on energy efficiency and fault tolerance through multi-sensor data fusion, which ensures continuity of data collection even when individual devices fail. These innovations are particularly relevant for humanitarian applications, where infrastructure damage and sensor failure risks are heightened. Moreover, Mizrak and Yaşar (2025) demonstrated the potential of piezoelectric energy harvesting within urban infrastructure, allowing smart sensors to function without traditional energy inputs—a necessity for long-term sustainability in post-disaster regions.

Artificial intelligence has increasingly become embedded in IoT sensor networks to enhance performance, especially in constrained environments. Namatherdhala et al. (2023) introduced a meta-heuristic algorithm embedded in artificial neural networks for disease prediction via smart health sensors. Their work illustrates the potential for real-time diagnostics, which can be repurposed for health surveillance in humanitarian crises. Aarif KO et al. (2025) reiterated the significance of precision sensing for environmental variables, showing how AI-enhanced sensors are essential in agriculture and by extension, food distribution monitoring in disaster-hit areas. The fusion of meta-heuristics, machine learning, and embedded intelligence is now foundational in modern sensor networks designed for rapid deployment and minimal human oversight.

Operational efficiency and logistical resilience are core to IoT's contribution to supply chains. Öztürk and Akkartal (2024) emphasized the value of IoT in last-mile delivery systems, focusing on vehicle tracking, route optimization, and load monitoring—all of which are vital in emergency aid logistics. Abdelhadi and Akkartal (2019) added depth by discussing the challenges of IoT implementation in warehouse management, including network reliability, sensor calibration, and integration with existing ERP systems. Their findings support the argument that IoT-driven logistics are not only feasible but essential for modernizing humanitarian response operations. Similarly, Özkanlısoy and Akkartal (2021) identified digital transformation frameworks where IoT plays a pivotal role in achieving visibility and agility across supply chains, characteristics that are indispensable during chaotic relief efforts.

Parallel to the evolution of IoT and smart sensors, advancements in predictive maintenance and data-driven logistics have transformed industrial and humanitarian asset management. Lawrence and Durana (2021) discussed how AI-powered big data platforms have redefined real-time logistics, enabling systems to predict equipment failure and reallocate resources efficiently. Their findings are echoed by Chen et al. (2023), who outlined the implementation challenges of data-driven structural monitoring, particularly in hostile environments. The combination of predictive algorithms and sensor-generated datasets now supports anticipatory supply chain management, which is critical during time-sensitive disaster response operations. Celestin (2023) further supported this by demonstrating how predictive maintenance reduced operational downtime in logistics fleets, ensuring the uninterrupted delivery of essential supplies.

From a strategic perspective, data-driven logistics has enabled organizations to shift from reactive to proactive operations. Tran-Dang et al. (2025) presented a framework for shaping logistics through digital technologies and strategic integration, highlighting benefits such as enhanced visibility, lower emissions, and demand-responsive planning. In alignment with this, Ojadi et al. (2024) explored the role of big data analytics in optimizing sustainable transportation and reducing environmental footprints. Their work directly informs the structuring of green humanitarian supply chains, where operational sustainability and social impact converge. Additionally, Kanu et al. (2025) emphasized predictive maintenance for gas distribution systems, a lesson that translates to logistics systems managing volatile or sensitive goods in disaster zones.

The literature also reflects a growing emphasis on resilience and adaptability in supply chain systems through smart integration. Mızrak (2023, 2024, 2025) in a trilogy of works, explored how the triple nexus of smart, secure, and sustainable supply chains supports resilience in the post-pandemic era. These studies converge on a few key insights: the integration of cybersecurity frameworks into IoT logistics systems, the necessity of scenario-based planning for disruption management, and the prioritization of strategic investments in digital resilience. His 2025 study especially emphasizes cybersecurity-aware logistics supported by sensor technologies and cloud-based predictive platforms, reinforcing the idea that digital tools are not merely operational enablers but strategic imperatives for humanitarian actors.

Furthermore, case-specific insights from Türkiye's retail and distribution sectors help contextualize these technologies within a regional perspective. Abdelhadi and Akkartal (2024) provided structural analysis of supply chain efficiency in Türkiye, revealing how IoT and digital platforms improved inventory turnover, minimized stockouts, and enabled dynamic distribution in both urban and semi-urban areas. These insights are transferable to humanitarian logistics, particularly in contexts where national infrastructure must adapt rapidly in response to disasters. Their analysis illustrates that the deployment of smart logistics platforms, though initially complex, results in measurable gains in speed, coverage, and coordination.

In sum, the literature demonstrates a robust evolution of IoT and smart sensor systems from passive collectors to intelligent, energy-efficient, and interoperable agents embedded in complex decision-making environments. Through diverse applications—from urban infrastructure and agricultural monitoring to fleet logistics and predictive maintenance—these technologies offer profound opportunities to improve the efficiency, transparency, and responsiveness of humanitarian aid distribution. The convergence of sensor technologies, AI analytics, and strategic planning creates a multidimensional infrastructure that can respond to the operational demands of modern crises, offering scalable solutions for governments, NGOs, and international relief agencies. These research contributions collectively build a compelling case for the widespread and strategic use of IoT in humanitarian contexts.

3. SMART SENSORS AND REAL-TIME MONITORING IN HUMANITARIAN AID

The integration of smart sensor technologies into humanitarian logistics has redefined how aid is monitored, managed, and delivered in complex operational contexts. A wide array of sensors—ranging from GPS modules and RFID tags to environmental sensors measuring temperature and humidity—enable organizations to make evidence-based decisions and respond promptly to emerging needs. Sehrawat and Gill (2019) classified smart sensors into categories based on physical, chemical, and environmental parameters, highlighting their applicability across sectors, including healthcare, logistics, and agriculture. RFID technology, in particular, has emerged as a cornerstone of IoT-enabled aid operations. Costa et al. (2021) reviewed the evolution of RFID sensors and underscored their transformation into dynamic, information-rich systems capable of not only identification but also monitoring ambient conditions. These RFID-based sensors now integrate with passive tags that allow tracking of temperature-sensitive goods such as vaccines and perishable food during transport and storage. Similarly, Miao et al. (2023) proposed a novel RFID-integrated sensor that simultaneously detects humidity, light, and CO_2 levels, making it highly relevant for monitoring conditions within enclosed humanitarian warehouses or shipping containers. This multi-parameter approach significantly increases visibility across the supply chain and helps reduce spoilage and inefficiencies.

In the field of sustainable logistics, the role of smart sensors is becoming increasingly critical. Ikumapayi et al. (2024) emphasized how smart sensor systems can support real-time monitoring by collecting geospatial and status data for cargo, vehicles, and infrastructure components in transit. These functionalities enable humanitarian agencies to develop responsive strategies that minimize logistical delays, optimize delivery routes, and ensure resource allocation under uncertain conditions. Rayhana et al. (2021) and Soussi et al. (2024) echoed similar sentiments within the context of smart agriculture, where RFID and sensor platforms provide real-time status checks of crop conditions and logistics chains. Their findings are readily transferable to humanitarian food aid operations, where monitoring shelf life, humidity, and transportation time is crucial. These insights are especially important for crisis situations where deliveries may take place in high-temperature environments or over long distances without consistent refrigeration. Therefore, the technical evolution of sensors has enabled a shift from reactive to predictive logistics planning in humanitarian response scenarios.

Visibility and transparency are foundational elements of effective humanitarian logistics, and smart technologies have significantly enhanced both. Khan et al. (2022) conceptualized a model linking transparency as a mediating variable between emerging technologies and logistics sustainability, arguing that real-time data access fosters trust, operational efficiency, and donor confidence. RFID has proven particularly effective in this regard; Wagner et al. (2024) demonstrated its ability to support disaster relief operations by increasing inter-organizational coordination and reducing information asymmetries. Their empirical findings revealed that RFID-enabled systems improve real-time status reporting and reduce resource duplication during large-scale emergency responses. This was further supported by Midkiff (2021), who advocated a "control tower" approach in which centralized data platforms aggregate sensor inputs to monitor aid movement, predict inventory needs, and resolve delivery anomalies. In the context of refugee aid, Pascucci (2021) warned of the over-technologization of humanitarian systems but acknowledged that digitized supply chains reduce redundancy and improve oversight. Płaczek and Świtalska (2023) emphasized that these technologies help move humanitarian systems beyond ad hoc delivery to a more planned, reliable, and data-driven paradigm.

The ability to track shipments in real time and monitor environmental parameters like temperature and humidity is particularly valuable in cold chain management, especially for distributing heat-sensitive goods such as vaccines or blood supplies. Cil et al. (2022) illustrated this with a case study in a container port, where IoT-enabled cold chain monitoring ensured that container temperatures were continuously tracked and anomalies were flagged in real time to prevent spoilage. Similarly, Raffik et al. (2021) proposed an integrated system using industrial automation and IIoT tools for tracking inventory levels and maintaining temperature control in transit. These systems contribute significantly to operational continuity and quality assurance in humanitarian logistics. By combining sensor outputs with centralized dashboards, field operators can gain actionable insights without manual inspections. This automation reduces labor intensity, speeds up decision-making, and ensures that vulnerable populations receive uncontaminated and functional aid materials. Moreover, automated inventory management allows agencies to respond quickly to unexpected spikes in demand, such as during natural disasters or pandemic outbreaks, when cold chain infrastructure is strained.

Operational efficiency and risk mitigation are enhanced significantly by real-time monitoring capabilities. Ikumapayi et al. (2024) highlighted that real-time sensor data allows logistics planners to proactively re-route shipments based on road conditions, weather disruptions, or civil disturbances, thus reducing both operational delays and exposure to physical risks. Mızrak and Akkartal (2024) emphasized that these capabilities are essential for achieving the Sustainable Development Goals, particularly in terms of ensuring access to food, water, and medical supplies in fragile regions. Khan et al. (2022) added that the transparency enabled by real-time data reduces not only operational blind spots but also corruption risks, as each step in the logistics chain becomes traceable and auditable. Wagner et al. (2024) similarly found that RFID systems deter theft and misappropriation by creating a digital trail for every item. These improvements collectively foster a more secure, accountable, and adaptive humanitarian logistics system capable of maintaining continuity even in highly dynamic and unstable environments.

Overall, the integration of smart sensors and real-time monitoring tools into humanitarian logistics represents a transformative advancement in the way aid is distributed and managed. The technologies examined—from RFID and environmental sensors to GPS-enabled tracking and cold chain monitors—enable a high-resolution view of the entire logistics network, from warehouses to last-mile delivery. These tools not only increase transparency and operational efficiency but also play a crucial role in safeguarding the integrity and timeliness of aid, particularly in resource-scarce and volatile settings. As humanitarian organizations continue to digitize their supply chains, the ongoing refinement and deployment of sensor-based technologies will be pivotal in enhancing both the responsiveness and resilience of global aid systems.

4. IOT-ENABLED SUSTAINABLE AID DISTRIBUTION

The implementation of IoT-enabled technologies in humanitarian logistics is increasingly aligned with sustainability objectives, offering solutions that simultaneously enhance operational efficiency and reduce environmental impact. The integration of green logistics practices, real-time data systems, and predictive analytics supports a systemic transformation in how aid is distributed, especially under the growing pressure to meet climate goals and optimize resource use. Khairuddin and Rahman (2025) emphasize the role of IoT infrastructure in equipping humanitarian distribution centers with intelligent systems that improve responsiveness, minimize wastage, and support eco-friendly logistics. Their findings demonstrate that IoT not only enables real-time inventory visibility but also provides a foundation for energy-aware decision-making, leading to measurable improvements in environmental footprint and operational agility.

Green logistics and environmental monitoring are becoming integral to the sustainability agenda of humanitarian operations. As highlighted by Rout and Samantaray (2023), IoT-enabled systems in supply chains can monitor environmental parameters such as carbon emissions, energy consumption, and fuel efficiency, supporting more environmentally responsible operations. Pratap et al. (2024) explored how IoT and big data integration enhances the sustainability performance of smart supply chains, offering dynamic optimization of vehicle routing, warehouse energy usage, and material consumption. Similarly, Khan et al. (2022) noted that IoT applications in sustainable supply chain management allow for precise control and reporting of environmental indicators, which is crucial in ensuring that aid missions operate with minimal ecological disruption. These studies collectively indicate that green ICT solutions supported by IoT facilitate proactive environmental monitoring and compliance with global sustainability standards in logistics.

Predictive maintenance and energy optimization represent another domain in which IoT transforms humanitarian aid logistics into a more sustainable and resilient system. Erhueh et al. (2024) revealed how IoT sensors embedded in energy infrastructure contribute to real-time fault detection, load balancing, and predictive maintenance scheduling, reducing unplanned downtime and enhancing energy efficiency. Murdan (2023) provided a conceptual model of IoT-enabled smart grids tailored to humanitarian energy networks, where portable solar or hybrid power systems can be dynamically managed based on sensor feedback. Moreover, Sharma et al. (2024) examined energy management systems incorporating IoT and machine learning algorithms to balance energy consumption, reduce excess usage, and improve battery storage performance in logistics hubs and mobile aid units. These technologies reduce both cost and carbon emissions, providing dual benefits for sustainability and reliability in humanitarian response contexts.

Data-driven decision-making, empowered by IoT analytics, is now central to efficient resource allocation in aid distribution systems. Malik (2024) argued that IoT facilitates real-time monitoring and feedback loops in organizational behavior, enabling managers to assess the sustainability impact of operations and adjust strategies accordingly. Ratnam (2025) presented an IoT-based mapping framework that enables real-time water distribution planning in disaster zones, improving equity in resource allocation. Farjana et al. (2023) introduced an IoT-cloud hybrid architecture for e-waste management that integrates data-driven decision-making to enhance reclamation efficiency, demonstrating how the same logic can be applied to reverse logistics in humanitarian efforts. Furthermore, Bhavani and Gajendra (2024) emphasized the role of smart sensing platforms in monitoring environmental degradation and informing sustainable interventions. u Salam et al. (2025) extended these ideas to smart construction in urban humanitarian infrastructure, where big data and IoT together inform optimal resource deployment. These studies affirm that leveraging sensor-driven analytics provides humanitarian actors with granular, actionable insights for sustainable operations.

The convergence of IoT with blockchain and AI technologies is revolutionizing transparency and accountability in aid supply chains. Chauhan and Sahoo (2024) explored how these digital innovations provide secure, immutable records that trace aid from origin to beneficiary, reducing the risk of misallocation or corruption. Saidu et al. (2025) offered a comprehensive review on the convergence of blockchain, AI, and IoT, showing that such integrations enhance traceability systems by enabling multi-level verification, decentralized control, and real-time auditing. Similarly, Suman et al. (2024) examined how transparent agri-extension and aid distribution programs can be supported through blockchain-enabled IoT, allowing for tamper-proof data recording and equitable distribution monitoring. These emerging technologies increase donor trust, operational compliance, and public accountability—key pillars of effective humanitarian logistics in the digital age. The convergence of these tools signifies a paradigm shift in how humanitarian organizations design secure, ethical, and sustainable aid systems.

In sum, IoT-enabled sustainable aid distribution systems represent a fusion of environmental consciousness, operational efficiency, and technological innovation. Whether through optimizing energy use, improving predictive capabilities, enhancing visibility, or embedding accountability mechanisms, IoT applications are reshaping the logistics frameworks of humanitarian actors. These systems allow for dynamic, real-time responses to on-the-ground conditions while upholding the sustainability and transparency goals that are increasingly demanded by global humanitarian standards. As these technologies mature and become more accessible, their strategic deployment will be critical in scaling up sustainable impact in disaster relief and aid delivery efforts worldwide.

5. TECHNOLOGICAL INFRASTRUCTURE AND IMPLEMENTATION CHALLENGES

The implementation of Internet of Things (IoT) and smart sensor systems in humanitarian aid logistics, particularly in disaster-prone or resource-scarce regions, involves a complex interplay of technological, organizational, and ethical challenges. These issues must be addressed holistically to ensure scalable, sustainable, and equitable technology deployment.

One of the most pressing concerns is connectivity and power availability in remote or disaster-affected regions. Humanitarian emergencies often damage terrestrial telecommunications and electrical grids, rendering conventional communication and energy systems inoperable. In such scenarios, satellite-based communication systems and solar-powered routers offer immediate solutions for reestablishing connectivity and power. Organizations like NetHope and Télécoms Sans Frontières have deployed satellite kits in post-disaster contexts (e.g., Haiti 2010, Nepal 2015, and Ukraine 2022) to restore vital communication links for coordination and logistics (Wikipedia, 2024; Télécoms Sans Frontières, 2024). Similarly, portable solar-powered network hubs and edge computing devices have been integrated into field operations to facilitate offline data processing and synchronization once connectivity is restored (WebbyLab, 2025). These innovations are crucial because many IoT-based logistics systems rely on continuous sensor data transmission, GPS tracking, and mobile dashboards. The use of low-power wide-area networks (LPWAN), such as LoRaWAN and NB-IoT, has also grown in popularity due to their energy efficiency and ability to transmit small packets over long distances with minimal infrastructure (Mishra et al., 2022).

Closely related to connectivity is the issue of data management platforms and visualization tools. With the proliferation of sensor-generated data—from RFID tracking tags to temperature and humidity sensors—humanitarian organizations must adopt integrated platforms capable of real-time monitoring, predictive analysis, and automated alerts. Platforms such as FIWARE and open-source SHM (structural health monitoring) dashboards have been developed to enable semantic modeling, visualization, and decision-making across various infrastructure nodes (Arxiv, 2020; Chen et al., 2024). These tools allow humanitarian actors to visualize logistics flows, identify disruptions, and reallocate resources accordingly. However, integration remains a key challenge. Many aid organizations operate with legacy systems or bespoke solutions that do not support interoperability with newer IoT platforms, thereby creating data silos and inhibiting cross-agency collaboration (Mızrak & Yaşar, 2025). Furthermore, local field staff often lack adequate training in data analytics or dashboard interpretation, reducing the effectiveness of such tools during high-stress operations.

Security, privacy, and ethical considerations are also paramount in IoT-based humanitarian interventions. The convergence of cyber-physical systems, big data, and AI introduces new vectors of cybersecurity risk, particularly in fragile settings where devices are hastily deployed and under-monitored (Abdullahi & Lazarova-Molnar,2025). Poorly configured devices, default passwords, and lack of encryption make IoT ecosystems vulnerable to interception, spoofing, or denial-of-service attacks. In humanitarian scenarios, where personal identifiable information (PII)—such as health data, GPS locations, or family relationships—is collected and transmitted, data breaches can have serious consequences for individual safety and organizational credibility. Moreover, ethical implications surrounding data collection, consent, and usage transparency are especially salient when working with vulnerable populations such as displaced persons or children. As Mızrak (2025) argues, incorporating privacy-by-design principles, decentralized identity management, and blockchain-enabled traceability can enhance both system integrity and public trust. Additionally, aligning deployments with GDPR-like standards and frameworks such as the Sphere Standards ensures ethical data handling in emergency settings.

Equally important are challenges related to scalability, interoperability, and organizational readiness. Scaling IoT solutions beyond pilot programs often reveals systemic constraints, including hardware maintenance, firmware updating, battery replacement logistics, and cost limitations. Without standards for data exchange and modular architecture, organizations often struggle to scale pilots into full operational systems. For example, the lack of interoperability between UN cluster agencies or NGOs using different platforms (e.g., Red Cross's Sahana Eden versus UNICEF's RapidPro) creates redundancies and bottlenecks (Płaczek & Świtalska, 2023). Additionally, organizational readiness is frequently overlooked. Many humanitarian organizations face barriers such as limited IT infrastructure, low digital literacy, and underdeveloped procurement pathways for smart technologies. As noted by Khan et al. (2022), successful IoT integration requires not only technological infrastructure but also institutional alignment—such as trained personnel, governance mechanisms, and long-term funding models.

To overcome these implementation bottlenecks, experts suggest a layered strategy. First, hybrid edge-cloud systems should be used to support both online and offline operation modes. Second, cyber-physical security audits and resilience assessments must be incorporated into the design phase of any humanitarian IoT initiative. Third, data ethics training should be institutionalized, especially for field staff. Finally, capacity-building initiatives—including partnerships with universities, private tech firms, and donor agencies—should focus on developing local technical expertise and ensuring that humanitarian innovation is both context-sensitive and sustainable (Saidu et al., 2025; Intelsat, 2024).

6. CASE INSIGHTS FROM HUMANITARIAN ORGANIZATIONS

World Food Programme (WFP): Blockchain & AI in Supply Chains

The World Food Programme (WFP) has made significant strides in modernizing humanitarian aid through its Building Blocks platform, a blockchain solution enabling multiple agencies to distribute cash or food via a shared digital wallet. As of 2022, Building Blocks was supporting over one million refugees—mostly in Jordan and Bangladesh—and managing more than $555 million in assistance, while reportedly saving $3.5 million in bank fees (WFP, 2022). In crisis scenarios, it has proven indispensable: for instance, following the 2020 Beirut port explosion, Building Blocks facilitated approximately $59 million in aid to 130,000 individuals, and during the 2022 Ukraine crisis, it helped 18 organizations coordinate $35 million in assistance by sharing real-time distribution data (WFP, 2023). WFP has also rolled out SCOUT, an AI-powered optimization tool that models its global food supply network. A 2024 pilot in West Africa demonstrated $2 million in savings from better route planning for a single commodity, while maintaining food access for 270,000 individuals during a funding shortfall. WFP projects future logistics savings of approximately 5% (~$15 million) by scaling SCOUT across operations (WFP Innovation, 2024). These systems underscore the transformative effect of digital tools—especially AI and blockchain—in enhancing transparency, efficiency, and timeliness in humanitarian logistics.

UNICEF: Wearable Nutrition Sensors & Cold Chain Digitalization

UNICEF's innovative blend of IoT and sensor technology is reshaping aid delivery, particularly in nutrition and vaccine distribution. In Ethiopia, wearable "smart bands" have been used to monitor children's weight, height, and body fat in real-time, allowing health workers to detect and respond to malnutrition earlier and more precisely. Early findings from this program indicate a 40% reduction in malnutrition risk among participants (UNICEF, 2023). Additionally, UNICEF equipped vaccine refrigerators in Kyrgyzstan with temperature sensors that relay real-time data to central dashboards in Bishkek. This deployment ensures continuous cold chain monitoring and immediate alerts for temperature deviations, safeguarding vaccine efficacy in remote regions (UNICEF Supply Chain, 2023). Beyond sensors, UNICEF is piloting drone delivery and sample transport in Malawi, utilizing UAVs and mobile apps to bridge long-distance, road-inaccessible routes (Matternet, 2022). These implementations reflect a growing commitment to technologically enabled aid—prioritizing data-driven, reliable delivery mechanisms in complex environments.

Red Cross/Red Crescent: Community Currencies & Digital Tools

The Red Cross movement—including the IFRC and national societies—has employed digital solutions to enhance cash assistance and operational visibility. A standout initiative is the **Sarafu Community Inclusion Currency**, a blockchain-based voucher launched in Kenya by the Kenya Red Cross in partnership with the Danish Red Cross. The system provides USSD/SMS-based digital credits that users can spend at local participating merchants, even offline, with transactions recorded on a blockchain for transparency. By 2021, over 40,000 users had effectively traded millions of Kenyan shillings worth of goods, improving access to essentials in informal settlements. Surveys reported 80% active engagement and 68% improved access to necessities (Red Social Innovation, 2021). This program integrates digital currency features—local issuance, embedded smart contracts to prevent hoarding, and training to foster trust—showing how blockchain can reinforce both financial access and market resilience (Red Social Innovation, 2021). The Red Cross also routinely uses data dashboards for logistics visualization and explores digital identities for beneficiaries, alongside trialing UAVs for remote medicine delivery (IFRC Logistics, 2022).

Médecins Sans Frontières (MSF): Drones & Digital Freight Management

MSF has adopted diverse digital tools in healthcare delivery, especially in remote and fragile regions. In Papua New Guinea, MSF tested autonomous 'cargo' drones to transport tuberculosis test samples from remote clinics to urban labs equipped with GeneXpert devices. The initiative reduced delivery times significantly, accelerating diagnosis and treatment, despite initial challenges with regulatory approvals and prototype limitations (Reach Alliance, 2021). MSF also deployed drones to deliver HIV test kits in Malawi and emergency medical kits in conflict-hit zones. Complementing these front-line innovations, MSF introduced OptiTrans, a Transport Management System announced in 2022 to streamline logistics workflows across European supply centers and field projects. OptiTrans integrates with MSF's ERP to enable end-to-end tracking, automated freight booking, and optimized routing. Early data showed reduced lead times, more efficient load consolidation, and decreased carbon emissions, prompting further extensions beyond the pilot locations (MSF, 2023). MSF combines on-ground IoT-enabled transport (drones) with back-end digital logistics, illustrating the dual importance of field and systems-level innovation.

Save the Children: Smart Cards & Mobile Cash Transfers

Save the Children has advanced digital financial inclusion via e-transfer technologies like smart cards and mobile wallets. A key initiative in Somalia (2018–2019) involved distributing $20 million via contactless smart cards issued through a fintech partner, redeemable at over 130 POS-enabled shops. Recipients were empowered with choice, local vendors saw increased economic activity, and the aid distribution achieved an impressive 99.9% delivery rate, reaching approximately 62,000 households over nine months (Save the Children, 2019). Nearly 151,000 food baskets were purchased, and digital dashboards allowed real-time monitoring of spending, improving transparency (Save the Children, 2019). Beneficiary feedback highlighted the importance of training and support structures in enabling effective adoption. Building on its success in Somalia, Save the Children expanded e-voucher and mobile money initiatives to Yemen, Liberia, and beyond, achieving secure, dignified, and adaptable aid delivery in diverse operational contexts (CALP, 2020).

GeoSeals Pilot in Ethiopia: IoT Asset Tracking

The **GeoSeals** pilot (2022–2024) is a practical IoT-based response to address "last-mile" visibility issues for nutrition supplies. Implemented by UNICEF, WFP, and the Frontier Technologies Hub (funded by FCDO), the pilot deployed ultra-low-cost RFID tags ($0.10–0.18 each) on Ready-to-Use Therapeutic Food (RUTF) boxes and installed six GeoSeal Hubs in strategic warehouses and clinics. Each hub included RFID and motion sensing, location-awareness, and cellular/Wi-Fi connectivity. When tagged boxes passed through, the hub logged the event and transmitted data via MQTT to a centralized dashboard accessible to logisticians (Frontier Tech Hub, 2024). Over a four-month period, the system consistently captured movements at all nodes, reduced reporting delays from weeks to <1 day, and proved resilient against intermittent connectivity through local buffering. Challenges included ensuring consistent tag reads within metallic packaging, powering hubs with solar/battery, and designing enclosures for environmental resilience. The system's low cost and scalability demonstrate that sophisticated IoT solutions can be deployed in austere environments to improve stock accuracy and responsiveness, reducing risks of stock-outs among vulnerable populations (Frontier Tech Hub, 2024).

Collective Lessons and Deployment Challenges

Across these diverse implementations—from blockchain to drones and smart tags—several cross-cutting themes and challenges emerge. First, technology alignment with local context is fundamental: initiatives like Sarafu and GeoSeals succeeded by blending high-tech tools with low-tech accessibility (USSD, passive RFID) and local agency. Second, capacity and trust-building—via training and community engagement—is essential to ensure uptake and sustainability, as demonstrated by WFP, Save the Children, and Red Cross programs. Third, interoperability and data sharing across agencies (WFP's shared ledger, Red Cross dashboards) enhances coordination but depends on open-standards and privacy safeguards. Fourth, maintenance and reliability—from drone durability to tag reading robustness—must be prioritized, particularly when hardware is deployed in harsh, remote settings. Lastly, ethical and financial transparency—through donor-facing dashboards, blockchain audit trails, and secure digital currency—enhances accountability and trust among beneficiaries and funders. These insights provide a roadmap for future humanitarian IoT initiatives prioritizing local integration, ethical design, and collaborative systems.

7. CONCLUSION

The strategic integration of IoT and smart sensor systems into humanitarian logistics requires a careful balance between technological advancement, financial feasibility, and contextual adaptability. A cost-benefit assessment must begin with quantifying the initial investment in infrastructure, including sensor devices, connectivity modules, cloud-based data platforms, and training costs. While these technologies entail significant upfront capital, their long-term advantages—such as reducing delivery delays, improving cold chain management, and enhancing supply chain transparency—contribute to greater operational efficiency and resource optimization (Khairuddin & Rahman, 2025; Rout & Samantaray, 2023). For instance, RFID-enabled inventory and cold chain monitoring systems have been shown to prevent vaccine spoilage and reduce inventory shrinkage in UNICEF-led logistics (UNICEF Supply Division, 2023), illustrating a clear return on investment over time.

Long-term sustainability in developing regions depends not only on the affordability of these technologies but also on their adaptability to local contexts. Regions prone to infrastructure fragility—due to conflict, natural disasters, or poor electrification—require lightweight, modular IoT systems with alternative energy sources such as solar-powered smart devices (Malhotra et al., 2021; Mizrak & Yaşar, 2025). Moreover, scalability becomes a crucial metric. Platforms must be interoperable with existing humanitarian information systems while remaining customizable to the local socio-technical landscape (Chen et al., 2024; Darabkh & Al-Akhras, 2025). Efforts like the WFP's Building Blocks and SCOUT initiatives demonstrate how blockchain and AI-enabled platforms can support scale and trust simultaneously by decentralizing data and enabling predictive routing in complex supply environments (WFP, 2022; WFP Innovation, 2024).

Strategic expansion should also consider regional training programs to build local technological capacity and avoid over-reliance on external contractors. Collaborative partnerships—especially public-private engagements—can reduce the financial and operational burdens on humanitarian actors and promote innovation ecosystems in underserved areas. The GeoSeals pilot in Ethiopia, which integrated wearable sensors and data dashboards into food aid delivery, underscores the importance of integrating national government systems and local logistics actors into early deployment stages (Frontier Technologies Hub, 2024).

In conclusion, the future of IoT in humanitarian logistics is closely tied to trust, collaboration, and adaptive governance frameworks. Ensuring ethical use, securing data privacy, and promoting transparency are fundamental to scaling these technologies without undermining vulnerable communities' autonomy (Chauhan & Sahoo, 2024; Saidu et al., 2025). Furthermore, fostering interoperability across NGOs, local governments, and donors is essential for developing a unified response framework that can respond to crises with agility and resilience. As the humanitarian landscape becomes increasingly data-driven, IoT technologies—when deployed strategically—hold the potential to transform aid delivery into a smarter, more responsive, and sustainable system.

REFERENCES

Aarif, K. O. M., Alam, A., & Hotak, Y. (2025). Smart sensor technologies shaping the future of precision agriculture: Recent advances and future outlooks. *Journal of Sensors*, *2025*(1), 2460098. DOI: 10.1155/js/2460098

Abdelhadi, A., & Akkartal, E. (2019). A framework of IoT implementations and challenges in Warehouse Management, Transportation and Retailing. *Eurasian Business & Economics Journal*, *18*, 25–41.

Abdullahi, S. M., & Lazarova-Molnar, S. (2025). On the adoption and deployment of secure and privacy-preserving IIoT in smart manufacturing: A comprehensive guide with recent advances. *International Journal of Information Security*, *24*(1), 53. DOI: 10.1007/s10207-024-00951-8

Alaba, F. A. (2024). The Evolution of the IoT. In *Internet of Things: A Case Study in Africa* (pp. 1–18). Springer Nature Switzerland. DOI: 10.1007/978-3-031-67984-1_1

Arxiv. (2020). *FIWARE-based semantic modeling and interoperability in disaster response IoT systems*. https://arxiv.org/abs/2005.02788

Bauer, M., Sanchez, L., & Song, J. (2021). IoT-enabled smart cities: Evolution and outlook. *Sensors (Basel)*, *21*(13), 4511. DOI: 10.3390/s21134511 PMID: 34209436

Bhavani, K., & Gajendra, N. (2024). Smart data-driven sensing: New opportunities to combat environmental problems. In *Bio-Inspired Data-driven Distributed Energy in Robotics and Enabling Technologies* (pp. 17–47). CRC Press. DOI: 10.1201/9781003530077-2

CALP. (2020). *Scaling electronic cash and voucher assistance: case study comparisons*. Cash Learning Partnership. Retrieved from https://www.calpnetwork.org/publication/scaling-electronic-cash-and-voucher-assistance-case-study-comparisons/

Celestin, M. (2023). How Predictive Maintenance in Logistics Fleets Is Reducing Equipment Downtime and Operational Losses. *Brainae Journal of Business* [BJBST]. *Sciences and Technology*, *7*(10), 1023–1033.

Chauhan, M., & Sahoo, D. R. (2024). Towards a greener tomorrow: Exploring the potential of AI, blockchain, and IoT in sustainable development. *Nature Environment and Pollution Technology*, *23*(2), 1105–1113. DOI: 10.46488/NEPT.2024.v23i02.044

Chen, J., Reitz, J., Richstein, R., Schröder, K. U., & Roßmann, J. (2024). IoT-based SHM using digital twins for interoperable and scalable decentralized smart sensing systems. *Information (Basel)*, *15*(3), 121. DOI: 10.3390/info15030121

Chen, Q., Cao, J., & Zhu, S. (2023). Data-driven monitoring and predictive maintenance for engineering structures: Technologies, implementation challenges, and future directions. *IEEE Internet of Things Journal*, *10*(16), 14527–14551. DOI: 10.1109/JIOT.2023.3272535

Cil, A. Y., Abdurahman, D., & Cil, I. (2022). Internet of Things enabled real time cold chain monitoring in a container port. *Journal of Shipping and Trade*, *7*(1), 9. DOI: 10.1186/s41072-022-00110-z

Costa, F., Genovesi, S., Borgese, M., Michel, A., Dicandia, F. A., & Manara, G. (2021). A review of RFID sensors, the new frontier of internet of things. *Sensors (Basel)*, *21*(9), 3138. DOI: 10.3390/s21093138 PMID: 33946500

Darabkh, K. A., & Al-Akhras, M. (2025). Evolutionary Cost Analysis and Computational Intelligence for Energy Efficiency in Internet of Things-Enabled Smart Cities: Multi-Sensor Data Fusion and Resilience to Link and Device Failures. *Smart Cities*, *8*(2), 64. DOI: 10.3390/smartcities8020064

Erhueh, O. V., Elete, T., Akano, O. A., Nwakile, C., & Hanson, E. (2024). Application of Internet of Things (IoT) in energy infrastructure: Lessons for the future of operations and maintenance. *Comprehensive Research and Reviews in Science and Technology*, *2*(2), 28–54. DOI: 10.57219/crrst.2024.2.2.0036

Farjana, M., Fahad, A. B., Alam, S. E., & Islam, M. M. (2023). An IoT-and cloud-based e-waste management system for resource reclamation with a data-driven decision-making process. *IoT*, *4*(3), 202–220. DOI: 10.3390/iot4030011

Frontier Technologies Hub. (2024). *GeoSeals pilot: Improving supply visibility for nutrition programmes in Ethiopia*. Retrieved from https://frontiertechhub.org/geoseals-ethiopia-supply-visibility/

IFRC. (2022). *How data dashboards and drones are helping the Red Cross improve logistics*. Retrieved from https://www.ifrc.org/article/how-data-dashboards-and-drones-are-helping-red-cross-improve-logistics

Ikumapayi, O. M., Laseinde, O. T., Elewa, R. R., Ogedengbe, T. S., & Akinlabi, E. T. (2024). Smart Sensors for Real-time Monitoring in a Sustainable Logistics. In *E3S Web of Conferences* (Vol. 552, p. 01079). EDP Sciences.

Innovation, W. F. P. (2024). *AI in action: SCOUT pilot results for supply chain optimization*. Retrieved from https://innovation.wfp.org/news/scout-ai-supply-chain-optimization-2024

Intelsat. (2024). Expanding rapid response connectivity capabilities ahead of the 2025 hurricane season. https://www.intelsat.com/resources/blog

Kanu, M. O., Ogu, E., Egbumokei, P. I., Digitemie, W. N., & Dienagha, I. N. (2025). Enhancing Asset Management in Gas Distribution Predictive Maintenance and Data-Driven Decision Making.

Khairuddin, M. M., & Rahman, N. A. A. (2025). Empowering Humanitarian Efforts: IoT-Enabled Solutions for Distribution Center. In *Supply Chain in Humanitarian Operations: Managing Disruption Through Intervention and Innovation* (pp. 77–84). Springer Nature Singapore. DOI: 10.1007/978-981-96-4426-1_7

Khan, M., Parvaiz, G. S., Ali, A., Jehangir, M., Hassan, N., & Bae, J. (2022). A model for understanding the mediating association of transparency between emerging technologies and humanitarian logistics sustainability. *Sustainability (Basel)*, *14*(11), 6917. DOI: 10.3390/su14116917

Khan, Y., Su'ud, M. B. M., Alam, M. M., Ahmad, S. F., Ahmad, A. Y. B., & Khan, N. (2022). Application of internet of things (IoT) in sustainable supply chain management. *Sustainability*, *15*(1), 694. DOI: 10.3390/su15010694

Lawrence, J., & Durana, P. (2021). Artificial Intelligence-driven Big Data Analytics, Predictive Maintenance Systems, and Internet of Thingsbased Real-Time Production Logistics in Sustainable Industry 4.0 Wireless Networks. *Journal of Self-Governance & Management Economics*, *9*(4).

Malhotra, P., Singh, Y., Anand, P., Bangotra, D. K., Singh, P. K., & Hong, W. C. (2021). Internet of things: Evolution, concerns and security challenges. *Sensors (Basel)*, *21*(5), 1809. DOI: 10.3390/s21051809 PMID: 33807724

Malik, S. (2024). Data-driven decision-making: Leveraging the IoT for real-time sustainability in organizational behavior. *Sustainability (Basel)*, *16*(15), 6302. DOI: 10.3390/su16156302

Matternet. (2022). *UNICEF and Matternet: Drones to deliver critical supplies in Malawi*. Retrieved from https://mttr.net/unicef-matternet-drones-malawi/

Médecins Sans Frontières (MSF). (2023). *OptiTrans: MSF's transport management system pilot*. Retrieved from https://www.msf.org/opti-trans-digital-logistics-management

Miao, F., Han, Y., Tian, P., Tao, B., Zang, Y., & Chu, P. K. (2023). Integrated sensor for humidity, temperature, light, and carbon dioxide based on passive RFID. *Sensors and Actuators. B, Chemical, 390*, 133913. DOI: 10.1016/j.snb.2023.133913

Midkiff, C. (2021). Using a control tower approach to drive visibility, aid planning and improve supply chain reliability. *Journal of Supply Chain Management. Logistics and Procurement, 4*(1), 70–78. DOI: 10.69554/DHRY3082

Mishra, P., Kumar, N., & Godfrey, W. W. (2022). An evolutionary computing-based energy-efficient solution for IoT-enabled software-defined sensor network architecture. *International Journal of Communication Systems, 35*(8), e5111. DOI: 10.1002/dac.5111

Mishra, P., Kumar, N., & Godfrey, W. W. (2022). An evolutionary computing-based energy-efficient solution for IoT-enabled software-defined sensor network architecture. *International Journal of Communication Systems, 35*(8), e5111. DOI: 10.1002/dac.5111

Mızrak, F. (2023). Managing Risks and Crises in the Logistics Sector: A Comprehensive Analysis of Strategies and Prioritization Using AHP Method. *Meriç Uluslararası Sosyal ve Stratejik Araştırmalar Dergisi, 7*(Özel Sayı), 114-148.

Mızrak, F. (2024). Resilience and Innovation Strategies: How Businesses Adapt to Supply Chain Disruptions in the Post-Pandemic Era. *Politik Ekonomik Kuram, 8*(3), 581–600. DOI: 10.30586/pek.1497718

Mızrak, F. (2025). The Triple Nexus of Smart, Secure, and Sustainable Supply Chains: Strategies for Resilience in the Digital Age. In *Utilizing Cybersecurity to Foster Business Innovation and Resiliency* (pp. 189-218). IGI Global Scientific Publishing.

Mızrak, F. (2025). The triple nexus of smart, secure, and sustainable supply chains: Strategies for resilience in the digital age. In Mızrak, F. (Ed.), *Utilizing cybersecurity to foster business innovation and resiliency* (pp. 189–218). IGI Global. DOI: 10.4018/979-8-3693-6417-8.ch009

Mızrak, F., & Akkartal, E. (Eds.). (2024). *Effective Logistics for Sustainable Development Goals*. IGI Global. DOI: 10.4018/979-8-3693-7071-1

Mizrak, F., & Yaşar, O. (2025). Strategic deployment of piezoelectric energy harvesting in smart urban infrastructure: A hybrid QPFRS, M-SWARA, K-means clustering, and PROMETHEE evaluation for sustainable advantage. *Energy Reports, 13*, 2565–2582. DOI: 10.1016/j.egyr.2025.02.005

Murdan, A. P. (2023, August). Powering the future: IoT-enabled smart grids for sustainable energy systems. In *International Conference on Electrical and Electronics Engineering* (pp. 273-285). Singapore: Springer Nature Singapore.

Namatherdhala, B., Mistry, J., Mallikarjunaradhya, V., & Logeshwaran, J. (2023, September). Meta-Heuristic Algorithm Enabled Artificial Neural Network for Heart Disease Diagnosis Using IoT Smart Sensors. In *2023 Third International Conference on Ubiquitous Computing and Intelligent Information Systems (ICUIS)* (pp. 418-425). IEEE. DOI: 10.1109/ICUIS60567.2023.00075

Ojadi, J. O., Odionu, C., Onukwulu, E., & Owulade, O. (2024). Big data analytics and AI for optimizing supply chain sustainability and reducing greenhouse gas emissions in logistics and transportation. *International Journal of Multidisciplinary Research and Growth Evaluation*, *5*(1), 1536–1548. DOI: 10.54660/.IJMRGE.2024.5.1.1536-1548

Özkanlısoy, Ö., & Akkartal, E. (2021). Digital transformation in supply chains: Current applications, contributions and challenges. *Bus. Manag. Stud. Int. J*, *9*, 32–55.

Öztürk, S., & Akkartal, E. (2024). Internet of Things (IoT) Applications in Last Mile Delivery. In *Strategic Innovations for Dynamic Supply Chains* (pp. 193–215). IGI Global Scientific Publishing. DOI: 10.4018/979-8-3693-3575-8.ch009

Pascucci, E. (2021). More logistics, less aid: Humanitarian-business partnerships and sustainability in the refugee camp. *World Development*, *142*, 105424. DOI: 10.1016/j.worlddev.2021.105424

Płaczek, E., & Świtalska, A. (2023). New technologies in humanitarian logistics. *Journal of Public Governance*, *65*(3), 48–58. DOI: 10.15678/PG.2023.65.3.04

Płaczek, E., & Świtalska, A. (2023). New technologies in humanitarian logistics. *Journal of Public Governance*, *65*(3), 48–58. DOI: 10.15678/PG.2023.65.3.04

Pratap, S., Jauhar, S. K., Gunasekaran, A., & Kamble, S. S. (2024). Optimizing the IoT and big data embedded smart supply chains for sustainable performance. *Computers & Industrial Engineering*, *187*, 109828. DOI: 10.1016/j.cie.2023.109828

Raffik, R., Rakesh, D., Venkatesh, M., & Samvasan, P. (2021, October). Supply Chain Control and Inventory Tracking System using Industrial Automation Tools and IIoT. In *2021 International Conference on Advancements in Electrical, Electronics, Communication, Computing and Automation (ICAECA)* (pp. 1-5). IEEE. DOI: 10.1109/ICAECA52838.2021.9675774

Ratnam, M. (2025). Water Supply Mapping for a Sustainable Future: Data-Driven Efforts in Decision Making. *Smart Internet of Things*, *2*(1), 1–10.

Rayhana, R., Xiao, G., & Liu, Z. (2021). RFID sensing technologies for smart agriculture. *IEEE Instrumentation & Measurement Magazine*, *24*(3), 50–60. DOI: 10.1109/MIM.2021.9436094

Reach Alliance. (2021). *Last mile health delivery via drone: A case study from Papua New Guinea.* Retrieved from https://reachalliance.org/project/drones-for-tuberculosis-papua-new-guinea/

Red Social Innovation. (2021). *Sarafu Community Currency: Inclusive blockchain-based humanitarian financing.* Retrieved from https://www.red-social-innovation.com/en/innovation/sarafu-community-currency/

Rout, S., & Samantaray, S. (2023, December). Green ICT: Exploring the Role of IoT-Enabled Technologies in Small-Scale Businesses. In *International Conference on Information and Communication Technology for Competitive Strategies* (pp. 309-321). Singapore: Springer Nature Singapore.

Saidu, Y., Shuhidan, S. M., Aliyu, D. A., Aziz, I. A., & Adamu, S. (2025). Convergence of blockchain, IoT, and AI for enhanced traceability systems: A comprehensive review. *IEEE Access : Practical Innovations, Open Solutions*, *13*, 16838–16865. DOI: 10.1109/ACCESS.2025.3528035

Saidu, Y., Shuhidan, S. M., Aliyu, D. A., Aziz, I. A., & Adamu, S. (2025). Convergence of blockchain, IoT, and AI for enhanced traceability systems: A comprehensive review. *IEEE Access : Practical Innovations, Open Solutions*, *13*, 16838–16865. DOI: 10.1109/ACCESS.2025.3528035

uSalam, M. H., Rathore, S. A., Maken, F. H., Janjua, J. I., & Irfan, M. (2025). Harnessing Big Data and IoT for Enhanced Resource Optimization in Sustainable Construction within Smart Cities. *The Journal of Research Review*, *2*(01), 90–104.

Save the Children. (2019). *Somalia: Smart card cash transfer pilot impact report.* Retrieved from https://resourcecentre.savethechildren.net/pdf/smartcard_somalia_report.pdf/

Sehrawat, D., & Gill, N. S. (2019, April). Smart sensors: Analysis of different types of IoT sensors. In *2019 3rd International Conference on Trends in Electronics and Informatics (ICOEI)*(pp. 523-528). IEEE.

Sharma, K. K., Verma, P. K., & Garg, P. (2024). IoT-Enabled Energy Management Systems For Sustainable Energy Storage: Design, Optimization, And Future Directions. *Frontiers in Health Informatics*, *13*(8).

Soussi, A., Zero, E., Sacile, R., Trinchero, D., & Fossa, M. (2024). Smart sensors and smart data for precision agriculture: A review. *Sensors (Basel)*, *24*(8), 2647. DOI: 10.3390/s24082647 PMID: 38676264

Suman, S., Deb, A., Prusty, A. K., Sameer, S., Divya, B. S., & Saha, S. (2024, December). Utilizing blockchain, IoT and machine learning for transparent agri-extension and resource distribution: A review. In *2024 2nd International Conference on Signal Processing, Communication, Power and Embedded System (SCOPES)* (pp. 1-6). IEEE.

Télécoms Sans Frontières. (2024). Emergency communication deployments and VSAT-based learning centers. https://en.wikipedia.org/wiki/Télécoms_Sans_Frontières

Tran-Dang, H., Kim, J. W., Lee, J. M., & Kim, D. S. (2025). Shaping the future of logistics: Data-driven technology approaches and strategic management. *IETE Technical Review*, *42*(1), 44–79. DOI: 10.1080/02564602.2024.2445513

UNICEF. (2023). *Leveraging smart sensors and wearables to combat malnutrition.* Retrieved from https://www.unicef.org/innovation/stories/smart-bands-fighting-malnutrition-ethiopia

UNICEF Supply Division. (2023). *Digital cold chain monitoring in Kyrgyzstan: Improving vaccine delivery*. Retrieved from https://www.unicef.org/supply/stories/kyrgyzstan-digital-cold-chain

Wagner, S. M., Ramkumar, M., Kumar, G., & Schoenherr, T. (2024). Supporting disaster relief operations through RFID: Enabling visibility and coordination. *International Journal of Logistics Management*, *35*(6), 1681–1712. DOI: 10.1108/IJLM-12-2022-0480

Wang, J., Lim, M. K., Wang, C., & Tseng, M. L. (2021). The evolution of the Internet of Things (IoT) over the past 20 years. *Computers & Industrial Engineering*, *155*, 107174. DOI: 10.1016/j.cie.2021.107174

WebbyLab. (2025). IoT data management: From edge to cloud. https://webbylab.com/blog/iot-data-management

WFP. (2022). *Building Blocks: A better way to deliver aid.* World Food Programme. Retrieved from https://innovation.wfp.org/project/building-blocks

Wikipedia. (2024). NetHope (NGO). https://en.wikipedia.org/wiki/NetHope

Chapter 5
Blockchain Technology in Humanitarian Logistics Enhancing Transparency, Accountability and Real-Time Decision Making

Mehmet Emin Aktas
https://orcid.org/0009-0008-8052-9866
Yeditepe University, Ataşehir, Turkey

Selin Nur Eroğlu
Yeditepe University, Ataşehir, Turkey

ABSTRACT

This chapter explores the transformative potential of blockchain technology in humanitarian logistics, focusing on its ability to enhance transparency, accountability, and decentralized decision-making. Traditional aid supply chains often struggle with inefficiencies, information asymmetry, and limited traceability—challenges that blockchain addresses through secure, real-time, and tamper-proof data infrastructure. The integration of blockchain with digital identity systems, smart contracts, IoT, and AI enables more adaptive, ethical, and inclusive aid delivery. Case studies, including Oxfam's UnBlocked Cash program and blockchain-based cash transfers in Ukraine, illustrate both the opportunities and the practical barriers to implementation. The chapter concludes with strategic policy recommendations aligned with Sustainable Development Goals (SDGs 8, 16, and 17), emphasizing the importance of cross-sector collaboration, digital capacity-building, and ethical governance.

DOI: 10.4018/979-8-3373-3643-5.ch005

1. INTRODUCTION

Humanitarian logistics has become a critical pillar of global disaster response, conflict relief, and long-term development support in an era marked by overlapping global crises. The frequency and scale of emergencies—ranging from protracted armed conflicts and displacement to climate-induced disasters and pandemics—have stressed traditional aid systems beyond their limits (Christensen & Ma, 2020; Kapucu & Hu, 2022). In this dynamic landscape, the humanitarian supply chain must not only be responsive and efficient but also transparent, accountable, and adaptable to rapidly evolving field conditions.

Despite decades of institutional learning, traditional humanitarian supply chains often suffer from chronic inefficiencies, fragmented information sharing, weak donor visibility, and vulnerability to corruption and mismanagement (Baharmand, Maghsoudi, & Coppi, 2021; Hunt, Narayanan, & Zhuang, 2022). These challenges are amplified in contexts of extreme uncertainty, where aid must traverse difficult geographies, political instability, and complex stakeholder networks. In many cases, beneficiaries remain disconnected from tracking the flow of aid, while donors demand greater transparency on how their contributions are utilized—creating a persistent trust gap across the chain.

Amid these challenges, digital innovations have begun to reshape the contours of humanitarian logistics. Among these, blockchain technology has emerged as a particularly promising solution to address information asymmetries, data integrity issues, and coordination deficits across multi-stakeholder environments (Ozdemir et al., 2021; Khan et al., 2021). Blockchain's decentralized ledger system enables immutable, real-time documentation of aid flows, digital identity verification for displaced populations, and smart contract-based automation of fund disbursement, offering a novel approach to building trust and efficiency in humanitarian operations. Furthermore, the integration of blockchain with other frontier technologies such as IoT, geospatial data, and AI opens new horizons for responsive and data-driven logistics systems (Mızrak, 2025; Gudala et al., 2022).

This chapter aims to explore the transformative potential of blockchain in humanitarian logistics by focusing on its ability to enhance transparency, accountability, and decentralized decision-making. Drawing from both academic literature and real-world case studies—including the WFP's Building Blocks project and blockchain-based aid delivery mechanisms in Ukraine and Haiti—it provides a comprehensive analysis of how blockchain reshapes operational, ethical, and strategic paradigms in humanitarian settings. By synthesizing cross-disciplinary insights and mapping practical implementations, the chapter contributes to a nuanced understanding of blockchain's strengths, limitations, and future pathways for integration in complex humanitarian environments.

Moreover, this work aligns with several Sustainable Development Goals (SDGs), particularly SDG 8 (Decent Work and Economic Growth) through the promotion of secure digital infrastructure, SDG 16 (Peace, Justice, and Strong Institutions) through improved transparency and trust, and SDG 17 (Partnerships for the Goals) through enhanced multi-stakeholder collaboration enabled by interoperable technologies. As global crises increasingly demand coordinated, accountable, and agile responses, blockchain stands out not only as a technical innovation but as a tool for institutional and ethical transformation in the service of humanity.

2. BLOCKCHAIN IN HUMANITARIAN LOGISTICS: CAPABILITIES AND TRANSFORMATIONS

2.1 Transparency and Traceability in the Aid Chain

Transparency in humanitarian logistics is more than a managerial best practice—it is a critical enabler of ethical and effective crisis response. It refers to the full visibility of actions, decisions, and resource flows across all stages of the humanitarian supply chain. In environments marked by resource scarcity, urgency, and overlapping actors, transparency ensures that aid reaches those in need without leakage, corruption, or inefficiencies. Hunt, Narayanan, and Zhuang (2022) argue that blockchain technology introduces a structural reconfiguration of transparency by offering immutable records, decentralized validation, and synchronized access to information across stakeholders. This is particularly valuable in humanitarian settings, where centralized systems often fail to deliver timely and verifiable data. By embedding traceability and openness into digital infrastructures, blockchain enhances not only logistical accountability but also moral credibility, restoring donor trust and safeguarding the dignity of recipients.

A core functionality of blockchain in this context is real-time monitoring, which transforms humanitarian logistics from a reactive to a proactive discipline. The integration of blockchain with Internet of Things (IoT) sensors enables continuous data collection on environmental conditions, locations, and supply chain performance metrics. Khan et al. (2021) demonstrate how this integration supports temperature-controlled medical supply chains, tracking pharmaceuticals through crisis regions with real-time updates on integrity and status. This synergy between IoT and blockchain allows humanitarian organizations to detect bottlenecks early, reroute deliveries when disruptions occur, and automate alerts for time-sensitive shipments. Similarly, Akkartal and Abdelhadi (2019) emphasize the value of IoT-enabled transparency in warehouse and transport systems, where human error and system fragmentation often lead to stockouts or duplications. When combined with blockchain's immutable ledgers, sensor-based data recording provides a multidimensional traceability mechanism that enhances both visibility and verifiability across logistics chains.

Another major challenge that blockchain helps overcome is information asymmetry—a common barrier in traditional humanitarian systems where vital data is siloed, delayed, or selectively shared. Baharmand, Maghsoudi, and Coppi (2021) explain that blockchain enables a single, shared ledger where all authorized actors—donors, implementing agencies, local partners—can access identical real-time information. This transparency eliminates discrepancies in decision-making, enables rapid consensus, and creates operational agility in high-pressure scenarios. In this regard, Ozdemir et al. (2021) note that blockchain also reduces the negative effects of bureaucratic and logistical barriers by replacing hierarchical approvals with consensus-driven smart contracts and tamper-proof validations. These changes are not merely technical—they represent a shift in power dynamics toward more democratic and inclusive aid coordination. By ensuring that data is universally accessible and simultaneously updated, blockchain builds a foundation for multi-actor trust and responsiveness.

One of the most compelling field implementations of blockchain in humanitarian logistics is the World Food Programme's (WFP) Building Blocks project in Jordanian refugee camps. This project integrated blockchain-based digital wallets with biometric iris scans to enable traceable, fraud-resistant cash transfers. Each transaction is recorded on a decentralized ledger, which donors and supervisors can audit in real time (Hadjisophocleous, Syed, & Lee, 2021). Beneficiaries can independently purchase food at designated supermarkets, without the need for paper vouchers, bank accounts, or intermediaries. The project reportedly reduced transaction costs by 98%, improved distribution speed, and empowered refugees through choice and dignity (WFP, 2019; Mızrak, 2025). As Mızrak (2025) further points out, the system represents a model for "smart, secure, and sustainable" aid, where technology not only optimizes efficiency but also aligns aid delivery with human rights principles and user empowerment. Building Blocks demonstrates that traceability is not just about tracking goods—it is about tracking fairness, inclusion, and respect in humanitarian action.

However, achieving this level of transparency and traceability is not without implementation challenges. According to Memarpour Ghiaci et al. (2024), key barriers to blockchain adoption in humanitarian contexts include limited digital infrastructure, organizational inertia, and poor integration with existing data systems. These factors can be particularly problematic in low-resource settings where reliable internet access, power, and device availability are scarce. Negi (2024) cautions that even when blockchain systems are technically sound, the absence of digital literacy among frontline workers or local NGOs can lead to misuse, underuse, or exclusion of critical actors. This may result in unintended transparency gaps or new forms of inequality. Hence, transparency initiatives must be accompanied by capacity-building, digital access provisioning, and inclusive governance structures. As Mızrak (2025) and Akkartal & Abdelhadi (2019) stress, the success of blockchain in humanitarian logistics depends not only on the robustness of the technology itself but also on the alignment of systems with the socio-technical context—human skills, organizational values, and infrastructural realities.

In conclusion, blockchain technology offers a transformative framework for enhancing transparency and traceability in humanitarian logistics. It replaces fragmented, opaque, and hierarchical systems with decentralized, verifiable, and inclusive architectures. Through its integration with IoT, real-time analytics, and biometric systems, blockchain can automate monitoring, reduce fraud, and improve decision-making at every stage of the aid chain. Yet its successful deployment demands more than just technical installation; it requires context-sensitive implementation, stakeholder training, and ethical design. By addressing both operational and ethical dimensions of traceability, blockchain has the potential to reimagine humanitarian logistics not only as a matter of supply but also of justice, dignity, and shared accountability.

2.2 Secure Identity Verification and Data Privacy

One of the most pressing vulnerabilities in humanitarian logistics arises from the limitations of traditional identity verification systems. These systems typically rely on centralized databases, physical documents, or paper-based registries—all of which are susceptible to forgery, loss, manipulation, and cyberattacks. Aslan et al. (2023) emphasize that centralized digital identity repositories are high-value targets for cybercriminals and suffer from single points of failure, making them prone to data breaches. Similarly, Ghelani, Hua, and Koduru (2022) underscore how the reuse of weak authentication mechanisms—such as password-based credentials or unencrypted IDs—exposes both personal information and institutional data to attack vectors like phishing, credential stuffing, and man-in-the-middle intrusions. These weaknesses are even more pronounced in humanitarian contexts, where affected populations such as refugees and internally displaced persons may lack formal documentation or reside in conflict zones with poor cybersecurity infrastructure. Husnain et al. (2022) further highlight that in IoT-enabled environments, including those used for supply monitoring in aid chains, the MQTT protocol and similar systems often lack built-in security, opening the door for identity spoofing and data tampering. These vulnerabilities not only endanger sensitive information but also threaten equitable access to life-saving aid, creating systemic exclusion and undermining the credibility of humanitarian operations. As Mızrak (2025) asserts, in a digital age where data has become a new form of currency and power, securing identity systems is not only a technical challenge but a strategic and ethical imperative.

Blockchain technology offers a structural solution to these challenges through decentralized digital identity frameworks. Unlike traditional ID systems, blockchain-enabled identity platforms allow users to own, manage, and share their credentials without depending on a central authority. Samunnisa and Gaddam (2023) describe how blockchain ensures that each identity record is cryptographically linked, time-stamped, and distributed across a peer-to-peer network, making unauthorized changes virtually impossible. This decentralization reduces the risk of mass data compromise and increases the resilience of humanitarian identity verification systems. Gudala et al. (2022) emphasize that blockchain integration with biometric data (e.g., iris scans, fingerprints) significantly enhances accuracy in authentication processes and prevents identity fraud in resource-constrained environments. In particular, self-sovereign identity (SSI) models—where individuals maintain control over which credentials they disclose and to whom—have become an ethical gold standard for privacy-centric aid delivery. Stockburger et al. (2021) illustrate this model's success in public transportation, which can be translated to humanitarian contexts where mobility, inclusivity, and auditability are essential. Yu et al. (2025) expand this argument by introducing blockchain-based privacy protection mechanisms for IoT-linked digital identity systems, reinforcing the trustworthiness of data exchanges even in volatile field conditions. Khaund (2025) similarly supports decentralized identity's potential in safeguarding sensitive information, noting its advantage in minimizing institutional overreach and promoting user-centric verification. Through blockchain, identity becomes portable, secure, and self-controlled—qualities essential for protecting vulnerable populations during crises.

The integration of smart contracts, zero-knowledge proofs (ZKPs), and biometric technologies further strengthens the security architecture of blockchain-based identity systems in humanitarian logistics. Smart contracts—programmable protocols that automatically execute actions when pre-set conditions are met—can be deployed to validate identities and trigger aid distribution without requiring human mediation. Das, Dasgupta, and Biswas (2023) demonstrate how these mechanisms allow seamless vehicle identification and tracking in transportation logistics, a model that can be adapted for verifying aid recipients or field staff. More importantly, zero-knowledge proofs provide a sophisticated privacy-enhancing solution. Ajayi et al. (2024) explain that ZKPs allow one party to prove that they meet a requirement (e.g., being over 18, or residing in a designated aid zone) without disclosing the underlying data. This ensures that even when beneficiaries are authenticated, their sensitive personal information remains protected—a crucial feature in environments where data misuse could result in surveillance, discrimination, or exploitation. Mızrak and Akkartal (2024) further assert that in aviation and defense-related logistics, the synergy of ZKPs with biometric identifiers has significantly improved the accuracy and accountability of access management, reducing insider threats and information leakage. Applied to humanitarian logistics, these tools not only secure identity verification but also reduce reliance on paper trails or manual vetting processes that are often inefficient or biased. The automation of aid delivery via smart contracts ensures fairness, consistency, and auditability—turning identity verification from a bottleneck into a safeguard for equitable assistance.

Beyond technical performance, the ethical dimensions of data ownership and user control are central to the responsible use of blockchain-enabled identity systems in humanitarian settings. Traditional identity models often strip individuals—especially displaced or undocumented people—of agency over their data, exposing them to systemic marginalization. Blockchain introduces a paradigm shift by allowing individuals to retain sovereignty over their credentials, choosing what to share and with whom. Mizrak (2024) emphasizes that ethical cybersecurity frameworks must integrate data dignity, ensuring that users are not only protected but empowered by digital systems. In this respect, humanitarian organizations must balance transparency with privacy by adopting privacy-by-design principles, consent-based verification flows, and opt-out mechanisms that respect personal autonomy. As Samunnisa and Gaddam (2023) argue, decentralized identity systems must not replicate the same surveillance hierarchies they seek to replace. Furthermore, the ethical success of such systems hinges on inclusive governance—ensuring that communities involved in humanitarian operations have a voice in how digital identity tools are designed, deployed, and monitored. Gudala et al. (2022) advocate for participatory feedback loops and adaptive standards to prevent technocratic decision-making and foster accountability. In the humanitarian context, where power imbalances are often stark, blockchain should not merely secure data but redistribute control—turning identity verification into a platform for human dignity and equitable access.

2.3 Donation Management and Fund Accountability

In humanitarian logistics, donation management and fund accountability represent a persistent challenge. Traditional donation tracking systems often rely on centralized, opaque structures that leave significant gaps between donor contributions and the actual delivery of aid. These systems may involve complex bureaucratic intermediaries and inconsistent reporting standards, which can hinder real-time monitoring and increase the risk of mismanagement or fraud. Shaheen et al. (2021) identify these systemic issues as key motivations for adopting blockchain-enabled donation tracking. Blockchain's core attributes—immutability, decentralization, and time-stamped record keeping—provide a transformative alternative. By enabling every donation transaction to be securely recorded on a distributed ledger, stakeholders gain immediate access to an auditable trail of funds. Almaghrabi and Alhogail (2022) emphasize that blockchain not only facilitates donation traceability from donor to beneficiary but also allows for the verification of purpose alignment—ensuring funds are used as intended. This enhances both operational clarity and ethical accountability in humanitarian financing, particularly in disaster-prone or politically unstable regions.

Transparency is a cornerstone of donor trust, and blockchain plays a critical role in reinforcing that trust. The real-time auditability of blockchain records reduces the information asymmetry that typically exists between donors and aid organizations. As Nairi, Cicioğlu, and Çalhan (2024) argue, the evolution toward Web 3.0 platforms offers an even more decentralized and user-empowered model of donation tracking, allowing donors to monitor not only the disbursement of funds but also the impact generated by their contributions. In their framework, blockchain serves as both a technical and symbolic mechanism—bridging the gap between intent and outcome. Rangone and Busolli (2021) reinforce this view through their Charity 4.0 analysis, showing that during the COVID-19 pandemic, blockchain applications significantly improved donor retention by providing evidence-based reassurance about fund utilization. This is particularly relevant in an era where donor skepticism and fatigue are rising due to widespread reports of inefficiency and misuse of humanitarian funds. When donors have access to transparent, immutable records, they are more likely to contribute, engage, and advocate for humanitarian causes over time.

A compelling real-world example of blockchain's role in donation transparency is Oxfam's UnBlocked Cash project. Piloted in Vanuatu and later expanded to other crisis-affected regions, this initiative leverages blockchain and Near Field Communication (NFC) technology to distribute digital cash directly to beneficiaries. According to Oxfam (2022), recipients receive a tap-and-pay card linked to a blockchain-based wallet, which they can use at authorized local vendors. Each transaction is recorded on the blockchain in real time, enabling donors, program managers, and financial auditors to monitor fund flows instantly. The system eliminates the need for banks or mobile connectivity—critical in remote or disrupted areas. As documented in Oxfam's own operational reports, this approach has significantly reduced delivery costs, increased response speed, and improved recipient dignity by allowing them to choose how to spend aid. Smart and Shrestha (2022) note that beyond technical efficiency, the system fostered greater community inclusion, vendor participation, and donor engagement. The UnBlocked Cash model exemplifies how digital innovation can reshape aid delivery into a transparent, efficient, and empowering process.

In addition to traceability, blockchain enhances accountability through smart contracts—self-executing protocols that automate fund disbursement based on predefined conditions. This innovation enables the transformation of passive donations into dynamic, event-driven resources. Trotter et al. (2020) introduce the concept of "smart donations," where contributions are only released if specific criteria are met (e.g., number of people vaccinated, shelters constructed, or food packets delivered). These contracts operate without human interference, reducing the possibility of fraud or discretion-based allocation. Wu, Lu, and Xu (2022) extend this logic in construction logistics by demonstrating how smart contracts can control payment freezing and conditional release—ensuring milestones are verified before disbursing funds. When applied to humanitarian contexts, such mechanisms can enhance the efficiency and fairness of aid distribution. For instance, conditional contracts could be used to trigger emergency funds only after satellite-verified disasters or biometric confirmation of recipient eligibility. These innovations promote a model of financial governance where accountability is embedded in the digital infrastructure itself—driving both cost-effectiveness and ethical rigor in humanitarian logistics.

In summary, blockchain technology fundamentally reconfigures how donations are tracked, verified, and disbursed in humanitarian operations. By providing a transparent and tamper-proof environment for financial transactions, it mitigates long-standing risks related to fraud, inefficiency, and donor disengagement. The Oxfam UnBlocked Cash initiative illustrates how blockchain can move beyond theory to practice, demonstrating scalable, inclusive, and ethical approaches to digital aid. Coupled with smart contracts, blockchain also enables conditional donations that align funds with measurable outcomes, enhancing trust and transparency across the donation lifecycle. As the humanitarian sector continues to confront funding constraints and public scrutiny, blockchain stands out as both a technological and moral innovation capable of restoring legitimacy and fostering resilience in aid financing.

3. BLOCKCHAIN AS A COORDINATION TOOL IN CRISIS MANAGEMENT

3.1 Inter-Organizational Data Sharing and Synchronization

Humanitarian crises often expose the limitations of existing coordination mechanisms among aid organizations, governmental bodies, and international actors. Coordination challenges arise from fragmented data systems, overlapping mandates, and inconsistent communication protocols, all of which can delay critical decision-making. Christensen and Ma (2020) highlight the complexity of inter-agency coordination in China, where overlapping bureaucratic jurisdictions during crisis response impede rapid information flow and resource allocation. Similar challenges were noted in the U.S. during the COVID-19 pandemic; Kapucu and Hu (2022) observe that the lack of a unified information-sharing platform among federal, state, and local agencies led to disjointed responses, resource duplication, and weakened public trust. Kuhlmann and Franzke (2022) report that Germany faced comparable issues in its multi-level governance structure, where differences in data access and procedural autonomy between federal and local entities complicated pandemic coordination. In such contexts, time-sensitive operations—such as the allocation of vaccines, shelter, or food—become vulnerable to administrative friction. These findings underscore the urgent need for a shared, tamper-proof data infrastructure that can synchronize decision-making across diverse institutional levels.

Blockchain technology offers a robust solution to this long-standing problem by functioning as a common data infrastructure that supports synchronized, real-time information sharing. Unlike traditional databases, blockchain enables decentralized record-keeping, where all participating nodes can view and verify identical transaction histories. Fu and Zhu (2021) frame blockchain as a "trusted data layer" ideal for crisis-oriented smart city governance, due to its integrity, availability, and interoperability. In the context of humanitarian logistics, Özkanlısoy and Akkartal (2021) emphasize that digital transformation efforts must go beyond automation to embrace shared digital platforms that reduce inter-organizational silos. Their earlier work (2020) calls for blockchain-integrated risk assessment frameworks in supply chains that not only track goods but also synchronize risk data across partners, suppliers, and responders. Moreover, Tao et al. (2024) demonstrate the operational feasibility of smart contracts embedded in blockchain systems that enforce data standards and automate compliance checking—an approach that can be repurposed to ensure consistent reporting across humanitarian agencies. Heo and Doh (2024) further propose combining blockchain with differential privacy techniques to allow secure multi-stakeholder data collaboration without compromising individual confidentiality. Collectively, these studies position blockchain as not just a technological upgrade, but a foundational infrastructure capable of addressing the systemic breakdowns in information synchronization during crises.

A key benefit of this decentralized architecture is its inherent trust-building capability, particularly in multi-actor crisis environments where institutional trust may be fragile or absent. Each blockchain node maintains an independent yet synchronized copy of the data, which reduces reliance on any single authority for verification or decision-making. This feature is especially important when coordination involves NGOs, UN agencies, local governments, and private-sector actors with differing governance frameworks and risk tolerances. According to Özkanlısoy and Akkartal (2021), blockchain fosters "platform neutrality," which democratizes data access and reduces disputes over data ownership or manipulation. In humanitarian operations, where real-time decisions must often be made across dispersed geographies, decentralized transparency becomes a trust enabler. Fu and Zhu (2021) also argue that blockchain's tamper-proof history provides a verifiable audit trail, enabling retrospective analysis and performance accountability. These features are critical not only for improving operational efficiency but also for enhancing transparency and compliance with humanitarian principles such as neutrality, impartiality, and equity.

A practical illustration of blockchain's role in inter-agency synchronization is seen in the World Food Programme's (WFP) collaborative initiatives with other development actors such as the International Fund for Agricultural Development (IFAD). As Nnachi (2019) describes in her doctoral research, this collaboration in regions like Nepal, El Salvador, and Ethiopia integrated humanitarian aid and climate resilience efforts through shared data systems, joint planning frameworks, and feedback loops. While blockchain was not originally a core component of this collaboration, recent extensions of WFP's digital strategies—such as the Building Blocks project—indicate a growing interest in leveraging blockchain to manage complex, multi-actor operations. The principle remains the same: creating a unified information environment where donors, implementers, and beneficiaries can access accurate, real-time data for decision-making. This ensures that aid is delivered efficiently, duplications are avoided, and accountability is enhanced. Blockchain, in this context, serves as the backbone for data harmonization across policy levels and operational units, bridging the gap between emergency response and long-term development planning.

In conclusion, effective inter-organizational coordination during crises depends on more than goodwill and institutional mandates—it requires an infrastructure that supports synchronized, secure, and transparent data sharing. Blockchain addresses this need by enabling decentralized data governance, ensuring that all actors operate from a shared, verifiable source of truth. Supported by smart contracts, privacy-preserving tools, and platform-neutral protocols, blockchain can transform fragmented crisis responses into cohesive, trust-based operations. The WFP's evolving collaborations exemplify how such systems can bridge humanitarian and development goals, and set the foundation for smarter, more resilient humanitarian governance.

3.2 Multi-Stakeholder Trust and Decentralized Decision Making

Crisis environments demand swift, inclusive, and trustworthy decision-making mechanisms among diverse stakeholders—governments, NGOs, private entities, donors, and local actors. Traditional centralized models often falter under the pressure of fragmented communication, uneven power dynamics, and competing interests. Alfantoukh, Ruan, and Durresi (2018) propose a multi-stakeholder consensus decision-making framework grounded in trust, where each actor's input is evaluated not just by authority or hierarchy, but by trustworthiness and contribution to the collective goal. Such frameworks are critical in humanitarian logistics, where coordination must be both agile and equitable. Fleischmann et al. (2024) emphasize the importance of "human-in-the-loop" decision-making algorithms, arguing that even in highly automated systems, stakeholder sentiment, trustworthiness scores, and social accountability must inform final outcomes. Similarly, Tariq (2025) underscores that in Industry 4.0-driven supply chains, multi-stakeholder collaboration enhances sustainability and responsiveness only when consensus and transparency are embedded in technology governance. Blockchain systems can facilitate such collaboration by removing the need for a central authority and offering a consensus-driven, decentralized environment for decision-making.

A central advantage of blockchain in multi-stakeholder crisis contexts is its ability to provide real-time data visibility to all actors, regardless of their location, technical capacity, or organizational affiliation. This democratization of information is particularly valuable when time-sensitive decisions—such as distributing medical supplies or allocating shelter—must be made collaboratively. Dadhich et al. (2024) identify social networks and inter-organizational trust as key mediators in the blockchain-social sustainability relationship, noting that blockchain's immutable, shared ledgers reduce the need for actors to rely solely on interpersonal trust or legacy relationships. Novak (2024) extends this by arguing that blockchain replaces "social trust" with "technological trust," allowing institutions that have never collaborated to act on shared data confidently. This is especially useful in humanitarian environments characterized by high turnover, new partnerships, and institutional fragmentation. Ding, Herbaut, and Negru (2024) introduce a conceptual model where blockchain-based trust mechanisms establish consistency and auditability across digital ecosystems, enabling organizations to respond cohesively to crises. When blockchain becomes the platform for real-time transparency, decision-making becomes less about persuasion or political positioning and more about evidence-based, ethically aligned consensus.

The importance of decentralized decision-making becomes even more pronounced in high-stakes emergency responses such as the Haiti earthquake and the ongoing Ukraine crisis. The Haiti relief effort faced widespread criticism for fragmented coordination, inconsistent aid delivery, and lack of local stakeholder inclusion. Although blockchain was not yet mature at the time, the absence of a transparent, distributed decision-making system led to duplicated efforts and resource mismanagement. By contrast, in Ukraine, emerging blockchain initiatives have begun to support more agile humanitarian aid flows. According to Chumachenko and Chumachenko (2022), the sheer speed and scale of displacement in Kharkiv necessitated decentralized platforms for registering refugees and tracking relief efforts. Ociepa-Kicińska and Gorzałczyńska-Koczkodaj (2022) highlight that in Poland, hosting millions of Ukrainian refugees, aid coordination improved through data-sharing protocols between NGOs, government agencies, and volunteers—an environment where blockchain could further enhance traceability and trust. Abay et al. (2022) and Rewizorski (2025) also describe how the Ukraine conflict destabilized global food systems, requiring multilayered coordination among states, donors, and international organizations to manage cascading humanitarian effects. In such polycentric settings, centralized command models are insufficient; instead, distributed, data-integrated frameworks like blockchain enable real-time verification, reduce bureaucratic delays, and help maintain accountability across sectors.

In summary, blockchain technology fosters an environment where trust becomes infrastructural rather than relational. In multi-stakeholder humanitarian operations, where time, integrity, and inclusion are critical, blockchain ensures that all actors have equal access to accurate data and the ability to participate in decentralized, consensus-driven decision-making. By automating trust through immutability and transparency, blockchain substitutes human judgment with codified rules—especially useful in situations with limited coordination history or fragmented authority. Drawing lessons from the Haiti coordination breakdown and the digitally adaptive response in Ukraine, blockchain emerges not merely as a tool for logistics, but as a paradigm shift in how decisions are shared, trusted, and implemented in crisis governance.

3.3 Challenges and Implementation Barriers

While blockchain technology offers substantial potential to transform humanitarian coordination and logistics, its implementation is not without significant structural and contextual challenges. One of the most persistent barriers is the deficit in digital infrastructure, particularly in crisis-affected and low-resource settings. Manny et al. (2021) argue that the digital transformation of infrastructure sectors—including logistics, public utilities, and communication networks—is hampered by institutional rigidity, underinvestment in ICT systems, and a lack of scalable digital standards. These limitations are compounded in humanitarian contexts, where operations often take place in remote or politically unstable regions with minimal internet connectivity and unreliable power supply. Del Carpio et al. (2022) stress that disparities in digital infrastructure amplify inequality and create a digital divide, especially post-COVID-19, where digital tools became essential for service delivery. Humanitarian organizations operating in areas without the foundational infrastructure for blockchain—such as distributed computing, cloud storage, and high-speed networks—face steep technical and financial obstacles to adoption. Moreover, as Albaroodi and Anbar (2025) caution, even when such infrastructure exists, its vulnerabilities—particularly in cloud-based blockchain deployments—pose security risks that can undermine system reliability. Oluwafemi (2023) adds that digital trust is also tied to infrastructural visibility and public perception; without trustworthy and inclusive systems, even technologically sound platforms may fail to gain legitimacy or adoption in the field.

Another major challenge lies in the high costs of integration and the shortage of human capital with blockchain-specific expertise. Developing a blockchain-based humanitarian platform requires more than just deploying a technical system; it involves integrating with existing logistics workflows, training personnel, establishing new data protocols, and continuously maintaining decentralized systems across a wide range of stakeholders. These tasks demand specialized skills in cryptography, smart contract design, distributed ledger management, and cybersecurity—capabilities that are often scarce within traditional humanitarian agencies. While private tech firms may possess this expertise, outsourcing to external actors can raise issues around ownership, ethical alignment, and long-term sustainability. Furthermore, the initial setup and operationalization costs of blockchain systems, including licensing, hardware, digital identity verification tools, and integration with IoT or biometric devices, can be prohibitive for many NGOs operating under donor constraints. These financial and skill-based barriers significantly slow down adoption and can result in fragmented or experimental deployments that fail to scale.

The absence of harmonized legal and regulatory frameworks further complicates the implementation of blockchain in humanitarian operations. Blockchain's decentralized and borderless architecture often conflicts with national laws on data sovereignty, financial transactions, and identity verification. Humanitarian actors frequently operate across multiple jurisdictions, each with its own interpretation of data privacy, contract enforceability, and institutional authority. This patchwork of legal regimes creates compliance uncertainty, deterring investment and innovation. For example, a blockchain-based identity system may be compliant with GDPR in Europe but incompatible with local data regulations in African or Asian countries. Furthermore, questions around accountability—such as who bears responsibility for erroneous or malicious transactions—remain unresolved in many legal systems, creating significant liability risks. Albaroodi and Anbar (2025) also note that regulatory frameworks for blockchain infrastructure security remain nascent, and current standards do not sufficiently address emergent threats like cryptographic breaches, protocol exploits, or the misuse of smart contracts. Until these legal ambiguities are addressed through global standards or bilateral agreements, humanitarian blockchain applications will remain limited to pilot projects rather than sector-wide transformations.

Finally, user experience (UX), digital literacy, and trust issues present significant field-level barriers to successful blockchain adoption. Many intended beneficiaries of humanitarian services—such as displaced populations, rural communities, and individuals with limited formal education—may struggle to interact with blockchain-enabled platforms, especially those requiring mobile apps, digital wallets, or biometric verification. As Oluwafemi (2023) emphasizes, digital trust must be earned through accessible design, transparent governance, and culturally appropriate engagement strategies. A system that is overly complex or opaque may alienate users and result in underutilization or outright rejection. Additionally, local implementing partners such as community-based organizations or field logistics teams may lack familiarity with blockchain processes, leading to operational delays or misuse. Literacy and UX barriers are not simply matters of interface design—they reflect broader issues of digital exclusion and technocratic control, which can erode community trust and ethical legitimacy. For blockchain to succeed in humanitarian contexts, it must be accompanied by robust capacity-building, iterative testing with local actors, and human-centered design principles that prioritize inclusion, simplicity, and transparency.

In sum, while blockchain holds great promise for decentralized coordination and secure data sharing in humanitarian logistics, its real-world implementation is constrained by a complex web of infrastructural, organizational, legal, and human challenges. Overcoming these barriers requires not only technical innovation but also policy reform, inclusive planning, and long-term investments in digital equity.

3.4 Case Spotlight: Blockchain-Based Cash Aid in Ukraine

In response to the humanitarian crisis in Ukraine, the United Nations High Commissioner for Refugees (UNHCR), in collaboration with the Stellar Development Foundation (SDF), Circle, and MoneyGram, launched a blockchain-based cash assistance pilot in late 2022. This initiative exemplifies the integration of decentralized finance into emergency aid systems, allowing displaced individuals to receive and use digital assets securely and efficiently (Stellar Development Foundation [SDF], 2023a).

The project operated through a tri-layered architecture:

- Stellar Blockchain Network, chosen for its energy efficiency, near-zero transaction fees, and rapid settlement capability;
- USDC Stablecoin, issued by Circle, ensuring low volatility and compliance with financial regulations;
- MoneyGram's on/off-ramp network, allowing recipients to convert USDC into local fiat currency at over 4,500 branches in Ukraine without needing a bank account (SDF, 2023b).

Beneficiaries received their funds via mobile wallets (e.g., Vibrant or Vesseo Assist), which were linked to unique digital identities verified during onboarding.

Recipients had the freedom to either retain the funds digitally or cash them out instantly at local MoneyGram centers (SDF, 2023c).

UNHCR reported that the program successfully delivered digital cash to more than 1,500 individuals, totaling over $1.1 million in humanitarian assistance (UNHCR, 2023). An independent pilot led by the International Rescue Committee (IRC) for 278 individuals showed 100% satisfaction with fund receipt and 94% reporting the process as easy (SDF, 2023a). Real-time delivery, financial autonomy, and cross-border usability were cited as major advantages (Swissinfo.ch, 2023).

Ethical considerations were also a cornerstone of the program. The use of USDC, a regulated stablecoin, addressed concerns around volatility and anti-money laundering (AML) compliance. Furthermore, by bypassing traditional banking structures and enabling beneficiaries to maintain full control over their aid, the program upheld the principles of humanitarian dignity and agency (Coindesk, 2023).

To ensure inclusive access, onboarding was done through SMS invitations, with multilingual training materials and support available both online and through in-person community hubs. This approach helped bridge digital literacy gaps among vulnerable populations (SDF, 2023a). The digital wallet's user-friendly design, combined with extensive user support, enabled the system to function effectively in the field even among populations unfamiliar with blockchain technology (Swissinfo.ch, 2023).

4. FUTURE TRENDS AND STRATEGIC OUTLOOK

4.1 Emerging Applications

As the field of humanitarian logistics evolves in tandem with rapid technological advances, blockchain is increasingly intersecting with broader digital ecosystems to support proactive, data-driven interventions. One of the most promising applications is in climate-disaster logistics. Given the increasing severity and frequency of climate-induced disasters, blockchain's immutable and decentralized data systems can help ensure continuity, accountability, and secure coordination across stakeholders during natural catastrophes. By integrating real-time data from distributed weather sensors, satellite feeds, and climate modeling systems with blockchain-led registries, humanitarian actors can automate resource mobilization before disasters strike—thus reducing loss of life and economic damage (Mızrak, 2025; Baharmand et al., 2021). Smart contracts could be triggered by thresholds such as early flood warnings or drought indexes, disbursing funds or repositioning supplies automatically—a practice that aligns with anticipatory action frameworks now promoted by WFP and IFRC (Negi, 2024).

Another important convergence lies between blockchain and predictive analytics powered by artificial intelligence. AI models can forecast the timing and location of humanitarian needs based on historical patterns, mobility data, and social media signals (Khan et al., 2021). When embedded in blockchain infrastructure, these forecasts become verifiable and traceable, providing both transparency and machine-aided responsiveness. For instance, predictive supply chain algorithms can automatically place procurement orders or alert distribution centers based on demand surges. This autonomous decision-making can dramatically reduce human error and enable agile relief cycles (Hunt et al., 2022; Mızrak & Akkartal, 2024). Such predictive capabilities, underpinned by distributed ledger trust systems, are especially crucial in fragile regions where bureaucratic delays or institutional mistrust undermine timely humanitarian action.

The integration of geospatial intelligence and Internet of Things (IoT) connectivity with blockchain further enhances supply chain visibility and security. By equipping relief shipments with GPS-enabled sensors and IoT tags that continuously transmit location, temperature, and humidity data, blockchain networks can create tamper-proof logs that ensure aid integrity throughout the supply journey (Akkartal & Abdelhadi, 2019; Baharmand et al., 2021). In highly complex supply chains, such as vaccine delivery or refugee camp provisioning, geospatial blockchain records also help mitigate losses from theft, spoilage, or diversion. These records not only enhance operational efficiency but also serve as audit trails for donors and regulators, who increasingly demand proof of impact and transparency (Memarpour Ghiaci et al., 2024).

4.2 Towards Global Interoperability and Ethical Governance

ooking ahead, one of the most critical requirements for blockchain's large-scale adoption in humanitarian contexts is global interoperability. As aid flows increasingly span multiple countries, jurisdictions, and organizations, blockchain platforms must be able to communicate across technical, legal, and institutional boundaries. This means developing shared protocols, open APIs, and modular data standards that allow different blockchain systems—whether run by NGOs, governments, or private donors—to exchange verified information in real time (Fu & Zhu, 2021; Tao et al., 2024). Without such interoperability, the promise of end-to-end traceability and shared situational awareness will remain siloed, undermining the full potential of blockchain to create cohesive global aid ecosystems (Özkanlısoy & Akkartal, 2021).

Ethical considerations are also at the forefront of future outlooks. Algorithmic accountability, especially in smart contract execution, is essential to prevent unjust or opaque fund disbursements. For instance, humanitarian actors must ensure that algorithms built into blockchain do not replicate bias or exclude vulnerable populations due to rigid eligibility rules or technological inaccessibility (Ajayi et al., 2024; Ding et al., 2024). This calls for "privacy by design" architectures that embed consent, minimal data exposure, and user control at every level of the system (Samunnisa & Gaddam, 2023; Yu et al., 2025). Moreover, systems must comply with global data protection regulations such as GDPR, which can be challenging in blockchain's inherently decentralized model. Solutions such as zero-knowledge proofs and decentralized identifiers offer pathways forward but require careful policy calibration (Gudala et al., 2022; Khaund, 2025).

To navigate these technological and governance frontiers, collaborative partnerships are indispensable. Future blockchain-based humanitarian solutions must be co-designed by technologists, local NGOs, and affected communities, rather than imposed as top-down tools. This co-production model not only ensures cultural appropriateness and usability but also builds trust and buy-in among field-level actors (Tariq, 2025; Fleischmann et al., 2024). Strategic alliances between private-sector blockchain firms (e.g., Circle, Stellar, Polygon), humanitarian organizations (e.g., WFP, IFRC, Oxfam), and governments can accelerate standards development, scale pilot implementations, and support capacity-building in under-resourced settings (Christensen & Ma, 2020; Rewizorski, 2025). In this collaborative spirit, the future of humanitarian logistics will not be merely digital—but also inclusive, transparent, and ethically resilient.

5. POLICY RECOMMENDATIONS FOR SCALABLE AND INCLUSIVE BLOCKCHAIN ADOPTION

For blockchain to meaningfully transform humanitarian logistics and supply chain operations, its adoption must be guided by robust policy frameworks that address legal, infrastructural, human, and ethical dimensions. The following strategic policy recommendations aim to ensure the scalability, inclusivity, and sustainability of blockchain solutions in the humanitarian domain.

Legal Frameworks, GDPR Compliance, and Regulatory Clarity

The first policy imperative is the establishment of coherent legal and regulatory frameworks that explicitly account for the unique architecture of blockchain systems. Unlike traditional databases, blockchain systems distribute data across nodes without a central authority, raising complex legal questions about data ownership, jurisdiction, and liability. Policymakers must work toward international harmonization of blockchain regulations to prevent fragmentation that hampers cross-border humanitarian efforts (Heo & Doh, 2024; del Carpio et al., 2022). Additionally, blockchain implementations in humanitarian settings must be designed in compliance with data protection laws such as the European Union's General Data Protection Regulation (GDPR), which mandates data minimization, user consent, and the right to be forgotten. Solutions such as zero-knowledge proofs and self-sovereign identity frameworks can reconcile blockchain's transparency with privacy obligations (Ajayi et al., 2024; Samunnisa & Gaddam, 2023). Legal clarity must also extend to the enforceability of smart contracts, which are now critical in automating donation disbursement and resource allocation but often lack formal legal standing (Wu et al., 2022).

Infrastructure Investment in Digital Access and Connectivity

A second critical pillar is the investment in digital infrastructure, particularly in low-resource and crisis-prone areas. As highlighted by Manny et al. (2021), digital transformation efforts frequently stall due to infrastructure deficits, including limited internet connectivity, unreliable electricity supply, and lack of digital interfaces. For blockchain to scale in humanitarian logistics, foundational investments must be made in cloud services, edge computing, and secure internet access at field distribution points, refugee camps, and remote healthcare facilities (Albaroodi & Anbar, 2025; Oluwafemi, 2023). Moreover, partnerships between governments, donors, and telecommunications firms can support the deployment of mobile-first blockchain platforms that work in low-bandwidth environments. This ensures that blockchain-based transparency and traceability mechanisms are not only technologically viable but also practically accessible to end-users in the field.

Capacity-Building for Local Actors

A technology is only as effective as the people empowered to use it. Thus, capacity-building and skills training for local NGOs, volunteers, logistics coordinators, and community members are essential. According to Mızrak (2025) and Baharmand et al. (2021), one of the primary barriers to adoption is the lack of technical literacy and institutional readiness among humanitarian actors. Training programs should include modules on digital identity systems, data protection principles, blockchain fundamentals, and practical applications such as aid registration or voucher distribution. Special attention must be given to gender and inclusion dimensions, ensuring that marginalized groups—including women, people with disabilities, and refugees—are not excluded from digital systems due to lack of digital literacy (Negi, 2024; Novak, 2024). International agencies like UNHCR and WFP should consider deploying mobile training units and gamified learning tools to reach rural and underserved areas.

Open-Source and Interoperable System Designs

Another major policy recommendation is the promotion of open-source blockchain tools and interoperable architectures. Closed, proprietary blockchain systems risk reinforcing silos rather than breaking them down. Instead, humanitarian organizations should advocate for permissioned, open-source platforms with standardized APIs and compliance with global data-sharing frameworks (Fu & Zhu, 2021; Tao et al., 2024). As demonstrated in blockchain-based collaborations such as Building Blocks by WFP, interoperability allows for real-time data exchange between different actors, including NGOs, governments, and private suppliers, thereby enhancing situational awareness and coordination (Baharmand et al., 2021; Nnachi, 2019). Moreover, modular and interoperable systems allow for scalability without lock-in, enabling organizations to integrate blockchain functionalities such as payment rails, supply chain audits, or ID management without overhauling existing platforms.

Ethical Audit Mechanisms and Digital Rights Safeguards

Finally, blockchain deployment in humanitarian contexts must be governed by strong ethical principles and digital rights safeguards. Given that vulnerable populations are often the subjects of data collection during crises, there is an urgent need for digital humanitarian charters that emphasize informed consent, data minimization, and user sovereignty (Mızrak, 2024; Ding et al., 2024). Independent ethical audit bodies should be established to monitor blockchain implementations, evaluating them against benchmarks for transparency, equity, and human rights. Blockchain systems must embed features such as opt-out options, pseudonymization, and audit logs to uphold user autonomy and institutional accountability (Khaund, 2025; Stockburger et al., 2021). Furthermore, collaboration with civil society watchdogs can ensure that blockchain does not become a technocratic tool that overrides community agency or reinforces power asymmetries in the aid ecosystem.

To ensure the successful integration of blockchain technologies in humanitarian logistics, a structured and inclusive approach is essential. As shown in Figure 1, this roadmap outlines a five-phase strategy beginning with the foundational need for digital infrastructure and internet accessibility, followed by targeted capacity-building for stakeholders, the establishment of regulatory frameworks and ethical oversight, the development of interoperable systems, and ultimately, the deployment of inclusive, people-centered solutions. This progression not only addresses current implementation barriers but also ensures long-term scalability, trust, and alignment with global humanitarian goals.

Figure 1. Roadmap for Scalable and Inclusive Blockchain Adoption

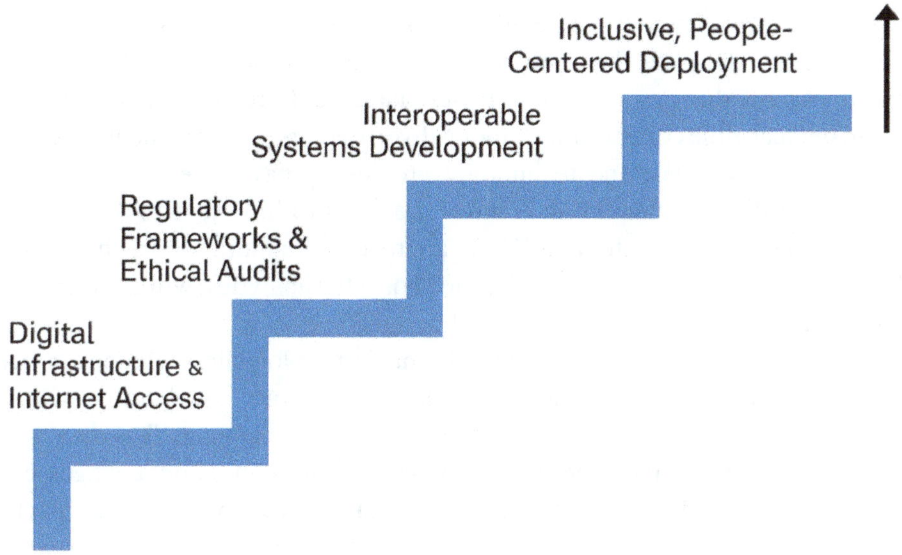

6. CONCLUSION

Blockchain technology presents a transformative paradigm shift for humanitarian logistics, offering a new architecture for transparency, accountability, and real-time decision-making. Across various domains—ranging from identity management and secure fund disbursement to multi-actor coordination and decentralized governance—blockchain offers novel mechanisms to address chronic inefficiencies and trust deficits that have historically hampered aid delivery. By digitizing the provenance of goods, securing digital identities, automating conditional aid through smart contracts, and enabling interoperable data environments, blockchain redefines what is technologically feasible in crisis contexts.

However, the transformative promise of blockchain is not purely technical. Its disruptive power also lies in its ethical and governance implications. Unlike traditional centralized models that consolidate control and obscure accountability, blockchain promotes a decentralized ethos grounded in transparency, auditability, and user sovereignty. This dual role—as a technical enabler and as an ethical scaffold—positions blockchain as a uniquely suitable tool for reshaping the humanitarian aid ecosystem. Nevertheless, realizing this dual potential demands vigilance: algorithmic decision-making must be carefully calibrated to avoid unintended exclusion, privacy risks must be mitigated through cryptographic safeguards, and digital rights must remain at the core of system design.

As global crises—from armed conflicts to climate-induced disasters—grow more frequent and complex, the humanitarian sector must move toward inclusive, trust-based systems that empower both beneficiaries and providers. Blockchain's ability to foster real-time collaboration among diverse actors—governments, NGOs, donors, local communities, and technology providers—paves the way for more equitable and resilient humanitarian architectures. But to fully realize this vision, stakeholders must adopt a systems-thinking approach, integrating blockchain with complementary technologies like AI, IoT, and geospatial analytics, while grounding every innovation in ethical, people-centered design.

Ultimately, the success of blockchain in humanitarian logistics will depend not solely on its cryptographic robustness or scalability, but on the collective will to ensure that technology serves humanity—not the other way around. This demands cross-sector collaboration, inclusive policy frameworks, and continuous engagement with those most affected by crisis and displacement. As we move forward, blockchain must not be viewed as a technological silver bullet, but as part of a broader ecosystem of tools, values, and practices committed to safeguarding dignity, fostering resilience, and rebuilding trust in humanitarian action.

REFERENCES

Abay, K. A., Breisinger, C., Glauber, J. W., Kurdi, S., Laborde Debucquet, D., & Siddig, K. (2022). *The Russia-Ukraine crisis: Implications for global and regional food security and potential policy responses* (Vol. 39). Intl Food Policy Res Inst. DOI: 10.2499/p15738coll2.135913

Ajayi, A. A., Emmanuel, I. G. B. A., Soyele, A. D., & Enyejo, J. O. (2024). Enhancing digital identity and financial security in decentralized finance (DeFi) through zero-knowledge proofs (ZKPs) and blockchain solutions for regulatory compliance and privacy. *Iconic Research and Engineering Journals*, *8*(4), 373–394.

Akkartal, E., & Abdelhadi, A. (2019). *A framework of IoT implementations and challenges in Warehouse Management, Transportation and Retailing*. Eurasian Business & Economics Journal.

Akkartal, E., & Abdelhadi, A. (2019). *A framework of IoT implementations and challenges in Warehouse Management, Transportation and Retailing*. Eurasian Business & Economics Journal.

Albaroodi, H. A., & Anbar, M. (2025). Security Issues and Weaknesses in Blockchain Cloud Infrastructure: A Review Article. *Journal of Applied Data Sciences*, *6*(1), 155–177. DOI: 10.47738/jads.v6i1.324

Alfantoukh, L., Ruan, Y., & Durresi, A. (2018, October). Multi-stakeholder consensus decision-making framework based on trust: A generic framework. In *2018 IEEE 4th International Conference on Collaboration and Internet Computing (CIC)* (pp. 472-479). IEEE. DOI: 10.1109/CIC.2018.00012

Almaghrabi, A., & Alhogail, A. (2022). Blockchain-based donations traceability framework. *Journal of King Saud University. Computer and Information Sciences*, *34*(10), 9442–9454. DOI: 10.1016/j.jksuci.2022.09.021

Aslan, Ö., Aktuğ, S. S., Ozkan-Okay, M., Yilmaz, A. A., & Akin, E. (2023). A comprehensive review of cyber security vulnerabilities, threats, attacks, and solutions. *Electronics (Basel)*, *12*(6), 1333. DOI: 10.3390/electronics12061333

Baharmand, H., Maghsoudi, A., & Coppi, G. (2021). Exploring the application of blockchain to humanitarian supply chains: Insights from Humanitarian Supply Blockchain pilot project. *International Journal of Operations & Production Management*, *41*(9), 1522–1543. DOI: 10.1108/IJOPM-12-2020-0884

Christensen, T., & Ma, L. (2020). Coordination structures and mechanisms for crisis management in China: Challenges of complexity. *Public Organization Review*, *20*(1), 19–36. DOI: 10.1007/s11115-018-0423-9

Chumachenko, D., & Chumachenko, T. (2022). Ukraine war: The humanitarian crisis in Kharkiv. *BMJ (Clinical Research Ed.)*, •••, 376. DOI: 10.1136/bmj.o796 PMID: 35338030

Dadhich, M., Opoku-Mensah, E., Kant Hiran, K., Akwasi Gyamfi, B., Tuffour, P., & Mahmoud, A. (2024). Exploring the mediating roles of social networks and trust in the blockchain-social sustainability nexus. *Journal of Economic Policy Reform*, *27*(3), 293–315. DOI: 10.1080/17487870.2024.2364649

Das, D., Dasgupta, K., & Biswas, U. (2023). A secure blockchain-enabled vehicle identity management framework for intelligent transportation systems. *Computers & Electrical Engineering*, *105*, 108535. DOI: 10.1016/j.compeleceng.2022.108535

del Carpio, X., Cuesta, J. A., Kugler, M. D., Hernández, G., & Piraquive, G. (2022). What effects could global value chain and digital infrastructure development policies have on poverty and inequality after COVID-19? *Journal of Risk and Financial Management*, *15*(2), 43. DOI: 10.3390/jrfm15020043

Ding, Y., Herbaut, N., & Negru, D. (2024, June). A Conceptual Model for Blockchain-Based Trust in Digital Ecosystems (Short Paper). In *International Conference on Advanced Information Systems Engineering* (pp. 18-24). Cham: Springer Nature Switzerland. DOI: 10.1007/978-3-031-61003-5_2

Fleischmann, M., Ramachandran, G., Koleilat, T., & Jurdak, R. (2024). Cyber-Social Consensus: Proposing a Human-in-the-Loop Algorithm for Automated Decision-Making in Multi-Stakeholder Settings. In *Proceedings of the 35th Australasian Conference on Information Systems (ACIS 2024)*. Association for Information Systems (AIS).

Fu, Y., & Zhu, J. (2021). Trusted data infrastructure for smart cities: A blockchain perspective. *Building Research and Information*, *49*(1), 21–37. DOI: 10.1080/09613218.2020.1784703

Ghelani, D., Hua, T. K., & Koduru, S. K. R. (2022). Cyber security threats, vulnerabilities, and security solutions models in banking. *Authorea Preprints*. DOI: 10.22541/au.166385206.63311335/v1

Gudala, L., Reddy, A. K., Sadhu, A. K. R., & Venkataramanan, S. (2022). Leveraging biometric authentication and blockchain technology for enhanced security in identity and access management systems. *Journal of Artificial Intelligence Research, 2*(2), 21–50.

Hadjisophocleous, O. N., Syed, T. A., & Lee, H. (2021, June). Blockchain-enabled humanitarian aid: A case study of the World Food Programme. In *PACIS* (p. 213).

Heo, G., & Doh, I. (2024). Blockchain and differential privacy-based data processing system for data security and privacy in urban computing. *Computer Communications, 222*, 161–176. DOI: 10.1016/j.comcom.2024.04.027

Hunt, K., Narayanan, A., & Zhuang, J. (2022). Blockchain in humanitarian operations management: A review of research and practice. *Socio-Economic Planning Sciences, 80*, 101175. DOI: 10.1016/j.seps.2021.101175

Husnain, M., Hayat, K., Cambiaso, E., Fayyaz, U. U., Mongelli, M., Akram, H., Ghazanfar Abbas, S., & Shah, G. A. (2022). Preventing MQTT vulnerabilities using IoT-enabled intrusion detection system. *Sensors (Basel), 22*(2), 567. DOI: 10.3390/s22020567 PMID: 35062536

Kapucu, N., & Hu, Q. (2022). An old puzzle and unprecedented challenges: Coordination in response to the COVID-19 pandemic in the US. *Public Performance & Management Review, 45*(4), 773–798. DOI: 10.1080/15309576.2022.2040039

Khan, M., Imtiaz, S., Parvaiz, G. S., Hussain, A., & Bae, J. (2021). Integration of internet-of-things with blockchain technology to enhance humanitarian logistics performance. *IEEE Access : Practical Innovations, Open Solutions, 9*, 25422–25436. DOI: 10.1109/ACCESS.2021.3054771

Khaund, B. (2025). Decentralized Identity Using Blockchain: Enhancing Security and Privacy in Digital Identity Management. *Journal of Computer Science and Technology Studies, 7*(6), 858–866.

Kuhlmann, S., & Franzke, J. (2022). Multi-level responses to COVID-19: Crisis coordination in Germany from an intergovernmental perspective. *Local Government Studies, 48*(2), 312–334. DOI: 10.1080/03003930.2021.1904398

Manny, L., Duygan, M., Fischer, M., & Rieckermann, J. (2021). Barriers to the digital transformation of infrastructure sectors. *Policy Sciences, 54*(4), 943–983. DOI: 10.1007/s11077-021-09438-y PMID: 34751195

Memarpour Ghiaci, A., Abbasi, M., Piri, M., & Akhavan, P. (2024). Barriers to blockchain adoption in humanitarian logistics in an uncertain environment. *Business Intelligence Management Studies, 12*(47), 153–184.

Mızrak, F. (2024). Enhancing Cybersecurity risk management through conceptual analysis of Hrm integration. *Yönetim Bilimleri Dergisi*, *22*(51), 96–118. DOI: 10.35408/comuybd.1342408

Mızrak, F. (2024). Resilience and Innovation Strategies: How Businesses Adapt to Supply Chain Disruptions in the Post-Pandemic Era. *Politik Ekonomik Kuram*, *8*(3), 581–600. DOI: 10.30586/pek.1497718

Mızrak, F. (2025). Cybersecurity and Strategic Innovation in the Digital Economy. In *Utilizing Cybersecurity to Foster Business Innovation and Resiliency* (pp. 1–30). IGI Global Scientific Publishing. DOI: 10.4018/979-8-3693-6417-8.ch001

Mızrak, F. (2025). The Triple Nexus of Smart, Secure, and Sustainable Supply Chains: Strategies for Resilience in the Digital Age. In *Utilizing Cybersecurity to Foster Business Innovation and Resiliency* (pp. 189-218). IGI Global Scientific Publishing.

Mizrak, F., & Akkartal, G. R. (2024). Prioritizing cybersecurity initiatives in aviation: A dematel-QSFS methodology. *Heliyon*, *10*(16), e35487. DOI: 10.1016/j.heliyon.2024.e35487 PMID: 39687858

Nairi, C., Cicioğlu, M., & Çalhan, A. (2024). Smart blockchain networks: Revolutionizing donation tracking in the Web 3.0. *Computer Communications*, *228*, 107972. DOI: 10.1016/j.comcom.2024.107972

Negi, S. (2024). A blockchain technology for improving financial flows in humanitarian supply chains: benefits and challenges. *Journal of Humanitarian Logistics and Supply Chain Management*, (ahead-of-print)

Nnachi, U. (2019). Linking humanitarian and development interventions into a joint resilience continuum: World food programme (wfp) and international fund for agricultural development (ifad) collaboration on building climate resilience in nepal. *El Salvador and Ethiopia (Doctoral dissertation, NUI Galway).*

Novak, M. (2024). Crypto altruism: Applying blockchain to charitable and humanitarian activities. *Chinese Public Administration Review*, *15*(1), 11–23. DOI: 10.1177/15396754231175173

Ociepa-Kicińska, E., & Gorzałczyńska-Koczkodaj, M. (2022). Forms of aid provided to refugees of the 2022 Russia–Ukraine war: The case of Poland. *International Journal of Environmental Research and Public Health*, *19*(12), 7085. DOI: 10.3390/ijerph19127085 PMID: 35742349

Oluwafemi, V. W. (2023). Globalisation and Digital Trust: Leveraging Blockchain to Decentralise Diaspora Investment and Public Procurement. *International Journal of Technology. Management and Humanities*, *9*(04), 49–71.

Oxfam (2022). UnBlocked Cash: Using blockchain to revolutionize humanitarian aid delivery. Retrieved from https://oxfam.app.box.com/s/5wh1dv0n80evv7lbqfs43xbqcpq0gxut/file/1241237853877

Ozdemir, A. I., Erol, I., Ar, I. M., Peker, I., Asgary, A., Medeni, T. D., & Medeni, I. T. (2021). The role of blockchain in reducing the impact of barriers to humanitarian supply chain management. *International Journal of Logistics Management*, *32*(2), 454–478. DOI: 10.1108/IJLM-01-2020-0058

Özkanlısoy, Ö., & Akkartal, E. (2021). Digital transformation in supply chains: Current applications, contributions and challenges. *Business & Management Studies: An International Journal*, *9*(1), 32–55.

Rangone, A., & Busolli, L. (2021). Managing charity 4.0 with Blockchain: A case study at the time of Covid-19. *International Review on Public and Nonprofit Marketing*, *18*(4), 491–521. DOI: 10.1007/s12208-021-00281-8

Rewizorski, M. (2025). Bound to Abstain?: The BRICS Response to the Russia-Ukraine Crisis. In *Global Governance and The Political South* (pp. 75-89). Routledge.

Samunnisa, K., & Gaddam, S. V. K. (2023). Blockchain-Based Decentralized Identity Management for Secure Digital Transactions. *Synthesis: A Multidisciplinary Research Journal, 1*(2), 22-29.

Shaheen, E., Hamed, M. A., Zaghloul, W., Al Mostafa, E., El Sharkawy, A., Mahmoud, A., . . . Attiya, G. (2021, July). A track donation system using blockchain. In *2021 international conference on electronic engineering (ICEEM)* (pp. 1-7). IEEE. DOI: 10.1109/ICEEM52022.2021.9480649

Smart, K., & Shrestha, S. (2022). Delivering Better together: Standard Operating Procedures for Oxfam's Approach to Cash and Voucher Assistance.

Stockburger, L., Kokosioulis, G., Mukkamala, A., Mukkamala, R. R., & Avital, M. (2021). Blockchain-enabled decentralized identity management: The case of self-sovereign identity in public transportation. *Blockchain: Research and Applications*, *2*(2), 100014.

Tao, X., Wu, Z., Xu, Y., Zheng, C., Fang, Y., Das, M., Liu, H., Gong, X., & Cheng, J. C. (2024). Smarter smart contracts for automatic BIM metadata compliance checking in blockchain-enabled common data environment. *Advanced Engineering Informatics*, *62*, 102627. DOI: 10.1016/j.aei.2024.102627

Tariq, M. U. (2025). Integrating Advanced Technologies for Multi-Stakeholder Collaboration: Driving Sustainability in Supply Chains Through Industry 4.0. In *Multi-Stakeholder Collaboration for Sustainable Supply Chain* (pp. 313-334). IGI Global Scientific Publishing.

Trotter, L., Harding, M., Shaw, P., Davies, N., Elsden, C., Speed, C., & Hallwright, J. (2020, December). Smart donations: Event-driven conditional donations using smart contracts on the blockchain. In *Proceedings of the 32nd Australian Conference on Human-Computer Interaction* (pp. 546-557). DOI: 10.1145/3441000.3441014

Wu, L., Lu, W., & Xu, J. (2022). Blockchain-based smart contract for smart payment in construction: A focus on the payment freezing and disbursement cycle. *Frontiers of Engineering Management*, *9*(2), 177–195. DOI: 10.1007/s42524-021-0184-y

Yu, H., Wang, G., Dong, A., Han, Y., Wang, Y., & Yu, J. (2025). Blockchain-enabled privacy protection scheme for IoT digital identity management. *High-Confidence Computing*, •••, 100320. DOI: 10.1016/j.hcc.2025.100320

Chapter 6
Redesigning Humanitarian Logistics with Intelligent Systems: From Chaos to Coordination

İlknur Yardımcı-Coşkun
https://orcid.org/0000-0002-7183-6142
Faculty of Business and Management Sciences, Maltepe University, Turkey

ABSTRACT

Sudden and destructive disasters such as earthquakes create complex and uncertain logistical needs that challenge traditional humanitarian response systems. This chapter explores how smart technologies such as artificial intelligence (AI), predictive analytics, cloud computing, Internet of Things (IoT), drone systems, and Geographic Information Systems (GIS) can enhance earthquake-based humanitarian logistics by improving speed, coordination, and decision-making. A thematic literature review, a technology–value matrix, and five real-world-inspired scenarios are used to evaluate these technologies' effectiveness across logistics functions. Additionally, an Integrated Smart Technology Ecosystem model is introduced to demonstrate how these tools can work collectively. The study highlights that successful implementation depends not only on technical capability but also on ethical governance, data quality, interoperability, and institutional readiness. Strategic recommendations are offered for humanitarian actors, emphasizing holistic planning and future research directions.

DOI: 10.4018/979-8-3373-3643-5.ch006

1. INTRODUCTION

The accelerating frequency, severity, and complexity of disasters driven by environmental degradation, socio-political instability, and global technological interdependencies—have drastically reshaped the landscape of humanitarian crises. Earthquakes, floods, pandemics, wars, forced migrations, and the escalating climate emergency not only increase the number of people requiring urgent assistance but also expose the structural limitations of conventional response systems. Humanitarian logistics, in particular, has become increasingly challenged by unpredictable demand patterns, infrastructure disruptions, information asymmetries, and multi-actor coordination gaps.

In such environments, the capacity of logistics systems to function rapidly, flexibly, efficiently, and sustainably is no longer a luxury but a matter of survival. Yet, the majority of existing humanitarian logistics infrastructures continue to rely on fragmented coordination mechanisms, operate with limited real-time data, and lack anticipatory planning capabilities. As a result, decision-making remains reactive and often delayed, leading to critical inefficiencies in the distribution of aid, allocation of resources, and overall situational awareness.

Traditionally, humanitarian logistics has been organized around manual operations and static contingency plans. However, over the past two decades, major global disasters such as the 2004 Indian Ocean tsunami, the 2010 Haiti earthquake, and more recently the 2023 Türkiye–Syria earthquake have served as catalysts for digital innovation in humanitarian operations. These events have underscored the urgent need for transformation toward proactive, data-informed, and digitally integrated response systems.

At the forefront of this transformation are smart technologies including Artificial Intelligence (AI), predictive analytics, Internet of Things (IoT), cloud computing, Geographic Information Systems (GIS), and autonomous platforms such as drones and robotic agents. These tools collectively offer unprecedented opportunities to enhance the agility, scalability, and responsiveness of humanitarian supply chains. They facilitate dynamic decision-making, disaster forecasting, real-time monitoring, route optimization, needs assessment, and improved access to vulnerable and hard-to-reach populations.

In the case of high-impact, time-critical disasters such as earthquakes, where minutes can determine the difference between life and death, technology-driven logistics solutions become essential. The ability to capture and process data in real time, to anticipate cascading failures, and to coordinate multi-stakeholder actions rapidly is vital to achieving life-saving outcomes. Smart systems thus represent a critical enabler of situational awareness, operational coherence, and resource effectiveness in humanitarian contexts.

This book chapter investigates how chaotic, fragmented, and delay-prone humanitarian logistics systems can be reconfigured into more coordinated, predictive, and resilient structures by leveraging intelligent technologies. The study systematically identifies key digital tools through an extensive literature review and assesses their functional contributions across the three core disaster phases preparedness, response, and recovery and within critical logistics functions such as evacuation planning, damage assessment, early warning, route design, data exchange, and service delivery.

Beyond descriptive analysis, the chapter introduces an original Technology–Value Matrix, which offers a comparative evaluation of each smart technology based on its contribution level, ease of implementation, operational impact, potential benefits, and limitations. To contextualize these findings, five realistic application scenarios are presented, drawing from both historical disaster cases and simulation-based modeling. These scenarios aim to demonstrate how selected technologies can be mobilized to address real-time logistical challenges during earthquake emergencies.

Recognizing that individual technologies cannot function in isolation under complex disaster conditions, the chapter also proposes an Integrated Smart Technology Ecosystem model. This framework synthesizes the role of interconnected Technologies such as IoT-based early warning systems, AI-powered analytics, drone imaging, GIS-enabled spatial planning, and cloud-based coordination platforms—into a unified operational architecture. The model highlights the importance of interoperability, data governance, and synchronized decision-making in enabling fast and targeted response actions.

Ultimately, this chapter advances the argument that digital transformation in humanitarian logistics is not merely a matter of technological adoption. It is equally a question of institutional readiness, ethical responsibility, policy innovation, and human-centered design. By offering strategic insights and practical frameworks for humanitarian organizations, local governments, and global policy actors, the chapter contributes to the ongoing discourse on building disaster response systems that are not only faster and smarter but also fairer, more transparent, and more resilient in the face of future uncertainties.

The primary objective of this book chapter is to comprehensively examine how artificial intelligence (AI), predictive analytics, and autonomous systems can be utilized in earthquake-oriented humanitarian logistics operations. The study aims to identify which intelligent technologies are most suitable for enhancing the effectiveness, speed, and coordination of humanitarian logistics systems in the face of sudden and large-scale disasters such as earthquakes. Within this scope, a literature review will identify AI-based solutions, predictive systems, and autonomous technologies that are currently used or proposed for use in earthquake scenarios. The roles of these technologies across the phases of preparedness, response, and recovery will be explored. Additionally, the expected benefits, challenges encountered, and ethical or infrastructural limitations of these solutions will be analyzed.

Accordingly, this chapter focuses on the following research questions:

- Which artificial intelligence, predictive analytics, and autonomous system technologies are currently used or have the potential to be used in earthquake-based disaster logistics?
- At which phases and within which logistics functions (e.g., supply procurement, route planning, resource allocation, information management, last-mile delivery) are these technologies applied?
- How can the integration of these systems impact response speed, resource efficiency, and coordination effectiveness?
- What are the key challenges, ethical considerations, and data security issues associated with the implementation of these technologies?
- How can hybrid models, where human and AI-based systems work collaboratively, contribute to more effective responses during earthquake crises?

The increasing integration of technology in disaster management has necessitated the redesign of humanitarian logistics processes, particularly in sudden and destructive crises such as earthquakes. In this context, the literature review conducted for this chapter systematically outlines how artificial intelligence (AI), predictive analytics, and autonomous systems are applied in disaster logistics and in which domains they create value.

The reviewed studies (see Table 1) generally cluster around four main thematic axes:

(i) decision support systems,
(ii) route planning and resource allocation,
(iii) communication and information-sharing infrastructures,
(iv) damage assessment and response speed.

In the context of Decision Support Systems, Hobeika et al. (1988) and Lechtenberg et al. (2017) emphasize the necessity of digital decision support systems to meet urban transportation needs following a disaster. These systems play a crucial role in directing response vehicles, dynamically adjusting networks in real time, and prioritizing cleanup operations. Similarly, Chang et al. (2024) and Mousazadeh & Aminpour (2025) propose two-stage stochastic models to optimize the location of post-disaster distribution centers and vehicle assignments. Regarding Resource Allocation and Route Planning, GIS-based decision support systems stand out. Qi et al. (2019) and Yılmaz et al. (2019) demonstrate that real-time optimization of warehouse selection and emergency routes significantly shortens response times. These technologies are tailored to actual disaster conditions such as rough terrain and damaged infrastructure, thereby increasing their applicability. In terms of Information Sharing and Coordination, cloud-based systems provide critical benefits. Banisakher et al. (2018) and Niyazi & Behnamian (2023) propose architectures that enable real-time data sharing and decision support, ensuring accurate resource allocation. Khan et al. (2022) further highlight how digitalization adds value to humanitarian logistics by enhancing accountability, transparency, and speed. In the domain of Imaging and Damage Assessment, AI-assisted satellites, drones, and sensor technologies are effectively used. Oliveira et al. (2024) and Estêvão (2024) report high accuracy in classifying post-earthquake building damage using these technologies. Ozturkcan (2023) and Nazlıoğlu et al. (2024) show how innovative solutions such as social media, WhatsApp bots, and crowdsourced platforms improve post-disaster information flow and contribute to resource coordination.

Several studies emphasize that post-disaster humanitarian logistics processes must be supported not only through digital decision systems but also through multi-faceted solutions that include physical infrastructure. For example, in a study previously conducted by the author, a modular pole system was proposed to simultaneously meet lighting, energy, and communication needs under post-disaster conditions (Aksoy & Yardımcı Coşkun, 2025). Such applications serve as tangible examples of how smart systems evaluated in the technology–value matrix can contribute to infrastructure sustainability in the field.

These findings align closely with the objectives of this chapter: smart systems can indeed accelerate response processes, optimize resource use, and make decision-making more predictable during destructive earthquakes. However, the literature also reveals critical gaps. There is a limited number of empirical studies focusing on human–AI collaboration, ethical data usage, the field applicability of hybrid systems, and the infrastructure requirements for sustainable implementation. This underlines the importance of this chapter's original contribution through its gap analysis and the use of the technology–value matrix framework.

In conclusion, the existing literature highlights the strategic value of smart systems in earthquake-based humanitarian logistics. However, it falls short of providing holistic and comparative answers to key questions such as how these technologies can be integrated into different logistics functions during crises, under what conditions they yield the highest benefit, and what ethical or systemic risks may arise. Accordingly, this chapter aims both to fill these gaps in a systematic manner and to offer strategic guidance for both academic research and practical applications.

Table 1. Overview of Relevant Literature

Author/Year	Summary of the Study
Eren et al., 2007	This study highlights the application of geospatial and communication technologies in post-earthquake operations. It identifies the use of Global Navigation Satellite Systems (GNSS) for precise location tracking, Remote Sensing (RS) for damage assessment, and satellite communication systems to enhance coordination and logistics during emergency response and recovery phases.
Hobeika et al., 1988	This study highlights the implementation of the Transportation Emergency Decision Support System (TEDSS) as a digital solution for logistics decision-making in urban disasters. It focuses on addressing post-earthquake transportation needs through real-time network adjustment, emergency vehicle dispatch algorithms, and prioritization of clean-up operations, thereby improving the efficiency of response and recovery efforts.
Lechtenberg et al., 2017	The paper emphasizes the need for tailored decision support systems in disaster relief logistics, advocating for integrated decision problems and simulation techniques to enhance decision-making processes during sudden, high-impact catastrophes like earthquakes, rather than relying solely on optimization methods.
Ochoa et al., 2017	The paper discusses redesigning Humanitarian Logistics through Multi-agent Systems and Artificial Intelligence, offering interdisciplinary perspectives and innovative techniques to enhance efficiency and effectiveness in disaster prevention and response, addressing various real-world applications and methodologies.
Banisakher et al., 2018; Alazawi et al., 2011; Dubey et al., 2018; Niyazi, and Behnamian, 2023	These studies have utilized cloud computing technologies to enhance coordination, data sharing, and decision-support mechanisms in disaster management, achieving benefits such as rapid response, resource optimization, and real-time information access.
Khademi Zareh et al., 2018	The paper proposes a mathematical model for redesigning humanitarian logistics networks to enhance preparedness and response to earthquakes, integrating rehabilitation strategies and debris clearance scheduling, ultimately improving accessibility and performance in delivering relief to evacuees compared to existing networks.
Bray et al., 2019	This study outlines the use of advanced geospatial technologies in post-earthquake contexts, including Light Detection and Ranging (LIDAR), Structure-from-Motion (SfM) image processing, and Unmanned Aerial Vehicles (UAVs) for data collection. These are employed alongside traditional methods such as differential GPS to enable detailed mapping and surveying of earthquake-induced damage.
Qi et al., 2019	The paper presents a Geographic Information System (GIS) based decision support system for emergency logistics, optimizing material allocation and transportation routes post-earthquake, enhancing timely assistance, and minimizing casualties through efficient decision-making processes in sudden, high-impact disasters.
Yılmaz et al., 2019	The paper presents a GIS-based framework for optimizing depot selection and routing in sudden-onset disasters like earthquakes, considering infrastructure survivability, legal speed limits, and real-life conditions to enhance emergency logistics decision-making and minimize response times.
Coan et al., 2020	The paper focuses on the digitalization of humanitarian supply chains, specifically through an inventory management system for health equipment, enhancing visibility of stocks and consumption, rather than directly addressing the redesign of humanitarian logistics with intelligent systems.

continued on following page

Table 1. Continued

Author/Year	Summary of the Study
Garrido and Aguirre, 2020	The paper presents a modeling framework for emergency logistics in earthquake scenarios, incorporating spatio-temporal demand correlation, resource allocation, and transportation capacity, enabling effective decision-making under budget constraints and demand uncertainty for rapid relief operations.
Göçmen and Kuvvetli, 2020	The paper focuses on an inventory routing model for post-earthquake logistics, emphasizing efficient distribution and inventory management. It highlights the importance of intelligent systems in minimizing costs and improving response times during humanitarian operations after disasters like the Van earthquake.
Paudel, 2020	The paper discusses the application of AI in reconstruction governance post-2015 Nepal earthquakes, utilizing data on loss, grievances, and infrastructure to inform policy decisions. However, challenges like institutional issues and financial gaps hindered timely reconstruction efforts.
Wu and Xu, 2020	The paper discusses using intelligent system engineering methods to enhance humanitarian logistics through accurate prediction, optimal planning, rapid decision-making, and real-time control, ultimately improving resource utilization and material security effectiveness in emergency logistics support.
Sánchez-Partida et al., 2021	In this study, Information and Communication Technologies (ICTs) played a predominant role in coordinating logistics activities between volunteers and victims during the 19S earthquake in Puebla, Mexico, facilitating timely communication and efficient resource allocation among various humanitarian actors.
Bačić et al., 2022	The article discusses the use of remote sensing sensors from space (EO) and geoinformation (GI) technologies to rapidly collect and process information about earthquakes and their consequences, enhancing crisis management efforts following catastrophic events such as the 2020 earthquakes in Croatia.
Hernández-Leandro et al., 2022	The paper focuses on a bi-objective model for post-earthquake logistics, emphasizing the location of temporary distribution centers and balancing aid distribution. It utilizes an exact AUGMECON method and a genetic algorithm to optimize time and cost in humanitarian logistics.
Khan et al., 2022	The paper emphasizes that digitalization enhances humanitarian logistics (HL) effectiveness by improving accountability, security, trust, transparency, and promptness, crucial for managing sudden, high-impact disasters like earthquakes, ultimately saving lives and alleviating suffering through timely resource distribution.
Hackathon, 2023	The paper discusses leveraging AI in disaster management post the 2023 Moroccan earthquake, highlighting its role in improving preparedness, response, and recovery through innovative projects developed during a hackathon, addressing challenges like data scarcity and interdisciplinary collaboration.
Oguntola and Ülkü, 2023	This study emphasizes the potential of artificial intelligence (AI) to enhance humanitarian logistics by optimizing operational processes through advanced algorithms and data-driven decision-making. It highlights AI's contribution to sustainable humanitarian logistics by addressing cultural, economic, environmental, and societal dimensions. Furthermore, it underscores the importance of human–AI collaboration in saving lives during disasters.

continued on following page

Table 1. Continued

Author/Year	Summary of the Study
Ozturkcan, 2023	This study identifies a diverse range of technologies utilized in the aftermath of earthquakes. These include social media platforms for communication, AI-powered satellite imagery for damage assessment, cryptocurrencies for facilitating donations, WhatsApp-based helplines and chatbots for assistance, whistle applications for distress signaling, and crowdsourced platforms for resource coordination and information dissemination.
Paz-Orozco et al., 2023	The study presents a methodology combining deterministic mathematical modeling and simulation to enhance logistics decision-making in earthquakes, improving supply delivery time by 30% and increasing equitable coverage by 25%, thus effectively addressing sudden, high-impact disaster scenarios.
Chang et al., 2024	The paper proposes a two-stage stochastic programming model for logistics decision-making in sudden-onset disasters, optimizing relief goods distribution center locations and vehicle allocation, while addressing uncertainties in post-disaster conditions, enhancing efficiency in response to catastrophic events like earthquakes.
Dindarik and Atabey, 2024	This study addresses the role of digitally supported solutions in logistics decision-making during earthquakes. Artificial intelligence for optimizing resource allocation, data analytics for disaster forecasting, and automation technologies such as drones for rapid damage assessment and aid distribution are identified as key factors that enhance the efficiency and effectiveness of response operations.
Estêvão, 2024	The study highlights the use of Generative AI models for rapid post-earthquake damage assessment, improving classification accuracy of structural damage, which aids emergency response, resource allocation, and resilience planning, ultimately enhancing humanitarian aid efforts in disaster scenarios.
Nazlıoğlu et al., 2024	The study identifies 89 unique digital solutions used after the February 2023 earthquake in Türkiye, focusing on web-based platforms for information dissemination and mobile platforms for communication, with strong involvement from private organizations in developing these technologies.
Oliveira et al., 2024	This study emphasizes the use of technologies such as video recordings, drone footage, and satellite imagery following earthquakes. These tools support the documentation and analysis of destruction, providing critical data to experts in seismology, earthquake engineering, and disaster management, thereby contributing to improved understanding and societal resilience.
Küçük and Yardımcı Coşkun, 2025	This study applies the Dijkstra algorithm for route planning in the context of disaster logistics, specifically focusing on transportation management from civil defense unit warehouses. It provides recommendations to ensure that emergency interventions are timely and sufficient by optimizing delivery routes within constrained environments.
Moonesar, 2025	The paper emphasizes predictive analytics and data-informed insights to enhance humanitarian logistics. By fostering public-private partnerships and focusing on readiness, rapid responses, and resilience, intelligent systems can optimize resource allocation and tailor relief strategies effectively during crises.
Mousazadeh and Aminpour, 2025	The paper presents a two-stage stochastic model for redesigning humanitarian supply chains, focusing on strategic and tactical decisions during earthquakes, specifically in Tehran. It optimizes facility locations, allocation patterns, and material flows to enhance efficiency and minimize costs.

A general evaluation of the findings derived from the Table 1 reveals that the integration of smart systems within disaster management significantly enhances operational awareness and decision support capacity. In this context, Information and Communication Technologies (ICT) provide a foundational infrastructure for managing several critical processes, including access to detailed mapping of the disaster area, real-time communication, data sharing, and resource coordination (Summer, 2010). Specifically, drone and satellite imaging systems (Oliveira et al., 2024), IoT-based early warning applications (Naik et al., 2024), and AI-supported rescue analyses (Öztürkcan, 2023) contribute to the speed, accuracy, and inclusiveness of response operations.

Moreover, prominent approaches in the literature such as stochastic modeling, inventory routing, and reconfiguration strategies (Paz-Orozco et al., 2023; Mousazadeh & Aminpour, 2025; Khademi Zareh et al., 2018) offer valuable practical insights for the strategic redesign of logistics networks. However, real-time data integration, the development of systems adaptable to various disaster scenarios, and the ethical boundaries of human–machine interaction remain major challenges in current applications. At this point, the broader, safer, and more inclusive integration of advanced digital solutions into humanitarian response systems emerges as a critical focus area for future research.

Although several studies propose technical frameworks, few adopt a comparative or integrated perspective that assesses interoperability, ethical implications, and real-world feasibility of smart technologies in crisis environments. Moreover, limited attention has been given to hybrid human–AI coordination models, particularly in resource-constrained or politically unstable regions.

2. METHODOLOGY ANALYTICAL FRAMEWORK

This study is structured to evaluate the role of artificial intelligence (AI), predictive analytics, and autonomous systems in the redesign of earthquake-based humanitarian logistics processes. Recognizing the increasing complexity and urgency of disaster response operations, the study aims to provide a holistic understanding of how intelligent technologies can improve decision-making, coordination, and resource efficiency in time-critical scenarios. The methodological approach adopted in this research comprises two interrelated components: (1) a thematic literature review, designed to systematically identify and classify the smart technologies applied in humanitarian logistics, and (2) the development of a technology–value matrix to comparatively evaluate these technologies across multiple operational dimensions. This dual framework enables both a comprehensive synthesis of the existing academic and practical knowledge base and a structured assessment of each technology's contribution level, ease of implementation, functional scope, and potential benefits and limitations. By integrating qualitative insights with conceptual mapping, the methodology supports a more grounded and strategic perspective on the digital transformation of humanitarian supply chains in the context of earthquakes.

In the first phase, a thematic literature review was conducted to identify intelligent technologies that are used or proposed in earthquake-related humanitarian logistics. The review covered academic databases such as Scopus, Web of Science, and Google Scholar. Keywords included terms such as *"earthquake humanitarian logistics," "disaster response technologies," "AI in disaster logistics," "predictive analytics," "emergency routing,"* and *"digital disaster management."*

The selected studies were filtered based on publication year, disaster type (earthquakes), type of technology, and corresponding logistics functions (preparedness, response, recovery). Considering the most cited and relevant contributions in the literature, 13 distinct technologies were identified. Inclusion criteria for selecting the technologies involved: (1) relevance to earthquake-related logistics operations, (2) citation frequency in disaster studies, and (3) availability of empirical or simulation-based evidence. Studies that focused solely on general ICT systems without application to logistics operations were excluded. These include: artificial intelligence, drone/satellite systems, Internet of Things (IoT), cloud computing, Geographic Information Systems (GIS), robotic systems, generative AI, blockchain/cryptocurrency solutions, social media/crowdsourcing platforms, stochastic modeling, multi-agent systems, LIDAR/SfM/GNSS technologies, and SMS/ICT-based tools.

These technologies were first classified with brief summaries in a table (see Table 2) and then visually and conceptually mapped through Figure 2.

The technology value matrix is a conceptual framework designed to help organizations assess and leverage technology to create value across multiple dimensions. It has been applied in contexts such as technology scouting, welfare technology, software architecture, and IT business value each emphasizing different aspects of value creation and stakeholder engagement (Peter et al., 2019).

The technology value matrix aims to analyze the contribution of a specific technology to an organization, system, or process across several dimensions. It enables a comprehensive comparison not only in terms of technical feasibility but also strategic relevance, operational utility, ease of implementation, and potential risks. The matrix is commonly employed in areas such as strategic technology planning, innovation management, digital transformation, and disaster management. It facilitates decision-making by helping prioritize technologies based on their impact and implementation readiness.

Methodologically, the matrix is structured around the following core dimensions:

- **Technological Contribution** (impact/contribution)

- **Ease of Implementation** (infrastructure requirements, cost, and expertise)
- **Functional Scope** (extent of operational applicability)
- **Potential Benefits** (cost-effectiveness, speed, accessibility)
- **Risks and Challenges** (ethical concerns, data security, social acceptance)

Such matrices are particularly useful in disaster and crisis environments, where high levels of uncertainty demand careful evaluation of risk–return trade-offs and efficient resource allocation.

In the second phase of this study, a customized technology–value matrix was developed to comprehensively assess the contributions of identified smart technologies to humanitarian logistics processes. Each technology was evaluated across five dimensions:

1. **Contribution**: The degree to which the technology contributes to the logistics process (High, Medium, Low).
2. **Ease of Implementation**: Evaluation based on infrastructure requirements, cost, and required expertise.
3. **Applicability**: Identification of the logistics phase(s) (preparedness, response, recovery) in which the technology is applied.
4. **Benefits**: Operational gains such as time efficiency, cost reduction, accessibility, and improved information sharing.
5. **Challenges**: Potential risks including ethical concerns, data security, regulatory issues, and public acceptance.

The evaluations in the matrix were based on findings from the literature and insights derived from scenario-based interpretations. Comparative analysis was performed between multi-functional technologies (e.g., cloud computing, artificial intelligence) and more narrowly focused but strategically relevant solutions (e.g., blockchain, robotic systems). The completed matrix is presented in Table 3, where the strengths and weaknesses of each technology are visually represented.

The matrix approach adopted in this study builds upon multidimensional evaluation frameworks previously proposed by Lan (2000), Mendonça (2003), and Chang & Pires A. (2015). Technologies were not assessed solely on their technical contributions but were systematically analyzed based on implementation feasibility, benefit potential, and foreseeable risks. This method provides a strategic lens for selecting and prioritizing technologies, particularly in high-uncertainty environments such as disaster response.

To contextualize the technology evaluation with field-based relevance, five application scenarios were developed, each incorporating one or more smart technologies. These scenarios were inspired by real-world disaster cases (e.g., the 2023

Türkiye–Syria earthquake, the 2015 Nepal earthquake) and simulation-based fictional models. The aim is to demonstrate the potential contribution of each technology within the decision-making context during a crisis.

The scenarios are visualized in the infographic in Figure 2, with each scenario aligned with the specific logistics function it supports (e.g., artificial intelligence, evacuation planning, drones, damage assessment).

One of the methodological innovations of this study is the evaluation of key smart technologies in disaster-based humanitarian logistics not only in terms of their individual contributions, but also in terms of their interoperability. While the literature typically focuses on the standalone benefits of specific technologies, the interaction and integration of different systems are often overlooked. However, in practice, crisis management processes require simultaneous data flows, multi-layered decision-making, and inter-organizational collaboration. Therefore, based on the multidimensional evaluation offered by the technology–value matrix, this study develops an "Integrated Smart Technology Ecosystem" model that emphasizes functional and data-based integration among technologies.

The key strength of this methodological approach lies in its dual focus: not only on technology assessment, but also on function-based and comparative analysis. Aligning the applicability of technologies with specific operational processes allowed the study to move beyond a purely theoretical analysis and develop a practical framework.

Moreover, one of the notable advantages of this methodology is its adaptability to evolving disaster contexts and emerging technologies. The technology–value matrix provides a flexible structure that can be updated as new data becomes available or as field-level priorities shift. This makes it particularly valuable for policymakers and humanitarian organizations seeking to maintain responsive and evidence-based strategies in dynamic environments. Furthermore, the integration of scenario analysis enhances the real-world relevance of the framework by illustrating how different technologies may interact under specific logistical constraints. This combined approach facilitates more nuanced planning and fosters technology adoption that is not only theoretically sound but also operationally viable.

However, the approach also presents some limitations. The evaluation criteria are primarily qualitative in nature and are not supported by quantitative weighting methods such as AHP or TOPSIS. Additionally, since the technology–value matrix is based on literature findings and scenario-driven insights, it requires further empirical validation for robustness.

3. SMART TECHNOLOGIES AND VALUE ASSESSMENT

In this section, smart technologies that emerged from the literature review as prominent in earthquake-based humanitarian logistics are identified and classified based on their potential use across different phases (see Figure 1). Table 2 summarizes the use cases of these technologies in the literature, thereby providing the technological framework that underpins the development of the technology–value matrix in the next stage.

Figure 1. Key Smart Technologies in Earthquake Humanitarian Logistics

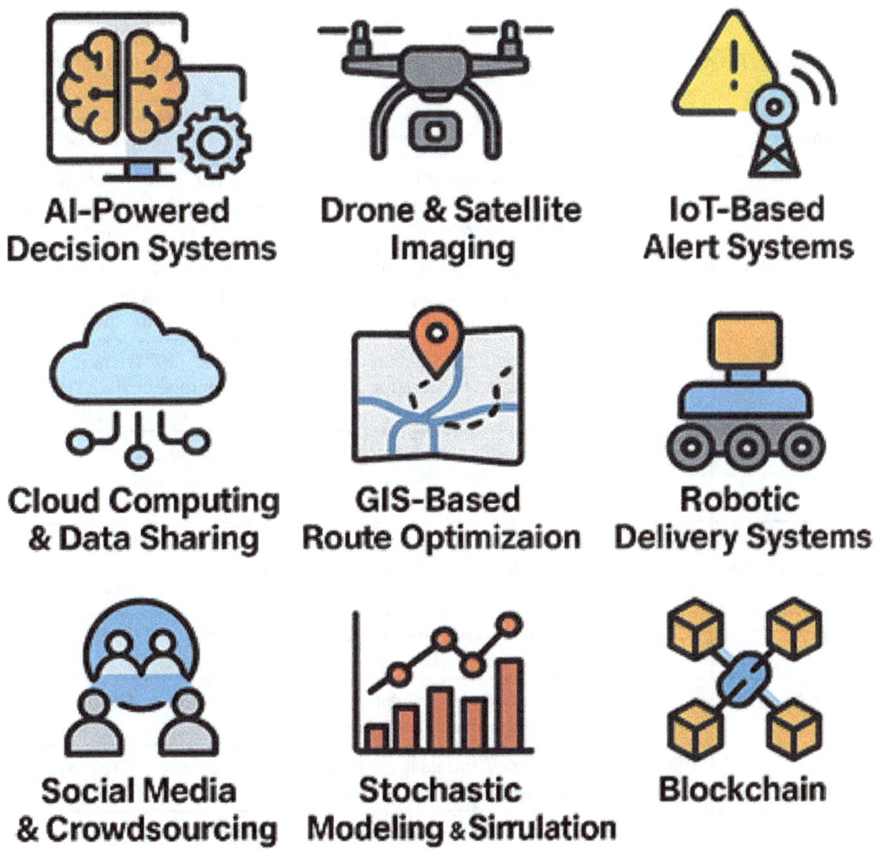

This figure presents the core smart technologies examined throughout the study, which are increasingly integrated into humanitarian logistics operations in response to earthquake-related disasters. The technologies include AI-powered decision systems, drone and satellite imaging, IoT-based alert systems, cloud computing, GIS-based route optimization, robotic delivery systems, social media and crowdsourcing platforms, stochastic modeling and simulation, and blockchain solutions. Each of these technologies addresses a distinct operational challenge ranging from early warning and damage assessment to resource coordination and last-mile delivery. Collectively, they form a foundational digital toolkit that supports agility, transparency, and efficiency in crisis response. The figure also highlights the technological diversity and multifunctionality required for modern disaster logistics, providing a visual framework for the comparative analysis conducted in the subsequent sections of the study.

Table 2. Smart Technologies Identified in the Literature and Summary of Their Applications

Technology	Summary of Use in the Literature	Reference(s)
Artificial Intelligence (AI)	Route optimization, decision support, resource allocation, data-driven management of rescue operations	Wu & Xu, 2020; Dindarik & Atabey, 2024; Hassan & Sofia 2025; Jagirdar & Pathak, 2025; lo Conte 2025;
Drones and Satellite Systems	Damage assessment, access to high-risk areas, image analysis, mapping	Bray et al., 2019; Oliveira et al., 2024; Igwenagu et al., 2025; Kumari et al., 2025.
Internet of Things (IoT)	Early warning systems, field monitoring, sensor-based automated information flow	Naik et al., 2024; Chitra et al., 2025; Choosumrong et al., 2025; Pahuriray & Cerna, 2025.
Cloud Computing	Real-time data sharing, inter-agency coordination, data backup	Banisakher et al., 2018; Dubey et al., 2018; Ravisankar et al., 2025; Sowmya et al., 2025.
Geographic Information Systems (GIS)	Route and warehouse optimization, spatial analysis, accessibility and path selection	Qi et al., 2019; Yılmaz et al., 2019; Tian & Jiang, 2025; Thakare et al., 2025.
Robotic Systems	Physical intervention in search and rescue missions, access to unreachable areas	Öztürkcan, 2023; Sebastian 2025.
Generative AI	Visual data analysis, structural damage classification, rapid situation assessment	Estêvão, 2024; Ahmad et al., 2025.
Blockchain / Cryptocurrency	Donation transparency, traceable resource management, decentralized financial systems	Nazlıoğlu et al., 2024; Abraha 2025.
Social Media / Crowdsourcing	Information dissemination, aid coordination, volunteer management, distress signaling applications	Ozturkcan, 2023; Su et al., 2025.
Stochastic Modeling	Warehouse location planning, transportation network design, two-stage decision support systems, scenario-based planning	Paz-Orozco et al., 2023; Mousazadeh & Aminpour, 2025; Küçük & Yardımcı Coşkun, 2025.

continued on following page

Table 2. Continued

Technology	Summary of Use in the Literature	Reference(s)
Multi-agent Systems	Distributed decision-making, autonomous task allocation, multi-stakeholder coordination	Ochoa et al., 2017; Acharya et al., 2025; Pathak & Pandey, 2025.
LIDAR / SfM / GNSS Technologies	High-resolution mapping, surface deformation measurement, structural inspection	Eren et al., 2007; Bray et al., 2019; Sestras et al., 2025.
SMS Systems / ICT-Based Tools	Crisis communication, early warning messages, real-time communication infrastructure	Summer, 2010; Kalogiannidis et al., 2025; Terande 2025.

Table 2 provides a comprehensive overview of smart technologies identified in the literature as relevant to earthquake-related humanitarian logistics. The table categorizes each technology based on its key applications, such as route optimization, early warning, damage assessment, information coordination, and resource allocation. It includes a diverse set of tools ranging from artificial intelligence (AI) and cloud computing to drones, blockchain, and Geographic Information Systems (GIS). By mapping these technologies to their operational functions, the table highlights their respective contributions to various stages of disaster management. In addition, references to seminal studies and recent empirical research are provided to support the evidence base for each technology's applicability. This structured summary serves as the foundation for subsequent analysis in the study, including the development of the technology–value matrix and scenario modeling.

Figure 2. Mapping Smart Technologies to Disaster Response Stages and Logistics Functions in Earthquake Scenarios

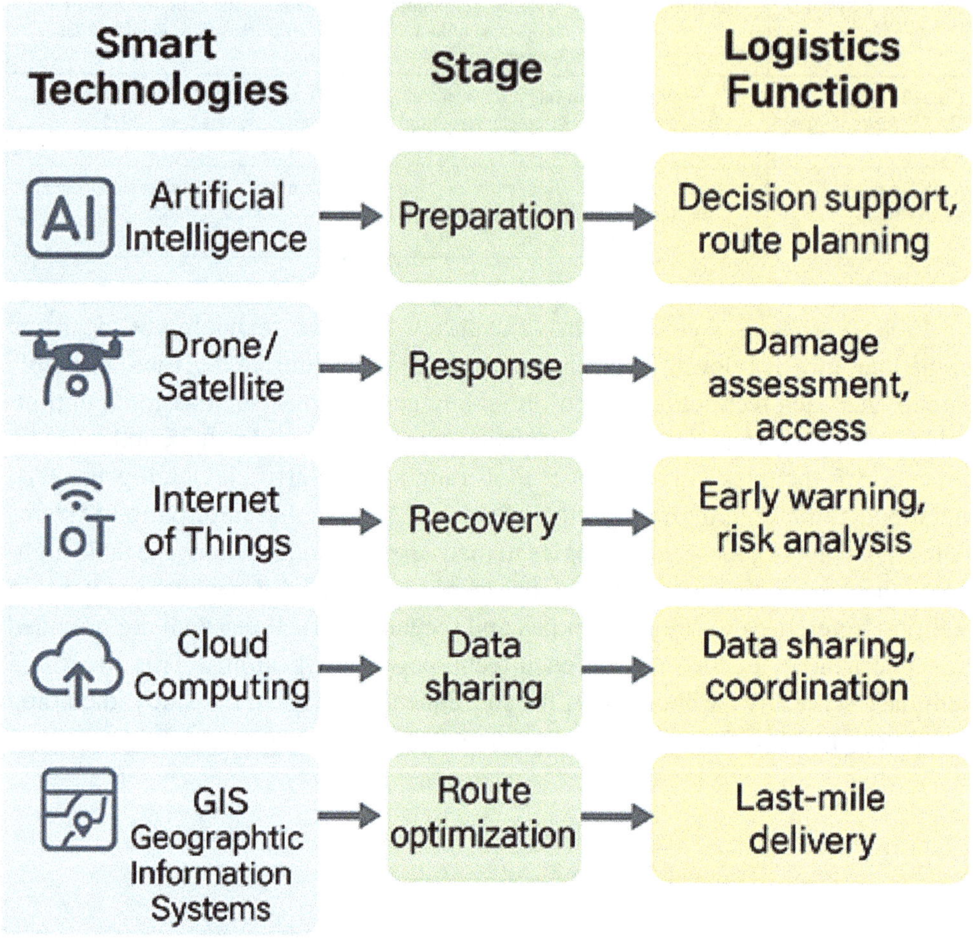

(developed by the author)

This figure presents the alignment of five smart Technologies; Artificial Intelligence (AI), drone/satellite systems, the Internet of Things (IoT), cloud computing, and Geographic Information Systems (GIS), with specific disaster management stages and corresponding logistics functions. Each technology is mapped to a distinct phase of the disaster cycle (e.g., preparation, response, recovery, data sharing, and optimization), illustrating its role in decision support, damage assessment, risk analysis, coordination, and last-mile delivery. The model highlights the sequential and functional contributions of these technologies in enhancing the speed, accuracy, and efficiency of humanitarian logistics during earthquake emergencies.

To evaluate the functional contributions of key technologies in earthquake-based humanitarian logistics processes, a comprehensive technology–value matrix was developed based on the smart technologies classified in Table 2. These Technologies, including artificial intelligence, drone/satellite systems, the Internet of Things (IoT), cloud computing, and Geographic Information Systems (GIS), represent the most frequently encountered systems in both theoretical and applied studies in the literature. The matrix systematically analyzes each technology in terms of its contribution to logistics processes, ease of implementation, operational scope, potential benefits, and associated limitations.

The technologies were assessed based on the following five core criteria:

1. **Contribution to Logistics Processes**: The extent to which the technology contributes to essential humanitarian logistics functions (e.g., procurement, transportation, coordination, delivery) categorized as High, Medium, or Low.
2. **Ease of Implementation**: The feasibility of implementing the technology in the field, considering infrastructure and technical expertise requirements categorized as Easy, Moderate, or Difficult.
3. **Operational Scope**: The disaster management phases in which the technology is effective; Preparedness, Response, and Recovery.
4. **Potential Benefits**: The advantages provided in terms of time efficiency, cost reduction, accessibility, and information sharing.
5. **Risks and Limitations**: Challenges related to ethical concerns, data security, and social acceptability.

Table 3. Technology Value Matrix

Technology	Contribution Level	Ease of Implementation	Operational Scope	Potential Benefits	Risks / Limitations
AI-Based Decision Support Systems	High	Moderate	Preparedness, Response	Rapid decision-making, resource optimization	Data quality, algorithmic bias
Drone and Satellite Imaging	High	Easy	Response, Recovery	Damage assessment, road condition analysis, access to risk zones	Flight permissions, image interpretation errors
IoT-Based Early Warning Systems	Moderate	Difficult	Preparedness	Early warnings, risk analysis	Infrastructure dependency, security vulnerabilities
Cloud Computing and Data Sharing	High	Easy	All Phases	Real-time information flow, coordination	Cybersecurity, data ownership

continued on following page

Table 3. Continued

Technology	Contribution Level	Ease of Implementation	Operational Scope	Potential Benefits	Risks / Limitations
GIS-Based Route Optimization	High	Moderate	Response	Shortest path routing, fuel and time savings	Need for up-to-date data, technical capacity requirements
Robotic Delivery Systems	Low–Moderate	Difficult	Response	Facilitation of last-mile delivery	Physical barriers, high cost
Social Media and Crowdsourcing	Moderate	Easy	Response, Recovery	Information dissemination, volunteer mobilization	Misinformation, lack of data verification
Stochastic Modeling and Simulation	High	Difficult	Preparedness	Logistics scenario analysis, preparedness planning	Need for large datasets, academic expertise requirements

(developed by the author)

The technology–value matrix developed in this study enables a multidimensional evaluation of the strategic contributions, implementation feasibility, operational scope, and potential challenges of smart technologies used in earthquake-based humanitarian logistics (see Table 3). A general analysis of the matrix reveals that while some technologies offer both high impact and ease of implementation, others, despite their strategic potential, face significant technical, ethical, and infrastructural constraints.

AI-based decision support systems provide critical contributions in complex operations such as route planning, resource allocation, and evacuation strategies, particularly during the preparedness and response phases. These systems process large datasets to deliver rapid, optimized, and multi-criteria decision-making. However, their effectiveness is often limited by algorithmic biases, high dependency on data quality, and the end users' ability to interpret system outputs—factors that may hinder the realization of their full potential.

Drone and satellite imaging systems rank among the highest-impact technologies during the response and recovery phases due to their ability to rapidly assess damage and evaluate inaccessible areas. Their ease of deployment provides a key advantage in early response efforts, enabling rapid action in situations such as road closures or infrastructure collapse. Nonetheless, effective operation depends on external factors such as weather conditions and flight permissions, as well as risks like image misinterpretation.

IoT-based early warning systems have the potential to deliver early detection and risk analysis prior to a disaster. In rapidly evolving crises such as earthquakes, even a few seconds of early warning can save lives. However, large-scale deployment of these systems depends heavily on infrastructure investments, continuous energy supply, and regional coverage. Cybersecurity risks—such as exposure to network breaches or external interference—also pose serious concerns.

Cloud-based data sharing systems are among the most widely applied technologies across all phases of humanitarian logistics. They enable real-time data exchange among multiple institutions, reducing duplication of efforts and resource waste. However, issues related to data ownership, privacy, and cybersecurity remain critical limitations to the secure and sustainable use of these technologies.

Geographic Information Systems (GIS) are particularly effective during the response phase, providing optimized routing, warehouse siting, and spatial analysis. GIS supports the development of efficient logistics strategies by incorporating variables such as terrain, road conditions, and population density. Yet, the need for high-resolution, up-to-date data and technical expertise is essential for the effective use of these systems.

Robotic systems offer potential for last-mile delivery and physical intervention during post-disaster distribution. However, widespread application is hindered by high infrastructure costs and physical obstacles in disaster-affected environments. As such, despite their theoretical appeal, these technologies are currently considered to have limited practical applicability.

Social media and crowdsourcing platforms offer innovative solutions for information dissemination and volunteer mobilization following a disaster. The rapid mapping of citizen-generated data can significantly support needs assessment and response coordination. However, misinformation, data noise, and verification challenges undermine the reliability of such platforms, emphasizing the need for controlled and supervised integration.

Lastly, **stochastic modeling and simulation techniques** provide significant benefits in the preparedness phase by allowing the evaluation of various disaster scenarios and enabling strategic planning. These models are especially valuable for decisions involving warehouse location, transportation network design, and logistics capacity planning. However, their reliance on large datasets and the need for specialized expertise limit widespread adoption. Unless user-friendly interfaces are developed for field personnel, these tools risk remaining confined to academic settings.

Overall, none of the technologies analyzed offer a "perfect" standalone solution; however, when combined, they can form a robust technology ecosystem. For instance, integrating AI-based decision systems with drone imagery or combining cloud infrastructure with crowdsourced data can produce synergistic effects that significantly enhance the performance of humanitarian logistics. Ultimately, the effectiveness of these technologies depends not only on their technical capabilities, but also on institutional adaptation, user training, and the quality of data management policies.

According to the general analysis of the matrix:

- AI-based systems provide high value in route planning, resource allocation, and crisis decision-making; however, their effectiveness must be supported by ethical considerations such as data quality and transparency.
- Drone and satellite technologies have become indispensable for on-site damage assessment and access planning in disaster zones.
- Cloud-based solutions support all stages of humanitarian logistics by enabling secure, fast, and decentralized information sharing.
- IoT and robotic systems offer potential benefits particularly in the preparedness and response phases, yet their adoption remains limited due to implementation challenges and infrastructure dependencies.

4. APPLICATION SCENARIOS: FIELD-LEVEL POTENTIAL OF TECHNOLOGIES

This section presents example scenarios developed to illustrate the practical use of different smart technologies in earthquake-based humanitarian logistics processes. Drawing from both real-world applications and simulation-based models, these scenarios aim to demonstrate the potential contributions of these technologies in the field and highlight the challenges encountered during their implementation.

Scenario 1: Evacuation Planning with AI-Based Decision Support System

Following a devastating earthquake, significant delays were observed in the evacuation processes. In response, an AI-powered decision support system was activated. The system analyzed multilayered data sets, including traffic density, road conditions, population distribution, and weather forecasts, to optimize the safest and fastest evacuation routes. As a result, evacuation times were substantially reduced, coordination among response teams improved, and logistics resources were utilized more efficiently.

Scenario 2: Damage Assessment Using Drone and Satellite Imaging

After the 2023 earthquake on the Türkiye–Syria border, ground transportation was severely disrupted, prompting the use of drones and satellite imaging systems for damage assessment. These images were analyzed using AI algorithms to identify critical areas in need of assistance and to prioritize aid delivery. Compared to traditional on-site surveys, this approach significantly shortened the response time.

Scenario 3: School Evacuation via IoT-Based Early Warning System

An IoT-based early warning system equipped with seismic sensors detected pre-shock signals and automatically transmitted alerts to connected schools. This allowed students to be directed to safe zones within seconds before the tremor, helping prevent potential casualties. The scenario demonstrates the life-saving role of early warning technologies in the preparedness phase.

Scenario 4: Data Sharing and Coordination through Cloud Computing

During the 2015 Nepal earthquake, a cloud-based data sharing platform was employed to facilitate communication between local governments, NGOs, and international aid organizations. With real-time updates, the system enabled a more balanced distribution of relief supplies and prevented redundant shipments. Reports indicated that this solution led to more than a 20% increase in resource utilization efficiency.

Scenario 5: Mobile Clinic Deployment with GIS-Based Route Optimization

In a region where healthcare infrastructure was severely damaged following an earthquake, Geographic Information Systems (GIS) were used to manage the distribution of mobile health services. Based on data on road conditions, population density, and structural damage, the placement of mobile clinics was optimized. As a result, thousands of people received basic healthcare within the first 24 hours, expanding service reach and reducing intervention time.

These scenarios collectively highlight not only the functional relevance of individual technologies but also their strategic value in enabling timely, targeted, and resource-efficient humanitarian responses. Importantly, each case demonstrates that the success of smart technology applications depends on contextual alignment with field conditions. For instance, the efficacy of AI in evacuation planning is contingent upon access to real-time and accurate data, while the success of drone-based assessments hinges on airspace regulations and image interpretation capacity. Moreover, the seamless coordination enabled by cloud computing illustrates the critical need for interoperable systems across organizational boundaries. These insights affirm that scenario-based planning is essential for designing adaptive digital strategies tailored to specific geographical, infrastructural, and social conditions. The integration of such field-informed scenarios into preparedness planning can significantly improve disaster response readiness and resilience.

Figure 3. Application Scenarios of Smart Technologies in Earthquake Response

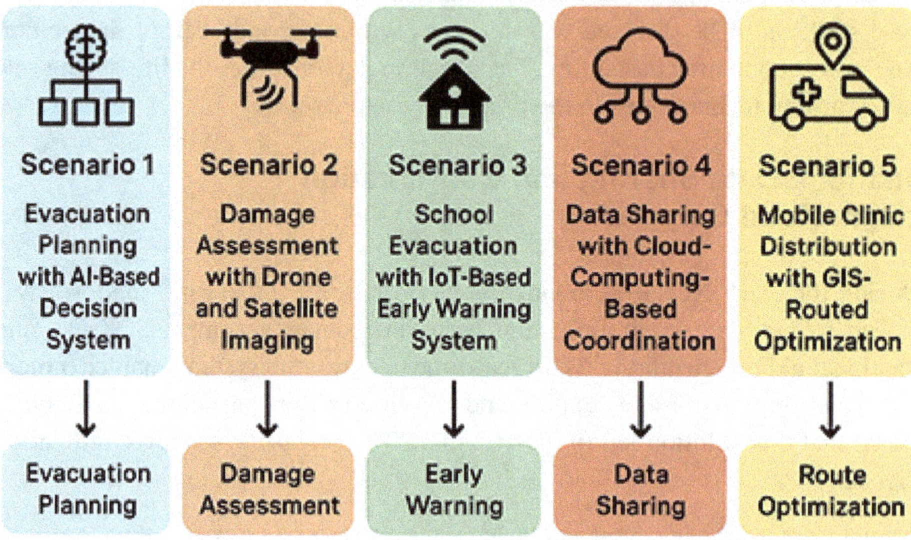

(developed by the author)

Figure 3 visualizes the application of five different smart technologies within earthquake-based humanitarian logistics scenarios and illustrates the corresponding logistics functions addressed in each case (e.g., evacuation, damage assessment, early warning, etc.).

5. INTEGRATED TECHNOLOGY ECOSYSTEM MODEL

The technology–value matrix enabled an individual analysis of the contributions of smart technologies in humanitarian logistics processes. However, real-world field conditions and disaster response realities demand that these technologies function not in isolation, but in an integrated and synchronized manner. Therefore, developing a holistic approach based on the interactive use of smart systems is of strategic importance for the success of crisis management.

In this context, an "Integrated Smart Disaster Response Technology Ecosystem" is proposed, involving the coordinated operation of artificial intelligence, drone/

satellite imaging, Geographic Information Systems (GIS), cloud computing, and Internet of Things (IoT) technologies. The model systematically structures the relationships among these technologies in terms of data generation, processing, interpretation, and decision support.

The technological ecosystem model emphasizes the interconnectivity of technologies and suggests viewing them as parts of a larger system rather than in isolation (Adomavicius et al., 2008). Similar to the technology–value matrix approach developed by Ismail and Ghani (2022), this model evaluates not only the individual effectiveness of technologies but also their capacity for integration. Supporting this view, studies such as Qi et al. (2019) and Mousazadeh & Aminpour (2025) also highlight the need for planning multi-component digital systems collectively in disaster logistics.

The first component of the ecosystem, IoT-based early warning systems, initiates data generation through sensors that detect seismic activity prior to the onset of a disaster. These signals are transmitted in real time to a cloud-based infrastructure. The cloud environment not only stores the data but also allows simultaneous access by various actors such as local authorities, humanitarian organizations, and healthcare services. Once the data stream begins, AI-powered decision support systems analyze the data to generate forecasts about the potential impacts of the disaster. These predictions are used to prioritize high-risk areas, trigger evacuation plans, and optimize resource allocation decisions.

After the event occurs, drone and satellite imaging systems are deployed to rapidly map damage in the field. The captured imagery is analyzed using AI-based visual recognition algorithms to determine which areas suffered the most severe damage, road conditions, and access priorities. This data is then transformed into spatial analyses via Geographic Information Systems (GIS) to support route planning, mobile clinic deployment, and the optimization of aid distribution points.

All of this data is consolidated on a cloud-based platform to ensure inter-agency coordination. Additionally, citizen-generated information gathered through social media and crowdsourcing tools is integrated into the system, creating a dynamic decision-support environment that combines both formal and informal data sources. Thus, the system enables not only data transfer among technologies, but also functional integration.

The practical impact of this model becomes particularly evident in the following ways:

- It establishes a seamless digital flow from early warning to emergency response.
- It integrates visual, spatial, and statistical data into a unified decision-making platform.

- It enables decision-makers to develop more robust plans under multi-stakeholder and uncertain conditions.
- It coordinates inter-agency data sharing without centralized control.
- It enables participatory crisis management by integrating public engagement (via crowdsourcing) with technology.

This integration model aligns with the scenarios presented in the previous section. For example, AI-supported evacuation decisions validated through drone imagery, risk-prone areas reported via social media mapped with GIS, and shared through cloud systems, exemplify this synergistic operation in real-life settings.

From an implementation perspective, the effective functioning of this model depends on three key enablers: (1) **interoperability** of technological infrastructures, (2) **open protocols** for data sharing between institutions, and (3) a **trained human workforce** capable of managing these technologies. Without these elements, information flow is interrupted, decision support mechanisms operate inefficiently, and the technological potential fails to translate into field impact.

In conclusion, disaster management is driven not only by individual technologies but also by their integration capacity when systematically brought together. Therefore, the technologies identified as high-contribution in the technology–value matrix should be designed to support one another and be implemented through a "technology ecosystem" approach. This perspective will enhance not only operational efficiency but also resilience, agility, and data-driven coordination in humanitarian logistics.

The proposed ecosystem model is adaptable across urban and rural contexts. In metropolitan areas, high connectivity facilitates real-time synchronization, whereas in rural settings, localized offline systems with delayed synchronization may be more feasible. This necessitates the development of tiered ecosystem designs that balance immediacy and resilience.

Table 4. Technology Integration Scenarios in Earthquake Humanitarian Logistics

Scenario	Integrated Technologies	Key Function
Evacuation Planning	AI + GIS	Decision Support, Real-time Routing
Early Warning System	IoT + Cloud	Sensing, Data Sharing, Early Alert
Damage Assessment	Drone + AI	Image Analysis, Accessibility Mapping
Community Coordination	Crowdsourcing + Cloud	Location Tagging, Feedback Flow

(developed by the author)

Table 4 presents selected integration scenarios involving smart technologies used in earthquake-based humanitarian logistics operations. Each scenario illustrates how the combination of complementary Technologies, such as AI, GIS, IoT, cloud computing, drones, and crowdsourcing, supports key logistics functions including evacuation planning, early warning, damage assessment, and community coordination. The scenarios emphasize how integrated digital solutions enhance decision-making, responsiveness, and resource allocation in disaster contexts.

6. DISCUSSION

This chapter systematically evaluated the role of smart technologies in the restructuring of earthquake-based humanitarian logistics processes. The findings derived from the technology–value matrix and application scenarios reveal that while certain technologies offer high operational value, they also face distinct challenges in terms of implementation conditions, data infrastructure, and ethical considerations. In particular, AI-based decision support systems demonstrate high effectiveness in route planning, resource allocation, and evacuation processes due to their capacity for multi-criteria evaluation and large-scale data analytics. However, successful field implementation of these systems requires high-quality and real-time data sources, transparent algorithms, and user-friendly interfaces that enable decision-makers to interpret system outputs. Ethical concerns such as algorithmic bias and lack of transparency must also be addressed. Drone and satellite imaging systems emerge as indispensable tools for damage assessment and needs analysis in inaccessible areas, especially during the response and recovery phases. While these technologies offer ease of deployment and rapid initial response, logistical limitations such as flight permissions, image interpretation capacity, and energy constraints should be taken into account. IoT-based early warning systems present a significant opportunity for early intervention. Nevertheless, their applicability remains limited in many regions due to infrastructure dependency and the need for extensive seismic sensor networks. Similarly, although robotic systems hold critical potential in last-mile delivery and search and rescue operations, they face barriers in the form of high costs and demanding technical maintenance. Cloud computing and data-sharing systems have proven highly effective in enhancing post-disaster coordination and managing decentralized information flows. However, issues related to data security, privacy, and access control may influence the long-term sustainability of these systems. Social media and crowdsourcing-based solutions serve as dynamic tools for volunteer mobilization and information dissemination. However, weaknesses such as information overload, the spread of inaccurate/incomplete data, and manipulation risks must be carefully managed. In summary, the effectiveness of smart technologies in humanitarian logistics is shaped not only by their technical capabilities but also by institutional alignment, public acceptance, ethical integrity, and infrastructural readiness. Therefore, the development of holistic models that promote technologies that are not only *effective*, but also *applicable* and *responsibly implemented*, is essential for achieving sustainable impact.

7. CONCLUSION

This study was designed to evaluate the potential contributions of artificial intelligence, predictive analytics, and autonomous systems in earthquake-based humanitarian logistics, and to discuss their applicability in the field within a multidimensional framework. The findings obtained through the literature review, the technology–value matrix, application scenarios, and the integrated technology ecosystem model clearly demonstrate the digital transformation potential of disaster management.

In sudden and destructive disasters such as earthquakes, rapid decision-making, equitable and efficient resource distribution, access route analysis, and reliable information sharing are of critical importance. Relying solely on traditional methods for these processes may lead to delays, resource waste, and coordination failures. Smart technologies play not only a supporting but also a transformative role in bridging these gaps.

As shown in the technology–value matrix analysis, technologies such as AI systems, drone/satellite imaging, cloud-based data sharing, Geographic Information Systems (GIS), IoT-based early warning systems, and crowdsourcing solutions offer significant contributions across various phases of humanitarian logistics. However, their applicability is shaped less by their potential benefits and more by factors such as system integration, user capability, data quality, and ethical frameworks. The technology–value matrix provides a comparative assessment of these factors, offering a strategic technology map to guide decision-makers.

Emerging technologies such as digital twins and AI-driven simulations have the potential to revolutionize preparedness planning by modeling infrastructure behavior under seismic stress. Future research should explore how these technologies can be ethically integrated into humanitarian supply chains.

The application scenarios aimed to demonstrate how theoretical findings translate into real-world operations. These examples illustrated how specific technologies can reduce response times, increase accessibility, and accelerate information flow. As shown in the scenarios, when technologies work in an integrated manner (e.g., AI + drone + cloud + GIS), response operations become not only faster but also more targeted and effective.

In this context, "integration capacity" stands out as one of the core contributions of this study. The effectiveness of smart technologies depends not only on their individual performance but also on interoperability, data-sharing protocols, inter-agency coordination, and user-friendly interfaces. The Integrated Technology Ecosystem Model was developed to address this need, schematically demonstrating how technologies can work together, which data flows are critical, and how decision support processes can be strengthened through smart systems.

The key findings of this study reveal that smart technologies have the potential to significantly improve the speed, precision, and flexibility of humanitarian logistics. These technologies support different functions across all stages of crisis management, including preparedness, response, and recovery. For instance, IoT systems are prominent in early warning mechanisms, GIS plays a vital role in response route planning, and blockchain technology is valuable for tracking resources during the recovery phase. The highest strategic value is found in AI systems, cloud-based data-sharing platforms, and drone/satellite systems. Furthermore, the success of technological solutions depends not only on technical proficiency but also on socio-technical factors such as data security, ethical responsibilities, user acceptance, and institutional collaboration. Finally, the study highlights that synergistic benefits are more likely to emerge from the integrated use of technologies—such as combining AI, drone, GIS, and cloud systems—rather than from isolated applications.

This study offers comprehensive policy and strategic recommendations tailored to the needs of key stakeholders in the humanitarian logistics ecosystem. For humanitarian aid organizations, it is imperative that technology investments are directed not only towards infrastructure development, but also towards strengthening human capacity. This includes the expansion of training programs, the provision of detailed user manuals, and the incorporation of field-specific simulations to ensure that staff are equipped with the necessary skills for effective technology utilization. Moreover, instead of relying on standardized, one-size-fits-all solutions, organizations should develop scenario-based technology portfolios that are sensitive to varying local contexts. For instance, it is recommended that low-cost IoT systems be prioritized for rural areas with limited connectivity, while advanced technologies such as drones should be deployed for rapid damage assessment in densely populated urban centers. In addition, the adoption and integration of crowdsourcing platforms for rapid data collection is encouraged, with the aim of linking these systems to broader digital infrastructures to enhance overall responsiveness and situational awareness.

Local governments, on the other hand, are urged to establish clear and robust regulatory frameworks as well as data-sharing protocols governing the use of IoT, drones, and AI in disaster management. Municipalities should take proactive steps to form digital disaster response teams that can effectively integrate smart technologies into local emergency planning and ensure seamless coordination with both national and international systems. To further facilitate effective disaster management, the development of open data infrastructures is essential, as these will support inter-agency collaboration throughout both the preparedness and response phases of disaster scenarios.

For policymakers, the formulation of ethical, transparent, and accountable standards for disaster technologies—particularly those involving artificial intelligence—remains a priority. Fundamental questions such as data ownership, data access rights, and data processing mechanisms must be addressed with clarity to build trust and ensure compliance with ethical standards. It is also crucial that disaster management policies incorporate a strong digitalization component, providing targeted support for rural and low-income regions to bridge technological gaps and reduce inequalities. Furthermore, national crisis management strategies should be designed to foster the creation of multi-stakeholder platforms focused on technology interoperability and to promote effective public–private partnerships that drive innovation and resource sharing.

Looking ahead, the study identifies several promising directions for future research. Although this chapter presents a qualitative analysis grounded in theoretical frameworks, thematic literature findings, a technology–value matrix, and practical application scenarios, further empirical validation is required. Future studies should undertake comparative field research to evaluate the real-world performance of the technologies discussed in diverse disaster contexts, with a particular focus on measurable outcomes such as user experience, time and cost efficiency, and operational success rates. The integration of system dynamics-based modeling is suggested as a valuable tool to explore how multi-technology systems—such as combinations of AI, GIS, drones, and IoT—function in real-time disaster response environments. Additionally, further research should examine critical issues surrounding data privacy, algorithmic bias, and the dynamics of human–AI trust, ultimately contributing to the development of an ethical governance framework for digital disaster management. Finally, there is a need to investigate the institutional adaptation capacity of local governments, non-governmental organizations, and disaster coordination centers, with particular attention to identifying barriers to technology adoption and the most effective capacity-building strategies.

REFERENCES

Abraha, D. T. (2025). Blockchain-based solution for addressing refugee management in the Global South: Transparent and accessible resource sharing in humanitarian organizations. *Frontiers in Human Dynamics*, *6*, 1391163. DOI: 10.3389/fhumd.2024.1391163

Acharya, D. B., Kuppan, K., & Divya, B. (2025). Agentic AI: Autonomous Intelligence for Complex Goals–A Comprehensive Survey. *IEEE Access: Practical Innovations, Open Solutions*, *13*, 18912–18936. DOI: 10.1109/ACCESS.2025.3532853

Adomavicius, G., Bockstedt, J., Gupta, A., & Kauffman, R. J. (2008). Understanding evolution in technology ecosystems. *Communications of the ACM*, *51*(10), 117–122. DOI: 10.1145/1400181.1400207

Ahmad, M., Ho, W. Y., Robalino, A. P. G., & Maqsood, M. (2025). Theoretical Implications of Generative AI for Content Generation in Geoinformatics Training. In Integration Strategies of Generative AI in Higher Education (pp. 101-130). IGI Global.

Aksoy, L., & Yardımcı Coşkun, İ. (2025). Afetlerde aydınlatma, haberleşme ve enerji ihtiyacının tek noktadan karşılanması için şebeke ve direk tasarımı. *Doğal Afetler ve Çevre Dergisi*, *11*(1), 206–219. DOI: 10.21324/dacd.1563581

Alazawi, Z., Altowaijri, S., Mehmood, R., & Abdljabar, M. B. (2011, Aug). Intelligent disaster management system based on cloud-enabled vehicular networks. In *2011 11th international conference on its telecommunications* (pp. 361-368). IEEE. DOI: 10.1109/ITST.2011.6060083

Bačić, Ž., Šugar, D., Poslončec-Petrić, V., & Nevistić, Z. (2022, Nov). Providing rapid earthquake information using EO/GI technology. *IOP Conference Series. Earth and Environmental Science*, *1109*(1), 012006. DOI: 10.1088/1755-1315/1109/1/012006

Banisakher, M., Mohammed, D., & Omar, M. (2018). A Cloud-Based Computing Architecture Model of Post-Disaster Management System. *International Journal of Simulation—Systems. Science & Technology*, *19*(5), 638–644.

Bray, J. D., Frost, J. D., Rathje, E. M., & Garcia, F. E. (2019). Recent advances in geotechnical post-earthquake reconnaissance. *Frontiers in Built Environment*, *5*, 5. DOI: 10.3389/fbuil.2019.00005

Chang, K. H., Chiang, Y. C., & Chang, T. Y. (2024). Simultaneous location and vehicle fleet sizing of relief goods distribution centers and vehicle routing for post-disaster logistics. *Computers & Operations Research, 161*, 106404. DOI: 10.1016/j.cor.2023.106404

Chang, N. B., & Pires, A. (2015). Technology Matrix for Solid Waste Management. In *Sustainable Solid Waste Management: A Systems Engineering Approach* (pp. 19–97). IEEE. DOI: 10.1002/9781119035848.ch2

Chitra, P., Acharjya, K., Ojha, V., Das, P., Faiz, A., & Rao, S. B. (2025, Mar). IOT and Sensor-Based Flood Monitoring and Warning Systems for Disaster Management. In *2025 International Conference on Automation and Computation (AUTOCOM)* (pp. 471-476). IEEE. DOI: 10.1109/AUTOCOM64127.2025.10956605

Choosumrong, S., Piyathamrongchai, K., Hataitara, R., Soteyome, U., Konkong, N., Chalongsuppunyoo, R., ... & Nemoto, T. (2025). Development of an IoT-Based Flood Monitoring System Integrated with GIS for Lowland Agricultural Areas.

Dindarik, N., & Atabey, A. (2024). Future of Earthquake-Based Disaster Logistics and Futuristic Approaches. *Journal of Social Sciences And Education, 7*(2), 257–278. DOI: 10.53047/josse.1536068

Dubey, S., Dahiya, M., & Jain, S. (2018, Feb). Application of distributed data center in logistics as cloud collaboration for handling disaster relief. In *2018 3rd International Conference On Internet of Things: Smart Innovation and Usages (IoT-SIU)* (pp. 1-11). IEEE. DOI: 10.1109/IoT-SIU.2018.8519865

Eren, A. M., Peeters, W., & Farrow, J. (2007, Jun). The use of space technologies to monitor and respond to earthquakes economic perspective. In *2007 3rd International Conference on Recent Advances in Space Technologies* (pp. 24-28). IEEE. DOI: 10.1109/RAST.2007.4283985

Estêvão, J. M. (2024). Effectiveness of generative ai for post-earthquake damage assessment. *Buildings (Basel, Switzerland), 14*(10), 3255. DOI: 10.3390/buildings14103255

Garrido, R. A., & Aguirre, I. (2020). Emergency logistics for disaster management under spatio-temporal demand correlation: The earthquakes case. *Journal of Industrial and Management Optimization, 16*(5), 2369–2387. DOI: 10.3934/jimo.2019058

Göçmen, E., & Kuvvetli, Y. (2020). Humanitarian Logistics Management After A Disaster: An Earthquake Case. *Dicle Üniversitesi Mühendislik Fakültesi Mühendislik Dergisi, 11*(2), 679–688.

Hackathon, M. S. (2023). Leveraging AI for natural disaster management: Takeaways from the Moroccan earthquake. arXiv. https://arxiv.org/abs/2311.08999

Hassan, A. F., & Sofia, D. (2025). Augmented Reality and AI in Remote Geospatial Analysis Enhancing Decision-Making in Crisis Management. American Journal of Engineering. *Mechanics and Architecture*, *3*(3), 129–144.

Hernández-Leandro, N. A., Ibarra-Rojas, O., & Camacho-Vallejo, J. F. (2022). A bi-objective humanitarian logistics model considering equity in the affected zones: Application to a recent earthquake in Mexico. *Operations Research*, *56*(3), 1737–1762. DOI: 10.1051/ro/2022067

Hobeika, A. G., Ardekanı, S. A., & Han, D. L. (1988). Logistics decisions following urban disasters. *Computer-Aided Civil and Infrastructure Engineering*, *3*(1), 13–27. DOI: 10.1111/j.1467-8667.1988.tb00153.x

Igwenagu, U. T. I., Debnath, R., Ahmed, A. A., & Alam, M. J. B. (2025). An Integrated Approach for Earth Infrastructure Monitoring Using UAV and ERI: A Systematic Review. *Drones (Basel)*, *9*(3), 225. DOI: 10.3390/drones9030225

Jagirdar, R., & Pathak, C. (2025). AI-Driven Transportation Solutions: Lessons From Developed Nations For Emergıng Economies. *Journal of Public Transportation*, *4*(1).

Kalogiannidis, S., Kalfas, D., Kontsas, S., Papaevangelou, O., & Chatzitheodoridis, F. (2025). Evaluating the Effectiveness of Early Warning Systems in Reducing Loss of Life in Natural Disasters: A case study of Greece. *Journal of Risk Analysis and Crisis Response*, *15*(1), 33–33. DOI: 10.54560/jracr.v15i1.547

Khademi Zareh, H., Rezaei, H., Bashiri, M., & Fakhrzad, M. B. (2018). A humanitarian reconfiguration and rehabilitation model for preparedness and response to earthquakes using a scheduled reopening of links. *Journal of Industrial and Systems Engineering*, *11*(4), 96–115.

Khan, M., Khan, M., Ali, A., Khan, M. I., Ullah, I., & Iqbal, M. (2022). Digitalization for fast, fair, and safe humanitarian logistics. *Logistics (Basel)*, *6*(2), 31. DOI: 10.3390/logistics6020031

Küçük B., Yardımcı Coşkun İ. (2025). Afet Lojistiği'nde Araç Rotalama Probleminin Optimizasyonu: İstanbul İli Anadolu Yakası Örneği. Maltepe Üniversitesi Akademik Bakış Dergisi, 1 (1).

Kumari, S., Agarwal, S., Agrawal, N. K., Agarwal, A., & Garg, M. C. (2025). A Comprehensive Review of Remote Sensing Technologies for Improved Geological Disaster Management. *Geological Journal*, *60*(1), 223–235. DOI: 10.1002/gj.5072

Lan, P. (2000). The technology-component matrix: A tool for analysing and managing knowledge. *International Journal of Technology Management*, *20*(5-8), 670–683. DOI: 10.1504/IJTM.2000.002887

Lechtenberg, S., Widera, A., & Hellingrath, B. (2017, Dec). Research directions on decision support in disaster relief logistics. In *2017 4th International Conference on Information and Communication Technologies for Disaster Management (ICT-DM)* (pp. 1-8). IEEE. DOI: 10.1109/ICT-DM.2017.8275681

lo Conte, D. L. (2025). Enhancing decision-making with data-driven insights in critical situations: impact and implications of AI-powered predictive solutions.

Mendonca, J. A. (2003). A model and sample case for teaching the business value of information technology. *Journal of Information Technology Education*, *2*(1), 61–72. DOI: 10.28945/313

Moonesar, I. A. (2025). Humanitarian Logistics and Health Response. In *Anticipatory Governance: Shaping a Responsible Future* (pp. 345-360). DOI: 10.1142/9789811296000_0023

Mousazadeh, M., & Aminpour, M. H. (2025). Humanitarian supply chain redesign using a GIS-based two-stage stochastic model: A case study of earthquake in Tehran. *Operations Research*, *59*(1), 1–31. DOI: 10.1051/ro/2024217

Naik, G. M., Kumari, R., Thejaswini, E., Lokesh, A., Badiger, M., & Kripa, T. (2024). Disaster Management and Humanitarian Aid. *Advances in Computational Intelligence and Robotics*, *5*(0), 274–297. DOI: 10.4018/979-8-3693-2093-8.ch015

Nazlıoğlu, S., Kalem, G., & Yazıcı, A. (2024). Digital Solutions for Disaster Management: Analyzing the Impact of the February 2023 Earthquake in Türkiye. *Afet ve Risk Dergisi*, *7*(1), 158–171. DOI: 10.35341/afet.1336337

Niyazi, M., & Behnamian, J. (2023). Application of cloud computing and big data in three-stage dynamic modeling of disaster relief logistics and wounded transportation: A case study. *Environmental Science and Pollution Research International*, *30*(13), 38121–38140. DOI: 10.1007/s11356-022-24770-3 PMID: 36575255

Ochoa, A. A., Vargas-Solar, G., Espinosa-Oviedo, J. A., & Rudomín, I. (2017). Humanitarian Logistics based on Multiagent Systems for the prevention of a plethora of disasters related with crowds.

Oguntola, I. O., & Ülkü, M. A. (2023). Artificial intelligence for sustainable humanitarian logistics. *In Encyclopedia of Data Science and Machine Learning*, pp. 2970–2983

Oliveira, C. S., Ferreira, M. A., & O'Neill, H. (2024). The Role of Video Cameras and Emerging Technologies in Disaster Response to Increase Sustainability of Societies: Insights on the 2023 Türkiye–Syria Earthquake. *Sustainability (Basel), 16*(17), 7618. DOI: 10.3390/su16177618

Ozturkcan, S. (2023). Technology and disaster relief: The Türkiye-Syria earthquake case study. *Ozturkcan, S.(2023). Technology and disaster relief: The Türkiye-Syria earthquake case study*. In Aldieri, L. (Ed.), *Innovation-Research and development for human, economic and institutional growth.*

Pahuriray, A. V., & Cerna, P. D. (2025). IoT-Enabled Flood Monitoring and Early Warning Systems. *Systematic Reviews.*

Pathak, G., & Pandey, D. (2025). AI Agents in Recruitment: A Multi-Agent System for Interview, Evaluation, and Candidate Scoring. Evaluation, and Candidate Scoring (May 01, 2025).

Paudel, N. R. (2020). Applications of Artificial Intelligence in Reconstruction Governance Lessons from Nepal Earthquakes. *AI and Robotics in Disaster Studies*, 167-181.

Paz-Orozco, H., de Brito, I.Jr, Chong, M., Anacona-Mopan, Y., Segura Dorado, J. A., & Moyano, M. (2023). Earthquake Decision-Making tool for humanitarian logistics network: An application in Popayan, Colombia. *Logistics (Basel), 7*(4), 68. DOI: 10.3390/logistics7040068

Peter, M., Gatziu Grivas, S., Horn, D., Rüegg, F., Barba, R., & Graf, M. (2019). The technology matrix—A tool-based method for technology scouting. In *12th IADIS International Conference on Information Systems.* Utrecht, The Netherlands. DOI: 10.33965/is2019_201905L017

Qi, C., Fang, J., & Sun, L. (2019). Implementation of emergency logistics distribution decision support system based on GIS. *Cluster Computing, 22*(S4), 8859–8867. DOI: 10.1007/s10586-018-1983-8

Ravisankar, S., Ramachandran, V., & Shankar, S. R. (2025, Mar). Virtual Disaster Management Systems for Real-Time Response and Aid. In *2025 International Conference on Data Science, Agents & Artificial Intelligence (ICDSAAI)* (pp. 1-5). IEEE.

Sánchez-Partida, D., Martínez-Flores, J. L., Caballero-Morales, S. O., Cano-Olivos, P., Fon-Galvez, M. J., Sánchez-Partida, D., ... & Caballero-Morales, S. O. (2021). 19S Earthquake in Puebla, Mexico: Intervention of the Different Actors in Humanitarian Aid. Disaster Risk Reduction in Mexico: Methodologies, Case Studies, and Prospective Views, 141-167.

Sebastian, A. (2025). Soft Robotics for Search and Rescue: Advancements, Challenges, and Future Directions. arXiv preprint arXiv:2502.12373.

Sestras, P., Badea, G., Badea, A. C., Salagean, T., Ro ca, S., Kader, S., & Remondino, F. (2025). Land surveying with UAV photogrammetry and LiDAR for optimal building planning. *Automation in Construction*, *173*, 106092. DOI: 10.1016/j.autcon.2025.106092

Sowmya, G., Sridevi, R., & Rao, K. S. (2025). Blockchain for Disaster Recovery: Enhancing Resilience, Coordination, and Trust in Crisis Management. In AI and Emerging Technologies for Emergency Response and Smart Cities (pp. 117-136). IGI Global Scientific Publishing.

Su, S., Zhou, J., Zhong, Z., & Zhang, J. (2025). How help-seeking information spreads on social media during disasters: The role of vulnerable groups and information features. *International Journal of Disaster Risk Reduction*, *120*, 105374. DOI: 10.1016/j.ijdrr.2025.105374

Summer, M. (2010). The value of information and communication technologies in humanitarian relief efforts. *Innovations: Technology, Governance, Globalization*, *5*(4), 55–68. DOI: 10.1162/INOV_a_00043

Terande, T. J. (2025). Leveraging Information and Communication Technology (ICT) Solutions for Food Security as Panacea for Hunger Alleviation in Nigeria. In Smart Technologies for Sustainable Development Goals (pp. 272-290). CRC Press.

Thakare, K. V., Tajne, K. M., THAKARE, K. V., & Tajne, K. (2025). A Comprehensive Review of Geographic Information Systems (GIS)-Based Methodologies for Urban Fire Risk Assessment. Cureus Journals, 2(1).

Tian, Y., & Jiang, Y. (2025). Research on urban landscape accessibility assessment model based on gis and spatial analysis. *GeoJournal*, *90*(2), 67. DOI: 10.1007/s10708-025-11310-y

Wu, L., & Xu, D. (2020). Research on Method and Technology of Emergency Logistics Intelligent System Engineering. In *Advances in Wireless Communications and Applications*. Smart Communic.

Yilmaz, Z., Aydemir-Karadag, A., & Erol, S. (2019). Finding optimal depots and routes in sudden-onset disasters: An earthquake case for Erzincan. *Transportation Journal*, *58*(3), 168–196. DOI: 10.5325/transportationj.58.3.0168

Chapter 7
Designing Green Digital Logistics for Post-Disaster Recovery Operations

Filiz Mızrak
https://orcid.org/0000-0002-3472-394X
Atlas University, Istanbul, Turkey

Gökçe Nur Durukan
https://orcid.org/0009-0002-3456-4587
Yeditepe University, Istanbul, Turkey

ABSTRACT

This chapter examines the intersection of digitization and green logistics in post-disaster recovery operations, focusing on how emerging tools—such as digital health kits, blockchain systems, and solar-powered communications—can be designed and deployed with minimal ecological impact. Drawing on recent field cases from UNICEF, the World Food Programme (WFP), and the Red Cross/Red Crescent Movement, the study highlights both the transformative potential and the unintended consequences of digital tools, including challenges in e-waste management, lifecycle tracking, and energy consumption. It explores circular logistics models, infrastructure barriers, and the role of digital sustainability assessment frameworks in guiding greener humanitarian innovation. This chapter contributes to advancing a new paradigm of eco-resilient digital logistics aligned with climate goals and social responsibility in humanitarian contexts.

DOI: 10.4018/979-8-3373-3643-5.ch007

1. INTRODUCTION

The increasing digitization of humanitarian logistics has reshaped the landscape of post-disaster response operations. Technologies such as drones for aerial damage assessment, IoT sensors for cold-chain monitoring, biometric verification systems for aid delivery, and digital health kits for remote diagnostics have enhanced operational efficiency, speed, and accountability in crises (Aghsami, Sharififar, Markazi Moghaddam, Hazrati, Jolai, & Yazdani, 2024; UNICEF, 2023). For example, the World Food Programme's blockchain-based Building Blocks platform now reaches over 1 million beneficiaries monthly, enabling real-time cash transfers and aid coordination (WFP, 2024). Likewise, Red Cross solar-powered communication hubs in disaster-prone areas have sustained critical services during blackouts (IFRC, 2023). However, while such technologies offer speed and precision, the environmental footprint they leave behind is often overlooked. According to the United Nations Environment Programme (UNEP), e-waste globally reached a record 59.4 million metric tons in 2022, with only 17.4% being formally recycled (UNEP, 2023). Humanitarian operations, though smaller in scale, are contributing to this growing challenge, particularly when donor-funded devices—such as tablets, sensors, and mobile phones—are deployed rapidly with little end-of-life planning.

Digital tools used in emergency settings—ranging from rugged laptops and health kits to solar-charged radios and cold chain monitoring systems—are not free from ecological consequences. These devices require rare-earth minerals like cobalt and lithium, whose extraction often involves environmentally damaging and exploitative labor practices, especially in conflict-prone regions (Byers, Bompa, Jin, De Wolf, & Bendiek-Laranjo, 2025). Additionally, the rapid turnover of hardware in humanitarian settings, driven by short project cycles and donor procurement timelines, leads to premature disposal and significant electronic waste. For example, UNICEF's own internal assessments revealed hotspots of e-waste in its field operations due to distributed devices not being recovered or recycled after use (UNEMG, 2023). Compounding the issue, disaster-affected regions often lack infrastructure for responsible recycling or disposal, leading to informal dumpsites that expose vulnerable populations, especially children, to toxic materials (Çetin & Kirchherr, 2025). While some agencies have begun integrating solar solutions to reduce reliance on diesel generators, the carbon footprint of manufacturing and distributing digital logistics infrastructure remains a critical blind spot in sustainability discussions.

In response to these challenges, this chapter explores the concept and practice of "green digital logistics" as a framework to align post-disaster digitization with environmental responsibility. The aim is to assess how humanitarian actors can design digital systems and supply chains that are both effective in crisis response and compliant with sustainability goals. The chapter draws on global cases—such as

UNICEF's device lifecycle programs in Zimbabwe, the Red Cross's solar-powered emergency shelters in Puerto Rico, and WFP's blockchain-led asset management in Jordan and Ukraine—to demonstrate best practices and identify critical gaps. It also engages with current academic literature on circular economy integration in humanitarian logistics (Pradhananga & ElZomor, 2023; Arnetoli & Bologna, 2022). Through this synthesis, the chapter argues for a systemic shift: digital humanitarian logistics must move beyond functionality toward circularity and climate resilience. Ultimately, the structure of the chapter moves from conceptual framing to real-world application, concluding with strategic recommendations to guide institutions, donors, and governments in embedding sustainability into future digital operations.

2. CONCEPTUAL FOUNDATIONS

2.1 Humanitarian Logistics in the Digital Era

Humanitarian logistics has undergone a significant transformation in the last decade, evolving from manual and paper-based processes to increasingly digitized, real-time, and data-driven systems. The adoption of emerging technologies—such as artificial intelligence (AI), blockchain, Internet of Things (IoT), and drones—has redefined how humanitarian aid is delivered, monitored, and evaluated. These technologies not only enhance the speed and efficiency of relief operations but also address challenges related to transparency, traceability, and equitable distribution. According to Khan et al. (2022), digitalization has become an indispensable enabler for creating humanitarian logistics systems that are fast, fair, and safe. In disaster-prone regions, where logistics operations often occur in volatile environments, the ability to deploy AI-enabled tools for demand forecasting and automated distribution planning ensures that critical resources reach vulnerable populations in a timely and need-based manner. Technologies such as drones for last-mile delivery and remote sensing for situational assessment have further extended the operational reach of humanitarian actors.

The World Food Programme (WFP) has been at the forefront of integrating digital innovation into its logistics operations, particularly in regions affected by food insecurity and natural disasters. For example, during the COVID-19 pandemic, WFP implemented blockchain-based platforms for supply chain tracking and introduced digital biometric systems for food voucher distribution, reducing fraud while increasing transparency and speed. Similarly, the United Nations High Commissioner for Refugees (UNHCR) employs biometric registration and digital identity systems in refugee camps to manage aid distribution more accurately and securely. These initiatives exemplify the growing reliance on digital tools to manage the complexity of humanitarian supply chains. As highlighted by Aćimović, Mijušković, and Đurović (2024), tools such as warehouse management systems (WMS), geolocation tracking, and real-time inventory dashboards are now essential in managing humanitarian logistics more effectively, replacing the previously reactive, manual methods with proactive and coordinated systems.

One of the most promising developments in recent years is the use of digital twins in humanitarian logistics. Digital twins are virtual replicas of physical systems, and when applied to humanitarian contexts, they allow for real-time simulation of logistics operations, resource flows, and infrastructure readiness. Cao et al. (2024) demonstrated how digital twin technology can be leveraged to model disaster zones, simulate different supply chain scenarios, and optimize logistics routes in near real-time. For instance, a digital twin of an emergency logistics hub can help humanitarian organizations assess capacity constraints, predict bottlenecks, and virtually test various response strategies before implementation. The use of such simulations was explored during cyclone responses in Southeast Asia, where agencies like IFRC collaborated with technology providers to pre-model evacuation routes and supply distributions using twin-based planning environments, resulting in better preparedness and fewer delays during actual deployment.

The rise of Industry 4.0 has also introduced a new set of capabilities and expectations for humanitarian logistics professionals. Digital competencies—such as data analytics, cybersecurity awareness, and systems thinking—are now critical for managing technologically integrated relief systems. Koh and Yuen (2022), through their comprehensive review, emphasized that the digital era requires logistics managers to shift from being operational enforcers to becoming strategic orchestrators of information flows and stakeholder coordination. The ability to interface with AI-driven decision support systems (DSS), manage interoperable digital platforms, and ensure ethical data handling practices has become central to modern humanitarian operations. Moreover, the pressure to act swiftly and accurately in life-threatening scenarios necessitates a workforce that is not only technologically adept but also capable of adapting to evolving digital infrastructures.

Despite these advancements, digitalization in humanitarian logistics remains uneven, especially in developing countries where infrastructure, digital literacy, and funding constraints hinder widespread adoption. Kurniawan (2025) points out that while many global organizations have begun integrating AI and blockchain into logistics workflows, many local NGOs still rely on spreadsheets and phone calls to manage critical operations. This creates an operational gap between digitally mature and digitally underserved actors within the same humanitarian response network. Bridging this divide requires systemic reform, including investments in infrastructure, policy alignment, and capacity-building. One such initiative is the WFP's Digital Logistics Capacity Strengthening Programme, which supports local partners by providing digital tools, mobile training modules, and open-source logistics software tailored for low-resource environments. Such efforts aim to create a more inclusive and digitally empowered humanitarian ecosystem.

Artificial intelligence, in particular, has shown great promise in enhancing resilience and sustainability in logistics operations. According to Christhia et al. (2025), AI-based decision support systems can be used to optimize resource allocation, prioritize distribution routes based on real-time crisis data, and forecast future aid needs based on predictive models. These systems are especially relevant in complex emergencies involving displacement, where accurate demand prediction is vital to avoid both oversupply and shortages. For example, in Syria and Yemen, humanitarian actors have tested AI-supported logistics tools that analyze satellite imagery and social media signals to estimate population movements and adjust supply routes accordingly. These interventions have not only improved responsiveness but also reduced waste, aligning digital logistics with broader sustainability goals.

As the digital transformation of humanitarian logistics continues to evolve, it is increasingly being shaped by sustainability imperatives. Chingono and Mbohwa (2023) assert that the intersection of Industry 4.0 and humanitarian logistics is not just a technical transition but a paradigm shift—one that demands new governance frameworks, stakeholder collaboration, and ethical use of data. Digital tools must be leveraged not only for operational excellence but also for environmental and social sustainability. Whether through AI-enabled emissions tracking, blockchain-secured procurement practices, or sensor-based cold chains that minimize spoilage, the humanitarian sector is gradually embracing digitalization as a conduit for sustainability. However, this shift requires a rethinking of not only technologies but also institutional mindsets, training protocols, and donor expectations. Humanitarian logistics in the digital era is no longer about simply delivering aid—it is about delivering it smarter, greener, and more equitably.

2.2 Sustainability in Humanitarian Supply Chains

Sustainability in humanitarian supply chains has emerged as a crucial concern, particularly in light of increasing environmental degradation and resource constraints in disaster-prone areas. While the primary objective of humanitarian logistics is to save lives and alleviate suffering, its operational footprint—especially during post-disaster relief—often carries unintended environmental consequences. These include the excessive use of diesel-powered transport, large-scale consumption of single-use plastics (e.g., water bottles, packaging), and mounting e-waste from rapidly deployed digital tools such as communication devices and portable solar panels. According to Karuppiah et al. (2021), the COVID-19 pandemic exposed the magnitude of such environmental challenges, revealing how the surge in PPE, packaging waste, and temporary shelter construction contributed significantly to environmental degradation. Relief organizations often rely on fast-response logistics models, which, while effective in short-term delivery, frequently overlook long-term environmental consequences. Consequently, there is a growing need to reconcile rapid emergency response with ecological responsibility in humanitarian contexts.

The literature increasingly calls for a transition toward sustainable humanitarian supply chains (SHSCs), built on the triple bottom line (TBL) framework—people, planet, and profit—which balances social welfare, environmental protection, and economic viability. Anjomshoae et al. (2025), in their comprehensive systematic review, emphasize that most humanitarian supply chain designs historically prioritized only the social dimension (people), with minimal regard for environmental and financial sustainability. However, the TBL approach advocates for integrating green logistics strategies—such as optimizing route planning to minimize fuel consumption, using biodegradable packaging, and deploying low-carbon vehicles—while still meeting the urgent needs of affected populations. For example, solar-powered cold chains for vaccine distribution in sub-Saharan Africa exemplify the overlap between environmental protection and life-saving operations. Additionally, economic sustainability in humanitarian logistics can be achieved by reducing waste and improving the efficiency of procurement and resource utilization, as discussed in Üstün and Akkartal (2024), who link logistics practices directly to Sustainable Development Goal 8 (Decent Work and Economic Growth).

Operationalizing sustainability in humanitarian logistics, however, is fraught with trade-offs and context-specific constraints. In their earthquake case study of Haiti, Shakibaei et al. (2024) propose a hybrid sustainable-resilient supply chain model that accounts for both long-term sustainability and short-term responsiveness. Their model demonstrates how infrastructure fragility, donor priorities, and supply volatility complicate sustainable practices in disaster zones. For example, while airlifting relief materials is often necessary during the initial response, it comes with a high carbon footprint. Similarly, mobile medical camps powered by diesel generators are critical for health delivery but are not environmentally benign. These realities underline the necessity of contextualized sustainability strategies—not one-size-fits-all approaches. Moreover, Nawazish et al. (2024) identify the lack of standardized sustainability metrics, fragmented stakeholder coordination, and insufficient training as systemic barriers to implementing sustainability in humanitarian operations. This gap calls for both theoretical advancement and empirical experimentation to create feasible and scalable SHSC models.

Cross-sectoral collaboration and logistics policy alignment are increasingly recognized as strategic enablers of sustainable humanitarian logistics. Larson (2021) underscores the critical link between security, sustainability, and collaboration in humanitarian supply chains. He argues that the sustainability of humanitarian operations cannot be realized without stakeholder integration, including NGOs, local governments, logistics providers, and the private sector. For instance, IFRC's Green Response initiative represents a collaborative approach to reduce the environmental footprint of humanitarian logistics by promoting clean energy use, local procurement, and waste minimization. In a similar vein, WFP and UNICEF have developed frameworks to align procurement and warehousing practices with carbon reduction goals. These initiatives are further supported by digital platforms that help track emissions, monitor energy usage, and map reverse logistics pathways for recycling or repurposing materials post-crisis. Such collaborations not only improve environmental performance but also enhance the transparency and legitimacy of humanitarian action in the eyes of donors and communities.

Emerging research has also emphasized the need to integrate sustainability into logistics planning tools and decision-making models. As highlighted in the edited volume by Mızrak and Akkartal (2024), logistics plays a pivotal role in achieving multiple Sustainable Development Goals (SDGs), not just emergency response. Their volume presents innovative logistics frameworks that simultaneously support SDG 9 (Industry, Innovation and Infrastructure), SDG 12 (Responsible Consumption and Production), and SDG 13 (Climate Action). Abdelhadi and Akkartal (2024) extend this logic through structural analysis in the retail sector of Türkiye, showcasing how logistics efficiency and sustainable development can be jointly optimized. Lessons from commercial logistics can be adapted to the humanitarian space by adopting green inventory management systems, eco-labeling for aid supplies, and life cycle cost analysis in procurement decisions. These strategies also promote local sourcing, which reduces transportation emissions and stimulates local economies, contributing to long-term resilience.

In summary, embedding sustainability into humanitarian supply chains is no longer a peripheral issue but a core requirement for ethical, effective, and future-ready humanitarian action. While traditional models have emphasized urgency and reach, contemporary frameworks now recognize the long-term impact of operations on the environment and economy. By adopting the TBL lens, designing hybrid sustainable-resilient systems, and leveraging collaborative policy platforms, humanitarian actors can redesign supply chains that serve both people and the planet without compromising effectiveness. However, translating sustainability rhetoric into practice requires overcoming entrenched structural challenges, investing in local capacity, and rethinking donor mandates to include environmental performance indicators. As the climate crisis intensifies and humanitarian needs grow more complex, the sustainability of the supply chain itself may become as important as the aid it delivers.

2.3 Digital Technologies and Sustainability Intersections

Digital technologies are no longer peripheral to logistics operations—they have become central enablers of both operational excellence and sustainability. In humanitarian contexts, where agility, resource constraints, and accountability are critical, the integration of digital tools such as Internet of Things (IoT) sensors, radio frequency identification (RFID) tags, blockchain systems, and remote sensing platforms has redefined the landscape of logistics planning and delivery. These technologies allow for unprecedented levels of visibility, real-time tracking, and predictive control across the entire supply chain. Barykin et al. (2021) argue that sustainable decision-making in digital logistics networks is made possible by real-time data ecosystems, where sensor-fed platforms help organizations reduce waste, optimize energy usage, and prevent overstocking or obsolescence. In humanitarian logistics, such functionality ensures that aid reaches beneficiaries without excess inventory that could spoil, expire, or be discarded—ultimately reducing environmental burden and enhancing trust.

One of the most transformative technologies in green digital logistics is the digital twin, which creates a real-time digital replica of logistics operations, enabling simulations of alternative delivery routes, warehouse configurations, and resource allocation strategies. Cebir and Akkartal (2024) explain how digital twin systems, when applied to post-disaster logistics, allow relief agencies to visualize infrastructure damage, simulate alternative supply paths, and evaluate fuel-efficient options before deployment. These simulations help organizations balance responsiveness with sustainability, such as selecting lower-emission ground transport instead of airlift when feasible. In Türkiye's emergency planning exercises, digital twins have been used to test the sustainability of cold-chain vaccine delivery in earthquake-prone zones, ensuring minimal energy consumption through route and load optimization. This integration of planning and environmental stewardship reflects the dual benefits of digitalization—not only streamlining operations but aligning them with sustainability goals.

The role of blockchain in humanitarian logistics is particularly salient in enhancing traceability and reducing duplication of aid resources. By offering a decentralized and tamper-proof record of transactions, blockchain prevents the overuse of resources, enhances the transparency of aid flows, and supports circular practices such as reusable packaging or reverse logistics. Zekhnini et al. (2022) highlight how combining blockchain with lean and green supply chain practices results in viable and measurable sustainability gains, especially when waste reduction, ethical sourcing, and emissions tracking are embedded into blockchain-based smart contracts. In contexts such as refugee camps or remote areas lacking strong oversight, blockchain ensures that donated goods are tracked from procurement to distribution and even disposal, facilitating more circular and less wasteful logistics loops.

IoT and RFID technologies also offer vital sustainability benefits in emergency logistics systems by enabling smart inventory and asset management. Liu et al. (2024) show how the integration of digital and physical logistics systems—referred to as *digital-real integration*—has accelerated the transformation of logistics networks toward sustainability. Through the use of RFID-enabled temperature sensors in cold chains, for instance, humanitarian actors can monitor vaccine integrity, reduce spoilage, and minimize redundant shipments. In sub-Saharan Africa, some WFP cold storage units now use IoT platforms to monitor internal temperatures and alert staff of anomalies in real time, thereby cutting energy usage and preventing loss. Özkanlısoy and Akkartal (2021) further emphasize that sensor-based platforms, when scaled with cloud analytics, support proactive decision-making and reduce resource misuse—especially important in crisis zones where every unit of aid must be justified and optimized.

Remote sensing technologies, often powered by satellites or drones, contribute to green logistics by enhancing situational awareness and reducing unnecessary transport activities. By analyzing aerial images of disaster-affected areas, logistics planners can make informed decisions about accessibility, damage severity, and optimal delivery points—minimizing the risk of misrouted or failed supply attempts. Nikseresht et al. (2024), in their bibliometric study, highlight the growing importance of remote sensing in *sustainable remanufacturing and recovery logistics*, especially as it relates to minimizing the carbon footprint of disaster response. In humanitarian operations in Syria and Yemen, remote sensing has been used to monitor flood zones and population movements, reducing the number of transport runs and enabling strategic pre-positioning of supplies. These insights help logistics actors avoid reactive, wasteful deployments and instead adopt precision-targeted and environmentally conscious delivery.

Fleet management is another area where digital tools intersect directly with sustainability goals. Akkartal and Aras (2021) explore how sustainability in fleet management is achieved by integrating telematics systems that optimize fuel efficiency, route selection, and maintenance schedules. These systems are increasingly used in humanitarian transport fleets to reduce emissions and extend vehicle lifecycles. For example, predictive maintenance alerts can prevent breakdowns in remote regions, reducing the need for emergency repairs and secondary shipments. Additionally, fleet monitoring dashboards offer agencies the ability to compare carbon footprints across routes, choose greener options, and report on emissions to donors. Such practices not only advance environmental performance but also strengthen accountability frameworks in humanitarian operations.

It is also essential to consider the human dimension of digital-sustainability integration. Čižiūnienė et al. (2025) argue that sustainable human resource management (HRM) plays a crucial role in embedding sustainability through digital tools in logistics systems, particularly during emergencies. In their study of the Lithuanian logistics sector, the authors found that equipping staff with digital competencies—such as using GIS dashboards, blockchain auditing tools, or AI-based inventory systems—correlated strongly with environmentally responsible practices. They stress the importance of training logistics workers not just to use digital systems, but to interpret data in ways that support sustainable choices. This is especially relevant in humanitarian logistics, where rapid decisions must also weigh long-term environmental impacts.

Finally, digital transformation must consider the rural and under-resourced contexts in which many humanitarian operations occur. Moazzeni and Sgarbossa (2025) highlight how collaborative logistics models, supported by digital platforms, are crucial for enabling sustainable operations in remote areas. Their systematic review shows that digital decision support tools tailored for rural settings—such as low-bandwidth routing apps, offline RFID readers, and modular cloud dashboards—can enhance sustainability without overburdening local capacity. In Ethiopia, pilot programs using mobile data collection paired with offline blockchain syncing have allowed humanitarian organizations to manage decentralized logistics while minimizing redundant trips and diesel use. Such applications show how technology can be adapted to serve both sustainability and equity in complex field environments. To better illustrate these impacts, Table 1 summarizes the typical environmental burdens associated with digital devices frequently used in humanitarian operations, including energy demands and e-waste contributions.

Table 1. Environmental Impacts of Common Digital Devices in Humanitarian Operations

Device Type	Primary Use Case	Key Environmental Risks	Lifecycle Challenges	End-of-Life Risk
Smartphones	Health reporting, coordination	Mining of cobalt/lithium, short replacement cycle	Difficult to retrieve post-deployment	Informal e-waste dumping
IoT Cold Chain Sensors	Vaccine/temp-sensitive aid	Embedded batteries, rare earths	Limited repairability	Toxic components
Drones	Aerial surveillance, mapping	High energy consumption, e-waste	Short operational lifespan	Battery disposal
Biometric Scanners	Refugee registration	Data server energy use	Data sensitivity, limited reuse	Limited recyclability

Source: UNEP (2023); Çetin & Kirchherr (2025); UNEMG (2023)

3. CHALLENGES IN GREEN DIGITAL LOGISTICS

3.1 Lack of Circular Systems for Emergency Digital Devices

Despite the rapid adoption of digital tools in humanitarian logistics—such as tablets for beneficiary registration, solar-powered lamps, GPS-enabled drones, and environmental sensors—very little attention has been paid to what happens to these devices after their use. In many post-disaster settings, emergency digital devices are deployed quickly to restore communication, improve coordination, and track aid deliveries. However, once their immediate utility is exhausted or the battery life ends, these devices often become electronic waste (e-waste) with no structured process for recovery, recycling, or safe disposal. According to Ramakrishna and Ramasubramanian (2024), the absence of reverse logistics systems for emergency electronics contributes to a growing volume of unmanaged e-waste, especially in fragile regions that lack national e-waste policies or recycling infrastructure. This is particularly problematic in low- and middle-income countries that host recurring humanitarian operations, where discarded electronics from aid agencies accumulate in informal waste streams, posing both environmental and health hazards.

The situation is exacerbated by the lack of formal take-back programs or circular economy frameworks tailored specifically for the humanitarian aid sector. Unlike the commercial electronics industry, which is increasingly pressured by regulations like the EU's Waste Electrical and Electronic Equipment (WEEE) Directive, humanitarian organizations are rarely bound by formal recovery mandates. As Bhattacharjee et al. (2025) note, e-waste contains toxic elements such as lead, cadmium, and mercury, and the improper disposal of these components—often through open-air burning or unregulated landfilling—leads to soil, water, and air contamination. Yet, in disaster-prone regions like Haiti, Yemen, and parts of the Sahel, post-crisis assessments rarely include an inventory of e-waste generated through relief operations. This gap stems from the fact that sustainability in humanitarian logistics has traditionally emphasized supply-side efficiency and responsiveness, without integrating end-of-life management for digital devices.

Advanced waste management models based on Industry 4.0 technologies offer promising pathways for closing this loop. Aydoğan et al. (2025) propose a decision-aided tool using continuous function-valued intuitionistic fuzzy sets to evaluate and optimize e-waste collection systems under uncertain conditions—conditions that are typical in post-disaster or conflict zones. Their framework, while originally applied to municipal contexts, can be adapted to humanitarian settings to assess risk zones for informal dumping, design modular e-waste bins, and generate routes for reverse logistics. Furthermore, Hayat (2023) discusses the integration of geospatial and AI tools in urban waste management, highlighting their potential for mapping hotspots of discarded electronics and forecasting e-waste generation patterns. If adapted to humanitarian camps or mobile health centers, such tools could help aid agencies plan for the sustainable decommissioning of their digital infrastructure.

Moreover, the digital transformation that brought sustainability benefits to commercial logistics has yet to penetrate the humanitarian sector in terms of circularity. Goel et al. (2024) argue that while digital transformation can offer environmental advantages, it also introduces new risks—especially when applied without an accompanying end-of-life strategy for devices. In many humanitarian missions, asset management systems lack tracking features for disposal or reuse. For example, tablets distributed for remote education during the COVID-19 crisis in refugee camps have not been retrieved or recycled in any organized manner, leading to both loss of value and ecological harm. The lack of cross-agency coordination and donor incentives for device retrieval further discourages circular approaches. Unlike food or medical aid, digital equipment often falls outside the scope of sustainability audits in humanitarian response evaluations.

In addition to the technical challenges, there are institutional and behavioral barriers. Ramakrishna and Ramasubramanian (2024) emphasize that e-waste management requires multi-actor cooperation, including manufacturers, governments, NGOs, and local recyclers. However, the fragmented nature of humanitarian logistics—where different agencies use different procurement systems and operate independently—makes such cooperation difficult. Moreover, logistical constraints such as remote geography, security risks, and customs restrictions hinder the ability to ship used equipment back to certified recycling centers. Even when take-back mechanisms are technically possible, lack of awareness among field staff and absence of donor guidelines often result in digital devices being left behind. As Hayat (2023) points out, circularity in e-waste requires more than technology—it demands institutional alignment, training, and incentive structures.

To address these gaps, future humanitarian logistics strategies must incorporate circularity as a design principle, not a post-hoc concern. This includes developing lightweight, modular, and repairable devices specifically designed for emergency contexts; embedding blockchain-based tagging to trace equipment across its lifecycle; and collaborating with local e-waste enterprises to create collection and refurbishing schemes. While such practices are rare today, pilot efforts in Kenya and India—where NGOs have partnered with social enterprises to refurbish solar kits and digital education tools—illustrate the feasibility of circular models even in low-resource environments. Ultimately, without embedding formal take-back programs and reverse logistics into the humanitarian digital supply chain, sustainability goals will remain incomplete, and the environmental costs of saving lives may become an overlooked but growing crisis.

3.2 Data Gaps and Infrastructure Barriers

Despite the growing push for digitalization in humanitarian logistics, many post-disaster regions face critical barriers in implementing green digital solutions due to persistent data gaps and inadequate infrastructure. In several low- and middle-income countries, digital transformation efforts are undermined by fragmented data ecosystems, where humanitarian agencies and government actors often operate on incompatible platforms, limiting the interoperability required for real-time coordination. For instance, as noted in the UNICEF digital health case in Zimbabwe, although smartphones and diagnostic devices improved medical reporting, the lack of unified data standards across clinics initially hampered the seamless integration of patient records into national health systems. Similarly, WFP's blockchain-based Building Blocks project in Jordan revealed that ensuring traceable and tamper-proof transactions was only possible after resolving identity verification challenges linked to missing biometric and registration data for displaced populations.

Moreover, connectivity infrastructure remains a major limitation in post-disaster areas. Solar-powered radio distribution by the Red Cross in Liberia during the Ebola outbreak exemplifies how digital outreach was hindered in communities lacking reliable electricity and telecommunications infrastructure. Even as mobile devices and IoT tools become more widespread, their functionality often depends on consistent access to power and mobile networks—both of which are among the first systems to collapse in disaster zones. Reports from IFRC (2023) underscore that while satellite solutions and portable network kits have become available, their cost and maintenance remain prohibitive for many local responders, especially when donor budgets prioritize immediate relief over long-term digital infrastructure investment.

Another overlooked barrier is the environmental mismatch between device durability and local recovery conditions. For example, the absence of local repair capacity or recycling pathways in affected regions often turns digital tools into short-lived interventions. The sustainability principle of circularity—as recommended by Çetin and Kirchherr (2025) in the Build Back Circular framework—is difficult to apply if logistical systems lack information about device end-of-life status or if there are no formal e-waste processing facilities. This emphasizes the need for not only digital capacity-building but also physical infrastructure investments such as solar-powered charging hubs, mobile data centers, and modular repair units to ensure continuous, eco-conscious functionality of digital logistics tools. Addressing these data and infrastructure gaps is critical to enabling the kind of interoperable, green, and resilient digital systems envisioned for future humanitarian operations.

3.3 Coordination and Accountability Issues

In the wake of a disaster, the ability to coordinate relief efforts depends not only on physical infrastructure but increasingly on the robustness of digital systems. However, many humanitarian operations continue to suffer from significant data gaps and infrastructural limitations that hinder the effective deployment and sustainability of digital logistics tools. A key issue lies in the poor traceability of digital assets deployed in the field—such as tablets, drones, IoT sensors, and communication nodes. In many post-disaster operations, these devices are rapidly deployed to enable situational awareness and communication, yet they are rarely tracked across their lifecycle. As Maghsoudi et al. (2023) highlight, even in digitally enhanced relief systems—such as cash and voucher assistance (CVA) platforms—donors and agencies lack clear visibility into how and where digital assets are stored, reused, or decommissioned. This opacity not only weakens sustainability but also reduces accountability in the long run, especially when device losses or misuse cannot be detected or reported.

These traceability challenges are compounded by inadequate digital infrastructure in many disaster-prone regions. In particular, limited bandwidth, intermittent connectivity, and constrained energy sources reduce the effectiveness of even the most advanced technological systems. Matracia et al. (2022) provide an in-depth analysis of the key architectural barriers to post-disaster communications, noting that many emergency communication hubs rely on fragile or outdated wireless networks that cannot support high-data transmission from UAVs, IoT sensors, or blockchain platforms. These limitations are particularly acute in rural or mountainous terrain, where terrestrial communications infrastructure is either absent or destroyed during disasters. As a result, digital logistics systems—such as those used for aid distribution monitoring or remote coordination—often fail to function when they are needed most, creating operational blind spots in the humanitarian response.

One of the most promising approaches to overcoming infrastructure limitations involves the deployment of UAV-assisted energy-efficient networks. Khalid et al. (2023) propose UAV-enabled Mobile Edge Computing (MEC) systems with energy harvesting capabilities to sustain digital communications in disaster-hit zones. These UAVs can serve as temporary communication relays, maintaining connectivity while also gathering data for damage assessments and logistics planning. Similarly, Hu et al. (2021) present an uplink optimization model that improves the throughput of UAV-enabled emergency networks in urban settings, allowing for faster information transfer and better coordination of digital assets. However, these systems remain energy-intensive and depend heavily on optimized path planning, which itself requires a level of data and digital literacy not always available among humanitarian field teams.

Energy constraints also present a persistent barrier to sustaining digital logistics platforms in disaster environments. Saif et al. (2021) address this issue by developing a clustering and energy-harvesting model for post-disaster communications, where emergency devices form decentralized communication clusters powered by ambient energy sources. These self-sustaining clusters reduce reliance on diesel generators or external power sources, offering a more environmentally sustainable and operationally resilient alternative. Yet, despite the technical promise of such solutions, their integration into actual humanitarian supply chains remains limited due to high setup costs, lack of training, and unclear interoperability with existing platforms. Moreover, Khan et al. (2022) emphasize that path planning in UAV networks must be dynamic and energy-aware, especially in 5G-assisted disaster zones, where energy efficiency and signal coverage must be constantly balanced against physical constraints and battery limitations.

The digital infrastructure gaps are not limited to communications systems alone—they extend to data collection, storage, and transfer capabilities. Many humanitarian logistics actors still rely on disconnected spreadsheets or standalone mobile apps that are not integrated into larger systems. Treiblmaier and Rejeb (2023) point out that blockchain applications in disaster logistics, while offering excellent transparency and security, are bandwidth-heavy and require synchronized consensus mechanisms—technologies that are difficult to implement in low-bandwidth post-disaster settings. In addition, many digital supply chain tools assume stable cloud connectivity, yet relief teams in field operations often operate without reliable access to cloud servers or national data repositories. This results in delayed or lost data transmission, eroding the potential benefits of digitalization in time-sensitive humanitarian environments.

Emerging solutions such as environmentally aware drone coordination, proposed by Qu et al. (2023), aim to bridge the bandwidth-energy-sustainability trade-off by optimizing drone deployment using AI-based multi-objective models. Their framework enables drone swarms to minimize redundant energy usage while maximizing communication and data relay capacity in real-time. However, this technology has been tested primarily in controlled environments and simulations—not in live humanitarian operations. Field trials and pilot deployments remain rare, partly due to regulatory restrictions and the complexity of integrating AI-driven systems with traditional logistics protocols. This gap highlights the need for scalable, user-friendly platforms that blend advanced features with the rugged, unpredictable realities of disaster relief.

Another challenge is the interoperability of digital systems across multiple humanitarian organizations, which often use proprietary technologies that cannot communicate with each other. This results in siloed data systems, where vital information on supply movements, beneficiary registration, or infrastructure assessments is not shared across agencies. As Maghsoudi et al. (2023) demonstrate in their cross-case analysis, this fragmentation undermines coordination and amplifies infrastructure inefficiencies. Without standard data protocols or centralized digital repositories, overlapping efforts occur, devices are lost or duplicated, and sustainable practices—such as circular recovery or shared usage—become nearly impossible.

In summary, while digital technologies have transformed humanitarian logistics, persistent data gaps and infrastructure barriers continue to restrict their full potential, especially in terms of sustainability and resilience. Poor asset traceability, limited energy and bandwidth availability, fragmented systems, and the high technical threshold for deployment all contribute to underutilization or failure in crisis settings. Bridging this gap will require not only technological innovation but also significant investments in local infrastructure, cross-agency digital standardization, and training programs to equip humanitarian staff with the skills to operate and maintain these systems in degraded environments. Only then can digital logistics platforms truly support sustainable, inclusive, and efficient humanitarian operations.

4. STRATEGIES FOR DESIGNING GREEN DIGITAL LOGISTICS

4.1 Eco-Design of Digital Equipment for Field Use

The growing reliance on digital tools in humanitarian logistics—ranging from tablets and GPS trackers to medical sensors and communication wearables—has raised urgent questions about their environmental impact and lifecycle sustainability. In crisis zones where infrastructure is often destroyed or degraded, these devices are essential for enabling real-time coordination, monitoring, and data collection. However, most are not designed for longevity, reuse, or environmental compatibility. The concept of eco-design offers a transformative solution by embedding environmental considerations directly into the design phase of digital equipment used in the field. This approach focuses on developing durable, modular, and recyclable devices that can withstand harsh environments while minimizing their ecological footprint. According to the Next Generation Mobile Networks (NGMN) Alliance (2021), network equipment and digital tools should follow end-to-end eco-design principles, encompassing not only energy efficiency during use but also material recovery, modular repairability, and low-impact manufacturing.

One key strategy in eco-design is the use of low-carbon energy systems to power digital field equipment. Ramasubramanian et al. (2022) emphasize the importance of replacing conventional lithium-ion power sources with sustainable energy alternatives such as bio-compatible batteries, flexible solar films, and self-charging supercapacitors. These innovations are especially relevant in humanitarian logistics where access to centralized power is limited, and energy generation must be both autonomous and sustainable. For instance, emergency medical kits equipped with self-powered diagnostic sensors can continuously operate without needing replacement batteries, reducing both operational waste and logistical burdens. Wearable devices for monitoring health or environmental conditions in the field can also incorporate low-power microcontrollers and flexible photovoltaics, extending their lifecycle and reducing emissions associated with recharging or disposal.

The development of solar-powered and low-energy consumption devices plays a vital role in enhancing both sustainability and resilience. Nordin et al. (2021), in their comprehensive review, propose the integration of photovoltaic solar cells and supercapacitors into compact field devices such as radios, sensors, and mobile terminals. These technologies can operate in extreme heat, high humidity, or remote locations without requiring fuel-based generators. This is particularly beneficial in refugee camps or disaster response hubs where fossil fuel logistics are often unstable or environmentally damaging. Moreover, solar-integrated devices can contribute to a reduced carbon footprint and foster energy independence for field teams operating under resource-constrained conditions.

In addition to energy innovations, material sustainability is an essential pillar of eco-design. Verma et al. (2025) discuss the potential of natural polymers and biodegradable composites in constructing digital devices that are both lightweight and environmentally friendly. By replacing traditional plastics and metals with renewable or recyclable materials, humanitarian organizations can reduce the long-term ecological impact of equipment disposal. Devices such as modular communication tablets or digital ID kits can be designed using bio-resins and plant-based casing, allowing for safe decomposition or easier recycling after decommissioning. This approach aligns with the principles of circular economy and is particularly effective when deployed alongside localized e-waste collection or repair infrastructure.

Another promising avenue is the application of nano-material innovations to enhance the energy efficiency and environmental performance of solar devices. Pradhan et al. (2024) present the use of nano-coatings and advanced semiconductor composites to improve photovoltaic conversion efficiency while lowering the embodied energy of production. In humanitarian contexts, where device weight and operational lifespan are critical, such innovations can drastically reduce emissions from equipment transport and increase usage cycles before replacement is needed. Lightweight solar-powered drones, for example, could be equipped with these nano-material enhancements to enable longer flight times with fewer battery replacements—a crucial advantage for real-time aerial assessments in remote or flood-affected regions.

Simplicity, scalability, and modular design also contribute to sustainable digital equipment deployment. As Pandey and Sharma (2024) explain, modular technologies enable the replacement of individual components—such as a faulty sensor or dead battery—without needing to discard the entire device. This not only reduces e-waste but also lowers costs and increases the autonomy of field teams who may lack access to full-scale technical support. Humanitarian actors can benefit from open-source hardware platforms that allow for plug-and-play upgrades, component swapping, and localized repair using 3D-printed or biodegradable parts. For example, a modular communication hub used in disaster response can be adapted to different environments simply by switching antennas, processors, or power modules, depending on the terrain and resource availability.

In conclusion, the eco-design of digital field equipment offers a crucial pathway toward more sustainable, resilient, and responsible humanitarian logistics. By prioritizing durability, low energy use, recyclability, and local adaptability in design processes, relief organizations can minimize the environmental footprint of their operations while enhancing device longevity and field performance. As donor expectations evolve and sustainability becomes a non-negotiable standard in global development, eco-designed digital equipment will play a pivotal role in shaping the next generation of humanitarian logistics technologies.

4.2 Circular Logistics Models in Post-Disaster Contexts

The aftermath of a disaster is often characterized by vast material flows into affected areas—temporary shelters, medical equipment, digital devices, and consumables are delivered at speed and scale. However, what remains largely unaddressed is the *exit strategy* for these materials once their immediate use concludes. This oversight results in growing volumes of e-waste, construction debris, and unusable aid products, particularly in fragile contexts where infrastructure for waste management is minimal or absent. The integration of circular logistics models into humanitarian operations offers a critical opportunity to redesign these post-disaster flows in alignment with sustainability, resilience, and resource efficiency. As Çetin and Kirchherr (2025) argue in their Build Back Circular Framework, humanitarian reconstruction should shift away from linear "use-and-dispose" models toward strategies that embrace reuse, remanufacturing, and material recovery from the earliest stages of disaster planning.

A central component of circular humanitarian logistics is the deployment of reverse logistics systems that recover digital devices and materials used during the emergency phase. These include solar-powered tablets, communication units, wearable medical sensors, drones, and temporary power kits. However, as Aghsami et al. (2024) emphasize, reverse logistics in post-disaster settings remains underdeveloped due to fragmented coordination, lack of standardized recovery protocols, and limited donor incentives. Humanitarian actors often prioritize inbound supply flows—delivering aid to beneficiaries—while neglecting the design of outbound flows for equipment retrieval, refurbishment, or recycling. For example, thousands of communication kits distributed for COVID-19 tracing or remote education remain unaccounted for in refugee camps, either abandoned, stored in non-functional condition, or improperly disposed of, resulting in long-term environmental impacts and lost economic value.

To enable functional reverse logistics systems, partnerships with local recycling enterprises and social innovators are essential. Pradhananga and ElZomor (2023) highlight that community-based circular economy models, where local organizations are trained and resourced to collect, repair, and upcycle relief assets, have proven successful in accelerating sustainability outcomes while fostering local economic development. In Nepal, for instance, local NGOs collaborated with e-waste startups to recover unused solar kits after the 2015 earthquake, dismantling them safely and reintegrating components into new energy systems for community schools. These models not only prevent environmental degradation but also create livelihood opportunities for crisis-affected populations, turning recovery logistics into a mechanism for empowerment. Such partnerships also contribute to post-disaster resilience by reducing reliance on new imports and enabling resource continuity using already deployed materials.

Designing temporary settlements and logistics hubs with circularity in mind further strengthens post-disaster sustainability. Arnetoli and Bologna (2022) propose design scenarios that incorporate reuse loops in materials and modular systems in shelter planning. For example, portable solar units and modular communication shelters can be designed for disassembly and redeployment, ensuring that infrastructure built in one emergency can be retrieved and reused in future operations. These innovations are vital for international agencies like UNHCR and IFRC, which respond to recurring crises in multiple regions and require mobile, adaptable infrastructure. When digital assets and supporting hardware are designed with end-of-life scenarios in mind, organizations are better positioned to minimize waste and maximize the life cycle of valuable equipment.

Furthermore, the restoration of post-hazard infrastructure using circular principles can reduce the environmental and financial burden of recovery operations. Byers et al. (2025) assert that circular economy strategies—such as reusing salvaged building materials, recycling damaged electronic systems, and integrating renewable energy sources—enhance both resource efficiency and long-term resilience. In Turkey, some municipalities are piloting closed-loop logistics systems where digital tools used during flood response are returned to depots, refurbished, and redeployed to fire-prone regions, following a lifecycle-based inventory model. These practices not only reduce emissions and material waste but also facilitate data-driven forecasting of asset utility over time, enabling smarter procurement and leaner aid systems in future crises.

The success of circular logistics models ultimately depends on their institutionalization across the humanitarian supply chain. That means including device recovery clauses in supplier contracts, creating inventory systems that track end-of-life status, and encouraging donors to support extended asset lifecycles beyond the emergency phase. Çetin and Kirchherr (2025) recommend embedding circularity indicators in emergency procurement policies, such as percentage of recoverable materials, CO_2 savings from reused goods, and number of recovered units per operation. When these performance metrics are integrated into logistics planning tools and donor reporting frameworks, circular strategies gain both visibility and legitimacy within the operational culture of humanitarian aid.

In summary, post-disaster contexts present a valuable opportunity to implement circular logistics models that simultaneously reduce waste, optimize resource use, and promote local engagement. By prioritizing reverse logistics, investing in recovery partnerships, and embedding circularity into the design and governance of emergency supply chains, humanitarian actors can move beyond reactive models and contribute to long-term sustainability and resilience in disaster-affected regions.

4.3 Blockchain and IoT for Asset Traceability

The convergence of blockchain and Internet of Things (IoT) technologies has significantly transformed asset traceability in humanitarian logistics, particularly under post-disaster conditions. These tools are essential for managing the growing inventory of digital humanitarian assets—such as solar-powered identity kits, biometric scanners, field communication sensors, and wearable medical devices—where accurate tracking is critical for ensuring transparency, preventing theft or misuse, and extending operational life. IoT-enabled assets equipped with embedded GPS, RFID chips, and environmental sensors provide continuous, real-time monitoring of asset condition, performance, and location. This capability is vital for humanitarian field operations in challenging terrains, enabling more efficient planning and allocation (Nikseresht et al., 2024; Moazzeni & Sgarbossa, 2025).

Blockchain complements this traceability by recording every interaction or movement of assets in an immutable ledger. Each digital asset is linked to a unique digital identity on the blockchain, which tracks its deployment, use, transfer, and return. This ensures complete transparency across the asset's lifecycle, making it easier to identify losses or damages and simplifying auditing processes (Treiblmaier & Rejeb, 2023). For instance, digital identity kits deployed by NGOs in remote refugee settlements can be tracked on-chain from dispatch to field registration, ensuring they are not diverted or duplicated. Similarly, medical sensors distributed in mobile clinics can register temperature deviations or failures on blockchain, flagging them for urgent replacement or maintenance.

The use of smart contracts further enhances asset lifecycle traceability. These self-executing scripts automatically trigger actions when certain thresholds are reached—such as logging a usage alert when a battery drops below 20% or initiating a replacement order when a device surpasses its operating hour limit. This is particularly relevant for cold chain equipment and wearable sensors used in post-disaster disease surveillance, where reliability is time-sensitive and life-critical (Khalid et al., 2023; Christhia et al., 2025). For example, when a vaccine sensor in a solar-powered cold box detects abnormal heat spikes, a smart contract can execute logistics commands: alerting nearby health teams, issuing a replacement device, and updating the traceability record.

Moreover, by maintaining a verifiable chain of custody, blockchain and IoT enable reverse logistics strategies—returning expired, damaged, or underutilized devices for refurbishment or recycling. Through public-private partnerships, field assets can be transferred to certified e-waste handlers, where traceability records validate origin and condition, improving trust and compliance with local regulations (Ramakrishna & Ramasubramanian, 2024). This circular data infrastructure ensures accountability while supporting environmental and ethical mandates of humanitarian operations. Ultimately, integrating blockchain and IoT into logistics not only secures operational efficiency but also facilitates data-driven decision-making and sustainable asset stewardship in disaster-stricken environments.

4.4 Digital Sustainability Assessment Tools

In humanitarian logistics, digital sustainability assessment tools play a pivotal role in systematically evaluating the environmental impacts of technologies deployed in crisis response. These tools—ranging from life cycle assessment (LCA) frameworks to carbon tracking dashboards and predictive analytics models—enable organizations to understand and manage the ecological footprint of digital operations with a level of precision that was previously unattainable. One of the most widely used methodologies is LCA, which quantifies energy usage, emissions, and material throughput across each phase of a device's lifecycle—from manufacturing and deployment to disposal or recycling (Barykin et al., 2021; Verma et al., 2025).

For example, applying LCA to drones used in emergency mapping or tablets used for data registration can reveal embedded carbon and resource intensities. Humanitarian organizations can then compare models and prioritize procurement of equipment with lower cradle-to-grave environmental burdens. In parallel, carbon tracking tools can be used to monitor live operations. These tools, powered by IoT data and cloud-based systems, provide real-time feedback on emissions related to transport, storage, and digital communications. Cold chain infrastructure embedded with energy sensors, for instance, can record electricity consumption and correlate it with greenhouse gas output, alerting managers to opportunities for switching to solar or improving insulation (Liu et al., 2024; Özkanlısoy & Akkartal, 2021).

Alongside these technical frameworks, organizations must also define and monitor Key Performance Indicators (KPIs)that guide continuous improvement. Relevant KPIs for green digital logistics include: (1) percentage of field devices refurbished or recycled; (2) ratio of emissions per unit of aid delivered; (3) average energy consumption per digital asset per mission day; and (4) material composition scores assessing recyclability and toxicity. These indicators offer not only operational insights but also accountability tools that can be reported to funders and regulators (Akkartal & Aras, 2021). When aligned with strategic targets like the Sustainable Development Goals (e.g., SDG 12 on Responsible Consumption and SDG 13 on Climate Action), these KPIs frame sustainability as an integral outcome—not a secondary consideration.

Furthermore, advanced decision-aided tools now allow managers to simulate the sustainability impacts of different logistics choices before execution. By inputting contextual variables (e.g., energy source, distance, asset type), planners can compare emissions, cost, and recovery rates across scenarios. For instance, in the delivery of biometric kits to flood-prone regions, such simulation tools can weigh the carbon cost of air freight versus drone dispatch, helping organizations prioritize the lower-impact option (Hayat, 2023; Pandey & Sharma, 2024). As humanitarian operations grow more digital, embedding sustainability metrics into decision-making will be vital to building both effective and ethically grounded logistics systems.

5. CASE EXAMPLES AND GOOD PRACTICES

5.1 UNICEF's Digital Health Kits and E-Waste Management

UNICEF's deployment of digital health kits represents a significant stride toward modernizing healthcare delivery in remote and underserved regions. A key initiative in Zimbabwe between 2023 and 2025 involved equipping village health workers with smartphones and portable diagnostic devices such as thermometers and blood glucose monitors. These tools enabled real-time communication between community health workers and clinics, facilitating faster diagnosis and response to conditions like childhood diabetes and hypertension. Reporting lags that once stretched over several weeks were reduced to near-instant data transmission, significantly improving case management and early intervention (UNICEF, 2023). This digital transformation in humanitarian healthcare logistics also raises critical concerns around the end-of-life management of electronic devices. In response, UNICEF has initiated sustainability policies centered on the environmental footprint of its digital tools. According to the United Nations Environment Management Group (UNEMG, 2021), UNICEF conducts life-cycle analyses of its electronic assets to identify e-waste hotspots and formulates recovery and recycling strategies. These include designing devices for durability and repairability, as well as collaborating with suppliers and local recyclers to ensure safe disposal. UNICEF has also supported global e-waste mapping efforts to reduce the use of child labor and environmental hazards in informal recycling sites (UNEMG, 2021). In this way, UNICEF's strategy exemplifies a dual-focus humanitarian logistics model: enabling life-saving diagnostics while ensuring that these digital interventions do not become future environmental liabilities. This aligns with broader calls in the literature for circular e-waste systems, especially for solar-powered and digital health devices used in field operations (Ramakrishna & Ramasubramanian, 2024; Bhattacharjee et al., 2025).

5.2 Red Cross Initiatives Using Solar-Powered Communication Tools

The Red Cross and Red Crescent Movement has been a pioneer in integrating renewable energy—particularly solar power—into its humanitarian logistics framework. Following Hurricane Maria in Puerto Rico (2017–2019), the American Red Cross collaborated with local partners to install solar microgrids (50 kW capacity) and battery storage at critical community facilities such as schools and emergency shelters. These systems provided essential services—lighting, communications, refrigeration, and water pumping—without relying on fossil fuels, ensuring resilience against power outages and reducing carbon emissions (American Red Cross, 2019). In line with its Green Response strategy, the Movement has continued scaling solar integration across its operations. For instance, the ICRC installed solar panels at its Bogotá, Colombia facility in 2021, covering 40% of energy needs and delivering long-term cost savings (ICRC, 2022). Similarly, mobile communication hubs powered by solar panels have been deployed in emergency responses. During the Ebola outbreak in West Africa (2014–2016), the Liberian Red Cross used solar-charged mobile radio vans and distributed solar radios to maintain community engagement even in off-grid villages (IFRC, 2017). These efforts proved critical in dispelling misinformation and improving public trust during the epidemic. One of the most innovative examples is the solar-powered bloodmobile launched by the American Red Cross in 2024. This vehicle supports mobile blood donation drives with a fully solar-enabled system that powers refrigeration units, air filtration, and diagnostic devices, reducing noise and emissions compared to diesel generators. It is projected to collect over 4,500 units of blood annually in the U.S. Pacific Northwest, setting a new standard for green medical logistics (American Red Cross, 2024). Collectively, these examples highlight how solar power is being used not just to support Red Cross logistics hubs but also as a strategic enabler for resilient, low-carbon humanitarian service delivery in the field (Nordin et al., 2021).

5.3 WFP's Use of Blockchain for Digital Asset Management

The World Food Programme (WFP) has pioneered the use of blockchain in humanitarian logistics, developing scalable solutions for cash transfers, aid coordination, and supply chain traceability. Its "Building Blocks" system, launched in 2017, allows for real-time transaction tracking on a private Ethereum-based blockchain. Initially tested in Pakistan and later expanded to refugee operations in Jordan, Lebanon, Bangladesh, and Ukraine, the system facilitates biometric-verified transactions without storing personal data on-chain, safeguarding privacy while enhancing transparency (WFP Innovation Hub, 2023). In Jordan's Azraq camp, Building Blocks enabled food and cash aid management for over 100,000 Syrian refugees, with UN Women and WFP coordinating across a single digital ledger. This avoided duplication and cut banking fees, saving approximately $2.4 million. By 2024, the platform had processed over $500 million in aid transactions, serving more than a million beneficiaries monthly and streamlining inter-agency operations (WFP Innovation Hub, 2024). WFP has also piloted blockchain in physical supply chains. The "Blocks for Transport" initiative digitized transport documents for shipments between Djibouti and Ethiopia, reducing transit times and providing a tamper-proof audit trail for customs, port authorities, and logisticians (Applied Blockchain, 2023). In parallel, the "Decapolis" platform, launched in Jordan in 2020, allowed smallholder farmers to record the lifecycle of agricultural produce on blockchain, improving market access by verifying food safety and sustainability compliance (WFP Innovation Hub, 2022). These blockchain systems exemplify advanced traceability and auditability in digital humanitarian logistics, from aid disbursement to food quality certification. As Goel et al. (2024) emphasize, such innovations enable secure and coordinated data sharing across multiple actors, boosting operational efficiency and reducing resource duplication. WFP's case demonstrates how blockchain technologies, when properly contextualized, can transform both the speed and integrity of global relief logistics.

6. STRATEGIC RECOMMENDATIONS

6.1 Design Principles for Green Digital Logistics in Emergency Planning

Effective design of green digital logistics systems in post-disaster settings requires alignment between technological function and environmental responsibility. One critical principle is the integration of end-of-life planning from the outset, as illustrated by UNICEF's digital health kits in Zimbabwe. In this initiative, digital thermometers, smartphones, and glucose monitors were not only deployed for real-time health reporting but were also subject to e-waste lifecycle assessments and planned recovery (UNICEF, 2023; UNEMG, 2021). Design strategies included using durable, repairable equipment, and working with local repair technicians to extend device longevity—measures that mitigate environmental degradation and reduce procurement costs during protracted recovery efforts. Another design principle involves the use of renewable-powered logistics infrastructure, such as the Red Cross solar microgrids installed at emergency shelters in Puerto Rico following Hurricane Maria. These solar systems ensured continuous operation of lights, water pumps, and communication tools during outages, reducing reliance on fossil fuel generators (American Red Cross, 2019; ICRC, 2022). This experience highlights the necessity of embedding off-grid resilience and low-emission energy sources directly into the architecture of disaster response systems. Lastly, traceability-enabling technologies, such as WFP's Building Blocks blockchain platform, must be designed not only for real-time logistics tracking but also for data privacy and interoperability. In Jordan and Ukraine, WFP's blockchain infrastructure successfully tracked cash transfers, verified identities through iris scans, and avoided duplication of aid delivery, all while using anonymized IDs to protect beneficiary data (WFP Innovation Hub, 2024). These cases demonstrate how system design must balance operational visibility with ethical considerations.

6.2 Policy Proposals for Integrating Sustainability into Donor-Funded Tech Deployment

To mainstream environmental sustainability within donor-funded humanitarian technology programs, clear procurement and asset recovery policies must be established. As seen in UNICEF's approach, incorporating e-waste mitigation and circular procurement criteria into vendor contracts—such as device take-back commitments and recyclability standards—can ensure that environmental responsibilities are shared among suppliers, donors, and implementing agencies (UNEMG, 2021). Donors should also mandate carbon accounting frameworks and digital sustainability KPIs in funded programs. These could include metrics such as greenhouse gas emissions avoided (e.g., from replacing diesel generators with solar-powered cold chains), volume of e-waste recovered, or percentage of logistics devices refurbished rather than replaced. For instance, the solar-powered bloodmobile by the American Red Cross provides a replicable model where clean energy integration into mobile operations can be tracked for emissions savings (American Red Cross, 2024). Moreover, funding eligibility criteria could be revised to prioritize technologies and partners demonstrating sustainable design and reuse potential. WFP's blockchain traceability platforms, which have demonstrably reduced financial waste and increased aid equity in Lebanon and Ukraine, exemplify how digital innovations with high accountability and scalability can meet both operational and sustainability goals (WFP Innovation Hub, 2023).

To operationalize the strategic priorities discussed, Table 2 summarizes actionable policy and design principles for embedding green logistics into digital humanitarian operations. These principles align with international sustainability goals and reflect both field practices and institutional insights reviewed in this chapter.

Table 2. Policy and Design Principles for Green Digital Humanitarian Logistics

Principle	Description	Example in Practice
Durability and Repairability	Devices should be repairable and built to last	UNICEF sourcing durable kits with take-back plans
Renewable Energy Integration	Use of solar/battery hybrid systems instead of diesel	Red Cross solar-powered bloodmobiles
Circular Supply Chain Design	Plan for end-of-life recovery and reuse of digital assets	WFP's blockchain-tracked cash vouchers
Local Technician Training	Upskill local actors to maintain and refurbish devices	UNICEF training for village health workers
Data-Energy Tradeoff Optimization	Reduce data server loads to save energy and minimize emissions	WFP using off-chain anonymized IDs

Source: Pradhananga & ElZomor (2023); Arnetoli & Bologna (2022); UNEMG (2023)

6.3 Cross-Sector Partnerships and Public–Private Collaboration Models

Addressing the dual challenge of disaster resilience and environmental sustainability requires strategic cross-sector partnerships. One successful model is the collaboration between WFP and Applied Blockchain to streamline transport documentation via shared digital ledgers in East Africa. This partnership improved border clearance efficiency for relief shipments and reduced physical paperwork use—contributing to both faster aid delivery and lower environmental burden (Applied Blockchain, 2023). In the private sector, vehicle manufacturers partnered with the American Red Cross to retrofit bloodmobiles with solar panels, allowing medical-grade operations without fuel use. This cooperation shows how green innovation in vehicle design can be co-developed through humanitarian–industry linkages (American Red Cross, 2024). At the grassroots level, UNICEF's collaboration with local health ministries and technicians in Zimbabwe ensured that digital health tools were not only distributed but also locally supported, maintained, and sustainably decommissioned. This embedded approach fostered both technical capacity and environmental awareness within the affected communities (UNICEF, 2023).To scale such outcomes, it is recommended that agencies establish multi-stakeholder platforms for green logistics innovation—bringing together donors, government agencies, logistics firms, technology developers, and local actors. These platforms can help identify shared sustainability benchmarks, coordinate supply chain traceability, and pool investments in renewable-powered solutions that benefit all partners.

7. CONCLUSION

In an era where climate change and disaster frequency intersect with accelerating technological deployment, greening digital humanitarian logistics is not a luxury but an imperative. This chapter has illustrated how the integration of sustainable practices into digital logistics—ranging from UNICEF's life-cycle-conscious health kits to the Red Cross's solar-powered infrastructure and WFP's blockchain-led traceability—demonstrates the feasibility and necessity of aligning efficiency with environmental stewardship. These cases collectively reinforce the urgency of moving beyond traditional, carbon-intensive relief logistics toward systems that are resilient, renewable-powered, and digitally traceable. However, scaling such models requires embedding sustainability at the core of emergency planning and institutional strategy. Future research must focus on developing standardized circularity frameworks, quantifiable environmental metrics (such as digital carbon footprints), and robust methods for tracking the environmental return on digital logistics investments. In parallel, humanitarian organizations must rethink their operational paradigms by incorporating sustainable procurement criteria, fostering public–private collaborations, and supporting local innovation ecosystems for device repair, reuse, and solar integration. A systemic shift is needed—one that reimagines digital tools not as disposable interventions, but as part of a regenerative cycle that supports both human recovery and planetary health in post-disaster contexts.

REFERENCES

Abdelhadi, A., & Akkartal, E. (2024). Supply chain efficiency a structural analysis in Türkiye's retail sector. *Brazilian Journal of Operations & Production Management, 21*(3), 2150–2150. DOI: 10.14488/BJOPM.2150.2024

Aćimović, S., Mijušković, V. M., & Đurović, M. (2024). THE USAGE OF CHOSEN DIGITAL TOOLS IN THE PROCESS OF HUMANITARIAN LOGISTICS MANAGEMENT. *BUSINESS LOGISTICS IN MODERN MANAGEMENT*, 155.

Aghsami, A., Sharififar, S., Markazi Moghaddam, N., Hazrati, E., Jolai, F., & Yazdani, R. (2024). Strategies for humanitarian logistics and supply chain in organizational contexts: Pre-and post-disaster management perspectives. *Systems, 12*(6), 215. DOI: 10.3390/systems12060215

Akkartal, E., & Aras, G. Y. (2021). Sustainability in fleet management. *Journal of Advanced Research in Economics and Administrative Sciences, 2*(3), 13–39. DOI: 10.47631/jareas.v2i3.288

Alliance, N. G. M. N. (2021). Green Future Networks Network Equipment Eco-Design and End to End Service Footprint. *Version 1.0.*

American Red Cross. (2019). *Puerto Rico recovery report.* Retrieved from https://www.redcross.org/about-us/news-and-events/news/2019/puerto-rico-recovery.html

American Red Cross. (2024). *American Red Cross launches solar-powered bloodmobile in Pacific Northwest.* Retrieved from https://1059thebrew.iheart.com/featured/tanner/post/2024-04-10-american-red-cross-unveils-solar-bloodmobile/

Anjomshoae, A., Banomyong, R., Hossein Azadnia, A., Kunz, N., & Blome, C. (2025). Sustainable humanitarian supply chains: A systematic literature review and research propositions. *Production Planning and Control, 36*(3), 357–377.

Applied Blockchain. (2023). *WFP Blocks for Transport: Using blockchain to streamline humanitarian logistics.* Retrieved from https://appliedblockchain.com/case-studies/wfp-blocks-for-transport

Arnetoli, M. V., & Bologna, R. (2022, June). Design Scenarios for a Circular Vision of Post-disaster Temporary Settlements. In *International Conference on Technological Imagination in the Green and Digital Transition* (pp. 471-481). Cham: Springer International Publishing.

Aydoğan, B. E. D. İ. A., Özçelik, G. Ö. K. H. A. N., & Ünver, M. E. H. M. E. T. (2025). Developing Industry 4.0-based e-waste management: A decision-aided tool equipped with continuous function-valued intuitionistic fuzzy sets. *International Journal of Environmental Science and Technology*, *22*(8), 6595–6620. DOI: 10.1007/s13762-024-05977-y

Barykin, S. E., Borisoglebskaya, L. N., Provotorov, V. V., Kapustina, I. V., Sergeev, S. M., De La Poza Plaza, E., & Saychenko, L. (2021). Sustainability of management decisions in a digital logistics network. *Sustainability (Basel)*, *13*(16), 9289. DOI: 10.3390/su13169289

Bhattacharjee, J., De, A., Kamila, B., & Mandal, A. (2025). Recent scenario of e-waste recycling: Chemical engineering. *International Journal of Chemical Reactor Engineering*, *23*(6), 675–700. DOI: 10.1515/ijcre-2024-0058

Byers, B., Bompa, D., Jin, Q., De Wolf, C., & Bendiek-Laranjo, A. (2025). Circular Economy for Post-Hazard Infrastructure Restoration: Strategies for Resilience and Resource Efficiency. *Journal of Sustainability*, *1*(1). Advance online publication. DOI: 10.55845/jos-2025-117

Cao, C., Chou, M. C., Zhang, F., Leng, W., & He, Y. (2024). Leveraging digital twin to enhance humanitarian logistics operations. *Flexible Services and Manufacturing Journal*, •••, 1–33. DOI: 10.1007/s10696-024-09580-8

Cebir, Y., & Akkartal, E. (2024). Digital twin in logistics and supply chain management. In *Strategic Innovations for Dynamic Supply Chains* (pp. 170–192). IGI Global Scientific Publishing. DOI: 10.4018/979-8-3693-3575-8.ch008

Çetin, S., & Kirchherr, J. (2025). The Build Back Circular Framework: Circular Economy Strategies for Post-Disaster Reconstruction and Recovery. *Circular Economy and Sustainability*, •••, 1–38.

Chingono, T. T., & Mbohwa, C. (2023). Humanitarian Logistics in the Industry 4.0. In *Supply Networks in Developing Countries: Sustainable and Humanitarian Logistics in Growing Consumer Markets* (pp. 99-127). Emerald Publishing Limited.

Christhia, M. L., Timbayo, O. O., Wahidurrijal, A. A., & Putra, A. B. A. (2025). A Literature Review on AI and DSS for Resilient and Sustainable Humanitarian Logistics. *International Journal of Computer Science and Humanitarian AI*, *2*(1), 29–36. DOI: 10.21512/ijcshai.v2i1.13028

Čižiūnienė, K., Voronavičiūtė, G., Marinkovic, D., & Matijošius, J. (2025). Sustainable Human Resource Management in Emergencies: The Case of the Lithuanian Logistics Sector. *Sustainability (2071-1050)*, *17*(6).

Goel, A., Masurkar, S., & Pathade, G. R. (2024). An overview of digital transformation and environmental sustainability: Threats, opportunities, and solutions. *Sustainability (Basel), 16*(24), 11079. DOI: 10.3390/su162411079

Hayat, P. (2023). Integration of advanced technologies in urban waste management. In *Advancements in Urban environmental studies: Application of geospatial technology and artificial intelligence in Urban studies* (pp. 397–418). Springer International Publishing. DOI: 10.1007/978-3-031-21587-2_23

Hu, B., Wang, L., Chen, S., Cui, J., & Chen, L. (2021). An uplink throughput optimization scheme for UAV-enabled urban emergency communications. *IEEE Internet of Things Journal, 9*(6), 4291–4302. DOI: 10.1109/JIOT.2021.3103892

International Committee of the Red Cross (ICRC). (2022). *ICRC Bogotá delegation integrates solar energy into operations*. Retrieved from https://www.icrc.org/en/document/icrc-bogota-solar-energy

International Federation of Red Cross and Red Crescent Societies (IFRC). (2017). *Community engagement during Ebola response in West Africa*. Retrieved from https://communityengagementhub.org/resources/2017/10/10/ebola-case-study-liberia

Karuppiah, K., Sankaranarayanan, B., Ali, S. M., & Paul, S. K. (2021). Key challenges to sustainable humanitarian supply chains: Lessons from the COVID-19 pandemic. *Sustainability (Basel), 13*(11), 5850. DOI: 10.3390/su13115850

Khalid, R., Shah, Z., Naeem, M., Ali, A., Al-Fuqaha, A., & Ejaz, W. (2023). Computational efficiency maximization for UAV-assisted MEC networks with energy harvesting in disaster scenarios. *IEEE Internet of Things Journal, 11*(5), 9004–9018. DOI: 10.1109/JIOT.2023.3322001

Khan, A., Zhang, J., Ahmad, S., Memon, S., Qureshi, H. A., & Ishfaq, M. (2022). Dynamic positioning and energy-efficient path planning for disaster scenarios in 5G-assisted multi-UAV environments. *Electronics (Basel), 11*(14), 2197. DOI: 10.3390/electronics11142197

Khan, M., Khan, M., Ali, A., Khan, M. I., Ullah, I., & Iqbal, M. (2022). Digitalization for fast, fair, and safe humanitarian logistics. *Logistics (Basel), 6*(2), 31. DOI: 10.3390/logistics6020031

Koh, L. Y., & Yuen, K. F. (2022). Emerging competencies for logistics professionals in the digital era: A literature review. *Frontiers in Psychology, 13*, 965748. DOI: 10.3389/fpsyg.2022.965748 PMID: 36389597

Kurniawan, D. A. (2025). Enhancing Humanitarian Logistics Through Digital Innovation and Systemic Reform: A Narrative Review in Developing Countries. *Sinergi International Journal of Logistics*, *3*(1), 1–14. DOI: 10.61194/sijl.v3i1.735

Larson, P. D. (2021). Security, sustainability and supply chain collaboration in the humanitarian space. *Journal of Humanitarian Logistics and Supply Chain Management*, *11*(4), 609–622. DOI: 10.1108/JHLSCM-06-2021-0059

Liu, Z., Zhao, Y., Guo, C., & Xin, Z. (2024). Research on the impact of digital-real integration on logistics industrial transformation and upgrading under green economy. *Sustainability (Basel)*, *16*(14), 6173. DOI: 10.3390/su16146173

Maghsoudi, A., Harpring, R., Piotrowicz, W. D., & Kedziora, D. (2023). Digital technologies for cash and voucher assistance in disasters: A cross-case analysis of benefits and risks. *International Journal of Disaster Risk Reduction*, *96*, 103827. DOI: 10.1016/j.ijdrr.2023.103827

Matracia, M., Saeed, N., Kishk, M. A., & Alouini, M. S. (2022). Post-disaster communications: Enabling technologies, architectures, and open challenges. *IEEE Open Journal of the Communications Society*, *3*, 1177–1205. DOI: 10.1109/OJCOMS.2022.3192040

Mızrak, F., & Akkartal, E. (Eds.). (2024). *Effective Logistics for Sustainable Development Goals*. IGI Global. DOI: 10.4018/979-8-3693-7071-1

Moazzeni, S., & Sgarbossa, F. (2025). Collaborative logistics and digital technologies in rural contexts: a systematic review and a decision aid model for logistics decision-makers.

Nawazish, M., Nandakumar, M. K., & Mateen, A. (2024). Are humanitarian supply chains sustainable? A systematic review and future research themes. *Benchmarking*, *31*(8), 2565–2601. DOI: 10.1108/BIJ-01-2023-0036

Nikseresht, A., Golmohammadi, D., & Zandieh, M. (2024). Sustainable green logistics and remanufacturing: A bibliometric analysis and future research directions. *International Journal of Logistics Management*, *35*(3), 755–803. DOI: 10.1108/IJLM-03-2023-0085

Nordin, N. A., Ansari, M. N. M., Nomanbhay, S. M., Hamid, N. A., Tan, N. M., Yahya, Z., & Abdullah, I. (2021). Integrating photovoltaic (PV) solar cells and supercapacitors for sustainable energy devices: A review. *Energies*, *14*(21), 7211. DOI: 10.3390/en14217211

Nordin, N. A., Ansari, M. N. M., Nomanbhay, S. M., Hamid, N. A., Tan, N. M., Yahya, Z., & Abdullah, I. (2021). Integrating photovoltaic (PV) solar cells and supercapacitors for sustainable energy devices: A review. *Energies, 14*(21), 7211. DOI: 10.3390/en14217211

Özkanlısoy, Ö., & Akkartal, E. (2021). Digital transformation in supply chains: Current applications, contributions and challenges. *Business & Management Studies: An International Journal, 9*(1), 32–55.

Pandey, S., & Sharma, S. K. (2024, December). Green technologies for sustainable development: Innovations, modalities and possibilities. In. AIP Conference Proceedings: Vol. 3217. *No. 1* (p. 040021). AIP Publishing LLC. DOI: 10.1063/5.0234463

Pradhan, S. C., Kumar, M., Yadav, S., Hirwani, B., & Verma, A. (2024). Enhancing Efficiency, Reducing Environmental Impact, and Ensuring Life Cycle Sustainability in Sustainable Solar Energy through Nano-Material Innovations. *Educational Administration: Theory and Practice, 30*(11), 399–405.

Pradhananga, P., & ElZomor, M. (2023). Revamping sustainability efforts post-disaster by adopting circular economy resilience practices. *Sustainability (Basel), 15*(22), 15870. DOI: 10.3390/su152215870

Qu, C., Sorbelli, F. B., Singh, R., Calyam, P., & Das, S. K. (2023). Environmentally-aware and energy-efficient multi-drone coordination and networking for disaster response. *IEEE Transactions on Network and Service Management, 20*(2), 1093–1109. DOI: 10.1109/TNSM.2023.3243543

Ramakrishna, S., & Ramasubramanian, B. (2024). Circular Practices in E-waste Management and Transportation. In *Handbook of Materials Circular Economy* (pp. 131–165). Springer Nature Singapore. DOI: 10.1007/978-981-97-0589-4_5

Ramasubramanian, B., Sundarrajan, S., Rao, R. P., Reddy, M. V., Chellappan, V., & Ramakrishna, S. (2022). Novel low-carbon energy solutions for powering emerging wearables, smart textiles, and medical devices. *Energy & Environmental Science, 15*(12), 4928–4981. DOI: 10.1039/D2EE02695C

Saif, A., Dimyati, K., Noordin, K. A., G C, D., Shah, N. S. M., Abdullah, Q., & Mohamad, M. (2021). An efficient energy harvesting and optimal clustering technique for sustainable postdisaster emergency communication systems. *IEEE Access : Practical Innovations, Open Solutions, 9*, 78188–78202. DOI: 10.1109/ACCESS.2021.3083640

Shakibaei, H., Moosavi, S. A., Aghsami, A., & Rabbani, M. (2024). Designing a sustainable-resilient humanitarian supply chain for post-disaster relief process, an earthquake case study in Haiti. *Journal of Humanitarian Logistics and Supply Chain Management*, (ahead-of-print).

Treiblmaier, H., & Rejeb, A. (2023). Exploring blockchain for disaster prevention and relief: A comprehensive framework based on industry case studies. *Journal of Business Logistics*, *44*(4), 550–582. DOI: 10.1111/jbl.12345

UNICEF. (2023). *Digital health innovation in Zimbabwe: Empowering frontline workers with data tools*. Retrieved from https://www.unicefusa.org/stories/digital-health-kit-transforming-care-zimbabwe

United Nations Environment Management Group (UNEMG). (2021). *United Nations e-waste management policy framework: Towards a circular economy*. Retrieved from https://unemg.org/un-e-waste-framework

Üstün, K., & Akkartal, E. (2024). The Role of Logistics in Decent Work and Economic Growth. In *Effective Logistics for Sustainable Development Goals* (pp. 48–78). IGI Global. DOI: 10.4018/979-8-3693-7071-1.ch003

Verma, S. K., Gupta, S., Sharma, A., & Rajput, S. (Eds.). (2025). *Advanced Energy Materials: Natural Polymers, Renewable Energy, Sustainable Development*. Walter de Gruyter GmbH & Co KG. DOI: 10.1515/9783111289076

World Food Programme (WFP) Innovation Hub. (2022). *Decapolis: Blockchain-based food traceability in Jordan*. Retrieved from https://innovation.wfp.org/project/decapolis

World Food Programme (WFP) Innovation Hub. (2023). *Building Blocks: A blockchain solution for humanitarian aid*. Retrieved from https://innovation.wfp.org/project/building-blocks

World Food Programme (WFP) Innovation Hub. (2024). *Blockchain solutions for cash assistance and supply chain traceability*. Retrieved from https://innovation.wfp.org/stories/how-wfp-uses-blockchain-to-transform-aid

Zekhnini, K., Cherrafi, A., Bouhaddou, I., Chaouni Benabdellah, A., & Bag, S. (2022). A model integrating lean and green practices for viable, sustainable, and digital supply chain performance. *International Journal of Production Research*, *60*(21), 6529–6555. DOI: 10.1080/00207543.2021.1994164

Chapter 8
Sustainable and Eco-Friendly Solutions in Humanitarian Logistics

Eda Selen çebi
https://orcid.org/0009-0002-7261-2455
Yeditepe University, Istanbul, Turkey

ABSTRACT

This chapter examines how circular economy (CE) principles, renewable energy, green supply chain management (GSCM), and supportive governance frameworks can be used to integrate sustainability into humanitarian logistics. It draws attention to the transition from conventional, reactive logistics to eco-friendly strategies that lower carbon emissions, cut waste, and improve operational resilience. Modular infrastructure, solar-powered microgrids, material reuse, and environmentally responsible procurement are important tactics. In order to overcome implementation obstacles, the chapter also highlights the significance of cross-sector collaboration, policy alignment, and institutional learning. It comes to the conclusion that, in a world that is changing, ethical, successful crisis response depends on sustainable humanitarian logistics, which is both feasible and necessary.

1. INTRODUCTION

Due to the increasing frequency and severity of humanitarian crises around the world as a result of conflict, climate change, and sociopolitical instability, humanitarian groups are under increasing pressure to provide relief in a sustainable manner in addition to efficiently and quickly. Humanitarian logistics has always prioritized responsiveness to crises, cost-effectiveness, and speed. But these activities' increasing

DOI: 10.4018/979-8-3373-3643-5.ch008

environmental impact—from resource exploitation to waste production and carbon emissions—has made sustainability an unavoidable concern (Jilani, Ali, & Khan, 2018; Boostani, Jolai, & Bozorgi-Amiri, 2021).

The idea of Green Supply Chain Management (GSCM) has become more well-known in the humanitarian field as a result of these difficulties. GSCM entails incorporating environmental factors into the supply chain at every level, including waste management, distribution, storage, transportation, and procurement (Seifert, Kunz, & Gold, 2023). The application of green logistics techniques is both required and difficult in humanitarian contexts, as activities frequently occur in vulnerable areas with inadequate infrastructure. For instance, employing renewable energy technologies, procuring from nearby vendors, and using biodegradable materials can all greatly lessen the environmental effect of operations while simultaneously boosting local resilience (Mangla & Luthra, 2022; Karl & Scholz Karl, 2022).

Sustainable techniques are still not widely used in humanitarian logistics, despite these benefits. Their widespread adoption is hampered by a number of obstacles, including as high upfront expenditures, unpredictable operations, and insufficient policy frameworks (Zarei, Carrasco-Gallego, & Ronchi, 2019). Furthermore, humanitarian operations frequently take place in areas devoid of essential infrastructure, including waste disposal systems, potable water, or electricity—conditions that make the implementation of green technology more challenging (Remida, 2015). Additionally, there is a significant discrepancy between the strategic implementation of sustainability policies and their implementation in field operations (Lid & Petermann, 2023).

However, the industry is moving more and more in the direction of sustainability thanks to advancements in digital technologies, renewable energy, and circular economy strategies. The possibility of technologies like big data analytics, AI-based logistics optimization, and solar-powered cold chains to enhance operational effectiveness and environmental performance is being investigated (Saari, 2023; Khan et al., 2022; Allahham et al., 2023). Simultaneously, the incorporation of circular economy concepts—such as modular infrastructure, recycling, and repair—offers encouraging paths toward waste reduction and resource optimization in crisis situations (Bag, Gupta, & Wood, 2022; Seifert et al., 2023).

Importantly, multi-stakeholder cooperation and policy frameworks are becoming important facilitators of sustainable humanitarian logistics. To share resources, expertise, and technology, collaborative governance models involving business sector actors, NGOs, governments, and local communities are crucial (Pascucci, 2021; Kashav & Garg, 2024). How humanitarian organizations link their operations with global sustainability targets is also being influenced by international frameworks like the UN Sustainable Development Goals (SDGs) and the Paris Agreement (Li et al., 2019; Tatham & Christopher, 2018).

The integration of GSCM principles, the use of sustainable technologies and renewable energy, the adoption of circular economy practices, and the function of governance and policy frameworks are the four main facets that this chapter examines in order to examine the changing field of sustainable humanitarian logistics. It offers a thorough analysis of how sustainability may be included into humanitarian supply chains, converting them into systems that are not only quick and efficient but also socially and environmentally responsible by utilizing current research and field-based insights.

2. INTEGRATION OF GREEN SUPPLY CHAIN MANAGEMENT IN HUMANITARIAN OPERATIONS

The role of supply chain management and logistics in relief efforts has grown increasingly important and complex as natural catastrophes, and climate change cause humanitarian crises to occur more frequently and with greater intensity. Humanitarian supply chains have historically placed a high priority on effectiveness, cost containment, and quick reaction to urgent demands. Nonetheless, there is a rising need to incorporate sustainability concepts into these activities as the world society grows more conscious of environmental deterioration. A key idea in converting humanitarian logistics into a robust and ecologically conscious system is green supply chain management, or GSCM (Jilani, Ali, & Khan, 2018).

Environmental supply chain management, which includes product design, material sourcing and selection, manufacturing procedures, final product distribution to customers, and end-of-life management, is known as GSCM (Seifert, Kunz, & Gold, 2023). This entails implementing ecologically friendly procedures in the framework of humanitarian operations while preserving the flexibility and quickness needed for emergency assistance. GSCM offers humanitarian actors a framework to reduce environmental effect across all supply chain activities without sacrificing service delivery to vulnerable communities, as stressed by Seifert et al. (2023).

Sustainable procurement is one of the cornerstones of GSCM. Decisions about procurement in humanitarian contexts have a significant impact on the environment and local economies. Humanitarian organizations are increasingly implementing policies that give ethical and ecologically derived goods top priority. Waste and pollution can be decreased, for example, by investing in recycled products, biodegradable packaging, and low-emission machinery. Additionally, purchasing from regional vendors promotes economic recovery in areas hit by disasters while reducing transportation-related emissions (Mangla & Luthra, 2022). This strategy is in line with the circular economy concept, which minimizes waste and reuses resources in an effort to lessen the environmental impact (Bag, Gupta, & Wood, 2022).

Additionally, there has been a notable increase in the use of green technologies in logistics operations, such as cold chains driven by renewable energy, energy-efficient storage systems, and solar-powered cars. The integration of green technologies into pre-disaster preparedness and post-disaster response, according to Boostani, Jolai, and Bozorgi-Amiri (2021), increases environmental sustainability while increasing logistical flexibility and autonomy in distant or infrastructure-deficient locations.

Despite these developments, there are still many obstacles to overcome when applying GSCM in humanitarian settings. The urgency of human need might sometimes take precedence over long-term sustainability objectives in the uncertain and high-pressure settings in which humanitarian logistics frequently operate. According to Zarei, Carrasco-Gallego, and Ronchi (2019), many relief groups struggle internally with the conflict between sustainable planning and quick reaction. Additionally, green solutions like electric automobiles or renewable energy grids are frequently not supported by the infrastructure in conflict or disaster-affected areas (Remida, 2015). Implementing and scaling sustainable methods is challenging due to these restrictions, which are further compounded by a lack of technical skills and financial constraints.

Progress is also hampered by institutional and policy-related issues in addition to inadequacies in environmental infrastructure. The scattered implementation of GSCM is a result of several factors, including a lack of defined sustainability measures, a lack of funding for green initiatives, and a lack of cooperation between government agencies and humanitarian actors. According to Lid and Petermann (2023), sustainability continues to be a secondary goal in many humanitarian efforts in the absence of unified frameworks and governmental mandates.

However, the advantages of incorporating GSCM are starting to become more obvious. Blockchain, big data analytics, and artificial intelligence (AI) are examples of emerging technologies that provide effective instruments to improve sustainability. Blockchain, for instance, can make procurement records transparent and impenetrable, guaranteeing supply chain accountability and traceability (Khan et al., 2022). By increasing the precision of demand forecasts and delivery scheduling, AI-driven forecasting models can streamline inventory management and cut waste. Additionally, by enabling real-time carbon emission monitoring, these technologies can assist enterprises in meeting environmental regulations and goals.

In humanitarian logistics, private sector cooperation has also been a major force behind GSCM. Humanitarian groups can gain access to cutting-edge technologies, eco-friendly supplies, and operational know-how that would not otherwise be possible through public-private collaborations. According to Pascucci (2021), the introduction of resource optimization strategies and commercial best practices by private organizations in refugee camps, for example, has resulted in more sustainable logistical operations. To guarantee that sustainability pledges and humanitarian ideals are not jeopardized in the name of efficiency or financial gain, such partnerships must be properly overseen.

Many humanitarian actors are now actively coordinating their logistical operations with frameworks like the Sustainable Development Goals (SDGs) of the United Nations in order to support global sustainability initiatives. SDGs like SDG 12 (responsible consumption and production) and SDG 13 (climate action) give relief organizations a strategic and moral obligation to reduce environmental damage while increasing the effectiveness of aid. According to Banomyong, Varadejsatitwong, and Oloruntoba (2019), humanitarian actors can make a significant contribution to long-term development and environmental conservation goals by incorporating GSCM into the SDG framework.

GSCM is also strongly tied to the localization of humanitarian supply chains, which is a strategy that encourages the participation and empowerment of local stakeholders in logistics planning and execution. Community-based waste management initiatives, local workforce training, and local sourcing all lessen environmental impacts while promoting resilience and self-sufficiency in places hit by crises (Li et al., 2019). In addition to upholding the GSCM tenets, localization increases the acceptability and relevance of humanitarian assistance.

In conclusion, even if there are still many obstacles in the way of fully implementing GSCM in humanitarian logistics, such as organizational inertia, financial limits, and infrastructure limitations, the road to sustainability is gradually gathering momentum. A solid basis for sustainable change is created by the combination of public-private cooperation, technical innovation, and conformity to international policy frameworks such as the SDGs. Stakeholder capacity building, ongoing investment in green technologies, and the institutionalization of sustainability concepts into humanitarian governance systems are crucial for removing the remaining obstacles. In a world dealing with more complicated and climate-related crises, greener humanitarian supply chains not only protect the environment but also boost the effectiveness, legitimacy, and resilience of humanitarian aid delivery.

3. RENEWABLE ENERGY AND SUSTAINABLE TECHNOLOGIES IN FIELD LOGISTICS

The shift to operations that are both resilient and ecologically conscious, the integration of sustainable technologies and renewable energy sources into humanitarian field logistics has become increasingly vital. The need for dependable, efficient, and environmentally friendly energy solutions in off-grid and high-risk contexts is greater than ever, especially as natural disasters, conflicts, and climate change continue to intensify humanitarian crises. This aligns with the broader global push toward decarbonization and green transformation, as emphasized by Mızrak, Polat, and Tasar (2024), who stress the strategic significance of renewable integration in large-scale operational frameworks such as airports.

Historically, humanitarian operations have relied heavily on fossil fuels, particularly diesel, to power field shelters, mobile medical units, lighting systems, and communication equipment. Diesel generators, while offering rapid deployment and high power density, pose severe logistical and security challenges due to fuel transport in unstable regions, and contribute significantly to noise pollution and greenhouse gas emissions (Remida, 2015; Saari, 2023). These issues exacerbate operational costs and increase vulnerability in disaster or conflict-prone areas while worsening environmental impacts (Mızrak, 2022).

In response, humanitarian organizations are increasingly embracing renewable energy technologies to fulfill dual objectives: minimizing environmental impact and enhancing operational efficiency. Saari (2023) underscores the transformative potential of solar-powered systems within medical cold chains—an essential element of humanitarian aid. Solar refrigeration units ensure reliable temperature control for vaccines and medications, safeguarding their efficacy without the high emissions or logistical complications of diesel systems. Stability and reliability in energy supply directly correlate with improved public health outcomes in remote or crisis-affected regions, where energy availability is often a matter of survival.

Solar photovoltaic (PV) systems, often complemented by energy storage batteries, are among the most prevalent renewable solutions in field logistics. These systems can be scaled to power everything from large field hospitals to small medical tents, depending on operational requirements. Hybrid microgrids incorporating solar, wind, and backup diesel generators have demonstrated significant promise in more complex settings, offering redundancy and continuous power supply during periods of low solar insolation or high demand (Seifert, Kunz, & Gold, 2023; Mızrak, 2023).

Renewable microgrids are particularly advantageous in mobile humanitarian setups and refugee camps due to their scalability and adaptability. Seifert et al. (2023) highlight successful implementations in refugee camps where energy access fosters safety through lighting, and supports economic activity, education, and communication. Such sustainable infrastructure strengthens the long-term resilience and dignity of displaced communities, as discussed by Üstün and Akkartal (2024), who emphasize the critical intersection between logistics, decent work, and economic growth.

Furthermore, modular and mobile energy systems have emerged as vital innovations. Remida (2015) describes plug-and-play renewable systems that can be quickly deployed in dynamic and unpredictable environments, such as conflict zones where infrastructure is severely damaged or nonexistent. Their ease of installation and transport reduces ecological footprints and eliminates the logistical burden of fuel convoys, empowering rapid humanitarian response (Mızrak, 2024).

Beyond electricity, renewable energy is transforming water and sanitation services in humanitarian logistics. Traditional water supply methods often rely on diesel-powered pumps and single-use plastics, which exacerbate environmental burdens. Innovations such as solar-powered purification systems, gravity-fed water networks, and UV sterilization offer decentralized, clean water alternatives, reducing fuel use, plastic waste, and reliance on bottled water (Karl & Scholz Karl, 2022; Danisman & Akkartal, 2023). These approaches align with circular economy principles by integrating resource reuse and minimizing waste, as highlighted in Mızrak (2022).

Another promising technology is the use of biogas digesters for cooking and waste management. By converting organic and human waste into clean-burning gas, these systems mitigate indoor air pollution, decrease deforestation by reducing wood fuel dependence, and manage sanitation challenges in densely populated humanitarian contexts. They contribute to both environmental preservation and public health, reflecting the kind of innovative, resource-conscious logistics models envisioned by Akkartal, Akkartal, and Yıldırım (2019).

Despite clear benefits, the adoption of sustainable technologies and renewable energy faces significant challenges. High upfront costs remain a major barrier, as humanitarian organizations often operate under financial constraints that prioritize immediate emergency needs over long-term sustainability investments (Zarei, Carrasco-Gallego, & Ronchi, 2019; Mızrak, 2023). Short-term funding cycles can discourage strategic investments in systems that ultimately lower lifecycle costs and increase resilience (Özkanlısoy & Akkartal, 2022).

Technical limitations further impede widespread adoption. There is frequently a shortage of skilled personnel to install, maintain, and repair renewable systems, leading to potential disruptions in essential services. Khan et al. (2022) highlight the critical role of digital solutions—including artificial intelligence, IoT sensors, and predictive maintenance platforms—in addressing these gaps by enabling real-time monitoring, fault detection, and energy optimization. Such technologies enhance system intelligence and reliability while reducing dependence on human expertise (Allahham et al., 2023).

In addition, aligning humanitarian logistics with global policy frameworks such as the UN Sustainable Development Goals (SDGs) has accelerated green technology deployment. Goals 7 (Affordable and Clean Energy), 12 (Responsible Consumption and Production), and 13 (Climate Action) are especially relevant. Partnerships with academic institutions and private sector actors have been instrumental in developing and scaling renewable solutions through knowledge transfer, technical innovation, and co-financing mechanisms (Pascucci, 2021; Khan et al., 2022).

Emerging policy frameworks and evolving donor requirements increasingly mandate environmental impact assessments and sustainability plans within grant proposals. This trend represents a shift towards more responsible and forward-looking humanitarian operations. The integration of renewable and sustainable technologies thus becomes not only an operational advantage but also a strategic imperative for organizations seeking continued support and legitimacy in the global humanitarian landscape (Waqas, Khan, & Al-Amin, 2023).

In summary, renewable energy and sustainable technologies are revolutionizing field logistics in the humanitarian sector. While financial, institutional, and technical barriers persist, the operational and environmental benefits of these solutions are too substantial to ignore. Cleaner, more resilient, and more cost-effective alternatives to traditional fossil-fuel-based approaches enhance mission efficacy and align humanitarian efforts with global sustainability agendas. Realizing the full potential of green logistics will require collective action focused on governance, innovation, capacity building, and cross-sector collaboration, ultimately transforming humanitarian assistance into a more sustainable and ethically responsible endeavor.

4. WASTE MINIMIZATION AND CIRCULAR ECONOMY APPROACHES

In disaster-affected and resource-constrained environments, waste accumulation—from food scraps and human waste to packaging materials, medical disposables, and expired medications—can seriously strain the local environment and infrastructure. This is why waste management in humanitarian logistics has become a crucial sustainability challenge. The need to provide life-saving assistance and the obligation to reduce their environmental impact must be balanced by humanitarian groups. The hazards of ecological deterioration, public health emergencies, and wasteful resource use increase as operations scale up during emergencies (Karl & Scholz Karl, 2022). The incorporation of circular economy (CE) ideas and waste minimization measures has become more prominent in humanitarian logistics discourse as a means of addressing these issues.

A change from the conventional linear "take-make-dispose" manufacturing paradigm to one that emphasizes resource reduction, reuse, recycling, and repurposing is encouraged by the circular economy model. This strategy fits very nicely with the principles and limitations of humanitarian logistics, where flexibility, resilience, and efficiency are essential. By prolonging the life cycle of products and materials, CE practices in humanitarian supply chains can limit waste generation, cut operating costs, and lessen reliance on virgin materials (Bag, Gupta, & Wood, 2022). Reusable packaging for food and medical supplies, easily repairable modular equipment, and reverse logistics for gathering and repurposing abandoned goods are a few examples of how to support sustainable operations in the field (Zarei, Carrasco-Gallego, & Ronchi, 2019).

The use of compostable and biodegradable packaging in emergency food delivery is one real-world example. If infrastructure permits, such materials can be utilized in composting systems or safely decompose in the environment rather than producing plastic garbage. Deploying mobile recycling units or waste-sorting centers in sizable refugee settlements is another creative use that helps keep recyclables out of landfills and creates jobs locally (Seifert, Kunz, & Gold, 2023). Similarly, to avoid contamination and encourage responsible stewardship of pharmaceutical products, hazardous materials and expired medications can be safely processed through on-site incinerators or returned through reverse supply chains for appropriate disposal (Boostani, Jolai, & Bozorgi-Amiri, 2021).

Changes in inventory and procurement procedures are also necessary for waste reduction. Excess stock is frequently the result of overordering or ill-planned deliveries, and a large portion of it is wasted because it spoils or becomes obsolete. Improved inventory control systems, just-in-time delivery techniques, and demand forecasting tools can all help cut down on wasteful stock and waste production. Blockchain and artificial intelligence-powered digital platforms are intriguing instruments for enhancing supply chain visibility and monitoring the lifecycle of products from production to consumption and disposal (Khan et al., 2022). In addition to increasing operational effectiveness, these tools facilitate data-driven choices that put sustainability first.

There are challenges associated with the humanitarian sector's shift to circular and waste-minimizing logistics systems, nevertheless. The fundamental infrastructure needed to support CE methods, such as recycling facilities, composting units, and hazardous waste treatment centers, is often lacking in humanitarian contexts. Furthermore, because of their simplicity and lower short-term dangers, disposable, single-use products are frequently preferred due to the urgency of catastrophe response (Lid & Petermann, 2023). These facts call for a planned, incremental strategy in which CE concepts are integrated into long-term recovery and preparedness initiatives rather than being restricted to emergency reaction.

Moreover, facilitating circularity in humanitarian supply chains requires cross-sectoral cooperation. Bridge capacity gaps and promote the development of local circular ecosystems through collaborations with private waste management companies, recycling businesses, local governments, and technology suppliers. For example, local business owners can be hired to fix kitchen appliances or renovate used tents, promoting local livelihoods and waste reduction. These collaborations support community resilience and economic development in addition to environmental objectives (Mangla & Luthra, 2022).

In conclusion, there is a significant chance to improve the long-term efficacy of relief efforts and the environmental sustainability of humanitarian logistics by implementing waste minimization strategies and circular economy concepts. Humanitarian actors can create supply chains that are not only responsive but also regenerative by using proactive strategies backed by innovation, cooperation, and policy reform, even while operational and infrastructure issues still exist. Humanitarian activities are guaranteed to be in line with global sustainability goals and not unintentionally worsen the very problems they are intended to alleviate when circular techniques are incorporated into logistical planning, procurement, and implementation.

There are several ways that waste minimization techniques can be used in humanitarian logistics. Boostani, Jolai, and Bozorgi-Amiri (2021) point out a number of waste reduction strategies, such as local material sourcing, modular logistics, and effective packaging. Humanitarian organizations can significantly cut down on the waste produced by single-use packaging materials by using reusable containers and packaging solutions. Over time, this lessens environmental pollution in environments with limited resources and eases the strain on waste disposal systems. Additionally, in order to track and monitor the environmental impact of logistics operations supply chain transparency is a necessity.

By enabling more accurate inventory control through technologies like radio-frequency identification (RFID) and barcode tracking, product waste from overstocking, spoiling, or expiration is decreased. Humanitarian organizations can ensure that aid reaches those in need without needlessly accumulating unused or damaged goods by improving inventory management, which also helps them generate less waste.

5. MODELS OF THE CIRCULAR ECONOMY IN HUMANITARIAN LOGISTICS OPERATIONS

When it comes to field logistics, the circular economy concept holds great promise, especially when it comes to waste and physical asset management. Reusable and modular infrastructure in disaster relief settings is one context where this has been successfully applied. In order to drastically lessen the environmental impact of temporary housing solutions, Remida (2015) explores the idea of modular shelters and facilities that can be put together and taken apart for reuse in various settings and events.

Key elements of the circular economy include material recycling and reuse in addition to modular infrastructure. Seifert et al. (2023), for instance, describe how 3D printing is used in refugee camps to recycle plastic waste into useful materials like tools and building components. These developments lessen dependency on outside vendors for raw materials and support the development of regional economies centered on material recovery and waste processing. Humanitarian organizations not only solve the waste problem but also generate jobs and promote economic resilience by enabling local communities to participate in these processes. Repair and renewal is another important circular economy strategy. Donated items that are frequently thrown away after little use, such as cars, medical devices, and electronics, are frequently given to humanitarian organizations.

In disaster-prone areas, Karl & Scholz Karl (2022) support the opening of neighborhood repair shops, which could prolong the useful life of donated items and cut down on waste. In addition to offering technical training and a way to get involved with the community, these workshops help local populations develop their skill set and become more resilient in long term.

The concepts of the circular economy are also being used more and more in the fields of biodegradable materials and alternative waste processing techniques. The distribution of humanitarian aid produces large volumes of organic waste in many refugee camps and isolated disaster areas, which is usually burned or dumped in landfills. However, this process may release methane and particulate matter into the atmosphere, among other detrimental effects on the environment and human health.

The potential of biogas technologies in humanitarian operations is highlighted by Karl & Scholz Karl (2022), specifically in the transformation of organic waste into cooking fuel. Organizations can use biogas digesters to convert agricultural residues, human waste, and food scraps into methane gas for heating or cooking. This ease the need for conventional cooking fuels like firewood and tackles the problem of deforestation, which is prevalent in places where firewood is the main energy source.

Also, organic waste can be turned into useful fertilizer in disaster areas and refugee camps by using composting techniques. By improving soil quality and encouraging sustainable farming methods, this strategy not only keeps waste from piling up but also helps local agriculture. Organizations can cut waste, carbon footprints, and develop sustainable, locally based solutions that promote self-sufficiency by incorporating these circular systems into humanitarian operations.

There are major obstacles preventing the circular economy from being widely used in humanitarian logistics, despite the fact that it has obvious advantages in terms of waste reduction and sustainability promotion. According to Zarei, Carrasco-Gallego, and Ronchi (2019), a significant obstacle in many field settings is the absence of infrastructure. Recycling systems, for example, frequently call for specific tools and skilled workers, both of which may be hard to find or deploy in disaster-affected areas.

In addition, Pascucci (2021) points out that because organizations are frequently more concerned with short-term relief than long-term sustainability, the short-term focus of many humanitarian missions can impede the adoption of circular economy practices. Because of this urgency, decisions may be made that put speed ahead of environmental concerns, such as distributing aid in single-use packaging or throwing away items before determining whether they can be reused. Also, Lid and Petermann (2023) wants to highlight logistical and cultural obstacles that come with influencing perspectives of local communities and humanitarian workers. Although the advantages of recycling and waste reduction are becoming more widely acknowledged, changing long-standing customs that may be rooted in the way aid is provided takes time, leadership, and education.

6. GOVERNANCE, COLLABORATION, AND POLICY FRAMEWORKS FOR SUSTAINABILITY

Achieving sustainability in humanitarian logistics requires strong governance, teamwork, and well-structured policy frameworks. These components serve as the cornerstone for guaranteeing that humanitarian operations are not only successful and efficient in providing aid, but also socially inclusive, environmentally conscious, and financially sustainable. Natural disasters, pandemics, and other global crises are becoming more complex, necessitating coordinated efforts from a range of stakeholders, including governments, private companies, humanitarian organizations, and local communities. In order to promote sustainability in field logistics operations, this section examines the function of governance, cooperative mechanisms, and policy frameworks.

The structures, procedures, and decision-making tools that direct the operational execution, strategic direction, and accountability of humanitarian operations are collectively referred to as governance. To guarantee that sustainability objectives are given top priority and incorporated into daily logistics operations, effective governance is essential.

According to Pascucci (2021), in order to match the priorities of different humanitarian actors with sustainability goals, it is imperative that governance structures be clear. These players could be governments, private sector partners, non-governmental organizations (NGOs), and United Nations agencies. A clear governance framework can encourage resource sharing, lessen conflicting interests, and make it easier for various sectors to coordinate their efforts. In order to guarantee that social and environmental effects are taken into account when organizing logistics operations, governance frameworks should also include sustainability criteria in decision-making procedures.

According to Seifert, Kunz, and Gold (2023), governance mechanisms ought to promote transparency and accountability, especially when it comes to allocating aid and managing resources in areas affected by disasters or conflicts. When paired with audits and impartial assessments, transparent reporting systems can assist in locating inefficiencies and potential improvement areas. Effective governance can promote positive change and the adoption of socially and environmentally responsible practices by making sure that humanitarian organizations are held accountable for their sustainability practices.

In humanitarian logistics, cooperation is essential to attaining sustainability. Because the scope of contemporary humanitarian operations frequently surpasses the capabilities of any one sector or organization, cooperation amongst multiple stakeholders is crucial to optimizing impact. This cooperation takes place on several levels, including between local communities, private sector partners, local governments, and humanitarian organizations.

In order to overcome logistical obstacles and achieve sustainable results, Mangla and Luthra (2022) emphasize the significance of cross-sector collaboration. For example, the creation and implementation of renewable energy technologies or the installation of recycling and waste management systems in refugee camps are just two examples of how public-private partnerships (PPPs) have been crucial in offering creative answers to humanitarian logistics problems. These collaborations guarantee that humanitarian objectives and values are upheld while simultaneously utilizing the resources and experience of the private sector.

According to Karl and Scholz Karl (2022), the cooperation between local governments and humanitarian organizations in overseeing waste-to-energy projects in refugee camps is a noteworthy illustration of effective cooperation. These programs help the local community and the environment by turning waste materials into valuable resources like compost and energy. The localization of aid can also be facilitated by working with regional companies on procurement procedures, which guarantees that resources are sourced responsibly and that logistics operations do not jeopardize local economies.

Information sharing is another essential component of teamwork. By giving humanitarian organizations access to real-time data on infrastructure requirements, sustainability metrics, and aid delivery, shared data platforms can enhance decision-making and resource allocation. Organizations can minimize waste, prevent duplication of effort, and make sure that resources are allocated to the most critical areas with the aid of these collaborative data systems.

6.1 Frameworks for Sustainable Humanitarian Logistics Policy

In order to create policy frameworks that support the adoption of sustainable practices in humanitarian logistics, governments and international organizations are essential. Clear policies aid in the establishment of the regulatory framework, provide incentives for sustainability, and offer direction for tackling the problems of resource conservation, waste management, and the use of renewable energy.

Effective policy frameworks for sustainability in humanitarian logistics, according to Khan et al. (2022), should incorporate both local and global viewpoints. Globally, nations and organizations can align their logistics operations with climate goals by using frameworks provided by international agreements like the Paris Climate Agreement. Local resources, infrastructure, and environmental issues should all be taken into consideration when developing policies that are specific to the needs and circumstances of areas affected by disasters.

For example, Kashav and Garg (2024) talk about how policy frameworks can help integrate big data, blockchain, and artificial intelligence (AI), three emerging technologies in logistics, into sustainable humanitarian operations. By enhancing supply chain operations, cutting waste, and enhancing the transparency and traceability of aid distribution, policies that encourage the adoption of these technologies can facilitate more effective and ecologically friendly logistics.

Also, Tatham and Christopher (2018) stress the significance of sustainable procurement practices that promote the sourcing of products and materials that satisfy social and environmental sustainability standards. Humanitarian organizations can encourage the use of environmentally friendly products, support ethical labor practices, and lessen the carbon footprint of their supply chains by incorporating sustainability into their procurement procedures.

However, a major obstacle still exists in the implementation gap between policy creation and actual practices. Lid and Petermann (2023) note that although policies are frequently created at the national or international level, problems like a lack of funding, unstable political environments, and a lack of local capacity can make it difficult to implement them in field operations. Policies must be created with a clear emphasis on long-term sustainability, local adaptability, and practicality in order to close this gap.

6.2 Opportunities and Difficulties in Governance and Policy

There are still significant governance and policy obstacles to overcome despite significant advancements in the integration of sustainability into humanitarian logistics. A complex and frequently fragmented environment with several players with differing interests and capacities is the setting in which humanitarian supply chains function. These actors include affected communities, donor governments, host nations, private-sector partners, United Nations agencies, and local and international non-governmental organizations (NGOs). Zarei, Carrasco-Gallego, and Ronchi (2019) assert that the lack of a cohesive governance structure that unifies the aims and methods of operation of different stakeholders frequently leads to redundant work, mismatched sustainability objectives, and decreased overall effectiveness.

Implementing coordinated and environmentally friendly procedures is hampered by fragmentation across humanitarian operations' many levels. For example, whereas implementing organizations concentrate on logistical execution and host governments promote long-term development, donors may prioritize accountability and quick response when allocating funds. This discrepancy results in a fragmented governance environment where sustainability factors—like lowering carbon emissions or integrating renewable energy sources—are not consistently included into all decision-making processes (Karl & Scholz Karl, 2022). The short funding cycles that are common in humanitarian settings add to the complexity and deter long-term investments in green infrastructure and policymaking.

The absence of policy coherence between humanitarian logistics plans and more general national or regional development and environmental policies is a serious governance issue. Humanitarian logistics frequently operate in silos, separate from national policies on waste management, renewable energy development, and climate change adaptation, as noted by Li et al. (2019). This gap undercuts attempts to increase resilience in disaster-affected areas and makes it more difficult to match emergency relief logistics with sustainable development routes. Although national governments may have zero-waste plans or renewable energy targets, these are rarely included into humanitarian supply chain procedures, which results in inefficiencies and lost synergy potential.

Nonetheless, there are chances to strengthen the integration of sustainability into the governance of humanitarian logistics. The increasing understanding of the value of cooperative policymaking including both development and humanitarian actors is one such possibility. According to Khan et al. (2022), new technologies like artificial intelligence (AI) and big data can facilitate more integrated governance by facilitating real-time environmental effect monitoring, encouraging openness, and influencing decision-making at all levels. By bridging the knowledge gap between field practitioners and policy strategists, these technologies can help guarantee that sustainability remains a top concern throughout the humanitarian response cycle.

Additionally, cross-sector collaborations with the corporate sector offer yet another way to innovate policies and enhance governance. According to Pascucci (2021), business-humanitarian collaborations have progressively contributed financial models, supply chain efficiencies, and technical advancements that promote green logistics. Thus, scalable and sustainable logistics solutions can be sparked by efficient governance structures that promote public-private cooperation, particularly when supported by accountability and regulatory incentives.

Aligning humanitarian logistics with global sustainability goals is also made possible by international frameworks like the UN Sustainable Development Goals (SDGs), the Paris Agreement, and the Sendai Framework for Disaster Risk Reduction. Goals 13 (Climate Action) and 17 (Partnerships for the Goals), for instance, specifically address the necessity of concerted, climate-aware action. However, robust governance support, capacity-building initiatives, and customized policy interventions that take into account local realities are still necessary for the operationalization of such global goals at the local level (Tatham & Christopher, 2018).

Donor organizations have a significant impact on how governance and policy systems are shaped. As part of funding agreements, donors can require lifecycle evaluations, environmental reporting, and green buying practices. Although this could encourage behavior change, if it is not accompanied by sufficient support systems for implementing agencies, it also poses the risk of overbureaucratization (Banomyong, Varadejsatitwong, & Oloruntoba, 2019). Therefore, in order to effectively adapt sustainability principles to various humanitarian contexts, effective governance must strike a balance between responsibility and flexibility.

The discrepancy between policy creation and implementation on the ground is one of the more complex challenges in policy implementation. Environmental sustainability goals are frequently poorly translated into field-level processes due to a lack of capacity, awareness, or technical assistance, even when they are incorporated into high-level strategic papers. According to Boostani, Jolai, and Bozorgi-Amiri (2021), logistics personnel working in emergency situations might not be properly trained in sustainable practices or might not have access to the equipment and facilities required to put these policies into action.

In the end, attaining sustainability in humanitarian logistics is a governance and policy issue that necessitates systemic change rather than just being a technological challenge. To match operational actions with sustainability goals, governance structures including multi-stakeholder decision-making bodies and inter-agency coordination platforms must be strengthened. Furthermore, policy frameworks need to be both solid enough to guarantee accountability and long-term environmental stewardship and flexible enough to take into account local situations.

In conclusion, there are many governance and policy obstacles that prevent sustainability from being widely incorporated into humanitarian logistics, but there are also a lot of chances for significant advancement. The industry may progress toward more efficient and sustainable logistics operations by enhancing stakeholder cooperation, coordinating humanitarian logistics with national and international environmental goals, and cultivating creative partnerships. Therefore, closing the governance and policy gaps is essential for both increasing the effectiveness of humanitarian operations and making sure that they have a good impact on long-term environmental and social outcomes.

7. CONCLUSION

Given the growing environmental issues, the frequency of disasters, and the growing demands for responsible relief distribution, incorporating sustainability into humanitarian logistics is becoming increasingly important. In order to lessen environmental impact, improve operational efficiency, and create long-term resilience, this chapter has given a thorough overview of how sustainable principles—specifically through the use of Green Supply Chain Management (GSCM), renewable energy adoption, circular economy practices, and governance frameworks—can be applied successfully in humanitarian contexts.

In humanitarian operations, green supply chain management focuses on reducing environmental damage while preserving the agility and speed needed for disaster response. GSCM encourages a comprehensive strategy that balances logistical effectiveness with environmental awareness, from local sourcing and eco-friendly buying to the use of green technologies. However, there are major implementation obstacles because humanitarian emergencies are unpredictable and high-pressure situations. Short-term results are frequently given precedence over long-term sustainability by organizations due to a shortage of resources, inadequate infrastructure, and the urgency of help delivery. Innovations like solar-powered transport fleets, AI-driven logistics systems, and eco-packaging solutions are demonstrating that responsiveness and sustainability may coexist in spite of these limitations.

The chapter also looked at how field logistics are changing as a result of sustainable technology and renewable energy. In rural and off-grid areas, solar PV systems, modular hybrid microgrids, and solar refrigeration units improve energy security while reducing carbon emissions. In refugee camps and catastrophe areas, these technologies are especially helpful in maintaining medical supplies, guaranteeing access to clean water, and enhancing general living conditions. However, the switch to renewable energy necessitates a large financial outlay as well as technical know-how, which are sometimes limited in humanitarian contexts.

An further route to sustainability is provided by circular economy strategies, which encourage material reuse, repair, and recycling. Utilizing biodegradable materials, 3D printing recycled plastics, and establishing mobile repair units are examples of waste minimization techniques that help decrease environmental degradation and reliance on outside resources. By facilitating skill development and generating jobs, these programs help boost regional economies. Their widespread implementation is still hampered, though, by cultural hurdles, a lack of community involvement, and inadequate waste management infrastructure.

Collaboration, policy, and governance are the cornerstones of any system for sustainable logistics. While strong policy frameworks provide the direction and incentives required for expanding sustainable practices, effective governance guarantees accountability and strategic alignment. Leveraging knowledge, resources, and creativity requires multi-stakeholder cooperation between governments, commercial sector partners, humanitarian organizations, and impacted communities.

In summary, attaining sustainability in humanitarian logistics is a challenging yet crucial task. Although structural and operational obstacles still exist, they can be overcome. It is essential to pursue a systematic and dedicated approach that incorporates policy integration, technology innovation, capacity building, and stakeholder collaboration. Humanitarian organizations can enhance assistance efficacy and make a permanent and transformative contribution to global environmental and social well-being by adopting sustainability as a fundamental value rather than a secondary issue.

REFERENCES

Akkartal, G. R., Akkartal, E., & Yıldırım, C. (2019). The Management Of Innovation In Supply Chain. *Eurasian Business & Economics Journal, 17*(17), 43–52.

Allahham, M. A. H. M. O. U. D., Sharabati, A. A. A., Hatamlah, H. E. B. A., Ahmad, A. Y. B., Sabra, S., & Daoud, M. K. (2023). Big data analytics and AI for green supply chain integration and sustainability in hospitals. *WSEAS Transactions on Environment and Development, 19*, 1218–1230. DOI: 10.37394/232015.2023.19.111

Bag, S., Gupta, S., & Wood, L. (2022). Big data analytics in sustainable humanitarian supply chain: Barriers and their interactions. *Annals of Operations Research, 319*(1), 721–760. DOI: 10.1007/s10479-020-03790-7

Banomyong, R., Varadejsatitwong, P., & Oloruntoba, R. (2019). A systematic review of humanitarian operations, humanitarian logistics and humanitarian supply chain performance literature 2005 to 2016. *Annals of Operations Research, 283*(1-2), 71–86. DOI: 10.1007/s10479-017-2549-5

Boostani, A., Jolai, F., & Bozorgi-Amiri, A. (2021). Designing a sustainable humanitarian relief logistics model in pre-and postdisaster management. *International Journal of Sustainable Transportation, 15*(8), 604–620. DOI: 10.1080/15568318.2020.1773975

Danisman, M., & Akkartal, E. (2023). Defining a new business model for sustainable biomass production from forestry residues in Türkiye by using TRIZ. *International Journal of Energy Economics and Policy, 13*(3), 243–253. DOI: 10.32479/ijeep.13985

Jilani, A., Ali, Y., & Khan, M. W. (2018). Greening of humanitarian supply chain with focus on logistics. *International Journal of Business Performance and Supply Chain Modelling, 10*(1), 49–66. DOI: 10.1504/IJBPSCM.2018.093319

Karl, A. A., & Scholz Karl, J. (2022). Human rights for refugees: Enhancing sustainable humanitarian supply chain to guarantee a health environment in refugee settlements. *Journal of Humanitarian Logistics and Supply Chain Management, 12*(3), 382–403. DOI: 10.1108/JHLSCM-11-2020-0104

Kashav, V., & Garg, C. P. (2024). Fortifying humanitarian supply chains: evaluating sustainability enablers for strengthened resilience of humanitarian supply chains during calamities and pandemics. *Journal of Humanitarian Logistics and Supply Chain Management.*

Khan, M., Khan, M., Ali, A., Khan, M. I., Ullah, I., & Iqbal, M. (2022). Digitalization for fast, fair, and safe humanitarian logistics. *Logistics (Basel), 6*(2), 31. DOI: 10.3390/logistics6020031

Khan, M., Parvaiz, G. S., Ali, A., Jehangir, M., Hassan, N., & Bae, J. (2022). A model for understanding the mediating association of transparency between emerging technologies and humanitarian logistics sustainability. *Sustainability (Basel), 14*(11), 6917. DOI: 10.3390/su14116917

Li, C., Zhang, F., Cao, C., Liu, Y., & Qu, T. (2019). Organizational coordination in sustainable humanitarian supply chain: An evolutionary game approach. *Journal of Cleaner Production, 219*, 291–303. DOI: 10.1016/j.jclepro.2019.01.233

Lid, I., & Petermann, K. A. (2023). *Challenges to environmental sustainability in humanitarian logistics activities* (Master's thesis, Handelshøyskolen BI).

Mangla, S. K., & Luthra, S. (2022). When challenges need an evaluation: For operational excellence and sustainability orientation in humanitarian supply and logistics management. *Production Planning and Control, 33*(6-7), 539–557. DOI: 10.1080/09537287.2020.1834129

Mızrak, F. (2022). An Evaluation for the Use of Alternative Vehicle Technologies and Energy Resources in Logistic Sector with a Strategic Approach. In *Circular Economy and the Energy Market: Achieving Sustainable Economic Development Through Energy Policy* (pp. 159–171). Springer International Publishing. DOI: 10.1007/978-3-031-13146-2_13

Mızrak, F. (2023). Managing Risks and Crises in the Logistics Sector: A Comprehensive Analysis of Strategies and Prioritization Using AHP Method. *Meriç Uluslararası Sosyal ve Stratejik Araştırmalar Dergisi, 7*(Özel Sayı), 114-148.

Mızrak, F. (2024). Strategies for Sustainable Business Growth in Maritime Logistics. In *Trends, Challenges, and Practices in Contemporary Strategic Management* (pp. 108-125). IGI Global Scientific Publishing. DOI: 10.4018/979-8-3693-1155-4.ch006

Mizrak, F., Polat, L., & Tasar, S. A. (2024). Applying Entropy Weighting and 2-Tuple Linguistic T-Spherical Fuzzy MCDM: A Case Study of Developing a Strategic Sustainability Plan for Istanbul Airport. *Sustainability (Basel), 16*(24), 11104. DOI: 10.3390/su162411104

Özkanlısoy, Ö., & Akkartal, E. (2022). The effect of Suez Canal blockage on supply chains. *Dokuz Eylül Üniversitesi Denizcilik Fakültesi Dergisi, 14*(1), 51–79. DOI: 10.18613/deudfd.933816

Pascucci, E. (2021). More logistics, less aid: Humanitarian-business partnerships and sustainability in the refugee camp. *World Development, 142*, 105424. DOI: 10.1016/j.worlddev.2021.105424

Remida, A. (2015). A systemic approach to sustainable humanitarian logistics. *Humanitarian Logistics and Sustainability*, 11-29.

Saari, S. (2023). Enhancing the environmental sustainability of emergency humanitarian medical cold chains with renewable energy sources. *Journal of Humanitarian Logistics and Supply Chain Management, 13*(2), 157–172. DOI: 10.1108/JHLSCM-09-2021-0095

Seifert, L., Kunz, N., & Gold, S. (2023). Sustainable innovations for humanitarian operations in refugee camps. *International Journal of Operations & Production Management, 43*(10), 1554–1586. DOI: 10.1108/IJOPM-05-2022-0302

Tatham, P., & Christopher, M. (Eds.). (2018). *Humanitarian logistics: Meeting the challenge of preparing for and responding to disasters*. Kogan Page Publishers.

Üstün, K., & Akkartal, E. (2024). The Role of Logistics in Decent Work and Economic Growth. In *Effective Logistics for Sustainable Development Goals* (pp. 48–78). IGI Global. DOI: 10.4018/979-8-3693-7071-1.ch003

Waqas, M., Khan, S. A. R., & Al-Amin, A. Q. (Eds.). (2023). *Emerging Trends in Sustainable Supply Chain Management and Green Logistics*. DOI: 10.4018/978-1-6684-6663-6

Zarei, M. H., Carrasco-Gallego, R., & Ronchi, S. (2019). To greener pastures: An action research study on the environmental sustainability of humanitarian supply chains. *International Journal of Operations & Production Management, 39*(11), 1193–1225. DOI: 10.1108/IJOPM-12-2018-0703

Chapter 9
Understanding the Role of HVAC Systems in Türkiye's Disaster Relief and Emergency Aid Operations

Turhan Karakaya
https://orcid.org/0000-0003-0818-8522
Dogus University, Istanbul, Turkey

ABSTRACT

This chapter explores the strategic role of HVAC systems in humanitarian logistics, using Türkiye's disaster response as a central case—particularly in light of the 2023 Kahramanmaraş earthquakes. It emphasizes the often-overlooked importance of HVAC in ensuring thermal comfort, indoor air quality, and cold chain continuity across emergency shelters, mobile hospitals, and refugee settlements. By analyzing Türkiye's institutional coordination between AFAD and the Turkish Red Crescent, and incorporating lessons from the COVID-19 pandemic and ongoing Syrian refugee support, the chapter illustrates how HVAC systems enhance health, resilience, and operational efficiency. Türkiye's experience serves as a scalable model for disaster-prone regions, advocating for HVAC-inclusive planning, policy development, and innovation in humanitarian aid delivery. In doing so, the chapter calls for cross-sectoral collaboration, sustainable infrastructure investment, and greater integration of HVAC technologies in global emergency preparedness strategies.

DOI: 10.4018/979-8-3373-3643-5.ch009

1. INTRODUCTION

Türkiye occupies a geostrategic and geophysical position that renders it particularly vulnerable to natural disasters, especially earthquakes, climate-induced heatwaves, and cold spells. With over 20 significant earthquakes recorded in the past century and the devastating Kahramanmaraş-centered earthquakes of February 2023 leaving more than 50,000 dead and millions displaced, the country's disaster exposure continues to challenge its infrastructure, emergency planning, and humanitarian response systems (Zemitis et al., 2021; Chester et al., 2021). Beyond seismic activity, Türkiye has also experienced extreme climatic variability, further complicating the delivery of humanitarian aid and the design of climate-resilient shelter systems in both sudden-onset and protracted crises.

In such contexts, the built environment—including temporary shelters, modular field hospitals, mobile cold chain units, and storage hubs—plays a vital role in determining the speed, efficiency, and sustainability of humanitarian operations (Conzatti et al., 2022; Matracia et al., 2022). Infrastructure is no longer merely a passive recipient of relief materials but a dynamic determinant of operational success. Emergency shelters must ensure thermal comfort for vulnerable populations, field hospitals must guarantee air quality and infection control, and storage units must maintain temperature-sensitive pharmaceuticals under extreme environmental conditions. These built systems are not isolated; they are part of a broader humanitarian logistics network that requires climate adaptation and engineering foresight.

Despite their importance, Heating, Ventilation, and Air Conditioning (HVAC) systems remain an underexplored yet essential component in this humanitarian infrastructure landscape. HVAC technologies determine whether shelters become survivable, whether vaccines reach populations potent, and whether hospitals can function in disease-prone zones (Fahrni et al., 2022; Morawska et al., 2024). In disaster scenarios, where logistics chains are often fragmented, energy is scarce, and weather extremes are intensified, HVAC systems directly influence morbidity, mortality, and psychological well-being (Hassan et al., 2024; Cheshmehzangi, 2021). The strategic integration of HVAC into humanitarian planning is no longer optional—it is foundational.

This chapter seeks to bridge the fragmented understanding between humanitarian logistics, climate-responsive systems, and emergency management by foregrounding HVAC technologies as critical enablers in disaster resilience. Using Türkiye as a focal case, the chapter explores the post-2023 earthquake response, mobile hospital infrastructure during the COVID-19 pandemic, long-term HVAC applications in refugee camps, and the coordination between key actors such as the Turkish Red Crescent and AFAD. It draws upon interdisciplinary research in humanitarian engineering, sustainability, disaster logistics, and healthcare infrastructure to highlight

HVAC's multifaceted role in relief operations. The scope also extends to evaluating energy-efficient and off-grid HVAC solutions, air quality management, and the thermal needs of displaced populations—emphasizing innovation, local capacity, and sustainability.

By contextualizing Türkiye's initiatives within broader humanitarian and infrastructural debates, this chapter contributes not only to academic discourse but also offers practical insights for policymakers, engineers, and humanitarian agencies aiming to integrate HVAC into future disaster preparedness and response strategies.

2. LITERATURE REVIEW

2.1. HVAC in Emergency and Mobile Applications

Heating, Ventilation, and Air Conditioning (HVAC) systems have become increasingly critical in the context of emergency response and mobile infrastructure, especially during humanitarian crises. Whether deployed in temporary shelters, field hospitals, or refrigerated logistics units, HVAC systems ensure the thermal comfort, air quality, and temperature stability that are essential to human health, medicine preservation, and operational functionality in volatile environments. The role of HVAC becomes especially pronounced in disaster scenarios where populations are displaced and infrastructure is either destroyed or inadequate. In such conditions, HVAC systems are no longer auxiliary technologies but rather foundational to the viability of relief operations. As Moultanovsky (2014) notes, innovations in mobile HVAC systems—such as modular units, rapid-deployment kits, and compact air handling units—have been specifically designed for mobile environments where space, energy, and time are limited resources. These technologies address challenges related to heat stress, hypothermia, humidity, and air contamination, which are common in shelters set up after natural disasters like earthquakes or floods. The strategic use of HVAC systems in such environments enables continuity in healthcare, sanitation, and logistical operations that are often otherwise compromised.

One of the most promising areas of research and application involves off-grid HVAC systems, especially relevant in rural or devastated regions where electricity and fuel supply may be unreliable. Zajecs, Lebedeva, and Odineca (2022) provide a compelling analysis of off-grid HVAC solutions tailored to temporary shelters deployed in extreme Latvian climate conditions. Their study emphasizes the integration of renewable energy sources (e.g., solar power) and smart control technologies to reduce reliance on fossil fuels and centralized grids. This approach holds immense potential for humanitarian logistics, especially in geographically isolated disaster zones such as southeastern Türkiye following the 2023 Kahramanmaraş earthquakes.

The scalability and energy autonomy of off-grid HVAC units allow for the rapid deployment of climate-controlled environments without placing additional strain on local infrastructure. This is particularly important when emergency teams are racing against time to stabilize affected populations, prevent the spread of diseases, and protect medical and food supplies. In such contexts, the effectiveness of off-grid HVAC systems becomes a determinant of operational success and human survival.

Another dimension in the advancement of HVAC systems for emergency applications is the integration of smart technologies and indoor localization, enabling automated response and adaptive control. For instance, Khoche et al. (2021) investigated occupancy detection models that support emergency HVAC management by adjusting ventilation and temperature settings based on real-time data about room usage. This approach is especially useful in mobile hospitals or quarantine zones where energy efficiency must be balanced with strict air circulation protocols. By using Wi-Fi signals and indoor localization methods, smart HVAC systems can prioritize airflow in crowded spaces, reduce unnecessary energy expenditure in unused zones, and enhance safety through controlled environments. These features also facilitate compliance with health and safety standards, particularly in scenarios such as COVID-19 mobile response units or infectious disease outbreaks in refugee camps. The growing fusion of HVAC technologies with sensor-based decision systems supports agile and responsive relief strategies, further embedding HVAC systems into the core of humanitarian logistics infrastructure.

Furthermore, the use of Building Information Modeling (BIM) and digital twins in HVAC system design is transforming the way temporary and mobile hospitals are planned and managed in real time. Jiang et al. (2025) highlight how digital twin technologies, when linked to HVAC controls, can simulate energy flows, thermal comfort levels, and usage patterns, enabling on-the-fly adjustments during emergency situations. This is particularly valuable when field hospitals undergo operational changes—such as repurposing rooms or accommodating unexpected surges in patient numbers—common occurrences during pandemics or large-scale disasters. For Türkiye's mobile hospital initiatives post-earthquake, digital twin-enabled HVAC systems can be employed to monitor and manage critical care environments, ensuring optimal conditions for patients, healthcare providers, and equipment. Moreover, the use of such intelligent systems enables predictive maintenance and early failure detection, reducing downtime and improving the reliability of operations in highly volatile environments. Integrating BIM and digital twins into emergency HVAC planning thus enhances both strategic foresight and operational efficiency.

Lastly, the integration of edge computing with mobile HVAC systems offers a pathway toward decentralized, autonomous, and highly responsive relief infrastructure. Pramanik et al. (2024) demonstrate a proof-of-concept where smart HVAC units utilize mobile crowd computing and edge-based data processing to optimize energy consumption and indoor environmental quality. In humanitarian settings, this would mean that each HVAC unit can make localized decisions—such as adjusting airflow or switching to battery mode—without relying on a central server or cloud system, which may be inaccessible during disasters. Such resilience is crucial in regions where digital and electrical infrastructures are compromised. In Türkiye, where mountainous terrain and infrastructure vulnerability can hinder centralized coordination, edge-enabled HVAC systems would allow local relief teams to maintain operational control, even in disconnected zones. These systems also support real-time monitoring and adaptation, making them suitable for both short-term disaster relief and long-term refugee accommodation. The convergence of edge computing and HVAC technologies represents a strategic evolution in emergency preparedness and mobile climate control systems.

2.2. Humanitarian Logistics and Infrastructure Support

The increasingly complex nature of humanitarian crises—ranging from climate-induced disasters to conflict-related displacements—has underscored the necessity of integrating engineering systems with humanitarian response strategies. At the heart of this intersection is the concept of humanitarian engineering, which involves the design and deployment of technological and infrastructural solutions tailored to vulnerable populations in high-risk environments. Schismenos et al. (2021) emphasize the critical role of mapping both vulnerability and capability factors when designing such systems, particularly for communities exposed to water-based disasters. Their study illustrates how sustainable infrastructure—such as mobile water filtration units, modular sanitation systems, and climate-responsive shelter solutions—can be adapted to meet local needs through participatory approaches. In Türkiye, regions prone to earthquakes and floods, such as the Black Sea or southeastern Anatolia, stand to benefit from these models, where engineering interventions must be strategically deployed to mitigate cascading vulnerabilities. The integration of HVAC systems into this landscape is not merely about comfort but about maintaining life-saving conditions in temporary infrastructure—ensuring clean air, safe temperatures, and disease control in emergency logistics hubs, mobile clinics, and refugee settlements.

The ethical and social dimensions of engineering solutions in humanitarian logistics are gaining prominence, particularly as AI and automation technologies are increasingly applied to disaster response planning. Pandey (2025) frames this as part of a broader discourse on ethical AI in humanitarian engineering, noting the dual imperative of innovation and responsibility. In remote deployment of critical systems—whether for HVAC, power generation, or emergency mobility—AI-powered tools are now helping to forecast demand, optimize routing, and manage resources in volatile environments. However, without culturally sensitive and ethically grounded design, such tools risk exacerbating inequalities or introducing systems that are technically impressive but practically unusable by the target population. For instance, an AI-enabled HVAC unit designed for humanitarian shelters must be not only efficient and low-energy but also easy to maintain, adaptable to different power sources, and operable by non-expert personnel. In Türkiye's disaster zones, this is especially crucial as many first responders and local stakeholders may lack the technical infrastructure or training to operate advanced systems. As such, the humanitarian engineering framework must account for local capacity, inclusivity, and sustainability, ensuring that infrastructure support aligns with the broader goals of equity and resilience.

An emerging area in humanitarian logistics is the Triple Nexus approach, which seeks to harmonize humanitarian aid, development cooperation, and peacebuilding within one strategic framework. This approach has significant implications for infrastructure support and supply chain design. Plesner Volkdal (2025) argues that development-oriented supply chains—traditionally focused on economic growth and long-term infrastructure—can be leveraged for humanitarian responseif reoriented to include principles of flexibility, decentralization, and conflict sensitivity. For Türkiye, which operates at the intersection of humanitarian response (e.g., Syrian refugee support), development investment (e.g., in eastern provinces), and regional stability efforts, this approach is especially relevant. Infrastructure systems such as mobile HVAC units, cold chains, water and sanitation logistics, and temporary housing must be designed not only for emergency use but for eventual integration into sustainable local systems. By embedding engineering innovation within development supply chains, humanitarian operations in Türkiye can shift from reactive crisis management to proactive resilience building. This strategic evolution also opens pathways for cross-sector collaboration between government agencies, NGOs, the private sector (including HVAC manufacturers), and community organizations.

2.3. Strategy and Innovation in Post-Disaster Response

Strategic responses to disasters increasingly depend on the ability to rapidly deploy modular infrastructure while maintaining sustainability and adaptability to evolving needs. Traditional linear approaches to disaster recovery—where relief, reconstruction, and development occur in rigid phases—are being replaced by more dynamic frameworks that emphasize modularity and innovation from the outset. As Mohan (2023) shows in his study of post-disaster recovery among Caribbean firms, organizations that invested in pre-disaster planning, flexible infrastructure, and scalable logistics were far more resilient and capable of restoring operations quickly. These findings have direct relevance for Türkiye, which frequently experiences earthquakes and floods, requiring systems such as mobile HVAC units, modular shelters, and cold-chain logistics to be deployed within hours rather than days. A key innovation is the use of prefabricated, easily transportable units equipped with self-sustaining systems (e.g., solar-powered HVAC), which align with sustainability goals while enabling fast-response capabilities. These systems are not only reusable and adaptable across different emergencies but can also be integrated into long-term community infrastructure, thereby bridging the gap between emergency response and sustainable development.

The importance of strategic Post-Disaster Needs Assessment (PDNA) has been emphasized as a foundation for building resilient infrastructure and allocating resources efficiently. Adekola and Adekola (2024) argue that PDNA serves as a structured, evidence-based process that guides both immediate recovery actions and long-term strategic planning. This involves not only damage evaluation but also understanding the evolving needs of affected populations and aligning recovery goals with sustainable infrastructure design. In the context of Türkiye's disaster-prone regions, a PDNA framework would prioritize technologies like modular HVAC systems that are adaptable, energy-efficient, and capable of operating in diverse environments. Strategic innovation, in this sense, is not limited to the technology itself but extends to how systems are selected, financed, deployed, and scaled. The incorporation of such technologies into PDNA processes helps reduce redundancies, optimize logistics chains, and ensure that post-disaster interventions are equitable, forward-looking, and grounded in local capabilities.

Another layer of strategic innovation lies in the integration of communications technologies into post-disaster logistics and infrastructure systems. Matracia et al. (2022) highlight how enabling technologies such as IoT sensors, satellite communications, and cloud-based coordination platforms are essential for managing dispersed relief operations, especially in environments with compromised infrastructure. When integrated with HVAC systems, such technologies can provide real-time data on internal climate conditions, energy usage, and equipment status—critical for maintaining safe environments in shelters, field hospitals, and logistics hubs. This smart infrastructure approach allows decision-makers to prioritize repairs, redirect resources, and ensure that aid is being used effectively. For Türkiye, investing in such integrated systems represents a significant opportunity to elevate post-disaster logistics to a new level of intelligence, enabling rapid scaling and cross-agency coordination in response to complex emergencies such as earthquakes, pandemics, and refugee influxes.

Strategic governance is also crucial in ensuring that innovations are embedded in institutional and community-level responses to disaster. Kong (2024) emphasizes the role of post-disaster governance in building resilient societies, pointing out that recovery is not merely a technical issue but a deeply political and social one. Decision-making about infrastructure deployment—including HVAC and other mobile systems—must consider the intersection of power dynamics, community trust, and inclusivity. In Türkiye, this means that disaster relief strategies must not only rely on centrally managed systems like AFAD (Disaster and Emergency Management Authority) but also incorporate local actors such as municipalities, NGOs, and affected communities. Innovation must therefore be paired with legitimacy, transparency, and participation. From a strategic perspective, HVAC deployment should be seen not just as a technical fix but as part of a broader resilience strategy that enhances safety, dignity, and long-term stability for displaced populations.

Lastly, the delivery of resilient infrastructure post-disaster requires a shift in both mindset and method. Chester et al. (2021) advocate for new delivery models that emphasize agility, decentralization, and pre-positioned modular units ready for deployment. Their study outlines how sustainability goals—such as minimizing carbon emissions, using renewable energy, and designing for disassembly—can be integrated into the design and delivery of emergency infrastructure. In Türkiye, this could involve the creation of regional depots that store HVAC-enabled modular shelters and field hospital components, ready to be mobilized within 24–48 hours. These facilities can work in tandem with predictive analytics to assess likely disaster zones and prepare tailored response kits accordingly. Furthermore, such strategies contribute to circular economy principles by enabling reuse, reducing waste, and minimizing environmental damage in already fragile contexts. The strategic alignment of sustainability, modularity, and rapid deployment in HVAC systems thus reflects an evolved approach to disaster response—one that anticipates, adapts, and integrates across short-term urgency and long-term resilience.

2.4. Research Gap and Theoretical Framing

Despite the growing sophistication of humanitarian logistics and the increasing emphasis on rapid deployment, sustainability, and modular infrastructure, the role of HVAC systems remains significantly underrepresented in both academic literature and practical frameworks. Most studies in disaster logistics and emergency infrastructure tend to focus on supply chains, medical triage, shelter provision, or water and sanitation systems, often treating thermal comfort and air quality as secondary or incidental considerations. However, this oversight neglects the critical impact that temperature regulation, ventilation, and air purification have on human health, operational efficiency, and the resilience of mobile systems—particularly in extreme climates or high-density shelters. As recent disasters in Türkiye have shown, such as the 2023 Kahramanmaraş earthquakes, failure to provide climate-controlled environments in tents, field hospitals, and logistics hubs can exacerbate vulnerability, hinder medical interventions, and degrade the overall quality of aid delivery. The research gap lies not only in the absence of dedicated studies on HVAC deployment in post-disaster settings, but also in the lack of systemic integration—where HVAC is strategically embedded into logistics planning, design specifications, and recovery frameworks from the outset.

To address this gap, a comprehensive theoretical lens is required—one that transcends isolated technological evaluation and instead frames HVAC as an embedded component within the humanitarian engineering ecosystem. Drawing from systems thinking, the chapter positions HVAC systems as infrastructural subcomponents whose performance and reliability are interdependent with other relief systems, such as energy supply, shelter architecture, health service delivery, and environmental control. This perspective aligns with resilience theory, which emphasizes the capacity of systems to absorb disruption, adapt to changing conditions, and reorganize while retaining core functionality. Within this framework, HVAC technologies are not peripheral but vital contributors to systemic robustness and adaptive capacity. Furthermore, the analysis incorporates aspects of the Triple Nexus framework (humanitarian–development–peace), arguing that sustainable and modular HVAC systems offer continuity across emergency relief, long-term development, and regional stabilization—particularly in protracted crisis contexts such as Türkiye's southeastern border zones. By framing HVAC not as a standalone utility but as a strategic enabler within humanitarian logistics, this chapter lays the groundwork for a new research agenda—one that calls for interdisciplinary collaboration between disaster studies, engineering design, public health, and logistics management to ensure equitable, efficient, and climate-responsive aid delivery.

3. THE ROLE OF HVAC IN EMERGENCY RELIEF OPERATIONS

3.1. Thermal Comfort and Health Outcomes in Temporary Shelters

Thermal comfort is a foundational element of human well-being, particularly in post-disaster scenarios where displaced populations are relocated to temporary shelters that are often poorly ventilated, inadequately insulated, and exposed to harsh environmental conditions. HVAC systems, when appropriately integrated, play a central role in regulating indoor temperatures, ensuring air quality, and mitigating both direct and indirect health risks. A case study by Zemitis et al. (2021) investigating thermal comfort levels in Latvian emergency shelters revealed that poor insulation and limited air exchange led to significant discomfort among occupants, contributing to increased susceptibility to respiratory infections and a decline in sleep quality. The study further emphasized that even basic HVAC interventions—such as low-energy heating and localized ventilation—substantially improved occupant well-being.

These findings hold direct relevance for Türkiye, where rapid shelter deployment often precedes HVAC planning, especially during winter or in high-altitude regions like Elbistan or Malatya. Addressing thermal inadequacy from the outset can reduce cold-related illnesses, improve recovery for vulnerable populations such as children and the elderly, and restore dignity to displaced individuals during times of crisis.

The relationship between shelter design and health outcomes is even more profound when considering prolonged displacement, where shelters transition from temporary solutions to semi-permanent living environments. Conzatti et al. (2022) offer a systematic review demonstrating that thermally suboptimal shelters contribute to a rise in both physical health issues (e.g., hypothermia, heat stroke, respiratory complications) and psychological stress, including anxiety and depression. The researchers highlight that inadequate ventilation and extreme indoor temperatures also affect the functionality of mobile clinics and disrupt the effectiveness of stored pharmaceuticals and food supplies. In this context, HVAC systems emerge not just as technical features but as life-supporting infrastructure that ensures a baseline of health, productivity, and social stability. Especially in Türkiye, where many Syrian refugee camps have evolved into long-term settlements, the incorporation of scalable and modular HVAC solutions is critical for preserving both public health and humanitarian integrity.

Furthermore, the COVID-19 pandemic has brought increased awareness to the role of indoor thermal comfort and air quality in disease control, especially in enclosed environments with high human density. Cheshmehzangi (2021) investigated thermal comfort and indoor satisfaction during lockdown conditions and found a direct correlation between perceived discomfort and increased symptoms of fatigue, irritability, and reduced cognitive function. In humanitarian shelters—often characterized by crowding, limited privacy, and poor air circulation—these stressors are magnified. HVAC systems, when equipped with HEPA filtration and humidity control, can significantly reduce the transmission of airborne pathogens and improve overall psychosocial conditions. For Türkiye's mobile quarantine shelters and COVID-19 response tents, the integration of adaptive HVAC systems with dynamic air regulation settings would have enhanced safety protocols and mitigated secondary health risks. This highlights the broader need to embed HVAC planning into emergency public health strategy, especially in anticipation of future pandemics or respiratory disease outbreaks.

The health implications of thermal discomfort are not limited to cold stress; extreme heat events—which are becoming more frequent due to climate change—pose equally severe risks. Flores-Larsen and Filippin (2021), in their study on low-income housing in Argentina, emphasize that inadequate cooling during heat waves resulted in elevated hospitalization rates, sleep disorders, and declines in work capacity. Their findings are particularly relevant for the summer conditions in Türkiye's southeastern regions, where daytime temperatures can exceed 40°C. Without appropriate HVAC infrastructure, temporary shelters in these areas become hazardous microenvironments, especially for children, pregnant women, and individuals with cardiovascular conditions. Passive cooling methods such as cross-ventilation or thermal shading are often insufficient without mechanical support. Therefore, deploying energy-efficient HVAC systems capable of maintaining thermal resilience during heat waves is not just a comfort-enhancing strategy but a public health imperative in disaster-prone settings.

Finally, indoor air quality and occupant health are also deeply intertwined with energy efficiency and thermal comfort outcomes. Hassan et al. (2024), in the ARDEN project in Ireland, evaluated deep energy renovations and found that improvements in building envelope insulation and HVAC upgrades significantly enhanced both air quality and thermal conditions. The study documented a measurable reduction in mold, dampness, and indoor pollutants, all of which are common issues in temporary shelters due to makeshift materials and insufficient maintenance. The researchers concluded that a holistic HVAC design—which balances thermal regulation, ventilation, and filtration—is essential in preserving respiratory health and overall indoor environmental quality. This reinforces the idea that HVAC systems should not be treated as isolated utilities, but as integral components of the humanitarian shelter ecosystem. In Türkiye's context, especially in densely populated disaster zones or long-term refugee facilities, incorporating such systems from the early planning phase can reduce future retrofitting costs, improve recovery conditions, and enhance the long-term sustainability of humanitarian operations.

3.2. Cold Chain Logistics for Medicine and Vaccines

Cold chain logistics represents one of the most critical yet fragile components of healthcare delivery during humanitarian crises. In the aftermath of disasters such as earthquakes, floods, or pandemics, the ability to maintain strict temperature control from storage to distribution becomes essential for preserving the integrity of thermolabile medicines and vaccines. Fahrni et al. (2022), in a comprehensive scoping review on COVID-19 vaccine logistics, emphasize that failures in cold chain systems—especially during emergencies—can lead to vaccine spoilage, potency loss, and public mistrust. Their findings show that maintaining a consistent temperature (typically 2–8°C for most vaccines, and up to -70°C for mRNA vaccines) is a non-negotiable requirement that must be factored into emergency preparedness plans. In Türkiye, the deployment of mobile vaccination units and refrigerated transport during the pandemic underscored both the potential and the logistical vulnerabilities of such systems, especially in rural or earthquake-affected regions where energy infrastructure may be unreliable or disrupted.

The importance of cold chain systems extends beyond pandemic response and applies equally to routine immunization and chronic disease management in post-disaster contexts. Ferman, Gonçalves, and Oliveira (2024) highlight how municipal primary care systems in Brazil have developed logistical frameworks to maintain cold chains for essential medicines and vaccines, often using portable refrigerators, solar-powered freezers, and route optimization strategies. These models are relevant for Türkiye, particularly in remote areas or within temporary shelters where the continuity of chronic treatments (e.g., insulin, antiretrovirals, biologics) must be ensured alongside routine immunization programs for displaced populations. The authors emphasize that cold chain systems must not only be technically robust but adaptable and modular, allowing them to function under fluctuating demand and resource constraints. This reinforces the need to include HVAC integration not only at storage hubs but also within mobile clinics, field hospitals, and transport vehicles, creating a multi-tiered and temperature-stable medical distribution network.

In many humanitarian contexts, challenges to cold chain effectiveness are not only technological but also systemic and organizational. Olutuase et al. (2022), in their review of medicines and vaccines supply chain challenges in Nigeria, identified key obstacles such as inconsistent electricity supply, lack of temperature monitoring, human resource shortages, and insufficient transport coordination. Although the study is based in West Africa, the systemic vulnerabilities mirror issues observed in Türkiye during times of mass displacement or disaster response—particularly in provinces with under-resourced health systems. These findings point to the importance of strategic cross-sector collaboration between public health institutions, logistics firms, and technology providers to ensure that cold chain integrity is preserved throughout the entire supply process. In this regard, the integration of HVAC systems with real-time monitoring technologies (e.g., IoT-enabled sensors, cloud-based dashboards) can enhance visibility, accountability, and risk mitigation throughout the cold chain.

Further highlighting the technological evolution of vaccine logistics, Manupati et al. (2021) propose a multi-echelon dynamic cold chain model that enables flexible, responsive distribution based on demand fluctuations, geospatial data, and emergency constraints. This dynamic approach is highly relevant for Türkiye's earthquake-prone regions where road access can be blocked and population densities shift rapidly due to evacuations. In such scenarios, centralized cold storage facilities may be rendered ineffective, necessitating decentralized models with mobile refrigeration units and smart deployment algorithms. The authors also advocate for the use of decision-support systems and simulation tools to optimize vaccine routing, minimize transit time, and preserve thermal stability—strategies that should be embedded into

Türkiye's national emergency response protocols. By linking predictive analytics with modular HVAC-powered cold storage, disaster response agencies can enhance both logistical precision and health outcomes in crisis settings.

Finally, Flores Ferman, Gonçalves, and Oliveira (2024) reemphasize the operational importance of last-mile delivery in cold chain logistics, particularly in decentralized municipal health services. Their study concludes that while national supply systems may function adequately, the weakest links often appear at the final delivery points—mobile clinics, refugee camps, or temporary health posts—where portable cold storage and HVAC infrastructure are most needed. In Türkiye, this highlights a pressing gap in the design of temporary healthcare infrastructure, which often prioritizes space and speed over thermal regulation and pharmaceutical protection. Addressing this issue requires not only investment in cold chain technology but also training for field health workers, standard operating procedures for equipment usage, and contingency plans for energy failure or logistical rerouting. Ultimately, the resilience and responsiveness of Türkiye's humanitarian health logistics can be substantially improved by recognizing HVAC-enabled cold chains as essential components of disaster-resilient public health infrastructure.

3.3. Air Quality, Ventilation, and COVID-19 Learnings

The COVID-19 pandemic catalyzed a global reevaluation of the importance of indoor air quality (IAQ) and ventilationin disease prevention and public health, especially in confined, high-density spaces such as classrooms, hospitals, and temporary shelters. Morawska, Li, and Salthammer (2024) assert that the airborne transmission of SARS-CoV-2 highlighted the systemic neglect of ventilation in building design and crisis response strategies. Their review in Scienceunderscores that proper ventilation is not just a thermal comfort measure but a first-line defense against respiratory infections, particularly in spaces where social distancing is difficult or impossible. For Türkiye, where temporary shelters and field hospitals were rapidly deployed during the 2023 earthquakes and the COVID-19 pandemic, the failure to incorporate high-efficiency HVAC systems with air filtration and controlled air exchange may have significantly contributed to secondary infections and poor occupant health outcomes. This emphasizes the urgent need to institutionalize ventilation standards into humanitarian infrastructure, recognizing clean indoor air as a core component of emergency healthcare.

The operational challenges of maintaining air quality in naturally ventilated or makeshift environments were particularly evident during the pandemic. Meiss et al. (2021), through a case study of naturally ventilated classrooms during COVID-19, observed that CO_2 levels routinely exceeded recommended thresholds, indicating insufficient air renewal and increased risk of airborne transmission. While windows and doors were often used for ventilation, this method proved inadequate in maintaining consistent airflow, especially during cold weather. Extrapolating these findings to post-disaster shelters in Türkiye—often constructed from non-breathable materials and clustered in close proximity—illustrates a major vulnerability in the country's emergency shelter strategy. Without mechanical ventilation supported by HVAC systems equipped with HEPA filters and demand-controlled airflow, these shelters may become incubators for disease, rather than safe havens. This calls for a shift from passive to active ventilation design, particularly in regions where mass displacement is likely and prolonged shelter occupancy is common.

Ventilation protocols introduced in the wake of COVID-19 have shown measurable effects on indoor air quality across different facility types. Eichholtz, Kok, and Sun (2024) examined ventilation upgrades in primary schools and found that mechanical interventions such as continuous air exchange, filtration, and CO_2 monitoring significantly improved IAQ while reducing absenteeism related to respiratory illness. These improvements demonstrate the broader value of strategic HVAC integration in public infrastructure—not only during pandemics but in maintaining long-term health outcomes. In the context of humanitarian logistics in Türkiye, such lessons are highly transferable. Field hospitals, mobile testing centers, and medical tents, which often lack proper HVAC design due to their temporary nature, should be redesigned to reflect this post-COVID standard. Portable air handling units, modular HEPA filters, and airflow zoning systems can and should be embedded into procurement frameworks and logistics plans for disaster response, ensuring that emergency health interventions are not undermined by poor environmental conditions.

Furthermore, HVAC systems must balance air quality with energy efficiency, especially in post-disaster scenarios where power supply is intermittent or limited. Buonomano et al. (2023) address this dual challenge by proposing new ventilation design criteria that integrate energy sustainability with indoor health requirements. Their model incorporates variable air volume systems, energy recovery ventilators, and renewable-powered HVAC units to ensure that IAQ is maintained without excessive energy demand. This is particularly relevant for Türkiye's mobile healthcare facilities and emergency shelters, which are often dependent on generators or limited grid access. Deploying HVAC systems that are energy-autonomous and sensor-driven can reduce operational costs while ensuring a safe indoor environment for both healthcare workers and displaced individuals. Moreover, such innovations contribute to the resilience of healthcare infrastructure, allowing operations to continue during power outages or supply chain disruptions common in disaster zones.

Finally, the seasonal and climatic dimensions of air quality and thermal comfort must not be overlooked. Alonso et al. (2021), in their study of primary schools in Mediterranean climates during the winter season, found that increased ventilation to prevent virus spread led to significant thermal discomfort and reduced occupant satisfaction. This trade-off is especially problematic in Türkiye, where regions like Eastern Anatolia face harsh winters, and indoor heating often competes with ventilation needs. The findings point to the necessity of holistic HVAC solutions that address both thermal comfort and infection control simultaneously—through technologies such as demand-based ventilation, hybrid heating-cooling units, and filtered air recirculation systems. Applying these integrated solutions to humanitarian shelters and mobile hospitals ensures that ventilation does not compromise comfort or energy efficiency. Ultimately, the post-COVID ventilation paradigm offers actionable insights for humanitarian logistics planners, emphasizing that safe air is no longer optional—it is essential infrastructure.

3.4. Energy Efficiency and Off-Grid HVAC Solutions

In disaster-affected or remote humanitarian contexts, reliable access to electricity is often severely limited or entirely absent—making energy-efficient and off-grid HVAC solutions essential for maintaining safe living conditions. Traditional HVAC systems typically rely on stable grid access, but such assumptions rarely hold in post-disaster settings, particularly in rural or mountainous areas of Türkiye where infrastructure may be damaged or undeveloped. Lee, Iacocca, and Joshi (2021) developed an energy usage model for heating and cooling of off-grid shelters, demonstrating that demand-side optimization—through insulation, thermal zoning, and selective equipment usage—can drastically reduce HVAC energy loads. Their study emphasizes that modular shelters equipped with pre-calculated thermal performance metrics can be paired with low-energy HVAC systems for optimized comfort and sustainability. For Türkiye's earthquake-prone regions, this approach enables not only immediate deployment but also long-term resilience, as such units can remain operational through multiple seasonal cycles without grid dependency.

A complementary strategy is the deployment of dedicated off-grid HVAC systems designed specifically for temporary shelters. Zajecs, Lebedeva, and Odineca (2022) investigated such systems in Latvia's harsh climate and found that hybrid HVAC units powered by solar or battery banks effectively maintained acceptable indoor temperatures despite ambient extremes. Their system integrated smart controllers, low-wattage compressors, and thermally adaptive materials to deliver a reliable and scalable solution. These findings are directly transferable to Türkiye's varied climate zones—where winter temperatures in eastern Anatolia and summer heat in the Mediterranean region both pose challenges for thermal comfort in disaster shelters. The advantage of off-grid HVAC systems is their portability, autonomy, and adaptability, which make them ideal for humanitarian operations requiring quick set-up, low maintenance, and environmental sustainability. Integrating such systems into Türkiye's national disaster inventory could greatly enhance the country's logistical preparedness and infrastructure resilience.

Recent advances in solar photovoltaic (PV) integration further enhance the viability of off-grid HVAC for humanitarian applications. Sedaghat et al. (2024), in their study on portable cabins in Kuwait, demonstrated the technical feasibility of combining solar PV with HVAC units to meet cooling loads efficiently under extreme heat. Their findings show that even in compact mobile structures, PV integration can yield up to 70% coverage of HVAC energy demands when coupled with thermal storage systems. This is particularly important for Türkiye's emergency shelters, especially in isolated or off-grid settings where fuel supply chains are disrupted. The incorporation of rooftop solar panels and battery systems provides shelters with autonomous energy, supporting not only HVAC operations but also lighting, refrigeration, and communication systems. Additionally, solar-PV HVAC solutions align with Türkiye's broader climate commitments and national targets for reducing greenhouse gas emissions in public infrastructure.

Further technological refinement is seen in solar-powered HVAC systems using natural refrigerants, which address both energy efficiency and environmental sustainability. Sulaiman et al. (2023) developed a solar off-grid air conditioning system that operates on low-GWP (global warming potential) natural refrigerants, reducing ecological impact while maintaining high thermal performance. Their experimental evaluation demonstrated that such systems are both technically viable and cost-effective in residential and temporary building applications. For Türkiye's humanitarian shelters, this offers a crucial innovation pathway: HVAC units that do not rely on synthetic refrigerants (e.g., HFCs), which are both costly and harmful to the environment. Integrating natural refrigerant-based systems reduces the long-term environmental footprint of emergency infrastructure while ensuring compliance with emerging global climate regulations.

From a systemic perspective, off-grid HVAC technologies must be embedded within broader Zero Energy Building (ZEB) and sustainable shelter frameworks. Kristiansen et al. (2021) explored container-based homes powered entirely by solar PV and supported by passive thermal design, confirming their feasibility as low-energy, autonomous living environments. The design considerations—such as insulation levels, ventilation control, and solar gain optimization—are highly relevant to Türkiye's modular shelter designs, which often use prefabricated container structures during large-scale displacements. These ZEB-style shelters, when equipped with energy-efficient HVAC, could serve not only for immediate relief but also as transitional housing for medium- to long-term recovery. Moreover, such infrastructure could be reused in future emergencies, offering a circular logistics model that aligns with both fiscal prudence and environmental responsibility.

Finally, Ghadirinejad et al. (2023) emphasize the importance of optimized system design through simulation-based planning and real-world case implementation. Their research outlines a framework for green and sustainable off-grid energy system design, integrating multi-objective optimization across energy efficiency, cost, emissions, and reliability. In Türkiye, applying such modeling tools in the planning stages of HVAC deployment for humanitarian purposes would enable policymakers and logistics agencies to evaluate multiple configurations before field deployment. This not only improves operational accuracy but also reduces the risk of underperforming systems in high-stakes environments. The transition toward data-driven, modular, and solar-integrated HVAC systems represents a paradigm shift in how emergency shelter and medical logistics are conceived—moving from reactive provision to proactive, sustainable design.

4. CASE STUDY: TÜRKIYE'S DISASTER RELIEF INITIATIVES

4.1. Post-2023 Earthquake HVAC Deployment

The twin earthquakes that struck southern Türkiye on February 6, 2023, registering magnitudes of 7.7 and 7.6, devastated provinces including Kahramanmaraş, Hatay, and Adıyaman during peak winter conditions. The humanitarian response faced an immediate dual challenge: large-scale displacement and subzero night temperatures. Emergency shelter efforts prioritized thermal protection, with Türkiye's Disaster and Emergency Management Authority (AFAD) and the Turkish Red Crescent (TRC) distributing over 175,000 tents and 1.5 million blankets across ten provinces in the initial days (Hürriyet Daily News, 2023a). Stadiums in Adıyaman were transformed into tent cities hosting 750–2,000 people each, while larger settlements for 6,000 were planned (Hürriyet Daily News, 2023b).

Local efforts complemented centralized distribution. Vocational schools manufactured improvised barrel stoves, and portable heaters were sourced through public donations and private partnerships (Hürriyet Daily News, 2023c). These ad hoc thermal measures were vital for survival in non-insulated shelters. As emergency relief transitioned to recovery, shelter conditions evolved. Tent cities gave way to modular container housing equipped with electricity, plumbing, and critically, air conditioning units. Each prefabricated container unit (approximately 21 m^2) offered enhanced insulation and environmental control compared to canvas tents, providing a more stable indoor climate (Red Cross Australia, 2023).

The establishment of mobile medical infrastructure was another priority. In Hatay alone, five modular field hospitals were delivered by international partners, outfitted with HVAC-supported utilities to facilitate continuous healthcare services

(Turmaks, 2023). The Ministry of Health deployed ten containerized mobile clinics in rural Hatay, each composed of three insulated shipping containers, equipped with HVAC, medical tools, and rest facilities for staff (Taipei Times, 2023). These facilities ensured climate stability essential for clinical procedures in volatile outdoor conditions.

Furthermore, by July 2023, the United Nations Development Programme (UNDP) noted temperatures exceeding 40 °C in the region and installed air conditioners in all 280 container homes at new settlements in Hatay and Kahramanmaraş (UNDP, 2023). Across Türkiye's container cities, AFAD reported the installation of more than 149,000 air conditioners and 105,000 ventilation units (UNECA, 2023). These upgrades reflect a shift from basic survival support to sustainable environmental conditioning. Ancillary facilities, including mobile laundry and shower units and social service centers, were also equipped with autonomous HVAC systems to support hygiene and psychosocial care services (Hürriyet Daily News, 2023d).

The HVAC deployment in the 2023 earthquake response in Türkiye followed a two-phase model: an initial phase centered on heating to prevent hypothermia, and a recovery phase involving integrated climate control systems for long-term habitability. This progression—ranging from makeshift stove heating in tents to climate-controlled modular living—illustrates how thermal resilience became a core component of disaster relief. The success of this model has implications for future humanitarian strategies in regions with extreme weather variability.

4.2. Turkish Red Crescent and AFAD Coordination

The coordination between Türkiye's Disaster and Emergency Management Authority (AFAD) and the Turkish Red Crescent (TRC) represents a cornerstone of the nation's disaster response framework. In the wake of the 2023 Kahramanmaraş-centered earthquakes, these two leading humanitarian organizations played pivotal roles in orchestrating rapid deployment of heating, ventilation, and air conditioning (HVAC) resources through institutional planning, equipment sourcing, and innovative public-private partnerships.

AFAD, operating under the Ministry of Interior, holds the statutory mandate for national disaster coordination. Its logistics plans, updated after the 1999 İzmit earthquake and further enhanced post-2011 Van earthquake, incorporate HVAC provisions under its *National Earthquake Strategy and Action Plan (UDSEP-2023)*, emphasizing environmental safety and thermal protection in mass shelters (AFAD, 2023). In the immediate aftermath of the 2023 disaster, AFAD initiated a multi-tiered deployment involving provincial warehouses, central stockpiles, and emergency contracts with local HVAC suppliers. Procurement strategies included pre-negotiated agreements with Turkish manufacturers and expedited customs clearance for international HVAC donations (TRT World, 2023a).

Simultaneously, the Turkish Red Crescent functioned as both a logistics operator and a service provider. With its Disaster Response Centers (DRCs) strategically located across the country, TRC activated mobile heating units and air-conditioned tents in coordination with AFAD's regional crisis centers (IFRC, 2023). The organizations shared a unified logistics information platform to optimize the distribution of generators, stoves, and HVAC-equipped containers. The coordinated logistics operations also extended to mobile blood donation buses, hygiene stations, and public kitchens—many of which required air purification and temperature stabilization systems to maintain health and food safety standards (TRC, 2023a).

Importantly, both agencies engaged private sector actors in delivering HVAC capacity. For example, Turkish HVAC industry leaders such as Alarko and DemirDöküm contributed modular heating systems and technical installation support under AFAD's emergency supplier protocol. These partnerships ensured not only the scale-up of supply but also technical accuracy in deploying HVAC systems suited to containerized and tent-based settings (KOSGEB, 2023).

In addition to industry collaboration, international NGOs such as Qatar Charity and Turkish NGOs like IHH Humanitarian Relief Foundation cooperated with AFAD and TRC to retrofit shelters with split-type air conditioning and forced-air heating units in Hatay and Malatya (ReliefWeb, 2023). The seamless coordination among institutions highlights Türkiye's maturing disaster logistics ecosystem, which leverages both centralized control (AFAD) and decentralized operational capacity (TRC), reinforced by civil society and private actors.

This case of institutional synergy demonstrates the strategic integration of HVAC into humanitarian infrastructure through structured planning, public-private partnerships, and cross-sector coordination. It provides a replicable model for other disaster-prone countries aiming to enhance climate-resilient emergency housing.

4.3. Syrian Refugee Camps in Türkiye

Since the onset of the Syrian civil war in 2011, Türkiye has hosted the largest refugee population in the world, with over 3.5 million registered Syrians under temporary protection as of 2024 (UNHCR, 2024). Managing long-term displacement has necessitated not only shelter and sanitation infrastructure but also sustainable heating, ventilation, and air conditioning (HVAC) solutions to ensure livability, particularly in Türkiye's southeastern provinces such as Gaziantep, Şanlıurfa, Kilis, and Hatay—regions that experience both scorching summers and freezing winters.

The Directorate General of Migration Management (DGMM), in collaboration with AFAD and the Turkish Red Crescent (TRC), has overseen the development of long-term HVAC strategies in refugee camps. In the early stages, temporary settlements were equipped with basic heating solutions, including portable stoves and gas heaters, which posed safety and ventilation challenges. Over time, the humanitarian strategy evolved to include modular container homes outfitted with integrated HVAC systems designed for year-round thermal comfort (AFAD, 2022; IFRC, 2021). These newer systems prioritize energy efficiency, indoor air quality, and climate adaptability. In camps such as Nizip and Elbeyli, renewable-energy-integrated HVAC models—such as solar-powered ventilation units and low-energy split ACs—have been piloted with support from international donors and private sector partners (UNDP Türkiye, 2023). These models aim to reduce dependency on grid electricity and fossil fuels while promoting environmental sustainability within humanitarian operations.

Crucially, HVAC design in these camps has shifted from an emergency response framework to a resilience-building paradigm. This includes predictive maintenance systems for air filters, cross-ventilation designs for minimizing airborne disease transmission, and mobile technical teams for HVAC servicing in high-density areas. Reports by the IOM (2022) and WHO (2021) highlight how poor ventilation and extreme temperatures exacerbate respiratory diseases, mental health issues, and overall morbidity in displaced populations, thereby reinforcing the centrality of HVAC in public health outcomes within refugee contexts. In addition, TRC has spearheaded training programs for refugees and local technicians on HVAC maintenance and basic repair skills, contributing to community-based resilience and vocational integration (TRC, 2023). These capacity-building initiatives not only ensure long-term system operability but also align with Türkiye's broader goals of empowering refugees through skills development and livelihood support.

Türkiye's experience with HVAC integration in refugee camps underscores the importance of transitioning from short-term climatic relief to a holistic, development-oriented approach that embeds environmental sustainability, health equity, and technological innovation in humanitarian logistics.

4.4. Lessons from Mobile Hospitals During the COVID-19 Crisis

The COVID-19 pandemic exposed critical vulnerabilities in global healthcare infrastructure, particularly in the context of rapid surge capacity. In Türkiye, one of the most notable responses to these challenges was the establishment of mobile and modular hospitals across urban and rural regions. These field hospitals were rapidly deployed to expand healthcare access, particularly during peak infection periods in 2020–2021. A vital but often overlooked component of their effectiveness was the adaptation and optimization of Heating, Ventilation, and Air Conditioning (HVAC) systems to meet stringent infection control requirements and thermal comfort standards (T.C. Sağlık Bakanlığı, 2021). In field hospitals established in cities like Istanbul, Ankara, and Gaziantep, specialized HVAC systems were tailored to ensure negative pressure in isolation rooms, high-efficiency particulate air (HEPA) filtration, and increased air changes per hour (ACH) to reduce the risk of airborne transmission. Studies have shown that inadequate ventilation can significantly amplify the spread of respiratory viruses like SARS-CoV-2 (Morawska et al., 2024; Meiss et al., 2021), making these adaptations crucial to healthcare delivery in temporary medical facilities.

The adaptation process was a joint effort coordinated by Türkiye's Ministry of Health, AFAD, and engineering contractors specializing in medical infrastructure. Design standards were based on World Health Organization (WHO) and Centers for Disease Control and Prevention (CDC) guidelines, which were customized for Türkiye's climatic and logistical conditions. Portable HVAC units with UV-C disinfection capabilities were deployed to ensure pathogen mitigation, while modular systems allowed for flexible zoning based on infection control protocols (Buonomano et al., 2023). Another innovation was the use of IoT-enabled HVAC monitoring systems in some field hospitals, which provided real-time feedback on temperature, humidity, and air quality. This data was integrated into centralized hospital dashboards to allow health administrators to adapt HVAC settings in response to patient loads and environmental variables, thereby enhancing operational resilience (Singh & Manoharan, 2025).

Post-crisis evaluations by the Turkish Medical Association (Türk Tabipleri Birliği) and public health researchers emphasized the role of HVAC in protecting both patients and frontline healthcare workers. Lessons from these deployments have since informed design guidelines for permanent healthcare facilities and pre-fabricated mobile clinics used in future emergencies, such as the 2023 Kahramanmaraş earthquakes (WHO, 2023; AFAD, 2023).

In sum, Türkiye's deployment of mobile hospitals during COVID-19 not only mitigated short-term public health risks but also catalyzed innovation in HVAC system design, maintenance, and remote control. These insights continue to inform preparedness strategies, emphasizing HVAC's strategic role in safeguarding public health in dynamic crisis environments.

5. STRATEGIC INTEGRATION OF HVAC IN HUMANITARIAN PLANNING

Effectively integrating HVAC systems into humanitarian planning requires a multidimensional strategy that aligns logistical foresight, cross-sectoral collaboration, local industry engagement, and intelligent decision-making. One foundational element is the pre-positioning of modular HVAC units within disaster-prone regions, ensuring that equipment can be deployed rapidly in the immediate aftermath of a crisis. Almadani, Aliyu, and Aliyu (2023) emphasize the importance of integrated operation centers in smart cities, where HVAC and other critical infrastructure are inventoried, monitored, and managed in real time. This approach facilitates faster response times and ensures interoperability between different relief components. Yang, Pan, and Pan (2022) extend this logistical paradigm by advocating for integrated offsite scheduling, particularly in modular construction environments. In humanitarian contexts, this translates into the coordinated staging of HVAC-equipped shelters and clinics, strategically located to minimize deployment lead times. Seifert, Kunz, and Gold (2023) reinforce this by calling for sustainable innovations in refugee camp operations—arguing that logistical models must incorporate energy-efficient HVAC systems as core components of health and safety infrastructure. Meanwhile, Alshalabi (2022) introduces a transitional shelter framework that emphasizes adaptable design, where HVAC functionality is not an add-on but embedded into the architectural and logistical DNA of humanitarian units. Together, these perspectives advocate for a holistic logistical ecosystem where HVAC systems are not reactive solutions, but pre-planned assets integrated across shelter, healthcare, and supply networks.

Strategic partnerships with HVAC manufacturers also play a pivotal role in ensuring that humanitarian operations have timely access to fit-for-purpose technologies. Srikandi et al. (2022) explore how HVAC firms can expand their global presence by adopting humanitarian-oriented business models, including rapid prototyping for off-grid environments and flexible production for emergency contracts. This shift encourages manufacturers to anticipate humanitarian demand, offering deployable units designed specifically for disaster contexts—lightweight, modular, and powered by renewable energy. Peruchi Pacheco da Silva et al. (2024) underscore the importance of sustainable practices among small- and medium-sized HVAC producers, noting that collaborative frameworks can incentivize these firms to produce low-energy systems tailored to mobile clinics, shelters, and temporary logistics centers. Such partnerships are vital for Türkiye's disaster preparedness efforts, particularly in enhancing domestic production capacity and ensuring local availability of HVAC systems during crises. Contractual frameworks with manufacturers, including contingency production clauses and adaptive supply agreements, further strengthen the resilience and responsiveness of humanitarian logistics.

In tandem with manufacturing capabilities, successful HVAC deployment in humanitarian operations requires rigorous training and capacity-building initiatives. Doody et al. (2021) demonstrate that pre-deployment programs for emergency responders significantly improve resilience, decision-making, and operational competence under high-stress conditions. Applying this to HVAC systems, technicians and logistics coordinators should be trained not only on installation and maintenance but also on fault detection, fuel management, and adaptive use in different environmental conditions. Noreen (2025) adds that capacity-building for healthcare workers—particularly at points of entry and during early disaster response—enhances institutional readiness and ensures HVAC systems are effectively utilized in high-stakes healthcare delivery. Hanna et al. (2021) draw parallels from the rapid deployment of climate technologies, emphasizing that interdisciplinary collaboration among engineers, public health experts, and NGOs is essential for scaling technical solutions like HVAC systems in emergency environments. In Türkiye, a national framework for cross-sectoral training would empower field personnel to operate HVAC units across diverse geographies and hazard scenarios, reducing downtime and maximizing impact.

Lastly, digital transformation through decision-making tools, artificial intelligence, and simulation modeling has the potential to revolutionize HVAC integration in humanitarian planning. Pu et al. (2025) highlight recent advancements in disaster response modeling, showing how optimization algorithms and simulation platforms can help planners identify optimal shelter locations, equipment distributions, and energy requirements. Rehan (2022) emphasizes the predictive power of AI in anticipating disaster impact zones and adjusting HVAC deployment accordingly. These tools can be especially useful in Türkiye, where seismic and climate data can be harnessed to build predictive HVAC deployment maps for different regions. Singh and Manoharan (2025) explore AI's role in enhancing smart city resilience, advocating for real-time HVAC monitoring systems that adapt based on occupancy, temperature, and air quality—critical factors in emergency shelters and mobile clinics. Kumar et al. (2025) further note that intelligent supply chain systems can support the delivery and lifecycle management of HVAC components under disaster conditions, ensuring sustained functionality. By combining AI-enabled decision-making with physical infrastructure, humanitarian planners can build agile, responsive, and sustainable HVAC systems that evolve with changing environmental and logistical realities.

6. CHALLENGES AND OPPORTUNITIES

The strategic integration of HVAC systems in humanitarian planning is fraught with both systemic challenges and emerging opportunities, particularly when viewed through the lens of infrastructure fragility, financial limitations, technological advancement, and environmental sustainability. One of the foremost barriers to effective HVAC deployment in disaster zones is the critical state of infrastructure in crisis-affected areas. Access to energy, the structural stability of buildings, and physical mobility are often compromised following large-scale disasters. Michalis and Vintzileou (2022) highlight how even minor infrastructural failures—such as undetected scour damage in bridges and foundations—can delay logistics operations, including the delivery and installation of HVAC equipment. Similarly, Burns (2019) stresses that energy security is a prerequisite for any climate control system, particularly in all-hazards disaster scenarios where multiple cascading failures—like fuel shortages and power outages—can simultaneously affect operational continuity. These concerns are not theoretical; Adhikari et al. (2017) documented severe healthcare service disruptions in Nepal during the dual burden of an earthquake and a fuel crisis, noting that prolonged power outages directly undermined refrigeration and indoor air control in makeshift hospitals. Majchrzak, Michalski, and Reginia-Zacharski (2021) further confirm that many national crisis management systems, including those in developed nations, remain unprepared for long-term blackouts, a vulnerability that directly impacts the reliability of HVAC systems in temporary shelters and mobile clinics. For Türkiye, which faces a similar mix of seismic, climatic, and infrastructural risks, these insights signal a pressing need for off-grid, rapidly deployable HVAC solutions supported by resilient logistics networks.

The interconnected strategies detailed above are visually synthesized in Figure 1. This Strategic HVAC Integration Model presents a phased framework from emergency deployment to long-term infrastructure planning, highlighting cross-sector coordination, modular technology use, and climate-responsive system integration.

Figure 1. Strategic HVAC Integration Model for Humanitarian Relief Operations

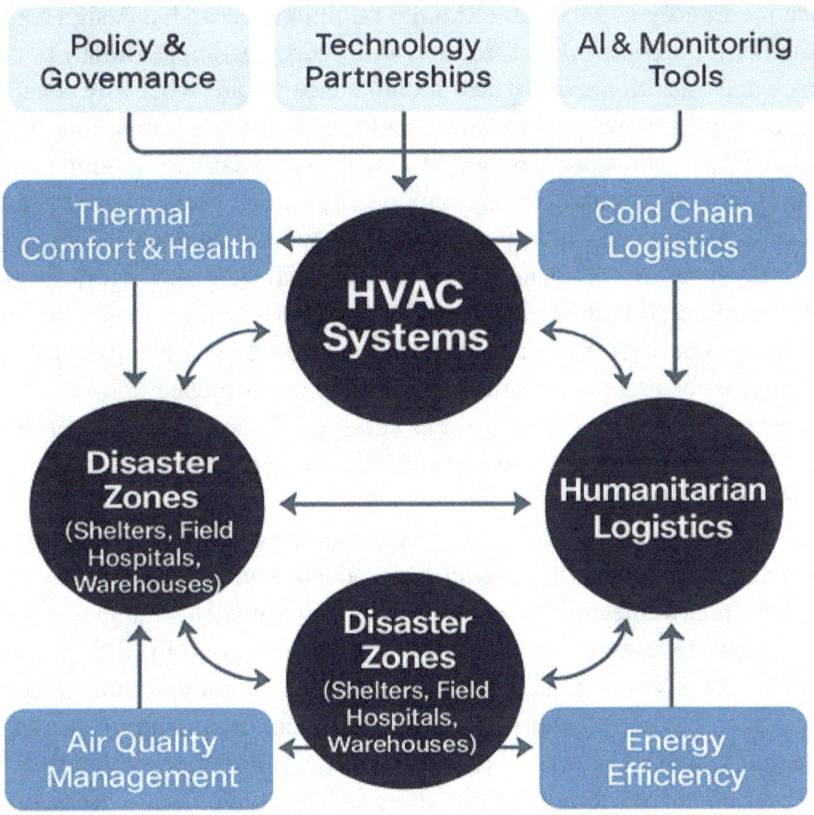

Equally pressing are the financial and procurement constraints associated with HVAC implementation in emergency settings. The urgency of disaster response often clashes with the budgetary rigidity of government and humanitarian organizations. Santoro, Mendoza, and Rincon (2021) propose a budget-constrained model predictive control system for HVAC applications, demonstrating how intelligent energy regulation can balance performance with economic limitations. Their research implies that resource-aware HVAC systems—particularly those that adjust output based on real-time environmental data—can maximize utility within strict financial constraints. However, this also requires agile funding mechanisms, rapid procurement processes, and pre-disaster investments in adaptable HVAC infrastructure. In the context of Türkiye's disaster response funding mechanisms, delays in budget allocation for technical assets like HVAC may hinder early-stage relief efforts and diminish the effectiveness of shelters, clinics, and command centers.

Despite these constraints, technological innovation offers promising solutions, especially in the form of portable, modular HVAC systems. Pless et al. (2022) introduce the Energy in Modular (EMOD) buildings method, a design framework that combines industrialized construction with energy-efficient climate systems for emergency and transitional use. These modular designs are especially beneficial for disaster zones where speed, scalability, and reusability are paramount. Likewise, Torres et al. (2021) showcase a plug-and-play façade system for modular buildings, highlighting how integrated HVAC components can be prefabricated and rapidly installed on-site. These technologies reduce setup times and enhance the adaptability of shelters to changing occupancy levels and external weather conditions. Baghi et al. (2021) reinforce this innovation trend through their analysis of solar-powered, net-zero energy houses from the Solar Decathlon, many of which utilized IoT-enabled HVAC systems for real-time climate control and performance optimization. Such systems are well suited for deployment in Türkiye's diverse terrain, offering energy independence and scalable design that can be tailored to both mountainous regions and densely populated urban shelters.

The evolution of HVAC in humanitarian settings is also increasingly tied to broader goals of sustainability and climate adaptation. Integrating low-emission technologies, renewable energy sources, and green logistics strategies is no longer aspirational but necessary. Shehadeh, Alshboul, and Tamimi (2025) conducted a quantitative analysis on climate-adaptive pavement technologies, underscoring the dual benefits of environmental performance and economic viability—a logic that applies equally to HVAC. Alabsi et al. (2021) argue for sustainable urban fabrics that integrate adaptive technologies in cities facing rapid climatic shifts, providing a conceptual basis for the development of resilient HVAC infrastructure in transitional shelter environments. Juaristi, Gómez-Acebo, and Monge-Barrio (2018) offer a qualitative evaluation of climate-adaptive façade materials, supporting HVAC systems by enhancing passive thermal regulation—an especially useful feature in temporary buildings where mechanical systems are limited. Bera (2025), though focusing on climate-adaptive clothing, contributes to this dialogue by illustrating how material science and behavioral design intersect to enhance human resilience against thermal extremes. Lastly, Shi et al. (2023) analyze the role of climate-adaptive innovation in agriculture, but their findings on carbon efficiency and economic heterogeneity offer transferable insights to HVAC systems, suggesting that localized, low-emission technologies can offer both climate mitigation and context-specific benefits in humanitarian deployments.

To consolidate the multifaceted insights discussed in this section, it is essential to map the critical enablers and barriers influencing the integration of HVAC systems into humanitarian logistics. While innovative technologies such as modular, solar-powered HVAC units and climate-adaptive designs present unprecedented opportunities, real-world constraints—ranging from infrastructure damage to budgetary and procurement hurdles—continue to challenge effective deployment. Türkiye's experience demonstrates that successful implementation relies not only on engineering solutions but also on coordinated governance, sustainable financing, and strategic foresight. Table 1 below provides a synthesized overview of these enablers and constraints, serving as a practical reference for policymakers, disaster planners, and humanitarian engineers seeking scalable, climate-responsive relief infrastructure.

Table 1. Strategic Enablers and Barriers for HVAC Integration in Humanitarian Logistics in Türkiye

Dimension	Enablers	Barriers
Institutional Coordination	AFAD–TRC partnership models; multi-agency drills	Overlapping mandates, lack of centralized HVAC logistics planning
Technology & Innovation	Modular HVAC units; solar-powered off-grid systems	Limited availability of portable, climate-resilient HVAC models
Finance & Procurement	Emergency budget reallocation; international aid funds	Budget constraints; delays in tender processes during crisis
Infrastructure Readiness	Container-based prefab deployment strategies	Damaged roads/buildings post-disaster impede HVAC system installation
Training & Human Capital	Field technician capacity-building; military-style deployment training	Lack of HVAC-specific disaster training for NGO/humanitarian personnel
Sustainability Focus	Climate-adaptive design; net-zero HVAC pilots in refugee camps	Weak integration of green logistics in emergency procurement guidelines

In summary, while HVAC systems hold significant potential to enhance the resilience, safety, and well-being of populations affected by disasters, their effective integration into humanitarian operations remains hampered by critical challenges. Infrastructure degradation, financial limitations, and gaps in technological readiness demand adaptive, scalable, and context-sensitive solutions. However, emerging innovations—ranging from modular HVAC units and IoT-enabled air quality monitoring to solar-powered off-grid systems—signal a transformative shift toward climate-adaptive, energy-efficient relief models. Türkiye's multifaceted experience illustrates both the barriers and breakthroughs possible when engineering ingenuity aligns with strategic planning and policy innovation. Recognizing HVAC not as an auxiliary service but as a core logistical asset is pivotal for future humanitarian frameworks capable of addressing the dual imperatives of emergency relief and sustainable development.

7. STRATEGIC RECOMMENDATIONS

To ensure that HVAC systems are systematically embedded into humanitarian aid and disaster response frameworks, a strategic set of policy, coordination, innovation, and evaluation measures must be adopted. One of the most urgent needs is the establishment of national policy frameworks that explicitly include HVAC technologies as core infrastructure within disaster response plans. In Türkiye—where earthquakes, floods, and prolonged displacement scenarios are increasingly common—disaster planning still tends to prioritize shelter, food, and basic healthcare, with HVAC systems often considered secondary. However, as evidenced in the findings of Fahrni et al. (2022) and Zemitis et al. (2021), the absence of reliable temperature control and air quality management in temporary shelters can severely compromise both public health and logistical performance. Integrating HVAC into Türkiye's national disaster preparedness strategies, including specific provisions for off-grid energy sources, modular deployment models, and portable air handling units, would formalize its role as essential infrastructure. This policy shift must be supported by updated procurement protocols, funding streams, and civil protection regulations to ensure HVAC units are pre-stocked, maintained, and rapidly deployable in all major hazard-prone regions.

A second recommendation concerns the need for multi-agency coordination and stakeholder alignment. Effective deployment of HVAC systems in disaster contexts requires the seamless collaboration of governmental disaster management agencies (such as AFAD), municipal governments, private-sector HVAC manufacturers, logistics providers, and humanitarian organizations like the Turkish Red Crescent. Studies such as those by Almadani et al. (2023) and Srikandi et al. (2022) emphasize the importance of collaborative platforms and integrated operation centers that bring these diverse actors together under shared objectives. Türkiye's humanitarian response capacity can be strengthened by developing stakeholder roadmaps that clarify roles, establish communication protocols, and promote interoperability in supply chains and infrastructure management. Such coordination must also extend to local communities and shelter occupants, whose insights can inform culturally appropriate and user-friendly HVAC designs. By embedding HVAC coordination into larger national and international disaster resilience strategies, Türkiye can significantly improve its operational efficiency and outcomes in future emergencies.

Encouraging technology development and innovation is the third pillar of a comprehensive strategy. To address the evolving nature of climate-related disasters, Türkiye must incentivize the development of HVAC systems tailored for humanitarian use—especially portable, solar-powered, and modular units. As highlighted by Sedaghat et al. (2024) and Pless et al. (2022), integrating photovoltaic technology with smart energy management can yield HVAC solutions that are both autonomous and energy efficient. Governmental and academic funding mechanisms should prioritize R&D in this field, especially projects that enable rapid prototyping and localization of HVAC technologies for Türkiye's diverse geographic and climatic conditions. Partnerships between universities, engineering firms, and humanitarian actors should also be strengthened to accelerate the commercialization of low-emission, climate-resilient HVAC systems. Tax incentives, public–private innovation grants, and regulatory fast-tracking could further stimulate progress in this space, aligning humanitarian needs with industrial capabilities.

Lastly, robust monitoring, evaluation, and impact assessment mechanisms are essential for optimizing the deployment and effectiveness of HVAC systems in the field. Current humanitarian infrastructure often lacks formal performance indicators for thermal comfort, air quality, energy usage, and occupant health—factors directly influenced by HVAC operations. Drawing on the frameworks proposed by Eichholtz et al. (2024) and Kumar et al. (2025), key performance indicators (KPIs) should be introduced into shelter and mobile health facility assessments, measuring metrics such as temperature stability, indoor CO_2 levels, equipment uptime, and energy autonomy. These KPIs can be integrated into existing disaster response monitoring platforms and supported by real-time IoT data collected from HVAC units in operation. In Türkiye, such systems would allow agencies to make evidence-based decisions, prioritize repairs or redeployments, and evaluate the long-term cost-effectiveness of different HVAC technologies under various disaster conditions. Transparent evaluation also supports accountability to donors, public authorities, and the communities served—ensuring that HVAC integration is not only technically sound but socially and operationally effective.

In sum, the strategic integration of HVAC systems into humanitarian planning requires a coordinated effort across policy design, institutional collaboration, technological advancement, and evidence-based evaluation. Türkiye, with its high exposure to natural hazards and evolving humanitarian responsibilities, stands to benefit greatly from adopting these recommendations—building a disaster response architecture that is not only reactive but anticipatory, inclusive, and resilient.

8. CONCLUSION

This chapter has explored the strategic role of Heating, Ventilation, and Air Conditioning (HVAC) systems in humanitarian logistics, with a particular focus on Türkiye's disaster relief initiatives. Drawing from multidisciplinary perspectives in humanitarian engineering, disaster logistics, thermal comfort research, and public health, the chapter has illuminated how HVAC systems function not merely as technical installations but as critical enablers of human dignity, safety, and operational efficiency in crisis environments.

The findings underscore that HVAC systems are integral to multiple dimensions of emergency aid operations—ensuring thermal comfort and health in temporary shelters, maintaining vaccine and medicine efficacy through cold chain logistics, safeguarding air quality and infection control in healthcare spaces, and supporting energy-efficient and climate-resilient infrastructure in off-grid scenarios. Türkiye's post-2023 earthquake response, COVID-19 mobile hospitals, and long-term refugee camp management all reveal how coordinated planning, adaptable technologies, and institutional integration of HVAC systems can significantly improve outcomes in humanitarian crises.

Türkiye stands out as a compelling case study of how a middle-income, disaster-prone nation can leverage public-private partnerships, centralized coordination mechanisms (through AFAD and the Turkish Red Crescent), and adaptive infrastructure models to embed HVAC into the heart of its humanitarian strategy. These practices offer transferable insights for other regions facing compound emergencies—be it due to natural disasters, pandemics, or conflict-induced displacement.

Strategically, the chapter highlights the importance of mainstreaming HVAC considerations into national disaster management frameworks, encouraging innovation through policy incentives, and investing in localized manufacturing and training capacity. The integration of artificial intelligence, modular systems, and renewable energy further represents a frontier for the evolution of HVAC in complex emergencies.

Future research should explore the intersection of HVAC deployment with gender-sensitive aid delivery, cross-cultural perceptions of thermal comfort, and real-time performance analytics using IoT and predictive maintenance. Practice-oriented studies could also investigate the cost-benefit dynamics of portable HVAC systems in rapid-onset versus protracted crises, as well as the resilience of supply chains delivering these systems under disrupted conditions.

In conclusion, HVAC systems must no longer be considered auxiliary to humanitarian infrastructure. They are essential, strategic assets—capable of mitigating human suffering, ensuring health and dignity, and enhancing the effectiveness of emergency response operations. Türkiye's evolving approach offers a valuable blueprint for integrating HVAC into future-ready humanitarian logistics worldwide.

REFERENCES

Adekola, O., & Adekola, J. (2024). Post-Disaster Needs Assessment as a strategic recovery planning process. In *Research Handbook on Flood Risk Management* (pp. 275–286). Edward Elgar Publishing. DOI: 10.4337/9781839102981.00028

Adhikari, B., Mishra, S. R., Marahatta, S. B., Kaehler, N., Paudel, K., Adhikari, J., & Raut, S. (2017). Earthquakes, fuel crisis, power outages, and health care in Nepal: Implications for the future. *Disaster Medicine and Public Health Preparedness*, *11*(5), 625–632. DOI: 10.1017/dmp.2016.195 PMID: 28416042

AFAD. (2022). *Annual report on shelter infrastructure in refugee camps*. https://www.afad.gov.tr

AFAD. (2023). *Post-disaster medical infrastructure assessment following the 2023 earthquakes*. https://www.afad.gov.tr

AFAD. (2023). *Ulusal Deprem Stratejisi ve Eylem Planı (UDSEP-2023)* [National Earthquake Strategy and Action Plan]. https://www.afad.gov.tr

Alabsi, A. A. N., Wu, Y., Koko, A. F., Alshareem, K. M., & Hamed, R. (2021). Towards climate adaptation in cities: Indicators of the sustainable climate-adaptive urban fabric of traditional cities in West Asia. *Applied Sciences (Basel, Switzerland)*, *11*(21), 10428. DOI: 10.3390/app112110428

Almadani, B., Aliyu, F., & Aliyu, A. (2023). Integrated Operation Centers in Smart Cities: A Humanitarian Engineering Perspective. *Sustainability (Basel)*, *15*(14), 11101. DOI: 10.3390/su151411101

Alonso, A., Llanos, J., Escandon, R., & Sendra, J. J. (2021). Effects of the COVID-19 pandemic on indoor air quality and thermal comfort of primary schools in winter in a Mediterranean climate. *Sustainability (Basel)*, *13*(5), 2699. DOI: 10.3390/su13052699

Alshalabi, W. M. W. (2022). *Holistic Transitional Approach of Humanitarian Shelters Through the Implementation of Adaptable Design Strategies* (Master's thesis, The British University in Dubai).

Baghi, Y., Ma, Z., Robinson, D., & Boehme, T. (2021). Innovation in sustainable solar-powered net-zero energy Solar Decathlon houses: A review and showcase. *Buildings (Basel, Switzerland)*, *11*(4), 171. DOI: 10.3390/buildings11040171

Bera, M. (2025). Innovations in climate-adaptive clothing design for promoting resilience and well-being in a changing climate: A review. *Design*, *2*(2), 8589. DOI: 10.36922/dp.8589

Buonomano, A., Forzano, C., Giuzio, G. F., & Palombo, A. (2023). New ventilation design criteria for energy sustainability and indoor air quality in a post Covid-19 scenario. *Renewable & Sustainable Energy Reviews*, *182*, 113378. DOI: 10.1016/j.rser.2023.113378 PMID: 37250178

Burns, M. G. (2019). *Managing energy security: an all hazards approach to critical infrastructure*. Routledge. DOI: 10.4324/9780429320071

Cheshmehzangi, A. (2021). Housing and health evaluation related to general comfort and indoor thermal comfort satisfaction during the COVID-19 lockdown. *Journal of Human Behavior in the Social Environment*, *31*(1-4), 184–209. DOI: 10.1080/10911359.2020.1817225

Chester, M., El Asmar, M., Hayes, S., & Desha, C. (2021). Post-disaster infrastructure delivery for resilience. *Sustainability (Basel)*, *13*(6), 3458. DOI: 10.3390/su13063458

Conzatti, A., Kershaw, T., Copping, A., & Coley, D. (2022). A review of the impact of shelter design on the health of displaced populations. *Journal of International Humanitarian Action*, *7*(1), 18. DOI: 10.1186/s41018-022-00123-0 PMID: 37519834

Doody, C. B., Robertson, L., Cox, K. M., Bogue, J., Egan, J., & Sarma, K. M. (2021). Pre-deployment programmes for building resilience in military and frontline emergency service personnel. *Cochrane Database of Systematic Reviews*, 12. PMID: 34870330

Eichholtz, P., Kok, N., & Sun, X. (2024). The effect of post-COVID-19 ventilation measures on indoor air quality in primary schools. *PNAS Nexus*, *3*(1), pgad429. DOI: 10.1093/pnasnexus/pgad429 PMID: 38145248

Fahrni, M. L., Ismail, I. A. N., Refi, D. M., Almeman, A., Yaakob, N. C., Saman, K. M., Mansor, N. F., Noordin, N., & Babar, Z. U. D. (2022). Management of COVID-19 vaccines cold chain logistics: A scoping review. *Journal of Pharmaceutical Policy and Practice*, *15*(1), 16. DOI: 10.1186/s40545-022-00411-5 PMID: 35236393

Ferman, P. M. F., Gonçalves, R. A. C., & Oliveira, A. J. B. D. (2024). Cold chain logistics: the pathways of vaccines and thermolabile medicines to patients in municipal primary care. *Acta sci., Health sci*, 65451-65451.

Flores-Larsen, S., & Filippin, C. (2021). Energy efficiency, thermal resilience, and health during extreme heat events in low-income housing in Argentina. *Energy and Building*, *231*, 110576. DOI: 10.1016/j.enbuild.2020.110576

Ghadirinejad, N., Ottermo, F., Nowzari, R., Alsaadi, N., & Ghadiri Nejad, M. (2023). Optimizing a green and sustainable off-grid energy-system design: A real case. *Sustainability (Basel), 15*(17), 12800. DOI: 10.3390/su151712800

Hanna, R., Abdulla, A., Xu, Y., & Victor, D. G. (2021). Emergency deployment of direct air capture as a response to the climate crisis. *Nature Communications, 12*(1), 368. DOI: 10.1038/s41467-020-20437-0 PMID: 33446663

Hassan, H., Mishra, A. K., Wemken, N., O'Dea, P., Cowie, H., McIntyre, B., & Coggins, A. M. (2024). Deep energy renovations' impact on indoor air quality and thermal comfort of residential dwellings in Ireland–ARDEN project. *Building and Environment, 259*, 111637. DOI: 10.1016/j.buildenv.2024.111637

Hürriyet Daily News. (2023a). Türkiye delivers tents, stoves, blankets to quake zone. *Hürriyet Daily News*. https://www.hurriyetdailynews.com

Hürriyet Daily News. (2023b). Tent cities rise in Adıyaman stadiums for earthquake survivors. *Hürriyet Daily News*. https://www.hurriyetdailynews.com

Hürriyet Daily News. (2023c). Barrel stove fabrication by schools supports heating efforts. *Hürriyet Daily News*. https://www.hurriyetdailynews.com

Hürriyet Daily News. (2023d). Mobile hygiene units serve displaced families. *Hürriyet Daily News*. https://www.hurriyetdailynews.com

IFRC. (2021). *Shelter and non-food item distribution in Türkiye: A 10-year perspective*. https://www.ifrc.org

IFRC. (2023). Türkiye: Earthquake Emergency Response. *International Federation of Red Cross and Red Crescent Societies*. https://www.ifrc.org

IOM. (2022). *The health-environment nexus in protracted displacement settings: Türkiye case study*. International Organization for Migration. https://www.iom.int

Jiang, F., Xie, H., Gandla, S. R., & Fei, S. (2025). Transforming Hospital HVAC Design with BIM and Digital Twins: Addressing Real-Time Use Changes. *Sustainability (Basel), 17*(8), 3312. DOI: 10.3390/su17083312

Juaristi, M., Gómez-Acebo, T., & Monge-Barrio, A. (2018). Qualitative analysis of promising materials and technologies for the design and evaluation of Climate Adaptive Opaque Façades. *Building and Environment, 144*, 482–501. DOI: 10.1016/j.buildenv.2018.08.028

Khoche, S., Chandrasekhar, K. V., Sasirekha, G. V. K., Bapat, J., & Das, D. (2021). Occupancy detection for emergency management of smart building based on indoor localization: A feasibility study. *SN Computer Science*, *2*(6), 419. DOI: 10.1007/s42979-021-00812-4

Kong, F. (2024). Post-Disaster Governance in Southeast Asia: Response, Recovery, and Resilient Societies. *Singapore Journal of Tropical Geography*, *45*(1).

KOSGEB. (2023). Emergency SME support for HVAC production. *Small and Medium Enterprises Development Organization of Türkiye*. https://www.kosgeb.gov.tr

Kristiansen, A. B., Zhao, B. Y., Ma, T., & Wang, R. Z. (2021). The viability of solar photovoltaic powered off-grid Zero Energy Buildings based on a container home. *Journal of Cleaner Production*, *286*, 125312. DOI: 10.1016/j.jclepro.2020.125312

Kumar, V., Goodarzian, F., Ghasemi, P., Chan, F. T., & Gupta, N. (2025). Artificial intelligence applications in healthcare supply chain networks under disaster conditions. *International Journal of Production Research*, *63*(2), 395–403. DOI: 10.1080/00207543.2024.2444150

Lee, D. S., Iacocca, M., & Joshi, Y. K. (2021). Energy usage modeling for heating and cooling of off-grid shelters. *Journal of Building Engineering*, *35*, 102054. DOI: 10.1016/j.jobe.2020.102054

Majchrzak, D., Michalski, K., & Reginia-Zacharski, J. (2021). Readiness of the polish crisis management system to respond to long-term, large-scale power shortages and failures (blackouts). *Energies*, *14*(24), 8286. DOI: 10.3390/en14248286

Manupati, V. K., Schoenherr, T., Subramanian, N., Ramkumar, M., Soni, B., & Panigrahi, S. (2021). A multi-echelon dynamic cold chain for managing vaccine distribution. *Transportation Research Part E, Logistics and Transportation Review*, *156*, 102542. DOI: 10.1016/j.tre.2021.102542 PMID: 34815731

Matracia, M., Saeed, N., Kishk, M. A., & Alouini, M. S. (2022). Post-disaster communications: Enabling technologies, architectures, and open challenges. *IEEE Open Journal of the Communications Society*, *3*, 1177–1205. DOI: 10.1109/OJCOMS.2022.3192040

Meiss, A., Jimeno-Merino, H., Poza-Casado, I., Llorente-Álvarez, A., & Padilla-Marcos, M. Á. (2021). Indoor air quality in naturally ventilated classrooms. Lessons learned from a case study in a COVID-19 scenario. *Sustainability (Basel)*, *13*(15), 8446. DOI: 10.3390/su13158446

Michalis, P., & Vintzileou, E. (2022). The growing infrastructure crisis: The challenge of scour risk assessment and the development of a new sensing system. *Infrastructures*, *7*(5), 68. DOI: 10.3390/infrastructures7050068

Mohan, P. S. (2023). Disasters, disaster preparedness and post disaster recovery: Evidence from Caribbean firms. *International Journal of Disaster Risk Reduction*, *92*, 103731. DOI: 10.1016/j.ijdrr.2023.103731

Morawska, L., Li, Y., & Salthammer, T. (2024). Lessons from the COVID-19 pandemic for ventilation and indoor air quality. *Science*, *385*(6707), 396–401. DOI: 10.1126/science.adp2241 PMID: 39052782

Moultanovsky, A. V. (2014). HVAC Systems, Mobile: Innovations. In *Encyclopedia of Energy Engineering and Technology-Four Volume Set (Print)* (pp. 891-908). CRC Press.

Noreen, N. (2025). Enhancing Healthcare Workers' Preparedness at points of Entry; role of capacity building Training. *International Journal of Infectious Diseases*, *152*, 107572. DOI: 10.1016/j.ijid.2024.107572

Olutuase, V. O., Iwu-Jaja, C. J., Akuoko, C. P., Adewuyi, E. O., & Khanal, V. (2022). Medicines and vaccines supply chains challenges in Nigeria: A scoping review. *BMC Public Health*, *22*(1), 11. DOI: 10.1186/s12889-021-12361-9 PMID: 34986820

Pandey, K. (2025). *Designing Ethical AI for Development: Challenges and Opportunities in Humanitarian Engineering and Electric Vehicles*. Designed for Adventure.

Peruchi Pacheco da Silva, R., Samadi, F., Losole, J., & Carpenter, J. (2024). Strategic Evaluation of Sustainable Practices for HVAC Systems in Small-and Medium-Sized US Manufacturers. *ASME Journal of Engineering for Sustainable Buildings and Cities*, *5*(3), 031002. DOI: 10.1115/1.4065961

Plesner Volkdal, C. (2025). Triple Nexus: Leveraging development supply chains for humanitarian aid and peace in Southeast Asia–a GBV focus. *Journal of Humanitarian Logistics and Supply Chain Management*, *15*(3), 210–237. DOI: 10.1108/JHLSCM-02-2024-0028

Pless, S., Podder, A., Kaufman, Z., Klammer, N., Dennehy, C., Muthumanickam, N. K., . . . Blazek, C. (2022). *The energy in modular (EMOD) buildings method: A guide to energy-efficient design for industrialized construction of modular buildings* (No. NREL/TP-5500-82447). National Renewable Energy Lab.(NREL), Golden, CO (United States).

Pramanik, P. K. D., Pal, S., Mukhopadhyay, M., & Choudhury, P. (2024). Sustainable edge computing with mobile crowd computing: A proof-of-concept with a smart HVAC use case. *The Journal of Supercomputing*, *80*(16), 23911–23994. DOI: 10.1007/s11227-024-06364-7

Pu, F., Li, Z., Wu, Y., Ma, C., & Zhao, R. (2025). Recent Advances in Disaster Emergency Response Planning: Integrating Optimization, Machine Learning, and Simulation. *arXiv preprint arXiv:2505.03979.*

Red Cross Australia. (2023). Türkiye earthquake: Container homes for survivors. *Red Cross Australia.* https://www.redcross.org.au

Rehan, H. (2022). Enhancing Disaster Response Systems: Predicting and Mitigating the Impact of Natural Disasters Using AI. *Journal of Artificial Intelligence Research*, *2*(1), 501.

ReliefWeb. (2023). Humanitarian HVAC retrofitting in Turkish shelters. *ReliefWeb.* https://www.reliefweb.int

Sağlık Bakanlığı, T. C. (2021). *Pandemi hastaneleri tasarım ve kullanım kılavuzu [COVID-19 Field Hospital Design and Use Manual].* https://www.saglik.gov.tr

Santoro, B. F., Mendoza, D. F., & Rincon, D. (2021). Budget-constrained economic model predictive control: A user-friendly proposal for HVAC. *Chemical Engineering Research & Design*, *176*, 229–242. DOI: 10.1016/j.cherd.2021.10.003

Schismenos, S., Stevens, G. J., Emmanouloudis, D., Georgeou, N., Shrestha, S., & Chalaris, M. (2021). Humanitarian engineering at the sustainability-development nexus: Mapping vulnerability and capability factors for communities at risk of water-based disasters. *Sustainability Science*, *16*(4), 1185–1199. DOI: 10.1007/s11625-020-00890-y PMID: 33425037

Sedaghat, A., Kalbasi, R., Narayanan, R., Mehdizadeh, A., Soleimani, S. M., Malayer, M. A., & Khan, M. M. K. (2024). Integrating solar PV systems for energy efficiency in portable cabins: A case study in Kuwait. *Solar Energy*, *277*, 112715. DOI: 10.1016/j.solener.2024.112715

Seifert, L., Kunz, N., & Gold, S. (2023). Sustainable innovations for humanitarian operations in refugee camps. *International Journal of Operations & Production Management*, *43*(10), 1554–1586. DOI: 10.1108/IJOPM-05-2022-0302

Shehadeh, A., Alshboul, O., & Tamimi, M. (2025). Quantitative Analysis of Climate-Adaptive Pavement Technologies: Mitigating Environmental Impact and Enhancing Economic Viability in Urban Infrastructure. *Journal of Construction Engineering and Management*, *151*(6), 04025064. DOI: 10.1061/JCEMD4.COENG-15682

Shi, R., Yao, L., Zhao, M., & Yan, Z. (2023). The role of climate-adaptive technological innovation in promoting agriculture carbon efficiency: Impact and heterogeneity in economic development. *Environmental Science and Pollution Research International*, *30*(60), 126029–126044. DOI: 10.1007/s11356-023-31205-0 PMID: 38010550

Singh, R., & Manoharan, G. (2025). AI Integration to Strengthen Disaster Resilience in Smart Cities. In *AI and Emerging Technologies for Emergency Response and Smart Cities* (pp. 1–30). IGI Global Scientific Publishing. DOI: 10.4018/979-8-3693-9770-1.ch001

Srikandi, D., Sutopo, W., Hisjam, M., & Istiqomah, S. (2022, August). Commercializing a Technology Use Global Business Strategy Approach: A Lesson Learned from HVAC Companies. In *Proceedings of the International Conference on Industrial Engineering and Operations Management* (pp. 3079-3090).

Sulaiman, A. Y., Obasi, G. I., Chang, R., Moghaieb, H. S., Mondol, J. D., Smyth, M., Kamkari, B., & Hewitt, N. J. (2023). A solar powered off-grid air conditioning system with natural refrigerant for residential buildings: A theoretical and experimental evaluation. *Cleaner Energy Systems*, *5*, 100077. DOI: 10.1016/j.cles.2023.100077

Taipei Times. (2023). Container clinics deployed with HVAC and equipment. *Taipei Times*. https://www.taipeitimes.com

Torres, J., Garay-Martinez, R., Oregi, X., Torrens-Galdiz, J. I., Uriarte-Arrien, A., Pracucci, A., Casadei, O., Magnani, S., Arroyo, N., & Cea, A. M. (2021). Plug and play modular façade construction system for renovation for residential buildings. *Buildings (Basel, Switzerland)*, *11*(9), 419. DOI: 10.3390/buildings11090419

TRC. (2023). *Community-based resilience and HVAC vocational programs*. Turkish Red Crescent. https://www.kizilay.org.tr

TRC. (2023a). Disaster response update—HVAC in shelter and service units. *Türk Kızılay (Turkish Red Crescent)*. https://www.kizilay.org.tr

Türkiye, U. N. D. P. (2023). *Sustainable energy solutions in refugee camp management*. United Nations Development Programme Türkiye. https://www.tr.undp.org

Turmaks. (2023). Modular hospitals delivered to Hatay. *Turmaks Medical Infrastructure*. https://www.turmaks.com

UNDP. (2023). Climate control in container cities. *United Nations Development Programme Türkiye*. https://www.tr.undp.org

UNECA. (2023). HVAC installations in Türkiye disaster shelters. *United Nations Economic Commission for Africa.* https://www.uneca.org

UNHCR. (2024). *Türkiye Operational Update – Refugee Response in 2023–2024.* United Nations High Commissioner for Refugees. https://www.unhcr.org/tr

WHO. (2021). *Environmental health risks in humanitarian settlements: Türkiye findings.* World Health Organization Regional Office for Europe. https://www.euro.who.int

WHO. (2023). *Guidance on temporary medical facilities and infection prevention in humanitarian settings.* World Health Organization. https://www.who.int

World, T. R. T. (2023a). Türkiye accelerates HVAC imports after quake. *TRT World.* https://www.trtworld.com

Yang, Y., Pan, M., & Pan, W. (2022). Integrated offsite logistics scheduling approach for high-rise modular building projects. *Journal of Construction Engineering and Management, 148*(6), 04022032. DOI: 10.1061/(ASCE)CO.1943-7862.0002280

Zajecs, D., Lebedeva, K., & Odineca, T. (2022). Application Possibilities of the Off-Grid HVAC System Operation Solution for Temporary Shelters in the Latvian Climate Conditions. *Latvian Journal of Physics and Technical Sciences, 59*(2), 55–63. DOI: 10.2478/lpts-2022-0011

Zemitis, J., Borodinecs, A., Bogdanovics, R., & Geikins, A. (2021). A case study of thermal comfort in a temporary shelter. *Journal of Sustainable Architecture and Civil Engineering, 29*(2), 139–149. DOI: 10.5755/j01.sace.29.2.29240

Chapter 10
Strategic Integration of Aviation, AI, and Predictive Analytics in Humanitarian Logistics

Kagan Cenk Mizrak
https://orcid.org/0000-0002-3472-394X
Nisantasi University, Istanbul, Turkey

ABSTRACT

This chapter examines the strategic role of aviation technologies, artificial intelligence (AI), and predictive analytics in enhancing humanitarian logistics. As crises grow more complex and unpredictable, aviation offers unmatched speed and flexibility, enabling timely aid delivery and real-time situational awareness. Case studies from the World Food Programme, UNHAS, and the Turkish Red Crescent illustrate the real-world application of these technologies in famine response, flight optimization, and post-disaster relief. The chapter also presents a phased roadmap for strategic technology integration and addresses ethical, regulatory, and governance challenges. By aligning emerging technologies with humanitarian values, the chapter provides actionable insights for leaders and policymakers seeking to build more resilient, data-informed humanitarian systems.

1. INTRODUCTION

In recent decades, the frequency, severity, and complexity of humanitarian crises have escalated significantly due to the compounded effects of armed conflicts, natural disasters, pandemics, and climate-induced displacements. The World Bank

DOI: 10.4018/979-8-3373-3643-5.ch010

(2023) estimates that over 100 million people are forcibly displaced globally, while climate-related hazards alone affect more than 200 million individuals each year. These crises often unfold in unpredictable, rapidly changing environments where logistical coordination is constrained by poor infrastructure, limited data availability, and fragmented institutional capacities. As humanitarian actors strive to deliver timely and effective aid under such volatile conditions, the demand for adaptive, agile, and foresight-driven operational strategies has never been greater.

Within this evolving landscape, aviation emerges as a pivotal enabler of strategic response, offering speed, reach, and flexibility that ground-based alternatives cannot match. Air transport can bypass infrastructural bottlenecks, deliver critical supplies to remote and inaccessible regions, and support aerial surveillance and assessment for real-time situational awareness. From drones delivering vaccines to cargo aircraft conducting emergency evacuations, aviation technologies are increasingly integrated into humanitarian logistics and decision-making frameworks. However, their effective deployment requires more than operational capability—it demands alignment with strategic objectives, risk governance mechanisms, and ethical imperatives. In this context, aviation must be understood not merely as a transportation modality but as a strategic asset embedded in a broader innovation ecosystem.

This chapter explores the strategic integration of aviation technologies—augmented by artificial intelligence (AI), predictive analytics, and autonomous systems—into humanitarian operations. Drawing from theoretical foundations in strategic management, including the Resource-Based View (RBV), Dynamic Capabilities Theory, and Stakeholder Theory, it critically examines how aviation and AI converge to support anticipatory logistics, scenario modeling, and real-time decision support. Through empirical insights and global case studies such as the World Food Programme's famine forecasting system, UNHAS's AI-powered flight planning, and the Turkish Red Crescent's post-earthquake drone operations, the chapter illustrates the operationalization of innovation for humanitarian impact.

Moreover, this chapter contributes to the literature by articulating a strategic roadmap for technology adoption in humanitarian logistics, incorporating key phases such as technology readiness assessment, capacity building, innovation alignment, cross-sector partnerships, and adaptive monitoring. It also addresses the governance, risk, and ethical challenges associated with AI and unmanned aerial systems in fragile environments—emphasizing the importance of value-sensitive design, regulatory compliance, and stakeholder engagement in mission-critical contexts.

Ultimately, the chapter argues for a paradigm shift in humanitarian strategy—one that centers on technologically informed decision-making, systems thinking, and ethically grounded foresight. As humanitarian organizations move toward digital transformation, they must not only invest in new tools but also reconfigure their strategic architecture to integrate those tools meaningfully, responsibly, and equitably. In doing so, they can enhance operational effectiveness while safeguarding the humanitarian principles that remain fundamental to their mission.

2. STRATEGIC MANAGEMENT FOUNDATIONS IN HUMANITARIAN CONTEXTS

The strategic management of humanitarian logistics, particularly within aviation-enabled operations, is increasingly framed by the Resource-Based View (RBV) of the firm. This perspective posits that sustainable competitive advantage arises from the possession and strategic deployment of rare, valuable, inimitable, and non-substitutable (VRIN) resources. In the context of humanitarian aviation logistics, such resources include specialized aircraft fleets, advanced air traffic systems, logistics coordination platforms, and embedded institutional knowledge. Ferreira and Ferreira (2025) emphasize that the RBV has evolved into a robust framework for analyzing how organizations leverage internal assets for strategic gain, especially under conditions of uncertainty. Applying this lens to humanitarian organizations reveals how air mobility capabilities—such as pre-positioned airbases, rapid deployment helicopters, or drone fleets—constitute strategic assets that offer speed, flexibility, and geographic reach not attainable through ground transportation. Wierzbiński et al. (2023), in their study on Polish aviation SMEs, similarly demonstrate that knowledge management orientation can enhance competitive performance, particularly when organizations actively mobilize their aviation-specific capabilities to serve niche logistics demands. This insight reinforces that in humanitarian logistics, the possession of aviation assets is not sufficient—strategic knowledge management and asset orchestration are equally essential for mission success. In disaster-prone regions, organizations with agile aviation resources outperform others due to their ability to rapidly access and deploy these capabilities, underlining the RBV's core thesis.

Complementing the RBV, the Dynamic Capabilities Theory (DCT) provides a more adaptive strategic lens, focusing on how organizations can reconfigure and renew their resources to respond to volatile environments—a constant feature of humanitarian crises. DCT emphasizes three interrelated capabilities: sensing opportunities and threats, seizing resources to address them, and reconfiguring existing operations to meet emergent demands. In humanitarian aviation logistics, this translates to using AI and predictive analytics to sense early disaster signals (e.g., forecasted floods or refugee movements), rapidly allocate aircraft and relief materials, and dynamically reroute based on real-time updates. Ayaz and Karademir (2021) reveal that organizational learning significantly enhances dynamic capabilities in aviation firms, allowing them to respond more effectively to disruptions. This is echoed by Roth, Rau, and Neyer (2023), who show that design thinking can strengthen dynamic managerial capabilities by fostering adaptive planning and cross-functional innovation. Within the humanitarian space, this means equipping crisis teams not only with predictive models but also with the managerial tools to interpret and act upon those insights. Durak and Sengur (2024) further argue that strategic flexibility—underpinned by dynamic capabilities—is critical for airlines managing uncertainty. This insight is particularly relevant to NGOs and intergovernmental agencies that must dynamically mobilize air assets and logistics resources during overlapping crises. Zahoor et al. (2022), in their COVID-19 study of Finnish SMEs, found that dynamic capabilities and strategic agility enabled rapid adaptation to changing demands, underscoring the need for similar adaptability in humanitarian contexts. These findings collectively support the idea that dynamic capabilities are indispensable for sustaining aviation-driven humanitarian operations in fluid and high-stakes environments.

Beyond internal capabilities, the external relational context of humanitarian logistics demands a rigorous application of Stakeholder Theory. Humanitarian organizations operate in a multi-actor ecosystem involving donors, national governments, military units, civil aviation authorities, local communities, and affected populations. Strategic decisions around aviation deployment, ethical data use, and sustainability must balance these stakeholders' priorities. Al Sarrah, Ajmal, and Mertzanis (2021) demonstrate that stakeholder perspectives are crucial in identifying sustainability indicators within Dubai's aviation sector, suggesting that inclusivity in planning enhances legitimacy and long-term viability. Similarly, Kivits and Sawang (2021) illustrate the dynamism of stakeholder engagement in aviation, showing that proactive, transparent, and adaptive interactions increase operational trust and coordination effectiveness. For humanitarian actors, this means cultivating open communication with local governments to ensure airspace access, collaborating with private sector logistics firms to co-deploy drones, and involving community organizations in last-mile distribution planning. Okafor (2022) expands this view through the lens of ethical sustainability accounting, proposing that strategic aviation decisions—such as carbon offsets, safety prioritization, and fair resource allocation—should be transparently reported to stakeholders to maintain legitimacy and ethical standing. In sum, Stakeholder Theory affirms that strategic success in aviation-enabled humanitarian logistics is contingent not only on technological and operational excellence but also on relational and ethical alignment with a diverse and often competing set of actors.

3. AVIATION AS A STRATEGIC LOGISTICS ASSET

Aviation serves as a cornerstone of strategic advantage in humanitarian logistics by enabling rapid, far-reaching, and flexible responses to complex emergencies. Air transport uniquely overcomes geographical and infrastructural barriers that often paralyze ground-based relief operations, especially in the immediate aftermath of natural disasters or armed conflict. Wu and Yang (2021) underscore that aviation logistics not only ensures speed but also strengthens the strategic responsiveness of relief agencies by reducing delivery lead times and supporting sustainability goals through optimized routing and multimodal integration. In humanitarian operations, the strategic value of aviation is amplified by its capacity to rapidly deploy life-saving supplies, personnel, and surveillance systems to remote or inaccessible locations. Haq and Faizan (2022) support this by identifying speed, dependability, and flexibility as critical performance indicators for gaining a competitive edge in the aviation sector—characteristics that are directly transferable to humanitarian contexts where time is synonymous with lives saved. Furthermore, air logistics provides organizations with the strategic flexibility to scale up or down operations in real time, reallocate aircraft based on changing priorities, and enable just-in-time responses through aerial cargo drops and medical evacuations. This makes aviation not just a mode of transport, but a mission-critical asset in humanitarian strategy.

Cost-benefit considerations are essential when evaluating the deployment of aviation assets in humanitarian operations. While aviation is often perceived as cost-intensive, its strategic utility in saving lives, maintaining supply chain continuity, and achieving donor expectations can outweigh its financial burden. Bråthen and Halpern (2012) analyze how targeted investments in air transport services for remote regions generate long-term economic and social returns by improving accessibility and resilience. Their findings suggest that when aviation is integrated as part of a broader strategic plan—including pre-positioned stockpiles, shared airspace agreements, and demand forecasting—it becomes a cost-effective enabler of logistics equity and disaster readiness. Mizrak and Akkartal (2024) further emphasize the cost-risk dimension from a cybersecurity standpoint, asserting that protecting aviation infrastructure from digital threats is critical for preserving its value as a secure and dependable logistics platform. Strategic innovation in aviation must therefore account not only for fuel and asset costs but also for the security and continuity of operations in increasingly digitized logistics environments. Mızrak (2025) expands this argument by highlighting how cybersecurity and resilience planning must be embedded in aviation's strategic business model to protect operational continuity, prevent data breaches, and avoid cascading failures in humanitarian supply chains—especially as AI and predictive analytics become integral to flight path optimization and cargo tracking systems.

The strategic deployment of aviation assets in humanitarian logistics follows a range of adaptive models, including pre-positioning hubs, modular fleet allocation, and just-in-time (JIT) aerial drops. Pre-positioning involves storing relief items near high-risk zones, enabling quick mobilization via air in early response phases. This model reduces dependency on damaged local infrastructure and accelerates the response window, a key factor in saving lives during acute emergencies. The strategic use of air corridors and temporary airfields further allows agencies to rapidly set up logistics pipelines in unpredictable or politically unstable contexts. Tatham, Neal, and Wu (2017) introduce the concept of hybrid cargo airships as a potential game-changer in this space, offering high payload capacity, low fuel consumption, and operational versatility in austere environments where conventional aircraft may be impractical. Dorn, Baird, and Owen (2018) echo this view in their analysis of airships in UN peace and humanitarian operations, highlighting their strategic deployment value in scenarios lacking formal runways or requiring persistent aerial presence. These emerging aviation technologies exemplify the shift toward more sustainable and strategically adaptive logistics systems, particularly in low-infrastructure settings. Whether through rotary-wing aircraft, fixed-wing planes, or autonomous drones, strategic deployment models must be informed by logistics intelligence, threat assessments, and situational awareness, thereby ensuring aviation assets are used not only effectively but also in alignment with humanitarian principles and strategic foresight.

4. AI AND PREDICTIVE ANALYTICS IN STRATEGIC HUMANITARIAN PLANNING

Artificial intelligence (AI) and predictive analytics have emerged as essential tools for demand forecasting, risk assessment, and inventory optimization in humanitarian logistics. In high-stakes disaster scenarios, where delays or resource misallocation can cost lives, AI-driven tools enable organizations to anticipate needs, pre-position supplies, and allocate assets with higher precision. Schneider, Jimenez, and Kyriazi (2023) detail the case of Project Jetson, developed by UNHCR to predict population movements in Somalia using machine learning algorithms that combine remote sensing data, conflict reports, and weather patterns. The predictive insights generated by Jetson enabled faster response planning and reduced dependency on static historical trends, demonstrating how humanitarian actors can leverage AI for agile crisis response. Similarly, Kondraganti, Narayanamurthy, and Sharifi (2024) emphasize that big data analytics allows real-time processing of unstructured data—such as social media feeds, satellite images, and sensor data—to forecast humanitarian demand more accurately. This capability significantly reduces blind spots in relief planning, especially in conflict zones and areas with disrupted communications. As the humanitarian sector evolves toward anticipatory action models, AI-enhanced demand forecasting and risk analysis are becoming strategic imperatives, moving organizations away from reactive logistics to preemptive planning grounded in data.

Beyond forecasting, AI also powers strategic dashboards and early warning systems that support organizational awareness and decision-making under uncertainty. Sudhi et al. (2025) highlight that AI-enabled emergency management platforms now integrate multimodal data—from drones, IoT devices, and mobile reporting applications—into real-time dashboards that visualize logistics flows, hotspot maps, and at-risk zones. These systems allow humanitarian managers to assess shifting operational landscapes at a glance and adapt strategies accordingly. The implementation of predictive dashboards enhances coordination between field units, headquarters, and donor agencies, fostering faster alignment on critical decisions such as flight routing, inventory dispatch, and medical triage. Bag, Gupta, and Wood (2022) further note that AI-enabled early warning systems help overcome systemic barriers in sustainable humanitarian supply chains by offering alerts on potential chokepoints, inventory expiration risks, and climate-exacerbated vulnerabilities. However, the success of these dashboards depends on data quality, interoperability, and the ability of humanitarian actors to interpret and trust algorithmic outputs. Coppi, Moreno Jimenez, and Kyriazi (2021) caution that explicability—the capacity for stakeholders to understand how AI arrives at its conclusions—is a fundamental principle for building ethical and accountable humanitarian AI systems. Without transparent AI design, predictive dashboards may introduce new uncertainties, especially in culturally sensitive or politically unstable environments.

AI also plays a growing role in scenario modeling and decision support systems (DSS) that help crisis leaders evaluate alternative strategies under uncertainty. Scenario-based modeling, powered by AI and simulation tools, enables humanitarian organizations to test logistical plans against a range of probable and extreme outcomes—such as disease outbreaks, infrastructure collapse, or refugee surges. De Boeck et al. (2023) argue that the collaboration between operations researchers and field practitioners is vital in building these complex yet context-aware decision models for humanitarian health supply chains. By incorporating real-time epidemiological and inventory data, such systems can recommend the most resilient and cost-effective strategies for medicine distribution, vaccination campaigns, and emergency airlifts. Moreover, Alipour (2025) notes that while AI offers transformative opportunities, it also introduces implementation challenges related to data governance, cross-organizational interoperability, and decision accountability. These challenges must be addressed through robust DSS design that combines human expertise with algorithmic intelligence in a transparent and participatory way. As the humanitarian sector transitions toward more digital and autonomous systems, the integration of AI-enabled scenario planning will not only enhance strategic foresight but also improve the agility and ethical quality of logistics decisions.

5. AUTONOMOUS SYSTEMS AND STRATEGIC AGILITY

Autonomous systems—particularly drones and unmanned aerial vehicles (UAVs)—have revolutionized last-mile delivery in humanitarian logistics by providing strategic flexibility, operational scalability, and unmatched access to remote or infrastructure-degraded environments. In disaster-prone or post-conflict regions where conventional vehicles face severe constraints, drones enable precision delivery of life-saving supplies, including vaccines, medical kits, and communication devices. Shuaibu, Mahmoud, and Sheltami (2025) emphasize that drone-based logistics models outperform traditional last-mile methods in terms of speed, terrain accessibility, and environmental adaptability. Their review identifies drone swarms, AI-based flight path optimization, and modular payload systems as game-changing technologies for humanitarian logistics. Eskandaripour and Boldsaikhan (2023) further highlight the maturation of drone systems, transitioning from experimental pilots to operational logistics frameworks that can support sustained relief efforts, particularly during floods, earthquakes, or disease outbreaks. Moradi, Wang, and Mafakheri (2024) extend this analysis to the broader concept of urban air mobility (UAM), arguing that drone integration should not be viewed as a short-term innovation but as a foundational layer in long-term sustainable humanitarian infrastructure. Tezei et al. (2024) add a strategic dimension by analyzing hybrid truck-drone models, which combine the reach of UAVs with the volume efficiency of ground vehicles—maximizing coverage while minimizing cost. These technologies redefine logistical agility and demonstrate that UAVs are no longer auxiliary tools but strategic assets critical to responsive and resilient humanitarian operations.

Strategic agility in humanitarian logistics also involves proactive risk mitigation through automation. Automation reduces human exposure to infectious environments, hostile territories, and physically hazardous areas, enabling organizations to maintain service delivery even under extreme conditions. He et al. (2024) address the energy-efficiency and regulatory trade-offs involved in integrating unmanned systems, particularly when organizations must balance environmental concerns with time-critical delivery mandates. This reflects the increasing need for strategic decision-making that incorporates not just logistics efficiency but also sustainability and compliance. As automation systems scale, their resilience against digital vulnerabilities, weather disruptions, and bandwidth limitations must be addressed to ensure reliable humanitarian outcomes. Mızrak and Akkartal (2024), in their edited volume on logistics for the Sustainable Development Goals (SDGs), assert that autonomous systems should be embedded into broader digital transformation agendas and supply chain governance frameworks. Similarly, Özkanlısoy and Akkartal (2021) emphasize the critical role of digital integration and interoperability in achieving automation at scale—highlighting that without unified data systems and strategic planning, autonomous technologies risk becoming fragmented solutions. Akkartal and Abdelhadi (2019) offer a complementary perspective by proposing an Internet of Things (IoT)-based framework for transportation and warehousing, where drones act as dynamic data nodes within an intelligent logistics ecosystem. Together, these studies affirm that automation not only enhances operational responsiveness but also provides a strategic risk buffer that enables humanitarian systems to adapt and respond more effectively to systemic shocks.

The strategic deployment of UAVs in health emergencies, such as the COVID-19 pandemic and Ebola outbreak, provides compelling evidence of their transformative potential. During these global crises, autonomous technologies were rapidly adopted to transport test kits, deliver vaccines, and support real-time monitoring in inaccessible areas. Lal et al. (2022) note that health information systems—when integrated with UAV logistics—enabled targeted interventions and accelerated pandemic preparedness. For example, during the Ebola outbreak, UAVs were used not only for delivery but also for aerial surveillance to monitor quarantine zones and optimize aid placement. These actions significantly improved response time and resource allocation. Mbunge, Chitungo, and Dzinamarira (2021) conducted a rapid review of drone and cognitive robotics applications during COVID-19 in sub-Saharan Africa, concluding that UAVs reduced the need for physical contact and helped bridge infrastructure gaps in overstretched healthcare systems. Their study underscores that the value of UAVs lies not only in physical delivery but also in data collection, thermal scanning, and broadcasting public health information. By acting as both transporters and sensors, drones became multifunctional agents of strategic health management. These cases illustrate how autonomous systems, when embedded into broader emergency response architectures, enhance situational awareness, reduce systemic delays, and support ethical, agile, and efficient humanitarian decision-making.

6. CASE STUDIES: STRATEGIC INNOVATION THROUGH AVIATION TECHNOLOGIES

6.1. WFP's Predictive Logistics System for Famine Response

The World Food Programme (WFP) has significantly advanced its operational foresight through the integration of predictive analytics into aviation logistics, particularly in responding to famine and displacement crises. One of the most notable innovations is the HungerMapLIVE platform, which combines near real-time data with geospatial modeling to anticipate food insecurity trends. This system integrates satellite imagery, market prices, conflict data, and climate indicators to generate alerts, enabling preemptive positioning of aviation assets and humanitarian cargo (WFP, 2023). It allows the WFP to shift from reactive to anticipatory logistics, dramatically enhancing the speed and precision of aerial supply drops in regions like the Horn of Africa.

The data pipeline for HungerMapLIVE supports scenario-based logistics planning. For instance, predictive models alerted WFP planners of escalating risk in Somalia during the 2022 drought cycle. This triggered the pre-deployment of aircraft and food stocks to Mogadishu and Garowe, facilitating emergency operations weeks earlier than in past crises (OCHA, 2022). These forecasts inform aviation routing, cargo loading strategies, and priority setting among vulnerable regions, aligning logistical decisions with data-driven humanitarian targets.

From a strategic management perspective, the system reflects principles of dynamic capabilities theory, enabling WFP to sense environmental changes, seize response opportunities, and reconfigure its aviation logistics network accordingly (Teece, 2007). Moreover, its alignment with stakeholder priorities—donors, local governments, and communities—supports an integrated resource-based and stakeholder-driven model. HungerMapLIVE also minimizes resource waste by preventing over-dispatch and redundant flights, thus enhancing operational cost-efficiency and reducing aviation carbon footprint (WFP, 2023). The system exemplifies how digital innovation in aviation logistics enhances organizational agility and strategic foresight in humanitarian operations.

6.2. UNHAS's AI-Driven Flight Planning for Fleet Optimization

The United Nations Humanitarian Air Service (UNHAS), managed by WFP Aviation, has implemented AI-powered flight planning systems to optimize fleet utilization, reduce fuel consumption, and maximize coverage in challenging environments. These systems were initially piloted in coordination with WFP's Aviation Safety Unit and the United Nations Office for Project Services (UNOPS), using advanced algorithms that analyze historical air traffic, mission urgency, weather data, and runway conditions (UNHAS, 2022). One such system is the Flight Planning Optimization Tool (FPOT), which relies on machine learning to suggest optimal flight schedules across multi-country air corridors.

This AI-driven scheduling is particularly critical in multi-agency coordination scenarios, where UNHAS operates over 60 aircraft across more than 15 humanitarian contexts—from South Sudan and the Central African Republic to Mali and

Afghanistan. By leveraging AI to reduce flight redundancies and increase payload efficiency, UNHAS achieved measurable improvements in cost-effectiveness. For example, in 2022, optimized routing resulted in a 12% reduction in flight hours and a 9% increase in passenger capacity utilization across East Africa (UNHAS, 2023).

Strategically, this case underscores how AI aligns with the principles of strategic agility and knowledge-based optimization in aviation logistics. The system not only adapts to real-time changes in humanitarian needs but also supports scenario-based simulations for risk mitigation. It also aids in long-term capacity planning—matching aircraft types, routes, and fuel types to changing topographical and political conditions. AI tools are also embedded within UNHAS's performance dashboard, used by field managers and regional coordinators to assess cost-benefit tradeoffs, regulatory constraints, and cargo prioritization. The use of AI in flight planning illustrates how strategic innovation in aviation technology translates into scalable, cross-operational efficiency.

6.3. Turkish Red Crescent's Drone Integration for Post-Earthquake Supply Drops

The Turkish Red Crescent (Kızılay) has emerged as a leader in deploying drone technology for disaster relief, particularly after major seismic events. In the aftermath of the 2023 Kahramanmaraş earthquake, which devastated large parts of southern Türkiye, Kızılay integrated fixed-wing and rotary drones into its logistics pipeline to conduct aerial assessments and deliver essential items—including medical kits, power banks, and water filtration devices—into isolated mountainous villages (TRC, 2023). Collaborating with the Turkish Technology Team Foundation (T3 Vakfı) and Aselsan, the Red Crescent deployed autonomous VTOL drones equipped with infrared cameras and real-time geospatial sensors.

The drones operated out of temporary logistics bases established near Gaziantep and Malatya, enabling just-in-time aerial drops in areas where roads were impassable. Drone missions were coordinated using a central command platform that integrated GIS layers, social media SOS signals, and survivor data. In several instances, the drone fleet enabled Kızılay to reach areas where manned helicopters had been grounded due to heavy fog or lack of landing zones (TRT Haber, 2023). This rapid delivery reduced mortality risks and provided time-sensitive aid before ground teams could arrive.

Strategically, the drone deployment reflects a hybrid model of strategic flexibility and automation. It aligns with the resource-based view by treating aviation drones not just as delivery tools but as modular, reconfigurable resources that augment resilience during crisis phases (Ferreira & Ferreira, 2025). The Red Crescent's integration of drones also contributed to its stakeholder legitimacy, enhancing public perception and donor trust due to the transparency of drone-enabled monitoring. Lessons from this response are now informing Türkiye's national disaster preparedness framework, where UAV integration is being formally institutionalized in Kızılay's standard operating procedures (AFAD, 2024).

Table 1 provides a comparative overview of the three analyzed case studies, highlighting the technological, strategic, and operational distinctions that underpin each organization's innovative use of aviation technologies in humanitarian logistics. By organizing these initiatives along dimensions such as technological tools, primary objectives, geographic scope, strategic frameworks, and achieved outcomes, the table facilitates a clear understanding of how aviation-based solutions are being strategically adapted to diverse crisis contexts. It also emphasizes the convergence of emerging technologies—such as predictive analytics, artificial intelligence, and autonomous systems—with core principles of strategic management including agility, dynamic capabilities, and stakeholder responsiveness. This synthesis enables a holistic appreciation of the varied, yet interconnected, ways aviation is being leveraged to advance timely, efficient, and accountable humanitarian interventions.

Table 1. Comparative Analysis of Strategic Innovations in Aviation Technologies for Humanitarian Logistics

Dimension	WFP – Predictive Aviation Logistics	UNHAS – AI Flight Planning	Turkish Red Crescent – Drone Deployment
Technology Used	Predictive Analytics (HungerMapLIVE)	AI Scheduling Algorithms (FPOT)	Autonomous Drones (VTOL, GIS-linked)
Primary Objective	Famine Anticipation & Pre-Deployment	Fleet Efficiency & Route Optimization	Post-Disaster Supply Drops & Surveillance
Geographic Scope	Horn of Africa, Yemen	Sub-Saharan Africa, Middle East	Türkiye (Kahramanmaraş Earthquake Response)
Strategic Framework	Dynamic Capabilities, Stakeholder Theory	Strategic Agility, Knowledge-Based View	Resource-Based View, Strategic Flexibility
Outcome/Impact	Reduced Response Time, Lowered Waste	12% Flight Time Reduction, Cost Savings	Access to Isolated Areas, Enhanced Legitimacy
Key Partners	FAO, OCHA, Local Gov'ts	UNOPS, ICAO	T3 Foundation, Aselsan, AFAD

7. STRATEGIC INTEGRATION ROADMAP

Successfully embedding aviation technologies, artificial intelligence (AI), and predictive analytics into humanitarian logistics requires a phased, strategically managed approach. The roadmap outlined below provides a structured progression for organizations aiming to achieve operational transformation while maintaining mission alignment, stakeholder legitimacy, and long-term adaptability. Each phase is informed by established strategic management principles, including resource-based planning, dynamic capabilities, stakeholder engagement, and continuous learning mechanisms.

Phase 1: Strategic Technology Assessment – Auditing Aviation and AI Readiness

The first step toward integration involves a comprehensive audit of existing technological assets and digital maturity within the organization. This phase focuses on assessing the current state of aviation logistics infrastructure, such as aircraft availability, telemetry capabilities, data collection platforms, and connectivity tools. Simultaneously, it evaluates AI readiness by identifying gaps in data governance, algorithmic literacy, cybersecurity posture, and ethical risk management. A diagnostic framework should include both technical and organizational readiness indicators, such as IT interoperability, decision support usage, and supply chain visibility. This strategic audit allows organizations to map their baseline and define realistic digital transformation objectives. It also supports prioritization of areas where AI and aviation innovation can yield the highest return in humanitarian terms—such as improved delivery times, reduced operational waste, or enhanced beneficiary targeting.

Phase 2: Organizational Capacity Building – Skills, Leadership, and Change Management

Technology adoption without adequate human capacity is unlikely to succeed in volatile humanitarian settings. This phase centers on equipping the workforce with interdisciplinary skills in aviation operations, data analytics, and AI ethics, while fostering leadership mindsets attuned to digital innovation. Strategic management literature emphasizes the importance of change agents and boundary-spanning leaders who can navigate organizational silos, align competing priorities, and mobilize support for new tools (Zhang & Saadé, 2025). Moreover, capacity building must address frontline staff, logistics managers, and regional coordinators—ensuring that all actors understand and trust the new systems. Training programs should combine simulation-based learning with real-time mission integration exercises. Change management strategies should also include feedback channels and incentive structures that reward experimentation and continuous learning.

Phase 3: Innovation Alignment – Integrating Tech with Mission and Performance Metrics

After initial capacity development, organizations must align innovation initiatives with core humanitarian mandates. This means ensuring that aviation and AI systems are not developed in isolation but rather embedded into planning cycles, mission objectives, and accountability frameworks. Key performance indicators (KPIs) should evolve to reflect not only efficiency outcomes—such as on-time deliveries or cost per flight—but also strategic enablers like anticipatory response capacity, supply chain resilience, and stakeholder trust. Integration at this stage also involves recalibrating standard operating procedures (SOPs) to incorporate data-driven decision-making, aerial delivery protocols, and machine-assisted scenario planning. Strategic alignment further entails conducting risk assessments to evaluate unintended consequences, such as technological exclusion of vulnerable populations or overdependence on automated systems.

Phase 4: Cross-Sector Partnerships – Collaborating with Private Sector, Tech Firms, and Military Aviation

Given the high costs and technical complexity of aviation and AI tools, strategic partnerships are critical for scalability and sustainability. This phase encourages humanitarian actors to build interoperable ecosystems with private tech companies, drone startups, aerospace firms, and military air support units. For instance, public-private collaborations can enable access to cutting-edge UAVs, AI cloud platforms, and satellite-linked flight systems. Partnerships with defense agencies may offer logistical expertise in conflict zones, while collaborations with academia and NGOs can enhance innovation legitimacy and shared learning. From a strategic management standpoint, such alliances reflect the application of networked resource strategies and open innovation models, which extend the organization's capabilities beyond internal boundaries. Governance models should be co-developed to ensure ethical deployment, data protection, and equitable access.

Phase 5: Adaptive Strategy Monitoring – Feedback Loops and KPI-Driven Review

In the final phase, organizations must institutionalize feedback mechanisms and performance monitoring systems to track the effectiveness of integrated aviation and AI solutions. Adaptive strategy frameworks call for iterative review cycles where lessons from deployments—both successes and failures—are systematically captured and used to recalibrate future strategies. Dashboards with real-time KPIs should be accessible to both operational staff and executive leadership, enabling dynamic course corrections and cross-level learning. Strategic foresight tools such as scenario modeling, stress testing, and horizon scanning can further guide decision-makers in preparing for emerging risks and technological disruptions. This continuous loop strengthens organizational resilience and ensures that aviation technologies evolve alongside changing humanitarian needs, geopolitical conditions, and stakeholder expectations.

8. GOVERNANCE, RISK, AND ETHICS IN STRATEGY EXECUTION

The strategic execution of aviation and artificial intelligence (AI) technologies in humanitarian logistics necessitates robust governance frameworks to mitigate emergent risks and ensure ethical compliance. As organizations increasingly rely on intelligent automation and autonomous systems, the complexity of associated ethical, legal, and strategic risks grows exponentially. Governance structures must therefore evolve in tandem with technological capabilities to uphold humanitarian values, prevent unintended harm, and foster accountability across global operations.

One of the most pressing challenges in the deployment of AI in humanitarian contexts is the management of extreme risks, including algorithmic bias, data privacy violations, autonomy failures, and misuse in fragile environments. Bengio et al. (2024) argue that as AI systems become more powerful and autonomous, the risk landscape shifts from operational failures to strategic-level threats, including the potential erosion of human oversight. Strategic governance must, therefore, incorporate robust safety protocols, alignment verification tools, and risk-informed deployment thresholdsto mitigate these systemic vulnerabilities. These measures are especially critical in contexts where predictive analytics and automated decision-making directly affect vulnerable populations.

Mutambara (2025) emphasizes that AI governance must be strategically framed to align with the UN Sustainable Development Goals (SDGs), particularly in fragile and data-sparse humanitarian environments. His framework underscores the need for strategic harmonization between technological innovation and ethical mandates, integrating value-based principles such as equity, transparency, and do-no-harm. Within aviation-supported humanitarian operations, this implies rigorous scrutiny of AI-driven flight routing algorithms, autonomous UAV behaviors, and real-time logistics optimization platforms. Ethical oversight must extend beyond system design to deployment scenarios, where unintended outcomes—such as exclusion of off-grid communities or profiling based on biased datasets—can have life-threatening consequences.

From a legal and humanitarian perspective, Broussard et al. (2019) provide a systematic review of how ethical obligations are frequently undermined in conflict and disaster settings. They highlight that organizational adherence to humanitarian principles such as impartiality, neutrality, and independence is often challenged by opaque technological systems and militarized partnerships. The integration of aviation technologies—particularly UAVs—into humanitarian supply chains risks blurring the line between civil and military logistics, thereby increasing suspicion among affected communities and jeopardizing operational legitimacy.

To address these risks, Smith, Pringle, and Hunt (2020) advocate for a value-sensitive design (VSD) approach, which embeds ethical reasoning and stakeholder engagement into the lifecycle of innovation. Their framework is particularly salient for humanitarian technologies, where user trust and ethical legitimacy are non-negotiable. Applying VSD to aviation and AI systems involves conducting contextual ethics assessments, incorporating diverse beneficiary perspectives, and enabling adjustable system parameters that respond to local moral concerns. This strategic alignment not only protects humanitarian credibility but also enhances user adoption and mission effectiveness.

Legal and regulatory frameworks surrounding unmanned aerial vehicles (UAVs) further complicate governance in international humanitarian operations. Tyshchuk (2024) explores how UAV usage at national borders and in conflict zones raises pressing questions around jurisdiction, sovereignty, and privacy. International humanitarian actors must navigate a fragmented legal landscape, where UAV regulations vary by country and are often reactive rather than anticipatory. Similarly, Fakhraian et al. (2023) note that emerging tools like digital twins—used to simulate UAV behavior—offer promising applications for safety assurance and regulatory compliance under the European Union's drone governance frameworks. These simulation-based methods can strategically inform pre-deployment risk assessments and enable adaptive flight strategies during missions.

Lastly, Singh (2024) provides a comprehensive analysis of the cybersecurity, surveillance, and regulatory dimensions of UAS (Unmanned Aircraft Systems), emphasizing the need for multilayered governance protocols. His study reveals that strategic risk management must address not only operational reliability but also data integrity, signal jamming, and dual-use risks—especially when UAVs are equipped with sensing, imaging, or payload delivery functions. These considerations necessitate a governance ecosystem that is both forward-looking and contextually grounded, combining international regulatory alignment, institutional transparency, and field-level ethical resilience.

In sum, effective governance of aviation and AI systems in humanitarian logistics requires multi-dimensional strategic integration—balancing technological potential with ethical safeguards, legal conformity, and mission-aligned values. As these technologies become more embedded in humanitarian infrastructures, organizations must adopt adaptive governance mechanisms that are capable of navigating uncertainty, engaging stakeholders, and maintaining trust amidst digital transformation.

9. CONCLUSION

As the humanitarian landscape becomes increasingly complex and technology-driven, strategic leadership must evolve to harness the transformative power of aviation, artificial intelligence (AI), and predictive analytics while maintaining ethical integrity and mission alignment. This chapter has examined how aviation technologies—combined with emerging data-driven capabilities—are reshaping humanitarian logistics from reactive supply models to anticipatory, agile, and precision-oriented systems. By grounding this transformation in established strategic management theories such as the Resource-Based View (RBV), Dynamic Capabilities, and Stakeholder Theory, humanitarian organizations can navigate uncertainty, leverage core assets, and maximize value for beneficiaries.

For humanitarian managers and policymakers, several key takeaways emerge. First, aviation is no longer a support function—it is a strategic enabler of humanitarian performance, offering unparalleled reach, speed, and flexibility in crisis response. Whether through unmanned aerial vehicles (UAVs) for last-mile delivery, cargo airships for remote access, or AI-optimized flight planning, air mobility has become integral to modern humanitarian strategy. Second, integrating AI into forecasting, needs assessment, and inventory optimization enables organizations to shift from static logistics chains to dynamic, data-informed ecosystems. However, as emphasized throughout this chapter, this integration must be accompanied by robust capacity building, governance structures, and ethical guardrails to avoid unintended consequences and protect vulnerable populations.

The evolving role of aviation extends beyond logistics. It contributes to strategic foresight, allowing humanitarian actors to anticipate threats, pre-position resources, and coordinate multilaterally with private, public, and military stakeholders. Aviation-supported systems are now instrumental in enabling real-time situational awareness, deploying autonomous relief systems, and building resilience in fragile regions. Importantly, their impact is amplified when deployed alongside AI, enabling multi-scenario modeling and adaptive resource allocation that traditional supply chains cannot achieve alone. For strategic leaders, the imperative is to treat aviation not merely as a tool, but as an integrated platform for innovation, coordination, and resilience.

Future research must continue to bridge the gap between operational technologies and strategic frameworks. First, systems thinking should be more deeply applied to humanitarian planning, recognizing interdependencies between actors, assets, information flows, and environmental factors. Second, the inclusion of Environmental, Social, and Governance (ESG) frameworks can enhance accountability, sustainability, and legitimacy in tech-driven humanitarian operations. This involves evaluating the ecological footprint of aviation technologies, ensuring equitable data use, and maintaining transparent governance mechanisms. Lastly, AI ethics should be treated as a cornerstone of strategic design rather than an afterthought. Research should focus on developing scalable methods for value-sensitive design, explicability standards, and inclusive stakeholder engagement to ensure technologies uphold the principles of humanity, impartiality, neutrality, and independence.

In conclusion, humanitarian leaders stand at a pivotal intersection of innovation and accountability. Those who can strategically integrate aviation and AI while navigating the ethical and governance complexities of modern humanitarian operations will be better positioned to respond effectively to crises, build resilient systems, and protect the dignity of those they serve.

REFERENCES

AFAD. (2024). *Türkiye Ulusal Afet Müdahale Planı 2024–2026*. Retrieved from https://www.afad.gov.tr

Akkartal, E., & Abdelhadi, A. (2019). *A framework of IoT implementations and challenges in Warehouse Management, Transportation and Retailing*. Eurasian Business & Economics Journal.

Al Sarrah, M., Ajmal, M. M., & Mertzanis, C. (2021). Identification of sustainability indicators in the civil aviation sector in Dubai: A stakeholders' perspective. *Social Responsibility Journal, 17*(5), 648–668. DOI: 10.1108/SRJ-06-2019-0203

Alipour, E. (2025). Challenges and Opportunities of Using Artificial Intelligence in Humanitarian Actions. *Quarterly Scientific Journal of Rescue and Relief, 17*(1), 1–3. DOI: 10.61186/jorar.17.1.1

Ayaz, S., & Karademir, S. (2021). Relationship between Organizational Learning and Dynamic Capabilities in Aviation Companies. *JOEEP: Journal of Emerging Economies and Policy*, *7*(2), 591–598.

Bag, S., Gupta, S., & Wood, L. (2022). Big data analytics in sustainable humanitarian supply chain: Barriers and their interactions. *Annals of Operations Research, 319*(1), 721–760. DOI: 10.1007/s10479-020-03790-7

Bengio, Y., Hinton, G., Yao, A., Song, D., Abbeel, P., Darrell, T., Harari, Y. N., Zhang, Y.-Q., Xue, L., Shalev-Shwartz, S., Hadfield, G., Clune, J., Maharaj, T., Hutter, F., Baydin, A. G., McIlraith, S., Gao, Q., Acharya, A., Krueger, D., & Mindermann, S. (2024). Managing extreme AI risks amid rapid progress. *Science, 384*(6698), 842–845. DOI: 10.1126/science.adn0117 PMID: 38768279

Bråthen, S., & Halpern, N. (2012). Air transport service provision and management strategies to improve the economic benefits for remote regions. *Research in Transportation Business & Management, 4*, 3–12. DOI: 10.1016/j.rtbm.2012.06.003

Broussard, G., Rubenstein, L. S., Robinson, C., Maziak, W., Gilbert, S. Z., & DeCamp, M. (2019). Challenges to ethical obligations and humanitarian principles in conflict settings: A systematic review. *Journal of International Humanitarian Action, 4*(1), 1–13. DOI: 10.1186/s41018-019-0063-x

Coppi, G., Moreno Jimenez, R., & Kyriazi, S. (2021). Explicability of humanitarian AI: A matter of principles. *Journal of International Humanitarian Action, 6*(1), 19. DOI: 10.1186/s41018-021-00096-6

De Boeck, K., Besiou, M., Decouttere, C., Rafter, S., Vandaele, N., Van Wassenhove, L. N., & Yadav, P. (2023). Data, analytical techniques and collaboration between researchers and practitioners in humanitarian health supply chains: A challenging but necessary way forward. *Journal of Humanitarian Logistics and Supply Chain Management, 13*(3), 237–248. DOI: 10.1108/JHLSCM-07-2022-0078

Dorn, W., Baird, N., & Owen, R. (2018). Airships in un humanitarian and peace operations: Ready for service? *Journal of Aviation/Aerospace Education Research, 27*(2), 41–58.

Durak, M. S., & Sengur, F. (2024). Managing Uncertainty in the Airline Industry: The Interaction of Strategic Flexibility, Organizational Learning, and Dynamic Capabilities. *International Journal of Aviation, Aeronautics, and Aerospace, 11*(3), 8. DOI: 10.58940/2374-6793.1931

Eskandaripour, H., & Boldsaikhan, E. (2023). Last-mile drone delivery: Past, present, and future. *Drones (Basel), 7*(2), 77. DOI: 10.3390/drones7020077

Fakhraian, E., Semanjski, I., Semanjski, S., & Aghezzaf, E. H. (2023). Towards safe and efficient unmanned aircraft system operations: Literature review of digital twins' applications and european union regulatory compliance. *Drones (Basel), 7*(7), 478. DOI: 10.3390/drones7070478

Ferreira, N. C., & Ferreira, J. J. (2025). The field of resource-based view research: Mapping past, present and future trends. *Management Decision, 63*(4), 1124–1153. DOI: 10.1108/MD-10-2023-1908

Haber, T. R. T. (2023). *Kızılay'dan Deprem Bölgesine Drone'lu Yardım*. Retrieved from https://www.trthaber.com

Haq, I., & Faizan, R. (2022). Role and Effectiveness of Five-Performance Indicators (Price, Dependability, Speed, Quality & Flexibility) in Attaining Competitive Edge in the Aviation Industry. *International Journal of Applied Business and Management Studies, 7*(2), 11–51.

He, C., Singh, P., P'yavka, S., Wolfe, L., Caldwell, K., Islam, T. M., . . . Mustafa, A. (2024). Balancing Trade-Offs: The Energy Efficiency of Unmanned Aircraft Systems Integration in Last-Mile Delivery and Operational Policy Restrictions. In *AIAA AVIATION FORUM AND ASCEND 2024* (p. 3646).

Kivits, R., & Sawang, S. (2021). *The dynamism of stakeholder engagement: A case study of the aviation industry*. Springer Nature. DOI: 10.1007/978-3-030-70428-5

Kondraganti, A., Narayanamurthy, G., & Sharifi, H. (2024). A systematic literature review on the use of big data analytics in humanitarian and disaster operations. *Annals of Operations Research, 335*(3), 1015–1052. DOI: 10.1007/s10479-022-04904-z PMID: 36846245

Lal, A., Ashworth, H. C., Dada, S., Hoemeke, L., & Tambo, E. (2022). Optimizing pandemic preparedness and response through health information systems: Lessons learned from Ebola to COVID-19. *Disaster Medicine and Public Health Preparedness, 16*(1), 333–340. DOI: 10.1017/dmp.2020.361 PMID: 33004102

Mbunge, E., Chitungo, I., & Dzinamarira, T. (2021). Unbundling the significance of cognitive robots and drones deployed to tackle COVID-19 pandemic: A rapid review to unpack emerging opportunities to improve healthcare in sub-Saharan Africa. *Cognitive Robotics, 1*, 205–213. DOI: 10.1016/j.cogr.2021.11.001

Mızrak, F. (2025). Cybersecurity and Strategic Innovation in the Digital Economy. In *Utilizing Cybersecurity to Foster Business Innovation and Resiliency* (pp. 1–30). IGI Global Scientific Publishing. DOI: 10.4018/979-8-3693-6417-8.ch001

Mızrak, F., & Akkartal, E. (Eds.). (2024). *Effective Logistics for Sustainable Development Goals*. IGI Global. DOI: 10.4018/979-8-3693-7071-1

Mizrak, F., & Akkartal, G. R. (2024). Prioritizing cybersecurity initiatives in aviation: A dematel-QSFS methodology. *Heliyon, 10*(16), e35487. DOI: 10.1016/j.heliyon.2024.e35487 PMID: 39687858

Moradi, N., Wang, C., & Mafakheri, F. (2024). Urban air mobility for last-mile transportation: A review. *Vehicles (Basel), 6*(3), 1383–1414. DOI: 10.3390/vehicles6030066

Mutambara, P. D. E. (2025). Strategic Framework for AI Deployment. In *Deploying Artificial Intelligence to Achieve the UN Sustainable Development Goals: Enablers, Drivers and Strategic Framework* (pp. 245–267). Springer Nature Switzerland. DOI: 10.1007/978-3-031-88423-8_11

OCHA. (2022). *Somalia Humanitarian Response Plan*. Retrieved from https://reliefweb.int/report/somalia

Okafor, U. I. (2022). Ethical Approach to Sustainability Accounting Practices and Financial Performance of Aviation Companies in Nigeria: A Conceptual Model. *Society & Sustainability, 4*(1), 25–42.

Özkanlısoy, Ö., & Akkartal, E. (2021). Digital transformation in supply chains: Current applications, contributions and challenges. *Business & Management Studies: An International Journal, 9*(1), 32–55.

Roth, K., Rau, C., & Neyer, A. K. (2023). Design thinking and dynamic managerial capabilities: A quasi-experimental field study in the aviation industry. *R & D Management*, *53*(5), 801–818. DOI: 10.1111/radm.12600

. Schneider, C., Jimenez, R. M., & Kyriazi, S. (2023). Artificial Intelligence-Based Predictive Analytics in the Humanitarian Sector: The Case of Project Jetson. *HARNESSING DATA INNOVATION FOR MIGRATION POLICY, 66.*

Shuaibu, A. S., Mahmoud, A. S., & Sheltami, T. R. (2025). A review of last-mile delivery optimization: Strategies, technologies, drone integration, and future trends. *Drones (Basel)*, *9*(3), 158. DOI: 10.3390/drones9030158

. Singh, B. (2024). Unmanned aircraft systems (UAS), surveillance, risk management to cybersecurity and legal regulation landscape: unraveling the future analysis, challenges, demand, and benefits in the high sky exploring the strange new world. *Unmanned aircraft systems*, 313-354.

Smith, A., Pringle, J., & Hunt, M. (2020). Value-sensitive design for humanitarian action: integrating ethical analysis for information and communication technology innovations. In *Ethics of Medical Innovation, Experimentation, and Enhancement in Military and Humanitarian Contexts* (pp. 105–124). Springer International Publishing. DOI: 10.1007/978-3-030-36319-2_7

Sudhi, M., Aishwarya, T. R., Shetty, D. K., Balakrishnan, J. M., Ahmad, S., & Sankaran, P. P. (2025). AI-DRIVEN INNOVATIONS IN EMERGENCY AND DISASTER RESPONSE: STRATEGIES FOR EFFECTIVE PLANNING. *Proceedings on Engineering*, *7*(2), 1293–1304. DOI: 10.24874/PES07.02C.009

Tatham, P., Neal, C., & Wu, Y. (2017). Hybrid cargo airships: A humanitarian logistic game changer? *Journal of Humanitarian Logistics and Supply Chain Management*, *7*(2), 102–125. DOI: 10.1108/JHLSCM-09-2016-0036

Tezei, J. F., de Freitas, C. R., Neto, A. L., Rodrigues, P. C. C., & Luche, J. R. D. (2024). Strategic analysis for a truck-drone hybrid model in last mile delivery. *International Contemporary Management Review*, *5*(1), 31–53. DOI: 10.54033/icmr-003

Tyshchuk, V. V. (2024). A review of legal regulation regarding the use of unmanned aerial vehicles for border security and the impact of global technologies. *International Comparative Jurisprudence*, *10*(1), 61–81.

UNHAS. (2022). *UNHAS Operational Brief: East Africa*. WFP Aviation Unit.

UNHAS. (2023). *WFP Aviation 2023 Annual Report*. Retrieved from https://www.wfp.org/publications

WFP. (2023). *HungerMapLIVE: Food Security Monitoring Platform.* Retrieved from https://hungermap.wfp.org

Wierzbiński, B., Zaborek, P., Wosiek, M., & Surmacz, T. (2023). Knowledge management orientation as a driver of competitive performance: Evidence from Polish SMEs in the aviation industry. *Entrepreneurial Business and Economics Review, 11*(1), 93–112. DOI: 10.15678/EBER.2023.110105

Wu, P. J., & Yang, C. K. (2021). Sustainable development in aviation logistics: Successful drivers and business strategies. *Business Strategy and the Environment, 30*(8), 3763–3771. DOI: 10.1002/bse.2838

Zahoor, N., Golgeci, I., Haapanen, L., Ali, I., & Arslan, A. (2022). The role of dynamic capabilities and strategic agility of B2B high-tech small and medium-sized enterprises during COVID-19 pandemic: Exploratory case studies from Finland. *Industrial Marketing Management, 105*, 502–514. DOI: 10.1016/j.indmarman.2022.07.006

Zhang, X., & Saadé, R. G. (2025). Towards a deeper understanding of strategic management factors in international non-governmental organizations. *Administrative Sciences, 15*(2), 34. DOI: 10.3390/admsci15020034

Chapter 11
Digitally Enabled Airbase Readiness and Strategic Airlift Planning for Humanitarian Crises Through Aviation Logistics Transformation

Cengiz Kerem Kutahya
https://orcid.org/0000-0002-7222-0921
Australian University Kuwait (AU), Turkey

ABSTRACT

This chapter explores how digital transformation can improve airbase readiness and strategic airlift planning in humanitarian logistics. It examines readiness factors such as runway infrastructure, fuel access, ICT systems, and cybersecurity, alongside airlift planning elements like aircraft types, cargo prioritization, and geography. Drawing from real-world cases—including NATO operations, UNHAS in Africa, and Türkiye's earthquake response—the study highlights the role of AI, blockchain, and digital twins in forecasting, coordination, and maintenance. A systems-based framework is proposed to digitally integrate air logistics, stressing ethical use, data protection, and global interoperability. The chapter concludes with strategic recommendations for policy reform, cross-sector collaboration, and scalable digital investment to build agile, transparent, and resilient humanitarian air logistics aligned with the SDGs.

DOI: 10.4018/979-8-3373-3643-5.ch011

1. INTRODUCTION AND CONCEPTUAL FOUNDATIONS

The increasing frequency, complexity, and severity of humanitarian crises—ranging from natural disasters and pandemics to protracted conflicts—have underscored the indispensable role of aviation in humanitarian logistics. In such rapidly evolving emergency scenarios, the ability to mobilize and deliver life-saving resources with speed and precision often hinges on the strategic readiness of airbases and the availability of efficient airlift capabilities. Whether in the immediate aftermath of an earthquake, during conflict-induced displacements, or in response to pandemics, aviation logistics enables access to remote or damaged regions, overcomes geographical bottlenecks, and ensures rapid deployment of personnel and supplies. Yet, these capabilities are only as effective as the systems that support them. The contemporary humanitarian landscape demands a shift from reactive to anticipatory logistics, a transformation that cannot be achieved without embracing digital technologies.

Digital transformation has thus become a necessity—not a luxury—for the future of humanitarian air logistics. As seen in various studies reviewed throughout this research (e.g., Mizrak & Akkartal, 2024; MoghadasNian, 2025; Woltjer et al., 2022), the integration of advanced technologies such as artificial intelligence (AI), blockchain, Internet of Things (IoT), and digital twin systems has the potential to drastically improve airbase preparedness, enable predictive maintenance, automate procurement processes, and enhance situational awareness through real-time data analytics. These digital enablers not only increase operational efficiency but also contribute to ethical governance and transparency, as evidenced in blockchain-based procurement platforms (Omar et al., 2021) and AI-driven decision support systems (Gupta et al., 2022). The concept of airbase readiness in this context extends beyond the physical state of infrastructure; it encapsulates human resource capabilities, ICT systems, cybersecurity resilience (Mızrak, 2024), and the ability to interoperate with diverse international stakeholders under unpredictable and high-pressure conditions.

Key concepts central to this study—airbase readiness, strategic airlift, and digital enablers—are examined with respect to crisis contexts including armed conflicts, sudden-onset natural disasters, and global pandemics. These contexts demand agility, interoperability, and coordination across multiple actors, including military units, non-governmental organizations (NGOs), UN agencies, and private-sector suppliers. For instance, operations like NATO's Enhanced Forward Presence demonstrate the necessity of airbase interoperability and resilience in conflict-prone regions, while the Turkish Air Force and Turkish Red Crescent's response after the 2023 earthquakes illustrates how airlift capacity and blockchain-enhanced logistics enabled rapid and accountable aid delivery. Furthermore, the alignment of such aviation-based humanitarian interventions with the Sustainable Development Goals (SDGs), particularly SDG 9 (Industry, Innovation, and Infrastructure), SDG 11 (Sustainable

Cities and Communities), and SDG 17 (Partnerships for the Goals), highlights their global relevance and ethical imperative.

To explore these dynamics, the research adopts a multi-method conceptual framework development approach. It synthesizes evidence from interdisciplinary sources—peer-reviewed studies, technical reports, and case-based observations—spanning logistics, aerospace systems, AI applications, and humanitarian operations. The methodology involves thematic integration of literature (e.g., Woltjer et al., 2022; Aladağ et al., 2023; Nicoletti, 2025), real-world field data (e.g., UNHAS digital operations in Africa, Turkish Red Crescent case studies), and cross-sectoral strategies to form a holistic understanding of digitally enabled aviation readiness. Through this synthesis, the study not only identifies the current limitations in digital air logistics but also proposes pathways for scaling innovation, enhancing coordination, and building resilient aviation infrastructures fit for the challenges of the 21st-century humanitarian landscape.

2. STRATEGIC FUNCTIONS OF AIRBASES AND AIRLIFT IN HUMANITARIAN LOGISTICS

2.1. Components of Airbase Readiness

Airbase readiness represents a multifaceted and dynamic capability essential for the successful deployment of strategic airlift during humanitarian crises. One of the most critical components is runway capability, which encompasses physical infrastructure resilience, maintenance scheduling, and adaptability under varying crisis scenarios. The functionality of runways must be assessed not only in terms of load-bearing strength and length but also in terms of rapid repairability, obstruction clearance, and weather resilience. As Aladağ, Demirdöğen, and Işık (2023) emphasize in their case study of Istanbul Grand Airport, infrastructure systems must be designed with contingencies in mind, including backup power generation and emergency runway extension protocols. Likewise, Ticas (2023) notes that agile combat environments require forward-deployed airfields to rapidly shift between takeoff and landing configurations, especially when supporting both military and humanitarian missions. The capacity to swiftly adapt to different aircraft types—from cargo jets to rotary-wing platforms—is paramount, particularly when airspace availability is constrained by geopolitical or environmental challenges. Runway systems must therefore be integrated with dynamic response plans, hazard detection mechanisms, and real-time communication tools to enable safe and efficient throughput during critical operations.

Another pillar of airbase readiness lies in fuel availability and refueling systems, which directly affect aircraft turnaround time and mission continuity. Fuel logistics are often vulnerable in humanitarian settings due to limited local supply chains and disrupted infrastructure. According to Woltjer et al. (2022), robust air transport system agility requires decentralized fueling points and mobile refueling systems that can be deployed with minimal reliance on host-nation capabilities. Fuel readiness also demands compatibility with various aircraft types and the incorporation of digital monitoring systems to track consumption, quality, and replenishment needs. As part of an operational readiness framework, Al-Mazrouie et al. (2021) stress that inadequate fuel infrastructure can lead to "transitional disastrous openings" in airport projects, especially during high-stakes activation phases. Furthermore, Mizrak and Akkartal (2024) highlight the cybersecurity vulnerabilities within fuel distribution networks, noting that these systems are increasingly targeted due to their digital interconnectivity. Consequently, modern airbases must implement both physical safeguards and cybersecurity protocols to protect critical refueling infrastructure against disruption and manipulation.

Human resources and personnel readiness constitute another cornerstone of airbase preparedness, encompassing technical training, psychological resilience, coordination skills, and cybersecurity literacy. Mızrak (2024) underlines the strategic role of human resources in aviation cybersecurity, particularly in crisis contexts where cyber-physical threats can destabilize operational systems. Personnel involved in logistics, command and control, and aircraft handling must undergo scenario-based training that integrates digital tools such as AI-supported simulations and decision-making platforms. According to Ticas (2023), transitions in airfield operations demand upskilling in agile combat employment (ACE) doctrines, where ground crews are expected to perform multifunctional roles across loading, fueling, and emergency repair tasks. Additionally, Woltjer et al. (2022) advocate for the establishment of cross-functional teams capable of managing both civilian and military logistics tasks under time-sensitive conditions. Effective personnel deployment thus hinges on comprehensive readiness programs that combine digital competencies with tactical agility, supported by institutional frameworks that promote continuous learning, rapid reallocation, and leadership adaptability.

The final and unifying component of modern airbase readiness is the integration of Information and Communication Technologies (ICTs) across logistics operations, infrastructure monitoring, and situational awareness systems. Digital platforms facilitate coordination between supply chain actors, real-time status reporting, and remote diagnostics for ground systems. Aladağ et al. (2023) demonstrate how ICT integration at Istanbul Grand Airport has enhanced its activation and transition capabilities by enabling digital twin modeling, predictive maintenance, and centralized resource allocation. Similarly, Mızrak (2024) emphasizes the role of AI-powered cybersecurity systems in safeguarding mission-critical ICT infrastructures from coordinated cyber threats. These tools not only protect sensitive data but also contribute to faster decision-making through automated threat detection and anomaly analysis. Woltjer et al. (2022) propose that air transport systems should embrace modular, scalable ICT architectures to maintain operational flexibility during crises. This digital backbone ensures that airbases remain responsive, resilient, and interoperable with international partners during multi-agency humanitarian deployments. Moreover, ICT integration underpins the ability to maintain a common operational picture across dispersed nodes, facilitating efficient communication, synchronized movements, and shared awareness of emerging risks.

In summary, airbase readiness is a holistic construct shaped by the interplay of runway operability, fuel logistics, personnel capabilities, and advanced ICT infrastructure. Each element is subject to external stressors and must be reinforced through adaptive planning, digital transformation, and institutional resilience. The convergence of physical and digital readiness components allows airbases to serve as pivotal hubs in the global humanitarian logistics network, ensuring that aid reaches affected populations swiftly, safely, and securely—even under the most challenging circumstances.

2.2. Airlift Planning in Humanitarian Operations

Strategic airlift planning plays a pivotal role in ensuring that humanitarian aid reaches affected populations swiftly, efficiently, and safely. A critical starting point in such planning is understanding aircraft typologies and how they influence cargo allocation and route planning. Different aircraft types—ranging from large-capacity jets like the Boeing C-17 or Antonov An-124 to smaller regional turboprops or rotary-wing aircraft—present varied advantages and limitations in humanitarian contexts. Arbuckle (2025) outlines that aircraft must be matched not only to cargo weight and volume but also to runway lengths, elevation conditions, and surrounding terrain. Aircraft used in disaster-stricken areas often require Short Take-Off and Landing (STOL) capabilities and may operate without fully functional airport infrastructure. Moreover, Mizrak, Mizrak, and Akkartal (2025) emphasize that the selection of aircraft must align with strategic priorities such as destination accessibility, geopolitical risks, and organizational capabilities. Hence, aircraft typology is not just an operational issue—it is deeply embedded in broader strategic logistics planning and national or NGO-level response frameworks.

Another fundamental aspect of airlift planning is the optimization of cargo prioritization, which is vital for maximizing payload utility and ensuring critical supplies are delivered first. Sahun, Sikirda, and Tymochko (2025) discuss the application of computer-based load optimization models that simulate cargo placement within aircraft holds to prevent imbalance, reduce fuel consumption, and comply with safety regulations. In humanitarian contexts, where time is a scarce resource, digital tools help determine not only what gets shipped but also how it is arranged to enable rapid unloading at remote airstrips. Complementing this, Kanmaz and Kütahya (2025) argue that risk mitigation strategies in air cargo operations—such as prioritizing perishable medical supplies or modular shelter units—must be built upon structured multi-criteria decision-making (MCDM) approaches. Their fuzzy TOPSIS model illustrates how logistics planners can systematically rank cargo types based on urgency, fragility, and logistical constraints. By integrating these computational and fuzzy logic techniques, humanitarian actors can achieve more reliable and ethically sound decisions in life-saving missions.

However, airlift planning must also account for numerous constraints, including weather patterns, geographic barriers, and political access limitations. Weather is perhaps the most dynamic and unpredictable constraint; severe storms, fog, or icy runways can ground aircraft and delay critical deliveries. According to Charnsethikul et al. (2025), the rise of Urban Air Mobility (UAM) and electric vertical takeoff and landing (eVTOL) aircraft introduces both potential and risks, especially when operating in volatile atmospheric conditions common in post-disaster settings. In such environments, planning must involve real-time weather forecasting tools and contingency routes to ensure safety and continuity. Geography further complicates operations—mountainous terrain, lack of navigable air corridors, or damaged infrastructure often demand mid-air adjustments and non-linear routing. Zhang and Chang (2025), in their intercontinental freight optimization study between China and Africa, highlight how diverse terrain and time windows complicate network reliability, a challenge mirrored in humanitarian missions across regions such as Sub-Saharan Africa, Southeast Asia, or the Middle East. Their study underscores the need for multi-aircraft-type scheduling and flexible hub-spoke designs to minimize disruption in long-distance humanitarian supply chains.

Lastly, political and regulatory access often determines the feasibility of strategic airlifts. Humanitarian missions frequently operate in conflict zones or politically sensitive regions where overflight rights, landing permissions, and customs protocols create friction. Mizrak, Polat, and Tasar (2024) show how strategic planning tools—such as entropy-weighted fuzzy MCDM—can support sustainability and resilience planning even in complex regulatory environments like that of Istanbul Airport. These tools help planners prioritize route alternatives, vendor partnerships, and regional hubs based on geopolitical risk exposure. Furthermore, Mizrak, Mizrak, and Akkartal (2025) argue that a robust destination selection strategy must incorporate political considerations alongside operational capacity and humanitarian urgency. As geopolitical tensions rise globally, humanitarian air corridors increasingly require negotiation with multiple stakeholders—including governments, military agencies, and civil aviation authorities—emphasizing the strategic, diplomatic, and logistical dimensions of airlift planning.

In summary, effective airlift planning in humanitarian operations hinges on the alignment of aircraft selection, cargo prioritization algorithms, and real-time constraint management strategies. Leveraging digital optimization tools, fuzzy logic models, and strategic foresight allows humanitarian logistics teams to enhance the speed, safety, and reach of air-based relief efforts. As disasters become more complex and time-sensitive, this comprehensive planning approach will remain essential to transforming aviation logistics into a resilient, data-informed pillar of global humanitarian response.

2.3. Coordination in Humanitarian Supply Chains

Effective coordination in humanitarian supply chains is essential to ensure that life-saving resources reach the most vulnerable populations, especially during crisis situations. One of the most challenging yet crucial aspects of coordination lies in last-mile delivery, which bridges the gap between central logistics hubs and remote or devastated communities. Öztürk and Akkartal (2024) emphasize that the last mile is often the most resource-intensive and time-critical stage of humanitarian logistics. In unpredictable terrains—such as post-disaster zones or refugee camps—traditional delivery methods are often insufficient. Instead, the integration of Internet of Things (IoT) technologies, such as GPS-enabled vehicles, drone surveillance, and real-time asset tracking, provides visibility and agility. These innovations help optimize route planning, monitor environmental disruptions, and reduce delays in critical deliveries. Moreover, last-mile delivery success hinges on mobile adaptability—transport units that can traverse damaged infrastructure, bypass bureaucratic checkpoints, and respond dynamically to emerging needs. As highlighted by Grange, Heaslip, and McMullan (2020), humanitarian supply chains must evolve from linear coordination models to more responsive, choreographed systems where frontline decision-making is supported by back-end digital intelligence.

A second key domain of coordination involves the management of cold chain logistics, which ensures the safe transportation and storage of temperature-sensitive goods such as vaccines, blood supplies, and perishable food. Cold chains in humanitarian contexts are particularly vulnerable to disruption due to energy shortages, infrastructure collapse, or misaligned planning. According to Larson (2021), sustainability and security in humanitarian cold chains require both technological infrastructure—like temperature-controlled storage units—and collaborative agreements among stakeholders for inventory synchronization. Industry 4.0 technologies can play a vital role in strengthening cold chain continuity. Kumar and Singh (2022) propose a strategic framework in which IoT sensors, RFID tags, and blockchain systems collectively enhance the traceability and integrity of cold-chain products. By ensuring that data on temperature thresholds and delivery timelines is shared across all nodes, organizations can minimize spoilage and maintain public trust during mass immunization or food security missions. Moghadam et al. (2022) further reinforce the role of IoT enablers by modeling their impact on humanitarian supply chains, suggesting that real-time environmental monitoring and remote diagnostics enhance cold chain reliability even in high-risk areas.

The third pillar of humanitarian coordination is inventory responsiveness, which reflects an organization's capacity to allocate and reallocate resources in response to rapidly shifting demands. In disaster-prone regions, demand patterns can fluctuate drastically within hours, requiring logistics systems that support adaptive planning and continuous stock monitoring. Akkartal, Akkartal, and Yıldırım (2019) argue that innovation management in supply chains—especially during humanitarian operations—must prioritize flexible inventory systems supported by scenario-based forecasting and agile procurement strategies. Effective inventory responsiveness is further tied to the strategic use of data analytics and interoperability standards that enable real-time updates between warehouses, field teams, and transportation units. Nawazish, Nandakumar, and Mateen (2024) identify responsiveness as a central theme in sustainable humanitarian supply chains, emphasizing that organizations must not only react quickly but also pre-position supplies based on predictive risk models. These insights align with Kumar and Singh's (2022) view that decentralized digital warehouses and predictive algorithms enable proactive resource allocation, thereby increasing supply chain resilience and reducing aid bottlenecks in times of crisis.

At the heart of successful humanitarian logistics lies stakeholder collaboration, where military forces, non-governmental organizations (NGOs), and UN agencies converge to form integrated operational networks. Coordination challenges often arise due to differing operational cultures, command structures, and data-sharing practices. Grange et al. (2020) suggest that transitioning from hierarchical to "choreographed" models of coordination allows each stakeholder to contribute autonomously while maintaining alignment with broader strategic goals. For example, while the military may provide infrastructure and airlift capabilities, NGOs offer localized knowledge and last-mile presence, and UN agencies ensure standardized procedures and compliance. Larson (2021) notes that collaborative logistics platforms—powered by secure digital systems—enhance information sharing, reduce duplication of effort, and support ethical transparency. Additionally, Moghadam et al. (2022) argue that stakeholder coordination is strengthened through IoT-mediated communication and real-time dashboards, enabling synchronized operations even across different jurisdictions. The need for integrated coordination mechanisms is further emphasized in the systematic review by Nawazish et al. (2024), which calls for governance frameworks that institutionalize cross-sector partnerships and mandate data interoperability.

In conclusion, coordination in humanitarian supply chains is not merely a logistical necessity but a strategic imperative. Achieving effective last-mile delivery, ensuring cold chain reliability, and maintaining inventory responsiveness all require the seamless integration of digital technologies and cross-sector collaboration. From IoT to Industry 4.0 solutions, modern tools are reshaping how aid is delivered under pressure. However, without clear coordination structures among military actors, NGOs, and UN agencies, even the most advanced systems risk fragmentation. A hybrid approach—combining digital innovation with organizational alignment—is thus essential to transforming humanitarian logistics into a responsive, sustainable, and people-centered enterprise.

3. DIGITAL TECHNOLOGIES TRANSFORMING AVIATION LOGISTICS

3.1. AI and Decision Support Systems

Artificial Intelligence (AI) has become a transformative force in aviation logistics, particularly in enabling more effective decision support systems for forecasting, routing optimization, and demand prediction. Traditional forecasting models are often limited by static assumptions and slow response to dynamic disruptions. However, AI-powered predictive analytics, fueled by large-scale real-time data, offer an adaptive capability that improves planning accuracy during humanitarian crises. MoghadasNian (2025) underscores the power of AI-driven predictive models in enhancing airline logistics operations by identifying early disruptions in demand patterns and predicting resource bottlenecks before they occur. These models incorporate deep learning and reinforcement learning to generate demand forecasts that consider weather anomalies, geopolitical developments, and supply shortages. Similarly, Gupta et al. (2022) review how machine learning and hybrid optimization models have reshaped the role of decision support systems in operations research, making them not only reactive tools but proactive strategic engines. The integration of AI into humanitarian aviation logistics enables organizations to anticipate population displacement patterns, emergency medical needs, and aid consumption rates—thus aligning strategic airlift planning with real-time demand fluctuations.

In the domain of routing optimization, AI systems significantly reduce inefficiencies in air logistics networks by automating route selection under complex constraints such as no-fly zones, air traffic congestion, or damaged infrastructure.

Nicoletti (2025) discusses how AI-enabled logistics platforms employ multi-agent systems and heuristic algorithms to optimize delivery paths in disaster-affected areas. These systems simulate thousands of potential routing scenarios and select the most time- and fuel-efficient solutions based on continuously updated environmental and operational data. Zhang (2024) further demonstrates the application of intelligent scheduling algorithms in civil aviation supply chains, showing how AI minimizes idle time for aircraft and reduces turnaround durations. In humanitarian operations, where every minute saved could translate to more lives saved, the ability of AI to adapt routing in real time is invaluable. Moreover, Hejji et al. (2021) highlight the importance of AI-based resource allocation models that simultaneously manage personnel deployment and aircraft utilization, thereby avoiding both underuse and overload in crisis conditions. These models not only optimize routing but also ensure that critical resources—pilots, medics, or cargo units—are assigned in the most impactful way.

Another critical area where AI and decision support systems intersect is in real-time load planning and flight scheduling, which directly influence the agility and efficiency of humanitarian air logistics. Load planning, traditionally reliant on static spreadsheets or manual calculations, has been revolutionized by AI systems that process cargo dimensions, weights, and priority codes in real time. MoghadasNian (2025) presents an AI-driven inventory optimization framework that enables dynamic adjustment of load configurations based on urgent medical supply requests or deteriorating weather conditions. AI-powered systems analyze aircraft capacity, fuel levels, destination constraints, and crew availability to generate optimal flight schedules in a matter of seconds. This allows for better synchronization between ground operations and airborne assets, particularly in fast-moving disaster zones. Zhang (2024) supports this by illustrating how big data and intelligent scheduling improve network efficiency and flight safety across complex aviation ecosystems. These intelligent planning systems are not isolated tools—they interact with AI-based forecasting models and IoT-enabled sensors to build a synchronized and responsive logistics infrastructure.

The human element remains critical in ensuring the successful deployment of AI in decision-making processes, especially in aviation logistics. Mızrak (2023) explores how fuzzy logic systems help human resource managers in aviation interpret ambiguous or conflicting information when making strategic decisions, such as staffing or scheduling. These systems complement AI tools by capturing the tacit knowledge and judgment of experienced personnel—an essential factor in crisis logistics where full data clarity is rarely available. Additionally, Mızrak (2024) highlights the strategic role of human resources in AI-integrated aviation cybersecurity, noting that system resilience relies on continuous staff training and awareness. As AI models grow more complex, human operators must interpret, verify, and fine-tune their recommendations, particularly in mission-critical environments like humanitarian aviation. This integration of AI with human decision-making and cybersecurity practices ensures that intelligent systems support—not replace—strategic thinking under pressure.

In sum, AI and decision support systems are redefining how aviation logistics operates under crisis conditions, from anticipatory demand forecasting to real-time load balancing and routing optimization. The combination of predictive analytics, intelligent scheduling, and human-centered decision modeling creates a logistics ecosystem that is not only efficient but also resilient and adaptable. As the humanitarian sector continues to face complex emergencies, the integration of AI tools—aligned with ethical governance and supported by trained personnel—offers a pathway toward more responsive, data-informed aviation logistics operations.

3.2. Blockchain for Transparency and Coordination

Blockchain technology, particularly through the use of smart contracts, has emerged as a powerful enabler of transparency and automation in humanitarian logistics. In crisis situations where procurement must be both fast and accountable, traditional bureaucratic methods often cause delays and inconsistencies. Smart contracts—automated, self-executing agreements coded on a blockchain—offer a solution by enabling decentralized procurement processes that execute only when predefined conditions are met. Omar et al. (2021) demonstrate the effectiveness of blockchain smart contracts in healthcare supply chains, where automated procurement dramatically improved contract compliance and delivery accuracy during emergencies. These programmable contracts reduce the need for manual oversight, lower the risk of corruption, and enhance auditability by maintaining immutable transaction logs. Xu, Chong, and Chi (2021) provide a broader procurement perspective, showing how blockchain facilitates secure bidding, real-time payment settlements, and dynamic contract adjustments across multiple industries, including aviation and civil infrastructure. The automation of contract terms ensures that aid suppliers receive payments only after verified delivery, reducing the potential for fraud and reinforcing donor trust.

Smart contracts not only streamline procurement but also improve coordination between actors by embedding logic for real-time delivery validation and approval. Rashid (n.d.) underscores how smart contracts improve compliance and operational efficiency by embedding procedural rules—such as temperature monitoring thresholds for medical supplies or time windows for emergency airlift missions—directly into the contract. This is particularly relevant in humanitarian aviation logistics, where mission-critical cargo (e.g., vaccines, shelter kits) must be delivered to precise locations at precise times. In such settings, automated contract enforcement helps align expectations between NGOs, government agencies, and vendors. Ezzati, Alizadeh, and Jokar (2024) further highlight the use of blockchain in supplier performance evaluation, where smart contracts transparently log delivery timeliness, quality metrics, and service level compliance. These performance records can be accessed and verified by all stakeholders in real time, supporting evidence-based procurement decisions and reducing disputes in high-pressure relief missions. The integration of smart contracts with AI forecasting tools also allows dynamic procurement—adjusting the order and delivery schedules based on evolving needs and verified field conditions.

In addition to streamlining procurement, blockchain enhances asset tracking and stakeholder coordination through decentralized and tamper-proof ledgers. In humanitarian operations, where multiple actors operate in fragmented supply chains across borders, having a single source of truth is invaluable. Omar et al. (2020) explore how blockchain-enabled Vendor Managed Inventory (VMI) systems allow for shared visibility of inventory levels, movement logs, and replenishment alerts between suppliers, airbase managers, and local distributors. These systems ensure timely refills of critical supplies and help coordinate stock rotation, even when operated by different agencies. The same infrastructure can track aircraft, mission logs, and equipment conditions across field sites in disaster zones. Ogunbiyi-Badaru et al. (2024) extend this view by examining blockchain-enabled asset management as a strategic tool for global humanitarian operations. They argue that blockchain reduces asset misuse by providing transparent custody chains, automated handoffs, and location tracking of equipment such as drones, fuel tanks, or mobile medical units. Importantly, the inclusion of all stakeholders—military, NGOs, and international organizations—on a shared blockchain network helps reduce friction, duplication, and risk of data silos.

Moreover, blockchain's immutability and decentralized nature strengthen trust and accountability across the humanitarian ecosystem. With real-time visibility into what resources are where, who is responsible, and when actions are taken, decision-makers gain a more accurate operational picture. This allows them to optimize airlift plans, align stakeholder actions, and monitor mission success with full traceability. In situations where corruption or aid diversion is a concern, blockchain serves not only as a logistics tool but as a governance mechanism. As Ogunbiyi-Badaru et al. (2024) emphasize, by embedding accountability at the infrastructure level, blockchain offers both transparency and resilience, even in fragile states or conflict zones where traditional oversight is difficult. Ultimately, the convergence of blockchain with aviation logistics platforms transforms fragmented operations into synchronized, data-driven networks capable of agile and ethical response.

3.3. Digital Twins and Predictive Maintenance

The adoption of digital twin technology in aviation logistics has opened new frontiers in simulating airbase readiness and proactively managing maintenance operations. A digital twin is a dynamic, real-time virtual representation of a physical system, allowing users to test scenarios, predict failures, and optimize performance before issues arise in the real world. Cebir and Akkartal (2024) emphasize the strategic application of digital twins in supply chain logistics, enabling organizations to simulate disruptions, optimize workflows, and reduce downtime. Within airbase environments, digital twins allow logistics planners to replicate entire operational setups—including aircraft parking configurations, refueling stations, ground personnel movements, and weather variability—to assess readiness under different crisis conditions. Luo et al. (2024) take this further by applying high-fidelity agent-based models to airport ground operations, showing how simulations using real-time data streams can anticipate delays, identify bottlenecks, and dynamically allocate resources. These simulations are not static—they adapt as conditions evolve, making them essential tools for humanitarian aviation hubs where environmental, geopolitical, and logistical factors change rapidly and unpredictably.

Beyond scenario testing, digital twins are increasingly central to predictive maintenance, enabling airbases to shift from reactive to proactive asset management. This transformation is critical in humanitarian aviation, where mission success often hinges on equipment reliability under constrained timelines. Candell et al. (2024) describe how health and asset management systems, when integrated with digital twin simulations, support intelligent decision-making across entire fleets of air vehicles. These systems use real-time condition monitoring and AI-driven anomaly detection to predict failures before they happen, thus improving safety and reducing maintenance-induced delays. For example, instead of adhering to rigid maintenance intervals, digital twins enable adaptive scheduling based on actual equipment usage and environmental stress factors. Kumari and Malhotra (2024) present a practical case in which digital twins were used to predict the fatigue life of aircraft main bearings, helping engineers avoid critical breakdowns and optimize component replacement cycles. In crisis scenarios, where aircraft must be ready to deploy at a moment's notice, such precision in predictive maintenance minimizes the risk of last-minute technical faults.

The ability of digital twins to enhance infrastructure readiness is also being recognized across next-generation airport and airbase planning initiatives. Alexandridis et al. (2024) explore how distributed AI modeling in smart airport systems allows for real-time monitoring of terminals, runways, and ground service equipment. Their framework incorporates environmental data, equipment telemetry, and historical failure trends to model infrastructure degradation over time. In a humanitarian context, this means base operators can anticipate the wear and tear of temporary airfields, mobile refueling systems, or portable communication towers and deploy preventative interventions well in advance. Toygar (2024), though focused on the maritime industry, offers a transferable model showing how digital twin integration supports sustainable asset control by reducing unnecessary maintenance actions and maximizing system longevity—an insight highly applicable to rapidly constructed field airbases. These systems help organizations balance short-term mission urgency with long-term operational sustainability, a vital consideration when humanitarian operations stretch over months or years.

To consolidate the applications of these transformative technologies in aviation logistics, Table 1 offers a comparative overview of AI, blockchain, and digital twin systems, summarizing their functions, use cases, and operational outcomes in humanitarian airbase and airlift context

Table 1. Digital technologies in aviation logistics

Technology	Function	Use Case	Outcome
AI Forecasting	Demand prediction, routing	MoghadasNian (2025)	Fuel savings, improved demand
Blockchain	Procurement, asset tracking	Omar et al. (2020, 2021)	Transparent delivery chains
Digital Twin	Asset health, base simulation	Luo et al. (2024); Cebir & Akkartal	Predictive maintenance

In summary, the convergence of digital twins and predictive maintenance is reshaping how airbases prepare for and respond to crises. From simulating operational scenarios to forecasting technical failures, these technologies allow aviation logistics teams to make smarter, faster, and more resilient decisions. Rather than relying on reactive responses, airbase managers can use digital replicas to test contingency plans, evaluate resource requirements, and optimize asset performance. As the humanitarian aviation landscape grows more complex and technologically integrated, digital twin systems offer a strategic advantage—merging virtual foresight with physical precision to ensure sustained mission readiness and infrastructure reliability.

3.4. Satellite, UAVs, and Remote Sensing Applications

The integration of remote sensing technologies and UAV (Unmanned Aerial Vehicle) platforms has revolutionized how humanitarian logistics teams evaluate base locations, assess post-disaster damage, and plan safe air corridors for relief operations. Base location selection is a critical first step in aviation-based humanitarian missions, especially in regions where terrain, infrastructure integrity, and population displacement must be dynamically assessed. UAV-based remote sensing offers high-resolution, real-time imagery that enables responders to evaluate elevation profiles, flood risks, accessibility, and proximity to affected communities. Feroz and Abu Dabous (2021) demonstrate how UAV imagery and LiDAR data were used for bridge condition assessment, an approach that can be directly applied to assessing airstrip readiness or approach routes for airbases in crisis zones. The ability to detect subtle surface degradation, debris, or load-bearing weaknesses informs safer landing and take-off planning in remote or damaged regions. These assessments are particularly valuable in environments where satellite coverage may be limited or delayed, offering a localized and scalable method of evaluating ground conditions prior to deployment.

UAVs also play an essential role in damage mapping following disasters such as earthquakes, landslides, or floods. Their capacity to rapidly scan large areas and produce geospatially accurate maps makes them ideal for building damage classification, infrastructure assessment, and identifying safe zones for airbase deployment or medical triage units. Nagasawa et al. (2021) present a model-based analysis where multi-UAV path planning was optimized for building damage surveys in post-disaster zones, demonstrating how simultaneous flight operations with coordinated flight paths improve coverage speed and mapping accuracy. Zocchi et al. (2023) extend this approach by integrating multi-sensor and multi-scale platforms—combining satellite and drone data to monitor slope instability along transportation and air access corridors. These methods help logistics teams anticipate potential secondary hazards, such as landslides or collapsing roads, that may impede cargo delivery or create risks for crew operations. In urban or densely populated informal settlements, UAVs can identify population concentrations and bottlenecks, enabling a better understanding of relief access needs. Olivatto, Inguaggiato, and Stanganini (2023) applied UAV mapping in Brazilian irregular settlements, demonstrating how high-resolution imaging supports socio-environmental risk analysis and improves emergency response planning in vulnerable areas.

A third critical use of UAV-enabled remote sensing in humanitarian aviation is air corridor planning—the design and validation of safe flight paths for cargo aircraft and medical evacuation missions. This involves identifying aerial hazards, visual obstructions, and no-fly zones while also ensuring that air routes intersect with areas of highest need. Zhang and Zhu (2023), in their comprehensive review of UAV remote sensing, emphasize the importance of aligning platform selection, sensor resolution, and data processing with the specific mission—whether terrain classification, obstacle detection, or route clearance. UAVs equipped with thermal, multispectral, and RGB sensors contribute to multi-layered data collection, which can be integrated into Geographic Information Systems (GIS) for predictive flight planning. Debnath et al. (2024) provide a detailed analysis of UAV path-planning algorithms and obstacle avoidance methods, showcasing how advanced AI-driven models are improving navigation safety in complex, cluttered airspaces. These capabilities are essential when planning low-altitude supply drops or operating in urban canyons, where line-of-sight limitations and infrastructure density increase risk. By simulating potential flight paths, identifying dynamic threats, and integrating environmental data, these UAV systems enhance the precision, reliability, and adaptability of humanitarian aviation logistics.

In summary, the deployment of UAV and remote sensing technologies provides humanitarian logistics teams with a real-time, data-rich toolkit for evaluating base sites, mapping disaster impacts, and designing safe aerial routes. Their speed, cost-effectiveness, and accessibility make them ideal for rapid assessment missions, particularly in environments with degraded infrastructure or limited situational awareness. As natural disasters and climate-driven emergencies intensify globally, the strategic use of UAV-based intelligence will become increasingly central to mission planning, risk mitigation, and efficient resource deployment in humanitarian aviation operations.

4. INTEGRATED FRAMEWORK AND CASE APPLICATIONS

4.1. A Systems Framework for Digitally-Enabled Readiness

The creation of a resilient and digitally-enabled readiness framework for humanitarian aviation logistics requires the seamless integration of airbase, logistics, and data systems. This integration aims to unify the physical infrastructure (runways, refueling stations, warehouses), operational logistics (fleet movement, inventory, personnel deployment), and digital tools (AI, blockchain, IoT) into a single responsive ecosystem. Srivastava, Srivastava, and Granata (2021) highlight the foundational importance of building "digitally enabled organizations" that leverage new-age technologies—such as cyber-physical systems and cloud-connected platforms—to increase agility, transparency, and real-time decision-making. For airbases, this means that runway status, aircraft availability, cargo readiness, and weather forecasts must all be processed through integrated dashboards that enable synchronized and automated responses to evolving crises. Özkanlısoy and Akkartal (2021) emphasize that digital transformation in supply chains demands interoperability between various systems—from ERP platforms to predictive maintenance modules—requiring robust data harmonization strategies. In aviation contexts, the absence of such integration often leads to communication breakdowns and redundant processes, particularly during high-tempo humanitarian missions.

Forward-operating bases (FOBs) used in humanitarian airlift scenarios must also incorporate logistics sustainability and long-term digital operability into their design. Marín and Marcos (2021) discuss logistical considerations in developing durable air units, noting that modularity, scalability, and real-time connectivity are essential for ensuring continuous functionality. Their research underscores that FOBs must evolve from isolated outposts to digitally connected nodes capable of interfacing with headquarters, local partners, and international coalitions. This necessitates the installation of sensor-equipped ground infrastructure, mobile satellite communications, and automated reporting systems—all of which feed into integrated situational awareness platforms. Burčiar, Kováč, and Važan (2024) provide further technical insights, proposing data integration strategies that allow proactive control of mission-critical production systems. In aviation logistics, these strategies translate into real-time alignment of supply chain functions with air mission schedules, allowing predictive resupply, intelligent rerouting, and precision timing for takeoff, refueling, and offloading activities.

To function effectively in multinational humanitarian contexts, the digitally-enabled readiness framework must also ensure interoperability and compliance with international standards, such as those established by ICAO, NATO, and IATA. Interoperability not only ensures smooth coordination across military, NGO, and civilian aviation actors but also supports data integrity, communication security, and air traffic safety in complex operating environments. Avtin et al. (2021) present principles of integrated airborne avionics that support standardized communication protocols, cross-platform data fusion, and situational data sharing between ground stations and aircraft. Applying these principles to humanitarian aviation systems means ensuring that flight management software, ground control systems, and UAV operation dashboards all follow globally recognized digital formats and encryption protocols. Srivastava et al. (2021) further emphasize that digitally mature organizations must adopt cross-compatible platforms that comply with both national regulations and international coalition requirements. As humanitarian logistics often involve multiple jurisdictions and rapid deployment across borders, adherence to globally accepted standards becomes essential not only for safety and efficiency but also for legal and diplomatic clearance.

In summary, building a digitally-enabled readiness system for humanitarian airbases entails the strategic integration of physical assets, digital systems, and interoperable communication platforms. Through a layered approach—merging logistics automation, predictive analytics, and compliance with international aviation standards—organizations can transform static bases into dynamic, resilient hubs capable of supporting agile, transparent, and data-informed airlift missions. This systems framework offers a blueprint for enhancing airbase readiness in increasingly complex and unpredictable humanitarian environments.

4.2. Cybersecurity, Risk Mitigation, and Ethics

The increasing reliance on digital systems in humanitarian aviation logistics raises significant challenges related to data protection, cyber-resilience, and cross-border privacy. As airbases and logistics networks adopt AI, IoT, blockchain, and cloud-based systems, the attack surface expands, making them more vulnerable to cyber threats such as data breaches, ransomware, and system hijacking. Perumal et al. (2024) emphasize that the integration of AI in aviation environments demands rigorous risk assessment frameworks, capable of identifying vulnerabilities in predictive analytics tools, autonomous scheduling systems, and decision support platforms. In cross-border humanitarian operations, where data flows between international agencies, local governments, and private logistics partners, the risks of unauthorized access or non-compliance with regional data protection laws become more severe. Mızrak (2025) underscores that achieving cyber-resilience in such environments requires layered defense strategies, including encryption standards, threat intelligence sharing, and real-time intrusion detection mechanisms. Furthermore, Adebayo et al. (2025) argue that machine learning algorithms can be leveraged to detect anomalies in data traffic and trigger automated containment protocols, reducing response time and minimizing mission disruption. These intelligent threat detection systems allow humanitarian aviation actors to maintain operational continuity even when under cyber duress, ensuring that critical aid flows are not compromised.

Alongside technical resilience, the deployment of digital technologies must be guided by robust ethical principles, especially in sensitive humanitarian zones where lives, rights, and geopolitical sensitivities are at stake. Kaushik et al. (2024) highlight the complex ethical dilemmas surrounding AI-based cybersecurity, including algorithmic bias, surveillance overreach, and lack of transparency in autonomous decision-making. In humanitarian contexts, these concerns are magnified by power asymmetries between aid recipients and operators, the potential misuse of collected data, and limited legal oversight in conflict zones. Devitt et al. (2023) advocate for the development of trusted human-AI networks, emphasizing that AI systems should augment—not replace—human judgment and empathy in mission-critical scenarios. A well-calibrated balance between automation and human control can reduce ethical blind spots while preserving speed and efficiency. Parmadi and Ramli (2025) provide field insights into how IoT-based humanitarian interventions in conflict areas often face barriers not just in infrastructure, but also in ethical governance. Their findings show that without local community engagement and culturally informed deployment, even well-intentioned digital systems risk creating distrust or unintended harm. Blockchain, often seen as a tool for transparency, also carries ethical considerations in humanitarian applications. Reghunadhan (2020) discusses how blockchain systems used in war zonescan inadvertently expose sensitive identities or transaction patterns, necessitating cautious implementation with strict data minimization and pseudonymization protocols.

The intersection of cybersecurity and ethics is especially critical in cross-border humanitarian logistics, where legal jurisdictions vary and operational urgency often trumps compliance protocols. Mızrak (2025) stresses that international humanitarian actors must adopt harmonized data governance models to ensure alignment with frameworks such as the GDPR, the UN's digital trust principles, and host-country cybersecurity laws. This is particularly important when handling biometric data for identity verification, real-time location tracking of aid workers, or sensitive health records during disaster responses. Kaushik et al. (2024) further note that ethical frameworks must be anticipatory rather than reactive—designed in advance to shape development, procurement, and implementation decisions. These frameworks should include clear guidelines for algorithmic accountability, data sovereignty, informed consent, and equitable access to AI tools. Finally, Devitt et al. (2023) argue that establishing a shared trust architecture between governments, NGOs, and technology providers is essential for legitimizing AI and blockchain systems used in the humanitarian domain. By embedding ethical considerations at the core of cybersecurity and digital innovation strategies, aviation logistics networks can become not only more secure but also more just and inclusive in their humanitarian mandate.

Table 2 outlines the key challenges and strategic solutions associated with digital transformation in aviation logistics for humanitarian operations. By categorizing barriers such as technical limitations, institutional resistance, and funding constraints alongside targeted recommendations—ranging from policy innovation to multi-sector collaboration—the table provides a concise framework for addressing systemic gaps. This overview supports forward-looking planning efforts by aligning actionable strategies with the broader goal of building resilient, interoperable, and digitally empowered air logistics systems.

Table 2. Risk categories in cyber-enabled airbase operations

Risk Category	Description	Ethical Concern	Mitigation Strategy
AI Overreliance	Undetected anomalies due to black-box AI	Bias, decision opacity	Explainable AI, human-in-the-loop systems
Cross-Border Data Flows	Conflict of jurisdiction/data breach	Privacy, sovereignty	Encrypted cloud with local data governance
Blockchain Vulnerabilities	Smart contract bugs	Tampering, false records	Auditing protocols and verification layers

In conclusion, cybersecurity in humanitarian aviation logistics extends beyond technological robustness—it is deeply intertwined with ethical responsibility and cross-border governance. As digital systems become integral to strategic airlift, remote coordination, and resource distribution, actors must prioritize both risk mitigation and ethical deployment. Leveraging AI for threat detection and blockchain for transparency offers tremendous potential—but only if implemented with foresight, accountability, and cultural sensitivity. Building digitally enabled airbases for humanitarian response means designing systems that are not just resilient to attack but also aligned with human rights, operational fairness, and international ethical standards.

4.3. Real-World Case Insights

4.3.1. NATO Enhanced Forward Presence (eFP) in Eastern Europe

Since 2020, NATO's Enhanced Forward Presence (eFP) has strengthened its aviation logistics and airbase readiness capabilities in Eastern Europe, particularly in response to increased geopolitical tensions. Aviation operations within the eFP framework, especially in countries like Poland, Estonia, Latvia, and Lithuania, have seen a marked increase in the deployment of rotary and fixed-wing aircraft for rapid air mobility, aerial resupply, and ISR (intelligence, surveillance, reconnaissance) missions. NATO has adopted modular airbase packages (ABPs) that include mobile command-and-control (C2) elements, tactical air navigation systems, and ICT platforms to ensure agile operations across dispersed bases. The use of AI-enabled logistics dashboards and predictive maintenance systems (aligned with NATO's FMN Spiral specifications) allowed multinational air units to synchronize asset management in real time, regardless of nation. Exercises like DEFENDER-Europe 2021 and BALTOPS 2022 illustrated the operational integration of drone-based surveillance and UAV-assisted logistics, especially for medical supplies and repair components. Enhanced air mobility corridors have also been simulated and rehearsed, including civil-military coordination for airspace deconfliction. Lessons learned include the necessity of cyber-resilient command networks, portable UAV launch platforms, and training for multinational digital interoperability under the NATO Standardization Office (NSO) directives.

4.3.2. UNHAS Digital Aviation Logistics in Africa

The United Nations Humanitarian Air Service (UNHAS) has expanded its digital aviation logistics footprint across Africa since 2020, operating in over 18 countries to support food aid, medical evacuations, and emergency supply drops. In nations like Chad, Mali, South Sudan, and the Central African Republic, UNHAS has piloted cloud-based flight scheduling and load optimization platforms that synchronize with WFP's digital logistics system (LESS - Logistics Execution Support System). These tools allow for real-time manifest updates, remote cargo visibility, and geofencing of airstrips. AI-driven demand forecasting has been implemented in Burkina Faso and Niger to optimize aircraft type selection and reduce fuel usage per ton-kilometer. UNHAS also adopted UAV-based pre-flight airstrip assessments using drone imagery to evaluate runway conditions post-conflict or disaster. Digital passenger tracking and biometric boarding systems have been trialed to enhance operational accountability in unstable regions. Blockchain is increasingly discussed for aid package tracking, although deployment remains limited due to connectivity constraints. Notably, during the Sudan humanitarian crisis (2023), UNHAS leveraged satellite internet to enable real-time coordination with WHO and UNICEF flights, delivering vaccines and medical teams to conflict-affected areas. Key takeaways include the importance of remote-enabled systems, modular airborne hubs, and decentralized command platforms to overcome bandwidth and terrain limitations.

4.3.3. Turkish Air Force and Turkish Red Crescent Post-Earthquake Airlift (2023)

Following the devastating Kahramanmaraş earthquakes in February 2023, the Turkish Air Force (TuAF) and the Turkish Red Crescent (Kızılay) jointly launched one of the largest post-disaster air logistics operations in the country's history. Over 120 military cargo and civilian charter aircraft were mobilized from major airbases like Etimesgut, Akinci, and Incirlik, transporting search-and-rescue teams, mobile hospitals, and humanitarian aid. The airlift relied on pre-established Air Movement Coordination Centers (AMCC) and integrated logistics planning software developed by the Turkish Armed Forces Command and Control Center (TAFCCC). AI-based load planning was deployed to optimize pallet configurations, and a digital twin model of the Incirlik base was activated to simulate throughput under high-volume emergency conditions. UAVs were used for post-quake damage mapping in regions like Hatay and Adıyaman, guiding where helicopters and fixed-wing craft could land. The Red Crescent operated a blockchain-based inventory management system (co-developed with Tubitak BILGEM), enabling traceable aid distribution from air drops to local warehouses. Interoperability with civilian authorities and NGO systems was facilitated through a centralized humanitarian logistics cloud, which also supported GIS-linked recipient verification. Critical insights included the value of having a digitized pre-disaster logistics plan, rapid airbase scalability, and flexible air corridor planning aligned with real-time seismic and weather data.

To further illustrate the diverse real-world implementations of digitally enabled aviation logistics, Table 3 presents selected case examples from global humanitarian and defense operations. Drawing from NATO's Enhanced Forward Presence, UNHAS digital deployments across Africa, and Türkiye's coordinated earthquake airlift response, the table highlights the integration of advanced technologies, the scope of operations, and the measurable impact on responsiveness and coordination. These case insights provide concrete evidence of how digital transformation enhances agility, transparency, and operational readiness in crisis logistics.

Table 3. Real-world case comparisons

Case Study	Geographic Scope	Digital Tools Used	Key Outcomes
NATO Enhanced Forward Presence	Eastern Europe	UAV surveillance, C2	Rapid logistics for deterrence
UNHAS Operations in Africa	Multiple (Chad, Sudan)	Blockchain, LESS, biometric	Improved tracking, reduced cargo loss
Turkish Air Force & Red Crescent	Türkiye (2023 quakes)	UAV mapping, AI logistics	Fast multi-corridor airlift coordination

5. FUTURE DIRECTIONS AND CONCLUSION

5.1. Challenges to Digital Transformation

The digital transformation of humanitarian aviation logistics presents a multitude of opportunities, but it is also hindered by several persistent and complex challenges. One major technical barrier is the lack of unified infrastructure across different airbases and logistic nodes, especially in conflict-prone or disaster-affected regions. Many humanitarian air logistics operations rely on legacy systems that lack interoperability with modern digital tools such as AI-driven demand forecasting or blockchain-based smart contracting. The adoption of these technologies often requires high-bandwidth connectivity, cloud infrastructure, and secure communication protocols — all of which may be unavailable or unreliable in remote or politically unstable regions.

Institutional resistance poses another significant hurdle. In both military and civilian humanitarian sectors, there are ingrained bureaucratic cultures that are slow to adapt to disruptive technologies. This is exacerbated by the lack of digital literacy among field personnel and decision-makers, many of whom are trained in traditional logistics practices and may not trust or fully understand automated planning systems or data-driven decision support. The transition to digital systems thus requires not only new tools but a significant cultural and operational shift.

The digital divide is also stark between organizations and regions. While actors like NATO and the UN have invested in advanced digital logistics systems, many national humanitarian agencies and NGOs in low-income countries lack the budget, expertise, or infrastructure to adopt similar capabilities. This inequality limits seamless coordination during multinational operations. Moreover, coordination gaps between various actors — including military forces, civil aviation authorities, NGOs, and UN agencies — often result in fragmented data sharing, duplicated efforts, or delayed responses. Funding limitations further aggravate the issue. Donor-driven humanitarian programs frequently prioritize direct relief over digital capacity-building, leaving critical areas like predictive analytics, IoT-based monitoring, and cyber-resilience underfunded. The lack of long-term investment planning also prevents sustained innovation in airbase readiness and aviation-based humanitarian logistics.

5.2. Strategic Recommendations

To address these challenges and unlock the full potential of digital transformation in aviation logistics for humanitarian response, a set of strategic interventions is necessary. First, **policy innovation** must focus on establishing regulatory frameworks that support technological experimentation, encourage interoperability, and facilitate the adoption of emerging technologies like AI, blockchain, and digital twin systems. Governments and international institutions such as ICAO, NATO, and the UN should collaborate to create adaptive regulatory environments that enable field-deployable digital tools while maintaining safety, accountability, and ethical standards.

Investment strategies must also shift from short-term project funding to long-term capacity development. This includes financing digital infrastructure in at-risk regions, such as high-frequency communication networks, satellite-based tracking systems, and autonomous UAV corridors for reconnaissance or supply. Additionally, funding mechanisms should incentivize the integration of digital logistics into national disaster response plans, ensuring that airbase readiness and digital coordination capabilities are prioritized alongside food and shelter in humanitarian budgets.

A particularly effective approach lies in fostering **public-private-academic partnerships**. These tri-sector collaborations can bridge knowledge gaps, provide innovative solutions, and scale best practices. For example, collaborations between universities and logistics firms can yield advanced simulation models or AI-based flight optimization tools tailored for humanitarian settings. Partnerships with technology providers can facilitate the customization and deployment of digital platforms like predictive maintenance dashboards or blockchain procurement chains. Public agencies can offer access to real-world operating environments for testing and feedback loops. This collaborative model also enhances the alignment of training programs, ensuring that future logisticians and humanitarian planners are equipped with both operational and digital competencies.

5.3. Concluding Reflections

In conclusion, the role of digitally enabled aviation logistics is no longer optional but essential in the current era of overlapping global crises. From conflict zones and pandemic outbreaks to climate-induced disasters, aviation provides unmatched speed, reach, and flexibility — but its effectiveness hinges increasingly on the integration of intelligent, secure, and adaptive digital systems. These systems not only improve coordination and transparency but also enable proactive and data-informed decision-making, which is critical for life-saving operations.

The transformation of airbase readiness and airlift planning into digital, interconnected, and resilient ecosystems is not without its challenges. Yet, the real-world case studies examined — such as NATO's digital logistics interoperability in Eastern Europe, UNHAS's AI-enabled coordination platforms in Africa, and Türkiye's blockchain-assisted airlift after the 2023 earthquakes — prove that innovation in this space is not only possible but already underway. These examples demonstrate the feasibility and necessity of transitioning toward a **resilient, agile, and accountable humanitarian air system**, one that can anticipate crises, adapt to dynamic field conditions, and ensure ethical and effective delivery of aid.

Looking ahead, the focus must be on sustained collaboration, ethical innovation, and strategic integration of technologies into every layer of the humanitarian aviation framework. This shift will redefine not only how humanitarian aid is delivered but also how we prepare, coordinate, and respond in a world where speed, information, and adaptability are the keys to saving lives.

REFERENCES

Adebayo, A. S., Chukwurah, N., & Ajayi, O. O. (2025). Artificial Intelligence and Machine Learning Algorithms for Advanced Threat Detection and Cybersecurity Risk Mitigation Strategies.

Akkartal, G. R., Akkartal, E., & Yıldırım, C. (2019). The Management Of Innovation In Supply Chain. *Eurasian Business & Economics Journal, 17*(17), 43–52.

Al-Mazrouie, J. R., Ojiako, U., Williams, T., Chipulu, M., & Marshall, A. (2021). An operations readiness typology for mitigating against transitional 'disastrous openings' of airport infrastructure projects. *Production Planning and Control, 32*(4), 283–302. DOI: 10.1080/09537287.2020.1730997

Aladağ, H., Demirdöğen, G., & Işık, Z. (2023). Fundamental Prerequisites of Operational Readiness, Activation, and Transition: Case Study of Istanbul Grand Airport. *Systems, 11*(9), 468. DOI: 10.3390/systems11090468

Alexandridis, K., Sabri, S., Smith, J., Logan, B., Bartfai-Walcott, K., & Migliori, D. (2024). Distributed AI modeling and simulation for smart airport digital twin applications. In *Digital Twins, Simulation, and the Metaverse: Driving Efficiency and Effectiveness in the Physical World through Simulation in the Virtual Worlds* (pp. 195–224). Springer Nature Switzerland. DOI: 10.1007/978-3-031-69107-2_9

Arbuckle, G. (2025). *Fundamentals of global air transport geography*. Taylor & Francis. DOI: 10.4324/9781003405351

Avtin, I. V., Baburov, V. I., Ponomarenko, B. V., & Shatrakov, Y. G. (2021). *Principles of Integrated Airborne Avionics*. Springer. DOI: 10.1007/978-981-16-0897-1

Burčiar, F., Kováč, S., & Važan, P. (2024). Check for updates Proactive Control of Production Systems Using Proposed Data Integration Strategies. *Software Engineering Methods in Systems and Network Systems: Proceedings of 7th Computational Methods in Systems and Software 2023, Vol. 2, 934*, 346.

Candell, O., Hällqvist, R., Olsson, E., Fransson, T., Thaduri, A., & Karim, R. (2024). Air vehicle system health and asset management: Modeling, simulation, and decision support. *International Journal of System Assurance Engineering and Management*, •••, 1–14. DOI: 10.1007/s13198-024-02481-x

Cebir, Y., & Akkartal, E. (2024). Digital twin in logistics and supply chain management. In *Strategic Innovations for Dynamic Supply Chains* (pp. 170–192). IGI Global Scientific Publishing. DOI: 10.4018/979-8-3693-3575-8.ch008

Charnsethikul, C., Silva, J. M., Verhagen, W. J., & Das, R. (2025). Urban Air Mobility Aircraft Operations in Urban Environments: A Review of Potential Safety Risks. [MDPI Publishing]. *Aerospace (Basel, Switzerland), 12*(4), 306. DOI: 10.3390/aerospace12040306

Debnath, D., Vanegas, F., Sandino, J., Hawary, A. F., & Gonzalez, F. (2024). A review of UAV path-planning algorithms and obstacle avoidance methods for remote sensing applications. *Remote Sensing (Basel), 16*(21), 4019. DOI: 10.3390/rs16214019

Devitt, S. K., Scholz, J., Schless, T., & Lewis, L. (2023). Developing a trusted human-AI network for humanitarian benefit. *Digital War, 4*(1), 1–17. DOI: 10.1057/s42984-023-00063-y

Ezzati, S. M., Alizadeh, R., & Jokar, M. R. A. (2024). Efficiency and Transparency in Supplier Performance Evaluation: A Blockchain-Powered Smart Contract Solution. *IEEE Access : Practical Innovations, Open Solutions.*

Feroz, S., & Abu Dabous, S. (2021). Uav-based remote sensing applications for bridge condition assessment. *Remote Sensing (Basel), 13*(9), 1809. DOI: 10.3390/rs13091809

Grange, R., Heaslip, G., & McMullan, C. (2020). Coordination to choreography: The evolution of humanitarian supply chains. *Journal of Humanitarian Logistics and Supply Chain Management, 10*(1), 21–44. DOI: 10.1108/JHLSCM-12-2018-0077

Gupta, S., Modgil, S., Bhattacharyya, S., & Bose, I. (2022). Artificial intelligence for decision support systems in the field of operations research: Review and future scope of research. *Annals of Operations Research, 308*(1), 215–274. DOI: 10.1007/s10479-020-03856-6

Hejji, D., Talib, M. A., Nassif, A. B., Nasir, Q., & Bouridane, A. (2021, November). AI-based models for resource allocation and resource demand forecasting systems in aviation: A survey and analytical study. In *2021 IEEE International Conference on Internet of Things and Intelligence Systems (IoTaIS)* (pp. 183-189). IEEE. DOI: 10.1109/IoTaIS53735.2021.9628555

Kanmaz, U., & Kütahya, C. K. (2025). Prioritizing Risk Mitigation Strategies in Air Cargo Freight Operations: A Fuzzy TOPSIS Approach. *Journal of Aviation, 9*(1), 181–195. DOI: 10.30518/jav.1599331

Kaushik, K., Khan, A., Kumari, A., Sharma, I., & Dubey, R. (2024). Ethical considerations in AI-based cybersecurity. In *Next-generation cybersecurity: AI, ML, and Blockchain* (pp. 437–470). Springer Nature Singapore. DOI: 10.1007/978-981-97-1249-6_19

Kumar, P., & Singh, R. K. (2022). Application of Industry 4.0 technologies for effective coordination in humanitarian supply chains: A strategic approach. *Annals of Operations Research, 319*(1), 379–411. DOI: 10.1007/s10479-020-03898-w PMID: 33531729

Kumari, U., & Malhotra, P. (2024). Use of digital twin in predicting the life of aircraft main bearing. *Simulation Techniques of Digital Twin in Real-Time Applications: Design Modeling and Implementation*, 261-288.

Larson, P. D. (2021). Security, sustainability and supply chain collaboration in the humanitarian space. *Journal of Humanitarian Logistics and Supply Chain Management, 11*(4), 609–622. DOI: 10.1108/JHLSCM-06-2021-0059

Luo, M., Fricke, H., Desart, B., Zapata, S. R., & Schultz, M. (2024). High-fidelity digital twin applied agent-based model for supporting predictable airport ground operations. *Available at SSRN* 4806351. DOI: 10.2139/ssrn.4806351

Marín, M. A. F. V., & Marcos, I. F. V. (2021). Logistical reflections on developing a forward operating base: Improving logistics sustainability in durable deployment of air units. In *Developments and Advances in Defense and Security* [Singapore: Springer Singapore.]. *Proceedings of MICRADS, 2021*, 421–431.

Mızrak, F. (2023). Analyzing Criteria Affecting Decision-Making Processes of Human Resource Management in the Aviation Sector-A Fuzzy Logic Approach. *Journal of Aviation, 7*(3), 376–387. DOI: 10.30518/jav.1331688

Mızrak, F. (2024). Integrating AI with aviation cybersecurity: The strategic role of human resources. *Business & Management Studies: An International Journal, 12*(3), 610–628. DOI: 10.15295/bmij.v12i3.2396

Mızrak, F. (2025). Cybersecurity and Strategic Innovation in the Digital Economy. In *Utilizing Cybersecurity to Foster Business Innovation and Resiliency* (pp. 1–30). IGI Global Scientific Publishing. DOI: 10.4018/979-8-3693-6417-8.ch001

Mizrak, F., & Akkartal, G. R. (2024). Prioritizing cybersecurity initiatives in aviation: A dematel-QSFS methodology. *Heliyon, 10*(16), e35487. DOI: 10.1016/j.heliyon.2024.e35487 PMID: 39687858

Mizrak, F., Mizrak, K. C., & Akkartal, G. R. (2025). Developing a strategic framework for airline destination selection: A multi-criteria decision-making approach applied to Turkish airlines. *Transportation Research Interdisciplinary Perspectives, 29*, 101322. DOI: 10.1016/j.trip.2025.101322

Mizrak, F., Polat, L., & Tasar, S. A. (2024). Applying entropy weighting and 2-tuple linguistic T-spherical fuzzy MCDM: A case study of developing a strategic sustainability plan for Istanbul Airport. *Sustainability (Basel), 16*(24), 11104. DOI: 10.3390/su162411104

Moghadam, M. R. S., Sahebi, I. G., Masoomi, B., Azzavi, M., Anjomshoae, A., Banomyong, R., & Ractham, P. (2022). Modeling IoT enablers for humanitarian supply chains coordination.

MoghadasNian., S. (2025). AI-Driven Inventory Optimization in Airline Logistics: Enhancing Efficiency, Sustainability, and Operational Performance. In *Proceedings of the International Conference on Artificial Intelligence in the Age of Digital Transformation. International Organization of Academic Studies, Tbilisi, Georgia. Language: English*

MoghadasNian., S. (2025). Digital transformation in airline logistics: Enhancing operational efficiency through AI-driven predictive analytics and blockchain integration. In *Proceedings of the International Conference on Artificial Intelligence in the Age of Digital Transformation.* International Organization of Academic Studies, Tbilisi, Georgia.

Nagasawa, R., Mas, E., Moya, L., & Koshimura, S. (2021). Model-based analysis of multi-UAV path planning for surveying postdisaster building damage. *Scientific Reports, 11*(1), 18588. DOI: 10.1038/s41598-021-97804-4 PMID: 34545140

Nawazish, M., Nandakumar, M. K., & Mateen, A. (2024). Are humanitarian supply chains sustainable? A systematic review and future research themes. *Benchmarking, 31*(8), 2565–2601. DOI: 10.1108/BIJ-01-2023-0036

Nicoletti, B. (2025). AI Transformation of Logistics. In *Artificial Intelligence for Logistics 5.0: From Foundation Models to Agentic AI* (pp. 107–131). Springer Nature Switzerland. DOI: 10.1007/978-3-031-94046-0_4

Ogunbiyi-Badaru, O., Alao, O. B., Dudu, O. F., & Alonge, E. O. (2024). Blockchain-enabled asset management: Opportunities, risks and global implications. *Comprehensive Research and Reviews in Multidisciplinary Studies, 2*(2), 14–22. DOI: 10.57219/crrms.2024.2.2.0042

Olivatto, T. F., Inguaggiato, F. F., & Stanganini, F. N. (2023). Urban mapping and impacts assessment in a Brazilian irregular settlement using UAV-based imaging. *Remote Sensing Applications: Society and Environment, 29*, 100911. DOI: 10.1016/j.rsase.2022.100911

Omar, I. A., Jayaraman, R., Debe, M. S., Salah, K., Yaqoob, I., & Omar, M. (2021). Automating procurement contracts in the healthcare supply chain using blockchain smart contracts. *IEEE Access : Practical Innovations, Open Solutions, 9*, 37397–37409. DOI: 10.1109/ACCESS.2021.3062471

Omar, I. A., Jayaraman, R., Salah, K., Debe, M., & Omar, M. (2020). Enhancing vendor managed inventory supply chain operations using blockchain smart contracts. *IEEE Access : Practical Innovations, Open Solutions*, *8*, 182704–182719. DOI: 10.1109/ACCESS.2020.3028031

Özkanlısoy, Ö., & Akkartal, E. (2021). Digital transformation in supply chains: Current applications, contributions and challenges. *Business & Management Studies: An International Journal*, *9*(1), 32–55.

Öztürk, S., & Akkartal, E. (2024). Internet of Things (IoT) Applications in Last Mile Delivery. In *Strategic Innovations for Dynamic Supply Chains* (pp. 193–215). IGI Global Scientific Publishing. DOI: 10.4018/979-8-3693-3575-8.ch009

Parmadi, B. D., & Ramli, K. (2025). Transforming Humanitarian Response with IoT in Conflict Zones: Field Insights, Ethical Frameworks, and Deployment Challenges. *International Journal of Electrical, Computer, and Biomedical Engineering*, *3*(1), 157–187. DOI: 10.62146/ijecbe.v3i1.112

Perumal, A. P., Chintale, P., Molleti, R., & Desaboyina, G. (2024). Risk Assessment of Artificial Intelligence Systems in Cybersecurity. *American Journal of Science and Learning for Development*, *3*(7), 49–60.

Rashid, H. (n.d.) Using Smart Contracts to Enhance Compliance and Efficiency in Procurement Operations. *IJLRP-International Journal of Leading Research Publication, 5*(8).

Reghunadhan, R. (2020). Ethical considerations and issues of blockchain technology-based systems in war zones: A case study approach. In *Handbook of research on blockchain technology* (pp. 1–34). Academic Press. DOI: 10.1016/B978-0-12-819816-2.00001-0

Sahun, Y., Sikirda, Y., & Tymochko, O. (2025). Application of Computer Load Optimization Model in an Aircraft Load Planning Process. In *Encyclopedia of Information Science and Technology* (6th ed., pp. 1–20). IGI Global.

Srivastava, Y. C., Srivastava, A., & Granata, C. (2021, December). Digitally Enabled Organizations-Leveraging New Age Technologies. In *Abu Dhabi International Petroleum Exhibition and Conference* (p. D012S159R001). SPE. DOI: 10.2118/207380-MS

Ticas, F. L. (2023). Agile Combat Employment (ACE) Readiness: Necessary Training Transitions For Airfield Operations Officers.

Toygar, A. (2024). Sustainability in the Maritime Industry: Integration of Digital Twin and Autonomous Control. In *Strategic Innovations for Dynamic Supply Chains* (pp. 31-49). IGI Global Scientific Publishing.

Woltjer, R., Johansson, B. J., Oskarsson, P. A., Svenmarck, P., & Kirwan, B. (2022). Air transport system agility: The Agile Response Capability (ARC) methodology for crisis preparedness. *Infrastructures*, *7*(2), 11. DOI: 10.3390/infrastructures7020011

Xu, Y., Chong, H. Y., & Chi, M. (2021). A review of smart contracts applications in various industries: A procurement perspective. *Advances in Civil Engineering*, *2021*(1), 5530755. DOI: 10.1155/2021/5530755

Zhang, H., & Chang, C. (2025). Freight network optimization for intercontinental long route with mixed time windows and multiple aircraft types-China-Africa case study. *Heliyon*, *11*(6), e42790. DOI: 10.1016/j.heliyon.2025.e42790

Zhang, P. (2024, September). Optimization and Implementation of Intelligent Scheduling Algorithms in the Civil Aviation Supply Chain. In *2024 International Conference on Industrial IoT, Big Data and Supply Chain (IIoTBDSC)* (pp. 314-318). IEEE. DOI: 10.1109/IIoTBDSC64371.2024.00063

Zhang, Z., & Zhu, L. (2023). A review on unmanned aerial vehicle remote sensing: Platforms, sensors, data processing methods, and applications. *drones*, *7*(6), 398.

Zocchi, M., Kasaragod, A. K., Jenkins, A., Cook, C., Dobson, R., Oommen, T., Van Huis, D., Taylor, B., Brooks, C., Marini, R., Troiani, F., & Mazzanti, P. (2023). Multi-sensor and multi-scale remote sensing approach for assessing slope instability along transportation corridors using satellites and uncrewed aircraft systems. *Remote Sensing (Basel)*, *15*(12), 3016. DOI: 10.3390/rs15123016

Chapter 12
Drones and UAVs for Rapid Emergency Relief and Last-Mile Delivery

Nazim Atluyev
https://orcid.org/0009-0002-2162-1108
Yeditepe University, Ataşehir, Turkey

ABSTRACT

This chapter explores the transformative role of Unmanned Aerial Vehicles (UAVs), commonly known as drones, in enhancing emergency relief logistics and last-mile delivery performance. As supply chains face increasing disruption from natural disasters, pandemics, and urban congestion, UAVs offer rapid, flexible, and contactless delivery solutions that improve reach, resilience, and sustainability. The chapter provides a comprehensive review of technological foundations, real-world applications, and strategic innovations, including digital twin systems, IoT integration, and AI-based optimization. Drawing on recent academic and operational literature, it critically examines key challenges such as regulatory constraints, technical limitations, and organizational barriers. The findings emphasize the need for harmonized policy frameworks, infrastructure readiness, and ethical design to support scalable and sustainable drone integration into future logistics systems.

1. INTRODUCTION

In recent years, unmanned aerial vehicles (UAVs), commonly known as drones, have emerged as transformative tools in logistics, offering promising applications in both emergency relief and last-mile delivery operations. As global supply chains continue to face disruption from natural disasters, pandemics, and growing urban-

DOI: 10.4018/979-8-3373-3643-5.ch012

ization, drones provide a responsive and flexible alternative to traditional delivery models. These aerial systems can traverse blocked infrastructure, bypass traffic congestion, and reach remote or underserved regions with greater speed and accuracy than conventional ground transport. Researchers have increasingly recognized the strategic value of drone deployment in logistics, particularly in addressing the "last-mile problem"—one of the most costly and complex stages of delivery (Shuaibu, Mahmoud, & Sheltami, 2025; Eskandaripour & Boldsaikhan, 2023).

The integration of UAVs into emergency response logistics has also demonstrated considerable potential in improving the timeliness and efficiency of critical aid distribution. Drones have been used to deliver medical supplies, vaccines, blood products, and surveillance data to areas affected by floods, earthquakes, or armed conflict, where access via land routes is limited or entirely unavailable (Gao et al., 2025; Yucesoy, Balcik, & Coban, 2025). These applications not only enhance the reach and resilience of humanitarian supply chains but also reduce risks to human responders operating in unstable or hazardous environments. UAV-supported emergency logistics represents a convergence of real-time data, predictive algorithms, and operational agility—offering an adaptable and scalable solution in increasingly unpredictable global contexts.

In parallel, the commercial logistics sector has also seen a surge in drone-assisted delivery models, particularly in dense urban areas where congestion and environmental concerns undermine traditional delivery methods. Optimized drone deployment has shown potential to reduce delivery times, cut emissions, and improve customer satisfaction through contactless and rapid services (Garg et al., 2023; Kumar et al., 2024). Numerical case studies from urban pilots such as Milan, Italy, highlight how route optimization, fleet scheduling, and hybrid vehicle-UAV coordination can significantly increase last-mile delivery performance while aligning with sustainability goals (Borghetti et al., 2022; Ghaffar et al., 2024). These operational improvements are further amplified by real-time analytics, IoT integration, and advanced geospatial mapping, which are now core components of drone logistics platforms.

Despite their advantages, drone deployment presents a range of challenges that must be addressed to support large-scale adoption. Regulatory constraints, including airspace access, flight altitude limits, and certification requirements, vary significantly across jurisdictions and often lag behind technological advancements (Shakhatreh et al., 2019; AL-Dosari, Hunaiti, & Balachandran, 2023). Issues related to cybersecurity, public safety, noise, and privacy further complicate implementation in populated areas. Moreover, infrastructure readiness, such as the availability of droneports, charging stations, and automated landing systems, remains uneven, particularly in developing regions (Hoffmann & Prause, 2018; Konert, Smereka, & Szarpak, 2019). Addressing these constraints requires coordinated action among policymakers, industry leaders, and technologists to ensure responsible and scalable UAV integration.

This chapter provides a comprehensive review of the evolving role of UAVs in emergency relief and last-mile delivery, highlighting technological foundations, strategic innovations, operational case studies, and critical barriers. Drawing from interdisciplinary literature and global examples, it explores how UAVs intersect with key themes such as digital transformation, sustainability, and supply chain resilience. The chapter also examines the implications of UAV adoption for infrastructure planning, policy development, and ethical logistics management. By synthesizing current insights and projecting future directions, this chapter aims to inform both academic research and practical decision-making in the rapidly advancing field of drone-assisted logistics.

2. TECHNOLOGICAL FOUNDATIONS OF UAVS IN LOGISTICS

Unmanned Aerial Vehicles (UAVs), widely known as drones, are emerging as vital tools in the transformation of logistics and supply chain management. Their unique ability to navigate challenging environments, deliver time-sensitive cargo, and operate semi-autonomously or fully autonomously makes them particularly suited for last-mile delivery and emergency response logistics. The main UAV types used in logistics include fixed-wing drones for long-range delivery, rotary-wing models for maneuverability in tight spaces, and hybrid vertical take-off and landing (VTOL) systems that combine both capabilities. The suitability of each UAV type depends on a variety of performance factors, including payload capacity, flight range, terrain adaptability, and delivery precision (Eskandaripour & Boldsaikhan, 2023; Pratelli et al., 2024).

A key enabler of drone performance in logistics is the advancement of navigation and automation systems. These systems leverage GPS, inertial measurement units (IMUs), and artificial intelligence to allow drones to follow optimal routes, avoid obstacles, and dynamically adjust to changing environmental conditions. UAVs equipped with AI-based flight planning tools are increasingly being deployed in urban settings to overcome traffic congestion, shorten delivery cycles, and minimize logistical costs. Recent research highlights how advanced routing algorithms and integrated vehicle-UAV frameworks have been utilized for vaccine transport, search-and-rescue missions, and aerial mapping in natural disaster zones (Garg et al., 2023; Ghaffar et al., 2024; Kumar et al., 2024).

Equally important is the role of connectivity and real-time data exchange. Drones now operate within complex digital ecosystems supported by 5G networks, satellite communications, and mesh routing protocols, which allow for continuous telemetry monitoring and system synchronization. The application of digital twin technology enables the real-time replication of drone logistics environments, allowing for scenario simulations, fleet performance tracking, and predictive maintenance strategies. Cebir and Akkartal (2024) note that digital twins are becoming essential in high-demand operations by improving operational foresight and resource efficiency. In parallel, the integration of Internet of Things (IoT) applications in drone delivery enhances traceability, condition monitoring, and cargo verification, especially in last-mile logistics, where transparency and responsiveness are paramount (Öztürk & Akkartal, 2024).

Energy systems continue to be one of the most pressing technological constraints in UAV logistics. While lithium-polymer batteries remain the most common energy source, they provide limited endurance, prompting the exploration of alternatives such as hydrogen fuel cells and solar-powered UAVs. These new energy models are increasingly viewed through the lens of environmental sustainability. For instance, optimized drone deployment has been shown to lower last-mile emissions, thereby supporting corporate green goals and urban air quality initiatives (Ahmed, 2025; Garg et al., 2023). In addition to their environmental benefits, drones have also proven essential in emergency and humanitarian logistics, especially in delivering medical supplies, vaccines, and relief goods to inaccessible or infrastructure-deficient areas. Numerous studies document their successful use during flood crises, pandemic lockdowns, and earthquakes, highlighting their rapid response capabilities and operational resilience (Gao et al., 2025; Yucesoy, Balcik, & Coban, 2025).

Despite these technological advancements, barriers such as regulatory fragmentation, airspace coordination, and data security remain significant. The lack of harmonized UAV legislation, particularly for cross-border or high-risk deployments, can limit scalability. Nonetheless, as Shuaibu, Mahmoud, and Sheltami (2025) argue, the convergence of AI, optimization models, and low-carbon technologies marks a strategic shift toward data-driven, decentralized logistics systems. These foundational capabilities are not just transforming tactical delivery processes but are also redefining how logistics systems are conceptualized, coordinated, and scaled in an increasingly complex global supply chain landscape.

3. APPLICATIONS IN EMERGENCY RELIEF AND LAST-MILE DELIVERY

The deployment of Unmanned Aerial Vehicles (UAVs) in both emergency response and commercial logistics has reshaped the operational boundaries of supply chain management. In emergency and disaster scenarios, drones have proven to be indispensable tools for delivering aid, conducting aerial assessments, and ensuring the continuity of logistics operations in environments where traditional infrastructure is damaged, blocked, or entirely absent. Natural disasters such as earthquakes, floods, and wildfires—as well as global health crises like the COVID-19 pandemic—have exposed the vulnerabilities of conventional supply chains and highlighted the critical need for rapid, flexible logistics responses. In this context, drones have filled a vital gap. As Mızrak (2023) emphasizes, effective risk and crisis management in logistics requires integrating agile delivery mechanisms, and UAVs provide an ideal solution for reaching affected populations with essential goods, including medical supplies, vaccines, and emergency equipment. UAVs also minimize the risks associated with human exposure during pandemics by enabling contactless delivery in quarantined or high-infection zones.

The use of drones in commercial last-mile delivery is equally transformative. With rising urban congestion and increasing consumer demand for fast, same-day delivery, traditional transportation models are reaching their limits. UAVs offer a solution by bypassing road traffic, reducing delivery times, and reaching areas where ground vehicles are inefficient or economically unfeasible. Their value is even more apparent in rural or geographically isolated areas, where logistics costs are typically high, and infrastructure development is limited. Mızrak et al. (2024) demonstrate how integrating UAVs into smart logistics planning—such as in the case of Istanbul Airport's strategic sustainability initiatives—can optimize route planning, reduce energy use, and contribute to broader environmental goals. Moreover, when coupled with digital and fuzzy multi-criteria decision-making models, drone logistics can be customized to meet dynamic operational needs in both commercial and humanitarian contexts.

Real-world case studies further illustrate the practical impact of UAV deployment. Zipline's drone delivery network in Rwanda and Ghana has become a benchmark for medical logistics innovation, consistently delivering blood, vaccines, and critical medications to remote health centers within minutes. Amazon Prime Air, while still in its pilot stages, reflects the ambition of integrating UAVs into mainstream e-commerce delivery, targeting efficiency gains in high-density urban areas. Similarly, organizations like UNICEF have utilized drones for vaccine transport in regions with difficult terrain or insufficient cold chain infrastructure, demonstrating the role of UAVs in enhancing health equity and access. These cases validate Özkanlısoy and Akkartal's (2022) assertion that the logistics sector must develop alternative delivery models to remain resilient in the face of geopolitical, infrastructural, and environmental disruptions—as highlighted during the Suez Canal blockage, where a single chokepoint paralyzed global supply chains.

Together, these examples underscore that UAV applications in logistics are not only operationally viable but strategically necessary. Whether responding to crisis conditions or reshaping the efficiency of last-mile delivery, drones are no longer peripheral technologies—they are central to the emerging architecture of responsive, sustainable, and digitally enhanced supply chains.

4. STRATEGIC INNOVATIONS IN DRONE-ENABLED SUPPLY CHAINS

The integration of drones into supply chains has introduced a wave of strategic innovations, reshaping how organizations manage delivery operations, respond to crises, and achieve sustainability goals. One of the most transformative developments is the adoption of digital technologies that enhance visibility, automation, and data-driven decision-making across logistics processes. Digital transformation in supply chains has expanded beyond conventional automation to include AI-supported routing, IoT-based tracking systems, and cloud-integrated analytics, which collectively enhance the efficiency and agility of UAV operations (Özkanlısoy & Akkartal, 2021). Internet of Things (IoT) technologies, in particular, play a pivotal role in last-mile delivery optimization, enabling real-time monitoring of package conditions, autonomous route updates, and seamless coordination with other transport modes (Öztürk & Akkartal, 2024).

One of the most promising innovations is the use of digital twin technology, which allows for real-time simulation and monitoring of drone operations. By creating digital replicas of physical delivery systems, companies can predict operational risks, optimize flight routes, and perform scenario analysis under uncertainty. Cebir and Akkartal (2024) emphasize that digital twin systems offer significant advantages for dynamic scheduling and infrastructure coordination, especially in volatile environments such as disaster zones or urban congestion. These systems also support predictive maintenance and fleet performance evaluation, which are crucial for scaling UAV-based logistics operations.

The adoption of drones is also accelerating the shift toward more sustainable logistics frameworks. Organizations are increasingly investing in electric UAV fleets to minimize fuel consumption and reduce emissions during last-mile delivery, aligning with the growing emphasis on green fleet management. Akkartal and Aras (2021) argue that integrating environmental criteria into fleet management strategies not only improves ecological performance but also contributes to long-term cost savings and operational resilience. Moreover, innovations in alternative energy sources, such as solar and hydrogen-powered drones, are becoming viable options for sustainable UAV deployment (Mızrak & Akkartal, 2024). These technological developments support broader efforts to transition toward low-emission logistics networks in urban and rural settings.

The emergence of flexible business models further enhances the strategic appeal of drone logistics. Drone-as-a-Service (DaaS) platforms and third-party UAV operators are making drone technology more accessible to small and medium-sized enterprises, especially in regions with limited infrastructure. Danışman and Akkartal (2023) demonstrate how innovation models like TRIZ can be applied to design sustainable logistics frameworks tailored to country-specific resource conditions. These models emphasize creative problem-solving, enabling the development of cost-effective and scalable solutions for regions with unique geographical and regulatory challenges.

Strategic management also plays a vital role in facilitating organizational transformation during drone integration. Change management frameworks must be in place to address resistance to new technologies and support the reskilling of logistics personnel. As Mızrak (2024) highlights, dynamic organizational models that embrace innovation, encourage cross-functional collaboration, and align with long-term strategic goals are essential for the successful adoption of UAV technologies. This is especially relevant in multi-stakeholder logistics ecosystems where private logistics firms, public authorities, and humanitarian organizations must coordinate across different regulatory, operational, and technological domains.

The strategic role of drones is also evident in supplier selection, reverse logistics, and green procurement practices. Akkartal and Mızrak (2023) outline how drones can support environmentally responsible supply chain structures by improving traceability and minimizing waste in returns processing. These capabilities are particularly valuable in industries such as healthcare and maritime logistics, where time sensitivity and sustainability are critical. Mızrak (2022) further demonstrates that alternative vehicle technologies and renewable energy sources, including drone-based systems, can support strategic transitions in the logistics sector toward more circular, resource-efficient operations.

The COVID-19 pandemic, along with high-impact events like the Suez Canal blockage, exposed the fragility of global supply chains and underscored the need for agile, diversified delivery solutions (Özkanlısoy & Akkartal, 2022). In response, UAVs have emerged as viable instruments for building resilience and responsiveness into logistics networks. Abdelhadi and Akkartal (2024) reinforce this view by identifying structural inefficiencies in Turkey's retail sector and recommending data-driven models that integrate UAVs and ground logistics to improve system performance.

Recent studies also highlight the operational benefits of UAV deployment from a technical, economic, and sustainability perspective. Optimized routing algorithms, AI-based scheduling, and multi-criteria decision models have been applied to improve delivery speed, reduce energy consumption, and ensure timely service in remote and congested areas (Shuaibu, Mahmoud, & Sheltami, 2025; Kumar et al., 2024; Garg et al., 2023). For example, hybrid models that integrate UAVs with ground vehicles have demonstrated significant reductions in delivery times and carbon emissions (Ghaffar et al., 2024). These approaches also enhance the flexibility of logistics systems by enabling reconfiguration based on changing weather, demand, or crisis conditions.

Operational studies and simulations reveal that drones are not only valuable for rapid delivery but also support real-time supply chain monitoring, inventory visibility, and dynamic warehouse-to-door coordination (Pratelli et al., 2024; Borghetti et al., 2022). In urban contexts, where delivery delays and environmental concerns are magnified, drone-assisted models are now being tested to improve traffic bypass and route efficiency. Research by Eskandaripour and Boldsaikhan (2023) and Shuaibu et al. (2025) confirms that the strategic use of UAVs leads to enhanced delivery responsiveness, particularly when supported by digital optimization and decentralized logistics architectures.

To ensure long-term viability, however, organizations must address several externalities, including regulatory uncertainty, airspace management, and data privacy. Studies have noted that fragmented legal frameworks and the absence of harmonized UAV guidelines remain among the most significant barriers to widespread adoption (Hoffmann & Prause, 2018; AL-Dosari et al., 2023). Furthermore, operational reliability under adverse conditions such as natural disasters requires robust system design, contingency planning, and stakeholder coordination (Konert, Smereka, & Szarpak, 2019; Johnson et al., 2021; Yucesoy, Balcik, & Coban, 2025). Integrating UAVs into these broader frameworks demands a multidimensional strategy that combines technological innovation with regulatory foresight, sustainability planning, and cross-sectoral collaboration.

In summary, the integration of drones into modern supply chains reflects a convergence of digital transformation, sustainability imperatives, and organizational innovation. By aligning emerging technologies with strategic business models, UAV-enabled logistics can support both resilience in crises and competitiveness in routine operations, making them a cornerstone of future-ready supply chain architectures.

5. CHALLENGES AND STRATEGIC IMPLICATIONS

Despite the growing momentum around the use of drones and UAVs in logistics and emergency delivery, several critical challenges continue to hinder their widespread adoption and operational scalability. One of the most prominent barriers is the lack of harmonized regulatory frameworks across countries and regions. The integration of drones into civilian airspace presents complex issues related to flight permissions, altitude restrictions, geofencing, and safety protocols. Many national aviation authorities have yet to develop comprehensive UAV policies that can balance innovation with public safety. Regulatory uncertainty particularly affects the scalability of UAV applications in last-mile delivery, as it complicates route planning, delays approvals, and increases operational risk. As Özkanlısoy and Akkartal (2022) note in their analysis of the Suez Canal blockage and its systemic effects, inflexible and reactive regulatory systems often aggravate existing logistical vulnerabilities rather than mitigate them. Similar regulatory rigidity can be seen in UAV deployment, where the absence of forward-looking policy frameworks limits the potential of drones to act as a strategic buffer in crisis scenarios.

Beyond regulatory issues, several **technical limitations** also pose major constraints. Drone endurance remains relatively limited due to current battery technologies, restricting range and payload capacity—factors especially problematic for high-volume delivery tasks or operations in remote regions. Weather conditions, including wind, rain, and extreme temperatures, can compromise drone flight stability and sensor functionality. Moreover, cybersecurity concerns are becoming increasingly important as UAVs become integrated into digital logistics infrastructures. The potential for signal jamming, data interception, or system hijacking raises serious questions about operational security and data privacy. Abdelhadi and Akkartal (2024) emphasize that these vulnerabilities are particularly significant in sectors with fragmented infrastructure and inconsistent digital capabilities, such as retail logistics in emerging economies. In such contexts, the successful deployment of UAVs requires not only technical readiness but also robust digital security frameworks.

In addition to technological and regulatory hurdles, organizational resistance remains a less visible but equally significant challenge. The transition toward UAV-supported logistics demands a cultural shift within organizations, as traditional logistics personnel may be hesitant to adopt unfamiliar technologies or workflows. Change resistance can stem from uncertainty around job security, skills mismatches, or a lack of clear strategic vision. As Mızrak (2024b) highlights, overcoming such resistance necessitates proactive change management strategies that incorporate staff training, leadership commitment, and cross-departmental collaboration. Without addressing internal resistance, even the most promising UAV innovations risk being underutilized or implemented ineffectively.

Given these constraints, strategic alignment between policy, infrastructure, and organizational capacity is essential. Effective UAV integration requires coordinated investment in drone-friendly infrastructure, such as designated takeoff/landing zones, air traffic management systems, and recharging stations. It also necessitates public-private partnerships to ensure that regulatory reforms keep pace with technological progress. Mızrak (2024b) argues that infrastructure readiness must be matched by institutional agility and strategic foresight, particularly in complex logistics environments like airports and seaports, where multiple stakeholders operate under overlapping jurisdictions. Finally, scalability depends on the ability to pilot, evaluate, and adapt UAV deployments in diverse operational contexts—ranging from urban e-commerce to rural healthcare supply chains—ensuring that drone solutions are both cost-effective and resilient.

In summary, while UAVs hold immense promise for the future of logistics, their full potential can only be realized through a coordinated approach that addresses regulatory, technical, organizational, and strategic dimensions. Integrating these elements into a unified roadmap will be critical for enabling safe, scalable, and sustainable drone operations in both commercial and emergency logistics ecosystems.

6. CONCLUSION

Unmanned Aerial Vehicles (UAVs) have rapidly transitioned from niche technologies to critical components of modern logistics systems, particularly in the domains of emergency response and last-mile delivery. Their ability to bypass physical infrastructure limitations, reduce delivery times, and operate in hazardous or inaccessible environments has made them indispensable in disaster relief operations, healthcare logistics, and urban e-commerce. UAVs offer a flexible and rapid alternative to conventional transport methods, filling critical gaps where speed, precision, and adaptability are required. Whether delivering life-saving medical supplies in flood zones or optimizing last-mile routes in congested urban centers, UAVs are redefining the operational boundaries of supply chains.

This transformation is occurring alongside two major global shifts: the acceleration of digital transformation and the rising imperative of sustainability. The convergence of these trends with UAV capabilities is reshaping logistics into a more intelligent, data-driven, and environmentally responsible domain. UAVs now operate within interconnected digital ecosystems that leverage artificial intelligence, Internet of Things (IoT), and digital twin technologies to enhance visibility, predictability, and responsiveness. At the same time, electric-powered drones and renewable energy integration support organizations' sustainability goals by lowering emissions and reducing dependence on fossil fuels. These synergies not only enhance efficiency but also contribute to broader environmental and social objectives.

Looking ahead, the successful integration of UAVs into logistics systems will depend on scalability, ethical implementation, and strategic alignment with evolving global needs. Ensuring broad and equitable access to drone technologies—especially in underserved or infrastructure-poor regions—will be essential to achieving inclusive development outcomes. Equally important is the development of ethical and regulatory frameworks that address concerns around airspace safety, data security, environmental impact, and labor transformation. As UAVs become embedded in core logistics infrastructures, balancing innovation with responsibility will be key to sustaining public trust and long-term viability.

To this end, several recommendations emerge for key stakeholders. Policymakers must prioritize the development of adaptive, harmonized regulations that facilitate safe UAV integration while encouraging innovation. Investment in drone-friendly infrastructure, real-time air traffic management systems, and intermodal hubs will be crucial for scaling operations. Supply chain leaders should proactively invest in workforce training, organizational change management, and technology partnerships to harness UAV capabilities effectively. Technology developers, in turn, must focus on enhancing drone reliability, energy efficiency, and interoperability with digital platforms while embedding robust cybersecurity and ethical design principles into their systems. Collectively, these actions will enable UAVs to move from experimental solutions to foundational tools in building future-ready, resilient, and sustainable supply chains.

REFERENCES

Abdelhadi, A., & Akkartal, E. (2024). Supply chain efficiency a structural analysis in turkey's retail sector. *Brazilian Journal of Operations & Production Management, 21*(3), 2150–2150. DOI: 10.14488/BJOPM.2150.2024

Ahmed, A. A. (2025). Drone Technology in Logistics Revolutionizing Last-Mile Delivery Solutions. *Eurasian Journal of Theoretical and Applied Sciences (EJTAS)*, 25-35.

Akkartal, E., & Aras, G. Y. (2021). Sustainability in fleet management. *Journal of Advanced Research in Economics and Administrative Sciences, 2*(3), 13–39. DOI: 10.47631/jareas.v2i3.288

Akkartal, G. R., & Mızrak, F. (2023). Defining reverse and green supplier selection criteria with a strategic management approach. In *Economic Development and the Environmental Ecosystem: The Role of Energy Policy in Economic Growth* (pp. 205–218). Springer Nature Switzerland. DOI: 10.1007/978-3-031-26596-9_17

AL-Dosari, K., Hunaiti, Z., & Balachandran, W.AL-Dosari. (2023). Systematic review on civilian drones in safety and security applications. *Drones (Basel), 7*(3), 210. DOI: 10.3390/drones7030210

Borghetti, F., Caballini, C., Carboni, A., Grossato, G., Maja, R., & Barabino, B. (2022). The use of drones for last-mile delivery: A numerical case study in Milan, Italy. *Sustainability (Basel), 14*(3), 1766. DOI: 10.3390/su14031766

Cebir, Y., & Akkartal, E. (2024). Digital twin in logistics and supply chain management. In *Strategic Innovations for Dynamic Supply Chains* (pp. 170–192). IGI Global. DOI: 10.4018/979-8-3693-3575-8.ch008

Danisman, M., & Akkartal, E. (2023). Defining a new business model for sustainable biomass production from forestry residues in Türkiye by using TRIZ. *International Journal of Energy Economics and Policy, 13*(3), 243–253. DOI: 10.32479/ijeep.13985

Eskandaripour, H., & Boldsaikhan, E. (2023). Last-mile drone delivery: Past, present, and future. *Drones (Basel), 7*(2), 77. DOI: 10.3390/drones7020077

Gao, J., Zhang, Y., Wu, Z., & Yu, L. N. (2025). Optimized collaborative scheduling of unmanned aerial vehicles for emergency material distribution in flood disaster management. *Mechatron. Intell Transp. Syst, 4*(1), 1–15. DOI: 10.56578/mits040101

Garg, V., Niranjan, S., Prybutok, V., Pohlen, T., & Gligor, D. (2023). Drones in last-mile delivery: A systematic review on Efficiency, Accessibility, and Sustainability. *Transportation Research Part D, Transport and Environment, 123*, 103831. DOI: 10.1016/j.trd.2023.103831

Ghaffar, M. A., Peng, L., Aslam, M. U., Adeel, M., & Dassari, S. (2024). Vehicle-UAV Integrated Routing Optimization Problem for Emergency Delivery of Medical Supplies. *Electronics (Basel), 13*(18), 3650. DOI: 10.3390/electronics13183650

Hoffmann, T., & Prause, G. (2018). On the regulatory framework for last-mile delivery robots. *Machines (Basel), 6*(3), 33. DOI: 10.3390/machines6030033

Johnson, A. M., Cunningham, C. J., Arnold, E., Rosamond, W. D., & Zègre-Hemsey, J. K. (2021). Impact of using drones in emergency medicine: What does the future hold? *Open Access Emergency Medicine : OAEM, 13*, 487–498. DOI: 10.2147/OAEM.S247020 PMID: 34815722

Konert, A., Smereka, J., & Szarpak, L. (2019). The use of drones in emergency medicine: Practical and legal aspects. *Emergency Medicine International, 2019*(1), 3589792. DOI: 10.1155/2019/3589792 PMID: 31871790

Kumar, G., Tanvir, O., Kumar, A., & Goswami, M. (2024). Optimal drone deployment for cost-effective and sustainable last-mile delivery operations. *International Transactions in Operational Research.*

Mızrak, F. (2022). An Evaluation for the Use of Alternative Vehicle Technologies and Energy Resources in Logistic Sector with a Strategic Approach. In *Circular Economy and the Energy Market: Achieving Sustainable Economic Development Through Energy Policy* (pp. 159–171). Springer International Publishing. DOI: 10.1007/978-3-031-13146-2_13

Mızrak, F. (2023). Managing Risks and Crises in the Logistics Sector: A Comprehensive Analysis of Strategies and Prioritization Using AHP Method. *Meriç Uluslararası Sosyal ve Stratejik Araştırmalar Dergisi, 7*(Özel Sayı), 114-148.

Mızrak, F. (2024). Effective change management strategies: Exploring dynamic models for organizational transformation. In *Perspectives on artificial intelligence in times of turbulence: Theoretical background to applications* (pp. 135–162). IGI Global.

Mızrak, F. (2024). Strategies for Sustainable Business Growth in Maritime Logistics. In *Trends, Challenges, and Practices in Contemporary Strategic Management* (pp. 108-125). IGI Global Scientific Publishing. DOI: 10.4018/979-8-3693-1155-4.ch006

Mızrak, F., & Akkartal, G. R. (2024). An Analysis of Alternative Energy Sources and Applications in Maritime Transportation with a Strategic Management Approach. *Decision Making in Interdisciplinary Renewable Energy Projects: Navigating Energy Investments*, 97-109.

Mizrak, F., Polat, L., & Tasar, S. A. (2024). Applying Entropy Weighting and 2-Tuple Linguistic T-Spherical Fuzzy MCDM: A Case Study of Developing a Strategic Sustainability Plan for Istanbul Airport. *Sustainability (Basel), 16*(24), 11104. DOI: 10.3390/su162411104

Özkanlısoy, Ö., & Akkartal, E. (2021). Digital transformation in supply chains: Current applications, contributions and challenges. *Business & Management Studies: An International Journal, 9*(1), 32–55.

Özkanlısoy, Ö., & Akkartal, E. (2022). The effect of Suez Canal blockage on supply chains. *Dokuz Eylül Üniversitesi Denizcilik Fakültesi Dergisi, 14*(1), 51–79. DOI: 10.18613/deudfd.933816

Öztürk, S., & Akkartal, E. (2024). Internet of Things (IoT) Applications in Last Mile Delivery. In *Strategic Innovations for Dynamic Supply Chains* (pp. 193–215). IGI Global. DOI: 10.4018/979-8-3693-3575-8.ch009

Pratelli, A., Brocchini, L., & Petri, M. (2024). Optimising drone-assisted logistics for urban last-mile delivery: An overview of applications, methodologies, and emerging trends. *J. Urban Dev. Manag, 3*(3), 188–197. DOI: 10.56578/judm030304

Shakhatreh, H., Sawalmeh, A. H., Al-Fuqaha, A., Dou, Z., Almaita, E., Khalil, I., Othman, N. S., Khreishah, A., & Guizani, M. (2019). Unmanned aerial vehicles (UAVs): A survey on civil applications and key research challenges. *IEEE Access : Practical Innovations, Open Solutions, 7*, 48572–48634. DOI: 10.1109/ACCESS.2019.2909530

Shuaibu, A. S., Mahmoud, A. S., & Sheltami, T. R. (2025). A review of last-mile delivery optimization: Strategies, technologies, drone integration, and future trends. *Drones (Basel), 9*(3), 158. DOI: 10.3390/drones9030158

Yucesoy, E., Balcik, B., & Coban, E. (2025). The role of drones in disaster response: A literature review of operations research applications. *International Transactions in Operational Research, 32*(2), 545–589. DOI: 10.1111/itor.13484

Chapter 13

Smart Aviation Solutions for Humanitarian Aid:

Integrating AI and Blockchain in WFP Air Logistics Operations

Tuncel Oz
https://orcid.org/0000-0001-6603-0841
Independent Researcher, Istanbul, Turkey

ABSTRACT

This chapter investigates the transformative potential of artificial intelligence (AI) and blockchain technologies in humanitarian aviation logistics, with a particular focus on the World Food Programme's (WFP) United Nations Humanitarian Air Service (UNHAS). As humanitarian crises demand faster, more transparent, and adaptive responses, digital tools offer promising solutions for optimizing flight routes, forecasting demand, automating procurement, and ensuring cargo traceability. The chapter analyzes how AI and blockchain can improve operational efficiency, vendor accountability, and service delivery verification. It also discusses key challenges related to system interoperability, data privacy, cybersecurity, and the digital divide. The chapter concludes with a phased roadmap for scaling digital adoption and provides strategic recommendations for humanitarian organizations, donors, and technology partners seeking to build more resilient, secure, and data-driven aviation logistics networks.

DOI: 10.4018/979-8-3373-3643-5.ch013

1. INTRODUCTION

1.1 Background and Context

The scale, frequency, and complexity of global humanitarian crises have escalated dramatically in recent years, driven by conflict, climate change, pandemics, and economic instability. These overlapping emergencies demand a logistical response that is not only rapid and reliable but also adaptive to uncertain and hostile environments. Among the key enablers of such responsiveness is humanitarian aviation, which plays a crucial role in delivering food, medical supplies, and personnel to hard-to-reach areas during emergencies. The United Nations Humanitarian Air Service (UNHAS)—managed by the World Food Programme (WFP)—is the world's leading provider of humanitarian air transport, operating in over 20 countries and supporting more than 400 aid organizations (WFP, n.d.-a). UNHAS bridges critical access gaps by flying into areas where land routes are impassable due to natural disasters, conflict, or infrastructural collapse (Landmann & Ślusarczyk, 2022; Dorn & Cross, 2016). To manage this vast operation, WFP relies on a complex network of charter flight contracts, airbases, ground handlers, and regulatory bodies. As detailed in its aviation policy reports, WFP uses digital procurement tools to manage charter flight operations, maintain air safety, and monitor delivery milestones in real time (WFP, n.d.-b). However, despite these digital foundations, traditional aviation logistics still faces major constraints, including limited visibility across partners, slow procurement processes, and weak integration between systems. In fragile states or conflict zones, these limitations can mean the difference between timely life-saving aid and missed opportunities (Patrick, 2018; Leiras et al., 2021).

1.2 The Promise of Smart Technologies

In response to these challenges, humanitarian organizations are increasingly exploring the integration of smart technologies, particularly artificial intelligence (AI) and blockchain, into their logistics and supply chain operations. In logistics, AI refers to data-driven systems capable of performing tasks such as demand forecasting, flight route optimization, and cargo prioritization through machine learning and real-time analytics (Hejji et al., 2021; Rosenow et al., 2022). Blockchain, by contrast, is a decentralized ledger system that enables the secure, tamper-proof recording of transactions and milestones, often through automated smart contracts that execute actions when predefined conditions are met (Ahmed, 2025; Morris, 2018). The integration of AI and blockchain offers compelling advantages for humanitarian aviation. AI can forecast crisis-induced demand surges, optimize aircraft allocation, and react in real-time to weather or security threats (Rehan, 2022; Shawon et al.,

2025). Blockchain, on the other hand, provides a verifiable audit trail for the entire delivery chain—from procurement to flight execution and final receipt—enhancing transparency and reducing fraud risks (Rahman et al., 2025; Ledger Insights, 2021). Together, these technologies promise a shift from reactive to predictive and adaptive logistics, allowing organizations like WFP to anticipate needs, validate services automatically, and allocate resources with precision and accountability.

1.3 Research Scope and Objectives

This chapter explores the digital transformation of aviation logistics in humanitarian aid delivery, with a specific focus on the World Food Programme (WFP) and its aviation division, UNHAS. Drawing from recent case studies in both humanitarian and commercial aviation, the chapter examines how emerging technologies—particularly AI and blockchain—can address longstanding logistical inefficiencies and risks. It investigates how WFP and its partners are beginning to incorporate these tools into operational processes, from charter flight contracting and air route planning to fuel logistics and cargo tracking.

The key research objectives are threefold:

1. To analyze the interoperability and integration challenges of AI and blockchain with existing humanitarian aviation systems.
2. To evaluate the ethical, regulatory, and cybersecurity implications of deploying smart technologies in fragile environments.
3. To propose a scalable roadmap for the adoption of AI and blockchain in humanitarian aviation, with recommendations tailored to donors, technology providers, and field actors.

Guiding questions include:

- How can AI improve the speed and precision of humanitarian air response?
- What role does blockchain play in improving procurement accountability and cargo visibility?
- What are the risks and limitations of digital transformation in data-poor, infrastructure-limited crisis zones?

By addressing these questions, the chapter aims to contribute to the broader discourse on digital resilience and innovation in humanitarian logistics, offering practical insights for international organizations, policymakers, and humanitarian technologists seeking to strengthen global emergency response systems.

2. DIGITALIZATION IN HUMANITARIAN AVIATION

2.1 Overview of Current WFP Air Logistics

The World Food Programme (WFP) operates one of the most expansive humanitarian logistics networks globally, with the United Nations Humanitarian Air Service (UNHAS) serving as its aviation arm. Structurally, WFP's air logistics is coordinated through a multi-tiered system involving the Global Logistics Cluster (GLC), which it leads, and regional or country-level logistics coordination hubs. As Landmann and Ślusarczyk (2022) describe, the WFP assumes a dual role: as both a direct implementer of humanitarian logistics services and as a facilitator coordinating efforts across NGOs, UN agencies, and host governments. Within this framework, UNHAS provides critical air transport in areas inaccessible by road or sea, especially during disasters or conflicts. The service supports over 400 humanitarian organizations through operations in nearly 20 countries, ensuring personnel, medical supplies, and food aid reach remote locations. The partnerships are diverse, including commercial air operators, government donors, and private-sector actors. However, the complexity of these inter-organizational relationships often generates challenges in alignment, particularly concerning service standardization, real-time information sharing, and harmonized airspace access. These coordination issues are compounded by limited infrastructure and regulatory hurdles in fragile and conflict-prone regions.

Since 2019, UNHAS has undergone substantial transformations in its operational scope and resilience-building strategies. As explored by Landmann and Ślusarczyk, 2024 in their recent analysis of UNHAS activities between 2019 and 2022, the service expanded its coverage during COVID-19 and post-disaster scenarios, delivering not only food but also personal protective equipment (PPE), diagnostic tools, and emergency medical teams to crisis zones. Notably, in the Democratic Republic of Congo, South Sudan, and parts of Mozambique, UNHAS ensured sustained humanitarian air corridors amid deteriorating ground conditions. Yet, these interventions were not without operational stress. Fuel shortages, unpredictable donor funding cycles, and aircraft maintenance in austere environments continually threaten flight consistency and safety. Furthermore, as the authors note, air fleet modernization and pilot retention are becoming increasingly urgent, given rising maintenance costs and the high turnover of skilled aviation personnel. The combination of environmental hazards—such as floods and sandstorms—and conflict dynamics further complicates route planning and airstrip usability, often requiring last-minute rerouting or deployment of alternative vertical lift assets like helicopters.

UNHAS's role is not limited to logistical mobility but extends to strategic humanitarian diplomacy, especially when navigating restricted or politically sensitive airspaces. According to Dorn and Cross (2016), the WFP—through UNHAS—has become a symbol of neutrality and humanitarian access, gaining special airspace permissions even in volatile zones like Darfur or northern Mali. This status allows the service to operate in conflict zones where commercial operators have withdrawn, enabling humanitarian actors to continue service delivery. The study highlights how aviation is more than a tool for delivery; it becomes a diplomatic instrument reinforcing humanitarian principles. However, Dorn and Cross also emphasize the fragility of this access, particularly when airspace management is militarized or when warring parties perceive humanitarian flights as political tools. This exposes UNHAS to both bureaucratic delays and security threats, requiring careful stakeholder engagement, strict operational neutrality, and transparent flight manifest protocols. The importance of such trust-building mechanisms underscores why structured coordination with local governments, rebel factions, and peacekeeping missions is essential for sustained aerial access.

The WFP's country-level logistics management also reflects localized operational challenges, as evidenced by Patrick (2018) in his case study on WFP's operations in Kampala, Uganda. The study underscores issues such as delayed customs clearance, inadequate ground handling services, and misaligned data systems between air and ground logistics. Although aviation operations are typically associated with speed and efficiency, Patrick demonstrates how downstream inefficiencies—like warehouse bottlenecks or manual inventory tracking—can erode the time saved through air transport. This integration gap between air delivery and last-mile distribution represents a critical vulnerability in the humanitarian logistics chain. Moreover, inefficient feedback loops between headquarters and field offices limit real-time decision-making, especially when aircraft are grounded due to evolving conditions on the ground. The study recommends a shift toward digitized, modular logistics systems that can better harmonize aviation inputs with distribution pipelines, reinforcing the need for smart technology integration discussed in later sections of this chapter.

Beyond delivery efficiency, sustainability in WFP aviation operations has become a growing concern. Hove-Sibanda, Awino, and Agyemang (2025) contextualize humanitarian air logistics within broader eco-logistics frameworks across Africa. They argue that while aviation is indispensable in time-sensitive operations, its carbon footprint, dependency on fossil fuels, and lack of recyclable materials in mobile logistics infrastructure raise long-term sustainability questions. The authors advocate for hybrid logistics models where air operations are strategically combined with rail and solar-powered cold chains for more sustainable aid delivery. They also stress the importance of climate risk assessments and resilience-building efforts, such as early warning systems and predictive weather analytics, to optimize air routes and cargo load efficiency. As the humanitarian sector seeks to align with the Sustainable Development Goals (SDGs), particularly SDG 13 (Climate Action), balancing urgency with environmental responsibility is likely to shape the future of WFP aviation strategies.

The WFP's collaborative model—especially through the Logistics Emergency Team (LET)—serves as an innovative partnership framework that strengthens its aviation logistics capacity. Stadtler and Van Wassenhove (2025) examine how LET, composed of leading private-sector logistics providers such as UPS, DHL, and Agility, supports WFP operations during crises by offering logistics assets, expertise, and warehousing infrastructure. While the LET primarily enhances ground-based logistics, its alignment with UNHAS operations creates scalable surge capacity, especially during complex emergencies like earthquakes or sudden refugee movements. The challenge, however, lies in institutionalizing these partnerships beyond ad-hoc crisis response. The study recommends the creation of joint aviation contingency protocols, shared training platforms, and a co-investment model for cargo aircraft pooling. By embedding these practices, the WFP can ensure more resilient and responsive aviation logistics, reducing dependency on unpredictable donor-funded charters and enabling faster mobilization.

Lastly, the integration of emerging technologies in conflict-zone logistics introduces both opportunities and barriers for WFP aviation. Ugwu et al. (2024) explore the application of digital tools in infectious disease responses, highlighting the role of drone delivery, GIS-based disease mapping, and AI-powered triage systems in supporting humanitarian missions. In air logistics, such innovations can transform how flight priorities are determined, how cargo is secured and tracked, and how humanitarian teams respond to real-time needs. However, the study cautions against techno-solutionism, noting persistent issues such as connectivity outages, data governance gaps, and lack of contextual adaptation in fragile states. In aviation, these challenges manifest through signal loss, cybersecurity threats, and the difficulty of integrating advanced tracking systems with existing analog equipment. Therefore, any technological leap in WFP air logistics must be underpinned by robust infrastructure, cross-sector training, and policy reform to ensure that innovation complements rather than complicates humanitarian operations.

2.2 Key Challenges in Traditional Operations

Despite the World Food Programme's extensive reach and critical role in humanitarian relief, its traditional logistics operations face numerous persistent challenges, especially in volatile and conflict-affected regions. One of the most pressing issues is systemic delays across the aid delivery chain, often caused by poor infrastructure, fluctuating security conditions, and bureaucratic border procedures. Hambagda et al. (2024), in their study of WFP operations in Boko Haram-controlled areas, demonstrate how the lead time between inventory planning and actual food delivery can stretch into weeks due to road blockages, airstrip closures, and local insurgent activity. Even when air logistics are used to circumvent land routes, delays still occur due to limited aircraft availability, fuel supply constraints, and approval requirements for flight operations over conflict zones. These delays significantly undermine the responsiveness of WFP's emergency interventions, particularly during famines or sudden-onset disasters. Furthermore, the paper notes that last-mile delivery suffers disproportionately, as air-dropped aid or warehouse-stored rations often struggle to reach mobile and displaced populations without secure and reliable distribution partnerships on the ground.

Another critical challenge is the fragmentation of data systems across the WFP's global and regional logistics operations. Landmann and Ślusarczyk (2022) highlight that although the WFP plays a leadership role in the Global Logistics Cluster, its coordination with partner NGOs, local authorities, and other UN agencies remains hindered by inconsistent digital infrastructures. The lack of interoperable data platforms results in siloed information flows, where supply tracking, demand assessments, and transportation planning are often carried out on separate systems without real-time synchronization. This not only leads to duplication of efforts and resource misallocation but also impedes visibility across the supply chain. For example, delayed updates on warehouse stocks or shipment statuses may cause misaligned dispatches or bottlenecks at transfer points. The authors suggest that a robust, shared digital architecture is essential to overcome these silos, especially when operating in remote regions where connectivity and bandwidth are limited. The absence of such integration continues to impact the WFP's ability to conduct predictive logistics and respond adaptively to dynamic field conditions.

Insecure regions further exacerbate the problem of fraud, theft, and manipulation of aid deliveries. Leiras et al. (2021), analyzing WFP food aid operations in Ethiopia, detail how insecurity not only affects physical delivery but also the integrity of distribution. In regions where humanitarian access is restricted by armed actors or politicized local intermediaries, aid consignments are often diverted, delayed, or seized. In some cases, corrupt local officials or criminal groups manipulate distribution lists or tamper with ration sizes, creating mistrust among recipients and reducing the efficacy of food security interventions. These challenges are especially common in regions with weak governance structures or contested territorial control. The study emphasizes the need for tamper-proof verification systems, stronger beneficiary authentication, and enhanced oversight mechanisms at every stage of the supply chain. Without these controls, the risk of resource leakage and reputational damage to WFP operations remains high, particularly in contexts where competition among aid actors intensifies operational pressure.

Lastly, coordination challenges across institutional and jurisdictional boundaries remain a major bottleneck in traditional WFP logistics. Afifi (2024), in a legal analysis of the international frameworks guiding food security, identifies a lack of operational cohesion among stakeholders involved in humanitarian logistics. Although treaties and multilateral protocols mandate cooperation during emergencies, practical implementation is often marred by jurisdictional overlaps, misaligned objectives, and fragmented responsibilities among national governments, donors, and humanitarian agencies. This disjointed landscape complicates the activation of air corridors, customs clearance for emergency cargo, and the rapid deployment of field teams. In many instances, the absence of standardized procedures or mutual recognition agreements results in duplicated reporting requirements, delayed permissions, and strategic misalignment between actors. Afifi argues that strengthening these legal and operational frameworks is essential to empowering the WFP and its partners to respond more effectively to global food security crises. Institutional reforms that promote real-time data sharing, unified response protocols, and joint accountability mechanisms are necessary to address these enduring coordination failures.

In summary, while the WFP has made significant strides in humanitarian logistics, the persistence of delays, data fragmentation, fraud risks, and coordination inefficiencies constrains the full realization of its mission. These traditional challenges reveal structural and systemic gaps that undermine the agility, transparency, and accountability of aid operations—especially in high-risk zones. As the next sections will explore, the integration of digital technologies such as artificial intelligence and blockchain presents a potential pathway to overcome these limitations and transform WFP's air logistics operations into a more responsive, data-informed, and resilient humanitarian system.

2.3 Digital Maturity and Readiness in Humanitarian Contexts

The transition to digitally enabled humanitarian logistics faces substantial structural and contextual barriers, especially in low-resource, crisis-prone environments. Humanitarian organizations like the World Food Programme (WFP) often operate in regions with limited digital infrastructure, inconsistent power supplies, and unreliable internet connectivity—all of which hinder the full deployment of advanced technologies. Namagembe and Ntayi (2025) explore how the organizational culture within humanitarian agencies interacts with the technology readiness of financial service providers to influence the adoption of digital cash-based assistance systems. Their findings indicate that while digital tools (e.g., e-vouchers, mobile transfers) offer speed and traceability, frontline staff often lack the necessary training, and local partners may not have the technological capacity to implement or maintain such systems. This mismatch in digital readiness leads to fragmented adoption, reinforcing reliance on manual processes and reducing scalability. Moreover, regulatory frameworks in many host countries either lag behind technological innovation or impose restrictions on data transfer and digital transactions, further impeding widespread deployment of digital logistics platforms.

In parallel, cost-related barriers remain a central concern in humanitarian technology adoption. As Özkanlısoy and Akkartal (2021) note, digital transformation in supply chains, particularly in humanitarian contexts, entails high upfront investment in software systems, data platforms, satellite infrastructure, and training programs. For resource-constrained organizations dependent on donor funding, such long-term investments may be deprioritized in favor of short-term, tangible relief outcomes. The lack of dedicated digital transformation budgets results in piecemeal implementation, often without sufficient integration across departments or geographies. Furthermore, staff resistance to change—driven by fears of obsolescence, low digital literacy, or over-reliance on legacy systems—compounds these financial and regulatory barriers. Alesani, Nasi, and Manni (2023) argue for a human-centered digital transformation approach in international organizations, emphasizing that sustainable change depends not only on technological tools but also on empowering employees through participatory design, co-learning, and leadership buy-in. Without addressing the human and organizational side of digital maturity, technical innovations risk remaining underutilized or misaligned with actual operational needs.

Despite these barriers, there are emerging opportunities for leapfrogging digital maturity through mobile connectivity, digital twins, and unmanned aerial vehicles (UAVs). Singh (2025) investigates how digital twin technology—virtual models of real-world logistics networks—can enhance the resilience and agility of humanitarian supply chains. In contexts such as disaster recovery or food relief, digital twins enable real-time monitoring, predictive planning, and scenario-based optimization. Although still in early stages of adoption in humanitarian settings, the WFP and similar organizations can benefit from pilot implementations in logistics hubs and flight planning for UNHAS operations. Similarly, Cebir and Akkartal (2024) highlight the integration of digital twins into air cargo operations, noting their potential to improve routing efficiency, monitor aircraft health, and track high-value or sensitive cargo in dynamic environments. As UAVs gain traction in last-mile delivery—especially in flood-prone or mountainous areas—mobile data and edge computing can be used to update logistics models in real time, allowing for dynamic adjustment to disrupted supply chains.

Another important enabler is mobile connectivity and data mobilization across regions with minimal fixed infrastructure. Maaß (2024), in her doctoral study on digital public health systems, introduces the Digital Public Health Maturity Index, which can be extended to assess humanitarian logistics readiness. She emphasizes the importance of cross-sector data integration, user access interfaces, and low-bandwidth adaptability in achieving digital inclusivity. These features are especially valuable in the humanitarian sector, where mobile devices are often the only point of data access for field workers. Mızrak (2025) further reinforces this perspective by framing the digital transformation of supply chains within a "Triple Nexus" of smart, secure, and sustainable systems. In her analysis, the adoption of smart logistics technologies—like IoT sensors on aircraft or blockchain-based cargo tracking—can be strategically aligned with cybersecurity frameworks and green logistics goals. This integrative perspective is crucial for organizations like WFP, which must balance digital innovation with concerns around data protection, system resilience, and climate-conscious logistics planning.

In summary, the digital maturity and readiness of humanitarian logistics systems are shaped by a complex interplay of infrastructural, financial, regulatory, and organizational factors. While the barriers remain significant, especially in fragile settings, the opportunities offered by emerging technologies—if aligned with human-centered strategies and sustainable policy frameworks—can transform traditional air logistics into agile, data-driven networks. Moving forward, a phased and inclusive approach to digital adoption, anchored in field realities and informed by capacity-building, will be essential for ensuring that innovations genuinely enhance the reach, reliability, and responsiveness of humanitarian air services like those of the WFP.

3. AI INTEGRATION IN WFP AIR LOGISTICS

3.1 AI for Predictive and Adaptive Operations

Artificial Intelligence (AI) is playing an increasingly transformative role in humanitarian aviation logistics by enabling more predictive, adaptive, and data-driven operations. One of the most impactful areas is flight route optimization, where AI algorithms help determine the most efficient, cost-effective, and safe flight paths under dynamic conditions. Rosenow, Lee, and Li (2022) emphasize that next-generation air routing models combine multi-objective optimizationand collaborative decision-making with AI to balance operational efficiency, environmental sustainability, and risk mitigation. This is particularly critical in humanitarian contexts where air logistics must navigate changing weather patterns, restricted airspaces, and emergent no-fly zones. The integration of AI allows for real-time adjustmentsbased on updated flight information, satellite inputs, and geopolitical developments. In WFP air operations, this can mean rerouting flights to avoid conflict zones while minimizing delays and fuel usage. As these technologies mature, AI-based routing systems can also incorporate predictive hazard detection, such as identifying likely flood paths or volcanic ash clouds, enhancing both safety and delivery reliability.

Beyond route planning, AI-driven demand forecasting is emerging as a core enabler for anticipatory humanitarian logistics. Hejji et al. (2021) present a comprehensive survey of AI-based models designed for resource allocation and demand prediction in aviation, highlighting their relevance in both commercial and humanitarian sectors. These models leverage historical delivery data, weather forecasts, regional crisis indicators, and satellite imagery to predict when and where humanitarian aid will be needed. For the World Food Programme (WFP), accurate demand forecasting can inform pre-positioning strategies, warehouse stocking decisions, and the timing of aircraft mobilization. In volatile regions such as the Sahel or Horn of Africa, where famines, floods, and displacement occur cyclically, AI models offer the potential to shift from reactive to anticipatory deployment. This reduces lead times, prevents resource wastage, and ensures faster response to emerging crises. Moreover, these models can be customized for various levels of granularity, from national trends to localized demand surges, offering scalable insights across operational tiers.

AI also supports cargo prioritization, enabling real-time decisions about what to load and deliver when resources—such as aircraft space, time, and funding—are constrained. Shawon et al. (2025) explore how AI can be used in sustainable logistics optimization, drawing parallels to eco-efficient supply chains where limited capacity must be allocated to maximize impact. Applying similar logic to humanitarian aviation, AI models can rank shipments by urgency, perishability, and beneficiary criticality, ensuring that medical supplies, ready-to-eat food, and personnel transport are prioritized appropriately. For example, during post-disaster response operations, AI algorithms can analyze recipient data, health needs, and local logistics access to decide whether antibiotics, shelter kits, or food rations take precedence on a UNHAS flight. These decisions, when made manually, are often subjective and time-intensive; AI introduces speed, transparency, and justifiability, enhancing operational efficiency and donor accountability.

Additionally, AI provides a foundation for learning-based adaptability, where past decisions inform future optimization. As Kumar (2022) notes, aviation sector AI applications benefit from continuous data inputs, which train machine learning models to refine performance over time. In the WFP's context, this could involve learning from previous missions—such as how much cargo a certain aircraft can safely carry in high-altitude or low-visibility environments—and feeding that intelligence back into planning systems. This iterative learning approach enhances the agility and precision of WFP air operations, particularly in multi-country deployments where terrain, regulations, and needs vary significantly. AI thus becomes a strategic asset that supports not only immediate operational goals but also long-term organizational learning and capacity building. The synergy of AI with logistics datasets, satellite analytics, and weather systems ensures that WFP can increasingly operate as a proactive, predictive, and performance-driven logistics provider in the humanitarian space.

3.2 Real-Time Situational Awareness

In the context of humanitarian air logistics, real-time situational awareness is essential for making informed decisions under volatile and high-stakes conditions. Artificial Intelligence (AI) enables continuous monitoring of natural disasters, climate conditions, and geopolitical volatility, thereby enhancing the World Food Programme's (WFP) capacity to respond quickly and accurately. Rehan (2022) emphasizes that AI-driven disaster prediction models—trained on historical and geospatial data—can anticipate the onset and severity of floods, earthquakes, and storms. By processing satellite imagery, weather forecasts, and seismic indicators in real time, these models support WFP in rerouting flights, allocating air assets more effectively, and reducing risks to personnel and cargo. For example, an AI system can alert air planners when a storm front threatens to cut off access to an airstrip, prompting them to deliver urgent supplies before the window closes. This predictive insight transforms traditional reactive models into anticipatory operations, which is particularly vital in fragile contexts where minutes can mean lives.

AI's role also extends to the detection of emerging geopolitical threats that may compromise air operations. Dugbartey (2025) frames geopolitical instability, climate-induced migration, and digital disruptions as systemic risks that increasingly overlap. AI tools—especially those used in predictive analytics and stress testing—can track political developments, social unrest, and conflict escalations across operational theaters. These systems scan news feeds, social media signals, and intelligence reports to flag risk zones, allowing humanitarian aviation managers to adjust delivery plans or avoid contested airspaces. Anwar (2025) further demonstrates this with AI-based early warning systems deployed in the Himalayan region, where terrain, geopolitical rivalries, and climate vulnerability intersect. These systems not only detect risk patterns but also produce geo-referenced alerts that inform strategic coordination between states and humanitarian actors. WFP's aviation units, especially in politically sensitive regions like South Sudan or Syria, can greatly benefit from this real-time political situational awareness to ensure flight safety, neutrality, and uninterrupted access to beneficiaries.

One of the most powerful, yet often underutilized, applications of AI in situational monitoring is its ability to process and analyze unstructured data from global media outlets and local information sources. Sufi and Alsulami (2025) present a model for AI-driven disaster intelligence based on news media, where natural language processing (NLP) techniques extract real-time event data from thousands of multilingual reports. These insights can complement traditional disaster databases by identifying non-quantified but actionable threats, such as rapidly deteriorating health conditions in refugee camps or unexpected security shifts near air corridors. For WFP operations, particularly UNHAS flights serving remote communities, such AI-enhanced information streams improve pre-flight briefings, cargo load decisions, and crew safety. Additionally, Bano (2025) explores how both the U.S. and China are using AI to predict and mitigate the effects of climate change on infrastructure and logistics. The comparative study highlights AI's role in identifying climate-induced logistical bottlenecks, which humanitarian air operations must increasingly navigate—such as rising temperatures affecting aircraft lift performance or thawing runways in permafrost zones.

From a compliance and governance perspective, AI also contributes to Environmental, Social, and Governance (ESG) risk monitoring, which is becoming relevant for donor-funded humanitarian operations. Ishrat, Khan, and Faisal (2025) discuss how AI can assess ESG indicators across operational regions, helping organizations remain accountable to both ethical and environmental standards. In aviation logistics, this might involve tracking emissions hotspots, monitoring ethical procurement practices in fuel logistics, or ensuring fair labor conditions at cargo handling facilities. The integration of ESG-aware AI tools aligns with WFP's broader sustainability commitments while helping maintain donor confidence in high-risk operations. Cao (2023) expands this view by highlighting how AI and data science foster smart disaster resilience, enabling dynamic scenario modeling and early decision-making based on multi-source data fusion. In practical terms, AI can synthesize satellite imagery, IoT data, and atmospheric simulations to offer an operational dashboard tailored for WFP logistics officers, providing a real-time map of vulnerabilities and recommended actions.

Lastly, AI-enabled situational awareness must be strategically integrated with aviation cybersecurity and organizational readiness, particularly as humanitarian air operations become more digitally dependent. Mızrak (2024) argues that the success of AI systems in aviation hinges on robust human resource strategies that balance algorithmic decision-making with human oversight. For instance, when AI detects a conflict-related cyber threat targeting flight navigation systems or warehouse databases, trained personnel must be equipped to assess and act on those alerts. This dual-layered approach is critical in ensuring operational continuity, especially when AI systems are deployed in decentralized, under-secured environments. Therefore, integrating AI for situational awareness must go beyond deploying software—it requires institutional preparedness, staff training, ethical safeguards, and continuous evaluation mechanisms to make AI tools a reliable partner in high-stakes humanitarian missions.

4. BLOCKCHAIN APPLICATIONS FOR TRANSPARENCY AND TRACEABILITY

4.1 Blockchain Fundamentals and Use Cases in Aid Delivery

Blockchain technology presents a transformative opportunity for enhancing transparency, efficiency, and accountability in humanitarian logistics. At its core, blockchain is a form of distributed ledger technology (DLT) that records transactions across a decentralized network, eliminating the need for a central authority while ensuring data immutability and traceability. In the context of humanitarian aid delivery—especially for air cargo operations carried out by the World Food Programme (WFP)—blockchain can secure the entire aid flow lifecycle, from procurement and flight manifests to final delivery confirmation. Rahman et al. (2025) offer a comprehensive review of blockchain applications in supply chains and emphasize how distributed ledgers enhance supply chain transparency, ensuring that all stakeholders—from donors to field operators—have access to a unified, tamper-proof record of transactions. This capability is particularly valuable in crisis zones, where accountability is paramount and documentation can easily be lost, manipulated, or destroyed.

One of the most impactful applications of blockchain in humanitarian logistics is the use of smart contracts—self-executing digital agreements that automatically enforce predefined conditions without human intervention. Alshahrani et al. (2024) propose a smart contract framework for transportation management that enables real-time decision-making based on shipment milestones, weather alerts, and routing constraints. When integrated into WFP's air cargo workflows, smart contracts can automate key processes such as aircraft loading permissions, payment releases to vendors, or customs clearance once digital proofs (e.g., sensor data or delivery receipts) are verified on-chain. Such automation not only reduces paperwork and manual bottlenecks but also lowers operational risk in fast-moving emergency scenarios. Furthermore, Liu et al. (2022) apply probabilistic model checking to validate smart contracts in port supply chains, highlighting how formal verification methods can ensure the reliability of automated decisions—an essential requirement when lives depend on the timely delivery of aid.

Distributed control is another critical advantage of blockchain systems, especially when coordinating among multiple humanitarian actors. Selvaprabhu (2023) emphasizes that decentralized networks offer trustworthy control across fragmented supply chains, making them ideal for cross-border aid missions that involve NGOs, UN agencies, and private contractors. In WFP air logistics, blockchain can serve as a shared digital infrastructure that all authorized parties can access to verify cargo origins, transfer custody, and confirm delivery—without relying on centralized databases that may be compromised or siloed. For example, a blockchain-enabled system could allow a donor country, WFP headquarters, regional air hubs, and local distribution centers to view and validate each step of a high-value medical cargo's journey, reducing the risk of loss, fraud, or diversion. This decentralized transparency also empowers affected communities by giving them visibility into aid delivery processes and minimizing opportunities for corruption or manipulation.

The integration of blockchain with Internet of Things (IoT) technologies further enhances its utility in last-mile delivery and in-flight cargo tracking. Öztürk and Akkartal (2024) explore how IoT sensors embedded in cargo containers or aircraft can feed real-time environmental data—such as temperature, humidity, shock, and location—into blockchain ledgers. These sensor readings can then trigger smart contracts that halt or redirect deliveries if cargo conditions fall outside acceptable ranges, such as with vaccines or perishable food. Akkartal and Abdelhadi (2019) reinforce this by discussing IoT-enabled warehouse and transportation systems, which, when linked to blockchain, can offer end-to-end visibility across multiple logistics nodes. For WFP's air logistics operations, this integration ensures that aid is not only delivered on time but also maintains quality and compliance standards, reducing wastage and increasing mission success.

Importantly, blockchain must be understood not as a standalone solution but as part of a broader digital transformation strategy that includes cybersecurity, data governance, and sustainability goals. Mızrak (2025) articulates this through the concept of the Triple Nexus of Smart, Secure, and Sustainable Supply Chains, arguing that blockchain can simultaneously strengthen operational efficiency, improve data protection, and align logistics with ethical and environmental standards. For instance, by ensuring full audit trails, blockchain reduces the potential for data breaches or false reporting, which is critical in conflict zones or politically sensitive operations. Furthermore, by reducing redundancies and administrative overhead, blockchain can contribute to greener logistics workflows, a priority for organizations like WFP that are seeking to meet both humanitarian and climate action targets under frameworks such as the SDGs.

In summary, blockchain offers a robust digital backbone for modern humanitarian logistics by embedding transparency, accountability, and automation into every layer of the aid delivery process. Through smart contracts, distributed ledgers, and IoT integrations, organizations like the WFP can elevate their air cargo operations to new standards of reliability and trust. As the humanitarian sector faces mounting demands for speed, security, and ethical governance, blockchain is poised to be a cornerstone of future-ready logistics systems that serve both people in crisis and the global community committed to their aid.

4.2 Secure Donor-to-Beneficiary Tracking

In humanitarian logistics—particularly for complex air operations carried out by organizations like the World Food Programme (WFP)—ensuring a transparent and accountable path from donor contributions to beneficiary delivery is essential. Blockchain technology offers an unprecedented mechanism for secure, verifiable, and immutable tracking of each transaction along this path. Omisola et al. (2023) propose a conceptual framework that combines blockchain and artificial intelligence to provide real-time visibility into supply chain flows. In the humanitarian context, such a system could track aid packages from the moment a donor commits funds, through procurement and international transit, to final delivery in remote or conflict-affected zones. This transparency mitigates common risks such as diversion of aid, unauthorized substitution of goods, or falsified delivery reports—challenges that have long plagued humanitarian missions. By providing a decentralized and tamper-proof ledger, blockchain enables end-to-end traceability, which improves operational credibility and reinforces trust among stakeholders, including governments, NGOs, and the beneficiaries themselves.

Procurement is often the first vulnerable point in the humanitarian supply chain, particularly in emergency contexts where goods must be sourced rapidly and often across borders. Ahmed (2025) highlights how blockchain can bring visibility to procurement contracts, ensuring vendor compliance, validating material authenticity, and preventing bid-rigging or invoice fraud. Smart contracts, once triggered by verified procurement data, can automatically approve payments or initiate shipping processes without manual intervention. For the WFP, this could streamline bulk procurement of food rations, medical supplies, or fuel, while ensuring alignment with ethical sourcing policies and compliance with donor conditions. In air logistics, these verified records can be directly linked to flight manifests, enabling aircraft to be loaded based on digitally confirmed orders, thus reducing errors and accelerating response times.

During the transit phase, blockchain plays a crucial role in maintaining the integrity of information flow across different transportation modes—whether by land to the airbase, by cargo flight to the destination, or by last-mile distribution to camps or relief centers. Bekrar et al. (2021) discuss the significance of blockchain in "closing the loop" of supply chains by ensuring that return flows—such as empty containers or feedback data—are also captured transparently. In WFP's case, blockchain could enable aircraft cargo to be monitored through geotagged checkpoints, with IoT sensors verifying real-time conditions such as temperature, humidity, and handling. These data points are written directly to the blockchain ledger, allowing donors to view cargo progress through a secure dashboard. Such visibility reduces information asymmetry between central offices and field operations and facilitates faster troubleshooting when disruptions occur. Additionally, the immutable nature of blockchain records supports logistical audits and compliance verification post-operation.

The final delivery stage is often the most sensitive, particularly in regions with security concerns or logistical complexity. Ahuja, Chugh, and Singh (2024), through their SeedChain model, illustrate how blockchain-enabled systems can ensure last-mile delivery verification, using digital tokens or QR-code-based validation by recipients. Applied to humanitarian aid, this could allow beneficiaries to confirm receipt of specific items using secure mobile devices or biometric IDs, thus creating a proof-of-delivery layer that closes the transparency gap. Sakthivel et al. (2024) further reinforce this by showing how blockchain can be used to digitally authenticate delivery records, capturing not only when and where goods were delivered but also by whom and under what conditions. These verified records can then be accessed by donors and oversight bodies, significantly strengthening accountability in areas where traditional reporting mechanisms are weak or susceptible to manipulation.

The implications of blockchain-enabled transparency extend beyond operational logistics to systemic trust-building and ethical governance. Channi, Sandhu, and Kumar (2025) stress the importance of transparency in building next-generation supply chains, especially in industries where public trust is fragile—such as pharmaceuticals. In the humanitarian sector, similar expectations are emerging, as donors and partners demand verifiable evidence of impact and responsible resource management. A blockchain-enabled humanitarian air logistics system, integrated across procurement, transit, and final delivery, would not only improve efficiency and reliability but also align WFP operations with global best practices in digital trust. It empowers donors with visibility into how their contributions are used, provides beneficiaries with assurance that aid is delivered as intended, and equips WFP with an intelligent infrastructure that can adapt to the speed and scale of future humanitarian needs.

In conclusion, blockchain offers a secure and transparent digital backbone for donor-to-beneficiary tracking in humanitarian logistics. Its ability to document procurement decisions, monitor real-time cargo transit, and authenticate delivery with immutable proof ensures that every stakeholder in the supply chain has access to a single source of verified truth. As the scale and complexity of humanitarian operations continue to grow, integrating blockchain across the aid delivery spectrum—from air cargo planning to on-ground receipt—will be essential for reinforcing trust, accountability, and operational excellence.

4.3 Case Example: Smart Contracting in Charter Flights and Fuel Logistics

4.3.1 Digital Contracting in Humanitarian Charter Flights (WFP/UNHAS)

International humanitarian organizations have increasingly adopted **digital procurement platforms** to manage charter air services. The World Food Programme (WFP), via its UN Humanitarian Air Service (UNHAS), utilizes an electronic tendering system—In-Tend—for contracting charter aircraft and related services, including fuel and ground handling (WFP, n.d.-a). This integrated e-contracting workflow connects service vendors (charter carriers, fuel suppliers, and others) from bidding and contract award through performance monitoring and delivery. The system enforces compliance checks, enabling real-time visibility of safety certifications and aircraft operational data, which must be reviewed by WFP's Air Transport Contracts Committee before contract finalization. By capturing flight milestones upon mission completion, the platform automatically validates contractual fulfillment and triggers payment processing within WFP's financial system. Although not blockchain-enabled, this digital contracting approach ensures standardized compliance, transparency, and auditability—and streamlines vendor integration by allowing electronic submission of orders, reports, and invoices (WFP, n.d.-b; WFP, n.d.-c).

4.3.2 Blockchain Smart Contracts for Aviation Fuel Logistics (Gazprom Neft & S7 Airlines)

In the commercial aviation sector, **smart contracts based on blockchain** have been deployed to automate fuel logistics, particularly into-plane transactions. The Aviation Fuel Smart Contract (AFSC) system, piloted by Gazprom Neft's aviation unit and S7 Airlines, incorporates the airline, fuel supplier, and banking partner into a blockchain-based workflow. Pre-flight, S7 submits estimated fuel volume and price into the system. The smart contract assigns a fuel truck and driver, and upon pilot confirmation of actual fuel quantity, an online bank authorization is triggered. Funds are held in escrow and released instantly once fueling is completed and digitally confirmed (Morris, 2018; "Gazpromneft Aero completes trial," 2021). This eliminates the need for pre-payments or bank guarantees, reduces administrative burden, and offers real-time settlement. Both airline and fuel supplier receive identical, tamper-proof transaction records detailing fuel volume, time, and location. The inaugural execution occurred at Novosibirsk's Tolmachevo airport, achieving settlement in seconds and significantly enhancing operational speed and accountability (Morris, 2018; Ledger Insights, 2021).

4.3.3 Integrated Digital Platforms for Fuel Procurement and Tracking

Beyond blockchain, many airlines now deploy **cloud-based procurement and fuel-tracking platforms** to replicate smart contracting benefits. Etihad Airways, for example, uses SAP Ariba as its integrated sourcing and contracting platform. Through the Ariba Network, Etihad and its fuel suppliers collaborate via a shared portal, where purchase orders, delivery confirmations, and invoices are exchanged electronically. This setup enables automatic validation of contract terms, real-time order status visibility, and alerts when deliveries are received or invoices approved. The shift to this system reduced processing costs and shortened Days Sales Outstanding for vendors (Etihad Airways, n.d.-a; AACO, n.d.). Additionally, specialized fuel management networks such as aFuel (Information Design One AG) and i6 enable real-time tracking of fueling milestones across over 150 airports. These platforms use IATA's AIDX standard for messaging: fuel orders, dispatch updates, progress status, and digitally signed fuel receipts are exchanged instantly among stakeholders. Once the digital fuel slip is signed at the wing tip, workflows automatically trigger payment processing—mirroring smart contract execution (Aircraft IT, n.d.; I6.io, n.d.).

4.3.4 Outcomes: Transparency, Speed, and Accountability

These real-world cases demonstrate that **smart and digital contracting systems** in aviation logistics deliver improved transparency, operational speed, and accountability. In S7's blockchain-enabled refueling pilot, the platform eliminated the need for bank guarantees, enabling near-instant payment upon service completion—thus resolving payment delays and reducing financial risk (Morris, 2018; Ledger Insights, 2021). For humanitarian charter flights, WFP's e-tendering system provides audit logs and verified completion milestones, giving donors and UN partners confidence in compliance and delivery integrity (WFP, n.d.-b). Etihad's adoption of SAP Ariba accelerated procurement cycles and improved supplier communication, enabling 24/7 processing and reducing manual errors (Etihad Airways, n.d.-a). Platforms like aFuel and i6 give both parties synchronized, timestamped records of fuel delivery, reducing disputes and providing clarity in shared operational data (Aircraft IT, n.d.; I6.io, n.d.). Whether through blockchain-based smart contracts or centralized digital procurement tools, aviation logistics is achieving end-to-end automation:

service validation triggers payment, all parties share a single truth, and operations are executed with compliance and speed.

To illustrate the varying degrees of digital maturity and innovation in aviation logistics, Table 1 presents a comparative overview of prominent platforms used in both humanitarian and commercial contexts. These platforms—ranging from WFP's centralized e-tendering system (In-Tend) to blockchain-enabled smart contracting (AFSC by S7 Airlines and Gazprom Neft)—demonstrate diverse approaches to improving transparency, automation, and accountability. While some platforms, such as SAP Ariba and aFuel/i6, rely on cloud-based procurement and messaging standards to optimize supplier integration and fuel tracking, others leverage blockchain to enforce real-time execution and settlement of services.

Table 1. Comparison of digital platforms in aviation logistics

Platform	Used By	Technology Type	Key Features	Outcome
In-Tend (WFP)	UNHAS	Centralized digital	Tendering, contract compliance	Improved auditability
AFSC (S7 Airlines)	S7, Gazprom Neft	Blockchain smart contract	Real-time fueling, instant payment	Faster turnaround
SAP Ariba	Etihad Airways	Cloud procurement	Supplier integration, invoice automation	Reduced admin cost
aFuel / i6	Multiple airlines	Digital messaging + API	Milestone tracking, e-signatures	Accurate fuel reconciliation

This comparison highlights how each system addresses key operational goals such as speed, auditability, and milestone verification, offering insights into the future of smart contracting in aviation logistics.

5. CONCLUSION

As humanitarian logistics evolves in response to increasing global crises, digital transformation is no longer optional—it is essential. This chapter has illustrated how the integration of artificial intelligence (AI) and blockchain technologies into humanitarian aviation logistics can significantly enhance efficiency, transparency, and accountability. Drawing on real-world examples from the World Food Programme (WFP), S7 Airlines, and Etihad Airways, we now conclude with key strategic insights related to system interoperability, ethical considerations, and a roadmap for scalable digital adoption.

5.1 Interoperability and System Design Considerations

Successful deployment of AI and blockchain in humanitarian contexts depends on interoperability with existing systems and the usability of digital tools by field-level operators. For the WFP and its UNHAS operations, integration with established platforms such as the In-Tend e-tendering system is critical (WFP, n.d.-a). AI systems for predictive analytics—like those for demand forecasting and route optimization (Hejji et al., 2021; Rosenow et al., 2022)—must be compatible with WFP's current logistics platforms and data infrastructures. Similarly, blockchain smart contracts for procurement and service validation (Morris, 2018; Ledger Insights, 2021) must align with the organization's financial workflows and vendor databases.

Moreover, digital solutions should be designed with user-centered principles to accommodate field staff working in low-resource, high-stress environments (Alesani et al., 2023). For instance, pilots in S7 Airlines' blockchain fuel system used tablet-based apps to input and verify data during refueling (Morris, 2018). Likewise, WFP's In-Tend platform enables field personnel to input operational data and access contract compliance checkpoints with minimal training (WFP, n.d.-c). This demonstrates the importance of intuitive interfaces, mobile compatibility, and low-bandwidth functionality in humanitarian settings, where digital literacy and infrastructure can vary widely (Maaß, 2024; Namagembe & Ntayi, 2025).

5.2 Ethical, Regulatory, and Security Considerations

The deployment of AI and blockchain must be underpinned by a firm commitment to ethical, legal, and cybersecurity standards. In humanitarian logistics, data privacy is especially sensitive due to the involvement of vulnerable populations, conflict zones, and donor transparency requirements (Anwar, 2025; Ishrat et al., 2025). AI-powered systems that process social media signals or geolocation data to predict disaster impacts (Rehan, 2022; Cao, 2023) must incorporate privacy-preserving algorithms, ensure informed consent, and comply with international data protection laws such as the GDPR. Blockchain systems, although secure by design, also raise regulatory and governance concerns, particularly regarding the legal recognition of smart contracts across jurisdictions (Ahmed, 2025). Additionally, cybersecurity threats must be addressed proactively—especially as aviation operations become more digitized and exposed to cyberattacks (Mızrak, 2024). WFP's systems must include encryption, role-based access controls, and contingency protocols for system breaches. The digital divide remains another significant barrier: without deliberate inclusion strategies, digital tools risk reinforcing inequalities between digitally connected headquarters and under-equipped field teams (Namagembe & Ntayi, 2025; Alesani et al., 2023).

As humanitarian aviation logistics embraces AI and blockchain technologies, several ethical, regulatory, and technical challenges must be addressed to ensure responsible and effective implementation. Table 2 outlines key risks that may arise in the process of digital transformation, including data privacy concerns, cybersecurity vulnerabilities, system integration issues, and the digital divide.

Table 2. Comparison of digital platforms in aviation logistics

Challenge	Description	Affected Area	Source
Data Privacy	Risk of exposing beneficiary identities	AI for demand forecasting	Rehan (2022); Ishrat et al. (2025)
Cybersecurity Risks	Vulnerable aviation systems under attack	Digital flight ops	Mızrak (2024)
Interoperability Gaps	Difficulty integrating legacy and new systems	Blockchain + ERP	Alesani et al. (2023)
Digital Divide	Low digital literacy or bandwidth limitations	Field team interface	Namagembe & Ntayi (2025)

These challenges impact not only the technological infrastructure but also the operational and ethical dimensions of aid delivery. For instance, AI systems used for demand forecasting may inadvertently compromise sensitive beneficiary data, while blockchain platforms may struggle to integrate with legacy humanitarian ERP systems. Understanding these barriers is crucial for developing inclusive, secure, and interoperable digital solutions tailored to the needs of field operations and crisis environments.

5.3 Roadmap for Scalable Digital Adoption

To ensure broad and effective deployment of AI and blockchain in humanitarian aviation, a phase-wise strategy is essential. The first phase involves pilot projects and sandbox testing—as seen in S7 Airlines' implementation of smart contracts for fuel logistics (Ledger Insights, 2021), or WFP's digital tendering workflows (WFP, n.d.-b). These pilots should focus on controlled environments with reliable infrastructure and active vendor collaboration.

The second phase should scale successful models across regions using modular, interoperable platforms. For instance, aFuel and i6 fuel management systems (Aircraft IT, n.d.; I6.io, n.d.) offer replicable blueprints for real-time service tracking and milestone validation. During this phase, technical partnerships with private-sector innovators and cloud providers (e.g., SAP Ariba for Etihad Airways) are crucial for bringing scalable platforms into humanitarian contexts. The third phase involves institutionalization and policy alignment. AI and blockchain must be embedded into WFP's standard operating procedures, budget frameworks, and donor reporting protocols. Mızrak (2025) emphasizes a "triple nexus" approach where smart, secure, and sustainable strategies are unified under a long-term digital governance model. For donors, this means funding not just hardware or software, but also training programs, ethical oversight, and system resilience planning. For technology partners, the focus should be on building low-code/no-code tools, localized support services, and open API architectures. Humanitarian actors must also invest in capacity building and co-design with affected communities to ensure that digital systems reflect the needs and realities of those they aim to serve (Alesani et al., 2023; Maaß, 2024).

In conclusion, AI and blockchain hold transformative potential for humanitarian aviation logistics, but realizing this potential requires more than technical innovation. It demands thoughtful integration with existing systems, ethical safeguards, and a collaborative, phased strategy that balances innovation with responsibility. The path forward must be as inclusive and transparent as the technologies themselves.

REFERENCES

I6.io. (n.d.). *i6: Digital fuel management solutions*. Retrieved from https://i6.io/

AACO (Arab Air Carriers Organization). (n.d.). *Etihad Airways to drive procurement efficiency with SAP Ariba*. Retrieved from https://www.aaco.org/media-center/news/aaco-members/etihad-airways-to-drive-procurement-efficiency-with-sap-ariba

Afifi, J. I. N. I. (2024). *Enhancing the Effectiveness of International Legal Frameworks on Food Security: Lessons From the World Food Programme's Efforts* (Master's thesis, Hamad Bin Khalifa University (Qatar)).

Ahmed, S. (2025). BLOCKCHAIN FOR SUPPLY CHAIN TRANSPARENCY: A DECENTRALIZED PATH TO TRUST AND TRACEABILITY. *Computer Science Bulletin*, *8*(01), 73–88.

Ahuja, R., Chugh, S., & Singh, R. (2024). SeedChain: A secure and transparent blockchain-driven framework to revolutionize the seed supply chain. *Future Internet*, *16*(4), 132. DOI: 10.3390/fi16040132

Aircraft, I. T. (n.d.). *aFuel: Digital fueling platform*. Retrieved from https://www.aircraftit.com/articles/afuel-platform-overview/

Akkartal, E., & Abdelhadi, A. (2019). *A framework of IoT implementations and challenges in Warehouse Management, Transportation and Retailing*. Eurasian Business & Economics Journal.

Alesani, D., Nasi, G., & Manni, S. (2023). Digital transformation in IOs–toward a human-centered approach. In *Management of International Institutions and NGOs* (pp. 406–431). Routledge. DOI: 10.4324/9781003289852-16

Alshahrani, A., Khedr, A., Belal, M., & Saleh, M. (2024). A Smart Contract Approach for Efficient Transportation Management. *International Journal of Advanced Computer Science and Applications*, *15*(10). Advance online publication. DOI: 10.14569/IJACSA.2024.0151074

Anwar, U. (2025). Artificial Intelligence Driven Early Warning Systems in the Himalayan Region: Strategic Implications for China, Pakistan, and Regional Stability in South Asia. *Review Journal of Social Psychology & Social Works*, *3*(3), 125–135.

Bano, S. (2025). The Role of AI in Predicting and Mitigating Climate Change: A Comparative Study of US and China's Approaches. *The Critical Review of Social Sciences Studies*, *3*(1), 664–675. DOI: 10.59075/dv9cmp29

Bekrar, A., Ait El Cadi, A., Todosijevic, R., & Sarkis, J. (2021). Digitalizing the closing-of-the-loop for supply chains: A transportation and blockchain perspective. *Sustainability (Basel)*, *13*(5), 2895. DOI: 10.3390/su13052895

Cao, L. (2023). AI and data science for smart emergency, crisis and disaster resilience. *International Journal of Data Science and Analytics*, *15*(3), 231–246. DOI: 10.1007/s41060-023-00393-w PMID: 37035277

Cebir, Y., & Akkartal, E. (2024). Digital twin in logistics and supply chain management. In *Strategic Innovations for Dynamic Supply Chains* (pp. 170–192). IGI Global Scientific Publishing. DOI: 10.4018/979-8-3693-3575-8.ch008

Channi, H. K., Sandhu, R., & Kumar, P. (2025). Enabling Transparent Supply to Build a Next-Generation Supply Chain. *Blockchain-Enabled Solutions for the Pharmaceutical Industry*, 207-231.

Dorn, A. W., & Cross, R. W. (2016). Flying Humanitarians: The UN Humanitarian Air Service. In *Air Power in UN Operations* (pp. 101-116). Routledge.

Dugbartey, A. N. (2025). Systemic financial risks in an era of geopolitical tensions, climate change, and technological disruptions: Predictive analytics, stress testing and crisis response strategies. *International Journal of Science and Research Archive*, *14*(02), 1428–1448. DOI: 10.30574/ijsra.2025.14.2.0563

Etihad Airways. (n.d.-a). *Sourcing & procurement – SAP Ariba integration*. Retrieved from https://www.etihad.com/en/about-us/supply-chain

Hambagda, B. M., Gupta, S., Srivastav, S., & Khurana, R.Buba M.T. Hambagda. (2024). Humanitarian Food Logistics: An Inventory Model for World Food Program (WFP) Operations in Boko Haram-Controlled Areas. *Communications on Applied Nonlinear Analysis*, *31*(6s), 380–387. DOI: 10.52783/cana.v31.1230

Hejji, D., Talib, M. A., Nassif, A. B., Nasir, Q., & Bouridane, A. (2021, November). AI-based models for resource allocation and resource demand forecasting systems in aviation: A survey and analytical study. In *2021 IEEE International Conference on Internet of Things and Intelligence Systems (IoTaIS)* (pp. 183-189). IEEE. DOI: 10.1109/IoTaIS53735.2021.9628555

Hove-Sibanda, P., Awino, Z. B., & Agyemang, E. (2025). Sustainable Food Supply Chains and Agricultural Logistics in Africa. In *Eco-Logistics and Sustainable Supply Chain Innovations* (pp. 267–320). IGI Global Scientific Publishing.

Ishrat, M., Khan, W., & Faisal, S. M. (2025). AI and risk forecasting: leveraging AI for environmental, social, and governance compliance. In *Artificial Intelligence for Financial Risk Management and Analysis* (pp. 307–334). IGI Global Scientific Publishing. DOI: 10.4018/979-8-3373-1200-2.ch015

Kumar, M. (2022). Optimized application of artificial intelligence (AI) in aviation market. *International Journal of Recent Research Aspects*, *9*(4).

Landmann, T., & Ślusarczyk, S. (2022). The World Food Program in the Global Logistics Cluster. *Systemy Logistyczne Wojsk*, *57*(2), 173–189. DOI: 10.37055/slw/163235

Landmann, T., & Ślusarczyk, S. (2024). The effects of the activities of The United Nations Humanitarian Air Service (UNHAS) in humanitarian logistics in 2019-2022 Efekty działań The United Nations Humanitarian Air Service (UNHAS) w logistyce humanitarnej w latach 2019-2022.

Ledger Insights. (2021, March 1). *Gazpromneft Aero completes trial of blockchain smart fueling system*. Retrieved from https://www.ledgerinsights.com/gazpromneft-aero-blockchain-aviation-fuel-s7-airlines/

Leiras, A., Gonçalves, P., Chawaguta, B., Brito, I. D., & Yoshizaki, H. T. Y. (2021). Food aid supply and distribution in insecure regions: World food programme operation analysis in Ethiopia. *Production*, *31*, e20210070. DOI: 10.1590/0103-6513.20210070

Liu, Y., Zhou, Z., Yang, Y., & Ma, Y. (2022). Verifying the smart contracts of the port supply chain system based on probabilistic model checking. *Systems*, *10*(1), 19. DOI: 10.3390/systems10010019

Maaß, L. (2024). *Multidisciplinary measuring of maturity and readiness in national digital public health systems: The digital public health maturity index* (Doctoral dissertation, Universität Bremen).

Mızrak, F. (2024). Integrating AI with aviation cybersecurity: The strategic role of human resources. *Business & Management Studies: An International Journal*, *12*(3), 610–628. DOI: 10.15295/bmij.v12i3.2396

Mızrak, F. (2025). The Triple Nexus of Smart, Secure, and Sustainable Supply Chains: Strategies for Resilience in the Digital Age. In *Utilizing Cybersecurity to Foster Business Innovation and Resiliency* (pp. 189-218). IGI Global Scientific Publishing.

Mızrak, F. (2025). The Triple Nexus of Smart, Secure, and Sustainable Supply Chains: Strategies for Resilience in the Digital Age. In *Utilizing Cybersecurity to Foster Business Innovation and Resiliency* (pp. 189-218). IGI Global Scientific Publishing.

Morris, N. (2018, August 27). *Russian airline S7 tests blockchain for aviation fuel.* Ledger Insights. Retrieved from https://www.ledgerinsights.com/s7-airlines-blockchain-aviation-fuel-gazpromneft/

Namagembe, S., & Ntayi, J. (2025). Humanitarian organization culture and humanitarian organization usage of digital cash-based assistance: The mediating role of financial service providers' technology readiness. *Journal of Electronic Business & Digital Economics, 4*(1), 88–111. DOI: 10.1108/JEBDE-04-2024-0010

Omisola, J. O., Bihani, D., Daraojimba, A. I., Osho, G. O., Ubamadu, B. C., & Etukudoh, E. A. (2023). Blockchain in supply chain transparency: A conceptual framework for real-time data tracking and reporting using blockchain and AI. *International Journal of Multidisciplinary Research and Growth Evaluation, 4.*

Özkanlısoy, Ö., & Akkartal, E. (2021). Digital transformation in supply chains: Current applications, contributions and challenges. *Business & Management Studies: An International Journal, 9*(1), 32–55.

Öztürk, S., & Akkartal, E. (2024). Internet of Things (IoT) Applications in Last Mile Delivery. In *Strategic Innovations for Dynamic Supply Chains* (pp. 193–215). IGI Global Scientific Publishing. DOI: 10.4018/979-8-3693-3575-8.ch009

Patrick, E. (2018). *Logistics management and service delivery in United Nations agencies: A case study of World Food Programme, Kampala Uganda* (Doctoral dissertation, Nkumba University).

Rahman, M. S., Hossain, M. S., Rahman, M. K., Islam, M. R., Sumon, M. F. I., Siam, M. A., & Debnath, P. (2025). Enhancing Supply Chain Transparency with Blockchain: A Data-Driven Analysis of Distributed Ledger Applications. *Journal of Business and Management Studies, 7*(3), 59–77. DOI: 10.32996/jbms.2025.7.3.7

Rehan, H. (2022). Enhancing Disaster Response Systems: Predicting and Mitigating the Impact of Natural Disasters Using AI. *Journal of Artificial Intelligence Research, 2*(1), 501.

Rosenow, D., Lee, T. T., & Li, Z. X. (2022). Next-generation air routing: Integrating AI, multi-objective optimization, and collaborative decision making for efficient and sustainable flight planning. *International Journal of Enterprise Modelling, 16*(3), 136–144.

Sakthivel, V., Periyaswamy, P., Lee, J. W., & Prabu, P. (2024). Enhancing transparency and trust in Agrifood supply chains through novel Blockchain-based architecture. [TIIS]. *KSII Transactions on Internet and Information Systems, 18*(7), 1968–1985.

Selvaprabhu, P. (2023). An examination of distributed and decentralized systems for trustworthy control of supply chains. *IEEE Access : Practical Innovations, Open Solutions, 11*, 137025–137052. DOI: 10.1109/ACCESS.2023.3338739

Shawon, R. E. R., Hasan, M. D., Rahman, M. A., Ghandri, M., Lamari, I. A., Kawsar, M., & Akter, R. (2025). Designing and Deploying AI Models for Sustainable Logistics Optimization: A Case Study on Eco-Efficient Supply Chains in the USA. *arXiv preprint arXiv:2503.14556.*

Singh, R. K. (2025). Transforming humanitarian supply chains with digital twin technology: A study on resilience and agility. *International Journal of Logistics Management, 36*(4), 1119–1135. DOI: 10.1108/IJLM-08-2024-0504

Stadtler, L., & Van Wassenhove, L. N. (2025). *The Logistics Emergency Team: Pioneering and Sustaining a New Partnership Model* (Doctoral dissertation, Grenoble Ecole de Management; INSEAD).

Sufi, F., & Alsulami, M. (2025). AI-Driven Global Disaster Intelligence from News Media. *Mathematics, 13*(7), 1083. DOI: 10.3390/math13071083

Ugwu, O. P. C., Alum, E. U., Ugwu, J. N., Eze, V. H. U., Ugwu, C. N., Ogenyi, F. C., & Okon, M. B. (2024). Harnessing technology for infectious disease response in conflict zones: Challenges, innovations, and policy implications. *Medicine, 103*(28), e38834. DOI: 10.1097/MD.0000000000038834 PMID: 38996110

World Food Programme (WFP). (n.d.-a). *UN Humanitarian Air Service (UNHAS).* Retrieved from https://www.wfp.org/un-humanitarian-air-service-unhas

World Food Programme (WFP). (n.d.-b). *Aviation Safety and Compliance – Tendering and Vendor Selection.* Retrieved from https://executiveboard.wfp.org/meetings-and-documents/2023/aviation-division-update

World Food Programme (WFP). (n.d.-c). *WFP Air Transport Contracts Committee.* Retrieved from https://docs.wfp.org/api/documents/WFP-0000139929/download/

Chapter 14

Integrating AI and Blockchain into Humanitarian Air Logistics:

A Case Study of Turkish Red Crescent's Aviation Response in Disaster Relief

Umit Kanmaz
https://orcid.org/0000-0003-2186-2737
Istanbul Ticaret University, Istanbul, Turkey

ABSTRACT

This chapter examines how the Turkish Red Crescent (TRC) has integrated artificial intelligence (AI) and blockchain technologies into aviation-based humanitarian logistics, with a focus on its response to the 2023 Kahramanmaraş earthquakes. It highlights how AI enhanced demand forecasting, route optimization, and real-time inventory tracking, while blockchain improved accountability through donation traceability and smart contracts. By comparing TRC's efforts with global actors like WFP and UNHAS, the chapter identifies transferable strategies for disaster-prone regions. It concludes with recommendations for digital literacy, ethical governance, and innovation scaling to support more resilient and transparent humanitarian operations.

DOI: 10.4018/979-8-3373-3643-5.ch014

1. INTRODUCTION

Aviation serves as a critical enabler in humanitarian relief logistics, offering unmatched speed, access, and operational flexibility in the face of widespread destruction or geographic isolation. When disasters strike—whether earthquakes, floods, pandemics, or conflict zones—air transport is often the only feasible means of delivering lifesaving supplies, deploying emergency responders, or evacuating survivors. As climate-related disasters increase in both frequency and severity, the logistical challenges confronting humanitarian actors have grown exponentially (Dube, Wedawatta, & Ginige, 2021). Compounding these challenges is the complexity of modern emergencies, which frequently involve multilayered coordination across agencies, time-sensitive decisions, and fragile or non-existent infrastructure. Traditional humanitarian supply chains, while resilient in many respects, often suffer from fragmented communication, delayed data flows, and inadequate visibility during crisis response (Matracia, Saeed, Kishk, & Alouini, 2022).

In this context, emerging technologies such as artificial intelligence (AI) and blockchain have demonstrated immense potential to enhance humanitarian logistics by addressing core vulnerabilities in real time. AI facilitates predictive analytics, resource allocation, and dynamic routing, allowing humanitarian organizations to forecast demand and optimize deliveries based on evolving field conditions (Beduschi, 2022; Dubey, Bryde, Dwivedi, Graham, & Foropon, 2022). Meanwhile, blockchain ensures data integrity and transactional transparency, enabling secure donation tracking, verification of aid distribution, and automation of supply chain contracts through smart contracts (Adediran et al., 2024; Baharmand, Maghsoudi, & Coppi, 2021). Together, these technologies can reshape the speed, accuracy, and accountability of air-based relief operations—transforming aviation logistics into a digitally driven ecosystem.

This chapter examines the Turkish Red Crescent (Türk Kızılay) as a leading national case of how AI and blockchain can be integrated into aviation-focused humanitarian response. As Türkiye's largest humanitarian organization and a member of the International Red Cross and Red Crescent Movement, TRC occupies a strategic role as both a first responder and a key component of the national disaster coordination mechanism alongside AFAD (IFRC, 2023). Its operational capacity spans national blood services, emergency shelter production, and psychosocial support, and was most recently tested during the 2023 Kahramanmaraş earthquakes. The organization's ability to rapidly activate air logistics—ranging from military helicopter missions to coordinated air cargo deliveries through Turkish Airlines and foreign donors—demonstrated the importance of aviation in bridging logistical gaps during large-scale disasters (Stat Times, 2023; DVIDS, 2023). Importantly, TRC's ongoing experimentation with AI for route optimization and blockchain for donation accountability positions it as a replicable model for other national humanitarian agencies operating in disaster-prone regions.

This chapter is organized into five main sections to explore the strategic integration of these technologies. Following this introduction, Section 2 lays the conceptual and technological foundation, covering the role of aviation in humanitarian logistics and the functional capabilities of AI and blockchain. Section 3 offers a detailed case study of the Turkish Red Crescent's aviation-based operations during the 2023 earthquakes, highlighting how technology supported speed, coordination, and transparency. Section 4 synthesizes the key benefits and limitations of TRC's approach, drawing comparisons with global actors such as WFP and UNHAS, and offering lessons for other regions. Finally, Section 5 presents policy recommendations and future directions for humanitarian organizations aiming to modernize their air logistics through digital transformation. By integrating theory, practice, and empirical insight, this chapter contributes to the evolving discourse on how technology can advance the effectiveness and equity of humanitarian relief in an era of complex emergencies.

2. THEORETICAL AND TECHNOLOGICAL FOUNDATIONS

2.1. Humanitarian Logistics and Air Mobility

The strategic role of air logistics in humanitarian operations has gained renewed prominence due to the increasing frequency and severity of disasters that disrupt conventional transportation infrastructure. In scenarios where roads, railways, and ports are either damaged or blocked, air mobility becomes not just a logistical advantage but a humanitarian necessity. Özkanlısoy and Akkartal (2020) emphasize that risk mitigation in digital and physical supply chains demands rapid and flexible mobility solutions, especially in emergency conditions where lead times are critical. Air logistics, particularly through the deployment of fixed-wing aircraft, helicopters, and increasingly unmanned aerial vehicles (UAVs), offers a means to bypass geographical constraints and deliver urgent aid such as medical supplies, food, and shelter materials directly to inaccessible regions. Mızrak (2023) further underscores the importance of proactive risk assessment in humanitarian logistics, noting that strategic airlift operations are essential in minimizing delay costs and sustaining life-saving interventions during crises. These capabilities allow humanitarian actors to maintain operational continuity, respond faster to volatile disaster environments, and improve the timeliness of aid delivery, which is often the most critical performance metric in relief logistics.

Air-based humanitarian supply chains possess unique characteristics that distinguish them from commercial or ground-based logistics systems. Unlike standard logistics operations, humanitarian air logistics are characterized by high uncertainty, sudden surges in demand, limited information flow, and constrained operational environments. As Rojas Trejos, Meisel, and Adarme Jaimes (2023) highlight in their systematic review, these supply chains must also contend with accessibility constraints, such as damaged airports or unpredictable weather, which necessitate dynamic and flexible delivery modes. This complexity is compounded by the imperative to coordinate among multiple stakeholders—including governments, non-governmental organizations (NGOs), military units, and private sector partners—each operating with different priorities and capacities. The recent COVID-19 pandemic illustrated how air logistics had to be adapted quickly for vaccine distribution and remote medical supply chains, often involving complex route planning under shifting regulatory environments (Mohamadi et al., 2023). These systems also require robust coordination platforms and decision-support tools that can manage real-time data and optimize scarce aviation assets in high-pressure scenarios. Therefore, air-based humanitarian logistics must not only be fast and agile but also resilient, data-driven, and ethically grounded in order to serve vulnerable populations effectively during times of crisis.

Technological advancements have further transformed the operational landscape of air logistics in humanitarian contexts. The integration of drones and UAVs into aid missions represents a disruptive innovation in last-mile delivery, particularly in remote or mountainous areas. Dhakal and Karunakaran (2023) describe how drone-based delivery systems have been successfully implemented for transporting medical supplies to rural regions, significantly reducing delivery times and bypassing terrain-related challenges. Aretoulaki et al. (2024) take this further by proposing a drone-enabled integrated humanitarian logistics platform that merges IoT and AI-based decision support for optimizing flight routes, payload configurations, and drop-off schedules. These systems can autonomously adjust to real-time data inputs, such as weather or demand fluctuations, enabling more adaptive and efficient operations. Moreover, the potential of drone swarms or coordinated fleets allows for parallel deliveries to multiple sites, enhancing coverage and responsiveness. According to Purtell, Hong, and Hiatt (2024), the field of advanced air mobility is evolving rapidly, with humanitarian applications among the most impactful and societally valuable use cases. These innovations not only enhance logistical reach but also contribute to the decentralization of relief efforts, empowering local units and improving last-mile effectiveness.

In addition to technology, the strategic integration of air logistics must also consider human-centric design and inter-agency cooperation. Aretoulaki (2024) emphasizes that the humanitarian value of UAV-based systems lies not only in their technical capabilities but also in their ability to be embedded within ethical, scalable, and interoperable frameworks. This means ensuring that UAV missions comply with humanitarian principles of neutrality, impartiality, and transparency, and that they are perceived as legitimate by affected communities. For example, integrating community feedback mechanisms into AI-based logistics platforms can help tailor deliveries to real needs and build trust in technological solutions. Likewise, partnerships with national civil aviation authorities are critical to navigating airspace restrictions and safety regulations, particularly in conflict or post-disaster zones. The success of the Turkish Red Crescent in navigating these challenges during recent earthquakes and refugee crises showcases the importance of institutional readiness and strategic coordination. As Mızrak (2023) argues, disaster preparedness is not merely about infrastructure but about the readiness of logistics systems to adapt to uncertainty, which makes the case for continued investment in agile and digitally enabled air logistics infrastructures.

Taken together, the evolution of humanitarian air logistics underscores its strategic importance as both an enabler and a transformer of disaster relief capabilities. From traditional cargo aircraft to AI-optimized UAVs, the sector reflects an ongoing shift toward more intelligent, decentralized, and adaptive operations. These systems are not only enhancing the speed and scale of aid distribution but also redefining how humanitarian supply chains are conceptualized and managed in the digital era. As Özkanlısoy and Akkartal (2020) caution, future humanitarian logistics must integrate both risk foresight and technological agility, particularly in volatile environments shaped by climate change, pandemics, and conflict. Therefore, air mobility is not just a logistical function but a strategic capability that underpins the effectiveness, equity, and resilience of global humanitarian efforts.

2.2. Artificial Intelligence in Humanitarian Operations

Artificial Intelligence (AI) is rapidly transforming humanitarian logistics, offering advanced capabilities for predictive analytics, resource optimization, and real-time decision-making under crisis conditions. At the forefront of this transformation is the ability of AI to enhance predictive analytics and demand forecasting, enabling organizations to better anticipate needs before disasters strike. Beduschi (2022) highlights the strategic potential of AI in forecasting demand surges and allocating resources in a timely manner, particularly in dynamic and unpredictable humanitarian scenarios. Predictive modeling supported by historical and real-time data empowers agencies to mobilize logistics assets more effectively, thereby reducing response delays and maximizing impact. Trusilo and Danks (2023) add that AI's role extends beyond efficiency, touching on moral and legal obligations in humanitarian contexts. Their work emphasizes that predictive systems must align with ethical standards, ensuring that AI does not introduce discrimination or exacerbate existing inequalities in aid distribution. In the context of air logistics, flight scheduling powered by AI can optimize route planning, fuel efficiency, and load balancing, all of which are essential for operating in time-critical environments where every minute counts.

AI-driven machine learning (ML) systems also play a vital role in optimizing supply distribution and improving response times across humanitarian operations. According to Dubey et al. (2022), embedding big data analytics and AI into the culture of humanitarian supply chains fosters greater agility and resilience. Machine learning algorithms can quickly process large volumes of diverse data—ranging from satellite images to weather forecasts—to generate actionable insights for logistics managers. Pasupuleti et al. (2024) explain how ML-based optimization techniques improve logistics and inventory management by dynamically adjusting to changing conditions, thus enhancing both sustainability and responsiveness. This is particularly valuable in disaster-prone regions where infrastructure may be compromised and needs evolve rapidly. As noted by Atieh (2025), AI also serves as a key enabler in achieving the Sustainable Development Goals (SDGs) by enhancing supply chain resilience and ensuring timely service delivery to vulnerable populations. Moreover, Efe (2022) underscores that AI's risk-reduction capacity lies in its ability to rapidly identify bottlenecks, predict resource shortages, and automate distribution processes—functions that were particularly critical during the COVID-19 pandemic and subsequent supply chain shocks.

The integration of AI into humanitarian logistics is not without its structural and philosophical challenges. Raikov and Pirani (2022) explore the tension between modern, efficiency-driven AI applications and the social-humanitarian goals of equity and inclusivity, arguing that unchecked algorithmic decision-making may risk sidelining human judgment. To bridge this gap, AI systems must be designed with human-in-the-loop protocols that allow for contextual decision-making and local adaptation. This aligns with the arguments made by Burkle Jr., Khorram-Manesh, and Goniewicz (2025), who advocate for AI-assisted decision-making frameworks that enhance, rather than replace, human expertise in complex emergencies. AI should serve as an augmentation tool, offering decision support under stress and uncertainty while maintaining accountability and ethical oversight. From a strategic management perspective, Mızrak (2025) argues that the integration of smart, secure, and sustainable supply chain systems—driven by AI—can significantly increase operational resilience in the face of global disruptions. Her earlier work (Mızrak, 2024) also emphasizes the role of AI in aviation cybersecurity, noting that the human resource dimension must be strategically aligned to ensure both technological proficiency and ethical governance in AI adoption.

In practical terms, successful AI deployment in humanitarian operations hinges on the digital maturity of logistics networks and the ability to manage transformation at scale. As Özkanlısoy and Akkartal (2021) observe, digital transformation in supply chains requires not only technological upgrades but also organizational readiness, capacity building, and cross-sector collaboration. Oguntola and Ülkü (2023) stress that sustainable humanitarian logistics models must embed AI capabilities within a broader ecosystem that includes data-sharing platforms, interoperability standards, and transparent performance metrics. This ecosystem approach enables real-time coordination between aid agencies, governments, and local actors, reducing duplication of efforts and improving aid targeting. Ultimately, AI's contribution to humanitarian logistics is not limited to technological innovation but extends to fostering systemic agility, strategic foresight, and ethical alignment with humanitarian values.

2.3. Blockchain Applications in Aid Delivery

Blockchain technology has emerged as a transformative tool in the humanitarian aid ecosystem, particularly for enhancing transparency, traceability, and accountability in the donation and distribution process. As humanitarian supply chains often involve multiple actors, fragmented data systems, and regions with limited oversight, the risk of misallocation, fraud, and inefficiency is significantly heightened. Blockchain, with its decentralized and immutable ledger system, offers a means to create a single source of truth accessible to donors, NGOs, and beneficiaries alike. Adediran et al. (2024) underscore the potential of blockchain to promote social good by ensuring that donations are tracked and verified at every stage—from origin to end-use—thus reducing corruption and boosting stakeholder confidence. Friday et al. (2023), in their systematic review, further emphasize that blockchain applications in international aid and public financial management have shown significant promise in resolving chronic issues of opacity, fund leakage, and bureaucratic delays. These attributes are particularly valuable in post-disaster scenarios where emergency resources need to be disbursed rapidly and accurately, and where traditional verification mechanisms often break down.

The application of blockchain to humanitarian supply chains has also enabled smart contract automation and digital identity solutions, which enhance operational efficiency and protect the dignity and privacy of aid recipients. Smart contracts—self-executing agreements coded onto a blockchain—enable the automation of complex tasks such as supplier payments, inventory releases, or conditional transfers of aid, based on predefined triggers like GPS coordinates or temperature thresholds for perishable goods. Gupta et al. (2022) demonstrate how smart contracts embedded in drone-based delivery systems (e.g., the GaRuDa model) can enable automatic verification and release of medical payloads in Healthcare 5.0 applications, which also hold strong relevance for remote disaster zones. Similarly, Kolhatkar et al. (2023) explore how blockchain-based systems in disaster management can automatically initiate emergency protocols and resource allocations without requiring manual intervention, thereby saving critical time and reducing human error. Meanwhile, the use of blockchain-enabled digital identity systems allows refugees and displaced populations—often lacking formal documentation—to access aid and essential services. Ruzafa (2021) notes that such systems can empower beneficiaries by assigning unique, secure, and portable identities, which facilitate eligibility checks without compromising privacy. This innovation not only prevents duplication and fraud but also supports the ethical imperative of treating recipients as rights-holders rather than passive aid subjects.

Governance structures built on blockchain frameworks also contribute to more equitable and efficient humanitarian operations. Jahankhani, Kendzierskyj, and Colin (2021) argue that blockchain technology fosters better governance by embedding transparency into the architecture of aid systems, enabling real-time auditing, and enhancing decision accountability. For instance, when integrated with GPS and IoT devices, blockchain can offer verifiable audit trails for transported goods, thereby reducing opportunities for diversion or theft. The Humanitarian Supply Blockchain pilot project, studied by Baharmand, Maghsoudi, and Coppi (2021), presents one of the earliest real-world implementations of blockchain in aid logistics. Their findings show that blockchain enhanced visibility across the supply chain, reduced transaction costs, and built trust between partner organizations by providing shared, tamper-proof data on inventory flows and performance metrics. These outcomes are critical for international agencies operating under donor scrutiny, where accountability is tied directly to funding sustainability and reputational integrity. Furthermore, the authors highlight that while blockchain cannot replace sound logistics planning or organizational competence, it acts as a digital enabler that amplifies coordination and reduces the cognitive and administrative burden during crisis response.

Despite its advantages, successful deployment of blockchain in humanitarian settings requires thoughtful integration with existing systems, legal compliance, and sensitivity to digital equity. As Kolhatkar et al. (2023) point out, the infrastructural prerequisites for blockchain adoption—such as internet access, energy supply, and digital literacy—must be addressed to avoid further marginalizing the very populations aid systems aim to support. This concern is echoed in Adediran et al. (2024), who caution that overly technical solutions can become exclusionary if not complemented by user-centered design and inclusive training. As such, blockchain should be understood not merely as a technical tool, but as a component of a broader digital humanitarian strategy aimed at systemic reform. In contexts like

Türkiye's earthquake and refugee responses, blockchain-enabled platforms could be instrumental in ensuring timely, equitable, and accountable air logistics operations, especially when integrated with AI, drones, and cloud-based dashboards for multi-stakeholder coordination.

2.4. Synergistic Use of AI and Blockchain

The convergence of Artificial Intelligence (AI) and blockchain technology presents a transformative opportunity for enhancing both the security and intelligence of automated systems within humanitarian operations. Their integration creates powerful synergies where AI contributes advanced analytics and decision-making capabilities, while blockchain ensures immutable data integrity, traceability, and trustless execution of operations. According to Aloun (2024), this union addresses one of the core challenges in humanitarian systems—how to make rapid, high-stakes decisions while maintaining accountability and transparency across fragmented stakeholder environments. In practical terms, interoperability between AI and blockchain allows for secure sharing of data between different entities, such as NGOs, logistics providers, and governmental agencies, without compromising privacy or control. Tyagi et al. (2024) emphasize that by embedding AI models within smart contracts, systems can autonomously execute tasks—such as verifying beneficiary eligibility, triggering UAV dispatch, or adjusting supply allocations—based on real-time data inputs. This level of automation not only accelerates decision-making but also reduces the potential for human bias or manipulation, especially in volatile disaster response scenarios.

From a systems architecture perspective, the conceptual framework for joint deployment of AI and blockchain rests on layered digital infrastructures that facilitate data capture, learning, verification, and execution. Mızrak (2024) outlines such a framework in the context of dynamic supply chains, where AI-enabled forecasting modules interact with blockchain-based traceability ledgers to orchestrate real-time, ethically governed decisions. For instance, AI may predict inventory shortages or demand spikes using historical and situational data, while blockchain ensures that such decisions are logged, auditable, and executed in compliance with pre-established humanitarian protocols. Zuo (2024) adds that this convergence is particularly powerful in IoT-intensive environments like smart supply chains, where physical assets (e.g., UAVs, cold chain sensors) interact continuously with cloud-based AI models and blockchain nodes. Through this interaction, operational integrity is preserved even in low-trust or decentralized contexts, as both human and machine decisions are verified and transparent. Li (2025) further argues that the organizational potential of AI–blockchain synergy lies in its ability to operationalize resilience: organizations can adapt faster to disruptions while maintaining ethical compliance and traceable accountability.

The collaborative functionality between these technologies also addresses important security and governance issues in digital humanitarian systems. AI models are often criticized for their opacity and vulnerability to adversarial attacks, while blockchain systems can be rigid or computationally inefficient when handling real-time data. Murugan et al. (2025) explore this complementarity by examining how AI enhances the flexibility and decision-making depth of blockchain systems, while blockchain secures AI outputs against tampering, data corruption, or unauthorized access. Applied to a humanitarian logistics context, this means that AI-generated recommendations—such as where to route emergency air deliveries—can be recorded immutably and validated in a distributed manner, reducing disputes and ensuring post-disaster audits are fully transparent. Tyagi et al. (2024) also point to cybersecurity as a major advantage of this dual-layered approach, particularly in regions where governance institutions are weak or communications infrastructure is compromised. By uniting AI's adaptive intelligence with blockchain's structural integrity, humanitarian actors can build platforms that are both smart and secure—capable of learning and adapting while remaining ethically and technically trustworthy.

As these integrated models move from theory to implementation, a number of practical and ethical considerations must also be addressed. While Aloun (2024) outlines several successful use cases in public health and logistics, scalability, energy efficiency, and ethical governance remain ongoing concerns. The success of these systems depends on not only technical design but also the degree to which end-users—including aid workers, local partners, and beneficiaries—are trained and empowered to interact with them. Mızrak (2024) underscores that in the humanitarian context, innovation should not be purely technology-driven but rather strategy-led and ethically anchored. This calls for the development of standardized frameworks for AI–blockchain interoperability in humanitarian logistics, possibly led by multi-stakeholder collaborations involving technology providers, humanitarian agencies, and regulators. Ultimately, the synergistic deployment of AI and blockchain offers not just operational improvements, but a paradigm shift toward more transparent, adaptive, and accountable aid systems—a critical transformation as humanitarian crises become more complex and frequent.

3. CASE STUDY: TURKISH RED CRESCENT'S AVIATION RESPONSE

3.1. Overview of the Turkish Red Crescent (TRC)

The Turkish Red Crescent (TRC), known as *Türk Kızılay*, is Türkiye's largest and oldest humanitarian organization. Founded in 1868, it is affiliated with the International Federation of Red Cross and Red Crescent Societies (IFRC) and serves as an auxiliary to the state in times of crisis, disaster, and conflict (IFRC, 2023). TRC's mandate includes emergency disaster relief, health services, shelter provision, refugee support, and blood donation coordination (Kızılay, 2023). With decades of operational experience, the organization has responded to numerous large-scale disasters both nationally and internationally, including the 2003 Bam earthquake in Iran, the 2004 Indian Ocean tsunami, the 2005 Pakistan earthquake, and the ongoing Syrian humanitarian crisis (Wikipedia, 2023a).

Within Türkiye's national emergency management system, TRC plays a critical role under the coordination of the Disaster and Emergency Management Authority (AFAD). According to Türkiye's Disaster Response Plan, TRC leads the Nutrition Service Group and participates in eight other coordination clusters, including logistics, shelter, health, psychosocial support, and international aid (IFRC, 2023). For example, TRC manages the national blood supply chain in coordination with the Ministry of Health, operates tent production facilities, and oversees large-scale relief warehouses (UNDRR, 2023). It also deploys psychosocial teams in collaboration with the Ministry of Family and Social Services to assist trauma-affected populations. Through these mechanisms, TRC serves as the operational engine of Türkiye's humanitarian response, often mobilizing thousands of trained staff and volunteers during emergencies and partnering with the UN, NGOs, and international donors for cross-border coordination (IFRC, 2023; Kızılay, 2023).

3.2. Aviation Logistics in Recent Disasters

During the February 2023 Kahramanmaraş earthquakes, the Turkish Red Crescent demonstrated its ability to rapidly integrate air logistics into its disaster response. The twin quakes, which struck 11 provinces in southeastern Türkiye, caused massive infrastructure damage. Roads and bridges collapsed, and harsh winter weather rendered many ground routes inaccessible (TRC, 2023a). These limitations, combined with fuel shortages and congestion, delayed the deployment of relief goods by land. To overcome this, TRC coordinated an airbridge operation in partnership with the Turkish Armed Forces and civil aviation authorities. Helicopters were used to airlift urgent supplies—including food parcels, blankets, hygiene kits, and tents—into remote and mountainous areas, such as Elbistan, where road access was blocked (Ajansturkhaber, 2023).

In addition to tactical helicopter drops, TRC supported the broader aerial aid supply chain through coordination at key air logistics hubs. Cargo aircraft from the Turkish Air Force, Turkish Airlines, and international donors transported shelter materials, medicine, and emergency equipment to staging airports such as Adana, Gaziantep, and Incirlik Air Base. At Incirlik, a high-volume "Ring of Fire" aid corridor was established, where hundreds of flights delivered humanitarian supplies around the clock (DVIDS, 2023). Turkish Airlines, working in coordination with AFAD and TRC, carried out over 1,300 aid flights and 156 cargo freighter missions. These flights transported more than 15,600 tons of humanitarian goods, including field hospitals and rescue equipment. Additionally, more than 230,000 disaster survivors were evacuated free of charge via Turkish Airlines flights to safer regions (Stat Times, 2023).

TRC's logistics staff played a key role in prioritizing cargo loads, clearing international shipments through customs, and distributing aid through its field depots. Coordination mechanisms such as airport-based joint operation centers, daily briefings with military and civil aviation partners, and deployment of TRC liaison officers at airfields enabled synchronized operations (Stat Times, 2023). By the end of the first month, TRC had facilitated the delivery of tens of thousands of tents, millions of food packages, and hygiene materials to over a dozen provinces through these aerial channels (TRC, 2023a). The use of air logistics during the Kahramanmaraş earthquakes illustrated how TRC utilizes aviation as a critical enabler of humanitarian access in severe disasters.

3.3. AI Implementation in Operations

In recent years, the Turkish Red Crescent (TRC) has taken steps to integrate artificial intelligence (AI) into its logistics operations to improve disaster response efficiency and accuracy. One of the primary applications has been in demand forecasting using machine learning algorithms. These tools allow humanitarian organizations to anticipate the types and quantities of relief items needed, as well as the geographic distribution of that need, based on damage reports, weather data, population movement, and prior response patterns (Beduschi, 2022; Atieh, 2025). During the 2023 Kahramanmaraş earthquakes, early-stage AI tools were reportedly used to analyze satellite imagery and drone footage to identify damaged infrastructure and inaccessible regions, helping TRC and its partners plan optimal air delivery routes (LinkedIn, 2023a). This reduced the need for slower manual assessments and enabled more precise targeting of air drops.

Beyond predictive analytics, AI has been used to support real-time tracking of inventory and personnel. TRC manages a national supply network, including warehouses and temporary depots across Türkiye. By integrating AI into its inventory management software, the organization can automatically monitor stock levels, detect shortages, and reroute supplies to where they are most urgently needed. UNICEF's experience with similar systems has shown that AI can reduce stock-outs and improve inventory accuracy by over 30% (LinkedIn, 2023b). TRC's Disaster Coordination Center in Ankara also uses real-time dashboards to monitor on-the-ground needs, volunteer deployments, and supply chains. These tools, when augmented with AI, can recommend optimal staffing strategies or predict surges in demand at specific field distribution sites using population flow data or social media signals (Dubey et al., 2022).

AI also aids in flight route optimization, especially during large-scale operations involving multiple helicopters and cargo aircraft. Algorithms can factor in weather forecasts, air traffic data, terrain obstructions, and fuel efficiency to generate real-time routing suggestions (Burkle Jr. et al., 2025). Studies suggest that AI-enabled humanitarian logistics systems can reduce delivery times by up to 40% and significantly reduce costs related to misallocated resources (Pasupuleti et al., 2024). However, TRC and other humanitarian organizations recognize that AI tools are not a replacement for human judgment. Rather, they are decision-support systems that must be supervised and fine-tuned continuously to ensure reliability, ethical use, and transparency (Beduschi, 2022; Raikov & Pirani, 2022). As TRC expands its digital capacity, its AI adoption will likely grow in sophistication, offering significant operational advantages for both routine and crisis interventions.

The Turkish Red Crescent's implementation of AI spans multiple operational areas, as summarized in Table 1, demonstrating how digital tools can enhance strategic responsiveness across the disaster lifecycle.

Table 1. AI applications in TRC operations

AI Functionality	Application Area	Expected Benefit
Demand prediction	Pre-positioning and resource allocation	Reduced delays, improved preparedness
Route optimization	Air and ground logistics planning	Shorter delivery times
Inventory management	Warehouse and depot visibility	Fewer stockouts, better replenishment

continued on following page

Table 1. Continued

AI Functionality	Application Area	Expected Benefit
Personnel deployment	Field operations	Efficient workforce use
Real-time monitoring dashboards	Crisis coordination	Faster decision-making

3.4. Blockchain Integration for Accountability

In the aftermath of the 2023 earthquakes and similar large-scale crises, the Turkish Red Crescent has increased interest in blockchain technology as a mechanism for improving transparency, traceability, and trust in humanitarian aid management. Blockchain's decentralized and tamper-proof structure makes it an ideal tool for ensuring that donations, supplies, and services reach intended recipients with minimal risk of fraud or mismanagement (Adediran et al., 2024). In a blockchain-based donation system, each financial or material transaction can be logged immutably on a shared ledger. This creates a verifiable audit trail from donor to distribution, enabling public stakeholders to see how resources are used in real time (Friday et al., 2023).

Several international organizations, including the Irish Red Cross and World Food Programme, have piloted blockchain-enabled donor transparency platforms that provide updates to contributors about how their funds are spent, and what items are purchased and delivered (Cointrust, 2023). The TRC is currently examining the feasibility of deploying similar platforms. For instance, a system could be developed where a donor's contribution is linked directly to a batch of tents or medical supplies that is then traceable through procurement, shipping, warehouse storage, and field delivery stages. This not only satisfies accountability requirements but also boosts donor trust, which is critical during high-profile national appeals.

Another application of blockchain in TRC operations involves smart contracts—self-executing agreements that trigger automatically when certain conditions are met. In a humanitarian airlift context, smart contracts could be used to coordinate with suppliers or logistics providers, automatically releasing payment when proof of delivery is recorded via digital signatures or IoT sensor scans (Baharmand et al., 2021). These systems reduce the need for intermediaries, speed up disbursement, and minimize disputes over contract fulfillment. According to Gupta et al. (2022), such automation has proven particularly useful in time-sensitive operations where rapid scaling and multi-party coordination are required.

Blockchain also strengthens supply chain transparency. Every shipment of aid materials—whether by air, land, or sea—can be tagged and recorded on the blockchain at each transfer point. This helps reduce loss, theft, and duplication of efforts by providing a single source of truth to all stakeholders involved (Jahankhani et al., 2021). In previous humanitarian blockchain pilots, including WFP's "Building Blocks" system, agencies were able to spot distribution gaps or overlaps in real-time and respond accordingly (WFP USA, 2023). With increasing public scrutiny over aid effectiveness, TRC's move toward blockchain adoption—including its acceptance of cryptocurrency donations as of 2023 (Binance Charity, 2023)—signals a commitment to full traceability and operational integrity. While the integration of such systems remains at a pilot stage, the long-term vision includes shared ledgers for procurement, warehousing, distribution, and financial reporting, potentially revolutionizing how the Turkish Red Crescent manages transparency and partner collaboration.

To ensure transparency, traceability, and trust in complex humanitarian logistics operations, blockchain technology has emerged as a powerful tool for end-to-end aid tracking. By recording each transaction or handoff in an immutable ledger, blockchain creates a visible and verifiable trail from donor contribution to last-mile delivery. In the context of the Turkish Red Crescent's (TRC) aviation-based disaster response, this technology enhances accountability, reduces fraud, and allows for real-time monitoring of aid distribution. Figure 1 presents a simplified blockchain workflow model that illustrates how TRC or similar agencies could implement a step-by-step mechanism—from donation input and smart contract issuance to delivery confirmation and open-access visibility for donors and stakeholders.

Figure 1. Blockchain workflow for humanitarian aid tracking

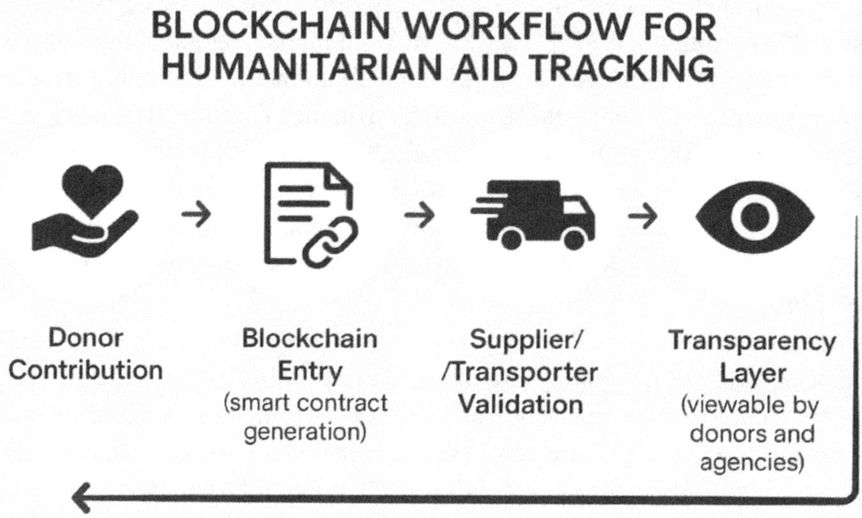

4. IMPLICATIONS

4.1. Benefits of Technology Integration

The integration of advanced technologies such as artificial intelligence, blockchain, cloud computing, and digital communication tools into humanitarian air logistics delivers measurable improvements in operational efficiency, transparency, and stakeholder trust. At the core of these benefits is the ability of digital systems to process and transmit real-time data across organizational boundaries, minimizing delays, reducing redundancies, and ensuring the right resources reach the right beneficiaries at the right time. Abdelhadi and Akkartal (2024) emphasize that structurally efficient supply chains—those characterized by lean resource use, responsive feedback loops, and robust digital infrastructure—consistently outperform traditional models, even under volatile conditions. In humanitarian contexts where stakes are high and resources constrained, such efficiency gains can directly translate into lives saved. Similarly, cloud-based business intelligence solutions allow for rapid data analytics, visualization, and decision-making across geographically dispersed teams. Aslan, Demirag, and Akkartal (2021) argue that selecting the right cloud-enabled intelligence platforms enables organizations to manage supply chain uncertainty more effectively and generate predictive insights that are essential for disaster readiness and real-time response.

Beyond efficiency, technology integration also enhances transparency and accountability, which are critical for building trust among stakeholders—especially in humanitarian settings where donor scrutiny, inter-agency cooperation, and public legitimacy are central to operational success. Mızrak (2024) illustrates this through the lens of aviation cybersecurity, demonstrating how artificial intelligence, when strategically aligned with human resources and governance frameworks, can deliver secure, traceable, and ethically compliant logistics operations. In the broader humanitarian logistics landscape, this means that all stakeholders—from local governments and NGOs to international donors—can access a unified view of logistics data, delivery schedules, and resource usage, thereby reducing information asymmetry and mitigating the risk of corruption or mismanagement. Trust, in this sense, is not just a relational asset but a digitally maintained infrastructure, facilitated by secure platforms and transparent data pipelines. This enables real-time auditing, performance tracking, and decision traceability, which in turn attract sustained donor engagement and inter-agency collaboration.

Furthermore, the use of digital platforms and communication tools significantly improves coordination between actors such as governments, humanitarian organizations, donors, and local communities. This is particularly crucial in complex emergencies where multiple entities must work in synchrony under severe time and resource constraints. Drawing from the education and public sector context, Dockendorff and Zaccarelli (2025) highlight how digital technology integration improves collaborative problem-solving and knowledge transfer across institutional silos—insights that are readily applicable to cross-agency humanitarian operations. Likewise, Ali et al. (2025) demonstrate that stakeholder engagement and outcome effectiveness increase when technology serves as a bridge, allowing for shared platforms, clearer role delineation, and consistent communication. In humanitarian logistics, this may manifest as interoperable dashboards, automated alerts, and data-sharing agreements that ensure alignment in objectives, timing, and responsibilities. When technologies are thoughtfully integrated—not merely as tools but as part of strategic coordination frameworks—they enable multi-stakeholder networks to move from fragmented action to synchronized response, improving both speed and impact in aid delivery missions.

4.2. Challenges and Risks

Despite the clear benefits of integrating technologies like AI, blockchain, and IoT into humanitarian air logistics, numerous challenges and risks persist—particularly related to data privacy and infrastructure limitations in disaster-prone zones. In the immediate aftermath of a disaster, communication networks are often disrupted, power supplies are unreliable, and digital infrastructure—if it existed at all—may be severely compromised. Matracia et al. (2022) emphasize that enabling resilient post-disaster communication requires advanced and context-sensitive architectures that can operate under degraded network conditions. These include satellite-based communications, mesh networks, and mobile edge computing; however, deploying such systems often requires prior investment, logistical access, and specialized personnel—resources that are scarce in crisis settings. Moreover, the very technologies that promise to enhance decision-making, such as digital twins or AI-driven platforms, require consistent data flows, computational power, and storage infrastructures that are often not available in emergency zones. Yu and He (2022) explore the use of digital twins in disaster prevention, acknowledging their powerful potential, but also highlighting critical infrastructure-related limitations in their real-time deployment and synchronization. These technical deficits not only hinder responsiveness but also pose serious concerns regarding data privacy, as emergency networks are frequently unsecured and vulnerable to breaches. Sensitive information—such as beneficiary identities, medical histories, or logistics plans—can be exposed or manipulated if robust data protection protocols are not embedded from the start.

In addition to physical infrastructure issues, interoperability between systems and institutions remains a persistent barrier to seamless coordination in humanitarian logistics. Effective disaster response relies on data exchange and collaboration among a multitude of actors—government agencies, military units, NGOs, private sector partners, and international organizations—each of which may use different technological platforms, data formats, and communication protocols. Khan et al. (2023) note that disaster management systems are often siloed, lacking standardized interfaces or integrated command structures, which leads to duplication of efforts, data inconsistencies, and delays in decision-making. For example, a blockchain ledger implemented by one NGO may not be compatible with the cloud system used by a government agency, undermining the visibility and traceability of aid flows. Krichen et al. (2024) also highlight that while technological advancements in disaster management—such as IoT sensors, AI models, and autonomous systems—have proliferated, their benefits are frequently diluted by institutional misalignment and weak data interoperability. These disconnects can manifest in conflicting datasets, delayed situational awareness, and logistical redundancies that ultimately impede the speed and effectiveness of aid delivery. Furthermore, the lack of shared digital governance frameworks exacerbates the challenge, especially in multi-jurisdictional operations where cybersecurity, data sharing regulations, and ethical standards differ significantly across borders. To overcome these risks, humanitarian systems must not only invest in infrastructure but also adopt common digital standards, protocols, and cross-sectoral training initiatives that promote adaptive and secure collaboration.

4.3. Comparative Reflections

The Turkish Red Crescent's (TRC) aviation-based disaster response strategy shares similarities with leading international humanitarian actors such as the World Food Programme (WFP) and the United Nations Humanitarian Air Service (UNHAS), but also reveals several context-specific strengths that make it a model for national disaster organizations. Like WFP and UNHAS, TRC leverages a multi-stakeholder logistics approach, combining government, military, civil aviation, and private sector resources to rapidly mobilize airlift capacity during emergencies. However, unlike WFP and UNHAS, which operate with more centralized international control, TRC functions as an embedded national institution with deep local networks, manufacturing capabilities (e.g., tents and mobile kitchens), and pre-existing agreements with ministries such as Health, Interior, and Transport. This allows TRC to act with speed and familiarity across Türkiye's vast geography and legal framework—an agility sometimes absent in multilateral organizations dependent on cross-border coordination or host-country permissions.

Another distinguishing feature is TRC's ability to scale rapidly due to its integrated role in Türkiye's Disaster Response Plan, its access to the Turkish Armed Forces for logistics, and the national carrier Turkish Airlines for civilian airlift. WFP and UNHAS are globally renowned for their rapid response logistics in Africa, the Middle East, and Asia; however, they often rely on UN clearance protocols, procurement delays, and fragile infrastructure. By contrast, TRC's deeply rooted partnerships and hybrid logistics capabilities (road, air, and rail) allowed it to airlift over 15,000 tons of aid within weeks of the 2023 earthquakes, aided by coordinated efforts with AFAD, municipalities, and NGOs. This capacity to blend national infrastructure with humanitarian standards positions TRC as a replicable model for other countries seeking to institutionalize rapid aviation-enabled disaster response within a national framework.

Lessons from TRC's approach can be meaningfully transferred to disaster-prone regions, particularly in low- and middle-income countries where national humanitarian capacity is still evolving. One key lesson is the importance of institutionalized disaster education and preparedness, especially at the community level. Studies show that disaster-resilient nations invest not only in physical logistics systems but also in education and training for local responders (Yusuf et al., 2022). TRC's integration of psychosocial support, public health coordination, and disaster literacy programs through schools and community centers mirrors successful models in China and Southeast Asia where disaster education has reduced trauma and improved resilience outcomes (Hu et al., 2023). Moreover, TRC's adaptive model aligns with "build-back-better" principles seen in post-disaster reconstruction cases like Zimbabwe's recovery from Cyclone Idai, where local ownership, logistical foresight, and inclusive coordination mechanisms played a vital role in successful recovery (Dube et al., 2021).

In essence, while WFP and UNHAS remain leaders in global air logistics for humanitarian aid, TRC's nationalized, scalable, and multi-sectoral model offers a complementary approach that can be localized in other countries. Governments aiming to strengthen their humanitarian infrastructure may look to TRC's hybrid logistics strategy, public-private partnerships, and integration into national emergency frameworks as a blueprint for building resilient, accountable, and swift disaster response systems.

4.4. Policy and Organizational Recommendations

To fully leverage emerging technologies such as artificial intelligence, blockchain, and IoT in disaster response, humanitarian agencies must invest in digital capacity building. The rapid digitalization of humanitarian logistics brings significant opportunities for operational efficiency and transparency, but also exposes structural weaknesses in digital literacy and readiness across many organizations. As Rai (2024) notes, in emergency settings—particularly those involving vulnerable populations—digital tools must be deployed with ethical considerations and supported by appropriate training to ensure they do not exacerbate inequalities or create unintended harms. This underscores the need for context-sensitive digital literacy programs that not only teach technical skills but also embed ethical frameworks, security awareness, and cultural relevance into training curricula.

Particularly in decentralized field operations, digital skills gaps can lead to poor implementation of life-saving tools like satellite mapping, biometric registration, or smart inventory systems. Abiddin, Ibrahim, and Aziz (2022) argue that community-based approaches to digital literacy—such as mobile learning units, peer mentoring, and multilingual content—can effectively build trust and long-term competence, especially in low-resource settings. These strategies are essential for local staff, volunteers, and partner organizations operating alongside institutions like the Turkish Red Crescent. Nanton, Doná, and Cestaro (2022) also highlight that digital equity is not just about access to devices but the ability to use them meaningfully—a concept that is critical when working with displaced populations and frontline responders in multilingual, high-stress environments. Moreover, AbdulKareem and Oladimeji (2024) emphasize that digital trust and user confidence in systems must be developed through sustained exposure, hands-on practice, and clear demonstrations of how digital tools improve humanitarian outcomes. Building such capacity will enable agencies like TRC and its peers to more effectively deploy and manage digital systems in both preparedness and crisis phases.

In parallel, strategic partnerships are essential for transferring technology and scaling innovation across humanitarian systems. Many national agencies lack the in-house capacity to develop or manage complex technologies like AI platforms, blockchain networks, or IoT-based warehousing systems. As Akkartal and Abdelhadi (2019) argue, private sector partnerships are crucial to bridge this technical gap, especially in domains like transportation, warehouse automation, and smart logistics. For instance, TRC's success during the 2023 earthquakes was partly due to coordinated efforts with Turkish Airlines, civil aviation authorities, and data-driven firms that facilitated rapid routing and distribution. Similar partnerships with fintech companies, software developers, and satellite imagery providers can enable agencies to adopt proven solutions without reinventing the wheel.

Furthermore, cross-sector consortia—involving governments, NGOs, universities, and tech firms—can foster collaborative research and pilot programs tailored to local contexts. These platforms support mutual learning, data-sharing protocols, and ethical design standards, thereby enabling technologies to scale responsibly. As Rai (2024) and AbdulKareem and Oladimeji (2024) emphasize, inclusive governance and co-design with end-users must accompany technology transfer to avoid digital divides. Whether through innovation hubs, shared infrastructure, or joint training platforms, strategic partnerships provide the foundation for scalable, resilient, and equitable adoption of emerging technologies in humanitarian logistics. For agencies like TRC, these recommendations offer a roadmap to transform from being merely digitally capable to digitally strategic—positioned to lead innovation in disaster preparedness and response on a national and international scale.

5. CONCLUSION

The case study of the Turkish Red Crescent (TRC) reveals a compelling narrative of how emerging technologies—particularly artificial intelligence (AI) and blockchain—can revolutionize aviation-based humanitarian logistics in ways that were previously inconceivable. Through the integration of AI-driven demand forecasting, flight route optimization, and real-time supply tracking, TRC significantly enhanced its operational agility and precision in responding to the 2023 Kahramanmaraş earthquakes. Simultaneously, the exploration and early implementation of blockchain for donation transparency, smart contracting, and aid traceability have laid the groundwork for a new era of accountability and stakeholder trust. When strategically combined, AI and blockchain do not merely augment existing logistics capacities—they create a synergistic infrastructure that enables real-time decision-making, predictive planning, and verifiable outcomes across complex, high-stakes humanitarian environments.

These technological innovations do not exist in isolation; their transformative potential lies in how they are strategically integrated into broader organizational frameworks. TRC's ability to rapidly mobilize air assets, synchronize with military and civilian actors, and engage in cross-sector collaboration underscores the critical importance of system-wide coordination and institutional readiness. Strategic integration empowers humanitarian agencies not only to respond faster but also to recover stronger and adapt continuously. The ability to anticipate need, automate distribution processes, and maintain transparent operations through technology contributes directly to building resilience in disaster-prone contexts. Moreover, TRC's embedded role in Türkiye's national disaster response ecosystem demonstrates that national agencies—when adequately equipped and digitally enabled—can act with the same speed and reach as global humanitarian giants, while maintaining cultural, legal, and logistical proximity to affected populations.

Looking forward, continuous digital transformation must become a core priority for humanitarian organizations worldwide. As climate-related disasters intensify in frequency and scale, there is an urgent need to move from reactive logistics to anticipatory logistics—leveraging AI for early warning and pre-positioning, and blockchain for real-time resource verification and decentralized coordination. Emerging technologies must be seen not just as tools but as integral components of humanitarian architecture. Yet realizing this vision requires deliberate investment in digital infrastructure, capacity building, and ethical design. AI and blockchain, while powerful, are only as effective as the systems in which they are embedded and the people who deploy them. Humanitarian agencies must therefore nurture digital fluency across all levels, from field workers to senior leadership, while ensuring systems are inclusive, accessible, and locally adaptable.

At the same time, ethical governance must remain a guiding principle in the deployment of these technologies. Algorithms and digital ledgers must be designed with transparency, data protection, and cultural sensitivity in mind, particularly when they affect vulnerable populations. The automation of humanitarian decision-making must always preserve the human element—allowing for empathy, discretion, and adaptability. Finally, this case study calls for more empirical research, pilot programs, and cross-national learning in the realm of humanitarian air logistics and digital innovation. As demonstrated by TRC's evolving model, the intersection of aviation, AI, and blockchain holds enormous potential for redefining emergency response capabilities. By documenting, evaluating, and iterating on such efforts, the global humanitarian community can move closer to a future where every response is faster, more transparent, and more equitable—no matter how severe the crisis or how remote the location.

REFERENCES

Abdelhadi, A., & Akkartal, E. (2024). Supply chain efficiency a structural analysis in Türkiye's retail sector. *Brazilian Journal of Operations & Production Management, 21*(3), 2150–2150. DOI: 10.14488/BJOPM.2150.2024

AbdulKareem, A. K., & Oladimeji, K. A. (2024). Cultivating the digital citizen: trust, digital literacy and e-government adoption. *Transforming Government: People. Process and Policy, 18*(2), 270–286.

Abiddin, N. Z., Ibrahim, I., & Aziz, S. A. (2022). Advocating digital literacy: Community-based strategies and approaches. *Academic Journal of Interdisciplinary Studies, 11*(1), 198–211. DOI: 10.36941/ajis-2022-0018

Adediran, F. E., Okunade, B. A., Daraojimba, R. E., Adewusi, O. E., Odulaja, B. A., & Igbokwe, J. C. (2024). Blockchain for social good: A review of applications in humanitarian aid and social initiatives. *International Journal of Science and Research Archive, 11*(1), 1203–1216. DOI: 10.30574/ijsra.2024.11.1.0184

Ajansturkhaber. (2023). Mehmetçik and Kızılay work together to deliver earthquake aid. Retrieved from https://www.ajansturkhaber.com

Akkartal, E., & Abdelhadi, A. (2019). *A framework of IoT implementations and challenges in Warehouse Management, Transportation and Retailing*. Eurasian Business & Economics Journal.

Ali, Z., Younis, S., Ahmad, N., Saba, F., & Ullah, N. (2025). Teachers' perspective of technology integration effects on students learning at university level. *J Rehabil Res Curr Updates, 1*(1), 01-06.

Aloun, M. S. (2024). Synergistic Integration of Artificial Intelligence and Blockchain Technology: Advancements, Applications, and Future Directions. *Journal of Intelligent Systems and Applied Data Science, 2*(2).

Aretoulaki, E. (2024). An Innovative Supply Chain & Logistics Model for Tackling Humanitarian Crises with the Support of Internet of Things (IoT) Technologies and Unmanned Aerial Vehicles (drones).

Aretoulaki, E., Ponis, S. T., & Plakas, G. (2024). Requirements Engineering for a Drone-Enabled Integrated Humanitarian Logistics Platform. *Applied Sciences (Basel, Switzerland), 14*(15), 6464. DOI: 10.3390/app14156464

Aslan, İ., Demirag, A., & Akkartal, E. (2021). *Collaboration of business intelligence and cloud computing and selecting the best cloud business intelligence solution* (Doctoral dissertation, Akademik Bilişim Araştırmaları Derneği).

Atieh, A. A. (2025). Enhancing Humanitarian Supply Chain Resilience Through AI: The Moderating Role of Artificial Intelligence in Achieving Sustainable Development Goals (SDGs) in Jordan. *International Journal of Sustainable Development and Planning, 20*(5), 2225–2234. DOI: 10.18280/ijsdp.200537

Baharmand, H., Maghsoudi, A., & Coppi, G. (2021). Exploring the application of blockchain to humanitarian supply chains: Insights from Humanitarian Supply Blockchain pilot project. *International Journal of Operations & Production Management, 41*(9), 1522–1543. DOI: 10.1108/IJOPM-12-2020-0884

Beduschi, A. (2022). Harnessing the potential of artificial intelligence for humanitarian action: Opportunities and risks. *International Review of the Red Cross, 104*(919), 1149–1169. DOI: 10.1017/S1816383122000261

Binance Charity. (2023). Turkish Red Crescent now accepts crypto donations. Retrieved from https://www.binance.charity

Burkle, F. M.Jr, Khorram-Manesh, A., & Goniewicz, K. (2025). Artificial Intelligence Assisted Decision-Making in Current and Future Complex Humanitarian Emergencies. *Disaster Medicine and Public Health Preparedness, 19*, e64. DOI: 10.1017/dmp.2025.63 PMID: 40111099

Cointrust. (2023). Irish Red Cross launches blockchain-based donations tracker. Retrieved from https://www.cointrust.com

Dhakal, S., & Karunakaran, K. (2023). Design and Implementation of Drone Technology for Medical Supplement Delivery Services in Rural Regions. *Int. Res. J. Eng. Technol, 10*, 545–550.

Dockendorff, M., & Zaccarelli, F. G. (2025). Successfully preparing future mathematics teachers for digital technology integration: A literature review. *International Journal of Mathematical Education in Science and Technology, 56*(5), 948–979. DOI: 10.1080/0020739X.2024.2309273

Dube, E., Wedawatta, G., & Ginige, K. (2021). Building-back-better in post-disaster recovery: Lessons learnt from Cyclone Idai-induced floods in Zimbabwe. *International Journal of Disaster Risk Science, 12*(5), 700–712. DOI: 10.1007/s13753-021-00373-3

Dubey, R., Bryde, D. J., Dwivedi, Y. K., Graham, G., & Foropon, C. (2022). Impact of artificial intelligence-driven big data analytics culture on agility and resilience in humanitarian supply chain: A practice-based view. *International Journal of Production Economics, 250*, 108618. DOI: 10.1016/j.ijpe.2022.108618

DVIDS. (2023). U.S. Air Force supports humanitarian aid flights at Incirlik. Retrieved from https://www.dvidshub.net

Efe, A. (2022). A review on risk reduction potentials of artificial intelligence in humanitarian aid sector. *Journal of the Humanities and Social Sciences, 5*(2), 184–205. DOI: 10.53048/johass.1189814

Friday, S. C., Lawal, C. I., Ayodeji, D. C., & Sobowale, A. (2023). Systematic review of blockchain applications in public financial management and international aid accountability. *International Journal of Multidisciplinary Research and Growth Evaluation, 4*(1), 1165–1180. DOI: 10.54660/.IJMRGE.2023.4.1.1165-1180

Gupta, R., Bhattacharya, P., Tanwar, S., Kumar, N., & Zeadally, S. (2022). GaRuDa: A blockchain-based delivery scheme using drones for healthcare 5.0 applications. *IEEE Internet of Things Magazine, 4*(4), 60–66. DOI: 10.1109/IOTM.001.2100045

Hu, X., Huang, P., Lv, Y., & Liu, M. (2023). Disaster education: Empowering resilience and mitigating PTSD in disaster-prone areas of China. *Environmental Research Communications, 5*(10), 105018. DOI: 10.1088/2515-7620/ad04f7

IFRC. (2023). Türkiye: Earthquakes 2023 – International Appeal Operations Update. Retrieved from https://adore.ifrc.org

Jahankhani, H., Kendzierskyj, S., & Colin, A. (2021). Blockchain as a tool for transparency and governance in the delivery of development aid. In *Strategy, Leadership, and AI in the Cyber Ecosystem* (pp. 93-111). Academic Press. DOI: 10.1016/B978-0-12-821442-8.00006-9

Khan, S. M., Shafi, I., Butt, W. H., Diez, I. D. L. T., Flores, M. A. L., Galán, J. C., & Ashraf, I. (2023). A systematic review of disaster management systems: Approaches, challenges, and future directions. *Land (Basel), 12*(8), 1514. DOI: 10.3390/land12081514

Kızılay. (2023). About Us. Retrieved from https://www.kizilay.org.tr

Kolhatkar, D., Jain, O., Patil, S., Shelke, P., Mirajkar, R., & Wawage, P. (2023, May). Blockchain applications in disaster management systems. In *2023 4th International Conference for Emerging Technology (INCET)* (pp. 1-7). IEEE. DOI: 10.1109/INCET57972.2023.10170452

Krichen, M., Abdalzaher, M. S., Elwekeil, M., & Fouda, M. M. (2024). Managing natural disasters: An analysis of technological advancements, opportunities, and challenges. *Internet of Things and Cyber-Physical Systems, 4*, 99–109. DOI: 10.1016/j.iotcps.2023.09.002

Krichen, M., Abdalzaher, M. S., Elwekeil, M., & Fouda, M. M. (2024). Managing natural disasters: An analysis of technological advancements, opportunities, and challenges. *Internet of Things and Cyber-Physical Systems, 4*, 99–109. DOI: 10.1016/j.iotcps.2023.09.002

Li, D. C. Y. (2025). The synergistic potential of AI and blockchain for organizations. *AI & Society, 40*(1), 221–222. DOI: 10.1007/s00146-023-01838-3

LinkedIn. (2023a). TRC's AI satellite analysis helps map quake damage. Retrieved from https://www.linkedin.com

LinkedIn. (2023b). UNICEF uses AI to improve disaster stock management. Retrieved from https://www.linkedin.com

Matracia, M., Saeed, N., Kishk, M. A., & Alouini, M. S. (2022). Post-disaster communications: Enabling technologies, architectures, and open challenges. *IEEE Open Journal of the Communications Society, 3*, 1177–1205. DOI: 10.1109/OJCOMS.2022.3192040

Mızrak, F. (2023). Managing Risks and Crises in the Logistics Sector: A Comprehensive Analysis of Strategies and Prioritization Using AHP Method. *Meriç Uluslararası Sosyal ve Stratejik Araştırmalar Dergisi, 7*(Özel Sayı), 114-148.

Mızrak, F. (2024). Integrating AI with aviation cybersecurity: The strategic role of human resources. *Business & Management Studies: An International Journal, 12*(3), 610–628. DOI: 10.15295/bmij.v12i3.2396

Mızrak, F. (2024). Integrating AI with aviation cybersecurity: The strategic role of human resources. *Business & Management Studies: An International Journal, 12*(3), 610–628. DOI: 10.15295/bmij.v12i3.2396

Mızrak, F. (Ed.). (2024). *Strategic Innovations for Dynamic Supply Chains*. IGI Global. DOI: 10.4018/979-8-3693-3575-8

Mızrak, F. (2025). The Triple Nexus of Smart, Secure, and Sustainable Supply Chains: Strategies for Resilience in the Digital Age. In *Utilizing Cybersecurity to Foster Business Innovation and Resiliency* (pp. 189-218). IGI Global Scientific Publishing.

Mohamadi, N., Bakhishi, H., Transchel, S., & Besiou, M. (2023). Impact of pandemics on humanitarian retailing operations: A voucher's case. *Production and Operations Management*, *32*(5), 1512–1528. DOI: 10.1111/poms.13690

Murugan, R., Yenduri, G., Maran, P., & Reddy Gadekallu, T. (2025). The synergy of artificial intelligence and blockchain in 6G spectrum management. *Intelligent Spectrum Management: Towards, 6G*, 237–262. DOI: 10.1002/9781394201235.ch10

Nanton, R., Doná, G., & Cestaro, C. (2022). Innovative Technologies and Digital Equity: Supporting Unaccompanied Asylum-Seeking and Refugee Children to Achieve Digital Literacy.

Oguntola, I. O., & Ülkü, M. A. (2023). Artificial intelligence for sustainable humanitarian logistics. *Encyclopedia of data science and machine learning*, 2970-2983.

ÖZKANLISOY, Ö., & Akkartal, E. (2020). Risk Assessment in Digital Supply Chains. *Journal of Economic & Social Research (2148-1407), 7*(14).

Özkanlısoy, Ö., & Akkartal, E. (2021). Digital transformation in supply chains: Current applications, contributions and challenges. *Business & Management Studies: An International Journal*, *9*(1), 32–55.

Pasupuleti, V., Thuraka, B., Kodete, C. S., & Malisetty, S. (2024). Enhancing supply chain agility and sustainability through machine learning: Optimization techniques for logistics and inventory management. *Logistics (Basel)*, *8*(3), 73. DOI: 10.3390/logistics8030073

Pasupuleti, V., Thuraka, B., Kodete, C. S., & Malisetty, S. (2024). Enhancing supply chain agility and sustainability through machine learning: Optimization techniques for logistics and inventory management. *Logistics (Basel)*, *8*(3), 73. DOI: 10.3390/logistics8030073

Purtell, C., Hong, S. J., & Hiatt, B. (2024). Bibliometric analysis on advanced air mobility and drones. *Journal of Air Transport Management*, *116*, 102569. DOI: 10.1016/j.jairtraman.2024.102569

Rai, M. S. (2024). Digitalization and Children in Humanitarian Emergencies: Addressing the challenges at the crossroads of Digital opportunities, Digital literacy and Child Trafficking. *Digital literacy and Child Trafficking (January 12, 2024).*

Raikov, A. N., & Pirani, M. (2022). Contradiction of modern and social-humanitarian artificial intelligence. *Kybernetes*, *51*(13), 186–198. DOI: 10.1108/K-01-2022-0057

Raikov, A. N., & Pirani, M. (2022). Contradiction of modern and social-humanitarian artificial intelligence. *Kybernetes*, *51*(13), 186–198. DOI: 10.1108/K-01-2022-0057

Rojas Trejos, C. A., Meisel, J. D., & Adarme Jaimes, W. (2023). Humanitarian aid distribution logistics with accessibility constraints: A systematic literature review. *Journal of Humanitarian Logistics and Supply Chain Management*, *13*(1), 26–41. DOI: 10.1108/JHLSCM-05-2021-0041

Ruzafa, M. C. (2021). *Blockchain as a chain for humanitarian aid: transforming the lives of refugees* (Master's thesis).

Stat Times. (2023). Turkish Airlines carried over 15,600 tons of aid for earthquake victims. Retrieved from https://www.stattimes.com

TRC. (2023a). Kahramanmaraş Earthquake Emergency Response Report. Retrieved from https://prddsgofilestorage.blob.core.windows.net

Trusilo, D., & Danks, D. (2023). Artificial intelligence and humanitarian obligations. *Ethics and Information Technology*, *25*(1), 12. DOI: 10.1007/s10676-023-09681-2

Tyagi, P., & Shrivastava, N. Sakshi, & Jain, V. (2024). Synergizing artificial intelligence and blockchain. In *Next-Generation Cybersecurity: AI, ML, and Blockchain* (pp. 83-97). Singapore: Springer Nature Singapore.

UNDRR. (2023). Türkiye national disaster plan and cluster responsibilities. Retrieved from https://www.preventionweb.net

WFP USA. (2023). Building Blocks: WFP's blockchain pilot for refugee cash transfers. Retrieved from https://www.wfpusa.org

Wikipedia. (2023a). Turkish Red Crescent. Retrieved from https://en.wikipedia.org/wiki/Turkish_Red_Crescent

Yu, D., & He, Z. (2022). Digital twin-driven intelligence disaster prevention and mitigation for infrastructure: Advances, challenges, and opportunities. *Natural Hazards*, *112*(1), 1–36. DOI: 10.1007/s11069-021-05190-x PMID: 35125651

Yusuf, R., Fajri, I., & Gani, S. A. (2022, June). Disaster education in disaster-prone schools: A systematic review. [). IOP Publishing.]. *IOP Conference Series. Earth and Environmental Science*, *1041*(1), 012034. DOI: 10.1088/1755-1315/1041/1/012034

Zuo, Y. (2024). Exploring the synergy: AI enhancing blockchain, blockchain empowering AI, and their convergence across IoT applications and beyond. *IEEE Internet of Things Journal*.

Compilation of References

AACO (Arab Air Carriers Organization). (n.d.). *Etihad Airways to drive procurement efficiency with SAP Ariba*. Retrieved from https://www.aaco.org/media-center/news/aaco-members/etihad-airways-to-drive-procurement-efficiency-with-sap-ariba

Aarif, K. O. M., Alam, A., & Hotak, Y. (2025). Smart sensor technologies shaping the future of precision agriculture: Recent advances and future outlooks. *Journal of Sensors*, *2025*(1), 2460098. DOI: 10.1155/js/2460098

Abay, K. A., Breisinger, C., Glauber, J. W., Kurdi, S., Laborde Debucquet, D., & Siddig, K. (2022). *The Russia-Ukraine crisis: Implications for global and regional food security and potential policy responses* (Vol. 39). Intl Food Policy Res Inst. DOI: 10.2499/p15738coll2.135913

Abdelhadi, A., & Akkartal, E. (2019). A framework of IoT implementations and challenges in Warehouse Management, Transportation and Retailing. *Eurasian Business & Economics Journal*, *18*, 25–41.

Abdelhadi, A., & Akkartal, E. (2024). Supply chain efficiency a structural analysis in turkey's retail sector. *Brazilian Journal of Operations & Production Management*, *21*(3), 2150–2150. DOI: 10.14488/BJOPM.2150.2024

AbdulKareem, A. K., & Oladimeji, K. A. (2024). Cultivating the digital citizen: trust, digital literacy and e-government adoption. *Transforming Government: People. Process and Policy*, *18*(2), 270–286.

Abdullahi, S. M., & Lazarova-Molnar, S. (2025). On the adoption and deployment of secure and privacy-preserving IIoT in smart manufacturing: A comprehensive guide with recent advances. *International Journal of Information Security*, *24*(1), 53. DOI: 10.1007/s10207-024-00951-8

Abdul, S., Adeghe, E. P., Adegoke, B. O., Adegoke, A. A., & Udedeh, E. H. (2024). AI-enhanced healthcare management during natural disasters: Conceptual insights. *Engineering Science & Technology Journal*, *5*(5), 1794–1816. DOI: 10.51594/estj.v5i5.1155

Abid, S. K., Chan, S. W., Sulaiman, N., Bhatti, U., & Nazir, U. (2023, October). Present and future of artificial intelligence in disaster management. In *2023 international conference on engineering management of communication and technology (EMCTECH)* (pp. 1-7). IEEE. DOI: 10.1109/EMCTECH58502.2023.10296991

Abiddin, N. Z., Ibrahim, I., & Aziz, S. A. (2022). Advocating digital literacy: Community-based strategies and approaches. *Academic Journal of Interdisciplinary Studies*, *11*(1), 198–211. DOI: 10.36941/ajis-2022-0018

Abid, S. K., Sulaiman, N., Chan, S. W., Nazir, U., Abid, M., Han, H., Ariza-Montes, A., & Vega-Muñoz, A. (2021). Toward an integrated disaster management approach: How artificial intelligence can boost disaster management. *Sustainability (Basel)*, *13*(22), 12560. DOI: 10.3390/su132212560

Aboualola, M., Abualsaud, K., Khattab, T., Zorba, N., & Hassanein, H. S. (2023). Edge technologies for disaster management: A survey of social media and artificial intelligence integration. *IEEE Access : Practical Innovations, Open Solutions*, *11*, 73782–73802. DOI: 10.1109/ACCESS.2023.3293035

Abraha, D. T. (2025). Blockchain-based solution for addressing refugee management in the Global South: Transparent and accessible resource sharing in humanitarian organizations. *Frontiers in Human Dynamics*, *6*, 1391163. DOI: 10.3389/fhumd.2024.1391163

Acharya, D. B., Kuppan, K., & Divya, B. (2025). Agentic AI: Autonomous Intelligence for Complex Goals–A Comprehensive Survey. *IEEE Access: Practical Innovations, Open Solutions*, *13*, 18912–18936. DOI: 10.1109/ACCESS.2025.3532853

Aćimović, S., Mijušković, V. M., & Đurović, M. (2024). THE USAGE OF CHOSEN DIGITAL TOOLS IN THE PROCESS OF HUMANITARIAN LOGISTICS MANAGEMENT. *BUSINESS LOGISTICS IN MODERN MANAGEMENT*, 155.

Adebayo, A. S., Chukwurah, N., & Ajayi, O. O. (2025). Artificial Intelligence and Machine Learning Algorithms for Advanced Threat Detection and Cybersecurity Risk Mitigation Strategies.

Adediran, F. E., Okunade, B. A., Daraojimba, R. E., Adewusi, O. E., Odulaja, B. A., & Igbokwe, J. C. (2024). Blockchain for social good: A review of applications in humanitarian aid and social initiatives. *International Journal of Science and Research Archive*, *11*(1), 1203–1216. DOI: 10.30574/ijsra.2024.11.1.0184

Adekola, O., & Adekola, J. (2024). Post-Disaster Needs Assessment as a strategic recovery planning process. In *Research Handbook on Flood Risk Management* (pp. 275–286). Edward Elgar Publishing. DOI: 10.4337/9781839102981.00028

Adhikari, B., Mishra, S. R., Marahatta, S. B., Kaehler, N., Paudel, K., Adhikari, J., & Raut, S. (2017). Earthquakes, fuel crisis, power outages, and health care in Nepal: Implications for the future. *Disaster Medicine and Public Health Preparedness*, *11*(5), 625–632. DOI: 10.1017/dmp.2016.195 PMID: 28416042

Adomavicius, G., Bockstedt, J., Gupta, A., & Kauffman, R. J. (2008). Understanding evolution in technology ecosystems. *Communications of the ACM*, *51*(10), 117–122. DOI: 10.1145/1400181.1400207

AFAD. (2022). *Annual report on shelter infrastructure in refugee camps*. https://www.afad.gov.tr

AFAD. (2023). *Post-disaster medical infrastructure assessment following the 2023 earthquakes*. https://www.afad.gov.tr

AFAD. (2023). *Ulusal Deprem Stratejisi ve Eylem Planı (UDSEP-2023)* [National Earthquake Strategy and Action Plan]. https://www.afad.gov.tr

AFAD. (2024). *Türkiye Ulusal Afet Müdahale Planı 2024–2026*. Retrieved from https://www.afad.gov.tr

Afifi, J. I. N. I. (2024). *Enhancing the Effectiveness of International Legal Frameworks on Food Security: Lessons From the World Food Programme's Efforts* (Master's thesis, Hamad Bin Khalifa University (Qatar)).

Aghsami, A., Sharififar, S., Markazi Moghaddam, N., Hazrati, E., Jolai, F., & Yazdani, R. (2024). Strategies for humanitarian logistics and supply chain in organizational contexts: Pre-and post-disaster management perspectives. *Systems*, *12*(6), 215. DOI: 10.3390/systems12060215

Ahatsi, E., & Olanrewaju, O. A. (2025). Enhancing Humanitarian Supply Chain Resilience: Evaluating Artificial Intelligence and Big Data Analytics in Two Nations. *Logistics (Basel)*, *9*(2), 64. DOI: 10.3390/logistics9020064

Ahmad, M., Ho, W. Y., Robalino, A. P. G., & Maqsood, M. (2025). Theoretical Implications of Generative AI for Content Generation in Geoinformatics Training. In Integration Strategies of Generative AI in Higher Education (pp. 101-130). IGI Global.

Ahmed, A. A. (2025). Drone Technology in Logistics Revolutionizing Last-Mile Delivery Solutions. *Eurasian Journal of Theoretical and Applied Sciences (EJTAS)*, 25-35.

Ahmed, I., Ahmad, M., Jeon, G., & Piccialli, F. (2021). A framework for pandemic prediction using big data analytics. *Big Data Research, 25*, 100190. DOI: 10.1016/j.bdr.2021.100190

Ahmed, S. (2025). BLOCKCHAIN FOR SUPPLY CHAIN TRANSPARENCY: A DECENTRALIZED PATH TO TRUST AND TRACEABILITY. *Computer Science Bulletin, 8*(01), 73–88.

Ahuja, R., Chugh, S., & Singh, R. (2024). SeedChain: A secure and transparent blockchain-driven framework to revolutionize the seed supply chain. *Future Internet, 16*(4), 132. DOI: 10.3390/fi16040132

Aiken, E., Bellue, S., Karlan, D., Udry, C., & Blumenstock, J. E. (2022). Machine learning and phone data can improve targeting of humanitarian aid. *Nature, 603*(7903), 864–870. DOI: 10.1038/s41586-022-04484-9 PMID: 35296856

Aircraft, I. T. (n.d.). *aFuel: Digital fueling platform.* Retrieved from https://www.aircraftit.com/articles/afuel-platform-overview/

Ajansturkhaber. (2023). Mehmetçik and Kızılay work together to deliver earthquake aid. Retrieved from https://www.ajansturkhaber.com

Ajayi, A. A., Emmanuel, I. G. B. A., Soyele, A. D., & Enyejo, J. O. (2024). Enhancing digital identity and financial security in decentralized finance (DeFi) through zero-knowledge proofs (ZKPs) and blockchain solutions for regulatory compliance and privacy. *Iconic Research and Engineering Journals, 8*(4), 373–394.

Akhyar, A., Zulkifley, M. A., Lee, J., Song, T., Han, J., Cho, C., & Hong, B. W. (2024). Deep artificial intelligence applications for natural disaster management systems: A methodological review. *Ecological Indicators, 163*, 112067. DOI: 10.1016/j.ecolind.2024.112067

Akkartal, E., & Abdelhadi, A. (2019). *A framework of IoT implementations and challenges in Warehouse Management, Transportation and Retailing*. Eurasian Business & Economics Journal.

Akkartal, E., & Aras, G. Y. (2021). Sustainability in fleet management. *Journal of Advanced Research in Economics and Administrative Sciences*, *2*(3), 13–39. DOI: 10.47631/jareas.v2i3.288

Akkartal, G. R., Akkartal, E., & Yıldırım, C. (2019). The Management Of Innovation In Supply Chain. *Eurasian Business & Economics Journal*, *17*(17), 43–52.

Akkartal, G. R., Barooti, A., & Akkartal, E. (2019). Gamification methods for teaching logistics and supply chain management. *Eurasian Business and Economic Journal*, *17*(5), 53–71.

Akkartal, G. R., & Mızrak, F. (2023). Defining reverse and green supplier selection criteria with a strategic management approach. In *Economic Development and the Environmental Ecosystem: The Role of Energy Policy in Economic Growth* (pp. 205–218). Springer Nature Switzerland. DOI: 10.1007/978-3-031-26596-9_17

Aksoy, L., & Yardımcı Coşkun, İ. (2025). Afetlerde aydınlatma, haberleşme ve enerji ihtiyacının tek noktadan karşılanması için şebeke ve direk tasarımı. *Doğal Afetler ve Çevre Dergisi*, *11*(1), 206–219. DOI: 10.21324/dacd.1563581

Al Sarrah, M., Ajmal, M. M., & Mertzanis, C. (2021). Identification of sustainability indicators in the civil aviation sector in Dubai: A stakeholders' perspective. *Social Responsibility Journal*, *17*(5), 648–668. DOI: 10.1108/SRJ-06-2019-0203

Alaba, F. A. (2024). The Evolution of the IoT. In *Internet of Things: A Case Study in Africa* (pp. 1–18). Springer Nature Switzerland. DOI: 10.1007/978-3-031-67984-1_1

Alabsi, A. A. N., Wu, Y., Koko, A. F., Alshareem, K. M., & Hamed, R. (2021). Towards climate adaptation in cities: Indicators of the sustainable climate-adaptive urban fabric of traditional cities in West Asia. *Applied Sciences (Basel, Switzerland)*, *11*(21), 10428. DOI: 10.3390/app112110428

Aladağ, H., Demirdöğen, G., & Işık, Z. (2023). Fundamental Prerequisites of Operational Readiness, Activation, and Transition: Case Study of Istanbul Grand Airport. *Systems*, *11*(9), 468. DOI: 10.3390/systems11090468

Alazawi, Z., Altowaijri, S., Mehmood, R., & Abdljabar, M. B. (2011, Aug). Intelligent disaster management system based on cloud-enabled vehicular networks. In *2011 11th international conference on its telecommunications* (pp. 361-368). IEEE. DOI: 10.1109/ITST.2011.6060083

Albahri, A. S., Khaleel, Y. L., Habeeb, M. A., Ismael, R. D., Hameed, Q. A., Deveci, M., Homod, R. Z., Albahri, O. S., Alamoodi, A. H., & Alzubaidi, L. (2024). A systematic review of trustworthy artificial intelligence applications in natural disasters. *Computers & Electrical Engineering, 118*, 109409. DOI: 10.1016/j.compeleceng.2024.109409

Albaroodi, H. A., & Anbar, M. (2025). Security Issues and Weaknesses in Blockchain Cloud Infrastructure: A Review Article. *Journal of Applied Data Sciences, 6*(1), 155–177. DOI: 10.47738/jads.v6i1.324

AL-Dosari, K., Hunaiti, Z., & Balachandran, W.AL-Dosari. (2023). Systematic review on civilian drones in safety and security applications. *Drones (Basel), 7*(3), 210. DOI: 10.3390/drones7030210

Alesani, D., Nasi, G., & Manni, S. (2023). Digital transformation in IOs–toward a human-centered approach. In *Management of International Institutions and NGOs* (pp. 406–431). Routledge. DOI: 10.4324/9781003289852-16

Alexandridis, K., Sabri, S., Smith, J., Logan, B., Bartfai-Walcott, K., & Migliori, D. (2024). Distributed AI modeling and simulation for smart airport digital twin applications. In *Digital Twins, Simulation, and the Metaverse: Driving Efficiency and Effectiveness in the Physical World through Simulation in the Virtual Worlds* (pp. 195–224). Springer Nature Switzerland. DOI: 10.1007/978-3-031-69107-2_9

Alfantoukh, L., Ruan, Y., & Durresi, A. (2018, October). Multi-stakeholder consensus decision-making framework based on trust: A generic framework. In *2018 IEEE 4th International Conference on Collaboration and Internet Computing (CIC)* (pp. 472-479). IEEE. DOI: 10.1109/CIC.2018.00012

Ali, Z., Younis, S., Ahmad, N., Saba, F., & Ullah, N. (2025). Teachers' perspective of technology integration effects on students learning at university level. *J Rehabil Res Curr Updates, 1*(1), 01-06.

Alipour, E. (2025). Challenges and Opportunities of Using Artificial Intelligence in Humanitarian Actions. *Quarterly Scientific Journal of Rescue and Relief, 17*(1), 1–3. DOI: 10.61186/jorar.17.1.1

Allahham, M. A. H. M. O. U. D., Sharabati, A. A. A., Hatamlah, H. E. B. A., Ahmad, A. Y. B., Sabra, S., & Daoud, M. K. (2023). Big data analytics and AI for green supply chain integration and sustainability in hospitals. *WSEAS Transactions on Environment and Development, 19*, 1218–1230. DOI: 10.37394/232015.2023.19.111

Alliance, N. G. M. N. (2021). Green Future Networks Network Equipment Eco-Design and End to End Service Footprint. *Version 1.0.*

Almadani, B., Aliyu, F., & Aliyu, A. (2023). Integrated Operation Centers in Smart Cities: A Humanitarian Engineering Perspective. *Sustainability (Basel)*, *15*(14), 11101. DOI: 10.3390/su151411101

Almaghrabi, A., & Alhogail, A. (2022). Blockchain-based donations traceability framework. *Journal of King Saud University. Computer and Information Sciences*, *34*(10), 9442–9454. DOI: 10.1016/j.jksuci.2022.09.021

Al-Mazrouie, J. R., Ojiako, U., Williams, T., Chipulu, M., & Marshall, A. (2021). An operations readiness typology for mitigating against transitional 'disastrous openings' of airport infrastructure projects. *Production Planning and Control*, *32*(4), 283–302. DOI: 10.1080/09537287.2020.1730997

Alonso, A., Llanos, J., Escandon, R., & Sendra, J. J. (2021). Effects of the COVID-19 pandemic on indoor air quality and thermal comfort of primary schools in winter in a Mediterranean climate. *Sustainability (Basel)*, *13*(5), 2699. DOI: 10.3390/su13052699

Aloun, M. S. (2024). Synergistic Integration of Artificial Intelligence and Blockchain Technology: Advancements, Applications, and Future Directions. *Journal of Intelligent Systems and Applied Data Science*, *2*(2).

Alshahrani, A., Khedr, A., Belal, M., & Saleh, M. (2024). A Smart Contract Approach for Efficient Transportation Management. *International Journal of Advanced Computer Science and Applications*, *15*(10). Advance online publication. DOI: 10.14569/IJACSA.2024.0151074

Alshalabi, W. M. W. (2022). *Holistic Transitional Approach of Humanitarian Shelters Through the Implementation of Adaptable Design Strategies* (Master's thesis, The British University in Dubai).

American Red Cross. (2019). *Puerto Rico recovery report*. Retrieved from https://www.redcross.org/about-us/news-and-events/news/2019/puerto-rico-recovery.html

American Red Cross. (2024). *American Red Cross launches solar-powered bloodmobile in Pacific Northwest*. Retrieved from https://1059thebrew.iheart.com/featured/tanner/post/2024-04-10-american-red-cross-unveils-solar-bloodmobile/

Amershi, S., Weld, D., Vorvoreanu, M., Fourney, A., Nushi, B., Collisson, P., & Horvitz, E. (2019, May). Guidelines for human-AI interaction. In *Proceedings of the 2019 chi conference on human factors in computing systems* (pp. 1-13).

Anjomshoae, A., Banomyong, R., Hossein Azadnia, A., Kunz, N., & Blome, C. (2025). Sustainable humanitarian supply chains: A systematic literature review and research propositions. *Production Planning and Control*, *36*(3), 357–377.

Anwar, U. (2025). Artificial Intelligence Driven Early Warning Systems in the Himalayan Region: Strategic Implications for China, Pakistan, and Regional Stability in South Asia. *Review Journal of Social Psychology & Social Works, 3*(3), 125–135.

Applied Blockchain. (2023). *WFP Blocks for Transport: Using blockchain to streamline humanitarian logistics*. Retrieved from https://appliedblockchain.com/case-studies/wfp-blocks-for-transport

Arbuckle, G. (2025). *Fundamentals of global air transport geography*. Taylor & Francis. DOI: 10.4324/9781003405351

Aretoulaki, E. (2024). An Innovative Supply Chain & Logistics Model for Tackling Humanitarian Crises with the Support of Internet of Things (IoT) Technologies and Unmanned Aerial Vehicles (drones).

Aretoulaki, E., Ponis, S. T., & Plakas, G. (2024). Requirements Engineering for a Drone-Enabled Integrated Humanitarian Logistics Platform. *Applied Sciences (Basel, Switzerland), 14*(15), 6464. DOI: 10.3390/app14156464

Arnetoli, M. V., & Bologna, R. (2022, June). Design Scenarios for a Circular Vision of Post-disaster Temporary Settlements. In *International Conference on Technological Imagination in the Green and Digital Transition* (pp. 471-481). Cham: Springer International Publishing.

Arxiv. (2020). *FIWARE-based semantic modeling and interoperability in disaster response IoT systems*. https://arxiv.org/abs/2005.02788

Aslan, İ., Demirag, A., & Akkartal, E. (2021). *Collaboration of business intelligence and cloud computing and selecting the best cloud business intelligence solution* (Doctoral dissertation, Akademik Bilişim Araştırmaları Derneği).

Aslan, Ö., Aktuğ, S. S., Ozkan-Okay, M., Yilmaz, A. A., & Akin, E. (2023). A comprehensive review of cyber security vulnerabilities, threats, attacks, and solutions. *Electronics (Basel), 12*(6), 1333. DOI: 10.3390/electronics12061333

Atieh, A. A. (2025). Enhancing Humanitarian Supply Chain Resilience Through AI: The Moderating Role of Artificial Intelligence in Achieving Sustainable Development Goals (SDGs) in Jordan. *International Journal of Sustainable Development and Planning, 20*(5), 2225–2234. DOI: 10.18280/ijsdp.200537

Avtin, I. V., Baburov, V. I., Ponomarenko, B. V., & Shatrakov, Y. G. (2021). *Principles of Integrated Airborne Avionics*. Springer. DOI: 10.1007/978-981-16-0897-1

Ayaz, S., & Karademir, S. (2021). Relationship between Organizational Learning and Dynamic Capabilities in Aviation Companies. *JOEEP: Journal of Emerging Economies and Policy*, *7*(2), 591–598.

Aydoğan, B. E. D. İ. A., Özçelik, G. Ö. K. H. A. N., & Ünver, M. E. H. M. E. T. (2025). Developing Industry 4.0-based e-waste management: A decision-aided tool equipped with continuous function-valued intuitionistic fuzzy sets. *International Journal of Environmental Science and Technology*, *22*(8), 6595–6620. DOI: 10.1007/s13762-024-05977-y

Ayers, J., Chadburn, O., & Hoque, K. A. (2024). *Behaviourally-Informed Early Warning and Anticipatory Action: Unleashing the Potential of Locally-Led Pre-emptive Response and the Forecast-Based Financing it Requires.* Current and Emerging Trends in the Management of International Disasters.

Bačić, Ž., Šugar, D., Poslončec-Petrić, V., & Nevistić, Z. (2022, Nov). Providing rapid earthquake information using EO/GI technology. *IOP Conference Series. Earth and Environmental Science*, *1109*(1), 012006. DOI: 10.1088/1755-1315/1109/1/012006

Baghi, Y., Ma, Z., Robinson, D., & Boehme, T. (2021). Innovation in sustainable solar-powered net-zero energy Solar Decathlon houses: A review and showcase. *Buildings (Basel, Switzerland)*, *11*(4), 171. DOI: 10.3390/buildings11040171

Bag, S., Gupta, S., & Wood, L. (2022). Big data analytics in sustainable humanitarian supply chain: Barriers and their interactions. *Annals of Operations Research*, *319*(1), 721–760. DOI: 10.1007/s10479-020-03790-7

Baharmand, H., Maghsoudi, A., & Coppi, G. (2021). Exploring the application of blockchain to humanitarian supply chains: Insights from Humanitarian Supply Blockchain pilot project. *International Journal of Operations & Production Management*, *41*(9), 1522–1543. DOI: 10.1108/IJOPM-12-2020-0884

Baharmand, H., Vega, D., Lauras, M., & Comes, T. (2022). A methodology for developing evidence-based optimization models in humanitarian logistics. *Annals of Operations Research*, *319*(1), 1197–1229. DOI: 10.1007/s10479-022-04762-9

Banisakher, M., Mohammed, D., & Omar, M. (2018). A Cloud-Based Computing Architecture Model of Post-Disaster Management System. *International Journal of Simulation—Systems. Science & Technology*, *19*(5), 638–644.

Banomyong, R., Varadejsatitwong, P., & Oloruntoba, R. (2019). A systematic review of humanitarian operations, humanitarian logistics and humanitarian supply chain performance literature 2005 to 2016. *Annals of Operations Research*, *283*(1-2), 71–86. DOI: 10.1007/s10479-017-2549-5

Bano, S. (2025). The Role of AI in Predicting and Mitigating Climate Change: A Comparative Study of US and China's Approaches. *The Critical Review of Social Sciences Studies*, *3*(1), 664–675. DOI: 10.59075/dv9cmp29

Barocas, S., Hardt, M., & Narayanan, A. (2023). *Fairness and machine learning: Limitations and opportunities*. MIT press.

Barykin, S. E., Borisoglebskaya, L. N., Provotorov, V. V., Kapustina, I. V., Sergeev, S. M., De La Poza Plaza, E., & Saychenko, L. (2021). Sustainability of management decisions in a digital logistics network. *Sustainability (Basel)*, *13*(16), 9289. DOI: 10.3390/su13169289

Bauer, M., Sanchez, L., & Song, J. (2021). IoT-enabled smart cities: Evolution and outlook. *Sensors (Basel)*, *21*(13), 4511. DOI: 10.3390/s21134511 PMID: 34209436

Beduschi, A. (2022). Harnessing the potential of artificial intelligence for humanitarian action: Opportunities and risks. *International Review of the Red Cross*, *104*(919), 1149–1169. DOI: 10.1017/S1816383122000261

Bekrar, A., Ait El Cadi, A., Todosijevic, R., & Sarkis, J. (2021). Digitalizing the closing-of-the-loop for supply chains: A transportation and blockchain perspective. *Sustainability (Basel)*, *13*(5), 2895. DOI: 10.3390/su13052895

Bengio, Y., Hinton, G., Yao, A., Song, D., Abbeel, P., Darrell, T., Harari, Y. N., Zhang, Y.-Q., Xue, L., Shalev-Shwartz, S., Hadfield, G., Clune, J., Maharaj, T., Hutter, F., Baydin, A. G., McIlraith, S., Gao, Q., Acharya, A., Krueger, D., & Mindermann, S. (2024). Managing extreme AI risks amid rapid progress. *Science*, *384*(6698), 842–845. DOI: 10.1126/science.adn0117 PMID: 38768279

Bera, M. (2025). Innovations in climate-adaptive clothing design for promoting resilience and well-being in a changing climate: A review. *Design*, *2*(2), 8589. DOI: 10.36922/dp.8589

Bhattacharjee, J., De, A., Kamila, B., & Mandal, A. (2025). Recent scenario of e-waste recycling: Chemical engineering. *International Journal of Chemical Reactor Engineering*, *23*(6), 675–700. DOI: 10.1515/ijcre-2024-0058

Bhavani, K., & Gajendra, N. (2024). Smart data-driven sensing: New opportunities to combat environmental problems. In *Bio-Inspired Data-driven Distributed Energy in Robotics and Enabling Technologies* (pp. 17–47). CRC Press. DOI: 10.1201/9781003530077-2

Binance Charity. (2023). Turkish Red Crescent now accepts crypto donations. Retrieved from https://www.binance.charity

Binns, R. (2018). Fairness in machine learning: Lessons from political philosophy. *Proceedings of the 2018 Conference on Fairness, Accountability and Transparency*, 149–159.

Bogoch, I. I., Watts, A., Thomas-Bachli, A., Huber, C., Kraemer, M. U., & Khan, K. (2020). Pneumonia of unknown aetiology in Wuhan, China: Potential for international spread via commercial air travel. *Journal of Travel Medicine*, *27*(2), taaa008. DOI: 10.1093/jtm/taaa008 PMID: 31943059

Boin, A., Ekengren, M., & Rhinard, M. (2020). *The European Union as crisis manager: Patterns and prospects*. Cambridge University Press.

Boostani, A., Jolai, F., & Bozorgi-Amiri, A. (2021). Designing a sustainable humanitarian relief logistics model in pre-and postdisaster management. *International Journal of Sustainable Transportation*, *15*(8), 604–620. DOI: 10.1080/15568318.2020.1773975

Borghetti, F., Caballini, C., Carboni, A., Grossato, G., Maja, R., & Barabino, B. (2022). The use of drones for last-mile delivery: A numerical case study in Milan, Italy. *Sustainability (Basel)*, *14*(3), 1766. DOI: 10.3390/su14031766

Bousdekis, A., Magoutas, B., Apostolou, D., & Mentzas, G. (2021). A review of data-driven crisis management. *Journal of Decision Systems*, *30*(1-2), 1–18. DOI: 10.1080/12460125.2020.1812014

Bråthen, S., & Halpern, N. (2012). Air transport service provision and management strategies to improve the economic benefits for remote regions. *Research in Transportation Business & Management*, *4*, 3–12. DOI: 10.1016/j.rtbm.2012.06.003

Bray, J. D., Frost, J. D., Rathje, E. M., & Garcia, F. E. (2019). Recent advances in geotechnical post-earthquake reconnaissance. *Frontiers in Built Environment*, *5*, 5. DOI: 10.3389/fbuil.2019.00005

Broussard, G., Rubenstein, L. S., Robinson, C., Maziak, W., Gilbert, S. Z., & DeCamp, M. (2019). Challenges to ethical obligations and humanitarian principles in conflict settings: A systematic review. *Journal of International Humanitarian Action*, *4*(1), 1–13. DOI: 10.1186/s41018-019-0063-x

Bughin, J., Seong, J., Manyika, J., Chui, M., & Joshi, R. (2018). Notes from the AI frontier: Modeling the impact of AI on the world economy. *McKinsey Global Institute*, *4*(1), 2–61.

Buonomano, A., Forzano, C., Giuzio, G. F., & Palombo, A. (2023). New ventilation design criteria for energy sustainability and indoor air quality in a post Covid-19 scenario. *Renewable & Sustainable Energy Reviews*, *182*, 113378. DOI: 10.1016/j.rser.2023.113378 PMID: 37250178

Burčiar, F., Kováč, S., & Važan, P. (2024). Check for updates Proactive Control of Production Systems Using Proposed Data Integration Strategies. *Software Engineering Methods in Systems and Network Systems: Proceedings of 7th Computational Methods in Systems and Software 2023, Vol. 2, 934*, 346.

Burkle, F. M.Jr, Khorram-Manesh, A., & Goniewicz, K. (2025). Artificial Intelligence Assisted Decision-Making in Current and Future Complex Humanitarian Emergencies. *Disaster Medicine and Public Health Preparedness, 19*, e64. DOI: 10.1017/dmp.2025.63 PMID: 40111099

Burns, M. G. (2019). *Managing energy security: an all hazards approach to critical infrastructure*. Routledge. DOI: 10.4324/9780429320071

Byers, B., Bompa, D., Jin, Q., De Wolf, C., & Bendiek-Laranjo, A. (2025). Circular Economy for Post-Hazard Infrastructure Restoration: Strategies for Resilience and Resource Efficiency. *Journal of Sustainability, 1*(1). Advance online publication. DOI: 10.55845/jos-2025-117

CALP. (2020). *Scaling electronic cash and voucher assistance: case study comparisons*. Cash Learning Partnership. Retrieved from https://www.calpnetwork.org/publication/scaling-electronic-cash-and-voucher-assistance-case-study-comparisons/

Candell, O., Hällqvist, R., Olsson, E., Fransson, T., Thaduri, A., & Karim, R. (2024). Air vehicle system health and asset management: Modeling, simulation, and decision support. *International Journal of System Assurance Engineering and Management*, •••, 1–14. DOI: 10.1007/s13198-024-02481-x

Cao, C., Chou, M. C., Zhang, F., Leng, W., & He, Y. (2024). Leveraging digital twin to enhance humanitarian logistics operations. *Flexible Services and Manufacturing Journal*, •••, 1–33. DOI: 10.1007/s10696-024-09580-8

Cao, L. (2023). AI and data science for smart emergency, crisis and disaster resilience. *International Journal of Data Science and Analytics, 15*(3), 231–246. DOI: 10.1007/s41060-023-00393-w PMID: 37035277

Cebir, Y., & Akkartal, E. (2024). Digital twin in logistics and supply chain management. In *Strategic Innovations for Dynamic Supply Chains* (pp. 170–192). IGI Global. DOI: 10.4018/979-8-3693-3575-8.ch008

Celestin, M. (2023). How Predictive Maintenance in Logistics Fleets Is Reducing Equipment Downtime and Operational Losses. *Brainae Journal of Business* [BJBST]. *Sciences and Technology, 7*(10), 1023–1033.

Çetin, S., & Kirchherr, J. (2025). The Build Back Circular Framework: Circular Economy Strategies for Post-Disaster Reconstruction and Recovery. *Circular Economy and Sustainability*, •••, 1–38.

Chang, K. H., Chiang, Y. C., & Chang, T. Y. (2024). Simultaneous location and vehicle fleet sizing of relief goods distribution centers and vehicle routing for post-disaster logistics. *Computers & Operations Research, 161*, 106404. DOI: 10.1016/j.cor.2023.106404

Chang, N. B., & Pires, A. (2015). Technology Matrix for Solid Waste Management. In *Sustainable Solid Waste Management: A Systems Engineering Approach* (pp. 19–97). IEEE. DOI: 10.1002/9781119035848.ch2

Channi, H. K., Sandhu, R., & Kumar, P. (2025). Enabling Transparent Supply to Build a Next-Generation Supply Chain. *Blockchain-Enabled Solutions for the Pharmaceutical Industry*, 207-231.

Charnsethikul, C., Silva, J. M., Verhagen, W. J., & Das, R. (2025). Urban Air Mobility Aircraft Operations in Urban Environments: A Review of Potential Safety Risks. [MDPI Publishing]. *Aerospace (Basel, Switzerland), 12*(4), 306. DOI: 10.3390/aerospace12040306

Chauhan, M., & Sahoo, D. R. (2024). Towards a greener tomorrow: Exploring the potential of AI, blockchain, and IoT in sustainable development. *Nature Environment and Pollution Technology, 23*(2), 1105–1113. DOI: 10.46488/NEPT.2024.v23i02.044

Chen, J., Cheng, Y., & Li, K. (2021). Data quality challenges in integrating AI for crisis management. *Journal of Information Systems and Crisis Response, 13*(1), 55–68.

Chen, J., Reitz, J., Richstein, R., Schröder, K. U., & Roßmann, J. (2024). IoT-based SHM using digital twins for interoperable and scalable decentralized smart sensing systems. *Information (Basel), 15*(3), 121. DOI: 10.3390/info15030121

Chen, Q., Cao, J., & Zhu, S. (2023). Data-driven monitoring and predictive maintenance for engineering structures: Technologies, implementation challenges, and future directions. *IEEE Internet of Things Journal, 10*(16), 14527–14551. DOI: 10.1109/JIOT.2023.3272535

Chen, S., Lin, H., & Yang, G. (2022). Efficient agricultural disaster financing using satellite data and artificial intelligence. *Computers & Electrical Engineering, 103*, 108394. DOI: 10.1016/j.compeleceng.2022.108394

Cheshmehzangi, A. (2021). Housing and health evaluation related to general comfort and indoor thermal comfort satisfaction during the COVID-19 lockdown. *Journal of Human Behavior in the Social Environment*, *31*(1-4), 184–209. DOI: 10.1080/10911359.2020.1817225

Chester, M., El Asmar, M., Hayes, S., & Desha, C. (2021). Post-disaster infrastructure delivery for resilience. *Sustainability (Basel)*, *13*(6), 3458. DOI: 10.3390/su13063458

Chingono, T. T., & Mbohwa, C. (2023). Humanitarian Logistics in the Industry 4.0. In *Supply Networks in Developing Countries: Sustainable and Humanitarian Logistics in Growing Consumer Markets* (pp. 99-127). Emerald Publishing Limited.

Chitra, P., Acharjya, K., Ojha, V., Das, P., Faiz, A., & Rao, S. B. (2025, Mar). IOT and Sensor-Based Flood Monitoring and Warning Systems for Disaster Management. In *2025 International Conference on Automation and Computation (AUTOCOM)* (pp. 471-476). IEEE. DOI: 10.1109/AUTOCOM64127.2025.10956605

Choosumrong, S., Piyathamrongchai, K., Hataitara, R., Soteyome, U., Konkong, N., Chalongsuppunyoo, R., ... & Nemoto, T. (2025). Development of an IoT-Based Flood Monitoring System Integrated with GIS for Lowland Agricultural Areas.

Christensen, T., & Ma, L. (2020). Coordination structures and mechanisms for crisis management in China: Challenges of complexity. *Public Organization Review*, *20*(1), 19–36. DOI: 10.1007/s11115-018-0423-9

Christhia, M. L., Timbayo, O. O., Wahidurrijal, A. A., & Putra, A. B. A. (2025). A Literature Review on AI and DSS for Resilient and Sustainable Humanitarian Logistics. *International Journal of Computer Science and Humanitarian AI*, *2*(1), 29–36. DOI: 10.21512/ijcshai.v2i1.13028

Chumachenko, D., & Chumachenko, T. (2022). Ukraine war: The humanitarian crisis in Kharkiv. *BMJ (Clinical Research Ed.)*, •••, 376. DOI: 10.1136/bmj.o796 PMID: 35338030

Cil, A. Y., Abdurahman, D., & Cil, I. (2022). Internet of Things enabled real time cold chain monitoring in a container port. *Journal of Shipping and Trade*, *7*(1), 9. DOI: 10.1186/s41072-022-00110-z

Čižiūnienė, K., Voronavičiūtė, G., Marinkovic, D., & Matijošius, J. (2025). Sustainable Human Resource Management in Emergencies: The Case of the Lithuanian Logistics Sector. *Sustainability (2071-1050), 17*(6).

Clark, A., & Chalmers, D. (1998). The extended mind. analysis, 58(1), 7-19.

Cointrust. (2023). Irish Red Cross launches blockchain-based donations tracker. Retrieved from https://www.cointrust.com

Comfort, L. K. (2007). Crisis management in hindsight: Cognition, communication, coordination, and control. *Public Administration Review*, *67*(s1), 189–197. DOI: 10.1111/j.1540-6210.2007.00827.x

Comfort, L. K., Boin, A., & Demchak, C. C. (Eds.). (2010). *Designing resilience: Preparing for extreme events*. University of Pittsburgh Pre. DOI: 10.2307/j.ctt5hjq0c

Comfort, L. K., Ko, K., & Zagorecki, A. (2004). Coordination in rapidly evolving disaster response systems: The role of information. *The American Behavioral Scientist*, *48*(3), 295–313. DOI: 10.1177/0002764204268987

Conzatti, A., Kershaw, T., Copping, A., & Coley, D. (2022). A review of the impact of shelter design on the health of displaced populations. *Journal of International Humanitarian Action*, *7*(1), 18. DOI: 10.1186/s41018-022-00123-0 PMID: 37519834

Coppi, G., Moreno Jimenez, R., & Kyriazi, S. (2021). Explicability of humanitarian AI: A matter of principles. *Journal of International Humanitarian Action*, *6*(1), 19. DOI: 10.1186/s41018-021-00096-6

Costa, F., Genovesi, S., Borgese, M., Michel, A., Dicandia, F. A., & Manara, G. (2021). A review of RFID sensors, the new frontier of internet of things. *Sensors (Basel)*, *21*(9), 3138. DOI: 10.3390/s21093138 PMID: 33946500

Cutter, S. L. (2018). Compound, cascading, or complex disasters: What's in a name? *Environment*, *60*(6), 16–25. DOI: 10.1080/00139157.2018.1517518

Dadhich, M., Opoku-Mensah, E., Kant Hiran, K., Akwasi Gyamfi, B., Tuffour, P., & Mahmoud, A. (2024). Exploring the mediating roles of social networks and trust in the blockchain-social sustainability nexus. *Journal of Economic Policy Reform*, *27*(3), 293–315. DOI: 10.1080/17487870.2024.2364649

Dall, K., & Schneider, S. (2023). Anticipatory humanitarian action. In *An Introduction to Humanitarian Action* (pp. 343–362). Routledge.

Danisman, M., & Akkartal, E. (2023). Defining a new business model for sustainable biomass production from forestry residues in Türkiye by using TRIZ. *International Journal of Energy Economics and Policy*, *13*(3), 243–253. DOI: 10.32479/ijeep.13985

Darabkh, K. A., & Al-Akhras, M. (2025). Evolutionary Cost Analysis and Computational Intelligence for Energy Efficiency in Internet of Things-Enabled Smart Cities: Multi-Sensor Data Fusion and Resilience to Link and Device Failures. *Smart Cities*, *8*(2), 64. DOI: 10.3390/smartcities8020064

Das, D., Dasgupta, K., & Biswas, U. (2023). A secure blockchain-enabled vehicle identity management framework for intelligent transportation systems. *Computers & Electrical Engineering*, *105*, 108535. DOI: 10.1016/j.compeleceng.2022.108535

Davenport, T. H., & Ronanki, R. (2018). Artificial intelligence for the real world. *Harvard Business Review*, *96*(1), 108–116.

De Boeck, K., Besiou, M., Decouttere, C., Rafter, S., Vandaele, N., Van Wassenhove, L. N., & Yadav, P. (2023). Data, analytical techniques and collaboration between researchers and practitioners in humanitarian health supply chains: A challenging but necessary way forward. *Journal of Humanitarian Logistics and Supply Chain Management*, *13*(3), 237–248. DOI: 10.1108/JHLSCM-07-2022-0078

Debnath, D., Vanegas, F., Sandino, J., Hawary, A. F., & Gonzalez, F. (2024). A review of UAV path-planning algorithms and obstacle avoidance methods for remote sensing applications. *Remote Sensing (Basel)*, *16*(21), 4019. DOI: 10.3390/rs16214019

del Carpio, X., Cuesta, J. A., Kugler, M. D., Hernández, G., & Piraquive, G. (2022). What effects could global value chain and digital infrastructure development policies have on poverty and inequality after COVID-19? *Journal of Risk and Financial Management*, *15*(2), 43. DOI: 10.3390/jrfm15020043

Dennehy, D., Oredo, J., Spanaki, K., Despoudi, S., & Fitzgibbon, M. (2021). Supply chain resilience in mindful humanitarian aid organizations: The role of big data analytics. *International Journal of Operations & Production Management*, *41*(9), 1417–1441. DOI: 10.1108/IJOPM-12-2020-0871

Devitt, S. K., Scholz, J., Schless, T., & Lewis, L. (2023). Developing a trusted human-AI network for humanitarian benefit. *Digital War*, *4*(1), 1–17. DOI: 10.1057/s42984-023-00063-y

Dhakal, S., & Karunakaran, K. (2023). Design and Implementation of Drone Technology for Medical Supplement Delivery Services in Rural Regions. *Int. Res. J. Eng. Technol*, *10*, 545–550.

Dijk, S. W., Krijkamp, E., Kunst, N., Labrecque, J. A., Gross, C. P., Pandit, A., Lu, C.-P., Visser, L. E., Wong, J. B., & Hunink, M. M. (2024). Making Drug Approval Decisions in the Face of Uncertainty: Cumulative Evidence versus Value of Information. *Medical Decision Making*, *44*(5), 512–528. DOI: 10.1177/0272989X241255047 PMID: 38828516

Dindarik, N., & Atabey, A. (2024). Future of Earthquake-Based Disaster Logistics and Futuristic Approaches. *Journal of Social Sciences And Education*, *7*(2), 257–278. DOI: 10.53047/josse.1536068

Ding, Y., Herbaut, N., & Negru, D. (2024, June). A Conceptual Model for Blockchain-Based Trust in Digital Ecosystems (Short Paper). In *International Conference on Advanced Information Systems Engineering* (pp. 18-24). Cham: Springer Nature Switzerland. DOI: 10.1007/978-3-031-61003-5_2

Dockendorff, M., & Zaccarelli, F. G. (2025). Successfully preparing future mathematics teachers for digital technology integration: A literature review. *International Journal of Mathematical Education in Science and Technology, 56*(5), 948–979. DOI: 10.1080/0020739X.2024.2309273

Doody, C. B., Robertson, L., Cox, K. M., Bogue, J., Egan, J., & Sarma, K. M. (2021). Pre-deployment programmes for building resilience in military and frontline emergency service personnel. *Cochrane Database of Systematic Reviews*, 12. PMID: 34870330

Dorn, A. W., & Cross, R. W. (2016). Flying Humanitarians: The UN Humanitarian Air Service. In *Air Power in UN Operations* (pp. 101-116). Routledge.

Dorn, W., Baird, N., & Owen, R. (2018). Airships in un humanitarian and peace operations: Ready for service? *Journal of Aviation/Aerospace Education Research, 27*(2), 41–58.

Doshi-Velez, F., & Kim, B. (2017). Towards a rigorous science of interpretable machine learning. *arXiv preprint arXiv:1702.08608.*

Dube, E., Wedawatta, G., & Ginige, K. (2021). Building-back-better in post-disaster recovery: Lessons learnt from Cyclone Idai-induced floods in Zimbabwe. *International Journal of Disaster Risk Science, 12*(5), 700–712. DOI: 10.1007/s13753-021-00373-3

Dubey, S., Dahiya, M., & Jain, S. (2018, Feb). Application of distributed data center in logistics as cloud collaboration for handling disaster relief. In *2018 3rd International Conference On Internet of Things: Smart Innovation and Usages (IoT-SIU)* (pp. 1-11). IEEE. DOI: 10.1109/IoT-SIU.2018.8519865

Dubey, R., Bryde, D. J., Dwivedi, Y. K., Graham, G., & Foropon, C. (2022). Impact of artificial intelligence-driven big data analytics culture on agility and resilience in humanitarian supply chain: A practice-based view. *International Journal of Production Economics, 250*, 108618. DOI: 10.1016/j.ijpe.2022.108618

Dubey, R., Luo, Z., Gunasekaran, A., Akter, S., Hazen, B. T., & Douglas, M. A. (2018). Big data and predictive analytics in humanitarian supply chains: Enabling visibility and coordination in the presence of swift trust. *International Journal of Logistics Management, 29*(2), 485–512. DOI: 10.1108/IJLM-02-2017-0039

Dugbartey, A. N. (2025). Systemic financial risks in an era of geopolitical tensions, climate change, and technological disruptions: Predictive analytics, stress testing and crisis response strategies. *International Journal of Science and Research Archive, 14*(02), 1428–1448. DOI: 10.30574/ijsra.2025.14.2.0563

Durak, M. S., & Sengur, F. (2024). Managing Uncertainty in the Airline Industry: The Interaction of Strategic Flexibility, Organizational Learning, and Dynamic Capabilities. *International Journal of Aviation, Aeronautics, and Aerospace, 11*(3), 8. DOI: 10.58940/2374-6793.1931

DVIDS. (2023). U.S. Air Force supports humanitarian aid flights at Incirlik. Retrieved from https://www.dvidshub.net

Efe, A. (2022). A review on risk reduction potentials of artificial intelligence in humanitarian aid sector. *Journal of the Humanities and Social Sciences, 5*(2), 184–205. DOI: 10.53048/johass.1189814

Eichholtz, P., Kok, N., & Sun, X. (2024). The effect of post-COVID-19 ventilation measures on indoor air quality in primary schools. *PNAS Nexus, 3*(1), pgad429. DOI: 10.1093/pnasnexus/pgad429 PMID: 38145248

Endsley, M. R. (2017). From here to autonomy: Lessons learned from human–automation research. *Human Factors, 59*(1), 5–27. DOI: 10.1177/0018720816681350 PMID: 28146676

Eren, A. M., Peeters, W., & Farrow, J. (2007, Jun). The use of space technologies to monitor and respond to earthquakes economic perspective. In *2007 3rd International Conference on Recent Advances in Space Technologies* (pp. 24-28). IEEE. DOI: 10.1109/RAST.2007.4283985

Erhueh, O. V., Elete, T., Akano, O. A., Nwakile, C., & Hanson, E. (2024). Application of Internet of Things (IoT) in energy infrastructure: Lessons for the future of operations and maintenance. *Comprehensive Research and Reviews in Science and Technology, 2*(2), 28–54. DOI: 10.57219/crrst.2024.2.2.0036

Eskandaripour, H., & Boldsaikhan, E. (2023). Last-mile drone delivery: Past, present, and future. *Drones (Basel), 7*(2), 77. DOI: 10.3390/drones7020077

Estêvão, J. M. (2024). Effectiveness of generative ai for post-earthquake damage assessment. *Buildings (Basel, Switzerland), 14*(10), 3255. DOI: 10.3390/buildings14103255

Etihad Airways. (n.d.-a). *Sourcing & procurement – SAP Ariba integration*. Retrieved from https://www.etihad.com/en/about-us/supply-chain

Eubanks, V. (2018). *Automating inequality: How high-tech tools profile, police, and punish the poor*. St. Martin's Press.

European Commission. (2021). *Proposal for a regulation laying down harmonised rules on artificial intelligence (Artificial Intelligence Act)*. Retrieved from: https://eur-lex.europa.eu/legal-content/EN/TXT/?uri=CELEX:52021PC0206

Ezzati, S. M., Alizadeh, R., & Jokar, M. R. A. (2024). Efficiency and Transparency in Supplier Performance Evaluation: A Blockchain-Powered Smart Contract Solution. *IEEE Access : Practical Innovations, Open Solutions*.

Fahrni, M. L., Ismail, I. A. N., Refi, D. M., Almeman, A., Yaakob, N. C., Saman, K. M., Mansor, N. F., Noordin, N., & Babar, Z. U. D. (2022). Management of COVID-19 vaccines cold chain logistics: A scoping review. *Journal of Pharmaceutical Policy and Practice*, *15*(1), 16. DOI: 10.1186/s40545-022-00411-5 PMID: 35236393

Fakhraian, E., Semanjski, I., Semanjski, S., & Aghezzaf, E. H. (2023). Towards safe and efficient unmanned aircraft system operations: Literature review of digital twins' applications and european union regulatory compliance. *Drones (Basel)*, *7*(7), 478. DOI: 10.3390/drones7070478

Fan, C., Zhang, C., Yahja, A., & Mostafavi, A. (2021). Disaster City Digital Twin: A vision for integrating artificial and human intelligence for disaster management. *International Journal of Information Management*, *56*, 102049. DOI: 10.1016/j.ijinfomgt.2019.102049

Farjana, M., Fahad, A. B., Alam, S. E., & Islam, M. M. (2023). An IoT-and cloud-based e-waste management system for resource reclamation with a data-driven decision-making process. *IoT*, *4*(3), 202–220. DOI: 10.3390/iot4030011

Ferman, P. M. F., Gonçalves, R. A. C., & Oliveira, A. J. B. D. (2024). Cold chain logistics: the pathways of vaccines and thermolabile medicines to patients in municipal primary care. *Acta sci., Health sci*, 65451-65451.

Feroz, S., & Abu Dabous, S. (2021). Uav-based remote sensing applications for bridge condition assessment. *Remote Sensing (Basel)*, *13*(9), 1809. DOI: 10.3390/rs13091809

Ferreira, N. C., & Ferreira, J. J. (2025). The field of resource-based view research: Mapping past, present and future trends. *Management Decision*, *63*(4), 1124–1153. DOI: 10.1108/MD-10-2023-1908

Fleischmann, M., Ramachandran, G., Koleilat, T., & Jurdak, R. (2024). Cyber-Social Consensus: Proposing a Human-in-the-Loop Algorithm for Automated Decision-Making in Multi-Stakeholder Settings. In *Proceedings of the 35th Australasian Conference on Information Systems (ACIS 2024)*. Association for Information Systems (AIS).

Flores-Larsen, S., & Filippin, C. (2021). Energy efficiency, thermal resilience, and health during extreme heat events in low-income housing in Argentina. *Energy and Building, 231*, 110576. DOI: 10.1016/j.enbuild.2020.110576

Floridi, L., Cowls, J., Beltrametti, M., Chatila, R., Chazerand, P., Dignum, V., Luetge, C., Madelin, R., Pagallo, U., Rossi, F., Schafer, B., Valcke, P., & Vayena, E. (2018). AI4People—an ethical framework for a good AI society: Opportunities, risks, principles, and recommendations. *Minds and Machines, 28*(4), 689–707. DOI: 10.1007/s11023-018-9482-5 PMID: 30930541

Friday, S. C., Lawal, C. I., Ayodeji, D. C., & Sobowale, A. (2023). Systematic review of blockchain applications in public financial management and international aid accountability. *International Journal of Multidisciplinary Research and Growth Evaluation, 4*(1), 1165–1180. DOI: 10.54660/.IJMRGE.2023.4.1.1165-1180

Frontier Technologies Hub. (2024). *GeoSeals pilot: Improving supply visibility for nutrition programmes in Ethiopia*. Retrieved from https://frontiertechhub.org/geoseals-ethiopia-supply-visibility/

Fu, Y., & Zhu, J. (2021). Trusted data infrastructure for smart cities: A blockchain perspective. *Building Research and Information, 49*(1), 21–37. DOI: 10.1080/09613218.2020.1784703

Gao, J., Zhang, Y., Wu, Z., & Yu, L. N. (2025). Optimized collaborative scheduling of unmanned aerial vehicles for emergency material distribution in flood disaster management. *Mechatron. Intell Transp. Syst, 4*(1), 1–15. DOI: 10.56578/mits040101

Garg, V., Niranjan, S., Prybutok, V., Pohlen, T., & Gligor, D. (2023). Drones in last-mile delivery: A systematic review on Efficiency, Accessibility, and Sustainability. *Transportation Research Part D, Transport and Environment, 123*, 103831. DOI: 10.1016/j.trd.2023.103831

Garrido, R. A., & Aguirre, I. (2020). Emergency logistics for disaster management under spatio-temporal demand correlation: The earthquakes case. *Journal of Industrial and Management Optimization, 16*(5), 2369–2387. DOI: 10.3934/jimo.2019058

Gevaert, C. M., Carman, M., Rosman, B., Georgiadou, Y., & Soden, R. (2021). Fairness and accountability of AI in disaster risk management: Opportunities and challenges. *Patterns (New York, N.Y.)*, *2*(11), 100363. DOI: 10.1016/j.patter.2021.100363 PMID: 34820647

Ghadirinejad, N., Ottermo, F., Nowzari, R., Alsaadi, N., & Ghadiri Nejad, M. (2023). Optimizing a green and sustainable off-grid energy-system design: A real case. *Sustainability (Basel)*, *15*(17), 12800. DOI: 10.3390/su151712800

Ghaffar, M. A., Peng, L., Aslam, M. U., Adeel, M., & Dassari, S. (2024). Vehicle-UAV Integrated Routing Optimization Problem for Emergency Delivery of Medical Supplies. *Electronics (Basel)*, *13*(18), 3650. DOI: 10.3390/electronics13183650

Ghelani, D., Hua, T. K., & Koduru, S. K. R. (2022). Cyber security threats, vulnerabilities, and security solutions models in banking. *Authorea Preprints*. DOI: 10.22541/au.166385206.63311335/v1

Göçmen, E., & Kuvvetli, Y. (2020). Humanitarian Logistics Management After A Disaster: An Earthquake Case. *Dicle Üniversitesi Mühendislik Fakültesi Mühendislik Dergisi*, *11*(2), 679–688.

Goel, A., Masurkar, S., & Pathade, G. R. (2024). An overview of digital transformation and environmental sustainability: Threats, opportunities, and solutions. *Sustainability (Basel)*, *16*(24), 11079. DOI: 10.3390/su162411079

Grange, R., Heaslip, G., & McMullan, C. (2020). Coordination to choreography: The evolution of humanitarian supply chains. *Journal of Humanitarian Logistics and Supply Chain Management*, *10*(1), 21–44. DOI: 10.1108/JHLSCM-12-2018-0077

Gudala, L., Reddy, A. K., Sadhu, A. K. R., & Venkataramanan, S. (2022). Leveraging biometric authentication and blockchain technology for enhanced security in identity and access management systems. *Journal of Artificial Intelligence Research*, *2*(2), 21–50.

Guha, S., Jana, R. K., & Sanyal, M. K. (2022). Artificial neural network approaches for disaster management: A literature review. *International Journal of Disaster Risk Reduction*, *81*, 103276. DOI: 10.1016/j.ijdrr.2022.103276

Gupta, R., Bhattacharya, P., Tanwar, S., Kumar, N., & Zeadally, S. (2022). GaRuDa: A blockchain-based delivery scheme using drones for healthcare 5.0 applications. *IEEE Internet of Things Magazine*, *4*(4), 60–66. DOI: 10.1109/IOTM.001.2100045

Gupta, S., Modgil, S., Bhattacharyya, S., & Bose, I. (2022). Artificial intelligence for decision support systems in the field of operations research: Review and future scope of research. *Annals of Operations Research, 308*(1), 215–274. DOI: 10.1007/s10479-020-03856-6

Haber, T. R. T. (2023). *Kızılay'dan Deprem Bölgesine Drone'lu Yardım*. Retrieved from https://www.trthaber.com

Hackathon, M. S. (2023). Leveraging AI for natural disaster management: Takeaways from the Moroccan earthquake. arXiv. https://arxiv.org/abs/2311.08999

Hadjisophocleous, O. N., Syed, T. A., & Lee, H. (2021, June). Blockchain-enabled humanitarian aid: A case study of the World Food Programme. In *PACIS* (p. 213).

Hambagda, B. M., Gupta, S., Srivastav, S., & Khurana, R.Buba M.T. Hambagda. (2024). Humanitarian Food Logistics: An Inventory Model for World Food Program (WFP) Operations in Boko Haram-Controlled Areas. *Communications on Applied Nonlinear Analysis, 31*(6s), 380–387. DOI: 10.52783/cana.v31.1230

Hanna, M. G., Pantanowitz, L., Jackson, B., Palmer, O., Visweswaran, S., Pantanowitz, J., Deebajah, M., & Rashidi, H. H. (2025). Ethical and bias considerations in artificial intelligence/machine learning. *Modern Pathology, 38*(3), 100686. DOI: 10.1016/j.modpat.2024.100686 PMID: 39694331

Hanna, R., Abdulla, A., Xu, Y., & Victor, D. G. (2021). Emergency deployment of direct air capture as a response to the climate crisis. *Nature Communications, 12*(1), 368. DOI: 10.1038/s41467-020-20437-0 PMID: 33446663

Haq, I., & Faizan, R. (2022). Role and Effectiveness of Five-Performance Indicators (Price, Dependability, Speed, Quality & Flexibility) in Attaining Competitive Edge in the Aviation Industry. *International Journal of Applied Business and Management Studies, 7*(2), 11–51.

Hassan, A. F., & Sofia, D. (2025). Augmented Reality and AI in Remote Geospatial Analysis Enhancing Decision-Making in Crisis Management. American Journal of Engineering. *Mechanics and Architecture, 3*(3), 129–144.

Hassan, H., Mishra, A. K., Wemken, N., O'Dea, P., Cowie, H., McIntyre, B., & Coggins, A. M. (2024). Deep energy renovations' impact on indoor air quality and thermal comfort of residential dwellings in Ireland–ARDEN project. *Building and Environment, 259*, 111637. DOI: 10.1016/j.buildenv.2024.111637

Hayat, P. (2023). Integration of advanced technologies in urban waste management. In *Advancements in Urban environmental studies: Application of geospatial technology and artificial intelligence in Urban studies* (pp. 397–418). Springer International Publishing. DOI: 10.1007/978-3-031-21587-2_23

He, C., Singh, P., P'yavka, S., Wolfe, L., Caldwell, K., Islam, T. M., . . . Mustafa, A. (2024). Balancing Trade-Offs: The Energy Efficiency of Unmanned Aircraft Systems Integration in Last-Mile Delivery and Operational Policy Restrictions. In *AIAA AVIATION FORUM AND ASCEND 2024* (p. 3646).

Hejji, D., Talib, M. A., Nassif, A. B., Nasir, Q., & Bouridane, A. (2021, November). AI-based models for resource allocation and resource demand forecasting systems in aviation: A survey and analytical study. In *2021 IEEE International Conference on Internet of Things and Intelligence Systems (IoTaIS)* (pp. 183-189). IEEE. DOI: 10.1109/IoTaIS53735.2021.9628555

Heo, G., & Doh, I. (2024). Blockchain and differential privacy-based data processing system for data security and privacy in urban computing. *Computer Communications*, *222*, 161–176. DOI: 10.1016/j.comcom.2024.04.027

Hernández-Leandro, N. A., Ibarra-Rojas, O., & Camacho-Vallejo, J. F. (2022). A bi-objective humanitarian logistics model considering equity in the affected zones: Application to a recent earthquake in Mexico. *Operations Research*, *56*(3), 1737–1762. DOI: 10.1051/ro/2022067

Heymann, D. L., & Rodier, G. (2004). SARS: lessons from a new disease. *Learning from SARS: Preparing for the next disease outbreak*, 234-245.

Hobeika, A. G., Ardekanı, S. A., & Han, D. L. (1988). Logistics decisions following urban disasters. *Computer-Aided Civil and Infrastructure Engineering*, *3*(1), 13–27. DOI: 10.1111/j.1467-8667.1988.tb00153.x

Hoffmann, T., & Prause, G. (2018). On the regulatory framework for last-mile delivery robots. *Machines (Basel)*, *6*(3), 33. DOI: 10.3390/machines6030033

Hove-Sibanda, P., Awino, Z. B., & Agyemang, E. (2025). Sustainable Food Supply Chains and Agricultural Logistics in Africa. In *Eco-Logistics and Sustainable Supply Chain Innovations* (pp. 267–320). IGI Global Scientific Publishing.

Hu, B., Wang, L., Chen, S., Cui, J., & Chen, L. (2021). An uplink throughput optimization scheme for UAV-enabled urban emergency communications. *IEEE Internet of Things Journal*, *9*(6), 4291–4302. DOI: 10.1109/JIOT.2021.3103892

Hunt, K., Narayanan, A., & Zhuang, J. (2022). Blockchain in humanitarian operations management: A review of research and practice. *Socio-Economic Planning Sciences*, *80*, 101175. DOI: 10.1016/j.seps.2021.101175

Hürriyet Daily News. (2023a). Türkiye delivers tents, stoves, blankets to quake zone. *Hürriyet Daily News*. https://www.hurriyetdailynews.com

Hürriyet Daily News. (2023b). Tent cities rise in Adıyaman stadiums for earthquake survivors. *Hürriyet Daily News*. https://www.hurriyetdailynews.com

Hürriyet Daily News. (2023c). Barrel stove fabrication by schools supports heating efforts. *Hürriyet Daily News*. https://www.hurriyetdailynews.com

Hürriyet Daily News. (2023d). Mobile hygiene units serve displaced families. *Hürriyet Daily News*. https://www.hurriyetdailynews.com

Husnain, M., Hayat, K., Cambiaso, E., Fayyaz, U. U., Mongelli, M., Akram, H., Ghazanfar Abbas, S., & Shah, G. A. (2022). Preventing MQTT vulnerabilities using IoT-enabled intrusion detection system. *Sensors (Basel)*, *22*(2), 567. DOI: 10.3390/s22020567 PMID: 35062536

Hu, X., Huang, P., Lv, Y., & Liu, M. (2023). Disaster education: Empowering resilience and mitigating PTSD in disaster-prone areas of China. *Environmental Research Communications*, *5*(10), 105018. DOI: 10.1088/2515-7620/ad04f7

I6.io. (n.d.). *i6: Digital fuel management solutions*. Retrieved from https://i6.io/

IFRC. (2021). *Shelter and non-food item distribution in Türkiye: A 10-year perspective*. https://www.ifrc.org

IFRC. (2022). *How data dashboards and drones are helping the Red Cross improve logistics*. Retrieved from https://www.ifrc.org/article/how-data-dashboards-and-drones-are-helping-red-cross-improve-logistics

IFRC. (2023). Türkiye: Earthquake Emergency Response. *International Federation of Red Cross and Red Crescent Societies*. https://www.ifrc.org

IFRC. (2023). Türkiye: Earthquakes 2023 – International Appeal Operations Update. Retrieved from https://adore.ifrc.org

Igwenagu, U. T. I., Debnath, R., Ahmed, A. A., & Alam, M. J. B. (2025). An Integrated Approach for Earth Infrastructure Monitoring Using UAV and ERI: A Systematic Review. *Drones (Basel)*, *9*(3), 225. DOI: 10.3390/drones9030225

Ikumapayi, O. M., Laseinde, O. T., Elewa, R. R., Ogedengbe, T. S., & Akinlabi, E. T. (2024). Smart Sensors for Real-time Monitoring in a Sustainable Logistics. In *E3S Web of Conferences* (Vol. 552, p. 01079). EDP Sciences.

Imran, M., Castillo, C., Lucas, J., Meier, P., & Vieweg, S. (2014, April). AIDR: Artificial intelligence for disaster response. In *Proceedings of the 23rd international conference on world wide web* (pp. 159-162).

Innovation, W. F. P. (2024). *AI in action: SCOUT pilot results for supply chain optimization*. Retrieved from https://innovation.wfp.org/news/scout-ai-supply-chain -optimization-2024

Intelsat. (2024). Expanding rapid response connectivity capabilities ahead of the 2025 hurricane season. https://www.intelsat.com/resources/blog

International Committee of the Red Cross (ICRC). (2022). *ICRC Bogotá delegation integrates solar energy into operations*. Retrieved from https://www.icrc.org/en/document/icrc-bogota-solar-energy

International Federation of Red Cross and Red Crescent Societies (IFRC). (2017). *Community engagement during Ebola response in West Africa*. Retrieved from https://communityengagementhub.org/resources/2017/10/10/ebola-case-study-liberia

IOM. (2022). *The health-environment nexus in protracted displacement settings: Türkiye case study*. International Organization for Migration. https://www.iom.int

Ishrat, M., Khan, W., & Faisal, S. M. (2025). AI and risk forecasting: leveraging AI for environmental, social, and governance compliance. In *Artificial Intelligence for Financial Risk Management and Analysis* (pp. 307–334). IGI Global Scientific Publishing. DOI: 10.4018/979-8-3373-1200-2.ch015

Jagirdar, R., & Pathak, C. (2025). AI-Driven Transportation Solutions: Lessons From Developed Nations For Emergıng Economies. *Journal of Public Transportation*, *4*(1).

Jahankhani, H., Kendzierskyj, S., & Colin, A. (2021). Blockchain as a tool for transparency and governance in the delivery of development aid. In *Strategy, Leadership, and AI in the Cyber Ecosystem* (pp. 93-111). Academic Press. DOI: 10.1016/B978-0-12-821442-8.00006-9

Jain, S., Meena, M. L., Kumar, V., & Detwal, P. K. (2022, November). Route Optimization as an Aspect of Humanitarian Logistics: Delineating Existing Literature from 2011 to 2022. In *Conference of Innovative Product Design and Intelligent Manufacturing System* (pp. 647–661). Springer Nature Singapore.

Jeble, S., Kumari, S., Venkatesh, V. G., & Singh, M. (2020). Influence of big data and predictive analytics and social capital on performance of humanitarian supply chain: Developing framework and future research directions. *Benchmarking*, *27*(2), 606–633. DOI: 10.1108/BIJ-03-2019-0102

Jiang, F., Xie, H., Gandla, S. R., & Fei, S. (2025). Transforming Hospital HVAC Design with BIM and Digital Twins: Addressing Real-Time Use Changes. *Sustainability (Basel)*, *17*(8), 3312. DOI: 10.3390/su17083312

Jilani, A., Ali, Y., & Khan, M. W. (2018). Greening of humanitarian supply chain with focus on logistics. *International Journal of Business Performance and Supply Chain Modelling*, *10*(1), 49–66. DOI: 10.1504/IJBPSCM.2018.093319

Jin, Z., Ng, K. K., Zhang, C., Chan, Y. Y., & Qin, Y. (2025). A multistage stochastic programming approach for drone-supported last-mile humanitarian logistics system planning. *Advanced Engineering Informatics*, *65*, 103201. DOI: 10.1016/j.aei.2025.103201

Johnson, A. M., Cunningham, C. J., Arnold, E., Rosamond, W. D., & Zègre-Hemsey, J. K. (2021). Impact of using drones in emergency medicine: What does the future hold? *Open Access Emergency Medicine : OAEM*, *13*, 487–498. DOI: 10.2147/OAEM.S247020 PMID: 34815722

Juaristi, M., Gómez-Acebo, T., & Monge-Barrio, A. (2018). Qualitative analysis of promising materials and technologies for the design and evaluation of Climate Adaptive Opaque Façades. *Building and Environment*, *144*, 482–501. DOI: 10.1016/j.buildenv.2018.08.028

Kalogiannidis, S., Kalfas, D., Kontsas, S., Papaevangelou, O., & Chatzitheodoridis, F. (2025). Evaluating the Effectiveness of Early Warning Systems in Reducing Loss of Life in Natural Disasters: A case study of Greece. *Journal of Risk Analysis and Crisis Response*, *15*(1), 33–33. DOI: 10.54560/jracr.v15i1.547

Kanmaz, U., & Kütahya, C. K. (2025). Prioritizing Risk Mitigation Strategies in Air Cargo Freight Operations: A Fuzzy TOPSIS Approach. *Journal of Aviation*, *9*(1), 181–195. DOI: 10.30518/jav.1599331

Kanu, M. O., Ogu, E., Egbumokei, P. I., Digitemie, W. N., & Dienagha, I. N. (2025). Enhancing Asset Management in Gas Distribution Predictive Maintenance and Data-Driven Decision Making.

Kapucu, N. (2008). Collaborative emergency management: Better community organising, better public preparedness and response. *Disasters*, *32*(2), 239–262. DOI: 10.1111/j.1467-7717.2008.01037.x PMID: 18380853

Kapucu, N., & Hu, Q. (2022). An old puzzle and unprecedented challenges: Coordination in response to the COVID-19 pandemic in the US. *Public Performance & Management Review*, *45*(4), 773–798. DOI: 10.1080/15309576.2022.2040039

Karl, A. A., & Scholz Karl, J. (2022). Human rights for refugees: Enhancing sustainable humanitarian supply chain to guarantee a health environment in refugee settlements. *Journal of Humanitarian Logistics and Supply Chain Management*, *12*(3), 382–403. DOI: 10.1108/JHLSCM-11-2020-0104

Karuppiah, K., Sankaranarayanan, B., Ali, S. M., & Paul, S. K. (2021). Key challenges to sustainable humanitarian supply chains: Lessons from the COVID-19 pandemic. *Sustainability (Basel)*, *13*(11), 5850. DOI: 10.3390/su13115850

Kashav, V., & Garg, C. P. (2024). Fortifying humanitarian supply chains: evaluating sustainability enablers for strengthened resilience of humanitarian supply chains during calamities and pandemics. *Journal of Humanitarian Logistics and Supply Chain Management.*

Kaushik, K., Khan, A., Kumari, A., Sharma, I., & Dubey, R. (2024). Ethical considerations in AI-based cybersecurity. In *Next-generation cybersecurity: AI, ML, and Blockchain* (pp. 437–470). Springer Nature Singapore. DOI: 10.1007/978-981-97-1249-6_19

Keisler, J. M., & Brodfuehrer, M. (2009). An application of value-of-information to decision process reengineering. *The Engineering Economist*, *54*(3), 197–221. DOI: 10.1080/00137910903108286

Khademi Zareh, H., Rezaei, H., Bashiri, M., & Fakhrzad, M. B. (2018). A humanitarian reconfiguration and rehabilitation model for preparedness and response to earthquakes using a scheduled reopening of links. *Journal of Industrial and Systems Engineering*, *11*(4), 96–115.

Khairuddin, M. M., & Rahman, N. A. A. (2025). Empowering Humanitarian Efforts: IoT-Enabled Solutions for Distribution Center. In *Supply Chain in Humanitarian Operations: Managing Disruption Through Intervention and Innovation* (pp. 77–84). Springer Nature Singapore. DOI: 10.1007/978-981-96-4426-1_7

Khalid, R., Shah, Z., Naeem, M., Ali, A., Al-Fuqaha, A., & Ejaz, W. (2023). Computational efficiency maximization for UAV-assisted MEC networks with energy harvesting in disaster scenarios. *IEEE Internet of Things Journal*, *11*(5), 9004–9018. DOI: 10.1109/JIOT.2023.3322001

Khan, A., Zhang, J., Ahmad, S., Memon, S., Qureshi, H. A., & Ishfaq, M. (2022). Dynamic positioning and energy-efficient path planning for disaster scenarios in 5G-assisted multi-UAV environments. *Electronics (Basel), 11*(14), 2197. DOI: 10.3390/electronics11142197

Khan, M., Imtiaz, S., Parvaiz, G. S., Hussain, A., & Bae, J. (2021). Integration of internet-of-things with blockchain technology to enhance humanitarian logistics performance. *IEEE Access : Practical Innovations, Open Solutions, 9*, 25422–25436. DOI: 10.1109/ACCESS.2021.3054771

Khan, M., Khan, M., Ali, A., Khan, M. I., Ullah, I., & Iqbal, M. (2022). Digitalization for fast, fair, and safe humanitarian logistics. *Logistics (Basel), 6*(2), 31. DOI: 10.3390/logistics6020031

Khan, M., Parvaiz, G. S., Ali, A., Jehangir, M., Hassan, N., & Bae, J. (2022). A model for understanding the mediating association of transparency between emerging technologies and humanitarian logistics sustainability. *Sustainability (Basel), 14*(11), 6917. DOI: 10.3390/su14116917

Khan, S. I., Qadir, Z., Munawar, H. S., Nayak, S. R., Budati, A. K., Verma, K. D., & Prakash, D. (2021). UAVs path planning architecture for effective medical emergency response in future networks. *Physical Communication, 47*, 101337. DOI: 10.1016/j.phycom.2021.101337

Khan, S. M., Shafi, I., Butt, W. H., Diez, I. D. L. T., Flores, M. A. L., Galán, J. C., & Ashraf, I. (2023). A systematic review of disaster management systems: Approaches, challenges, and future directions. *Land (Basel), 12*(8), 1514. DOI: 10.3390/land12081514

Khan, Y., Su'ud, M. B. M., Alam, M. M., Ahmad, S. F., Ahmad, A. Y. B., & Khan, N. (2022). Application of internet of things (IoT) in sustainable supply chain management. *Sustainability, 15*(1), 694. DOI: 10.3390/su15010694

Khaund, B. (2025). Decentralized Identity Using Blockchain: Enhancing Security and Privacy in Digital Identity Management. *Journal of Computer Science and Technology Studies, 7*(6), 858–866.

Khoche, S., Chandrasekhar, K. V., Sasirekha, G. V. K., Bapat, J., & Das, D. (2021). Occupancy detection for emergency management of smart building based on indoor localization: A feasibility study. *SN Computer Science, 2*(6), 419. DOI: 10.1007/s42979-021-00812-4

Kivits, R., & Sawang, S. (2021). *The dynamism of stakeholder engagement: A case study of the aviation industry*. Springer Nature. DOI: 10.1007/978-3-030-70428-5

Kızılay. (2023). About Us. Retrieved from https://www.kizilay.org.tr

Klein, G. (2008). Naturalistic decision making. *Human Factors, 50*(3), 456–460. DOI: 10.1518/001872008X288385 PMID: 18689053

Klein, G. A. (2017). *Sources of power: How people make decisions*. MIT press.

Koh, L. Y., & Yuen, K. F. (2022). Emerging competencies for logistics professionals in the digital era: A literature review. *Frontiers in Psychology, 13*, 965748. DOI: 10.3389/fpsyg.2022.965748 PMID: 36389597

Kolhatkar, D., Jain, O., Patil, S., Shelke, P., Mirajkar, R., & Wawage, P. (2023, May). Blockchain applications in disaster management systems. In *2023 4th International Conference for Emerging Technology (INCET)* (pp. 1-7). IEEE. DOI: 10.1109/INCET57972.2023.10170452

Kondraganti, A., Narayanamurthy, G., & Sharifi, H. (2024). A systematic literature review on the use of big data analytics in humanitarian and disaster operations. *Annals of Operations Research, 335*(3), 1015–1052. DOI: 10.1007/s10479-022-04904-z PMID: 36846245

Konert, A., Smereka, J., & Szarpak, L. (2019). The use of drones in emergency medicine: Practical and legal aspects. *Emergency Medicine International, 2019*(1), 3589792. DOI: 10.1155/2019/3589792 PMID: 31871790

Kong, F. (2024). Post-Disaster Governance in Southeast Asia: Response, Recovery, and Resilient Societies. *Singapore Journal of Tropical Geography, 45*(1).

KOSGEB. (2023). Emergency SME support for HVAC production. *Small and Medium Enterprises Development Organization of Türkiye*. https://www.kosgeb.gov.tr

Krichen, M., Abdalzaher, M. S., Elwekeil, M., & Fouda, M. M. (2024). Managing natural disasters: An analysis of technological advancements, opportunities, and challenges. *Internet of Things and Cyber-Physical Systems, 4*, 99–109. DOI: 10.1016/j.iotcps.2023.09.002

Kristiansen, A. B., Zhao, B. Y., Ma, T., & Wang, R. Z. (2021). The viability of solar photovoltaic powered off-grid Zero Energy Buildings based on a container home. *Journal of Cleaner Production, 286*, 125312. DOI: 10.1016/j.jclepro.2020.125312

Küçük B., Yardımcı Coşkun İ. (2025). Afet Lojistiği'nde Araç Rotalama Probleminin Optimizasyonu: İstanbul İli Anadolu Yakası Örneği. Maltepe Üniversitesi Akademik Bakış Dergisi, 1 (1).

Kuhlmann, S., & Franzke, J. (2022). Multi-level responses to COVID-19: Crisis coordination in Germany from an intergovernmental perspective. *Local Government Studies*, *48*(2), 312–334. DOI: 10.1080/03003930.2021.1904398

Kumar, G., Tanvir, O., Kumar, A., & Goswami, M. (2024). Optimal drone deployment for cost-effective and sustainable last-mile delivery operations. *International Transactions in Operational Research.*

Kumari, U., & Malhotra, P. (2024). Use of digital twin in predicting the life of aircraft main bearing. *Simulation Techniques of Digital Twin in Real-Time Applications: Design Modeling and Implementation*, 261-288.

Kumari, S., Agarwal, S., Agrawal, N. K., Agarwal, A., & Garg, M. C. (2025). A Comprehensive Review of Remote Sensing Technologies for Improved Geological Disaster Management. *Geological Journal*, *60*(1), 223–235. DOI: 10.1002/gj.5072

Kumar, M. (2022). Optimized application of artificial intelligence (AI) in aviation market. *International Journal of Recent Research Aspects*, *9*(4).

Kumar, P., & Singh, R. K. (2022). Application of Industry 4.0 technologies for effective coordination in humanitarian supply chains: A strategic approach. *Annals of Operations Research*, *319*(1), 379–411. DOI: 10.1007/s10479-020-03898-w PMID: 33531729

Kumar, V., Goodarzian, F., Ghasemi, P., Chan, F. T., & Gupta, N. (2025). Artificial intelligence applications in healthcare supply chain networks under disaster conditions. *International Journal of Production Research*, *63*(2), 395–403. DOI: 10.1080/00207543.2024.2444150

Kurniawan, D. A. (2025). Enhancing Humanitarian Logistics Through Digital Innovation and Systemic Reform: A Narrative Review in Developing Countries. *Sinergi International Journal of Logistics*, *3*(1), 1–14. DOI: 10.61194/sijl.v3i1.735

Lal, A., Ashworth, H. C., Dada, S., Hoemeke, L., & Tambo, E. (2022). Optimizing pandemic preparedness and response through health information systems: Lessons learned from Ebola to COVID-19. *Disaster Medicine and Public Health Preparedness*, *16*(1), 333–340. DOI: 10.1017/dmp.2020.361 PMID: 33004102

Landmann, T., & Ślusarczyk, S. (2024). The effects of the activities of The United Nations Humanitarian Air Service (UNHAS) in humanitarian logistics in 2019-2022 Efekty działań The United Nations Humanitarian Air Service (UNHAS) w logistyce humanitarnej w latach 2019-2022.

Landmann, T., & Ślusarczyk, S. (2022). The World Food Program in the Global Logistics Cluster. *Systemy Logistyczne Wojsk*, *57*(2), 173–189. DOI: 10.37055/slw/163235

Lan, P. (2000). The technology-component matrix: A tool for analysing and managing knowledge. *International Journal of Technology Management*, *20*(5-8), 670–683. DOI: 10.1504/IJTM.2000.002887

Larson, P. D. (2021). Security, sustainability and supply chain collaboration in the humanitarian space. *Journal of Humanitarian Logistics and Supply Chain Management*, *11*(4), 609–622. DOI: 10.1108/JHLSCM-06-2021-0059

Lawrence, J., & Durana, P. (2021). Artificial Intelligence-driven Big Data Analytics, Predictive Maintenance Systems, and Internet of Thingsbased Real-Time Production Logistics in Sustainable Industry 4.0 Wireless Networks. *Journal of Self-Governance & Management Economics*, *9*(4).

Lechtenberg, S., Widera, A., & Hellingrath, B. (2017, Dec). Research directions on decision support in disaster relief logistics. In *2017 4th International Conference on Information and Communication Technologies for Disaster Management (ICT-DM)* (pp. 1-8). IEEE. DOI: 10.1109/ICT-DM.2017.8275681

Ledger Insights. (2021, March 1). *Gazpromneft Aero completes trial of blockchain smart fueling system*. Retrieved from https://www.ledgerinsights.com/gazpromneft-aero-blockchain-aviation-fuel-s7-airlines/

Lee, D. S., Iacocca, M., & Joshi, Y. K. (2021). Energy usage modeling for heating and cooling of off-grid shelters. *Journal of Building Engineering*, *35*, 102054. DOI: 10.1016/j.jobe.2020.102054

Leiras, A., Gonçalves, P., Chawaguta, B., Brito, I. D., & Yoshizaki, H. T. Y. (2021). Food aid supply and distribution in insecure regions: World food programme operation analysis in Ethiopia. *Production*, *31*, e20210070. DOI: 10.1590/0103-6513.20210070

Leslie, D. (2020). Tackling COVID-19 through responsible AI innovation: Five steps in the right direction. *Harvard Data Science Review*, *10*, 1–78.

Li, C., Zhang, F., Cao, C., Liu, Y., & Qu, T. (2019). Organizational coordination in sustainable humanitarian supply chain: An evolutionary game approach. *Journal of Cleaner Production*, *219*, 291–303. DOI: 10.1016/j.jclepro.2019.01.233

Lid, I., & Petermann, K. A. (2023). *Challenges to environmental sustainability in humanitarian logistics activities* (Master's thesis, Handelshøyskolen BI).

Li, D. C. Y. (2025). The synergistic potential of AI and blockchain for organizations. *AI & Society, 40*(1), 221–222. DOI: 10.1007/s00146-023-01838-3

Li, G., Liu, Z., Zhang, J., Han, H., & Shu, Z. (2024). Bayesian model averaging by combining deep learning models to improve lake water level prediction. *The Science of the Total Environment, 906*, 167718. DOI: 10.1016/j.scitotenv.2023.167718 PMID: 37832688

Linardos, V., Drakaki, M., Tzionas, P., & Karnavas, Y. L. (2022). Machine learning in disaster management: recent developments in methods and applications. *Machine Learning and Knowledge Extraction, 4*(2).

LinkedIn. (2023a). TRC's AI satellite analysis helps map quake damage. Retrieved from https://www.linkedin.com

LinkedIn. (2023b). UNICEF uses AI to improve disaster stock management. Retrieved from https://www.linkedin.com

Liu, Y., Zhou, Z., Yang, Y., & Ma, Y. (2022). Verifying the smart contracts of the port supply chain system based on probabilistic model checking. *Systems, 10*(1), 19. DOI: 10.3390/systems10010019

Liu, Z., Zhao, Y., Guo, C., & Xin, Z. (2024). Research on the impact of digital-real integration on logistics industrial transformation and upgrading under green economy. *Sustainability (Basel), 16*(14), 6173. DOI: 10.3390/su16146173

lo Conte, D. L. (2025). Enhancing decision-making with data-driven insights in critical situations: impact and implications of AI-powered predictive solutions.

Luo, M., Fricke, H., Desart, B., Zapata, S. R., & Schultz, M. (2024). High-fidelity digital twin applied agent-based model for supporting predictable airport ground operations. *Available at SSRN* 4806351. DOI: 10.2139/ssrn.4806351

Maaß, L. (2024). *Multidisciplinary measuring of maturity and readiness in national digital public health systems: The digital public health maturity index* (Doctoral dissertation, Universität Bremen).

Maghsoudi, A., Harpring, R., Piotrowicz, W. D., & Kedziora, D. (2023). Digital technologies for cash and voucher assistance in disasters: A cross-case analysis of benefits and risks. *International Journal of Disaster Risk Reduction, 96*, 103827. DOI: 10.1016/j.ijdrr.2023.103827

Maiti, M., & Kayal, P. (2024). Exploring innovative techniques for damage control during natural disasters. *Journal of Safety Science and Resilience = An Quan Ke Xue Yu Ren Xing (Ying Wen), 5*(2), 147–155. DOI: 10.1016/j.jnlssr.2024.02.004

Majchrzak, D., Michalski, K., & Reginia-Zacharski, J. (2021). Readiness of the polish crisis management system to respond to long-term, large-scale power shortages and failures (blackouts). *Energies, 14*(24), 8286. DOI: 10.3390/en14248286

Malhotra, P., Singh, Y., Anand, P., Bangotra, D. K., Singh, P. K., & Hong, W. C. (2021). Internet of things: Evolution, concerns and security challenges. *Sensors (Basel), 21*(5), 1809. DOI: 10.3390/s21051809 PMID: 33807724

Malik, S. (2024). Data-driven decision-making: Leveraging the IoT for real-time sustainability in organizational behavior. *Sustainability (Basel), 16*(15), 6302. DOI: 10.3390/su16156302

Mangla, S. K., & Luthra, S. (2022). When challenges need an evaluation: For operational excellence and sustainability orientation in humanitarian supply and logistics management. *Production Planning and Control, 33*(6-7), 539–557. DOI: 10.1080/09537287.2020.1834129

Manny, L., Duygan, M., Fischer, M., & Rieckermann, J. (2021). Barriers to the digital transformation of infrastructure sectors. *Policy Sciences, 54*(4), 943–983. DOI: 10.1007/s11077-021-09438-y PMID: 34751195

Manupati, V. K., Schoenherr, T., Subramanian, N., Ramkumar, M., Soni, B., & Panigrahi, S. (2021). A multi-echelon dynamic cold chain for managing vaccine distribution. *Transportation Research Part E, Logistics and Transportation Review, 156*, 102542. DOI: 10.1016/j.tre.2021.102542 PMID: 34815731

Marín, M. A. F. V., & Marcos, I. F. V. (2021). Logistical reflections on developing a forward operating base: Improving logistics sustainability in durable deployment of air units. In *Developments and Advances in Defense and Security* [Singapore: Springer Singapore.]. *Proceedings of MICRADS, 2021*, 421–431.

Massimi, F., Ferrara, P., Petrucci, R., & Benedetto, F. (2024). Deep learning-based space debris detection for space situational awareness: A feasibility study applied to the radar processing. *IET Radar, Sonar & Navigation, 18*(4), 635–648. DOI: 10.1049/rsn2.12547

Matracia, M., Saeed, N., Kishk, M. A., & Alouini, M. S. (2022). Post-disaster communications: Enabling technologies, architectures, and open challenges. *IEEE Open Journal of the Communications Society, 3*, 1177–1205. DOI: 10.1109/OJCOMS.2022.3192040

Matternet. (2022). *UNICEF and Matternet: Drones to deliver critical supplies in Malawi*. Retrieved from https://mttr.net/unicef-matternet-drones-malawi/

Mbunge, E., Chitungo, I., & Dzinamarira, T. (2021). Unbundling the significance of cognitive robots and drones deployed to tackle COVID-19 pandemic: A rapid review to unpack emerging opportunities to improve healthcare in sub-Saharan Africa. *Cognitive Robotics, 1*, 205–213. DOI: 10.1016/j.cogr.2021.11.001

Médecins Sans Frontières (MSF). (2023). *OptiTrans: MSF's transport management system pilot*. Retrieved from https://www.msf.org/opti-trans-digital-logistics-management

Mehrabi, N., Morstatter, F., Saxena, N., Lerman, K., & Galstyan, A. (2021). A survey on bias and fairness in machine learning. *ACM Computing Surveys, 54*(6), 1–35. DOI: 10.1145/3457607

Meiss, A., Jimeno-Merino, H., Poza-Casado, I., Llorente-Álvarez, A., & Padilla-Marcos, M. Á. (2021). Indoor air quality in naturally ventilated classrooms. Lessons learned from a case study in a COVID-19 scenario. *Sustainability (Basel), 13*(15), 8446. DOI: 10.3390/su13158446

Memarpour Ghiaci, A., Abbasi, M., Piri, M., & Akhavan, P. (2024). Barriers to blockchain adoption in humanitarian logistics in an uncertain environment. *Business Intelligence Management Studies, 12*(47), 153–184.

Mendonca, J. A. (2003). A model and sample case for teaching the business value of information technology. *Journal of Information Technology Education, 2*(1), 61–72. DOI: 10.28945/313

Miao, F., Han, Y., Tian, P., Tao, B., Zang, Y., & Chu, P. K. (2023). Integrated sensor for humidity, temperature, light, and carbon dioxide based on passive RFID. *Sensors and Actuators. B, Chemical, 390*, 133913. DOI: 10.1016/j.snb.2023.133913

Michalis, P., & Vintzileou, E. (2022). The growing infrastructure crisis: The challenge of scour risk assessment and the development of a new sensing system. *Infrastructures, 7*(5), 68. DOI: 10.3390/infrastructures7050068

Midkiff, C. (2021). Using a control tower approach to drive visibility, aid planning and improve supply chain reliability. *Journal of Supply Chain Management. Logistics and Procurement, 4*(1), 70–78. DOI: 10.69554/DHRY3082

Mishra, P., Kumar, N., & Godfrey, W. W. (2022). An evolutionary computing-based energy-efficient solution for IoT-enabled software-defined sensor network architecture. *International Journal of Communication Systems, 35*(8), e5111. DOI: 10.1002/dac.5111

Mızrak, F. (2023). Managing Risks and Crises in the Logistics Sector: A Comprehensive Analysis of Strategies and Prioritization Using AHP Method. Meriç Uluslararası Sosyal ve Stratejik Araştırmalar Dergisi, 7(Özel Sayı), 114-148.

Mızrak, F. (2024). Strategies for Sustainable Business Growth in Maritime Logistics. In Trends, Challenges, and Practices in Contemporary Strategic Management (pp. 108-125). IGI Global Scientific Publishing. DOI: 10.4018/979-8-3693-1155-4.ch006

Mızrak, F. (2025). The Triple Nexus of Smart, Secure, and Sustainable Supply Chains: Strategies for Resilience in the Digital Age. In *Utilizing Cybersecurity to Foster Business Innovation and Resiliency* (pp. 189-218). IGI Global Scientific Publishing.

Mızrak, F., & Akkartal, G. R. (2024). An Analysis of Alternative Energy Sources and Applications in Maritime Transportation with a Strategic Management Approach. Decision Making in Interdisciplinary Renewable Energy Projects: Navigating Energy Investments, 97-109.

Mızrak, F. (2022). An Evaluation for the Use of Alternative Vehicle Technologies and Energy Resources in Logistic Sector with a Strategic Approach. In *Circular Economy and the Energy Market: Achieving Sustainable Economic Development Through Energy Policy* (pp. 159–171). Springer International Publishing. DOI: 10.1007/978-3-031-13146-2_13

Mızrak, F. (2023). Analyzing Criteria Affecting Decision-Making Processes of Human Resource Management in the Aviation Sector-A Fuzzy Logic Approach. *Journal of Aviation*, *7*(3), 376–387. DOI: 10.30518/jav.1331688

Mızrak, F. (2024). Effective change management strategies: Exploring dynamic models for organizational transformation. In *Perspectives on artificial intelligence in times of turbulence: Theoretical background to applications* (pp. 135–162). IGI Global.

Mızrak, F. (2024). Enhancing Cybersecurity risk management through conceptual analysis of Hrm integration. *Yönetim Bilimleri Dergisi*, *22*(51), 96–118. DOI: 10.35408/comuybd.1342408

Mızrak, F. (2024). Integrating AI with aviation cybersecurity: The strategic role of human resources. *Business & Management Studies: An International Journal*, *12*(3), 610–628. DOI: 10.15295/bmij.v12i3.2396

Mızrak, F. (2024). Resilience and Innovation Strategies: How Businesses Adapt to Supply Chain Disruptions in the Post-Pandemic Era. *Politik Ekonomik Kuram*, *8*(3), 581–600. DOI: 10.30586/pek.1497718

Mızrak, F. (2025). Cybersecurity and Strategic Innovation in the Digital Economy. In *Utilizing Cybersecurity to Foster Business Innovation and Resiliency* (pp. 1–30). IGI Global Scientific Publishing. DOI: 10.4018/979-8-3693-6417-8.ch001

Mızrak, F. (2025). The triple nexus of smart, secure, and sustainable supply chains: Strategies for resilience in the digital age. In Mızrak, F. (Ed.), *Utilizing cybersecurity to foster business innovation and resiliency* (pp. 189–218). IGI Global. DOI: 10.4018/979-8-3693-6417-8.ch009

Mızrak, F., & Akkartal, E. (Eds.). (2024). *Effective Logistics for Sustainable Development Goals*. IGI Global. DOI: 10.4018/979-8-3693-7071-1

Mizrak, F., & Akkartal, G. R. (2024). Prioritizing cybersecurity initiatives in aviation: A dematel-QSFS methodology. *Heliyon, 10*(16), e35487. DOI: 10.1016/j.heliyon.2024.e35487 PMID: 39687858

Mizrak, F., Mizrak, K. C., & Akkartal, G. R. (2025). Developing a strategic framework for airline destination selection: A multi-criteria decision-making approach applied to Turkish airlines. *Transportation Research Interdisciplinary Perspectives, 29*, 101322. DOI: 10.1016/j.trip.2025.101322

Mizrak, F., Polat, L., & Tasar, S. A. (2024). Applying Entropy Weighting and 2-Tuple Linguistic T-Spherical Fuzzy MCDM: A Case Study of Developing a Strategic Sustainability Plan for Istanbul Airport. *Sustainability (Basel), 16*(24), 11104. DOI: 10.3390/su162411104

Mizrak, F., & Yaşar, O. (2025). Strategic deployment of piezoelectric energy harvesting in smart urban infrastructure: A hybrid QPFRS, M-SWARA, K-means clustering, and PROMETHEE evaluation for sustainable advantage. *Energy Reports, 13*, 2565–2582. DOI: 10.1016/j.egyr.2025.02.005

Moazzeni, S., & Sgarbossa, F. (2025). Collaborative logistics and digital technologies in rural contexts: a systematic review and a decision aid model for logistics decision-makers.

Moghadam, M. R. S., Sahebi, I. G., Masoomi, B., Azzavi, M., Anjomshoae, A., Banomyong, R., & Ractham, P. (2022). Modeling IoT enablers for humanitarian supply chains coordination.

MoghadasNian., S. (2025). AI-Driven Inventory Optimization in Airline Logistics: Enhancing Efficiency, Sustainability, and Operational Performance. In *Proceedings of the International Conference on Artificial Intelligence in the Age of Digital Transformation. International Organization of Academic Studies, Tbilisi, Georgia. Language: English*

MoghadasNian., S. (2025). Digital transformation in airline logistics: Enhancing operational efficiency through AI-driven predictive analytics and blockchain integration. In *Proceedings of the International Conference on Artificial Intelligence in the Age of Digital Transformation.* International Organization of Academic Studies, Tbilisi, Georgia.

Mohamadi, N., Bakhishi, H., Transchel, S., & Besiou, M. (2023). Impact of pandemics on humanitarian retailing operations: A voucher's case. *Production and Operations Management, 32*(5), 1512–1528. DOI: 10.1111/poms.13690

Mohan, P. S. (2023). Disasters, disaster preparedness and post disaster recovery: Evidence from Caribbean firms. *International Journal of Disaster Risk Reduction, 92*, 103731. DOI: 10.1016/j.ijdrr.2023.103731

Moonesar, I. A. (2025). Humanitarian Logistics and Health Response. In *Anticipatory Governance: Shaping a Responsible Future* (pp. 345-360). DOI: 10.1142/9789811296000_0023

Moradi, N., Wang, C., & Mafakheri, F. (2024). Urban air mobility for last-mile transportation: A review. *Vehicles (Basel), 6*(3), 1383–1414. DOI: 10.3390/vehicles6030066

Morawska, L., Li, Y., & Salthammer, T. (2024). Lessons from the COVID-19 pandemic for ventilation and indoor air quality. *Science, 385*(6707), 396–401. DOI: 10.1126/science.adp2241 PMID: 39052782

Morley, J., Cowls, J., Taddeo, M., & Floridi, L. (2020). Ethical guidelines for COVID-19 tracing apps. *Nature, 582*(7810), 29–31. DOI: 10.1038/d41586-020-01578-0 PMID: 32467596

Morris, N. (2018, August 27). *Russian airline S7 tests blockchain for aviation fuel.* Ledger Insights. Retrieved from https://www.ledgerinsights.com/s7-airlines-blockchain-aviation-fuel-gazpromneft/

Morrison, K. (2002). *School leadership and complexity theory.* Routledge.

Moultanovsky, A. V. (2014). HVAC Systems, Mobile: Innovations. In *Encyclopedia of Energy Engineering and Technology-Four Volume Set (Print)* (pp. 891-908). CRC Press.

Mousazadeh, M., & Aminpour, M. H. (2025). Humanitarian supply chain redesign using a GIS-based two-stage stochastic model: A case study of earthquake in Tehran. *Operations Research, 59*(1), 1–31. DOI: 10.1051/ro/2024217

Munawar, H. S., Mojtahedi, M., Hammad, A. W., Kouzani, A., & Mahmud, M. P. (2022). Disruptive technologies as a solution for disaster risk management: A review. *The Science of the Total Environment*, *806*, 151351. DOI: 10.1016/j.scitotenv.2021.151351 PMID: 34740667

Munir, A., Aved, A., & Blasch, E. (2022). Situational awareness: Techniques, challenges, and prospects. *AI*, *3*(1), 55–77. DOI: 10.3390/ai3010005

Murdan, A. P. (2023, August). Powering the future: IoT-enabled smart grids for sustainable energy systems. In *International Conference on Electrical and Electronics Engineering* (pp. 273-285). Singapore: Springer Nature Singapore.

Murri, S., Bhoyar, M., Selvarajan, G. P., & Malaga, M. (2024). Transforming Decision-Making with Big Data Analytics: Advanced Approaches to Real-Time Insights, Predictive Modeling, and Scalable Data Integration. *International Journal of Communication Networks and Information Security*, *16*(5), 506–519.

Murugan, R., Yenduri, G., Maran, P., & Reddy Gadekallu, T. (2025). The synergy of artificial intelligence and blockchain in 6G spectrum management. *Intelligent Spectrum Management: Towards, 6G*, 237–262. DOI: 10.1002/9781394201235.ch10

Mutambara, P. D. E. (2025). Strategic Framework for AI Deployment. In *Deploying Artificial Intelligence to Achieve the UN Sustainable Development Goals: Enablers, Drivers and Strategic Framework* (pp. 245–267). Springer Nature Switzerland. DOI: 10.1007/978-3-031-88423-8_11

Nagasawa, R., Mas, E., Moya, L., & Koshimura, S. (2021). Model-based analysis of multi-UAV path planning for surveying postdisaster building damage. *Scientific Reports*, *11*(1), 18588. DOI: 10.1038/s41598-021-97804-4 PMID: 34545140

Nagendra, N. P., Narayanamurthy, G., & Moser, R. (2022). Management of humanitarian relief operations using satellite big data analytics: The case of Kerala floods. *Annals of Operations Research*, *319*(1), 885–910. DOI: 10.1007/s10479-020-03593-w

Naik, G. M., Kumari, R., Thejaswini, E., Lokesh, A., Badiger, M., & Kripa, T. (2024). Disaster Management and Humanitarian Aid. *Advances in Computational Intelligence and Robotics*, *5*(0), 274–297. DOI: 10.4018/979-8-3693-2093-8.ch015

Nairi, C., Cicioğlu, M., & Çalhan, A. (2024). Smart blockchain networks: Revolutionizing donation tracking in the Web 3.0. *Computer Communications*, *228*, 107972. DOI: 10.1016/j.comcom.2024.107972

Namagembe, S., & Ntayi, J. (2025). Humanitarian organization culture and humanitarian organization usage of digital cash-based assistance: The mediating role of financial service providers' technology readiness. *Journal of Electronic Business & Digital Economics*, *4*(1), 88–111. DOI: 10.1108/JEBDE-04-2024-0010

Namatherdhala, B., Mistry, J., Mallikarjunaradhya, V., & Logeshwaran, J. (2023, September). Meta-Heuristic Algorithm Enabled Artificial Neural Network for Heart Disease Diagnosis Using IoT Smart Sensors. In *2023 Third International Conference on Ubiquitous Computing and Intelligent Information Systems (ICUIS)* (pp. 418-425). IEEE. DOI: 10.1109/ICUIS60567.2023.00075

Nanton, R., Doná, G., & Cestaro, C. (2022). Innovative Technologies and Digital Equity: Supporting Unaccompanied Asylum-Seeking and Refugee Children to Achieve Digital Literacy.

Naudé, W. (2020). Artificial intelligence vs COVID-19: Limitations, constraints and pitfalls. *AI & Society*, *35*(3), 761–765. DOI: 10.1007/s00146-020-00978-0 PMID: 32346223

Nawazish, M., Nandakumar, M. K., & Mateen, A. (2024). Are humanitarian supply chains sustainable? A systematic review and future research themes. *Benchmarking*, *31*(8), 2565–2601. DOI: 10.1108/BIJ-01-2023-0036

Nazlıoğlu, S., Kalem, G., & Yazıcı, A. (2024). Digital Solutions for Disaster Management: Analyzing the Impact of the February 2023 Earthquake in Türkiye. *Afet ve Risk Dergisi*, *7*(1), 158–171. DOI: 10.35341/afet.1336337

Negi, S. (2024). A blockchain technology for improving financial flows in humanitarian supply chains: benefits and challenges. *Journal of Humanitarian Logistics and Supply Chain Management*, (ahead-of-print)

Nemitz, P. (2018). Constitutional democracy and technology in the age of artificial intelligence. *Philosophical Transactions. Series A, Mathematical, Physical, and Engineering Sciences*, *376*(2133), 20180089. DOI: 10.1098/rsta.2018.0089 PMID: 30323003

Nicoletti, B. (2025). AI Transformation of Logistics. In *Artificial Intelligence for Logistics 5.0: From Foundation Models to Agentic AI* (pp. 107–131). Springer Nature Switzerland. DOI: 10.1007/978-3-031-94046-0_4

Nikseresht, A., Golmohammadi, D., & Zandieh, M. (2024). Sustainable green logistics and remanufacturing: A bibliometric analysis and future research directions. *International Journal of Logistics Management*, *35*(3), 755–803. DOI: 10.1108/IJLM-03-2023-0085

Niyazi, M., & Behnamian, J. (2023). Application of cloud computing and big data in three-stage dynamic modeling of disaster relief logistics and wounded transportation: A case study. *Environmental Science and Pollution Research International, 30*(13), 38121–38140. DOI: 10.1007/s11356-022-24770-3 PMID: 36575255

Nnachi, U. (2019). Linking humanitarian and development interventions into a joint resilience continuum: World food programme (wfp) and international fund for agricultural development (ifad) collaboration on building climate resilience in nepal. *El Salvador and Ethiopia (Doctoral dissertation, NUI Galway).*

Nordin, N. A., Ansari, M. N. M., Nomanbhay, S. M., Hamid, N. A., Tan, N. M., Yahya, Z., & Abdullah, I. (2021). Integrating photovoltaic (PV) solar cells and supercapacitors for sustainable energy devices: A review. *Energies, 14*(21), 7211. DOI: 10.3390/en14217211

Noreen, N. (2025). Enhancing Healthcare Workers' Preparedness at points of Entry; role of capacity building Training. *International Journal of Infectious Diseases, 152*, 107572. DOI: 10.1016/j.ijid.2024.107572

Nosraty, N., Soroori Sarabi, A., Arsalani, A., Toosi, R., & Sharajsharifi, M. (2025). Artificial intelligence for disaster risk management in the beauty industry. *International Journal of Advanced Multidisciplinary Research and Studies, 5*(3), 1076–1086. DOI: 10.62225/2583049X.2025.5.3.4422

Novak, M. (2024). Crypto altruism: Applying blockchain to charitable and humanitarian activities. *Chinese Public Administration Review, 15*(1), 11–23. DOI: 10.1177/15396754231175173

OCHA. (2022). *Somalia Humanitarian Response Plan*. Retrieved from https://reliefweb.int/report/somalia

Ochoa, A. A., Vargas-Solar, G., Espinosa-Oviedo, J. A., & Rudomín, I. (2017). Humanitarian Logistics based on Multiagent Systems for the prevention of a plethora of disasters related with crowds.

Ociepa-Kicińska, E., & Gorzałczyńska-Koczkodaj, M. (2022). Forms of aid provided to refugees of the 2022 Russia–Ukraine war: The case of Poland. *International Journal of Environmental Research and Public Health, 19*(12), 7085. DOI: 10.3390/ijerph19127085 PMID: 35742349

Ogunbiyi-Badaru, O., Alao, O. B., Dudu, O. F., & Alonge, E. O. (2024). Blockchain-enabled asset management: Opportunities, risks and global implications. *Comprehensive Research and Reviews in Multidisciplinary Studies, 2*(2), 14–22. DOI: 10.57219/crrms.2024.2.2.0042

Oguntola, I. O., & Ülkü, M. A. (2023). Artificial intelligence for sustainable humanitarian logistics. *Encyclopedia of data science and machine learning*, 2970-2983.

Oguntola, I. O., & Ülkü, M. A. (2023). Artificial intelligence for sustainable humanitarian logistics. *In Encyclopedia of Data Science and Machine Learning*, pp. 2970–2983

Ojadi, J. O., Odionu, C., Onukwulu, E., & Owulade, O. (2024). Big data analytics and AI for optimizing supply chain sustainability and reducing greenhouse gas emissions in logistics and transportation. *International Journal of Multidisciplinary Research and Growth Evaluation*, *5*(1), 1536–1548. DOI: 10.54660/.IJMRGE.2024.5.1.1536-1548

Okafor, U. I. (2022). Ethical Approach to Sustainability Accounting Practices and Financial Performance of Aviation Companies in Nigeria: A Conceptual Model. *Society & Sustainability*, *4*(1), 25–42.

Olivatto, T. F., Inguaggiato, F. F., & Stanganini, F. N. (2023). Urban mapping and impacts assessment in a Brazilian irregular settlement using UAV-based imaging. *Remote Sensing Applications: Society and Environment*, *29*, 100911. DOI: 10.1016/j.rsase.2022.100911

Oliveira, C. S., Ferreira, M. A., & O'Neill, H. (2024). The Role of Video Cameras and Emerging Technologies in Disaster Response to Increase Sustainability of Societies: Insights on the 2023 Türkiye–Syria Earthquake. *Sustainability (Basel)*, *16*(17), 7618. DOI: 10.3390/su16177618

Olutuase, V. O., Iwu-Jaja, C. J., Akuoko, C. P., Adewuyi, E. O., & Khanal, V. (2022). Medicines and vaccines supply chains challenges in Nigeria: A scoping review. *BMC Public Health*, *22*(1), 11. DOI: 10.1186/s12889-021-12361-9 PMID: 34986820

Oluwafemi, V. W. (2023). Globalisation and Digital Trust: Leveraging Blockchain to Decentralise Diaspora Investment and Public Procurement. *International Journal of Technology. Management and Humanities*, *9*(04), 49–71.

Omar, I. A., Jayaraman, R., Debe, M. S., Salah, K., Yaqoob, I., & Omar, M. (2021). Automating procurement contracts in the healthcare supply chain using blockchain smart contracts. *IEEE Access : Practical Innovations, Open Solutions*, *9*, 37397–37409. DOI: 10.1109/ACCESS.2021.3062471

Omar, I. A., Jayaraman, R., Salah, K., Debe, M., & Omar, M. (2020). Enhancing vendor managed inventory supply chain operations using blockchain smart contracts. *IEEE Access : Practical Innovations, Open Solutions*, *8*, 182704–182719. DOI: 10.1109/ACCESS.2020.3028031

Omisola, J. O., Bihani, D., Daraojimba, A. I., Osho, G. O., Ubamadu, B. C., & Etukudoh, E. A. (2023). Blockchain in supply chain transparency: A conceptual framework for real-time data tracking and reporting using blockchain and AI. *International Journal of Multidisciplinary Research and Growth Evaluation, 4.*

Oxfam (2022). UnBlocked Cash: Using blockchain to revolutionize humanitarian aid delivery. Retrieved from https://oxfam.app.box.com/s/5wh1dv0n80evv7lbqfs43xbqcpq0gxut/file/1241237853877

Ozdemir, A. I., Erol, I., Ar, I. M., Peker, I., Asgary, A., Medeni, T. D., & Medeni, I. T. (2021). The role of blockchain in reducing the impact of barriers to humanitarian supply chain management. *International Journal of Logistics Management, 32*(2), 454–478. DOI: 10.1108/IJLM-01-2020-0058

ÖZKANLISOY, Ö., & Akkartal, E. (2020). Risk Assessment in Digital Supply Chains. *Journal of Economic & Social Research (2148-1407), 7*(14).

Özkanlısoy, Ö., & Akkartal, E. (2021). Digital transformation in supply chains: Current applications, contributions and challenges. *Bus. Manag. Stud. Int. J, 9*, 32–55.

Özkanlısoy, Ö., & Akkartal, E. (2021). Digital transformation in supply chains: Current applications, contributions and challenges. *Business & Management Studies: An International Journal, 9*(1), 32–55.

Özkanlısoy, Ö., & Akkartal, E. (2022). The effect of Suez Canal blockage on supply chains. *Dokuz Eylül Üniversitesi Denizcilik Fakültesi Dergisi, 14*(1), 51–79. DOI: 10.18613/deudfd.933816

Özmen, M., Çelik, R., Çelik, Ü. N., Teber, M., Aktaş, D. C., & Kaya, M. F. (2023). Last Mile Humanitarian Aid Delivery Model with Electric Vehicles to Disaster Areas. *Bitlis Eren Üniversitesi Fen Bilimleri Dergisi, 12*(4), 1275–1288. DOI: 10.17798/bitlisfen.1379840

Öztürk, S., & Akkartal, E. (2024). Internet of Things (IoT) Applications in Last Mile Delivery. In Strategic Innovations for Dynamic Supply Chains (pp. 193-215). IGI Global.

Ozturkcan, S. (2023). Technology and disaster relief: The Türkiye-Syria earthquake case study. *Ozturkcan, S.(2023). Technology and disaster relief: The Türkiye-Syria earthquake case study.* In Aldieri, L. (Ed.), *Innovation-Research and development for human, economic and institutional growth.*

Pahuriray, A. V., & Cerna, P. D. (2025). IoT-Enabled Flood Monitoring and Early Warning Systems. *Systematic Reviews.*

Pandey, K. (2025). *Designing Ethical AI for Development: Challenges and Opportunities in Humanitarian Engineering and Electric Vehicles*. Designed for Adventure.

Pandey, S., & Sharma, S. K. (2024, December). Green technologies for sustainable development: Innovations, modalities and possibilities. In. AIP Conference Proceedings: Vol. 3217. *No. 1* (p. 040021). AIP Publishing LLC. DOI: 10.1063/5.0234463

Papanagnou, C., Seiler, A., Spanaki, K., Papadopoulos, T., & Bourlakis, M. (2022). Data-driven digital transformation for emergency situations: The case of the UK retail sector. *International Journal of Production Economics*, *250*, 108628. DOI: 10.1016/j.ijpe.2022.108628

Parmadi, B. D., & Ramli, K. (2025). Transforming Humanitarian Response with IoT in Conflict Zones: Field Insights, Ethical Frameworks, and Deployment Challenges. *International Journal of Electrical, Computer, and Biomedical Engineering*, *3*(1), 157–187. DOI: 10.62146/ijecbe.v3i1.112

Pascucci, E. (2021). More logistics, less aid: Humanitarian-business partnerships and sustainability in the refugee camp. *World Development*, *142*, 105424. DOI: 10.1016/j.worlddev.2021.105424

Pasupuleti, V., Thuraka, B., Kodete, C. S., & Malisetty, S. (2024). Enhancing supply chain agility and sustainability through machine learning: Optimization techniques for logistics and inventory management. *Logistics (Basel)*, *8*(3), 73. DOI: 10.3390/logistics8030073

Pathak, G., & Pandey, D. (2025). AI Agents in Recruitment: A Multi-Agent System for Interview, Evaluation, and Candidate Scoring. Evaluation, and Candidate Scoring (May 01, 2025).

Patrick, E. (2018). *Logistics management and service delivery in United Nations agencies: A case study of World Food Programme, Kampala Uganda* (Doctoral dissertation, Nkumba University).

Paudel, N. R. (2020). Applications of Artificial Intelligence in Reconstruction Governance Lessons from Nepal Earthquakes. *AI and Robotics in Disaster Studies*, 167-181.

Paz-Orozco, H., de Brito, I.Jr, Chong, M., Anacona-Mopan, Y., Segura Dorado, J. A., & Moyano, M. (2023). Earthquake Decision-Making tool for humanitarian logistics network: An application in Popayan, Colombia. *Logistics (Basel)*, *7*(4), 68. DOI: 10.3390/logistics7040068

Pearson, C. M., & Clair, J. A. (1998). Reframing crisis management. *Academy of Management Review*, *23*(1), 59–76. DOI: 10.2307/259099

Peruchi Pacheco da Silva, R., Samadi, F., Losole, J., & Carpenter, J. (2024). Strategic Evaluation of Sustainable Practices for HVAC Systems in Small-and Medium-Sized US Manufacturers. *ASME Journal of Engineering for Sustainable Buildings and Cities*, *5*(3), 031002. DOI: 10.1115/1.4065961

Perumal, A. P., Chintale, P., Molleti, R., & Desaboyina, G. (2024). Risk Assessment of Artificial Intelligence Systems in Cybersecurity. *American Journal of Science and Learning for Development*, *3*(7), 49–60.

Peter, M., Gatziu Grivas, S., Horn, D., Rüegg, F., Barba, R., & Graf, M. (2019). The technology matrix—A tool-based method for technology scouting. In *12th IADIS International Conference on Information Systems*. Utrecht, The Netherlands. DOI: 10.33965/is2019_201905L017

Płaczek, E., & Świtalska, A. (2023). New technologies in humanitarian logistics. *Journal of Public Governance*, *65*(3), 48–58. DOI: 10.15678/PG.2023.65.3.04

Plesner Volkdal, C. (2025). Triple Nexus: Leveraging development supply chains for humanitarian aid and peace in Southeast Asia–a GBV focus. *Journal of Humanitarian Logistics and Supply Chain Management*, *15*(3), 210–237. DOI: 10.1108/JHLSCM-02-2024-0028

Pless, S., Podder, A., Kaufman, Z., Klammer, N., Dennehy, C., Muthumanickam, N. K., . . . Blazek, C. (2022). *The energy in modular (EMOD) buildings method: A guide to energy-efficient design for industrialized construction of modular buildings* (No. NREL/TP-5500-82447). National Renewable Energy Lab.(NREL), Golden, CO (United States).

Pradhananga, P., & ElZomor, M. (2023). Revamping sustainability efforts post-disaster by adopting circular economy resilience practices. *Sustainability (Basel)*, *15*(22), 15870. DOI: 10.3390/su152215870

Pradhan, S. C., Kumar, M., Yadav, S., Hirwani, B., & Verma, A. (2024). Enhancing Efficiency, Reducing Environmental Impact, and Ensuring Life Cycle Sustainability in Sustainable Solar Energy through Nano-Material Innovations. *Educational Administration: Theory and Practice*, *30*(11), 399–405.

Pramanik, P. K. D., Pal, S., Mukhopadhyay, M., & Choudhury, P. (2024). Sustainable edge computing with mobile crowd computing: A proof-of-concept with a smart HVAC use case. *The Journal of Supercomputing*, *80*(16), 23911–23994. DOI: 10.1007/s11227-024-06364-7

Pratap, S., Jauhar, S. K., Gunasekaran, A., & Kamble, S. S. (2024). Optimizing the IoT and big data embedded smart supply chains for sustainable performance. *Computers & Industrial Engineering*, *187*, 109828. DOI: 10.1016/j.cie.2023.109828

Pratelli, A., Brocchini, L., & Petri, M. (2024). Optimising drone-assisted logistics for urban last-mile delivery: An overview of applications, methodologies, and emerging trends. *J. Urban Dev. Manag*, *3*(3), 188–197. DOI: 10.56578/judm030304

Pu, F., Li, Z., Wu, Y., Ma, C., & Zhao, R. (2025). Recent Advances in Disaster Emergency Response Planning: Integrating Optimization, Machine Learning, and Simulation. *arXiv preprint arXiv:2505.03979.*

Purtell, C., Hong, S. J., & Hiatt, B. (2024). Bibliometric analysis on advanced air mobility and drones. *Journal of Air Transport Management*, *116*, 102569. DOI: 10.1016/j.jairtraman.2024.102569

Qi, C., Fang, J., & Sun, L. (2019). Implementation of emergency logistics distribution decision support system based on GIS. *Cluster Computing*, *22*(S4), 8859–8867. DOI: 10.1007/s10586-018-1983-8

Qu, C., Sorbelli, F. B., Singh, R., Calyam, P., & Das, S. K. (2023). Environmentally-aware and energy-efficient multi-drone coordination and networking for disaster response. *IEEE Transactions on Network and Service Management*, *20*(2), 1093–1109. DOI: 10.1109/TNSM.2023.3243543

Raffik, R., Rakesh, D., Venkatesh, M., & Samvasan, P. (2021, October). Supply Chain Control and Inventory Tracking System using Industrial Automation Tools and IIoT. In *2021 International Conference on Advancements in Electrical, Electronics, Communication, Computing and Automation (ICAECA)* (pp. 1-5). IEEE. DOI: 10.1109/ICAECA52838.2021.9675774

Rahman, M. S., Hossain, M. S., Rahman, M. K., Islam, M. R., Sumon, M. F. I., Siam, M. A., & Debnath, P. (2025). Enhancing Supply Chain Transparency with Blockchain: A Data-Driven Analysis of Distributed Ledger Applications. *Journal of Business and Management Studies*, *7*(3), 59–77. DOI: 10.32996/jbms.2025.7.3.7

Rahwan, I., Cebrian, M., Obradovich, N., Bongard, J., Bonnefon, J. F., Breazeal, C., Crandall, J. W., Christakis, N. A., Couzin, I. D., Jackson, M. O., Jennings, N. R., Kamar, E., Kloumann, I. M., Larochelle, H., Lazer, D., McElreath, R., Mislove, A., Parkes, D. C., Pentland, A. S., & Wellman, M. (2019). Machine behaviour. *Nature*, *568*(7753), 477–486. DOI: 10.1038/s41586-019-1138-y PMID: 31019318

Rai, M. S. (2024). Digitalization and Children in Humanitarian Emergencies: Addressing the challenges at the crossroads of Digital opportunities, Digital literacy and Child Trafficking. *Digital literacy and Child Trafficking (January 12, 2024).*

Raikov, A. N., & Pirani, M. (2022). Contradiction of modern and social-humanitarian artificial intelligence. *Kybernetes, 51*(13), 186–198. DOI: 10.1108/K-01-2022-0057

Ramakrishna, S., & Ramasubramanian, B. (2024). Circular Practices in E-waste Management and Transportation. In *Handbook of Materials Circular Economy* (pp. 131–165). Springer Nature Singapore. DOI: 10.1007/978-981-97-0589-4_5

Ramasubramanian, B., Sundarrajan, S., Rao, R. P., Reddy, M. V., Chellappan, V., & Ramakrishna, S. (2022). Novel low-carbon energy solutions for powering emerging wearables, smart textiles, and medical devices. *Energy & Environmental Science, 15*(12), 4928–4981. DOI: 10.1039/D2EE02695C

Rangone, A., & Busolli, L. (2021). Managing charity 4.0 with Blockchain: A case study at the time of Covid-19. *International Review on Public and Nonprofit Marketing, 18*(4), 491–521. DOI: 10.1007/s12208-021-00281-8

Rashid, H. (n.d.) Using Smart Contracts to Enhance Compliance and Efficiency in Procurement Operations. *IJLRP-International Journal of Leading Research Publication, 5*(8).

Ratnam, M. (2025). Water Supply Mapping for a Sustainable Future: Data-Driven Efforts in Decision Making. *Smart Internet of Things, 2*(1), 1–10.

Ravisankar, S., Ramachandran, V., & Shankar, S. R. (2025, Mar). Virtual Disaster Management Systems for Real-Time Response and Aid. In *2025 International Conference on Data Science, Agents & Artificial Intelligence (ICDSAAI)* (pp. 1-5). IEEE.

Rayhana, R., Xiao, G., & Liu, Z. (2021). RFID sensing technologies for smart agriculture. *IEEE Instrumentation & Measurement Magazine, 24*(3), 50–60. DOI: 10.1109/MIM.2021.9436094

Reach Alliance. (2021). *Last mile health delivery via drone: A case study from Papua New Guinea.* Retrieved from https://reachalliance.org/project/drones-for-tuberculosis-papua-new-guinea/

Red Cross Australia. (2023). Türkiye earthquake: Container homes for survivors. *Red Cross Australia.* https://www.redcross.org.au

Red Social Innovation. (2021). *Sarafu Community Currency: Inclusive blockchain-based humanitarian financing.* Retrieved from https://www.red-social-innovation.com/en/innovation/sarafu-community-currency/

Reghunadhan, R. (2020). Ethical considerations and issues of blockchain technology-based systems in war zones: A case study approach. In *Handbook of research on blockchain technology* (pp. 1–34). Academic Press. DOI: 10.1016/B978-0-12-819816-2.00001-0

Rehan, H. (2022). Enhancing Disaster Response Systems: Predicting and Mitigating the Impact of Natural Disasters Using AI. *Journal of Artificial Intelligence Research*, *2*(1), 501.

ReliefWeb. (2023). Humanitarian HVAC retrofitting in Turkish shelters. *ReliefWeb*. https://www.reliefweb.int

Remida, A. (2015). A systemic approach to sustainable humanitarian logistics. *Humanitarian Logistics and Sustainability*, 11-29.

Rewizorski, M. (2025). Bound to Abstain?: The BRICS Response to the Russia-Ukraine Crisis. In *Global Governance and The Political South* (pp. 75-89). Routledge.

Rojas Trejos, C. A., Meisel, J. D., & Adarme Jaimes, W. (2023). Humanitarian aid distribution logistics with accessibility constraints: A systematic literature review. *Journal of Humanitarian Logistics and Supply Chain Management, 13*(1), 26–41. DOI: 10.1108/JHLSCM-05-2021-0041

Rosenow, D., Lee, T. T., & Li, Z. X. (2022). Next-generation air routing: Integrating AI, multi-objective optimization, and collaborative decision making for efficient and sustainable flight planning. *International Journal of Enterprise Modelling*, *16*(3), 136–144.

Roth, K., Rau, C., & Neyer, A. K. (2023). Design thinking and dynamic managerial capabilities: A quasi-experimental field study in the aviation industry. *R & D Management*, *53*(5), 801–818. DOI: 10.1111/radm.12600

Rout, S., & Samantaray, S. (2023, December). Green ICT: Exploring the Role of IoT-Enabled Technologies in Small-Scale Businesses. In *International Conference on Information and Communication Technology for Competitive Strategies* (pp. 309-321). Singapore: Springer Nature Singapore.

Ruzafa, M. C. (2021). *Blockchain as a chain for humanitarian aid: transforming the lives of refugees* (Master's thesis).

Saari, S. (2023). Enhancing the environmental sustainability of emergency humanitarian medical cold chains with renewable energy sources. *Journal of Humanitarian Logistics and Supply Chain Management, 13*(2), 157–172. DOI: 10.1108/JHLSCM-09-2021-0095

Sağlık Bakanlığı, T. C. (2021). *Pandemi hastaneleri tasarım ve kullanım kılavuzu [COVID-19 Field Hospital Design and Use Manual]*. https://www.saglik.gov.tr

Sahun, Y., Sikirda, Y., & Tymochko, O. (2025). Application of Computer Load Optimization Model in an Aircraft Load Planning Process. In *Encyclopedia of Information Science and Technology* (6th ed., pp. 1–20). IGI Global.

Saidu, Y., Shuhidan, S. M., Aliyu, D. A., Aziz, I. A., & Adamu, S. (2025). Convergence of blockchain, IoT, and AI for enhanced traceability systems: A comprehensive review. *IEEE Access : Practical Innovations, Open Solutions*, *13*, 16838–16865. DOI: 10.1109/ACCESS.2025.3528035

Saif, A., Dimyati, K., Noordin, K. A., G C, D., Shah, N. S. M., Abdullah, Q., & Mohamad, M. (2021). An efficient energy harvesting and optimal clustering technique for sustainable postdisaster emergency communication systems. *IEEE Access : Practical Innovations, Open Solutions*, *9*, 78188–78202. DOI: 10.1109/ACCESS.2021.3083640

Sakthivel, V., Periyaswamy, P., Lee, J. W., & Prabu, P. (2024). Enhancing transparency and trust in Agrifood supply chains through novel Blockchain-based architecture. [TIIS]. *KSII Transactions on Internet and Information Systems*, *18*(7), 1968–1985.

Samunnisa, K., & Gaddam, S. V. K. (2023). Blockchain-Based Decentralized Identity Management for Secure Digital Transactions. *Synthesis: A Multidisciplinary Research Journal, 1*(2), 22-29.

Sánchez-Partida, D., Martínez-Flores, J. L., Caballero-Morales, S. O., Cano-Olivos, P., Fon-Galvez, M. J., Sánchez-Partida, D., ... & Caballero-Morales, S. O. (2021). 19S Earthquake in Puebla, Mexico: Intervention of the Different Actors in Humanitarian Aid. Disaster Risk Reduction in Mexico: Methodologies, Case Studies, and Prospective Views, 141-167.

Sandoval-Ríos, F., Gajardo-Poblete, C., & López-Núñez, J. A. (2025, March). Role of data literacy training for decision-making in teaching practice: A systematic review. [). Frontiers Media SA.]. *Frontiers in Education*, *10*, 1485821. DOI: 10.3389/feduc.2025.1485821

Santoro, B. F., Mendoza, D. F., & Rincon, D. (2021). Budget-constrained economic model predictive control: A user-friendly proposal for HVAC. *Chemical Engineering Research & Design*, *176*, 229–242. DOI: 10.1016/j.cherd.2021.10.003

Save the Children. (2019). *Somalia: Smart card cash transfer pilot impact report.* Retrieved from https://resourcecentre.savethechildren.net/pdf/smartcard_somalia_report.pdf/

Schismenos, S., Stevens, G. J., Emmanouloudis, D., Georgeou, N., Shrestha, S., & Chalaris, M. (2021). Humanitarian engineering at the sustainability-development nexus: Mapping vulnerability and capability factors for communities at risk of water-based disasters. *Sustainability Science*, *16*(4), 1185–1199. DOI: 10.1007/s11625-020-00890-y PMID: 33425037

Sebastian, A. (2025). Soft Robotics for Search and Rescue: Advancements, Challenges, and Future Directions. arXiv preprint arXiv:2502.12373.

Sedaghat, A., Kalbasi, R., Narayanan, R., Mehdizadeh, A., Soleimani, S. M., Malayer, M. A., & Khan, M. M. K. (2024). Integrating solar PV systems for energy efficiency in portable cabins: A case study in Kuwait. *Solar Energy*, *277*, 112715. DOI: 10.1016/j.solener.2024.112715

Sehrawat, D., & Gill, N. S. (2019, April). Smart sensors: Analysis of different types of IoT sensors. In *2019 3rd International Conference on Trends in Electronics and Informatics (ICOEI)*(pp. 523-528). IEEE.

Seifert, L., Kunz, N., & Gold, S. (2023). Sustainable innovations for humanitarian operations in refugee camps. *International Journal of Operations & Production Management*, *43*(10), 1554–1586. DOI: 10.1108/IJOPM-05-2022-0302

Selvaprabhu, P. (2023). An examination of distributed and decentralized systems for trustworthy control of supply chains. *IEEE Access : Practical Innovations, Open Solutions*, *11*, 137025–137052. DOI: 10.1109/ACCESS.2023.3338739

Sestras, P., Badea, G., Badea, A. C., Salagean, T., Ro ca, S., Kader, S., & Remondino, F. (2025). Land surveying with UAV photogrammetry and LiDAR for optimal building planning. *Automation in Construction*, *173*, 106092. DOI: 10.1016/j.autcon.2025.106092

Seyedan, M., Mafakheri, F., & Wang, C. (2022). Cluster-based demand forecasting using Bayesian model averaging: An ensemble learning approach. *Decision Analytics Journal*, *3*, 100033. DOI: 10.1016/j.dajour.2022.100033

Shaheen, E., Hamed, M. A., Zaghloul, W., Al Mostafa, E., El Sharkawy, A., Mahmoud, A., . . . Attiya, G. (2021, July). A track donation system using blockchain. In *2021 international conference on electronic engineering (ICEEM)* (pp. 1-7). IEEE. DOI: 10.1109/ICEEM52022.2021.9480649

Shakhatreh, H., Sawalmeh, A. H., Al-Fuqaha, A., Dou, Z., Almaita, E., Khalil, I., Othman, N. S., Khreishah, A., & Guizani, M. (2019). Unmanned aerial vehicles (UAVs): A survey on civil applications and key research challenges. *IEEE Access : Practical Innovations, Open Solutions*, *7*, 48572–48634. DOI: 10.1109/ACCESS.2019.2909530

Shakibaei, H., Moosavi, S. A., Aghsami, A., & Rabbani, M. (2024). Designing a sustainable-resilient humanitarian supply chain for post-disaster relief process, an earthquake case study in Haiti. *Journal of Humanitarian Logistics and Supply Chain Management*, (ahead-of-print).

Sharma, K. K., Verma, P. K., & Garg, P. (2024). IoT-Enabled Energy Management Systems For Sustainable Energy Storage: Design, Optimization, And Future Directions. *Frontiers in Health Informatics, 13*(8).

Sharma, P., & Joshi, A. (2020). Challenges of using big data for humanitarian relief: Lessons from the literature. *Journal of Humanitarian Logistics and Supply Chain Management, 10*(4), 423–446. DOI: 10.1108/JHLSCM-05-2018-0031

Shawon, R. E. R., Hasan, M. D., Rahman, M. A., Ghandri, M., Lamari, I. A., Kawsar, M., & Akter, R. (2025). Designing and Deploying AI Models for Sustainable Logistics Optimization: A Case Study on Eco-Efficient Supply Chains in the USA. *arXiv preprint arXiv:2503.14556.*

Shehadeh, A., Alshboul, O., & Tamimi, M. (2025). Quantitative Analysis of Climate-Adaptive Pavement Technologies: Mitigating Environmental Impact and Enhancing Economic Viability in Urban Infrastructure. *Journal of Construction Engineering and Management, 151*(6), 04025064. DOI: 10.1061/JCEMD4.COENG-15682

Shi, F., Wang, J., Shi, J., Wu, Z., Wang, Q., Tang, Z., He, K., Shi, Y., & Shen, D. (2021). Review of artificial intelligence techniques in imaging data acquisition, segmentation, and diagnosis for COVID-19. *IEEE Reviews in Biomedical Engineering, 14*, 4–15. DOI: 10.1109/RBME.2020.2987975 PMID: 32305937

Shi, R., Yao, L., Zhao, M., & Yan, Z. (2023). The role of climate-adaptive technological innovation in promoting agriculture carbon efficiency: Impact and heterogeneity in economic development. *Environmental Science and Pollution Research International, 30*(60), 126029–126044. DOI: 10.1007/s11356-023-31205-0 PMID: 38010550

Shneiderman, B. (2020). Human-centered artificial intelligence: Reliable, safe & trustworthy. *International Journal of Human-Computer Interaction, 36*(6), 495–504. DOI: 10.1080/10447318.2020.1741118

Shuaibu, A. S., Mahmoud, A. S., & Sheltami, T. R. (2025). A review of last-mile delivery optimization: Strategies, technologies, drone integration, and future trends. *Drones (Basel), 9*(3), 158. DOI: 10.3390/drones9030158

Singh, R. K. (2025). Transforming humanitarian supply chains with digital twin technology: A study on resilience and agility. *International Journal of Logistics Management, 36*(4), 1119–1135. DOI: 10.1108/IJLM-08-2024-0504

Singh, R., & Manoharan, G. (2025). AI Integration to Strengthen Disaster Resilience in Smart Cities. In *AI and Emerging Technologies for Emergency Response and Smart Cities* (pp. 1–30). IGI Global Scientific Publishing. DOI: 10.4018/979-8-3693-9770-1.ch001

Smart, K., & Shrestha, S. (2022). Delivering Better together: Standard Operating Procedures for Oxfam's Approach to Cash and Voucher Assistance.

Smith, A., Pringle, J., & Hunt, M. (2020). Value-sensitive design for humanitarian action: integrating ethical analysis for information and communication technology innovations. In *Ethics of Medical Innovation, Experimentation, and Enhancement in Military and Humanitarian Contexts* (pp. 105–124). Springer International Publishing. DOI: 10.1007/978-3-030-36319-2_7

Soussi, A., Zero, E., Sacile, R., Trinchero, D., & Fossa, M. (2024). Smart sensors and smart data for precision agriculture: A review. *Sensors (Basel), 24*(8), 2647. DOI: 10.3390/s24082647 PMID: 38676264

Sowmya, G., Sridevi, R., & Rao, K. S. (2025). Blockchain for Disaster Recovery: Enhancing Resilience, Coordination, and Trust in Crisis Management. In AI and Emerging Technologies for Emergency Response and Smart Cities (pp. 117-136). IGI Global Scientific Publishing.

Srikandi, D., Sutopo, W., Hisjam, M., & Istiqomah, S. (2022, August). Commercializing a Technology Use Global Business Strategy Approach: A Lesson Learned from HVAC Companies. In *Proceedings of the International Conference on Industrial Engineering and Operations Management* (pp. 3079-3090).

Srivastava, Y. C., Srivastava, A., & Granata, C. (2021, December). Digitally Enabled Organizations-Leveraging New Age Technologies. In *Abu Dhabi International Petroleum Exhibition and Conference* (p. D012S159R001). SPE. DOI: 10.2118/207380-MS

Stadtler, L., & Van Wassenhove, L. N. (2025). *The Logistics Emergency Team: Pioneering and Sustaining a New Partnership Model* (Doctoral dissertation, Grenoble Ecole de Management; INSEAD).

Stat Times. (2023). Turkish Airlines carried over 15,600 tons of aid for earthquake victims. Retrieved from https://www.stattimes.com

Stockburger, L., Kokosioulis, G., Mukkamala, A., Mukkamala, R. R., & Avital, M. (2021). Blockchain-enabled decentralized identity management: The case of self-sovereign identity in public transportation. *Blockchain: Research and Applications*, *2*(2), 100014.

Sudhi, M., Aishwarya, T. R., Shetty, D. K., Balakrishnan, J. M., Ahmad, S., & Sankaran, P. P. (2025). AI-DRIVEN INNOVATIONS IN EMERGENCY AND DISASTER RESPONSE: STRATEGIES FOR EFFECTIVE PLANNING. *Proceedings on Engineering*, *7*(2), 1293–1304. DOI: 10.24874/PES07.02C.009

Sufi, F. K., & Khalil, I. (2022). Automated disaster monitoring from social media posts using AI-based location intelligence and sentiment analysis. *IEEE Transactions on Computational Social Systems*.

Sufi, F., & Alsulami, M. (2025). AI-Driven Global Disaster Intelligence from News Media. *Mathematics*, *13*(7), 1083. DOI: 10.3390/math13071083

Sulaiman, A. Y., Obasi, G. I., Chang, R., Moghaieb, H. S., Mondol, J. D., Smyth, M., Kamkari, B., & Hewitt, N. J. (2023). A solar powered off-grid air conditioning system with natural refrigerant for residential buildings: A theoretical and experimental evaluation. *Cleaner Energy Systems*, *5*, 100077. DOI: 10.1016/j.cles.2023.100077

Suman, S., Deb, A., Prusty, A. K., Sameer, S., Divya, B. S., & Saha, S. (2024, December). Utilizing blockchain, IoT and machine learning for transparent agri-extension and resource distribution: A review. In *2024 2nd International Conference on Signal Processing, Communication, Power and Embedded System (SCOPES)* (pp. 1-6). IEEE.

Summer, M. (2010). The value of information and communication technologies in humanitarian relief efforts. *Innovations: Technology, Governance, Globalization*, *5*(4), 55–68. DOI: 10.1162/INOV_a_00043

Su, S., Zhou, J., Zhong, Z., & Zhang, J. (2025). How help-seeking information spreads on social media during disasters: The role of vulnerable groups and information features. *International Journal of Disaster Risk Reduction*, *120*, 105374. DOI: 10.1016/j.ijdrr.2025.105374

Taddeo, M., & Floridi, L. (2018). How AI can be a force for good. *Science*, *361*(6404), 751–752. DOI: 10.1126/science.aat5991 PMID: 30139858

Taipei Times. (2023). Container clinics deployed with HVAC and equipment. *Taipei Times*. https://www.taipeitimes.com

Tan, L., Guo, J., Mohanarajah, S., & Zhou, K. (2021). Can we detect trends in natural disaster management with artificial intelligence? A review of modeling practices. *Natural Hazards, 107*(3), 2389–2417. DOI: 10.1007/s11069-020-04429-3

Tao, X., Wu, Z., Xu, Y., Zheng, C., Fang, Y., Das, M., Liu, H., Gong, X., & Cheng, J. C. (2024). Smarter smart contracts for automatic BIM metadata compliance checking in blockchain-enabled common data environment. *Advanced Engineering Informatics*, *62*, 102627. DOI: 10.1016/j.aei.2024.102627

Tariq, M. U. (2025). Integrating Advanced Technologies for Multi-Stakeholder Collaboration: Driving Sustainability in Supply Chains Through Industry 4.0. In *Multi-Stakeholder Collaboration for Sustainable Supply Chain* (pp. 313-334). IGI Global Scientific Publishing.

Tatham, P., & Christopher, M. (Eds.). (2018). *Humanitarian logistics: Meeting the challenge of preparing for and responding to disasters*. Kogan Page Publishers.

Tatham, P., Neal, C., & Wu, Y. (2017). Hybrid cargo airships: A humanitarian logistic game changer? *Journal of Humanitarian Logistics and Supply Chain Management*, *7*(2), 102–125. DOI: 10.1108/JHLSCM-09-2016-0036

Télécoms Sans Frontières. (2024). Emergency communication deployments and VSAT-based learning centers. https://en.wikipedia.org/wiki/Télécoms_Sans_Frontières

Terande, T. J. (2025). Leveraging Information and Communication Technology (ICT) Solutions for Food Security as Panacea for Hunger Alleviation in Nigeria. In Smart Technologies for Sustainable Development Goals (pp. 272-290). CRC Press.

Tezei, J. F., de Freitas, C. R., Neto, A. L., Rodrigues, P. C. C., & Luche, J. R. D. (2024). Strategic analysis for a truck-drone hybrid model in last mile delivery. *International Contemporary Management Review*, *5*(1), 31–53. DOI: 10.54033/icmr-003

Thakare, K. V., Tajne, K. M., THAKARE, K. V., & Tajne, K. (2025). A Comprehensive Review of Geographic Information Systems (GIS)-Based Methodologies for Urban Fire Risk Assessment. Cureus Journals, 2(1).

Tian, Y., & Jiang, Y. (2025). Research on urban landscape accessibility assessment model based on gis and spatial analysis. *GeoJournal*, *90*(2), 67. DOI: 10.1007/s10708-025-11310-y

Ticas, F. L. (2023). Agile Combat Employment (ACE) Readiness: Necessary Training Transitions For Airfield Operations Officers.

Torres, J., Garay-Martinez, R., Oregi, X., Torrens-Galdiz, J. I., Uriarte-Arrien, A., Pracucci, A., Casadei, O., Magnani, S., Arroyo, N., & Cea, A. M. (2021). Plug and play modular façade construction system for renovation for residential buildings. *Buildings (Basel, Switzerland)*, *11*(9), 419. DOI: 10.3390/buildings11090419

Toygar, A. (2024). Sustainability in the Maritime Industry: Integration of Digital Twin and Autonomous Control. In *Strategic Innovations for Dynamic Supply Chains* (pp. 31-49). IGI Global Scientific Publishing.

Tran-Dang, H., Kim, J. W., Lee, J. M., & Kim, D. S. (2025). Shaping the future of logistics: Data-driven technology approaches and strategic management. *IETE Technical Review*, *42*(1), 44–79. DOI: 10.1080/02564602.2024.2445513

TRC. (2023). *Community-based resilience and HVAC vocational programs*. Turkish Red Crescent. https://www.kizilay.org.tr

TRC. (2023a). Disaster response update—HVAC in shelter and service units. *Türk Kızılay (Turkish Red Crescent)*. https://www.kizilay.org.tr

TRC. (2023a). Kahramanmaraş Earthquake Emergency Response Report. Retrieved from https://prddsgofilestorage.blob.core.windows.net

Treiblmaier, H., & Rejeb, A. (2023). Exploring blockchain for disaster prevention and relief: A comprehensive framework based on industry case studies. *Journal of Business Logistics*, *44*(4), 550–582. DOI: 10.1111/jbl.12345

Trotter, L., Harding, M., Shaw, P., Davies, N., Elsden, C., Speed, C., & Hallwright, J. (2020, December). Smart donations: Event-driven conditional donations using smart contracts on the blockchain. In *Proceedings of the 32nd Australian Conference on Human-Computer Interaction* (pp. 546-557). DOI: 10.1145/3441000.3441014

Trusilo, D., & Danks, D. (2023). Artificial intelligence and humanitarian obligations. *Ethics and Information Technology*, *25*(1), 12. DOI: 10.1007/s10676-023-09681-2

Tsamados, A., Aggarwal, N., Cowls, J., Morley, J., Roberts, H., Taddeo, M., & Floridi, L. (2022). The ethics of algorithms: Key problems and solutions. *AI & Society*, *37*(1), 215–230. DOI: 10.1007/s00146-021-01154-8

Türkiye, U. N. D. P. (2023). *Sustainable energy solutions in refugee camp management*. United Nations Development Programme Türkiye. https://www.tr.undp.org

Turmaks. (2023). Modular hospitals delivered to Hatay. *Turmaks Medical Infrastructure*. https://www.turmaks.com

Turoff, M., Chumer, M., de Walle, B. V., & Yao, X. (2004). The design of a dynamic emergency response management information system (DERMIS). [JITTA]. *Journal of Information Technology Theory and Application*, *5*(4), 3.

Tversky, A., & Kahneman, D. (1974). Judgment under Uncertainty: Heuristics and Biases: Biases in judgments reveal some heuristics of thinking under uncertainty. *science, 185*(4157), 1124-1131.

Tyagi, P., & Shrivastava, N. Sakshi, & Jain, V. (2024). Synergizing artificial intelligence and blockchain. In *Next-Generation Cybersecurity: AI, ML, and Blockchain* (pp. 83-97). Singapore: Springer Nature Singapore.

Tyshchuk, V. V. (2024). A review of legal regulation regarding the use of unmanned aerial vehicles for border security and the impact of global technologies. *International Comparative Jurisprudence*, *10*(1), 61–81.

Ugwu, O. P. C., Alum, E. U., Ugwu, J. N., Eze, V. H. U., Ugwu, C. N., Ogenyi, F. C., & Okon, M. B. (2024). Harnessing technology for infectious disease response in conflict zones: Challenges, innovations, and policy implications. *Medicine*, *103*(28), e38834. DOI: 10.1097/MD.0000000000038834 PMID: 38996110

UNDP. (2023). Climate control in container cities. *United Nations Development Programme Türkiye*. https://www.tr.undp.org

UNDRR. (2023). Türkiye national disaster plan and cluster responsibilities. Retrieved from https://www.preventionweb.net

UNECA. (2023). HVAC installations in Türkiye disaster shelters. *United Nations Economic Commission for Africa*. https://www.uneca.org

UNHAS. (2022). *UNHAS Operational Brief: East Africa*. WFP Aviation Unit.

UNHAS. (2023). *WFP Aviation 2023 Annual Report*. Retrieved from https://www.wfp.org/publications

UNHCR. (2024). *Türkiye Operational Update – Refugee Response in 2023–2024*. United Nations High Commissioner for Refugees. https://www.unhcr.org/tr

UNICEF Supply Division. (2023). *Digital cold chain monitoring in Kyrgyzstan: Improving vaccine delivery*. Retrieved from https://www.unicef.org/supply/stories/kyrgyzstan-digital-cold-chain

UNICEF. (2023). *Digital health innovation in Zimbabwe: Empowering frontline workers with data tools*. Retrieved from https://www.unicefusa.org/stories/digital-health-kit-transforming-care-zimbabwe

UNICEF. (2023). *Leveraging smart sensors and wearables to combat malnutrition*. Retrieved from https://www.unicef.org/innovation/stories/smart-bands-fighting-malnutrition-ethiopia

United Nations Environment Management Group (UNEMG). (2021). *United Nations e-waste management policy framework: Towards a circular economy*. Retrieved from https://unemg.org/un-e-waste-framework

uSalam, M. H., Rathore, S. A., Maken, F. H., Janjua, J. I., & Irfan, M. (2025). Harnessing Big Data and IoT for Enhanced Resource Optimization in Sustainable Construction within Smart Cities. *The Journal of Research Review*, *2*(01), 90–104.

Vaishya, R., Javaid, M., Khan, I. H., & Haleem, A. (2020). Artificial Intelligence (AI) applications for COVID-19 pandemic. *Diabetes & Metabolic Syndrome*, *14*(4), 337–339. DOI: 10.1016/j.dsx.2020.04.012 PMID: 32305024

Varsha, V. R., Naganandini, S., & Hariharan, C. (2024). Utilizing AI and machine learning for natural disaster management: predicting natural disasters with AI and machine learning. In *Internet of Things and AI for Natural Disaster Management and Prediction* (pp. 279–304). IGI Global.

Venkatasubbu, S., & Krishnamoorthy, G. (2022). Ethical considerations in AI addressing bias and fairness in machine learning models. *Journal of Knowledge Learning and Science Technology ISSN: 2959-6386 (online)*, *1*(1), 130-138.

Verma, S. K., Gupta, S., Sharma, A., & Rajput, S. (Eds.). (2025). *Advanced Energy Materials: Natural Polymers, Renewable Energy, Sustainable Development*. Walter de Gruyter GmbH & Co KG. DOI: 10.1515/9783111289076

Vinuesa, R., Azizpour, H., Leite, I., Balaam, M., Dignum, V., Domisch, S., Felländer, A., Langhans, S. D., Tegmark, M., & Fuso Nerini, F. (2020). The role of artificial intelligence in achieving the Sustainable Development Goals. *Nature Communications*, *11*(1), 233. DOI: 10.1038/s41467-019-14108-y PMID: 31932590

Voigt, P., & Von dem Bussche, A. (2017). *The EU General Data Protection Regulation (GDPR): A practical guide*. Springer International Publishing., DOI: 10.1007/978-3-319-57959-7

Wagner, S. M., Ramkumar, M., Kumar, G., & Schoenherr, T. (2024). Supporting disaster relief operations through RFID: Enabling visibility and coordination. *International Journal of Logistics Management*, *35*(6), 1681–1712. DOI: 10.1108/IJLM-12-2022-0480

Wang, J., Lim, M. K., Wang, C., & Tseng, M. L. (2021). The evolution of the Internet of Things (IoT) over the past 20 years. *Computers & Industrial Engineering, 155*, 107174. DOI: 10.1016/j.cie.2021.107174

Waqas, M., Khan, S. A. R., & Al-Amin, A. Q. (Eds.). (2023). *Emerging Trends in Sustainable Supply Chain Management and Green Logistics*. DOI: 10.4018/978-1-6684-6663-6

WebbyLab. (2025). IoT data management: From edge to cloud. https://webbylab.com/blog/iot-data-management

Weller, A. (2019). Transparency: motivations and challenges. In *Explainable AI: interpreting, explaining and visualizing deep learning* (pp. 23–40). Springer International Publishing. DOI: 10.1007/978-3-030-28954-6_2

WFP USA. (2023). Building Blocks: WFP's blockchain pilot for refugee cash transfers. Retrieved from https://www.wfpusa.org

WFP. (2022). *Building Blocks: A better way to deliver aid*. World Food Programme. Retrieved from https://innovation.wfp.org/project/building-blocks

WFP. (2023). *HungerMapLIVE: Food Security Monitoring Platform*. Retrieved from https://hungermap.wfp.org

WHO. (2021). *Environmental health risks in humanitarian settlements: Türkiye findings*. World Health Organization Regional Office for Europe. https://www.euro.who.int

WHO. (2023). *Guidance on temporary medical facilities and infection prevention in humanitarian settings*. World Health Organization. https://www.who.int

Wierzbiński, B., Zaborek, P., Wosiek, M., & Surmacz, T. (2023). Knowledge management orientation as a driver of competitive performance: Evidence from Polish SMEs in the aviation industry. *Entrepreneurial Business and Economics Review, 11*(1), 93–112. DOI: 10.15678/EBER.2023.110105

Wikipedia. (2023a). Turkish Red Crescent. Retrieved from https://en.wikipedia.org/wiki/Turkish_Red_Crescent

Wikipedia. (2024). NetHope (NGO). https://en.wikipedia.org/wiki/NetHope

Woltjer, R., Johansson, B. J., Oskarsson, P. A., Svenmarck, P., & Kirwan, B. (2022). Air transport system agility: The Agile Response Capability (ARC) methodology for crisis preparedness. *Infrastructures, 7*(2), 11. DOI: 10.3390/infrastructures7020011

World Food Programme (WFP) Innovation Hub. (2022). *Decapolis: Blockchain-based food traceability in Jordan*. Retrieved from https://innovation.wfp.org/project/decapolis

World Food Programme (WFP) Innovation Hub. (2023). *Building Blocks: A blockchain solution for humanitarian aid*. Retrieved from https://innovation.wfp.org/project/building-blocks

World Food Programme (WFP) Innovation Hub. (2024). *Blockchain solutions for cash assistance and supply chain traceability*. Retrieved from https://innovation.wfp.org/stories/how-wfp-uses-blockchain-to-transform-aid

World Food Programme (WFP). (n.d.-a). *UN Humanitarian Air Service (UNHAS)*. Retrieved from https://www.wfp.org/un-humanitarian-air-service-unhas

World Food Programme (WFP). (n.d.-b). *Aviation Safety and Compliance – Tendering and Vendor Selection*. Retrieved from https://executiveboard.wfp.org/meetings-and-documents/2023/aviation-division-update

World Food Programme (WFP). (n.d.-c). *WFP Air Transport Contracts Committee*. Retrieved from https://docs.wfp.org/api/documents/WFP-0000139929/download/

World, T. R. T. (2023a). Türkiye accelerates HVAC imports after quake. *TRT World*. https://www.trtworld.com

Wu, L., Lu, W., & Xu, J. (2022). Blockchain-based smart contract for smart payment in construction: A focus on the payment freezing and disbursement cycle. *Frontiers of Engineering Management*, *9*(2), 177–195. DOI: 10.1007/s42524-021-0184-y

Wu, L., & Xu, D. (2020). Research on Method and Technology of Emergency Logistics Intelligent System Engineering. In *Advances in Wireless Communications and Applications*. Smart Communic.

Wu, P. J., & Yang, C. K. (2021). Sustainable development in aviation logistics: Successful drivers and business strategies. *Business Strategy and the Environment*, *30*(8), 3763–3771. DOI: 10.1002/bse.2838

Xu, Y., Chong, H. Y., & Chi, M. (2021). A review of smart contracts applications in various industries: A procurement perspective. *Advances in Civil Engineering*, *2021*(1), 5530755. DOI: 10.1155/2021/5530755

Yang, Y., Li, W., Gulliver, T. A., & Li, S. (2019). Bayesian deep learning-based probabilistic load forecasting in smart grids. *IEEE Transactions on Industrial Informatics*, *16*(7), 4703–4713. DOI: 10.1109/TII.2019.2942353

Yang, Y., Pan, M., & Pan, W. (2022). Integrated offsite logistics scheduling approach for high-rise modular building projects. *Journal of Construction Engineering and Management*, *148*(6), 04022032. DOI: 10.1061/(ASCE)CO.1943-7862.0002280

Yilmaz, Z., Aydemir-Karadag, A., & Erol, S. (2019). Finding optimal depots and routes in sudden-onset disasters: An earthquake case for Erzincan. *Transportation Journal*, *58*(3), 168–196. DOI: 10.5325/transportationj.58.3.0168

Yucesoy, E., Balcik, B., & Coban, E. (2025). The role of drones in disaster response: A literature review of operations research applications. *International Transactions in Operational Research*, *32*(2), 545–589. DOI: 10.1111/itor.13484

Yu, D., & He, Z. (2022). Digital twin-driven intelligence disaster prevention and mitigation for infrastructure: Advances, challenges, and opportunities. *Natural Hazards*, *112*(1), 1–36. DOI: 10.1007/s11069-021-05190-x PMID: 35125651

Yu, H., Wang, G., Dong, A., Han, Y., Wang, Y., & Yu, J. (2025). Blockchain-enabled privacy protection scheme for IoT digital identity management. *High-Confidence Computing*, •••, 100320. DOI: 10.1016/j.hcc.2025.100320

Yusuf, R., Fajri, I., & Gani, S. A. (2022, June). Disaster education in disaster-prone schools: A systematic review. [). IOP Publishing.]. *IOP Conference Series. Earth and Environmental Science*, *1041*(1), 012034. DOI: 10.1088/1755-1315/1041/1/012034

Zahoor, N., Golgeci, I., Haapanen, L., Ali, I., & Arslan, A. (2022). The role of dynamic capabilities and strategic agility of B2B high-tech small and medium-sized enterprises during COVID-19 pandemic: Exploratory case studies from Finland. *Industrial Marketing Management*, *105*, 502–514. DOI: 10.1016/j.indmarman.2022.07.006

Zajecs, D., Lebedeva, K., & Odineca, T. (2022). Application Possibilities of the Off-Grid HVAC System Operation Solution for Temporary Shelters in the Latvian Climate Conditions. *Latvian Journal of Physics and Technical Sciences*, *59*(2), 55–63. DOI: 10.2478/lpts-2022-0011

Zarei, M. H., Carrasco-Gallego, R., & Ronchi, S. (2019). To greener pastures: An action research study on the environmental sustainability of humanitarian supply chains. *International Journal of Operations & Production Management*, *39*(11), 1193–1225. DOI: 10.1108/IJOPM-12-2018-0703

Zekhnini, K., Cherrafi, A., Bouhaddou, I., Chaouni Benabdellah, A., & Bag, S. (2022). A model integrating lean and green practices for viable, sustainable, and digital supply chain performance. *International Journal of Production Research*, *60*(21), 6529–6555. DOI: 10.1080/00207543.2021.1994164

Zemitis, J., Borodinecs, A., Bogdanovics, R., & Geikins, A. (2021). A case study of thermal comfort in a temporary shelter. *Journal of Sustainable Architecture and Civil Engineering*, *29*(2), 139–149. DOI: 10.5755/j01.sace.29.2.29240

Zhang, Z., & Zhu, L. (2023). A review on unmanned aerial vehicle remote sensing: Platforms, sensors, data processing methods, and applications. *drones, 7*(6), 398.

Zhang, H., & Chang, C. (2025). Freight network optimization for intercontinental long route with mixed time windows and multiple aircraft types-China-Africa case study. *Heliyon*, *11*(6), e42790. DOI: 10.1016/j.heliyon.2025.e42790

Zhang, P. (2024, September). Optimization and Implementation of Intelligent Scheduling Algorithms in the Civil Aviation Supply Chain. In *2024 International Conference on Industrial IoT, Big Data and Supply Chain (IIoTBDSC)* (pp. 314-318). IEEE. DOI: 10.1109/IIoTBDSC64371.2024.00063

Zhang, P., Liu, Y., Yang, G., & Zhang, G. (2022). A distributionally robust optimisation model for last mile relief network under mixed transport. *International Journal of Production Research*, *60*(4), 1316–1340. DOI: 10.1080/00207543.2020.1856439

Zhang, X., & Saadé, R. G. (2025). Towards a deeper understanding of strategic management factors in international non-governmental organizations. *Administrative Sciences*, *15*(2), 34. DOI: 10.3390/admsci15020034

Zhao, X. (2024). Network security situational awareness and early warning architecture based on big data. *International Journal of System Assurance Engineering and Management*, •••, 1–17. DOI: 10.1007/s13198-024-02522-5

Zocchi, M., Kasaragod, A. K., Jenkins, A., Cook, C., Dobson, R., Oommen, T., Van Huis, D., Taylor, B., Brooks, C., Marini, R., Troiani, F., & Mazzanti, P. (2023). Multi-sensor and multi-scale remote sensing approach for assessing slope instability along transportation corridors using satellites and uncrewed aircraft systems. *Remote Sensing (Basel)*, *15*(12), 3016. DOI: 10.3390/rs15123016

Zuo, Y. (2024). Exploring the synergy: AI enhancing blockchain, blockchain empowering AI, and their convergence across IoT applications and beyond. *IEEE Internet of Things Journal.*

About the Contributors

Erkut Akkartal is an academic and researcher specializing in econometrics, quantitative methods, and logistics management. He is a professor at Yeditepe University, where he has held various administrative roles, including department head and quality board member. With a Ph.D. in Econometrics from Istanbul University and additional master's degrees in Management Science and Statistics, he has an extensive academic background. His research interests encompass supply chain management, sustainability, digital transformation, and risk assessment. He has supervised numerous graduate theses, authored multiple books, and published extensively in peer-reviewed international journals. Before academia, he served in the Ministry of National Defense, gaining practical experience in logistics management. Prof. Akkartal continues to contribute to the field through teaching, research, and editorial responsibilities in scholarly publications.

Filiz Mızrak is an Assistant Professor at Beykoz University, specializing in logistics management, strategic management, and aviation studies. She holds a Ph.D. in Management Strategies from Istanbul Medipol University and has extensive experience in both academia and the logistics sector. Dr. Mızrak has authored numerous peer-reviewed journal articles and book chapters on topics such as cybersecurity in aviation, supply chain management, and strategic investment decisions. She has supervised master's theses and served as an editor for academic publications on logistics and strategic management. Her research contributions focus on integrating innovative methodologies like multi-criteria decision-making and fuzzy logic into business and aviation studies.

***

Gökçe Durukan is ambitious, hardworking, and an easily adapted person who loves learning new languages. She was on an Erasmus Program in Finland, Oulu.

She has a high honors degree in English Language and Literature from Yeditepe University and is currently doing her master's in International Trade and Logistics Management with 100% scholarship due to ranking first in her bachelor's department. She is working as a Research Assistant in the Logistics Management Department at Yeditepe University.

Toprak Kolsuz is a passionate logistics management student at Yeditepe University, currently working in the Customer Service Department at CMA CGM. He is driven by a deep commitment to growth, leadership, and impact. His career goal is to continuously push his own boundaries, become a stronger version of himself, and inspire those around him. He is building his career at the intersection of logistics, communication, and customer experience where every interaction is an opportunity to lead, learn, and leave a positive mark

İlknur Yardımcı Coşkun was born in 1989 in Istanbul. She completed her undergraduate studies in the Department of Industrial Engineering at Sakarya University, her master's degree in the Industrial Engineering Program at Marmara University, Institute of Science, and her doctoral studies in the Industrial Engineering Doctoral Program at Istanbul Technical University, Graduate Education Institute. In 2023, she was awarded the title of "Doctor." Her areas of expertise include logistics and supply chain management. She teaches courses such as operations research, production and inventory management, transportation management, and project management. She has published articles, conference papers, and book chapters on various topics related to logistics and supply chain management, as well as statistical and multi-criteria decision-making techniques and production management. She is currently a faculty member in the Department of International Trade and Logistics at Maltepe University, Faculty of Business and Management Sciences.

Index

A

B

C

D

E

G

H

I

L

P

R

S

T

V

W

www.ingramcontent.com/pod-product-compliance
Lightning Source LLC
LaVergne TN
LVHW062327300926
849161LV00007B/1608
* 9 7 9 8 3 3 7 3 3 6 4 3 5 *